UNDERSTANDING ART

FIFTH EDITION

Lois Fichner-Rathus

The College of New Jersey

Prentice Hall, Upper Saddle River, New Jersey 07458

Library of Congress Cataloging-in-Publication Data

Fichner-Rathus, Lois
Understanding art/Lois Fichner-Rathus – 5th ed.
p. cm.
Includes index.
ISBN: 0-13-645938-2
1. Visual perception. 2. Composition (Art) 3. Art – History.
I. Title.
N7430.5F5 1998
701'. 1–dc21

97-16039
CIP

Editorial Director: *Charlyce Jones Owen*
Acquisitions Editor: *Bud Therien*
Assistant Vice President of Production & Manufacturing: *Barbara Kittle*
Editorial/Production Supervision: *Harriet Tellem*
Manufacturing Manager: *Nick Sklitsis*
Prepress and Manufacturing Buyer: *Robert Anderson*
Marketing Manager: *Sheryl Adams*
Executive Manager, New Media: *Alison Pendergast*
Editorial Assistant: *Gianna Caradonna*
Creative Design Director: *Leslie Osher*
Art Direction and Design: *Anne Bonanno Nieglos* and *Maria Lange*
Cover Design: *Tom Nery*
Photo Researcher: *Francelle Carapetyan / Image Research*
Cover Photo Research: *Lois Fichner-Rathus*
Cover Photograph: *Francisco Hidalgo / The Image Bank*

This book was set in 9/13 New Century Schoolbook by Anne DeMarinis and
was printed and bound by R. R. Donnelley and Sons. The cover was printed
by The Lehigh Press Inc. Color separation and film were supplied by
Lehigh Press Colortronics.

Printed in the United States of America
10 9 8 7 6 5 4

ISBN 0-13-645938-2

Prentice-Hall International (UK) Limited, *London*
Prentice-Hall of Australia Pty. Limited, *Sydney*
Prentice-Hall Canada Inc., *Toronto*
Prentice-Hall Hispanoamericana, S.A., *Mexico*
Prentice-Hall of India Private Limited, *New Delhi*
Prentice-Hall of Japan, Inc., *Tokyo*
Pearson Education Asia Pte. Ltd., *Singapore*
Editora Prentice-Hall do Brasil, Ltda., *Rio de Janeiro*

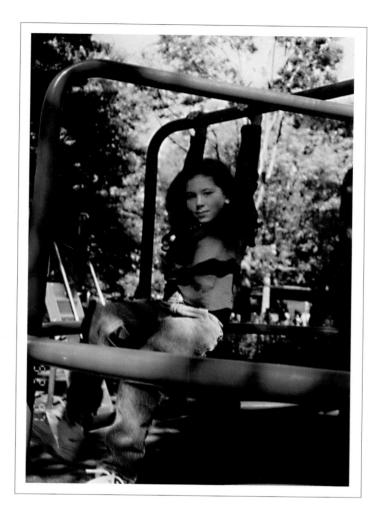

For Taylor,
my youngest,
who, after being dragged from
cathedral to cathedral and
museum to museum,
got to play in the
Stravinsky Fountain

BRIEF CONTENTS

CONTENTS

12 Christian Art: From Catacombs to Cathedrals

13 The Renaissance

SPECIAL FEATURES

PREFACE

"I will always remember when the stars fell down around me and lifted me up above the George Washington Bridge..."

—Faith Ringgold

Thus begins Faith Ringgold's joyful monologue, as written on her painted patchwork quilt, *Tar Beach.* Therein is the story of her life and her dreams on a tar-covered Harlem rooftop.

Ringgold's words say much about art and can perhaps lead us on our quest to understand something about art. A textbook on art is not like a textbook in other academic disciplines. Yes, there is a special vocabulary of art. Yes, this vocabulary is woven into a language that speaks of the principles of art. And yes, art has a history. All these things are the subject matter of this textbook. Yet there is another aspect of art that is also very much its subject matter—the wonderment, the mystery, the magic, and the ineffable beauty of art. These aspects of art are captured in Faith Ringgold's words, and they are also found throughout this book.

"Everyone wants to understand art," complained Pablo Picasso. "Why not try to understand the song of a bird? Why does one love the night, flowers, everything around one without trying to understand them? But in the case of a painting, people have to understand."

We shall take a chance in this volume. We shall gamble that we can learn to understand the songs of birds and still love them. We shall gamble that we can dissect the night and the flowers and still be captured by their beauty. We shall gamble that in trying to analyze art, we do not lose sight of its beauty and wonderment.

WHAT'S NEW IN THIS EDITION

1. A new feature, "Preliminary Sketch," stimulates student interest in the subject matter through chapter opening "teasers." Here are some examples:

Chapter 1:
- There is no agreed-upon definition of art.
- The *Mona Lisa* is a portrait of a banker's wife.
- One contemporary artist sold, as art, the concept of "A two-inch wide, one-inch deep trench, cut across a standard one car driveway".

Chapter 13:
- Shakespeare was born in the year that Michelangelo died.
- America was named after the cousin of the model who posed for Botticelli's *The Birth of Venus.*

Chapter 17:
- Jackson Pollock made drip paintings by placing huge canvases on the floor and then walking over them, splashing paint across their surfaces.
- Whereas many artists have strived to portray the beautiful, Pop art intentionally depicts commonplace, familiar, even boring images.

2. ***Understanding Art's* trademark Compare & Contrast feature** has been expanded in the fifth edition to offer in-depth perspectives on visual and critical issues surrounding the works in the features. Consider the following examples:

- In Chapter 2, Matisse's *Open Window, Collioure* with Aponovich's *Still Life: Penobscot Bay* and Fish's *Scaffolding*
- In Chapter 9, Compare and Contrast Stained Glass Windows, Medieval and Modern
- In Chapter 13, Compare and Contrast Leonardo da Vinci's *Mona Lisa,* Marcel Duchamp's *L.H.O.O.Q.,* G. Odutokun's *Dialogue with Mona Lisa,* and Sadie Lee's *Bona Lisa*
- In Chapter 14, *Judith and Holofernes* by Caravaggio, Gentileschi, and Donatello
- In Chapter 15, Ingres's *Grande Odalisque,* Delacroix's *Odalisque,* Cézanne's *A Modern Olympia,* and Sylvia Sleigh's *Philip Golub Reclining*

3. **Key terms and artist's names at the ends of the chapters.** The lists serve as outlines to help students review what they have learned.

4. **The fifth edition of *Understanding Art* has a dynamic interactive website.**

WHAT REMAINS

The fifth edition, like earlier editions, remains a textbook that is intended to work both for students and professors. *Understanding Art* continues to serve as a tool to help organize and enlighten this demanding, often whirlwind-like course. My goal has been to write a book that would do it all: to edify and inform students, and at the same time to keep them engaged, animated, inspired; to meet the desire of instructors for comprehensive exposition.

The fifth edition continues to balance discussions of media and methods with comprehensive coverage of art history—a balancing act that set earlier editions apart from other art appreciation textbooks.

The fifth edition also retains two successful features from earlier editions: "Compare and Contrast" and "A Closer Look."

COVERAGE

> *Languages like English and French have symbols such as letters or words that are combined according to rules of grammar to create a message. The visual arts have plastic elements that are composed according to principles of unity, balance, and rhythm, and so on.*
>
> —From Chapter 2

Understanding Art is comprehensive and balanced in coverage. It communicates the excitement, relevance, and beauty of art by combining stimulating discussions of the language and elements of art with extensive treatment of the history of art. The elements of art—media, methods, content, composition, style—and the purposes of art compose the first part of the book. Chapters 1–9 focus on what we respond to in a work of art and how artists go about their work. It was my intention to show that our lives are enriched not only by drawing, painting, sculpture, and architecture, but also by photography, cinematography, video art, craft, even graphic design.

To understand where we are, "what's happening," we must also understand where we have been. To provide such insight, the history of art is covered chronologically in the second part of the book.

Chapter 18, the final part of the book, tours the world of art beyond Europe and the United States. We examine the ethnographic art of Africa, the South Pacific, and the Americas. We visit the Islamic art of the Near, Middle, and Far East, Indian art, and the art of China and Japan. We see that artists from diverse periods and cultures use the same language and elements of art to commemorate their experiences, express their religious values, persuade their audiences—even to protest the social order.

PEDAGOGY AND STYLE

Art has the power to make us think profoundly, to make us feel deeply. Whether we gaze upon a landscape painting that reminds us of a vacation past, or an abstract work that challenges our grasp of geometry, or a quilt that evokes family ties and traditions, it is almost impossible to truly confront a work and remain unaffected.

—From Chapter 1

The pedagogy and style of *Understanding Art* were crafted to make students think profoundly, to make them feel deeply. I refused to allow students to experience a course in art appreciation and come away unaffected.

Most students who take art appreciation courses are nonmajors. Some are fulfilling a distribution requirement in the humanities. Their rendezvous with art may be superficial and brief, unless we seize the opportunity to reach them. *Understanding Art* therefore uses pedagogical and stylistic features to engage and enlighten the contemporary broad-based college population:

■ **Preliminary Sketches:** Interesting facts at the beginning of every chapter stimulate student interest in the subject matter.

■ **Introduction:** An introductory chapter, "What Is Art?", discusses the meanings, purposes, and styles of art.

■ **A Closer Look** features: These features motivate students by offering insights into artist's personalities and enlighten them by delving into various topics in greater depth. In Chapter 3, "Life, Death, and Dwelling in the Deep South" highlights an African-American artist's portrayal of the organic relationship between a woman and her home in South Carolina. In Chapter 3, "Paper Dolls for a Post-Columbian World" shows how a Native-American artist uses biting humor to display some of the "gifts" of European Americans to Native Americans. In Chapter 14, "Caravaggio's Police Blotter: The Art of Violence" reveals that the artist was as violent as many of his works. In Chapter 15, "Why Did van Gogh Cut Off His Ear?" offers a number of hypotheses, including psychodynamic hypotheses, about why the postimpressionist might have mutilated himself.

■ **Compare and Contrast** features: These features show two or more works of art side-by-side and phrase questions that help students focus on their stylistic and technical similarities and differences. They parallel the time-honored pedagogical technique in which professors compare and contrast slides of works in class.

As an example, in Chapter 2 we Compare and Contrast Lieberman's Photo of Picasso with Van Ness's *Summer Sunlight,* and ask students to compare the ways in which a photograph and a painting portray the hot light of summer. In Chapter 8 we Compare and Contrast Jiminez's *Border Crossing* with Hall's *The Border* and ask students to consider two very different perspectives on the problem of illegal immigration in the United States. In Chapter 12 we Compare and Contrast Savoldo's *St. Matthew* with Two Carolingian *St. Matthews* and have students consider stylistic differences among three works of the same era on the same subject.

■ **Facts about Art:** At the top of many pages are facts about works of visual art related to the sciences, the arts, and the social and political events of the day. These pieces of information—perhaps we can refer to them as "art bytes"—show that works of art, though they may be unique, are connected with the other arts and events of their times.

■ **Key terms and Artist's Names:** These lists are found at the end of every chapter and underscore for the student the significant material in the chapter.

■ **Glossary:** Key terms are boldfaced in the text and defined in an end-of-book glossary.

■ **Website:** *Arts and Humanities on the World Wide Web* (www.prenhall.com/artcentral) is a comprehensive website designed to augment *Understanding Art.* The website is designed for professors and students teaching and studying art. By utilizing the technology of "hypertext," the web allows users access to a vast array of historical, cultural, and general interest sites organized and correlated to chapters and content found in the text.

Arts and Humanities on the Web will have the following elements:
- Searchable database of worldwide museums with homepages on the WWW
- Searchable database of artist's homepages on the WWW
- Bulletin board features for professors and students
- Text specific homepages
- Links to WWW tutorials and other resources related to using the Web
- Links to resources for using the WWW in teaching art and culture
- Student toolbox with links to resources utilized by students studying art and culture

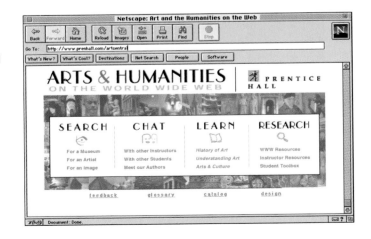

- **Style:**

  Art is a powerful tool, and the artist knows this well. It can be used to replicate reality in the finest detail, tricking the eye into perceiving truth in imitation. Artists have reached outward to describe truths about humanity and have reached inward to describe truths about themselves. Sometimes their pursuit has led them to beauty, at other times to shame and outrage. The "ugly truth," like the beautiful truth, provides commentary on the human condition.

  —From Chapter 1

  Style is a form of art. Style is also a powerful tool. The style of writing and the explanations of concepts are tailored to stimulate and enlighten students without compromising the complexity of the subject matter. To me, the test of good writing is that it communicate, that it teach, that it inspire. Professors who have used earlier editions of *Understanding Art* assure me that my goals as an author have been met.

- **The New York Times Supplement Program:** The New York Times and Prentice Hall are sponsoring Themes of the Times: a program designed to enhance access to current information or relevence in the classroom.

  Through this program, the core subject matter provided in the text is supplemented by a collection of time-sensitive articles from one of the world's most distinguished newspapers, The New York Times. These articles demonstrate the vital, ongoing connection between what is learned in the classroom and what is happening in the world around us.

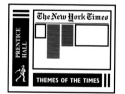

  To enjoy the wealth of information of The New York Times daily, a reduced subscription rate is available. For information, call toll-free: 1-800-631-1222.

  Prentice Hall and The New York Times are proud to co-sponsor Themes of the Times. We hope it will make the reading of both textbooks and newspapers a more dynamic, involving process.

ACKNOWLEDGMENTS

I consider myself fortunate to have studied with a fine group of artists, art historians, and art professionals who helped shape my love of art and my thinking about art throughout my career. Without the broad knowledge, skills, and dedication of these individuals, *Understanding Art* would not have taken its present form and might not have come into being. They include: James S. Ackerman, Wayne V. Anderson, Stanford Anderson, Whitney Chadwick, Michael Graves, George Heard Hamilton, Ann Sutherland Harris, Julius S. Held, Henry A. Millon, Sam Hunter, Konrad Oberhuber, John C. Overbeck, Michael Rinehart, Andrew C. Ritchie, Mark W. Roskill, Theodore Roszak, Miriam Schapiro, Bernice Steinbaum, and Jack Tworkov.

I'm going to say a few words about Bernice Steinbaum of the Steinbaum Krauss Gallery in New York. Bernice has dedicated herself to the support of women artists and artists of color. For many years, while the art world was immersed solely in the work of European and European-American males, Bernice spoke—a voice in the wilderness, as it were—about the works of women and artists of color. On behalf of the community of art historians and educators, I thank Bernice for helping bring them into the light.

I acknowledge with pleasure the fine group of publishing professionals at Prentice Hall and elsewhere, who helped bring this book into being. First are Bud Therien, Publisher, and J. Philip Miller, President, who brought this book to Prentice Hall when it was little more than a, forgive me, gleam in my eye. They have been there for me edition after edition. Thanks, guys. Then there's Harriet Tellem, who is new to the book, but who handled all the daily details that convert a typed manuscript and a list of illustrations into the beautiful bound book that you are holding in your hands.

I would like to thank my husband, Spence, for being my resident techie. And finally I would like to thank my kids, Allyn, Jordan, and Taylor for learning to use the microwave and order in pizza on their own, and for getting off America Online when Mom needed to work on the book.

—Lois Fichner-Rathus, Short Hills, N.J.
LoisFR@aol.com

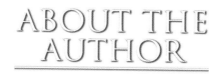

Lois Fichner-Rathus received her M.S. from the Williams College Graduate Program in the History of Art and her Ph.D. in the History, Theory, and Criticism of Art from the Massachusetts Institute of Technology. Her areas of specialization include the theory of art, feminist art history and criticism, ancient and classical art, and modern art and architecture. She has authored grants, contributed to books, written exhibition catalogue essays, and published numerous articles in professional journals including *ARTS Magazine* and the *The Print Collector's Newsletter.* She is currently Art Department Chair and a professor of art history and interdisciplinary studies at The College of New Jersey. She resides in Short Hills, New Jersey, with her husband, Spence Rathus, and their three daughters, Allyn, Jordan, and Taylor.

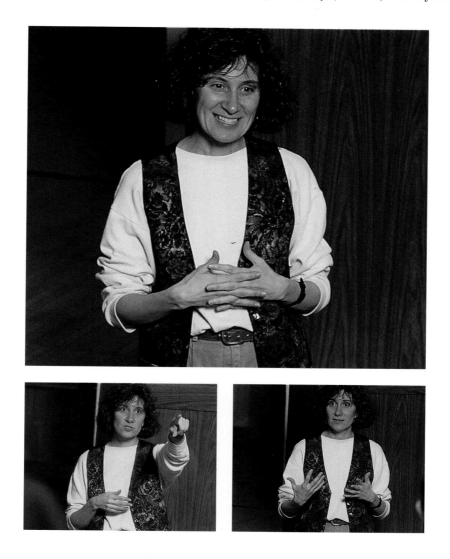

UNDERSTANDING
ART

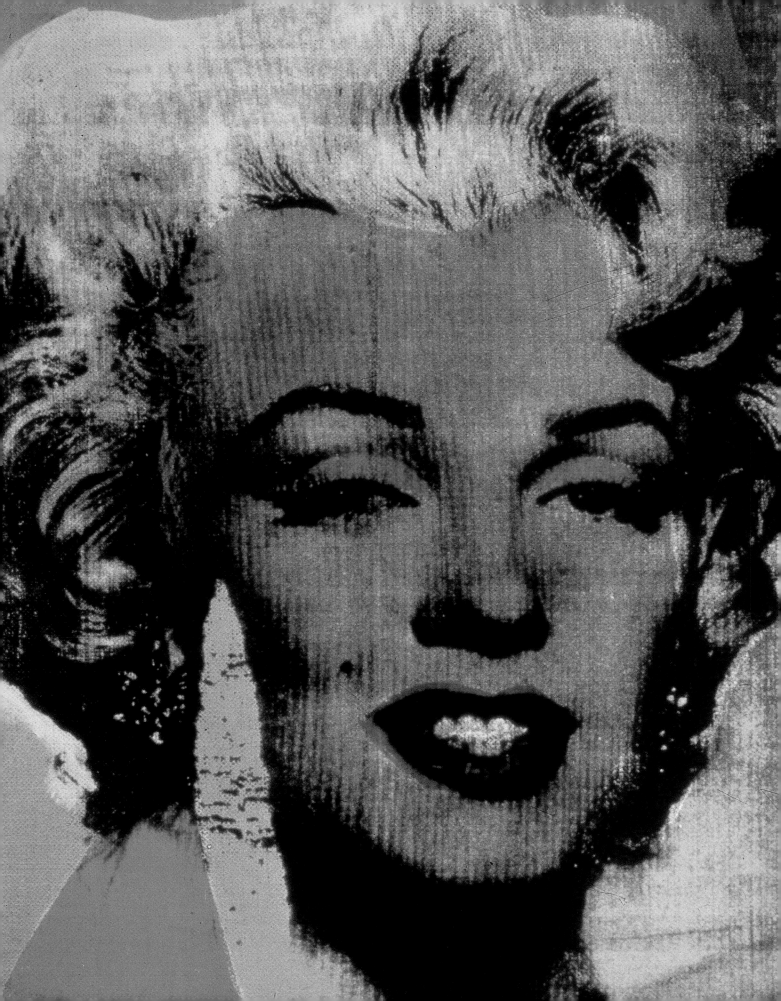

c h a p t e r

WHAT IS ART? MEANINGS, PURPOSES, STYLES

P R E L I M I N A R Y
Sketch

- ❏ There is no agreed-upon definition of art.

- ❏ The *Mona Lisa* is a portrait of a banker's wife.

- ❏ Art does not necessarily have to be beautiful.

- ❏ Art has been used to placate the gods, to record experience, to portray forces at work in the unconscious reaches of the mind, to protest injustice, and to create both order and chaos.

- ❏ One contemporary artist sold, as art, the concept of "A two-inch wide, one-inch deep trench, cut across a standard one-car driveway."

Andy Warhol, *Four Marilyns* (detail). See Figure 1–10.

Everyone wants to understand art. Why not try to understand the song of a bird? Why does one love the night, flowers, everything around one without trying to understand them? But in the case of a painting, people have to understand.

—*Pablo Picasso*

Beauty, truth, immortality, order, harmony—these concepts and ideals have occupied us since the dawn of history. They enrich our lives and encourage us to extend ourselves beyond the limits of flesh and blood. Without them, life would be but a mean struggle for survival, and the value of survival itself would be unclear.

It is in the sciences and the arts that we strive to weave our experiences into coherent bodies of knowledge and to communicate them. Many of us are more comfortable with the sciences than with the arts. Science teaches us that the universe is not ruled purely by chance. The sciences provide ways of observing the world and experimenting so that we can learn what forces determine the courses of atoms and galaxies. Even those of us who do not consider ourselves "scientific" recognize that the scientific method permits us to predict and control many important events on a grand scale.

The arts are more elusive to define, more difficult to gather into a conceptual net. We would probably all agree that the arts enhance daily experience; some of us would contend that they are linked to the very quality of life. **Art** has touched everyone, and art is all around us. Crayon drawings, paper cutouts, and the like are part of the daily lives of our children—an integral function of both magnet and refrigerator door. We all look for art to brighten our dormitory rooms, enhance our interior decor, beautify our cities, and embellish our places of worship. We are certain that we do not want to be without the arts, yet we are hard-pressed to define them and sometimes even to understand them. In fact, the very word *art* encompasses many meanings, including ability, process, and product. As ability, art is the human capacity to make things of beauty and things that stir us; it is creativity. As process, art encompasses acts such as drawing, painting, sculpting, designing buildings, and using the camera to create memorable works. This definition is ever-expanding, as materials and methods are employed in innovative ways to bring forth a creative product. As product, art is the completed work—an etching, a sculpture, a structure, a tapestry. If as individuals we do not understand science, we are at least comforted by the thought that others do. With art, however, the experience of a work is unique. Reactions to a work will vary widely according to the nature of the individual, the time, place, and culture. And although we may find ourselves saying, before a work of art that has us befuddled, "I hate it! I don't understand it!," we suspect that there is something about the very nature of art that transcends understanding.

This book is about the visual arts. Despite their often enigmatic nature, we shall try to share something of what is known about them so that understanding may begin. We do not aim to force our aesthetic preferences on you; if in the end you dislike a work as much as you did to start, that is completely acceptable. But we will aim to heighten awareness of what we respond to in a work of art and try to communicate why what an artist has done is important. In this way, you can counter, "I hate it, but at least I understand it."

As in many areas of study—languages, computers, the sciences—amassing a basic vocabulary is intrinsic to understanding the material. You will want to be able to describe the attributes of a work of art and be able to express your reactions to it. We shall see how the elements of art, such as line, color, and shape, are composed into works of art. We shall examine many media, including drawing, painting, printmaking, sculpture, architecture, the camera arts, ceramics, and fiber arts. We shall even look at graphic, industrial, and landscape design and see that the creative urges that stir the painter also stir the practitioner.

When asked why we should study history, the historian answers that we must know about the past in order to have a sense of where we are and where we may be going. This argument also holds true for the arts; there is more to art history than memorizing dates! Examining a work in its historical, social, political, and stylistic context will enable you to have a more meaningful dialogue with that work. You will be amazed and entertained by the ways in which the creative process has been intertwined with world events and individual personalities. We shall follow the journey of art, therefore, from the wall paintings of our Stone Age ancestors through the graffiti art of today's subway station. The media, the forms, the styles, and the subjects may evolve and change from millennium to millennium, from day to day, but uniting threads lie in the persistent quest for beauty, for truth, or for self-expression.

1–1 LEONARDO DA VINCI
MONA LISA (C. 1503). OIL ON PANEL. 30¼ × 21″.
LOUVRE MUSEUM, PARIS.

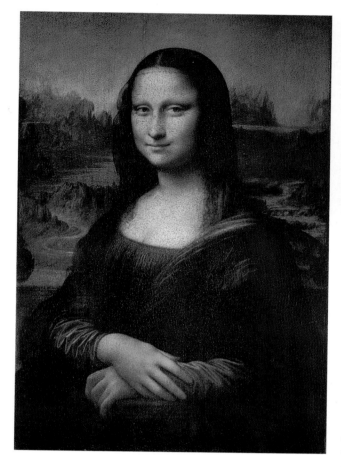

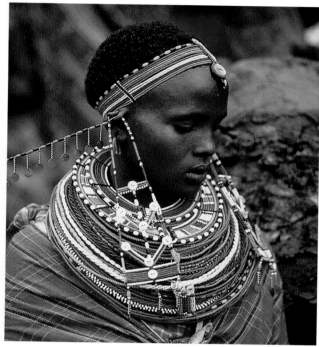

PURPOSES OF ART

Many philosophers have argued that art serves no function, that it exists for its own sake. Some have asserted that there is something about the essence of art that transcends the human occupation with usefulness. Others have held that in trying to analyze art too closely, one loses sight of its beauty and wonderment.

These may be valid points of view. Nevertheless, our understanding and appreciation of art often can be enhanced by asking the questions, "Why was this created?" "What is its purpose?" In this section we shall see that works of art come into existence for a host of reasons that are as varied as the human condition.

TO CREATE BEAUTY

The beautiful is in nature, and it is encountered in the most diverse forms of reality. Once it is found, it belongs to art, or, rather, to the artist who discovers it.
—Gustave Courbet

Art has always added beauty to our lives. At times, the artist has looked to nature as the standard of beauty, and thus imitated it. At other times the artist has aimed to improve upon nature, developing an alternate standard—an idealized form. Standards of beauty in and of themselves are by no means universal. The Classical Greeks were obsessed with their idea of beauty, and they fashioned mathematical formulas for rendering the human body in sculpture so that it would achieve a majesty and perfection unknown in nature. The sixteenth-century artist Leonardo da Vinci, in what is perhaps the most famous painting in the history of Western art, enchants generations of viewers with the eternal beauty and mysteriousness of the smiling *Mona Lisa* (Fig. 1–1). But appreciation of the stately repose and refined features of this Italian woman is tied to an affinity to a Western standard of beauty. Elsewhere in the world, these very features might seem alien, unattractive, or undesirable. On the other hand, the standard of beauty in some non-Western societies which holds scarification, body painting, tattooing and adornment (Fig. 1–2) both beautiful and sacred, may seem odd and unattractive to someone from the Western world. One art form need not be seen as intrinsically superior to the other; in these works, quite simply, beauty is in the eye of the society's beholder.

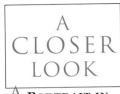

For centuries, artists have devoted their full resources, their lives, to their work. Orlan has also offered her pound of flesh—to the surgeon's scalpel.

Orlan (Fig. 1–3) is a French multimedia performance artist who has been undergoing a series of cosmetic operations to create, in herself, a composite sketch of what Western art has long set forth as the pinnacle of human beauty: the facial features that we find in classic works such as Botticelli's *Venus* (Fig. 1–4), Leonardo's *Mona Lisa* (Fig. 1–1), and eighteenth-century French Painter, François Boucher's *Europa*. Or, more specifically, *Venus's* chin, the *Mona Lisa's* forehead, and *Europa's* mouth.

Most people undergo cosmetic surgery in private, but not Orlan. Several of her operations have been performances or media events. Her first series of operations were carried out in France and Belgium. The operating rooms were filled with symbols of flowering womanhood in a form compatible with medicine: sterilized plastic fruit. There were huge photos of Orlan, and the surgeons and their assistants were decked out not in surgical greens, but in costumes created by celebrated couturiers. A recent operation was performed in the New York office of a cosmetic surgeon and transmitted, via satellite, to the Sandra Gering Gallery in the city's famed SoHo district. Orlan did not lie unconscious in a hospital gown. Rather she lay awake in a long black dress and read from a work on psychoanalysis while the surgeon implanted silicone in her face to imitate the protruding forehead of *Mona Lisa*.

When will it all end? Orlan says that "I will stop my work when it is as close as possible to the computer composite,"[1] as the lips of *Europa* split into a smile.

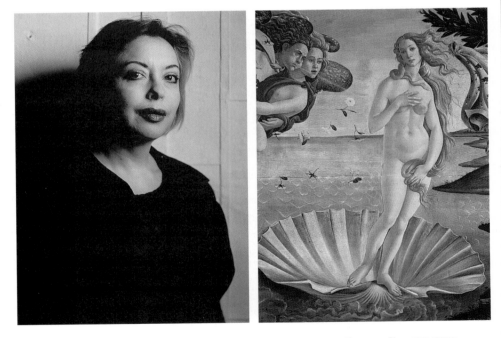

1–3 FRENCH PERFORMANCE ARTIST ORLAN, WHO HAS DEDICATED HERSELF TO ASSUMING THE APPEARANCE OF WESTERN CLASSIC BEAUTY AS FOUND IN THE WORKS OF LEONARDO, BOTTICELLI, AND BOUCHER.

1–4 DETAIL FROM ITALIAN RENAISSANCE ARTIST SANDRO BOTTICELLI'S OIL PAINTING, *THE BIRTH OF VENUS* (C. 1482). OIL ON CANVAS. 5'8⅞" × 9'1⅞".
UFFIZI GALLERY, FLORENCE.

[1]Margalit Fox, "A Portrait in Skin and Bone," *The New York Times*, November 21, 1993, p. V8.

1–5 *The Hunt of the Unicorn, VI: The Unicorn Is Killed and Brought to the Castle* (Franco-Flemish, 15th century). Silk, wood, silver, and silver-gilt threads. 12′1″ × 12′9″.
The Metropolitan Museum of Art, N.Y. Gift of John D. Rockefeller, Jr., The Cloisters Collection, 1937. (37.80.5).

1–6 JOYCE KOZLOFF
Galla Placidia in Philadelphia (1985). Mosaic installation. 13 × 16′.
Penn Center, Suburban Station, Philadelphia. Courtesy of the artist.

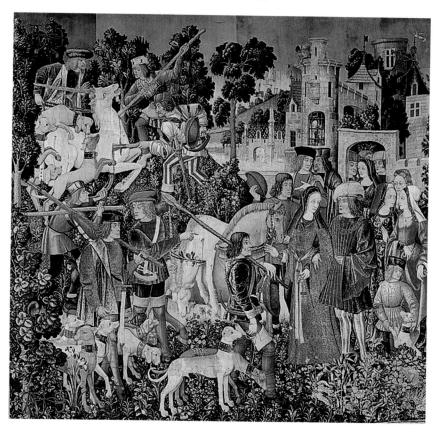

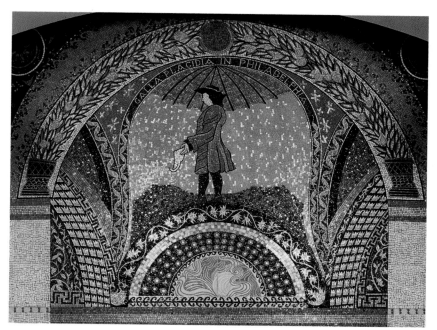

To Provide Decoration

We have all decided at one time or another to change the color of our bedrooms. We have hung a poster or painting here rather than there, and we have arranged a vase of flowers or placed a potted plant in just the right spot in the room. We may not have created works of art, but we did accomplish one thing: we managed to delight our senses and turn our otherwise ordinary environments into pleasurable havens.

Works of art have been used to create pleasing environments for centuries. Paintings are not only objects of beauty in themselves; they also hang on walls and can be painted directly on them. Sculptures find their way into rooms, courts, and gardens; photographs are found in books; and fiber arts are seen on walls and floors. Whatever other functions they may serve, many works of art are also decorative.

The Unicorn Tapestries (Fig. 1–5) were commissioned at the end of the sixteenth century as a wedding present to Anne of Brittany and King Louis XII, and were meant to adorn the walls of one of the King's chateaus. The tapestries are tightly woven from a rich palette of wools and silks and are highlighted by silver threads. Eighty-five varieties of plants are accurately portrayed. The subject of the tapestries, the hunt of the unicorn, appropriately symbolizes courtly love and marriage.

These lush tapestries seem completely at home in a royal residence, but one of art's pleasures is to be found in its unexpected incongruities. Joyce Kozloff's *Galla Placidia in Philadelphia* (Fig. 1–6), mosaic for the Penn Center Suburban Railroad

IN 1965, COLUMBIA PICTURES RELEASED *THE AGONY AND THE ECTASY*, A FILM ON THE LIFE OF MICHELANGELO AND HIS RELATIONSHIP WITH POPE JULIUS II. IT STARRED CHARLTON HESTON AND REX HARRISON.

1–7 FRIDA KAHLO
SELF-PORTRAIT WITH MONKEY (1940). OIL ON MASONITE.
21¾ × 19½″.
PRIVATE COLLECTION.

1–8 ROBERT MAPPLETHORPE
SELF-PORTRAIT (1988). GELATIN
SILVER PRINT.
©1988, ESTATE OF ROBERT MAPPLETHORPE.

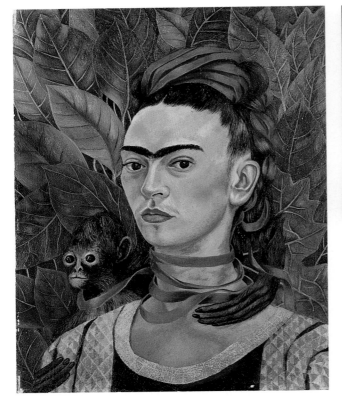

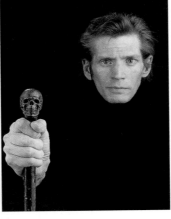

photorealist painter, all, in their way, pursued truth and attempted to reveal it. Truth about how the world looks; truth about how the world works. But artists have also reached outward to describe truths about humanity and have reached inward to describe truths about themselves. Sometimes their pursuit has led them to beauty, at other times to shame and outrage. The "ugly truth," just like the beautiful truth, provides a valid commentary on the human condition.

In her self-portraits, the Mexican painter Frida Kahlo used her tragic life as an emblem for human suffering. At the age of eighteen, she was injured when a streetcar slammed into a bus on which she was a passenger. The accident left her with many serious wounds, including a fractured pelvis and vertebrae, and chronic pain. Kahlo's marriage to the painter Diego Rivera was also painful. She once told a friend, "I have suffered two serious accidents in my life, one in which a streetcar ran over me. . . . The other accident was Diego."[2] Virtually all of her works reveal the anguish of her life. Kahlo typically presents herself alone, with objects that were meaningful to her, or, as in *Self-Portrait with Monkey* (Fig. 1–7), with her pets. Her face is always painted with extreme realism and set within a compressed space, requiring the viewer to confront the "true" Frida. When asked why she painted herself so often, she replied, "Porque estoy muy sola" (because I am all alone). Those who knew Kahlo conjecture that she painted self-portraits in order to "survive, to endure, to conquer death."

Another haunting portrayal of unvarnished truth can be seen in Robert Mapplethorpe's *Self-Portrait* (Fig. 1–8). The veracity of the photographic medium is inescapable; the viewer is forced to confront the artist's troublesome gaze. But the portrait also discloses the truth about

Station in that city, elevates decorative patterns to the level of fine art and raises the art historical consciousness of the casual commuter. The original Mausoleum of Galla Placidia is the fifth-century chapel and burial place of a Byzantine Empress, a landmark monument known for its complex and colorful mosaics (one of them can be seen on page 290). Kozloff's own intricate and diverse designs dazzle the eye and stimulate the intellect, providing an oasis of color in an otherwise humdrum city scene.

TO REVEAL TRUTH

> *It is the glory and good of Art,*
> *That Art remains the one way possible*
> *Of speaking truths, to mouths like mine at least.*
> —Robert Browning

Art is a powerful tool, and the artist knows this well. It can be used to replicate reality in the finest detail, tricking the eye into perceiving truth in imitation. The ancient Greeks, the Renaissance artist, the contemporary

[2]Martha Zamora, *Frida Kahlo: The Brush of Anguish*. San Francisco: Chronicle Books, 1990, p. 37.

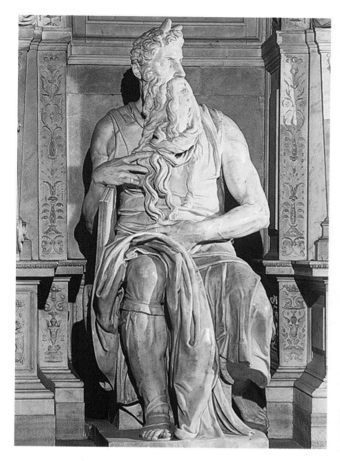

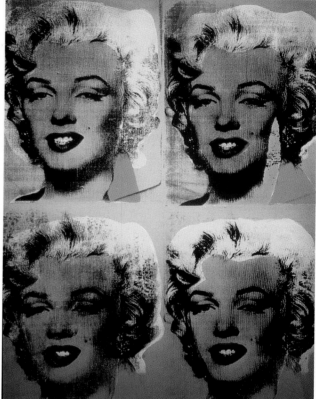

Mapplethorpe's battle with AIDS, and perhaps suggests
an attempt to reconcile his inevitable death. The artist's
skeletal head slips into a background haze while his
tightly clenched fist grips a cane with a skull and juts
forward into sharp focus. The anger and defiance of Mapplethorpe's whitened knuckles contrasts with the soft,
almost pained expression of the artist's face.

TO IMMORTALIZE

> *Blest be the art that can immortalize.*
> —William Cowper

> *All passes. Art alone*
>   *Enduring stays to us;*
> *The Bust outlasts the throne,*
>   *The coin, Tiberius.*
> —Henry Austin Dobson

In the face of certain death, an artist like Robert Mapplethorpe can defy mortality by creating a work that
will keep his talents and his tragedy in the public's
consciousness for decades. Human beings are the only
species conscious of death, and for millennia, they have
used art to overleap the limits of this life.

Many tales have been told of the struggles between
the Renaissance giant, Michelangelo, and his patron,
Pope Julius II, concerning the latter's tomb. The original
commission was to have been an ambitious tribute to
the pontiff—a two-story building with twenty-eight
sculptures. Both artist and patron saw the work as the
crowning achievement of his career. But funds were
diverted from the tomb for other pet projects during the
Pope's lifetime, and after his death, the project was
curtailed to eight works, the most prominent of which is
the majestic *Moses* (Fig. 1–9). Michelangelo's talents
were too much in demand, as the succeeding Pope
focused on his own bid for immortality.

In *Four Multicolored Marilyns* (Fig. 1–10), Pop
artist Andy Warhol participated in the cultural immor-
talization of a film icon of the 1960s by reproducing
a well-known photograph of Monroe on canvas. Proclaimed a "sex symbol" of the silver screen, she rapidly
rose to fame and shocked her fans by taking her own
life at an early age. In the decades since Monroe's
death, her image is still found on posters and calendars,
books and songs are still written about her, and the

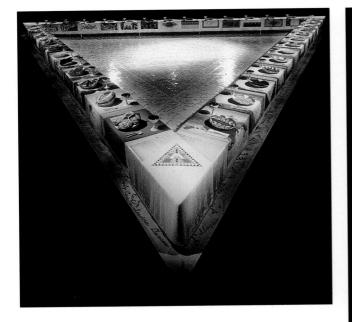

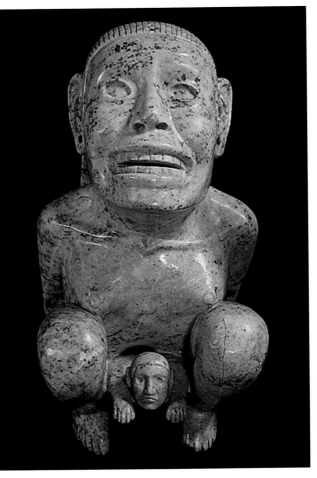

public's appetite for information about her early years
and romances remains insatiable. In other renderings,
Warhol arranged multiple images of the star as if lined
up on supermarket shelves, commenting, perhaps, on
the ways in which contemporary flesh peddlers have
packaged and sold her—in death as well as life.

The lines between life and death, between place
and time, are temporarily dissolved in the renowned
installation conceived by feminist artist Judy Chicago
called *The Dinner Party* (Fig. 1–11). Constructed to
honor and immortalize history's notable women, the
idea for this multimedia work revolves around a fantastic dinner party, where the guests of honor meet before
place settings designed to reflect their personalities and
accomplishments. Hundreds of collaborators—from
potters to embroiderers—helped to concretize Chicago's
vision of *The Dinner Party*. Chicago and numerous
other women artists have invested much energy in
alerting the public to the significant role of women in
the arts and society.

TO EXPRESS RELIGIOUS VALUES

The quest for immortality is the bedrock of organized
religion. From the cradle of civilization to the contemporary era, from Asia to the Americas and from the

Crimea to the Cameroon, human beings across time
and cultures have sought answers to the unanswerable
and have salved their souls with the notion of a life
after death. It is not surprising that, in the absence of
physical embodiments for the deities they fashioned,
humans developed art forms to visually render the unseen. Often the physical attributes granted to their
gods were a reflection of humans themselves. It has
been said, for example, that the Greeks made their
men into gods and their gods into men. In other
societies, deities were often represented as powerful
and mysterious animals, or composite men-beasts.
Ritual and ceremony grew alongside the establishment
of religions and the representation of deities, in actual
or symbolic form. Until modern times, one could

1–13 JESSIE OONARK
A Shaman's Helping Spirits (1971). Stonecut and Stencil. 37¹⁄₁₆ × 25¹⁄₁₆″.
ART GALLERY OF ONTARIO, TORONTO, CANADA; GIFT OF THE KLAMER FAMILY, 1978, 24/40.

1–14 AARON DOUGLAS
Noah's Ark (c. 1927). Oil on Masonite. 48 × 36″.
AFRO-AMERICAN COLLECTION OF ART, THE CARL VAN VECHTEN GALLERY OF FINE ARTS, FISK UNIVERSITY, NASHVILLE, TENN.

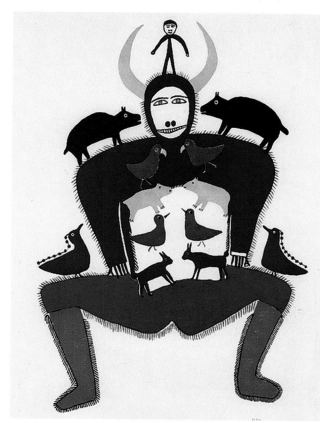

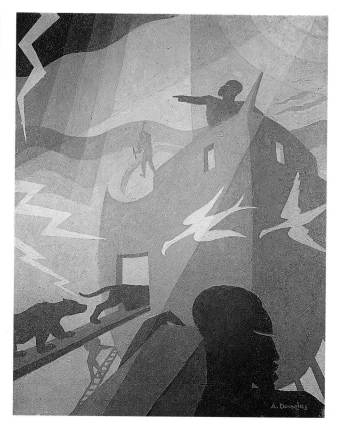

probably study the history of art in terms of works expressing religious values alone.

Art has been used to express hopes for fertility, to propitiate the gods, to symbolize great religious events and values, and to commend heavenward the souls of the departed. The small, gemlike sculpture of Tlazolteotl (Fig. 1–12), the Aztec goddess of childbirth, is a powerful image that binds the otherworld with common human experience. Tlazolteotl squats in the manner of childbirth in many societies, baring her teeth in pain as her son, the god of maize, is born.

Contemporary Inuit artist Jessie Oonark, who lived in the Canadian Arctic, created the image *A Shaman's Helping Spirits* (Fig. 1–13), as a symbol of the healing rituals associated with the medicine men of her culture. Shamanism is a religion based on a belief in good and evil spirits that can be controlled and influenced only by the power of the shaman, a kind of priest. The

strong, flat shapes and bright colors lend a directness and vitality to her expression.

Another artist of color, Aaron Douglas, translated a biblical story into a work that speaks to the African-American sensibility. In his *Noah's Ark* (Fig. 1–14), one of seven paintings based on James Weldon Johnson's book, *God's Trombones: Seven Negro Sermons in Verse*, Douglas expressed a powerful vision of the great flood. Animals enter the ark in pairs as lightning flashes about them and the sky turns a hazy grey-purple with the impending storm. African men, rendered in rough-hewn profile, ready the arc and direct the action in a dynamically choreographed composition that takes possession of and personalizes the biblical event for Douglas's race and culture.

We are not likely to think of a building as a vehicle for expressing beliefs and emotions, but some of the most illustrious expressions of religious values in the

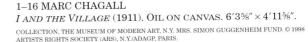

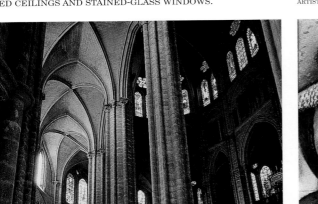

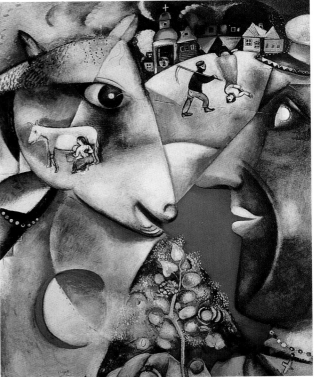

history of western culture are to be found in the gothic cathedral (Fig. 1–15). Here, everything from the structure to the stained glass was invested with symbolism, while chalices and reliquaries were bejeweled in utmost splendor. The physical light, which passed through the brightly colored windows and shone on the glistening surfaces of ceremonial objects, became divine light by analogy. The ultimate goal of the abbot and the architect was the creation of a celestial kingdom on earth.

TO EXPRESS FANTASY

Art also serves as a vehicle by which artists can express their inmost fantasies. Whereas some have labored to reconstruct reality and commemorate actual experiences, others have used art to give vent to their imaginary inner lives. There are many types of fantasies, such as those found in dreams and daydreams or simply the objects and landscapes that are conceived in the imagination. The French painter Odilon Redon once said that there is "a kind of drawing which the imagination has liberated from any concern with the details of reality in order to allow it to serve freely for the repre-

sentation of things conceived" in the mind. In an attempt to capture the inner self, many twentieth-century artists also have looked to the psychoanalytic writings of Sigmund Freud and Carl Jung, who suggested that primeval forces are at work in the unconscious reaches of the mind. These artists have sought to use their art as an outlet for these unconscious forces, as we shall see in Chapters 16 and 17.

Marc Chagall's self-portrait, *I and the Village* (Fig. 1–16), provides a fragmented image of the artist among fantasized objects that seem to float in and out of one another. Fleeting memories of life in his Russian village are pieced together like so many pieces of a dreamlike puzzle, reflecting the very fragmentary nature of memory itself. Chagall's world is a happy, though private one; the strange juxtaposition of images is reconciled only in the artist's own mind.

A similar process of fragmentation and juxtaposition was employed by German artist Max Beckmann in *The Dream* (Fig. 1–17), but with a very different effect. The suggestion of space and atmosphere in Chagall's

IN THE SUMMER OF 1937, ADOLF HITLER ARRANGED AN EXHIBITION FEATURING ARTISTS WHOSE WORK HE CALLED "DEGENERATE." MAX BECKMANN WAS AMONG THEM.

1–17 MAX BECKMANN
THE DREAM (1921). OIL ON CANVAS. 73⅛ × 35″.
THE ST. LOUIS ART MUSEUM. BEQUEST OF MORTON D. MAY. © 1998 ARTISTS RIGHTS SOCIETY (ARS), N.Y./VG BILD-KUNST, BONN.

1–18 GERTRUDE KÄSEBIER
THE MAGIC CRYSTAL (C. 1904). PLATINUM PRINT.
THE ROYAL PHOTOGRAPHIC SOCIETY, BATH, ENGLAND.

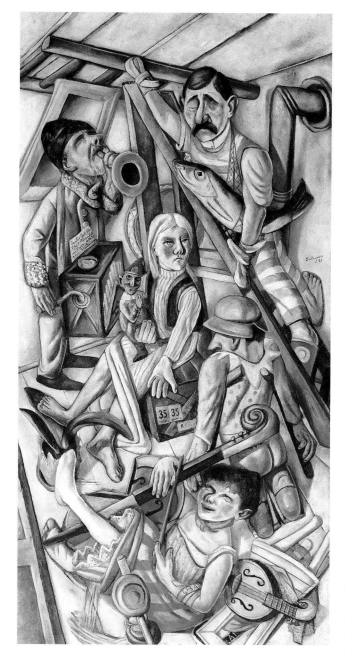

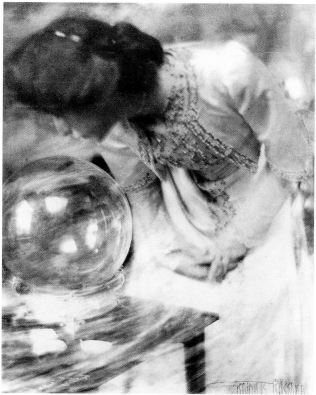

painting has given way to a claustrophobic room in which figures are compressed into a zigzag group. The soft, rolling hills and curving lines which gave the village painting its pleasant, dreamy quality have been forfeited for harsh, angular shapes and deformations. Horror hides in every nook and cranny, from the amputated and

bandaged hands of the man in red stripes, to the blinded street musician and maimed harlequin. Are these marionettes from some dark comedy, or human puppets locked in a world of manipulation and hopelessness?

Beckmann used line and shape and color to enhance the maudlin, nightmarish quality of his subject. Artists often capitalize on the technical effects of their chosen medium to complement the content of their works. The photographer Gertrude Käsebier added special materials to her printing paper to create the sensation of psychic forces connecting a woman to a crystal ball as she stares into its mesmerizing core (Fig. 1–18). The surroundings are airy and intangible; the experience is not of this world.

TO STIMULATE THE INTELLECT AND FIRE THE EMOTIONS

Art has the power to make us think profoundly, to make us feel deeply. Beautiful or controversial works of all media can trigger many associations for us. Whether we

1–19 JENNY HOLZER
INFLAMMATORY ESSAYS (DETAIL) (1980–84). OFFSET PRINT ON
COLORED PAPER. 20 PARTS, EACH 17 × 17″.
COURTESY OF JENNY HOLZER STUDIO, N.Y.

1–20 RYOANJI ZEN TEMPLE, JAPANESE GARDEN. KYOTO, JAPAN.

*DESTROY SUPERABUNDANCE. STARVE THE
FLESH, SHAVE THE HAIR, EXPOSE THE
BONE, CLARIFY THE MIND, DEFINE THE
WILL, RESTRAIN THE SENSES, LEAVE
THE FAMILY, FLEE THE CHURCH, KILL
THE VERMIN, VOMIT THE HEART, FORGET
THE DEAD. LIMIT TIME, FORGO
AMUSEMENT, DENY NATURE, REJECT
ACQUAINTANCES, DISCARD OBJECTS,
FORGET TRUTHS, DISSECT MYTH, STOP
MOTION, BLOCK IMPULSE, CHOKE SOBS,
SWALLOW CHATTER. SCORN JOY, SCORN
TOUCH, SCORN TRAGEDY, SCORN
LIBERTY, SCORN CONSTANCY, SCORN HOPE,
SCORN EXALTATION, SCORN REPRODUCTION,
SCORN VARIETY, SCORN EMBELLISHMENT,
SCORN RELEASE, SCORN REST, SCORN
SWEETNESS, SCORN LIGHT. IT'S A
QUESTION OF FORM AS MUCH AS FUNCTION.
IT IS A MATTER OF REVULSION.*

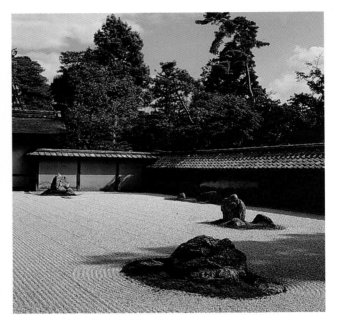

gaze upon a landscape painting that reminds us of a
vacation past, or an abstract work that challenges our
grasp of geometry, or a quilt that evokes family ties and
traditions, it is almost impossible to truly confront a work
and remain unaffected. We may think about what the
subjects are doing, thinking, and feeling. We may reflect
on the purposes of the artist. We may seek to trace the
sources of our own emotional response or advance our
self-knowledge and our knowledge of the outside world.

Consider Jenny Holzer's conceptual art work
Inflammatory Essays (Fig. 1–19). A conceptual work does
not necessarily represent external objects, but is more
likely fully conceived in the artist's mind. The artform
challenges the traditional view of the artist as creative
visionary, skilled craftsperson, and master of one's
media. The "art" lies in the artist's conception. **Word-
works,** such as this, seem to comment on the imper-
sonal information systems of modern times, while posing
a challenge to the formal premises of art, and stirring an
intellectual response in the viewer. Holzer's work draws
readers into a piercing feminist declaration. They are
provoked into defending their own views on the subject

of women's rights. Holzer's *Inflammatory Essay* series
consists of numerous issues—torture, poverty, freedom—
voiced in a volatile manner, but controlled by a constant
format of one hundred words arranged in twenty lines.

At its most extreme, the conceptual art product
may exist solely in the mind of the artist, with or without a physical embodiment. Consider these:
A wordwork by Robert Barry—

*All the things I know
but of which I am not
at the moment thinking—
1:36 PM; June 15, 1969*

or, a concept by artist Lawrence Weiner, sold to a patron,
who installed the work himself: "A two-inch wide, one-
inch deep trench, cut across a standard one-car driveway."

TO CREATE ORDER AND HARMONY

Art is harmony.
—Georges Seurat

*I try not to have things look as if chance had
brought them together, but as if they had a necessary bond between them.*
—Jean-François Millet

1–21 HENRI MATISSE
PIANO LESSON (1916). OIL ON CANVAS. 8′½″ × 6′11¾″.

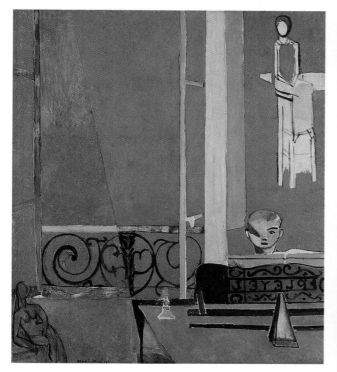

1–22 LAURIE SIMMONS
RED LIBRARY #2 (1983). COLOR PHOTOGRAPH. 48½ × 38¼″.

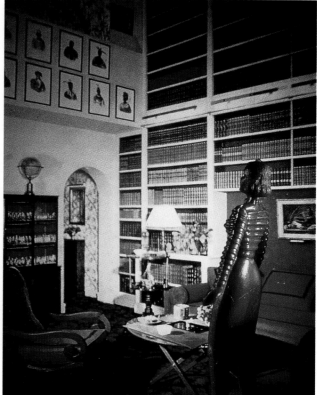

Artists and scientists have been intrigued by, and have ventured to discover and describe, the underlying order of nature. The Classical Greeks fine-polished the rough edges of nature by applying mathematical formulas to the human figure to perfect it; the nineteenth-century painter Paul Cézanne once remarked that all of nature could be reduced to the cylinder, the sphere, and the cone.

One of the most perfect expressions of order and harmony is found in the fragile Japanese sand garden (Fig. 1–20). These medieval gardens frequently accompany pavilions and are placed at the service of Zen, a Buddhist sect that seeks inner harmony through introspection and meditation. The gentle raked pattern of the sand symbolizes water and rocks, and mountains reaching heavenward. Such gardens do not invite the observer to mill about; their perfection precludes walking. They are microcosms, really—universes unto themselves.

Frequently an artist will use composition to impose order on the disparate content of a work. Composition refers to the aesthetic arrangement of elements within a work of art. At first glance, Henri Matisse's *Piano Lesson* (Fig. 1–21) may not impress the casual viewer as a

masterpiece of order and organization. Yet every object, every color, virtually every line has been chosen and placed to lead the eye to every section of the piece. The pea-green wedge of drapery at the window is repeated in the shape of the metronome atop the piano, the wrought iron grillwork is complemented by the curvilinear lines of the music desk, and the enigmatic figure in the upper right background finds her counterpart in a small sculpture placed diagonally across the canvas. By way of contrast and repetition, there is unity within the diversity of objects.

When can order pose a threat to harmony and psychological well-being? Perhaps this is the question that Laurie Simmons set out to answer in her color photograph called *Red Library #2* (Fig. 1–22). Here, in a compulsively organized library, where nothing is a hair out of place, a robot-like woman assesses her job well done. She has become one with her task; even her dress, hair, and skin match the decor.

1–23 JAUNE QUICK-TO-SEE SMITH
ECLIPSE (1987). OIL ON CANVAS. 60 × 60″.
COLLECTION OF THE ARTIST. COURTESY STEINBAUM KRAUSS GALLERY, N.Y.

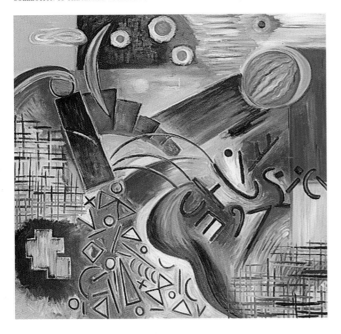

TO EXPRESS CHAOS

Just as beauty has its dark side and the intellect is balanced by the emotion, so too do order and harmony presume the existence of chaos. Artists have portrayed chaos in many ways throughout the history of art, seeking analogies in apocalyptic events such as war, famine, or natural catastrophe. But chaos can be suggested even in the absence of specific content. In *Eclipse* (Fig. 1–23), without reference to nature or reality, Native American artist Jaune Quick-To-See Smith creates an agitated, chaotic atmosphere of color, line, shape, and movement. The artist grew up on the Flathead Indian reservation in Montana and uses a full vocabulary of Native American geometric motifs and organic images from the rich pictorial culture of her ancestors.

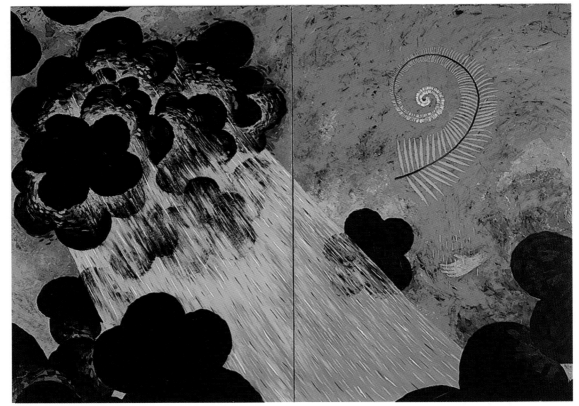

1–24 LOUISA CHASE
STORM (1981). OIL ON CANVAS. 90 × 120″.
DENVER ART MUSEUM; PURCHASED WITH FUNDS FROM NATIONAL ENDOWMENT FOR THE ARTS MATCHING FUND AND ALLIANCE FOR CONTEMPORARY ART. (1982.53).

1–25 ALFRED STIEGLITZ
THE STEERAGE (1907). PHOTOGRAPH.
COURTESY THE LIBRARY OF CONGRESS, WASHINGTON, D.C.

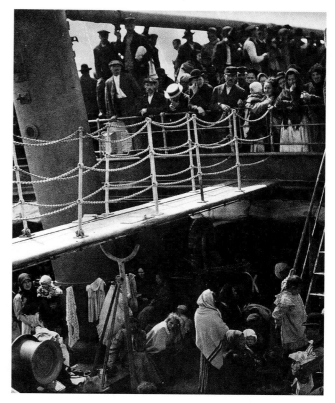

TO RECORD AND COMMEMORATE EXPERIENCE

Art is not a handicraft, it is the transmission of feeling the artist has experienced.
—Leo Tolstoy

From humanity's earliest days, art has served to record and communicate experiences and events. From prehistoric cave paintings, thought to record significant events in the history of paleolithic societies, to a work like the Vietnam Memorial in Washington, D.C., installed in honor of American service personnel who died during this country's involvement in that war, art has been used to inform future generations of what and who have gone before them. Art also serves to convey the personal experiences of an artist in ways that words cannot.

American painter Louisa Chase was inspired to paint nature's unbridled power as revealed in waves, waterfalls, and thunderstorms, though the intensity of her subjects is often tempered by her own presence in the piece. In *Storm* (Fig. 1–24), a cluster of thick, black clouds lets go a torrent of rain, which, in league with the decorative palette of pinks and purples, turns an artificial blue. The highly charged images on the left side of the canvas are balanced on the right by the most delicate of ferns, spiraling upward, nourished by the downpour. Beneath the sprig, the artist's hand cups the raindrops, becoming part of the painting, and part of nature's event as well. Chase said of a similar storm painting, "During the [marking] process I do become the storm—lost—yet not lost. An amazing feeling of losing myself yet remaining totally conscious."[3]

The photographer Alfred Stieglitz, who recognized the medium as a fine art as well as a tool for recording events, happened upon the striking composition of *The Steerage* (Fig. 1–25) on an Atlantic crossing aboard the Kaiser Wilhelm II. He rushed to his cabin for his camera, hoping that the upper and lower masses of humanity would maintain their balanced relationships to one another, to the drawbridge that divides the scene, to the stairway, the funnel, and the horizontal beam of the mast. The "steerage" of a ship was the

least expensive accommodation. Here the "huddled masses" seem suspended in limbo by machinery and by symbolic as well as actual bridges. Yet the tenacious human spirit may best be symbolized by the jaunty patch of light that strikes the straw hat of one passenger on the upper deck. Stieglitz was utterly fascinated and moved by what he saw:

I stood spellbound for a while, looking and looking. Could I photograph what I felt, looking and looking and still looking? I saw shapes related to each other. I saw a picture of shapes and underlying that the feeling I had about life. . . . Rembrandt came into my mind and I wondered would he have felt as I was feeling.[4]

Over eighty years after Stieglitz captured the great hope of immigrants entering New York harbor, African-American artist Faith Ringgold tells the story of life and

---

[3]Louisa Chase, journal entry for February 20, 1984, in *Louisa Chase* (New York: Robert Miller Gallery, 1984).

[4]Nathan Lyons, ed., *Foundations of Modern Photography,* (Englewood Cliffs: Prentice-Hall, 1966), p. 129.

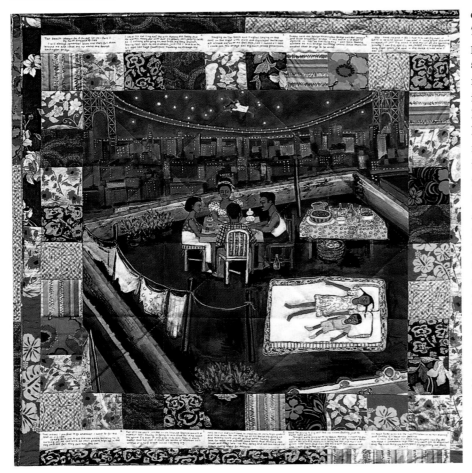

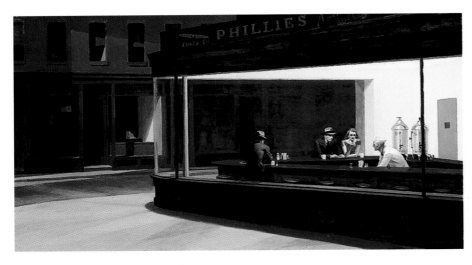

dreams on a tar-covered rooftop. *Tar Beach* (Fig. 1–26) is a painted patchwork quilt that stitches together the artist's memories of family, friends, and feelings while growing up in Harlem. Ringgold is noted for her use of materials and techniques associated with women's traditions, as well as her use of the narrative, or story-telling, a strong tradition in African-American families. A large, painted square with images of Faith, her brother, her parents, and neighbors dominates the quilt and is framed with brightly patterned pieces of fabric. Along the top and bottom are inserts crowded with Ringgold's written description of her experiences. This wonderfully innocent and joyful monologue begins:

I will always remember when the stars fell down around me and lifted me up above the George Washington Bridge . . .

TO REFLECT THE SOCIAL AND CULTURAL CONTEXT

Works of art all through the ages show us in the clearest fashion how mankind has changed, how a stage that has once appeared never reappears.
—Philipp Otto Runge

Faith Ringgold's *Tar Beach* tells us the story of a young girl growing up in Harlem. Her experiences take place within a specific social and cultural context. In recording experience, artists thus frequently record the activities and objects of their

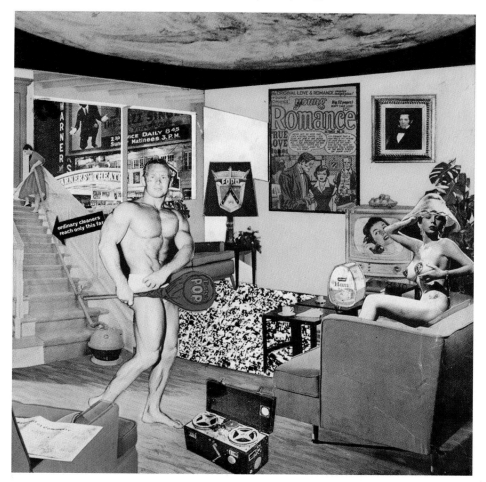

times and places, reflecting contemporary fashions and beliefs, as well as the states of the crafts and sciences.

The architecture, the hairstyles, hats and shoulder pads, even the price of cigars (only 5 cents), all set Edward Hopper's *Nighthawks* (Fig. 1–27) unmistakably in an American city during the late 1930s or 1940s. The subject is commonplace and uneventful, though somewhat eerie. There is a tension between the desolate spaces of the vacant street and the corner diner. Familiar objects become distant. The warm patch of artificial light seems precious, even precarious, as if night and all its troubled symbols are threatening to break in on disordered lives. Hopper uses a specific sociocultural context to communicate an unsettling, introspective mood of aloneness, of being outside the mainstream of experience.

In Richard Hamilton's *Just What Is It That Makes Today's Homes So Different, So Appealing?* (Fig. 1–28) the aims are identical, but the result is self-mocking, upbeat, and altogether fun. This little collage functions as a veritable time capsule for the 1950s, a decade during which the speedy advance of technology finds everyone buying pieces of the American dream. What is that dream? Comic books, TV, movies and tape recorders; canned hams and TV dinners; enviable physiques, tootsie-roll pops, vacuum cleaners that finally let the "lady of the house" clean all the stairs at once. Hamilton's piece serves as a memento of the time and the place and the values of the decade for future generations.

In a sense, Hamilton's work leaves nothing to the imagination. The images are devoid of symbolic content;

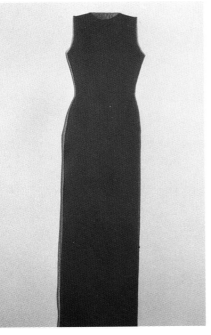

1–29 JUDITH SHEA
INAUGURAL BALL (1980). COTTON
ORGANDY. 67 × 24 × 1½".
JACK AND MARYON ADELAAR. MAX PROTETCH GALLERY.

they are what they are, as are their users. Quite the opposite is true of Judith Shea's *Inaugural Ball* (Fig. 1–29). On the surface, the red sheath gown seems spare and quite ordinary, something any woman might don for a special occasion. Yet the title of the work compels us to associate a specific time and place and individual with the garment. A quick look at the date places the inauguration at the beginning of Ronald Reagan's first term as President, and White House watchers will recall that First Lady Nancy's couture preference was for the color red. Is the artist suggesting that the

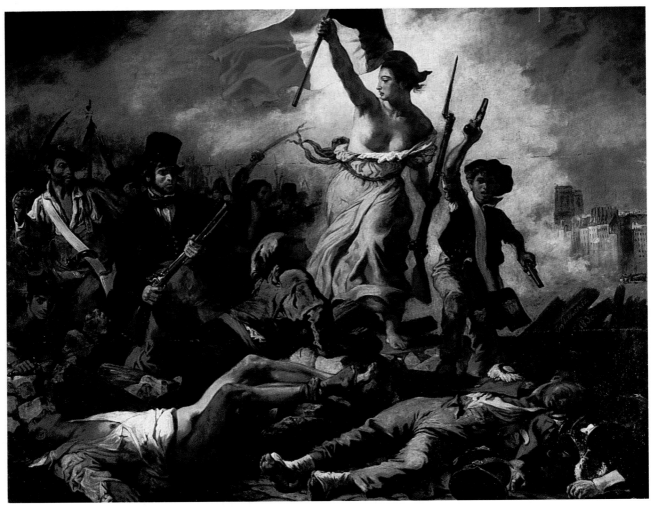

1–30 EUGÈNE DELACROIX
LIBERTY LEADING THE PEOPLE (1830). OIL ON CANVAS. 8'6" × 10'10".
LOUVRE MUSEUM, PARIS.

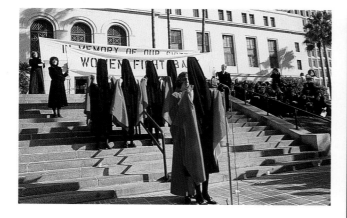

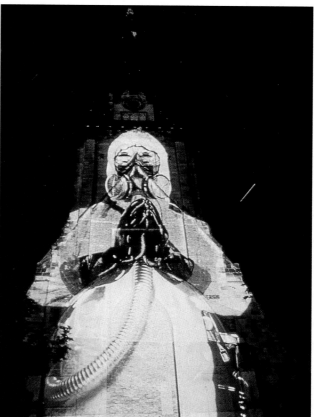

inauguration of a new President fills the people with hope, but that the First Lady can hope for little more than to fill the proper gown? When the people envision the President, perhaps they wonder, "What is he thinking? What will he do?" When the people envision the First Lady, perhaps they are more inclined to ask, "What is she wearing?"

To Protest Injustice and Raise Social Consciousness

> Art has always been employed by the different social classes who hold the balance of power as one instrument of domination—hence, a political instrument. One can analyze epoch after epoch—from the Stone Age to our own day—and see that there is no form of art which does not also play an essential political role.
> —Diego Rivera

Artists, like other people, have taken on bitter struggles against the injustices of their times. Like other people, they have tried to persuade others to join them in their causes, and it has been natural for them to use their creative skills to do so.

The nineteenth-century Spanish painter Francisco Goya used his art to satirize the political foibles of his day and to condemn the horrors of war (see Fig. 15–8). In the twentieth century another Spanish painter, Pablo Picasso, would condemn war in his masterpiece *Guernica* (Fig. 16–12).

Goya's French contemporary, Eugène Delacroix, painted the familiar image of *Liberty Leading the People* (Fig. 1–30) in order to keep the spirit of the French

Revolution alive in 1830. In this painting, people of all classes are united in rising up against injustice, led onward by an **allegorical** figure of liberty. Rifles, swords, a flag—even pistols—join in an upward rhythm, underscoring the classical pyramid shape of the composition.

Suzanne Lacy and Leslie Labowitz's performance, *In Mourning and in Rage* (Fig. 1–31), was a carefully orchestrated media event reminiscent of ancient public rituals. Members of feminist groups donned black robes to commemorate women who had been victims of rape-murders and to protest the shoddy media coverage usually given such tragedies.

Expatriate Polish artist Krzysztof Wodiczko projects huge slide images on public buildings to reveal their "true" function and to protest themes like authoritarianism and pollution. His *Projection on the Martin Luthur Kirche* (Fig. 1–32), a gigantic montage of a figure in gloves and a protective suit, focuses attention on industrial pollution.

WHEN THE *AMOROUS COUPLE* WAS CAPTURED IN CERAMIC BY A MESO-AMERICAN ARTIST, CHARLEMAGNE RULED THE HOLY ROMAN EMPIRE FROM HIS COURT IN WESTERN EUROPE.

1–33 MIRIAM SCHAPIRO
WONDERLAND (1983). ACRYLIC AND FABRIC COLLAGE ON CANVAS. 90 × 144″ (FRAMED)
COLLECTION: NATIONAL MUSEUM OF AMERICAN ART, SMITHSONIAN INSTITUTION, WASHINGTON D.C. COURTESY STEINBAUM KRAUSS
GALLERY, N.Y. © MIRIAM SCHAPIRO.

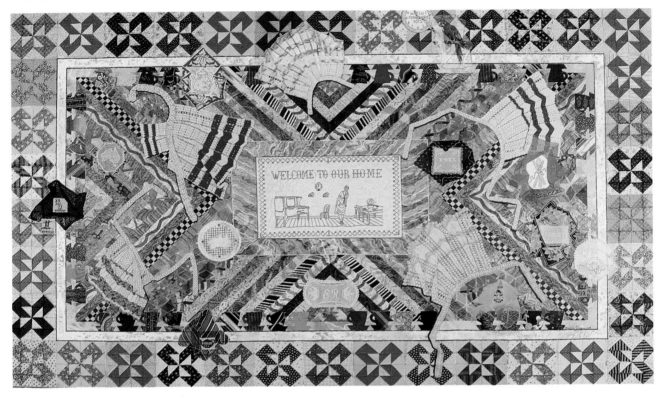

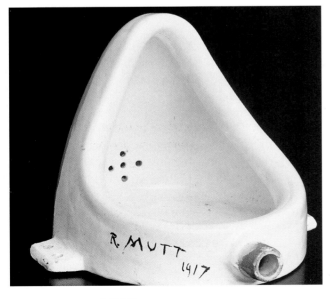

1–34 MARCEL DUCHAMP
FOUNTAIN (1917) (1951 VERSION AFTER LOST ORIGINAL).
PORCELAIN URINAL. 24″ HIGH.
COURTESY SIDNEY JANIS GALLERY, N.Y. © 1998 ARTISTS RIGHTS SOCIETY (ARS), N.Y./ADAGP,
PARIS. ESTATE OF MARCEL DUCHAMP.

TO ELEVATE THE COMMONPLACE

Have you come across embroidered dishtowels or aprons with the words "God Bless Our Happy Home" or "I Hate Housework"? Miriam Schapiro's *Wonderland* (Fig. 1–33) is a collage that reflects her "femmage" aesthetic—her interest in depicting women's domestic culture. The work contains ordinary doilies, needlework, crocheted aprons, handkerchiefs, and quilt blocks, all anchored to a geometric patterned background that is augmented with brushstrokes of paint. In the center is the most commonplace of the commonplace: an embroidered image of a housewife who curtsies beneath the legend, "Welcome to Our Home."

Some of the more interesting elevations of the commonplace to the realm of art are found in the **ready-mades** and **assemblages** of twentieth-century artists. Marcel Duchamp's *Fountain* (Fig. 1–34) is a urinal, turned upside down and labeled. Pablo Picasso's *Bull's Head* (Fig. 6-25) is fashioned from the seat and handlebars of an old bicycle. In **Pop art,** the dependence on commonplace objects and visual cliches

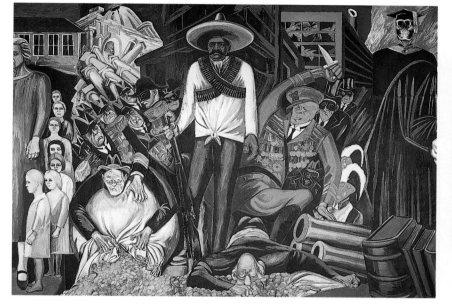

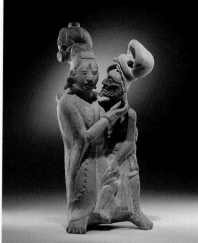

reaches a peak. Prepared foods, soup and beer cans, media images of beautiful women and automobile accidents—these became the subject matter of Pop art. As we saw in Figures 1–10 and 1–28, works of Pop art impel us to cast a more critical eye on the symbols and objects with which we surround ourselves.

TO MEET THE NEEDS OF THE ARTIST

Artists may have special talents and perceptive qualities, but they are also people. As people, they have a number of needs and are motivated to meet these needs.

The psychologist Abraham Maslow spoke of a hierarchy, or ordered arrangement, of needs, including (1) biological needs as for food and water; (2) safety needs; (3) needs for acceptance and love; (4) needs for achievement, recognition, approval, and prestige; and (5) the need for "self-actualization"—that is, the need to fulfill one's unique potential. Self-actualizing people have needs for novelty, exploration, and understanding, and they have aesthetic needs for art, beauty, and order.

In many cases, art permits the individual both to earn a living and to meet needs for achievement or self-actualization. Murals such as Jose Clemente Orozco's *Epic of American Civilization: Hispano-America* (Fig. 1–35) were created for a branch of the WPA, a federal work-relief program intended to help workers, including artists, survive the Great Depression. The WPA made it possible for many artists to meet basic needs as well as needs for achievement. Orozco, of course, also chose subject matter that enabled him to express his outrage at the financial and military injustices imposed upon the Mexican peasant.

Creating works of art that are accepted by one's audience can lead to an artist's social acceptance and recognition. In some quarters the very term "artist" elicits admiration and respect, although elsewhere it may arouse suspicion. Art can also provide the individual with an aesthetically stimulating opportunity to explore the underlying order in the external world and the limits of the mental world within.

STYLES OF ART

In the visual arts, **style** refers to the characteristic ways in which artists express themselves. Artists throughout history have portrayed familiar themes, but their works have differed not only in their social and cultural contexts, but also in their style.

Compare Figures 1–36 through 1–44. As a group, they are rich with similarities and differences. Of course, they are all works of art that portray couples. One way in which they differ, however, is in their sociocultural context—the Mayan ceramic couple (Fig. 1–36), for example, is an eighth- to tenth-century Pre-Columbian sculpture, whose garments, jewelry, and even facial features link it to that specific time and place. Those same tell-tale attributes are what link Roy Lichtenstein's

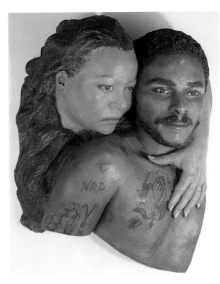

1–37 ROY LICHTENSTEIN

FORGET IT! FORGET ME! (1962). MAGNA AND OIL ON CANVAS.
79⅞ × 68".

ROSE ART MUSEUM, BRANDEIS UNIVERSITY, WALTHAM, MASS. GEVIRTZ-MINUCHIN PURCHASE FUND 1962.138. © ROY LICHTENSTEIN.

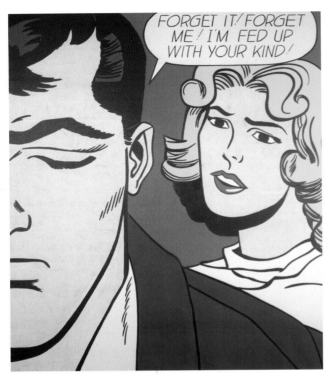

1–38 IDA APPLEBROOG

HAPPY BIRTHDAY TO ME (1982). ACRYLIC AND RHOPLEX ON CANVAS. 83 × 66½".

COURTESY RONALD FELDMAN FINE ARTS, N.Y.

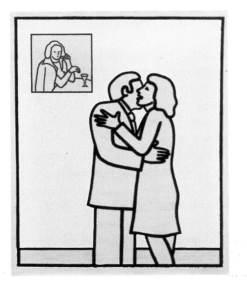

Forget It! Forget Me! (Fig. 1–37) to the United States in the decade of the sixties. Ida Applebroog's *Happy Birthday to Me* (Fig. 1–38), John Ahearn's *Mario and Norma* (Fig. 1–39), and Grant Wood's *American Gothic* (Fig. 1–40) all reflect aspects—rather diverse aspects—of modern America, whereas the tumult in Oskar Kokoschka's *The Whirlwind* (Fig. 1–43) reflects the location and era in which it was painted—Germany in the years leading to World War I. Constantin Brancusi's *The Kiss* (Fig. 1–41) could be said to be without context, while it may seem that the context of Jackson Pollock's *Male and Female* (Fig. 1–44) is not of this world. One could also speak of differences in the attitudes and behavior of the couples; some are kissing, one is arguing, one seems in danger of being swept away by the elements, one is very much a part of the element in which they dwell. Yet another way in which the works differ is in terms of *style*.

REALISTIC ART

The style of the Ahearn (Fig. 1–39) and Wood (Fig. 1–40) couples is described as **realistic.** The term *realism* has had many meanings in art; it is, for instance, the name of a specific school of art that flowered during the nineteenth century. But more broadly, realism refers to the portrayal of people and things as they are seen by the eye or really thought to be, without idealization, without distortion.

Ahearn's striking illusion of realism is achieved by first casting his models in plaster and then painting the surfaces with faithful flesh tones and exacting detail. The skin and hair color, distinctive facial features, and tattoos on Mario's arm add a sense of authenticity and personality to the piece.

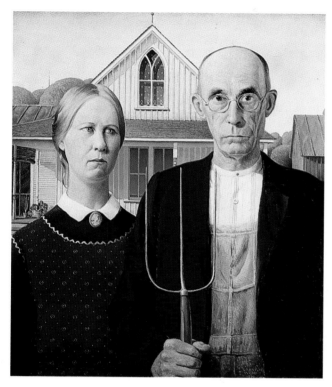

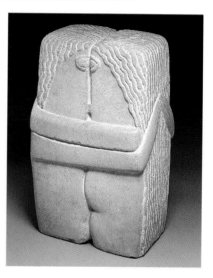

Grant Wood's familiar *American Gothic* is a painstakingly realistic portrait of the staid virtues of the rural life in America. It is also one of our more commercialized works of art; images derived from it have adorned boxes of breakfast cereal, greeting cards, and numerous other products. Note the repetition of the pitchfork pattern in the man's shirtfront, the upper-story window of the house, and the plant on the porch. He is very much tied to his environment; like the woman in Simmons's *Red Library #2* (Fig. 1–22), his identity has become one with his task. Were it not for the incongruously spry curl falling from the mistress's otherwise tucked-tight hairdo, we might view this composition—as well as the sitters therein—as solid, stolid, and monotonous.

REALISTIC VERSUS REPRESENTATIONAL ART The Applebroog and Lichtenstein couples are portrayed in a style that departs from strict realism, yet the observer clearly identifies the subject of each work as an interaction between a man and a woman. *Happy Birthday to Me* (Fig. 1–38) indicates that visual information in a work can be quite spare, but no less effective and suggestive. What is the connection between the embracing woman and her solitary counterpart (alone but for a drink) in the picture within the picture? Does time pass as we go from frame to frame? Is the estranged woman with the drink recalling past relationships, captured in

the bigger picture? Is the apparently happier woman doomed to aloneness—or alone within herself right now? Do we have a contemporary allegory about the fate that overhangs transient intimacies?

Lichtenstein's painting (Fig. 1–37), an example of Pop Art, also departs from realism, adopting instead the visual cliches of the comic strip. Both works can be described as **representational.**

The term *representational art,* often used synonymously with *figurative art,* is defined as art which portrays, however altered or distorted, things perceived in the visible world. One could also say that representational art refers to art that represents people or objects in something of a *recognizable form.* The people in the Lichtenstein may not be realistic, but they are clearly recognizable. The Mayan couple (Fig. 1–36) are similarly representational but not realistic.

A number of aspects of the Brancusi sculpture (Fig. 1–41) are recognizable. One can determine an upper torso, arms, eyes, and hair. Yet the artist seems to have been more interested in the independent relationships of the forms, or in expressing his own perceptions of the act of kissing, than in being true to the human form. For this reason many people would not characterize *The Kiss* as representational. As we shall later see, *The Kiss* is an example of abstract art.

EXPRESSIONISTIC ART

In **expressionistic** art, form and color are freely distorted by the artist in order to achieve a heightened emotional impact. **Expressionism** also refers to a

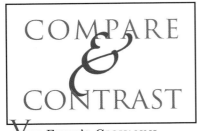

COMPARE & CONTRAST

Van Eyck's *Giovanni Arnolfini and His Bride* with Kokoschka's *The Whirlwind*

The style of a work of art refers to the characteristic ways in which artists express themselves and the times in which they live. As we can see in this section with the theme of couples, a full range of media, methods, and styles contribute to the uniqueness of each work. If you add to these the historical and cultural contexts of the works, you gain insight into the way in which art reflects society.

In this text's first Compare and Contrast feature, let us consider Jan van Eyck's *Giovanni Arnolfini and His Bride* (Fig. 1–42) and Oskar Kokoschka's *The Whirlwind* (Fig. 1–43). What are the *stylistic* differences between the paintings?

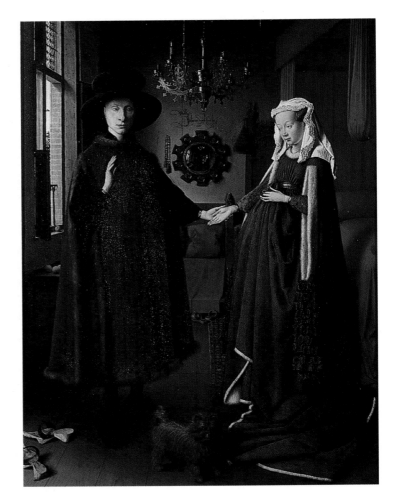

1–42 JAN VAN EYCK
Giovanni Arnolfini and His Bride (1434). Oil on wood. 33 × 22½″.

The Whirlwind is expressionistic; how would you describe the van Eyck? How do you think that the style of each work reflects the context in which it was created? How do the attitudes and behavior of the couples differ?

What can you say about each artist's brushwork? How do the brushstrokes contribute to the emotional tone of each painting? (Can you imagine the van Eyck being rendered with Kokoschka's brushwork, or vice versa?) As you contemplate the stylistic differences, it may be helpful to consider the functions of each painting. The van Eyck painting was more than a portrait; it was intended in part to serve as a record of a marriage vow. It contains a wealth of objects invested with symbolism that pertains to the marriage ceremony. The Kokoschka is bereft of such objects or symbols. What difference does the presence of symbols make in the viewer's understanding of each work?

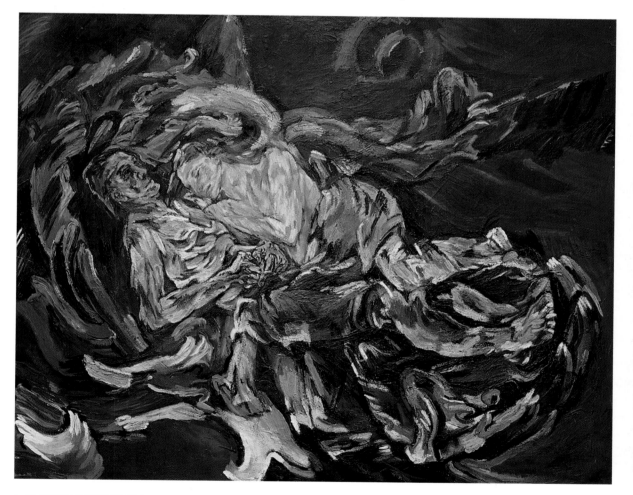

1–43 OSKAR KOKOSCHKA
THE WHIRLWIND (1914).
OIL ON CANVAS. 71½ × 86½".

1–44 JACKSON POLLOCK
MALE AND FEMALE. OIL ON CANVAS. 73¼ × 49″.
PHILADELPHIA MUSEUM OF ART, GIFT OF MR. AND MRS. H. GATES LLOYD. (74-232-1) © 1998
POLLOCK-KRASNER FOUNDATION/ARTISTS RIGHTS SOCIETY (ARS), N.Y.

1–45 JEAN ARP
HUMAN CONCRETION (1935). ORIGINAL PLASTER,
19½ × 18¾ × 25½″.
THE MUSEUM OF MODERN ART, N.Y. GIFT OF THE ADVISORY COMMITTEE. © 1998 ARTISTS RIGHTS
SOCIETY (ARS), N.Y./VG BILD-KUNST, BONN.

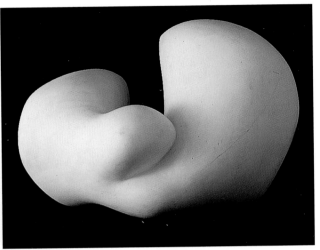

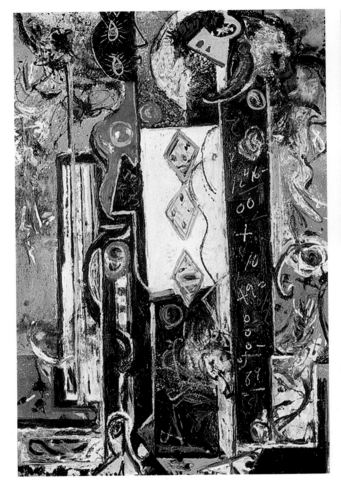

ABSTRACT ART

The term **abstract art** applies to art that departs significantly from the actual appearance of things. Such art may be completely **nonobjective,** or **non-representational,** or it may convert reality into forms that can be appreciated for their own sake. Brancusi created *The Kiss* in order to capture what, to him, was the essential nature of the act of kissing—the merging of the participants—not to recreate the actual forms of the human subjects. The independent relationships of the forms override the realities of the human figure. Brancusi's sculpture, though abstract, refers to realistic subject matter, that is, to people.

In *The Kiss,* we perceive the human torso reduced into a simple block form. Twentieth-century proponents of **Cubism,** such as Pablo Picasso and Georges Braque (see Figs. 16–8 to 16–12), also reduced natural forms into largely angular geometrical equivalents. To some degree, despite their reduction to geometrical forms, the figures of Picasso and Braque remain recognizable. We can pick them out if we work at it.

Jackson Pollock's *Male and Female* (Fig. 1–44) is yet another depiction of a couple, but the "figures" are a great deal more difficult to locate than Brancusi's. At the time of the painting, Pollock was undergoing psychoanalysis, and he was quite convinced that the unconscious played a major role in his art. Using a method called **psychic automatism,** Pollock attempted to clear his mind of purpose and concerns so that inner conflicts and ideas could find expression through his work.

modern art movement, but many earlier works are expressionistic in the broader sense of the term.

In *The Burial of Count Orgaz* (Fig. 13–13), El Greco's expressionistic elongation of the heavenly figures seems to emphasize their ethereal spirituality. **Postimpressionist** Vincent van Gogh relied on both an expressionistic palette and brushwork to transfer emotion to his canvases.

Kokoschka's expressionistic painting, *The Whirlwind* (Fig. 1–43), is marked by frenzied brushstrokes that mirror the torment of his inner life, as well as the impending darkness of war in Germany. Reclining figures occupy the center of a dark, imaginary landscape. Images of earth, water, and flesh merge in a common palette and bevy of strokes; little distinguishes one from another. All seem caught up in a churning sky, very much in danger of being swept away.

Pollock would have agreed with painter Edgar Degas's remark that "The artist does not draw what he sees, but what he must make others see. Only when he no longer knows what he is doing does the painter do good things."

Sometimes abstract art makes no reference to reality. We call such art nonobjective or non-representational. Many twentieth-century artists, such as Helen Frankenthaler, create nonobjective works. In *Magic Carpet* (Fig. 2–9), Frankenthaler poured rather than brushed her paint onto the canvas to create shapes that are evocative, but nonetheless non-representational. Viewers may find much that seems familiar in her composition—perhaps a landscape with accumulating cloud masses, but the content of the work is technically nonobjective.

Here is a twist: Consider the sculpture in Figure 1–45. Certainly it is abstract. Is it *nonobjective,* however? Were it not for the title, one could not be faulted for labeling it nonobjective. After all, the abstract forms are not necessarily derived from objects in the real world. But the title of the piece, *Human Concretion,*

suggests that the sculpture is after all derived from the human figure, or at least shares certain organic qualities with the human figure.

As we noted at the outset, the question "What is art?" has no single answer and raises many other questions. Our discussion of the meanings, purposes, and styles of art is meant to facilitate the individual endeavor to understand art, but is not intended to be exhaustive. Some people will feel that we have omitted several important meanings and purposes of art; others will disagree with our definitions of some of the styles of art. But these considerations hint at the richness and elusiveness of the concept of art.

In Chapter 2 we shall expand our discussion of the meanings and purposes of art to include the "language" of art. That chapter will not provide us with a precise definition of art either, but it will afford us insight into the ways in which artists use elements of art such as line, shape, color, and texture to create works of art. Even though art has always been with us, the understanding of art is in its infancy.

key terms

Art	Pop art	Figurative art	Non-representational
Allegorical	Style	Expressionistic art	art
Ready-made art	Realistic art	Abstract art	Psychic automatism
Assemblage	Representational art	Nonobjective art	

artists

Leonardo da Vinci	Jenny Holzer	Krzysztof Wodiczko
Sandro Botticelli	Henri Matisse	Miriam Schapiro
Joyce Kozloff	Laurie Simmons	Marcel Duchamp
Frida Kahlo	Jaune Quick-to-See Smith	Jose Clemente Orozco
Robert Mapplethorpe	Louisa Chase	Roy Lichtenstein
Michelangelo	Alfred Stieglitz	Ida Applebroog
Andy Warhol	Faith Ringgold	John Ahearn
Judy Chicago	Edward Hopper	Grant Wood
Jessie Oonark	Richard Hamilton	Jan van Eyck
Aaron Douglas	Judith Shea	Oskar Kokoschka
Marc Chagall	Eugène Delacroix	Constantin Brancusi
Max Beckmann	Suzanne Lacy	Jackson Pollock
Gertrude Käsebier	Leslie Labowitz	Jean Arp

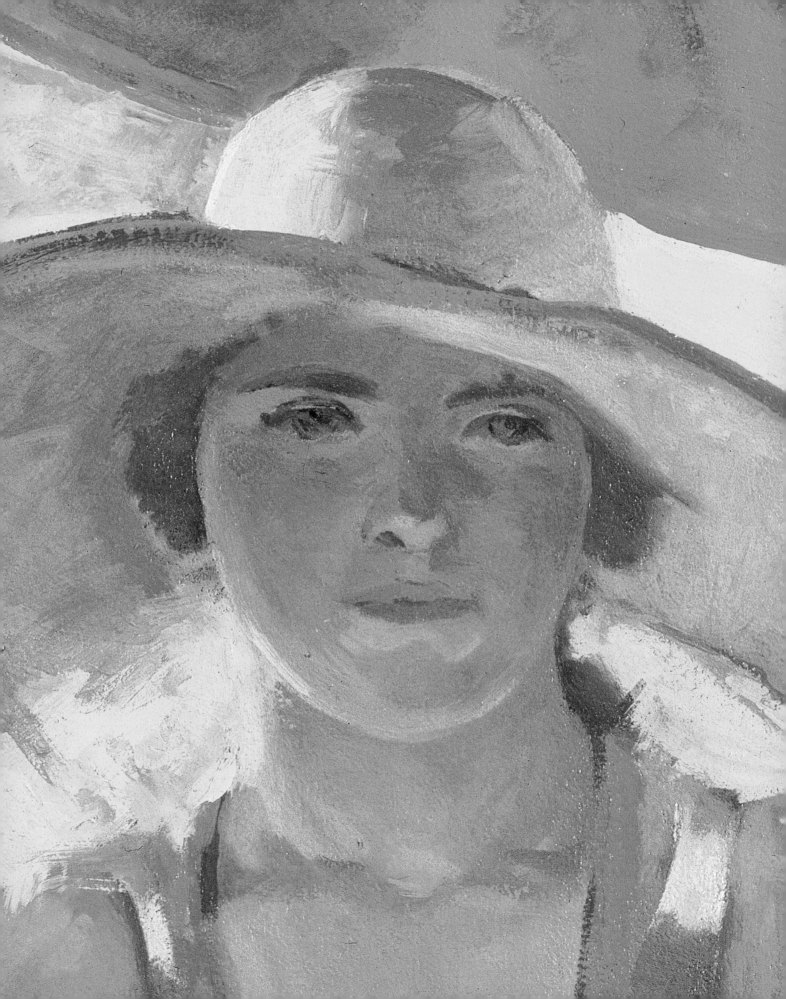

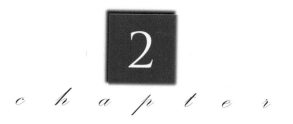

THE LANGUAGE OF ART: ELEMENTS, COMPOSITION, AND CONTENT

PRELIMINARY *Sketch*

- ❏ Light is a form of electromagnetic energy that stimulates the eyes and produces visual sensations.

- ❏ You obtain yellow light when you mix red and green light.

- ❏ The colors in a work of art evoke emotional responses from viewers.

- ❏ Warm colors such as oranges and yellows seem to advance toward the viewer, whereas cool colors such as blues and greens seem to recede from the viewer.

- ❏ We see plants as green because the pigment in chlorophyll absorbs other hues and reflects only green.

- ❏ Objects appear to change in color depending on their distance from us and lighting conditions.

- ❏ Part of the content of a work of art may be in you, not in the work itself.

Beatrice Whitney Van Ness, *Summer Sunlight* (detail). See Figure 2–20.

Teach me half the gladness
that thy brain must know—
such harmonious madness
from my lips would flow
the world should listen then,
as I am listening now.
          —*Percy Bysshe Shelley, "To a Skylark"*

2–1 ELIE NADELMAN
Head of a Woman (1907). Pen and ink and pencil on brown paper. 21 × 12⅝″.
ALBRIGHT-KNOX ART GALLERY, BUFFALO, N.Y.; CHARLES W. GOODYEAR FUND, 1953.

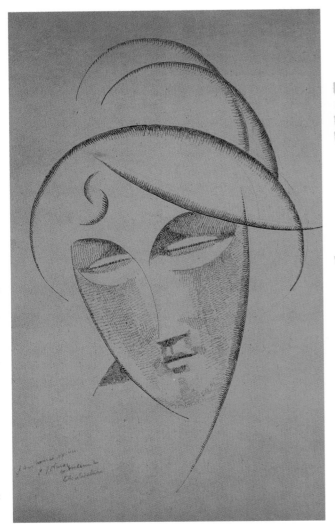

The communication between artist and viewer is something like the miraculous songs of the skylark falling on the ears of the poet. Artists project their experiences and their feelings—all the gladness and agony that their brains must know—into their artistic creations. But unlike the skylark, whose lyrical carols are instinctive, artists rely on their craft and talent to replicate nature or to make manifest that which is within.

Artists select from a variety of media, including, but by no means limited to, drawing, painting, sculpture, architecture, photography, textiles, ceramics. They then employ the **plastic elements** of art—line, shape, texture, shading, color, and so on—to express themselves in this medium. In their self-expression, they use the plastic elements to create **compositions** of a certain **content.**

ART AS LANGUAGE

Plastic elements, composition, and content—these three comprise what we refer to as the language of art. A **language** is a means of communicating thoughts and feelings. In spoken and written languages we communicate by means of sounds and symbols; in the visual arts we communicate through media.

Languages like English and French have symbols such as letters or words that are combined according to rules of grammar to create a message. The visual arts have plastic elements that are composed or organized according to principles of unity, balance, and rhythm, among others. The composition of the elements creates the content of the work—even if this content is an abstract image and not a natural **subject,** such as a human figure or a landscape.

In this chapter we explore the language of art and examine the ways in which artists organize the elements of art in their creations.

ELEMENTS OF ART

The elements in the language of art include line, shape, light, color, texture, mass, and space. Artists also use actual and implied time and motion as compositional elements.

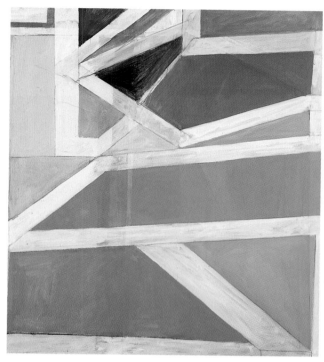

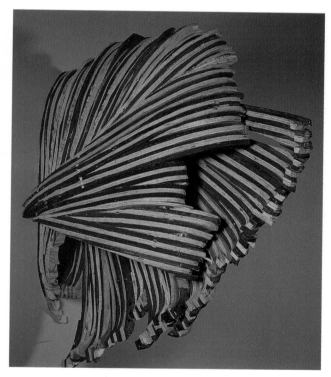

LINE

A **line** is the mark left by a moving point. Lines can be straight or curved. In geometry the line has no width, but in the visual arts lines may be light and slender or dark and thick. Lines imply action because they are created by action. In sculpture and other three-dimensional media, lines are perceived edges that define and contain forms. Lines may be perceived as delicate, tentative, elegant, assertive, forceful, or even brutal.

The line, as an element of art, is alive with possibilities. Artists use line to outline shapes, to evoke forms and movement, to imply solid mass, and even for its own sake. In groupings, lines can create shadows and even visual illusions.

Elie Nadelman's pen drawing, *Head of a Woman* (Fig. 2–1) uses a paucity of lines to evoke the major contours of the head and simple coiffure. Short, crosshatched lines are used to mold smaller contours, as in the delicate construction of the lips and the shadows beneath the eyebrows and nose.

In *Ocean Park # 22* (Fig. 2–2), Richard Diebenkorn separates color fields of blue and green with thick white lines that overlap and intersect to form the predominant pattern in the painting. The effect is akin to slats of wood nailed across an open window or supporting an architectural structure.

Heide Fasnacht's wooden construction, *Pell Mell II* (Fig. 2–3) consists of wooden rings stained with India ink to create a bold linear pattern that mimics the flowing shapes and the raw splintery surfaces of the material. Here line is used to highlight the structure and provide a directionality to the piece.

2–4 OGATA KORIN
RED AND WHITE PLUMS IN THE SPRING (TOKUGAWA PERIOD, LATE 17TH–EARLY 18TH CENTURY) (ONE OF A PAIR OF TWO-FOLD SCREENS).
MOA MUSEUM, ATAMI.PPS.

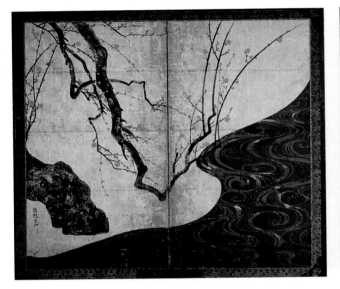
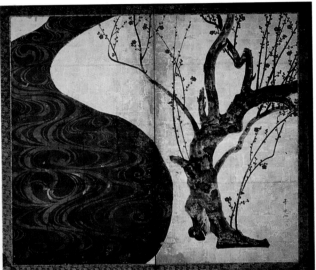

Red and White Plums in the Spring (Fig. 2–4) is a two-fold screen by Japanese decorative painter Ogata Korin (1658–1716). Here masterful lines serve their traditional functions of outlining shapes—in this case, some of the more strident shapes of nature. The rash diagonal of the branch plunges toward, then recoils from, the gentler ebb and flow of the waters beneath. The unnatural golden ground serves as a backdrop for the sparkling buds and blossoms.

SHAPE

During the early twentieth century, Gestalt psychologists studied human perception and developed a number of principles of perceptual organization. For example, we organize lines and shapes into figure-ground relationships. That is, we perceive figures against backgrounds. We also tend to integrate parts into meaningful wholes, even when there are gaps in sensory information. If it were not for the tendency to perceive meaningful forms

from shards of information, how would we interpret the hair of Nadelman's *Head of a Woman.*

Shape can be communicated in a number of ways. In *Red and White Plums in the Spring,* shape is clearly communicated by dominant lines that enclose specific areas of the painted screen. Shape can also be communicated through patches of color or texture. In three-dimensional works such as sculpture and architecture, shape is discerned when the work is viewed against its environment. The edges, colors, and textures of the work give it shape against the background.

The *Black Hummingbird Pattern Quilt* (Fig. 2–5) by an unknown Amish artist is a playful demonstration of figure-ground relationships. The quilt is constructed of octagonal and diamond-shaped pieces of cloth in black and primary colors. The viewer alternately focuses on the octagons and the diamond shapes, bringing each in turn to the foreground, because neither pattern is by its nature secondary to, or supportive of, the other.

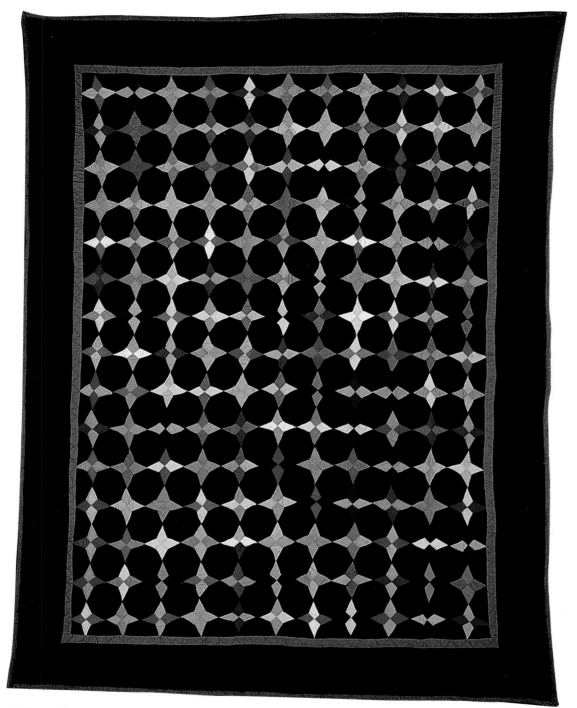

2–5 BLACK HUMMINGBIRD
PATTERN QUILT (C. 1925),
UNKNOWN ARTIST. (AMISH,
SHIPSHEWANA, INDIANA).
COTTON. 88 × 66″.

COLLECTION, MUSEUM OF AMERICAN
FOLK ART, N.Y. GIFT OF DAVID POTTINGER
(1980.37.69).

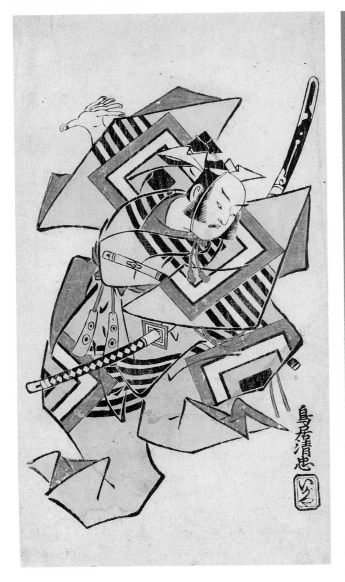

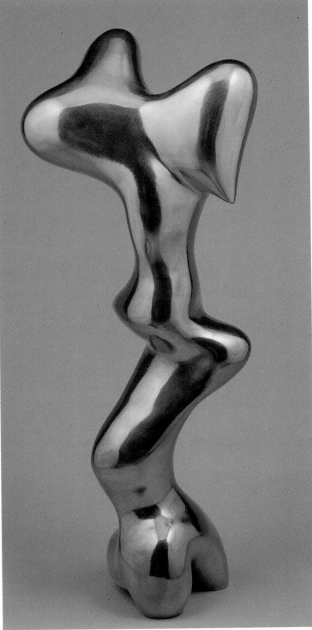

In Torii Kiyotada's (Fig. 2–6) portrait of an actor, a
veritable flurry of angular shapes weaves in and out of
one another in a complex fashion, creating a sense of
dynamic movement. The actor, while apparently fierce
and energetic, seems almost as much a prisoner to these
shapes as he is perpetrator of extreme posture and
movement. Here, too, our perspective shifts as we focus
now on the head or hand of the actor, now on his sword
and scabbard, which form a unified crescent arcing
through the composition.

Figure 2–10 also illustrates the variety of shapes
an artist might create from organic and geometric to
well-defined or amorphous. **Organic** shapes, like those
of the head and hand, reflect those found in nature.
Most of the organic shapes found in art are soft,

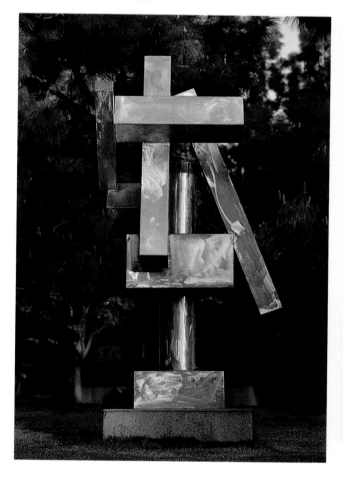

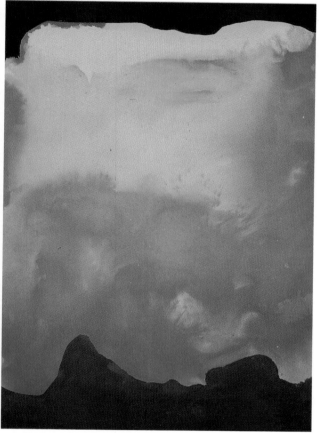

curvilinear, and irregular, although some natural shapes, such as those found in the structure of crystals, are harsh and angular. **Geometric** shapes are regular and precise, such as triangles, rectangles, and circles.

Jean Arp's bronze sculpture, aptly titled *Growth* (Fig. 2–7), has the semblance of skin wrapping bone. While it is natural in the sense of having an organic form, it is clearly not of nature, but of Arp's fantasy. In sharp contrast, the sculpture of David Smith (as in *CUBI XX,* Fig. 2–8) assembles machined cylinders, cubes, and other shapes into aesthetic geometric puzzles.

Shapes, however, need not be clearly defined shapes or derived from nature or the laws of geometry. Many artists, such as the contemporary painter

Helen Frankenthaler, create amorphous shapes. In *Magic Carpet* (Fig. 2–9), Frankenthaler literally poured paint onto her canvas, creating a nebulous work dense in form and rich in texture. The picture may evoke mountains against a sky of billowing cumulus clouds—indeed, it feels as though something is about to break loose—but the painting does not in fact represent reality.

LIGHT

According to the Bible, in the beginning light was set apart from darkness. Light was good and the potential for evil lay in darkness. We speak of the "light" of reason. In almost all cultures light symbolizes goodness and knowledge. What is this stuff called light? **Light** is electromagnetic energy of various wavelengths, that part of the spectrum that stimulates the eyes and produces visual sensations.

ONE YEAR BEFORE MALEVICH PAINTED HIS *SUPREMACIST COMPOSITION*, THE CZARIST
GOVERNMENT OF RUSSIA WAS OVERTURNED IN THE VIOLENT UPHEAVAL KNOWN AS THE
RUSSIAN REVOLUTION.

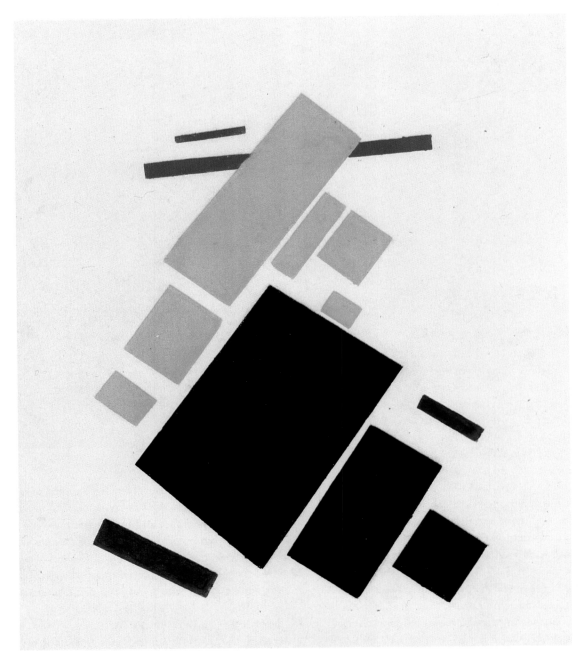

2–10 KASIMIR MALEVICH
SUPREMATIST COMPOSITION:
AEROPLANE FLYING (1915,
DATED 1914). 22⅞ × 19″.
THE MUSEUM OF MODERN ART, N.Y.,
PURCHASE.

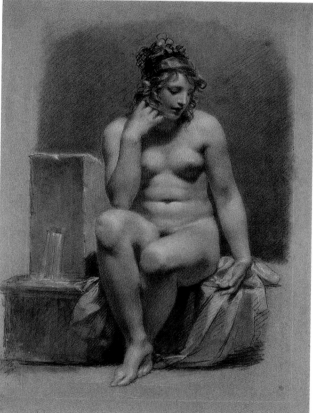

The **value** of a color of a surface is its lightness or darkness. The value is determined by the amount of light reflected by the surface: the greater the amount of light reflected, the lighter the surface. More light is reflected by a white surface than by a gray surface, and gray reflects more than black. White, therefore, is lighter than gray, and gray is lighter than black.

Pictures that strongly contrast light and dark often make forceful differentiations between figure and ground, as do the geometric shapes in Kasimir Malevich's *Suprematist Composition: Aeroplane Flying* (Fig. 2–10). In Malevich's *Suprematist Composition: White on White* (Fig. 2–11), a geometric shape is outlined, but there is no contrast in values between the figure and the background. Thus the work is subtle, not forceful. The viewer must work to perceive the form in the painting. Malevich wished to evoke a pure emotional response from the viewer by removing the content of his work from the world of natural forms. The foreground and background squares are both off-white, differentiated only by size, position, and slight variations in texture and hue.

By use of many gradations of value, objects portrayed on a flat surface can be given a rounded,

three-dimensional appearance. The method of gradually shifting from light to dark to create the illusion of a curved surface is called **chiaroscuro.**

In *La Source* (Fig. 2–12), Pierre-Paul Prud'hon creates the illusion of rounded surfaces on blue-gray paper by using black and white chalk to portray light gradually dissolving into shade. His subtle **modeling** of the nude is facilitated by the middle value of the paper and the gradation of tones from light to dark through a series of changing greys. Prud'hon's light source is not raking and harsh, but diffuse and natural. The forms are not sharply outlined; we must work to find outlining anywhere but in the drapery and in the hair. The softly brushed edges of the figure lead your eye to perceive three-dimensional form (continuing around into space) rather than flat, two-dimensional shape.

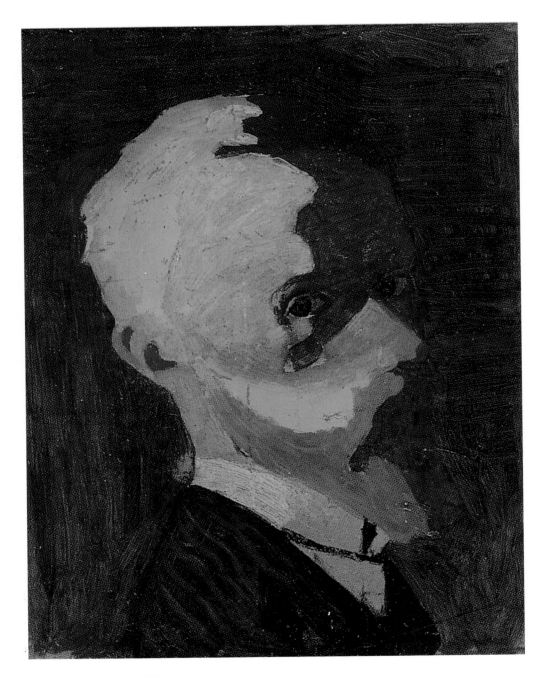

2–13 EDOUARD VUILLARD
SELF-PORTRAIT (1892).
OIL ON BOARD. 14½ × 11¼″.

2–14 DOROTHEA ROCKBURNE
ARENA IV (1978). VELLUM, MYLAR TAPE, VARNISH, ON
100% RAGBOARD. 54½ × 47″.

2–15 PRISM

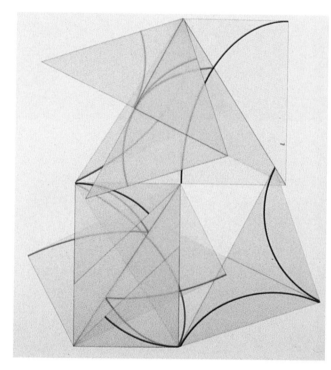

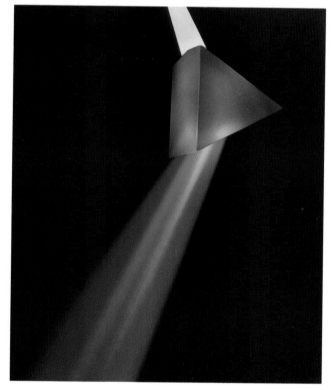

Edouard Vuillard's *Self-Portrait* (Fig. 2–13) is a harsh counterpoint to Prud'hon's drawing. A spotlighting effect creates strong contrasts between light and shadow, eliminating the gradual progression of tones used in chiaroscuro. The planes of the face turn into a dramatic relief. As in a high-contrast photograph, form leaps from blackness, and the stern lighting and unnatural palette flatten the portrait into abstract patterns.

Dorothea Rockburne's *Arena IV* (Fig. 2–14) is a meditative abstraction that suggests the artist's preoccupation with mathematical relationships and balance. Her *Arena* works, inspired by Giotto's Arena Chapel frescoes in Padua, consist of arcs of color that filter through overlapping shapes of translucent parchment. Much of the composition is built from this overlapping and the resultant implication of varying quantities of light.

COLOR

Color is a central element in our spoken language as well as in the language of art. We also connect emotion with color: We speak of being blue with sorrow, red with anger, green with envy. The poets paint a thoughtful mood as a brown study.

The color in works of art can also trigger strong emotional responses in the observer, working hand in hand with line and shape to enrich the viewing experience. The **Postimpressionist** Vincent van Gogh chose color more for its emotive qualities rather than for its fidelity to nature. In some amorphous abstract works, such as *Magic Carpet* (Fig. 2–9), color itself seems to be much of the "message" being communicated by the artist. The yellow form seems to billow and swell; the darker shading within is ominous. Subtle changes in tonality create a mysterious light that envelops the viewer.

And so, it is time for us to ask, What is color?

You have no doubt seen a rainbow or observed how light sometimes separates into several colors when it is filtered through a window. Sir Isaac Newton discovered that sunlight, or white light, can be broken down into different colors by a triangular glass solid called a **prism** (Fig. 2–15).

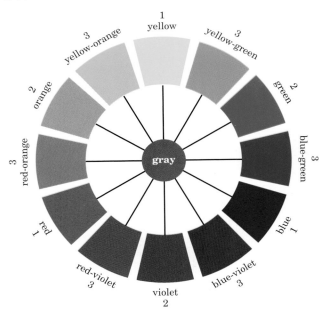

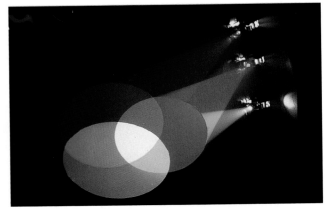

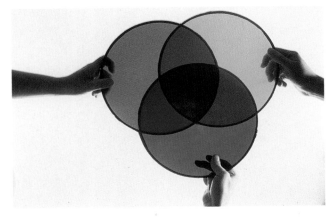

PSYCHOLOGICAL DIMENSIONS OF COLOR: HUE, VALUE, AND SATURATION   The wavelength of light determines its color, or **hue.** The visible spectrum consists of the colors red, orange, yellow, green, blue, indigo, and violet. The wavelength for red is longer than that for orange, and so on through violet.

The value of a color, like the value of any light, is its degree of lightness or darkness. If we wrap the colors of the spectrum around into a circle, we create a color wheel such as that shown in Figure 2–16. (Note that we must add some purples not found in the spectrum in order to complete the circle.) Yellow is the lightest of the colors on the wheel, and violet is the darkest. As we work our way around from yellow to violet, we encounter progressively darker colors. Blue-green is about equal in value to red-orange, but green is lighter than red.

The colors on the green-blue side of the color wheel are considered **cool** in "temperature," whereas the colors on the yellow-orange-red side are considered **warm.** Perhaps greens and blues suggest the coolness of the ocean or the sky, and hot things tend to burn red or orange. A room decorated in green or blue may appear more appealing on a hot day in July than a room decorated in red or orange. On a canvas, warm colors seem to advance toward the picture plane, a phenomenon that partly explains why the oranges and yellows of *Summer Sunlight* (see Fig. 2–20) appear to pulsate toward the viewer. Cool colors, on the other hand, seem to recede.

The **saturation** of a color is its pureness. Pure hues have the greatest intensity, or brightness. The saturation, and hence the intensity, decrease when another hue or black, gray, or white are added.

Artists produce **shades** of a given hue by adding black, and **tints** by adding white.

COMPLEMENTARY VERSUS ANALOGOUS COLORS   The colors opposite each other on the color wheel are said to be **complementary.** Red-green and blue-yellow are the major complementary pairs. If we mix complementary colors together, they dissolve into neutral gray.

Wait! you may say: Blue and yellow cannot be "complementary" because by mixing **pigments** of blue and yellow we create green, not gray. That is true, but we are talking about mixing *lights,* not pigments. Light is the source of all color; pigments reflect and absorb different wavelengths of light selectively. The mixture of lights is an *additive* process, whereas the mixture of pigments is *subtractive* (see Fig. 2–17).

Pigments attain their colors by absorbing light from certain segments of the spectrum and reflecting the rest. For example, we see most plant life as green because the pigment in chlorophyll absorbs most of the red, blue, and violet wavelengths of light. The remaining green is reflected. A red pigment absorbs most of the spectrum but reflects red. White pigment reflects all

ON JANUARY 2, 1776, THE FIRST FLAG OF THE UNITED STATES WAS RAISED IN CAMBRIDGE, MASS., BY GEORGE WASHINGTON. THE FLAG AS WE KNOW IT, WITH STARS FOR EVERY STATE, WAS SANCTIONED BY CONGRESS 18 MONTHS LATER. BETSY ROSS APPEARS TO HAVE HAD NOTHING TO DO WITH THE DESIGN, AFTER ALL.

2–18 JASPER JOHNS
FLAGS (1965). OIL ON CANVAS WITH RAISED CANVAS. 72 × 48″.
© JASPER JOHNS/LICENSED BY VAGA, N.Y. PHOTO COURTESY OF LEO CASTELLI GALLERY, N.Y.

2–19 VICTOR VASARELY
ORION (1956). PAPER ON PAPER MOUNTED ON WOOD.
6′ 10½″ × 6′ 6¾″.
HIRSHHORN MUSEUM AND SCULPTURE GARDEN, SMITHSONIAN INSTITUTION, WASHINGTON, DC.
GIFT OF JOSEPH H. HIRSHHORN, 1966. © 1998 ARTISTS RIGHTS SOCIETY (ARS), N.Y./ADAGP, PARIS.

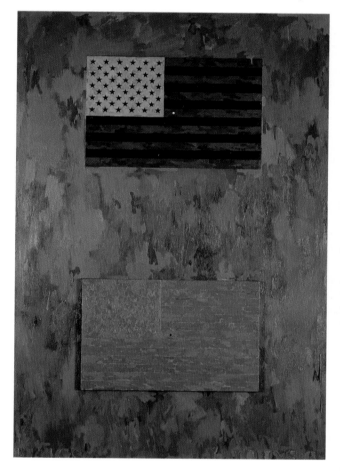

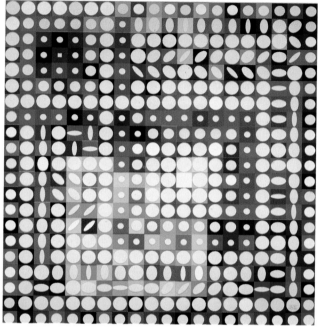

colors equally. Black pigment reflects very little light; it absorbs all wavelengths without prejudice. Black and white may be considered colors, but not hues. Black, white, and their mixture of gray are **achromatic,** or neutral, "colors," also referred to simply as **neutrals.**

The pigments of red, blue, and yellow are the **primary colors**, those that we cannot produce by mixing other hues. **Secondary colors** are created by mixing pigments of the primary colors. The three secondary colors are orange (derived from mixing red and yellow), green (blue and yellow), and violet (red and blue), denoted by the number 2 on the color wheel. **Tertiary colors** are created by mixing pigments of primary and adjoining secondary colors and are denoted by a 3 on the color wheel.

An interesting phenomenon occurs when we stare at colors for a while and then look away. Try this experiment:

Look at the light-colored dot in the center of the green, black, and yellow flag painted by Jasper Johns (Fig. 2–18) for about thirty seconds. Then gaze at the dot in the center of the rectangle below. If you have followed directions and are not color-blind, you should see the familiar red, white, and blue. The red, white, and blue flag is an **afterimage** of the green, black, and yellow. Why do afterimages occur? The eye is constructed so that prolonged sensations of color become opposed by perception of the complementary color. The same holds true for black and white; staring at one will create an afterimage of the other.

Hues that lie next to one another on the color wheel are **analogous.** They form families of color such as yellow and orange, orange and red, and green and blue. As we work our way around the wheel, the families intermarry, such as blue with violet and violet with red. Works that use closely related families of color seem harmonious, like the Japanese woodcut of the actor (Fig. 2–6). Works that juxtapose colors which lie across from one another on the color wheel will have the opposite effect. They will appear jarring and discordant rather than harmonious.

Victor Vasarely's *Orion* (Fig. 2–19) is an assemblage of paper cut-outs that take on different intensities depending on their backgrounds. Vasarely, an "Op Artist,"

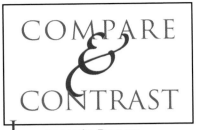
COMPARE & CONTRAST

LIBERMAN'S *PHOTO
OF PICASSO*
WITH
VAN NESS'S *SUMMER
SUNLIGHT*

The highly saturated and vibrant colors of Beatrice Whitney Van Ness's *Summer Sunlight* (Fig. 2–20) evoke the sense of a sultry summer day. Everything is bathed in a hot orange-yellow light that filters through the beach umbrella and the woman's hat to impart an intense orange glow to her face and body. Patches of cool blue offer the viewer's eye respite from the overall heat of reds and yellows, much as a swim is the only escape from the intense heat of the summer afternoon.

Compare and contrast Van Ness's painting with the photograph of Pablo Picasso by Alexander Liberman (Fig. 2–21). How do the colors in the photograph capture the sense of summer? What are some of the similarities between the painting and the photograph? What are some of the differences?

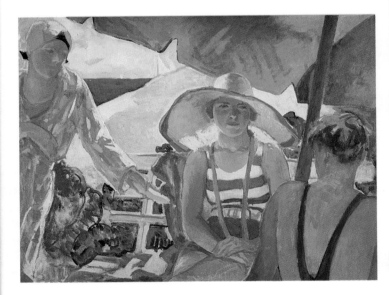

2–20 BEATRICE WHITNEY
VAN NESS
SUMMER SUNLIGHT (C. 1936).
OIL ON CANVAS. 39 × 49″.

NATIONAL MUSEUM OF WOMEN IN THE
ARTS, WASHINGTON, D.C. GIFT OF WALLACE
AND WILHELMINA HOLLADAY.

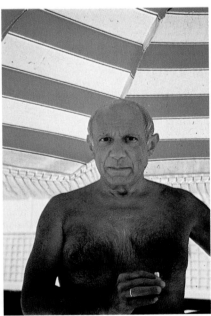

2–21 ALEXANDER
LIBERMAN
PHOTOGRAPH OF PABLO
PICASSO. FROM *THE ARTIST
IN HIS STUDIO.*

WYLIE, AITKEN & STONE, INC.

2–22 CLAUDE MONET
Haystack at Sunset Near Giverny (1891). Oil on canvas. 28⅞ × 36½″.

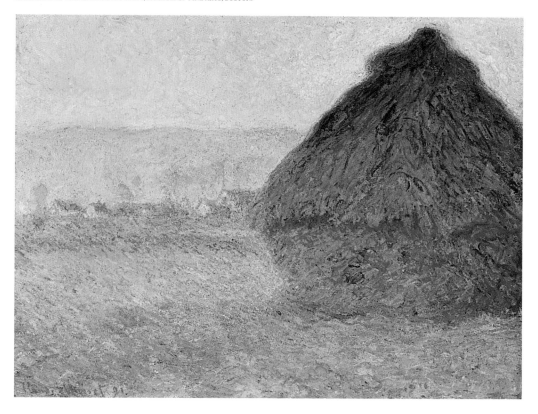

sought to create optical illusions in many of his works. In *Orion,* the shifts from warm to cool hues cause elements of the arrangement to move toward or away from the viewer. The progressions of circles and ellipses within lighter and darker squares contribute to the pulsating sense of the piece.

Many pictures show a balance of hues, although artists do not necessarily think in terms of complementary and analogous colors. Artists may simply experiment with their compositions until they find them pleasing, but our analyzing their use of color and other elements of art helps us to appreciate their work.

LOCAL VERSUS OPTICAL COLOR   Have you ever driven at night and wondered whether vague wavy lines in the distance outlined the peaks of hills or the bases of clouds? Objects may take on different hues as a function of distance or lighting conditions. The greenness of the trees on a mountain may make a strong impression from the base of the mountain, but from a distant van-

tage point the atmospheric scattering of light rays may dissolve the hue into a blue haze. Light-colored objects take on a dark appearance when lit strongly from behind. Hues fade as late afternoon wends its way to dusk and dusk to night. **Local color** is defined as the hue of an object as created by the colors its surface reflects under normal lighting conditions. **Optical color** is defined as our perceptions of color, which can vary markedly with lighting conditions.

Consider the *Haystack at Sunset Near Giverny* (Fig. 2–22) by the French **Impressionist** Claude Monet. Hay is light brown or straw-colored, but Monet's haystack takes on fiery hues, reflecting the angle of the light from the departing sun. The upper reach of the stack, especially, is given a forceful silhouette through flowing swaths of dark color. Surely the pigments of the surface of the haystack are no darker than the roofs of the houses that cling tenuously to an implied horizontal line across the center left of the picture. But the sun washes out their pigmentation. Nor can we with cer-

2–23 VINCENT VAN GOGH
THE NIGHT CAFÉ (1888). OIL ON CANVAS. 27½ × 35″.
YALE UNIVERSITY ART GALLERY, NEW HAVEN, CONN. BEQUEST OF STEPHEN C. CLARK, B.A. 1903.

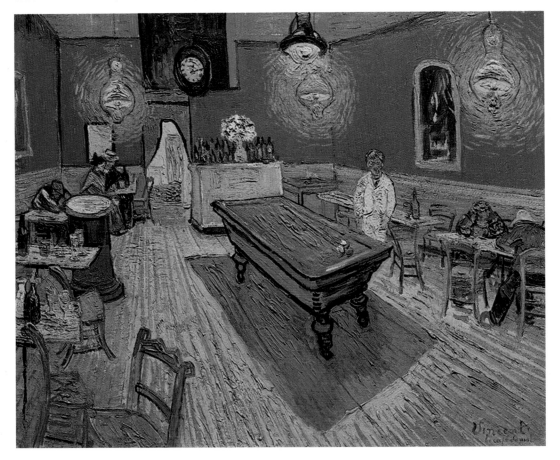

tainty interpret the horizontal above the roofs. Is it the top of a distant hill or the base of a cloud? Only in the visual sanctuary to the front of the haystack do a few possibly accurate greens and browns assert themselves. The amorphous shapes and pulsating color fields of *Haystack* lend the painting a powerful emotional impact.

In *The Night Café* (Fig. 2–23), Vincent van Gogh used color expressively rather than realistically. A café is generally seen as a place to unwind and relax in the company of friends, yet the artist chose this harsh palette to tell the world that this is a place where one "can ruin oneself." The red of the walls and the green of the ceiling clash, yet the billiard table and the floor, which both contain reds and greens, marry the two. The agitated swirls of local color that surround the lamps create lights that never were—a psychological display of brilliance and agitation.

In Judy Pfaff's *Voodoo* (Fig. 2–24), highly saturated colors determine the content and the spirit of the work. Though we may at first perceive naught but pure design, the title of the piece is suggestive of mysterious figures undulating in a Caribbean jungle undergrowth. The hues in this painting are so intense that they destroy the distinction between local color and optical color.

Texture is another element of art that can evoke a strong emotional response.

TEXTURE
The softness of skin and silk, the coarseness of rawhide and homespun cloth, the coolness of stone and tile, the warmth of wood—these are but a few of the **textures** that artists capture in their works. The word *texture* derives from the Latin for "weaving," and it is used to

2–24 JUDY PFAFF
VOODOO (1981). CONTACT-PAPER COLLAGE ON MYLAR, 98 × 60″ (FRAMED).
ALBRIGHT-KNOX ART GALLERY, BUFFALO; EDMUND HAYES FUND, 1983.

2–25 MAX ERNST
THE EYE OF SILENCE (1943–44). OIL ON CANVAS. 42½ × 55½″.
WASHINGTON UNIVERSITY GALLERY OF ART, ST. LOUIS. © 1998 ARTISTS RIGHTS SOCIETY (ARS), N.Y./ADAGP, PARIS.

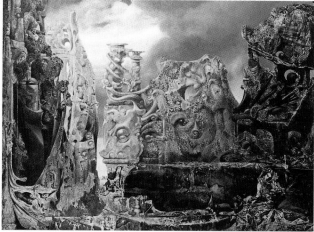

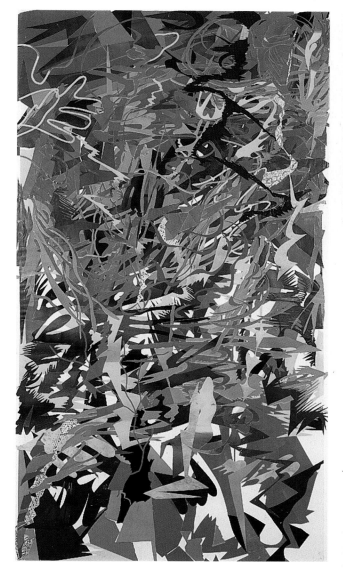

describe the surface character of woven fabrics and other materials as experienced primarily through the sense of touch.

Artists use line, color, and other elements of art to create the illusion of various textures in flat drawings and paintings. When the appearance of depicted objects differs from that of the paper, canvas, or other support, they are said to have **implied texture.** Sculptors and architects deal with the **actual textures** of their media of stone, wood, and other materials. In doing so, they

may create works that yield visual impressions quite different from the surface character of the material. Baroque sculptor Gianlorenzo Bernini (see Fig. 6–10) seemed to defy the very nature of marble in his illusions of textures of flesh and drapery.

The portraits by Rembrandt van Rijn (see Chapter 14) achieve a strong tactile quality through the artist's use of actual and implied texture. Rembrandt frequently used dabs of **impasto** to express the ways in which light can alternately construct and dissolve objects. The character of his brushstrokes lends reality to the visual impressions of skin, delicate lace, and here and there the impetuous emergence of a brilliant gem. He advised viewers not to stand too close to his canvases. When we do so, the art of his masterly illusion-making becomes apparent, and his subjects dissolve into the texture of his brush strokes.

Max Ernst believed that irrational impulses and chance arrangements should play an important role in art. In his *The Eye of Silence* (Fig. 2–25), Ernst used innovative methods of applying paint to generate forms that have the implied texture of geological formations that never were. His fantastic "landscapes"—or perhaps we should say, his intended vistas of the unconscious—achieve much of their emotional impact through texture. Soft, rounded, even voluptuously vulnerable organic forms grow out of, or are consumed by, harsh, rocklike entities.

2–26 ANA MENDIETA
ARBOL DE LA VIDA, NO. 294, FROM THE *ARBOL DE LA VIDA / SILUETA* (TREE OF LIFE/SILHOUETTE) SERIES (1977). COLOR PHOTOGRAPH, 20 × 13¼″. DOCUMENTATION OF EARTH-BODY SCULPTURE WITH ARTIST, TREE TRUNK, AND MUD, AT OLD MAN'S CREEK, IOWA CITY, IOWA.

© THE ESTATE OF ANA MENDIETA. COLLECTION IGNACIO C. MENDIETA, COURTESY GALERIE LELONG, NEW YORK.

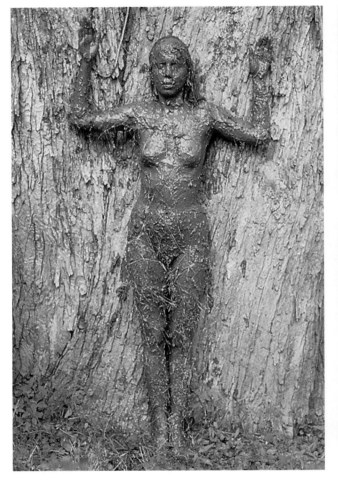

2–27 MERET OPPENHEIM
OBJECT (1936). FUR-COVERED CUP, SAUCER, AND SPOON. OVERALL HEIGHT: 2⅞″.

THE MUSEUM OF MODERN ART, N.Y. PURCHASE. © 1998 ARTIST'S RIGHTS SOCIETY (ARS), N.Y./PRO LITTERIS, ZURICH.

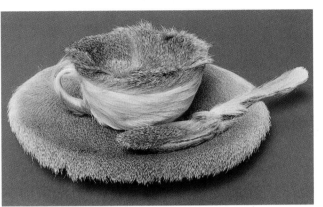

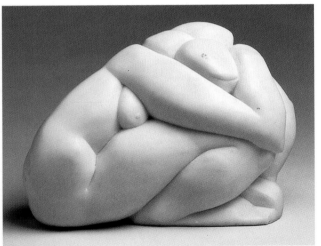

2–28 HENRI GAUDIER-BRZESKA
CROUCHING FIGURE (C. 1914). MARBLE. 8¾ × 12 × 4″.
COLLECTION WALKER ART CENTER, MINNEAPOLIS. ART CENTER ACQUISITION FUND, 1957.

The impact of *Arbol de la Vida* (Tree of Life), no. 294 (Fig. 2–26), is largely related to the shock value of its extraordinary contrasts of texture. Feminist artist Ana Mendieta presents her own body, draped in mud (an "earth-body sculpture"), against the craggy bark of a tree. Like some women artists, she shuns painting, especially abstract painting, as historically inundated with male values. Mendieta ties her flesh and blood, instead, across time and cultures, to the ancient myths of the mother earth goddesses.

Similar or identical materials can be manipulated to produce quite different textures. David Smith's steel sculptures (Fig. 2–8) frequently possess a smooth, satiny surface, whereas from a distance Richard Stankiewicz's

metal **assemblages** (see Fig. 6–23) often have a mottled, softer, organic look. Wood can be rough hewn, as in the African mask *Kagle* (Fig. 6–13), or as smooth as ivory, as in Fumio Yoshimura's *Dog Snapper* (Fig. 6–16). Contrast the smoothness of the Etruscan terracotta **sarcophagus** (Fig. 11–18) with the coarseness of Reuben Nakian's free-form clay sculpture (Fig. 6–3).

Textures can simultaneously attract and repel us. Meret Oppenheim's *Object* (Fig. 2–27) consists of a cup, saucer, and spoon covered with fur. The shape and function of the usually smooth teacup may trigger associations to utterly civilized and refined social

2–29 HENRY MOORE
RECLINING MOTHER AND CHILD (1960–61). CAST BRONZE. 86½ × 33¼ × 54″.
COLLECTION WALKER ART CENTER, MINNEAPOLIS. GIFT OF THE T. B. WALKER FOUNDATION. 1963.

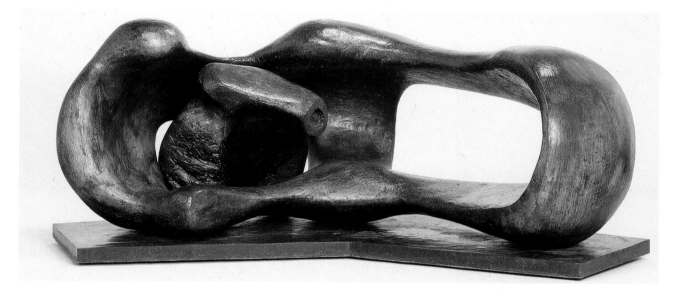

settings and occasions. The coarse primal fur, on the other hand, stimulates rather different ideas, and the thought—even fleeting—of drinking from this cup is repugnant.

MASS

In the science of physics, the **mass of a body is a reflection of its weight**. The larger its mass, the more difficult a body is to move. In art, the mass of a depicted object— or of a sculpture or work of architecture—is its implied or actual bulk, size, or magnitude. In a two-dimensional drawing or painting, the term *mass* usually refers to a large area or form of one color. For example, in the Frankenthaler painting (Fig. 2–9), we can speak of masses of colors as well as *fields* of colors. The large color fields of these paintings affords them an **implied mass** that is not generally found in paintings that are characterized by smaller forms of more varied colors.

Henri Gaudier-Brzeska's *Crouching Figure* (Fig. 2–28) is a small marble sculpture of both actual and implied mass. Marble is a dense material, and the figure is not easy to lift, even though it is only 8¾ inches tall. The form of the sculpture augments the denseness of the material to heighten the sense of massiveness. The limbs are compact. Nothing protrudes. When a wrestler flails his arms, he is easy to bring to the mat,

but a wrestler who assumes a compact position is hard to budge, difficult to topple.

The **actual mass** of Henry Moore's *Reclining Mother and Child* (Fig. 2–29) vastly outscales that of the Gaudier-Brzeska figure. Moore's bronze sculpture is more than 7 feet long and nearly 3 feet high. But Moore's lyrical wrapping of large spaces imparts a lightness to his figures that denies their massiveness. The easy flow of air and light integrates the work into its surroundings, whereas the Gaudier-Brzeska maintains a stubborn aloofness.

Similarly, the actual massiveness of the Egyptian Pyramids lends them their impact. Small models of these structures can accurately depict their shapes and colors, can suggest something of their textures, and can readily portray the harmony of the relationships among their parts. But without actual mass, the structures remain like toys: an essential element of their aesthetic character is lost.

On the other hand, the open interiors and skeletal support systems of massive Gothic cathedrals and contemporary skyscrapers imply a lightness and airiness that is not found in the Pyramids. How is it, the viewer may wonder, that these churches and urban structures of metal, stone, and glass can be supported by their "skeletons"? Their paradoxical lightness contributes to our appreciation of their massiveness.

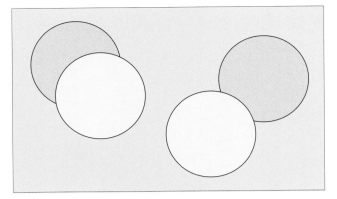

2–31 VALERIE JAUDON
TALLAHATCHEE (1984).
OIL AND GOLD LEAF ON
CANVAS. 80 × 96″.
COURTESY SIDNEY JANIS GALLERY, N.Y.
© VALERIE JAUDON/LICENSED BY VAGA, N.Y.

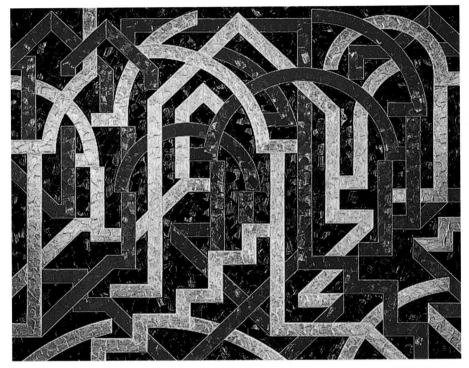

SPACE

"No man is an island, entire of itself," wrote the poet John Donne. If Donne had been speaking of art, he might have written, "No subject exists in and of itself." A building has a site, a sculpture is surrounded by space, and even artists who work in two-dimensional media such as drawing and painting create figures that bear relationships to one another and to their grounds. Objects exist in three-dimensional space. Artists either carve out or model their works within three-dimensional space, or else somehow come to terms with three-dimensional space through two-dimensional artforms.

In Chapters 6 and 7, which discuss the three-dimensional artforms of sculpture and architecture, we explore ways in which artists situate their objects in space and envelop space. In Chapter 7 we chronicle the age-old attempt to enclose vast reaches of space that began with massive support systems and currently focuses on lightweight steel-cage and shell-like structures. In this section we will examine ways in which artists who work in two dimensions create the illusion of depth—that is, the third dimension.

OVERLAPPING When nearby objects are placed in front of more distant objects, they obscure part or all of the distant objects. Figure 2–30 shows two circles and two arcs, but our perceptual experiences encourage us to interpret the drawing as showing four circles, two in the foreground and two in back. That is, our perceptual experiences allow an artist to create the illusion of depth by overlapping objects, or apparently placing one in front of another.

Valerie Jaudon's *Tallahatchee* (Fig. 2–31) is an intricate exercise in overlapping. The work is composed of an interlace pattern of straight and arcing ribbons, weaving in and out of shifting planes. Space is drastically

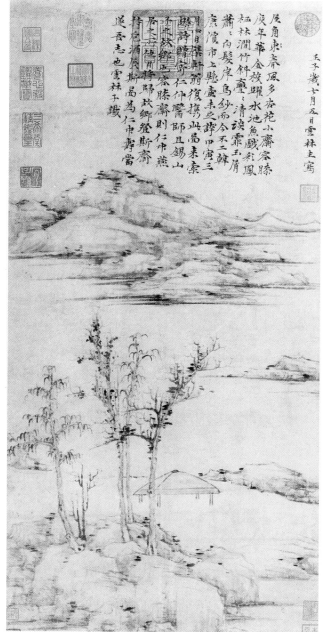

2–32 NI ZAN
RONGXI STUDIO. LATE YUAN/EARLY MING DYNASTY (1279–1368).
HANGING SCROLL; INK ON PAPER. HEIGHT: 29¼″.
NATIONAL PALACE MUSEUM, TAIEI, TAIWAN, REPUBLIC OF CHINA.

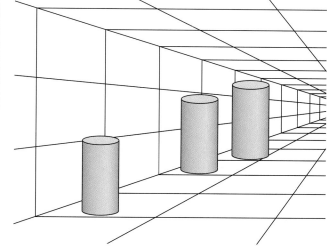

2–33 A VISUAL ILLUSION.

compressed, forcing the viewer's eye to trace the progression of lines through the mazelike configuration.

RELATIVE SIZE AND LINEAR PERSPECTIVE   The farther objects are from us, the smaller they appear to the eye. To recreate this visual phenomenon and to create the illusion of three-dimensionality on a two-dimensional surface, such as a canvas, artists employ a variety of techniques, among them **relative size** and **linear perspective.** For example, in the Bierstadt painting (Fig. 2–43) on page 56, objects in the foreground are smaller in size and scale relative to the mountains in the distance, making them look even more imperious. In Aponovich's *Still Life: Penobscot Bay* (Fig. 2–40), the landscape seen through the window seems very remote, in large part due to the relatively large scale of the still life in the foreground.

In the Chinese ink drawing shown in Figure 2–32, the natural elements in the top and bottom of the scroll are shown at the same size, as if they were seen from the same distance. Yet the viewer—particularly the schooled viewer—tends to perceive the hills at the top as being farther away. Again, objects depicted at the bottom of a work tend to be perceived as closer to the viewer.

Note how the cylinders in Figure 2–33 appear to grow larger toward the top of the composition. Why? For at least two reasons: (1) Objects at the bottom of a composition are usually perceived as being closer to the

2–34 ONE-POINT PERSPECTIVE.

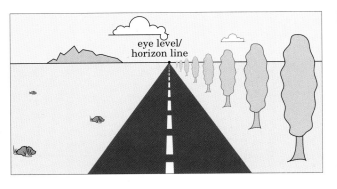

2–36 OBJECTS SET AT DIFFERENT ANGLES SHOWN IN PERSPECTIVE.

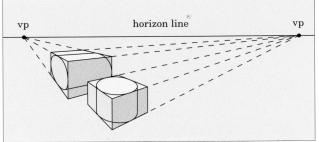

2–35 TWO-POINT PERSPECTIVE.

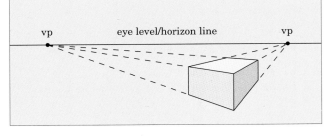

2–37 CURVED OBJECTS SHOWN IN PERSPECTIVE.

picture plane, and (2) the converging lines are perceived as being parallel, even when they are not. However, if they were parallel, then space would have to recede toward the center right of the composition, and the cylinder in that region would have to be farthest from the viewer. According to rules of perspective, a distant object that appears to be equal in size to a nearby object would have to be larger, and so we perceive the cylinder to the right as the largest, although it is equal in size to the others.

Figures 2–34 through 2–35 show that the illusion of depth can be created in art by making parallel lines come together, or converge, at one or more **vanishing**

points on an actual or implied **horizon.** The height of the horizon in the composition corresponds to the apparent location of the viewer's eyes, that is, the **vantage point** of the viewer. As we shall see in later chapters, the Greeks and Romans had some notion of linear perspective, but perspective was refined by Renaissance artists such as Leonardo da Vinci.

In **one-point perspective** (Fig. 2–34), parallel lines converge at a single vanishing point on the horizon. Renaissance artist Albrecht Dürer's woodcut *The Adoration of the Magi* (Fig. 2–38) functions very much like an exercise in one-point perspective. One can locate the vanishing point by following converging parallel

THE ADORATION OF THE MAGI (1511). WOODCUT. 11½ × 8⅝".
THE METROPOLITAN MUSEUM OF ART, N.Y. GIFT OF JUNIUS S. MORGAN, 1919 (19.73.163).

2–39 CONVERGING PARALLEL LINES INTERSECT AT THE VANISHING POINT.

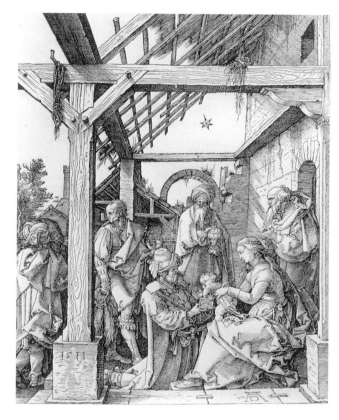

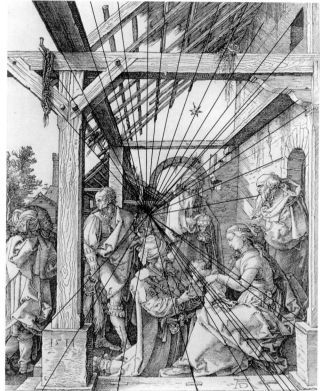

lines (Fig. 2–39) to where they intersect near the center of the composition. By placing the vanishing point near the eye level of the figures, Dürer gives the viewer a psychological sense of communicating with them.

In **two-point perspective** (Fig. 2–35), two sets of parallel lines converge at separate vanishing points on the horizon. Two-point perspective is appropriate for representing the recession of objects that are seen from an angle, or obliquely.

We can use additional sets of parallel lines to depict objects that are set at different angles, as shown in Figure 2–36. Figure 2–37 shows how curved objects may be "carved out" of rectangular solids.

ATMOSPHERIC PERSPECTIVE   In **atmospheric perspective** (also called *aerial perspective*), the illusion of depth is created by techniques such as texture gradients, brightness gradients, color saturation, and the manipulation of warm and cool colors.

A gradient is a progressive change. The effect of a **texture gradient** relies on the fact that closer objects are perceived as having rougher or more detailed surfaces. In the Dürer woodcut (Fig. 2–38), the grain of the wooden posts and beams in the foreground is more detailed than that of the posts and beams behind the figures, heightening the perception of depth. The effect of a **brightness gradient** is due to the lesser intensity of distant objects.

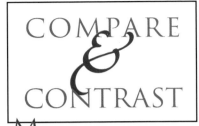

COMPARE & CONTRAST

MATISSE'S *OPEN WINDOW, COLLIOURE* WITH APONOVICH'S *STILL LIFE: PENOBSCOT BAY* AND FISH'S *SCAFFOLDING*

A room with a view. An ordinary set of circumstances, and yet, one that is rife with promise, with expectation, with potential revelation. Reflecting on the subject in this way will perhaps offer some clue as to why the still life before a window has intrigued artists over centuries. For the coupling of the two subjects creates a composition that far exceeds the sum of its parts.

Each of the works in this exercise is an oil painting on canvas. Describe the different ways in which the medium is handled. Does one work appeal more to the intellect, one more to the senses? Why? All three of the artists have been influenced by photography, but in different ways. Can you detect how? Aponovich's (Fig. 2–40) photorealistic detail awakens all of our senses. The flattened perspective in Matisse's (Fig. 2–41) early twentieth-century composition asserts the two-dimensionality of the canvas surface and collapses planes as does the lens of the camera. Janet Fish (Fig. 2–42) has likewise manipulated her painted surface to mimic a photograph by compressing the foreground and background. How do the artists literally play with perspective? How do they engage in spatial exploration?

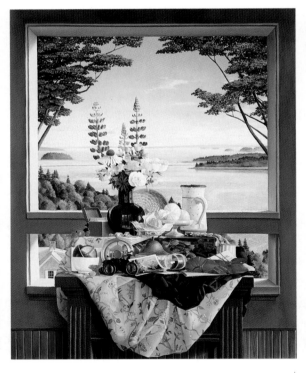

2–40 JAMES APONOVICH
STILL LIFE: PENOBSCOT BAY (1992).
OIL ON CANVAS. 60 × 48".

COURTESY TATISTCHEFF GALLERY, N.Y.

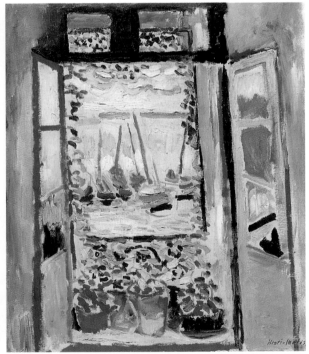

2–41 HENRI MATISSE
OPEN WINDOW, COLLIOURE (1905).
OIL ON CANVAS. 21¾ × 18⅛".

FROM THE COLLECTION OF MR. AND MRS. JOHN HAY WHITNEY, N.Y. © 1998 SUCCESSION H. MATISSE, PARIS/ARTISTS RIGHTS SOCIETY (ARS), N.Y.

How do they explore levels of reality, differences in perception? What role does the window play in how we view the still life arrangement? Conversely, how does the still life arrangement alter or define our relationship to the landscape?

Bringing together the window and the still life arrangement also evokes a narrative that pushes beyond the content cues. Who lives here? What do their possessions tell us about who they are? What are their thoughts as they look beyond the trappings of their interior to the outside world? What is our place, as viewers, in their reality?

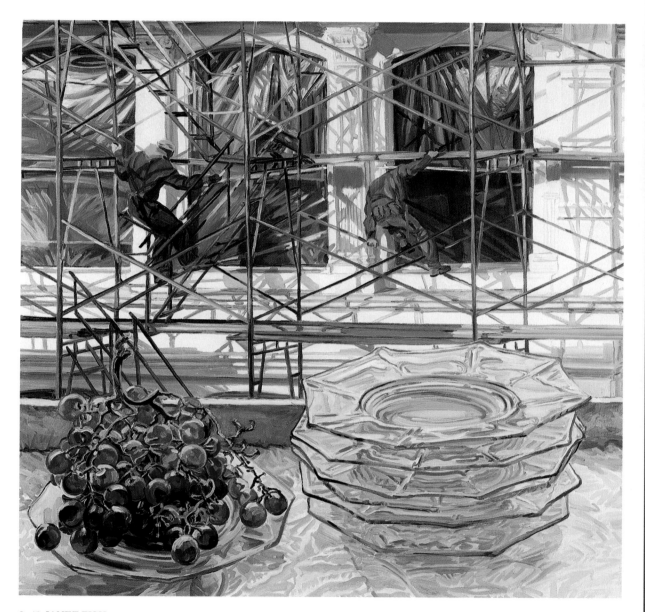

2–42 JANET FISH
SCAFFOLDING (1992). OIL ON CANVAS. 42 × 42″.
COURTESY D.C. MOORE GALLERY, N.Y. © BETH PHILLIPS.

2–43 ALBERT BIERSTADT
MERCED RIVER, YOSEMITE VALLEY (1866). OIL ON CANVAS. 36 × 50″.
THE METROPOLITAN MUSEUM OF ART, N.Y. GIFT OF THE SONS OF WILLIAM PATON, 1909 (09.214.1).

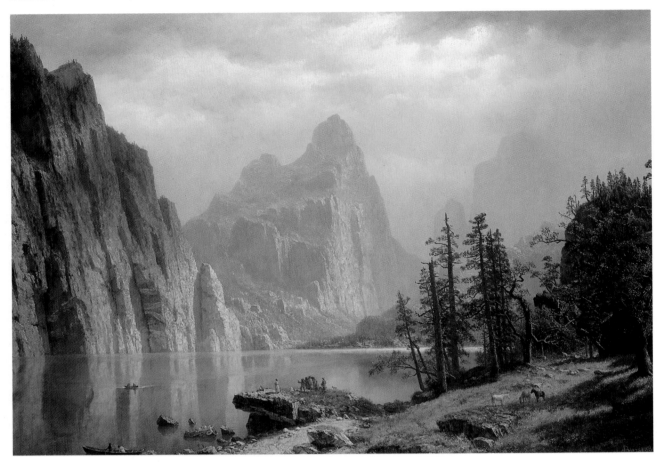

The romantic Albert Bierstadt landscape *Merced River, Yosemite Valley* (Fig. 2–43) relies in part on atmospheric perspective to create the illusion of deep vistas. The brighter clouds seem closer, as do the luminous rock walls reflected in the water. The nearby boulders and crags are more jagged than those in the distance. The distant looming mountains in the upper right part of the picture are barely discernible. The nearby trees are greener, brighter, and more finely detailed than the suggestions of vegetation on the distant shore. Vasarely's *Orion* (Fig. 2–19) uses some principles of atmospheric perspective to help create the illusion of movement through a vibrating effect. The brightest, most intense circles are perceived as being closest to the viewer, although, of course, all the mounted scraps of paper are right on the picture plane.

The haunting painting, *Schunnemunk Mountain* (Fig. 2–44), reveals Sylvia Plimack Mangold's fascina-

tion with the transitional moments of the day. Here in the evening of the Hudson River Valley, brightness gradients employing purple, navy, and cobalt set the hills beneath the sky. The dark foreground is rendered more vacant by twinkling lights that suggest habitation in the valley beyond.

TIME AND MOTION

Objects and figures exist and move not only in space, but also in the dimension of time. In its inexorable forward flow, time provides us with the chance to develop and grasp the visions of our dreams. Time also creates the stark limits beyond which none of us may extend.

Artists have sought not only to represent three-dimensional space in two-dimensional art forms, but also to represent the passage of time. Only recently have art forms been developed that involve *actual* time and

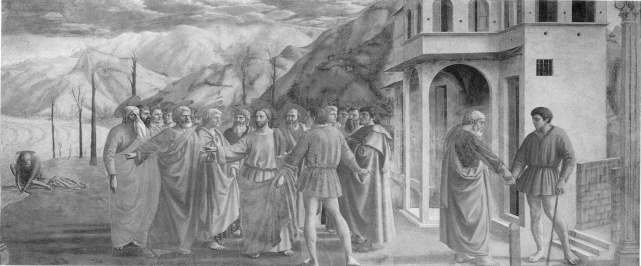

2–45 MASACCIO
THE TRIBUTE MONEY (C. 1427). FRESCO.
BRANCACCI CHAPEL, SANTA MARIA DEL CARMINE, FLORENCE.

actual movement. In the following chapters we shall discuss a number of them, including kinetic sculpture and motion pictures. In this chapter we confine our discussion to ways in which artists have represented time and motion in more traditional media such as painting, sculpture, architecture, and photography. Through these modes of expression, artists create **implied time** and **implied motion.**

The Italian Renaissance artist Masaccio told a three-part story in his fresco *The Tribute Money* (Fig. 2–45). In the center grouping, Jesus is advising St. Peter that he will find a coin to pay the tax collector in the mouth of a fish. At the left of the composition, St. Peter is extracting the coin from the fish's mouth. To the right, he is shown dutifully handing the coin to the tax collector. The viewer must know the story to interpret the painting, because

I Can't (1981). Ink and Rhoplex on vellum. Seven parts: 10½ × 9½″ (6); 9 × 9½″ (1).

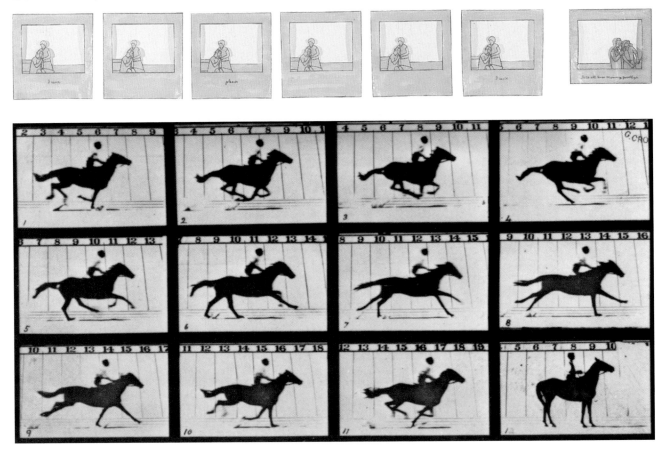

2–47 EADWEARD MUYBRIDGE
Galloping Horse (1878). Photograph.

the background is continuous, implying that the depicted events happen concurrently. Note, too, how dramatically the single-point perspective is defined by the horizontals of the building to the right.

In *I Can't,* Ida Applebroog (Fig. 2–46) implies the passage of time through a series of seven panels, not altogether dissimilar from the frames used to advance a narrative in comic books. Here a barren scene with two women—relationship unknown—is repeated, and the uncertain captions "Please" and "I can't" offer a rhythm to the mysterious theme. In the end we find an alarming, but still unclear, kidnaping at gunpoint, lending menace to the otherwise ordinary caption, "Let's all kiss Mommy goodbye."

Applebroog advances (and retreats) her narrative through a series of panels. The photographer Eadweard Muybridge told "stories" about the nature of motion through series of frames, each of which stopped rapid action. In *Galloping Horse* (Fig. 2–47), the motion of a running horse is implied in eleven frames, with the twelfth showing animal and rider at rest. In two dramatic frames, all hooves are in the air at once.

At the time Duchamp's *Nude Descending a Staircase #2* (Fig. 2–48) was first exhibited, a critic described the painting as "an explosion in a shingle factory." Certainly the intersecting, splintered planes can leave such an impression. But these planes do not burst forth uncontrolled from a central core. Instead, they are

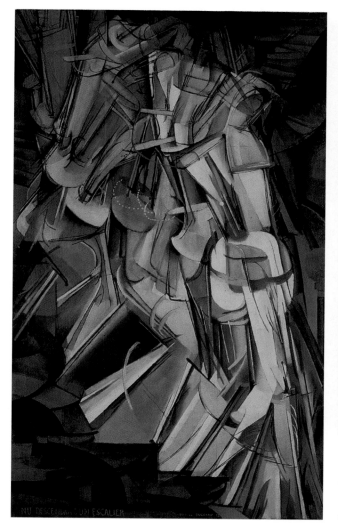

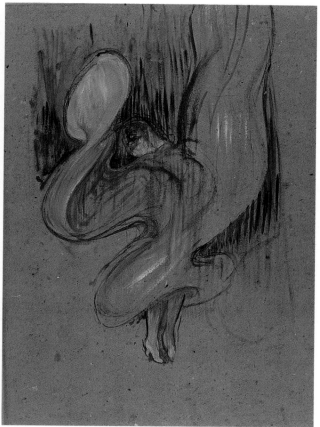

COMPOSITION

arranged in an orderly, coherent fashion that describes the multifaceted form of a human figure in motion down a flight of stairs. It could be said that *Nude* creates the illusion of movement through a progressive series of overlapping images, in a sense paralleling the effects of **stroboscopic motion** (see p. 182) in a painting.

In Henri de Toulouse-Lautrec's *Loïe Fuller in the Dance of Veils* (Fig. 2–49), billowing organic drapery is filled with air, implying a sweep of arms. A fleeting moment seems to have been arrested. The work grants permanence to a dynamic relationship between air and vessel that otherwise lasts but an instant.

Composition is a process—the act of composing or organizing the plastic elements of art. Composition can occur at random, exemplified by the old mathematical saw that an infinite number of monkeys pecking away at an infinite number of typewriters would eventually (though mindlessly) produce *Hamlet.* But artistic composition takes place according to aesthetic principles such as proportion and scale, unity, balance, and rhythm. When we use principles of organization such as these, beautiful works are created by a finite number of artists.

This is not to say that all artists try to apply these principles; some artists create stimulating works by purposefully violating them. Still others work without awareness of the names of these principles or their historical application.

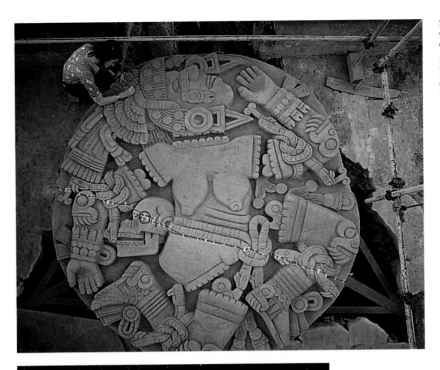

2–50 *Coyolxauhqui*, from
the Great Temple of
Tonochtitlán, Aztec,
Mexico City, Late
Postclassic
(c. 1400–1500). Stone.
Diameter approx. 11′.

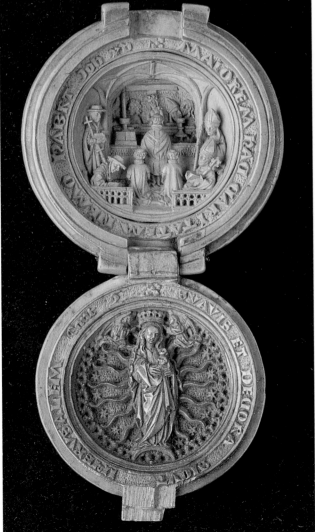

2–51 ANONYMOUS
Rosary Bead,
Netherlandish (ca.
1500–1510). Boxwood
diameter (closed): 1⅝″;
(open): 3⅜″ high.
SMITH COLLEGE MUSEUM OF ART,
NORTHHAMPTON, MASS., PURCHASED 1991.

The Aztec stone sculpture from the Great Temple of
Tenochtitlán (Fig. 2–50) is a gruesome, though oddly
beautiful, carving depicting the dismemberment of the
goddess Coyolxuahqui (don't feel sorry for her, she
killed her mother). The body fragments are arranged
with puzzle precision in a revolving pattern that echoes
the shape of the mammoth disk. Each piece is essential
to the composition; it is hard to imagine how one could
change anything without seriously compromising the
integrity of the whole. Balance and rhythm make the
overall design fluid, though circumscribed. Given the so-
phistication of the design, the horror of the content is
ironic; this relief stood at the base of a staircase leading
up to a shrine where human sacrifice took place. It was
one of the last things that the victim's eyes would have
gazed upon.

Another religious work, of a different time, place,
and system of beliefs, offers a somewhat different
solution to a compositional problem. The boxwood
rosary bead in Figure 2–51 is an extraordinary example
of technical skill. In the smallest of spaces, figures are

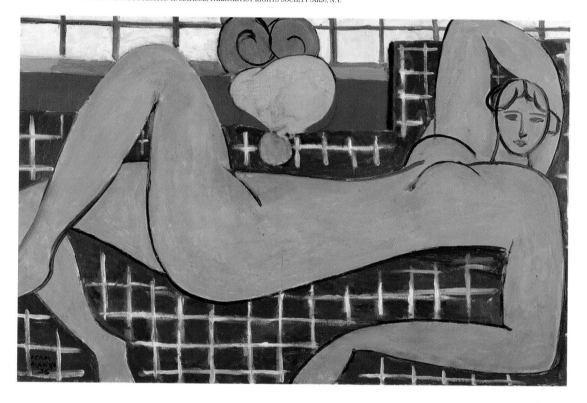

meticulously carved and precisely arranged. The top section is characterized by a strong symmetry: The central figures of a priest and two worshippers, whose backs are turned toward us, form a strong triangular shape. A total of four other figures flank the group—two to each side. The planes defining the space are numerous and there is even a suggestion of a vaulted ceiling that gives light and air to an otherwise crowded composition. The earthly figures of this sphere, complemented by their concrete and detailed environment, are contrasted with the otherworldly nature of the scene beneath it. Here the Virgin Mary, with the child Jesus in her arms, is surrounded by a complicated pattern of serpentine lines, stars, and a crescent moon, all symbolically connected to the the Virgin. The patterns, shapes, and body poses in both sections of the rosary bead also complement the spherical shape of the bead. The hallmark of this successful composition is its ability to remain clear and decipherable in spite of its complexity of detail.

PROPORTION AND SCALE

Proportion is the comparative relationship of the parts of a composition to each other and to the whole. The historic attempt of philosophers and artists to discover or establish mathematical rules of proportion that will lead to aesthetic compositions is older than the ancient Greeks.

The Classical Greek sculptor Polykleitos created noble athletic figures (see Fig. 11–11) in which the height of the body was precisely eight times the length of the head. This rule was not intended so much to reflect reality as to perfect it. Much of the Classical Greek Parthenon (Fig. 11–9) was constructed according to the principle of the **Golden Section,** which states that a small part must relate to a larger part as the larger part relates to the whole.

The beauty of a work like Titian's *Venus of Urbino* (Fig. 13–31) is inseparable from its classical proportions. Henri Matisse's voluptuous *Large Reclining Nude* (Fig. 2–52), reclines majestically in a similar

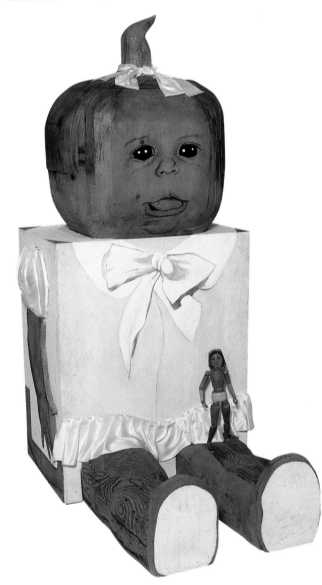

traditional pose, but unlike Titian, Matisse has toyed with the body's proportions. When viewed separately, each part is appealing, even sensuous, but in combination the proportions, and ultimately the whole, are unrealistic: the head is too small, the torso too long, the shoulders and arms too massive. Matisse's violation of realistic proportions is intentional. His interest in the interplay of patterns and lines led to distortions that infused the forms with emotion, personal meaning, and absorbing design.

Whereas proportion is the relationship of parts to each other to the work as a whole, **scale** is the relative size of an object compared with others of its kind, its setting, or human dimensions. The Pyramids of Giza and the skyscrapers of New York are imposing because of their scale, that is, their size compared with the size of other buildings, their sites, and people. Their overall size is essential to their impact.

It is in part the play on the viewer's sense of scale that creates the visual shock and sheer humor of Marisol's *Baby Girl* (Fig. 2–53). A wooden doll with adjustable limbs and torso—the sort used for drawing exercises in art classes—sports a portrait of Marisol herself. It is perched on the stocky thigh of the baby, who neither looks at nor touches the "toy." The baby girl, by any other definition a subject that suggests delicacy and softness, is transformed into a cumbersome hunk of a figure. Only the shirring of her puffy sleeves and frilly gathers of her white dress soften the harshness of the overall form. Marisol's manipulation of scale and our perception of it is confirmed by the fact that in looking at the illustration of this work in your book (without sneaking a peek at the dimensions), you would have no real sense of how large or small the work actually is. Scale also elevates Claes Oldenburg's *Clothespin* (Fig. 2–54) from the commonplace to the level of fine art.

UNITY

Unity is oneness or wholeness. A work of art achieves unity when its parts seem necessary to the composition. One way in which the Classical Greeks afforded their artistic works unity was through their exacting proportions.

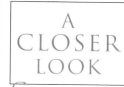
**CLAES
OLDENBURG:
ON CLOTHESPINS,
BASEBALL BATS,
AND OTHER
MONUMENTS**

When one drives around Philadelphia's Center Square, one is impressed by the broadness of the avenues, the classical columns and arches of City Hall, the steel and glass curtain walls of the new office buildings, and . . . by a 45–foot-tall clothespin (Fig. 2–54).

Why a clothespin? "I like everything about clothespins," reported Pop artist Claes Oldenburg, "even the name." The clothespin sculpture, aptly called *Clothespin* by its creator, was erected as a tribute to the 1976 Bicentennial. The line down the center of the pin suggests an updating of the cracked Liberty Bell, and the spring could be viewed as spelling out '76. Moreover, the clothespin consists of two structures clasped together, by a spring, in an embrace—an appropriate symbol for Philadelphia, the City of Brotherly Love. One might think that this symbolism was incidental, but in 1972 Oldenburg made a silkscreen comparing his clothespin to Brancusi's *The Kiss* (Fig. 1–41), which also depicts an embrace.

Clothespin is just one of the ordinary objects to which Oldenburg has lent monumentality by upgrading their scale. His 24-foot-high *Lipstick* rises serenely on a Yale University quadrangle, and the Houston Public Library sports an 18-foot-high mouse. The plaza of the Social Security Administration building in Chicago, a city that supports two major league baseball franchises, is punctuated by a 100-foot-tall baseball bat. Oldenburg has drawings of typewriter erasers and upside-down ice cream cones whose waffle patterns rival the faces of the Egyptian Pyramids.

It could be argued that the subjects of Oldenburg's monuments are trivial, but we must also admit that they have a certain symbolic meaning and depth for Americans. In centuries to come, they may say more about twentieth-century America than would a few more bronze riders on horseback.

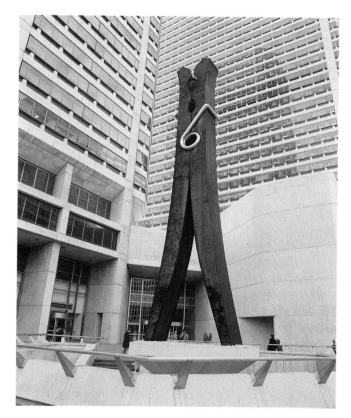

2–54 CLAES OLDENBURG
CLOTHESPIN (1976).
CORTEN STEEL WITH
STAINLESS STEEL BASE.
45′ HIGH.
COURTESY PACE WILDENSTEIN.

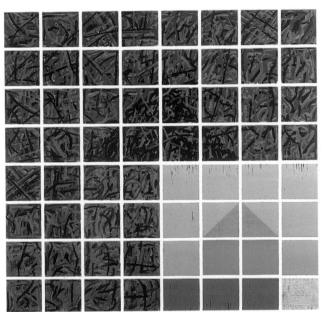

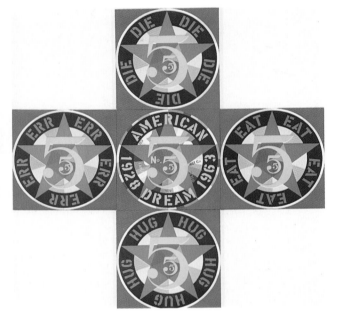

Artists frequently stir the viewer's interest by creating variety within unity, as found in Jennifer Bartlett's *2 Priory Walk* (Fig. 2–55) and in Robert Indiana's *The Demuth American Dream No. 5* (Fig. 2–56). *2 Priory Walk,* from the street address of the house that serves as Bartlett's subject, is rendered in sixty-four panels: emerging from an expressionistic landscape dominated by jarring reds and greens; carved geometrically from a blue field (fifteen of the sixteen panels in the lower right quadrant); and composed of dots in the lowest right-hand panel. The repetition in the panel format and in the images of the dwelling provide an overall unity.

Indiana's work is a tribute to Charles Demuth and his painting *I Saw the Figure 5 in Gold.* Indiana multiplies the older artist's work into five panels unified by the number 5 and the overall shape of the cross. The inscriptions and colors of the panels vary, extending the symbolic import of the imagery.

BALANCE

A work of art possesses **balance** when its visual or actual weights or masses (including color masses) are distributed in such a way that they achieve harmony. In Calder's **mobile** (Fig. 6–28), the actual weights are balanced and account for both physical and visual harmony.

The human body and many cathedrals and contemporary office buildings achieve balance through **bilateral symmetry,** in which the left side of the work is largely mirrored by the right. The balance of Oldenburg's *Clothespin* (Fig. 2–54) also stems from bilateral symmetry.

Asymmetrical balance is achieved when non-equivalent forms, masses, or other elements balance one another. For example, the massive dark rooflines of Le Corbusier's *Notre-Dame-du-Haut* (Fig. 7–22) are balanced by the whiteness of the walls and the vertical thrust of adjoining towers.

2–57 JOAN MIRÓ
THE BIRTH OF THE WORLD (MONTROIG, SUMMER, 1925). OIL ON CANVAS. 8′2¾″ × 6′6⅘″.

THE MUSEUM OF MODERN ART, N.Y. ACQUIRED THROUGH AN ANONYMOUS FUND, THE MR. AND MRS. JOSEPH SLIFKA AND ARMAND G. ERPF FUNDS AND BY GIFT OF THE ARTIST. © 1998 ARTISTS RIGHTS SOCIETY (ARS), N.Y./ADAGP, PARIS.

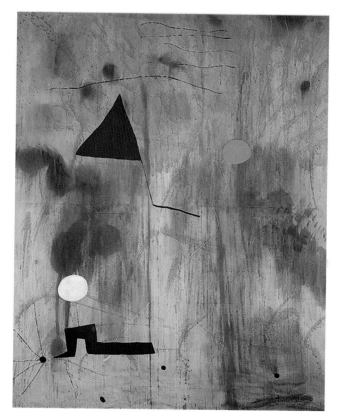

2–58 GERTRUDE KÄSEBIER
BLESSED ART THOU AMONG WOMEN (C. 1898). PHOTOGRAPH.

COURTESY THE LIBRARY OF CONGRESS, WASHINGTON, D.C.

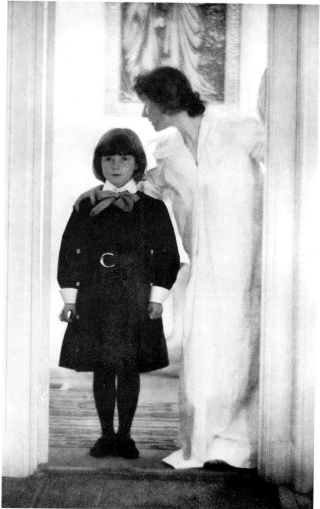

In *The Birth of the World* (Fig. 2–57), Joan Miró first allowed paint to run freely across his canvas. Then he placed emergent forms in black, white, and red against this background, suggesting a sort of primordial soup. Note how the red and white circular shapes balance one another. If you cover the white shape, the composition seems lopsided to the right; if you cover the red shape, it seems lopsided to the left. Although Miró claims to have placed his shapes at random, a strong sense of composition is evident.

What an exquisite sense of composition we find in Gertrude Käsebier's delicately textured photograph *Blessed Art Thou Among Women* (Fig. 2–58). Notice how the dark value of the girl's dress is balanced both by the dark wall to the left and by the woman's hair. Similarly, the stark light value of the vertical shaft of the doorway to the left and the light values of the right side of the composition are in equilibrium. The floor and painting in the background provide unifying middle values. If the composition of works such as these is instinctive, some artists' instincts are well schooled indeed.

RHYTHM

The world would be a meaningless jumble of sights and sounds were it not for the regular repetition of sensory impressions. Natural **rhythms,** or orderly

2–59 WAYNE THIEBAUD
PIE COUNTER (1963). OIL. 30 × 36″.
COLLECTION OF WHITNEY MUSEUM OF AMERICAN ART, N.Y. LARRY ALDRICH FOUNDATION FUND.

2–60 INTERIOR OF THE SANCTUARY OF THE MOSQUE AT CÓRDOBA, SPAIN (ISLAMIC) (786–987).

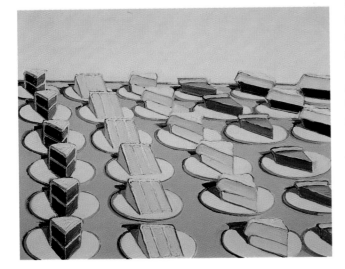

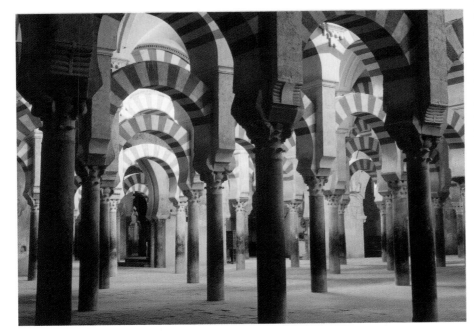

progressions, regulate events ranging from the orbits of the planets to the unfolding of the genetic code into flesh and blood. The rhythm of Muybridge's *Galloping Horse* (Fig. 2–47) elevates the series of photographs from a study of mechanical principles to the realm of art. Wayne Thiebaud's stately procession in *Pie Counter* (Fig. 2–59) seems to be a comment on the homogeneity of contemporary American society as fostered by the advertising designs of Madison Avenue.

Rhythms are found also in architecture. The architects of the Middle Ages (see Chapters 7 and 12) imbued the great cathedrals with a sense of rhythm by repeating their open spaces, or **bays,** very much as Robert Indiana did in *The Demuth American Dream No. 5* (Fig. 2–56). The roof of the mosque at Córdoba, Spain (Fig. 2–60) is supported by a rhythmic progression of arches that span the distances between the columns. Mosques built in this so-called **hypostyle** system could be expanded in any direction by adding columns and arches as the congregation grew. Many modern buildings are given rhythmic composition by the repetition of the elements of their steel skeletons. This structural rhythm is made evident in the Wainwright Building (Fig. 7–17) and Lever House (Fig. 7–18) by the equidistant vertical lines between the windows.

In contrast to the Wainwright Building and Lever House, the U.S. Air Force Academy Chapel at Colorado Springs (Fig. 2–61) wears its skeleton on the outside. Light and shade strongly affirm its advancing series of thrusting aluminum pylons. From the front, the building is a simple triangle. From the side it is a ribbed rectangle. Only from an oblique angle do we receive the dramatic impact of triangles within triangles, abstractions that echo the spikes of the chapel's Rocky Mountain setting.

2–61 SKIDMORE OWINGS AND MERRILL
U.S. AIR FORCE ACADEMY CHAPEL, COLORADO SPRINGS
(1956–1962).

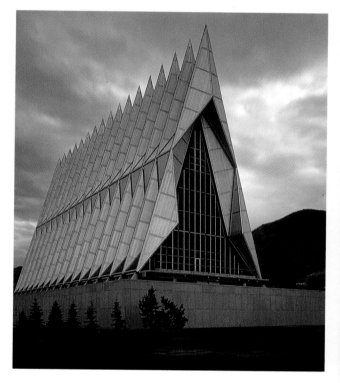

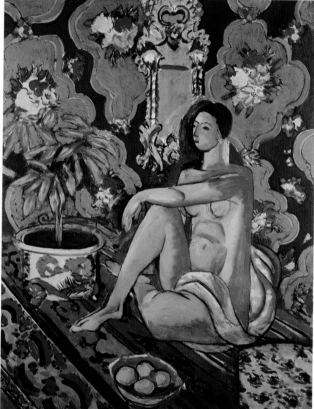

PATTERN

The **pattern** of a work of art is the arrangement of shapes within it, the design of its parts or elements. Beyond that, pattern usually refers to a highly decorative and repetitive motif. The bold and intricate floral patterns of the wallpaper, rug, and other features of Matisse's *Decorative Figure Against Ornamental Background* (Fig. 2–62) vie for attention with the draped nude. Because of overlapping (and logic), we see that the figure is seated between the viewer and the wallpaper. Yet when we focus on the large, colorful floral patterns, there are figure-ground reversals, so that the flowers leap into the foreground, thereby flattening the space.

CONTENT

The *content* of a work of art is everything that is contained in it. The content of a work refers not only to its lines or forms, but also to its subject matter and its underlying meanings or themes.

THE LEVELS OF CONTENT

We may think of works of art as containing three levels of content: (1) elements and composition, (2) subject matter, and (3) underlying or symbolic meanings or themes. In terms of its *elements* and *composition,* the content of Matisse's *Decorative Figure Against Ornamental Background* consists of balanced, highly patterned forms created by paint on canvas. The *subject matter* consists of a seated woman, a bowl of fruit, and a potted plant, all in a richly decorated room. The underlying or *symbolic meanings* or *themes* of the work surely have something to do with lushness, fullness, fertility, and related ideas. Altogether, then, there are three levels of content—as in many works of art.

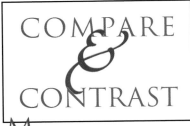

COMPARE
&
CONTRAST

Mondrian's
*Composition in Red,
Blue, and Yellow*
with
His *Broadway
Boogie-Woogie*

What is the subject matter and underlying meaning of **nonobjective** paintings? In nonobjective art it may be that the elements and composition are the entirety of the content. Any other content may originate with the viewer, not the artist. Still, perhaps much of the beauty of nonobjective art, as in so many instances of objective art, derives from its appearance as a rich, fertile ground for the viewer's imagination.

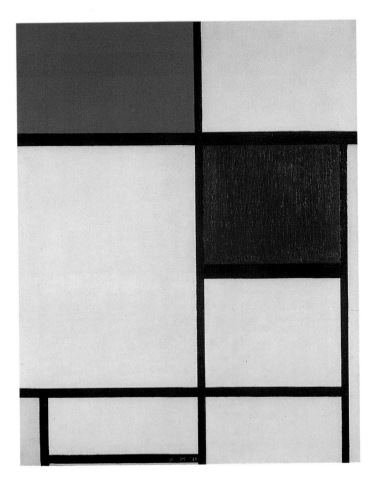

2–63 PIET MONDRIAN
Composition with Red, Blue, and Yellow (1930). Oil on canvas. 20 × 20".

COLLECTION MR. AND MRS. ARMAND P. BARTOS, N.Y. COPYRIGHT MODRIAN ESTATE/HOLTZMAN TRUST.

Piet Mondrian created numerous geometric abstract works, such as *Composition with Red, Blue, and Yellow* (Fig. 2–63) and *Broadway Boogie-Woogie* (Fig. 2–64). How are they alike, and how do they differ? Both contain rectangles; both contain primary colors, albeit with very different visual impacts. Perhaps the key issue has to do with their titles. Let me suggest that one of the works is nonobjective and the other is an abstraction of a pulsating metropolis. What do the titles suggest to you about the meanings of the works?

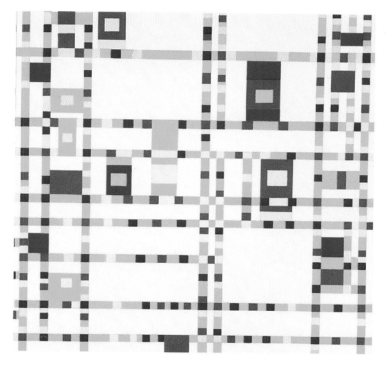

2–64 PIET MONDRIAN
BROADWAY BOOGIE-WOOGIE
(1942–43). OIL ON CANVAS. 50 × 50″.

THE MUSEUM OF MODERN ART, N.Y. GIVEN
ANONOMOUSLY. PHOTOGRAPH
© 1998 THE MUSEUM OF MODERN ART, N.Y.

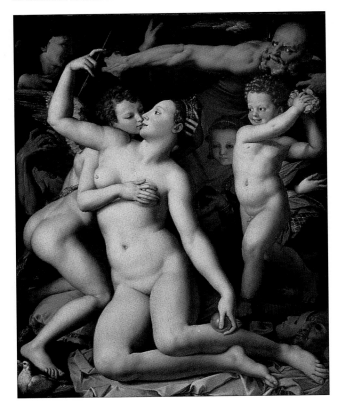

ICONOGRAPHY

Iconography is the study of the themes and symbols in the visual arts—the figures and images that lend works their underlying meanings. Bronzino's sixteenth-century masterpiece *Venus, Cupid, Folly, and Time (The Exposure of Luxury)* (Fig. 2–65) is a classic example of works in which there is much more than meets the eye. The painting weaves an intricate allegory, with many actors, many symbols. Venus, undraped by Time and spread in a languorous diagonal across the front plane, is fondled by her son Cupid. Folly prepares to cast roses on the couple, while Hatred and Inconstancy (with two left hands) lurk in the background. Masks, symbolizing falseness, and other objects, meanings known or unknown, complete the scene.

Works such as these offer iconographers a field day. Is Bronzino saying that love in an environment of hatred and inconstancy is foolish or doomed? Is something being suggested about incest? Self-love? Can one fully appreciate Bronzino's painting without being aware of its iconography? Is it sufficient to respond to the elements and composition, to the figure of a woman being openly fondled before an unlikely array of onlookers? No simple answer is possible, and a Mannerist artist like Bronzino would have intended this ambiguity. Certainly one could appreciate the composition and the subject matter for their own sake, but awareness of the symbolism enriches the viewing experience.

In many cases, artists supply the viewer with clear, familiar images, and frequently they intend to communicate certain underlying themes. But in some cases, the underlying themes may be at least in part the invention of the viewer. In Helen Frankenthaler's *Magic Carpet* (Fig. 2–9), for example, we may interpret the billowing yellow-orange masses as symbolic of the emotions that build within us and threaten our composure. Did the artist intend this symbolism, however, or is it our own invention? Many of us love a puzzle and are willing to spend a great deal of time attempting to decipher the possible iconography of a work of art. In other cases, any definition of the subject matter of a work is an invention of the viewer.

The language of art sometimes opens a direct line of communication with the symbolic systems of the observer. Since the ideas and symbols we use to make meaning of the world cannot overlap perfectly, art may trigger different associations in each of us.

key terms

Plastic elements
Composition
Content
Language
Subject
Line
Organic shape
Geometric shape
Light
Value
Chiaroscuro
Modeling
Prism
Hue
Cool color
Warm color

Saturation
Shade
Tint
Complementary
Pigment
Achromatic
Neutrals
Primary colors
Secondary colors
Tertiary colors
Afterimage
Analogous
Local color
Optical color
Texture
Implied texture

Actual texture
Impasto
Mass
Implied mass
Actual mass
Relative size
Linear perspective
Vanishing point
Horizon
Vantage point
One-point perspective
Two-point perspective
Atmospheric perspective
Aerial perspective
Texture gradient
Brightness gradient

Implied time
Implied motion
Stroboscopic motion
Proportion
Golden Section
Scale
Unity
Balance
Bilateral symmetry
Asymmetrical balance
Rhythm
Bay
Pattern
Iconography
Nonobjective

artists

Elie Nadelman
Richard Diebenkorn
Heide Fasnacht
Ogata Korin
Torii Kyotada
Jean Arp
David Smith
Helen Frankenthaler
Kasimir Malevich
Pierre-Paul Prud'hon
Edouard Vuillard
Dorothea Rockburne
Jasper Johns
Victor Vasarely
Beatrice Whitney van Ness
Alexander Liberman

Claude Monet
Vincent van Gogh
Judy Pfaff
Max Ernst
Ana Mendieta
Meret Oppenheim
Henri Gaudier-Brzeska
Henry Moore
Valerie Jaudon
Ni Zan
Albrecht Dürer
James Aponovich
Henri Matisse
Janet Fish
Albert Bierstadt
Sylvia Plimack Mangold

Masaccio
Ida Applebroog
Eadweard Muybridge
Marcel Duchamp
Henri de Toulouse-Lautrec
Marisol
Claes Oldenburg
Jennifer Bartlett
Robert Indiana
Joan Miró
Gertrude Käsebier
Wayne Thiebaud
Skidmore Owings and Merrill
Bronzino
Piet Mondrian

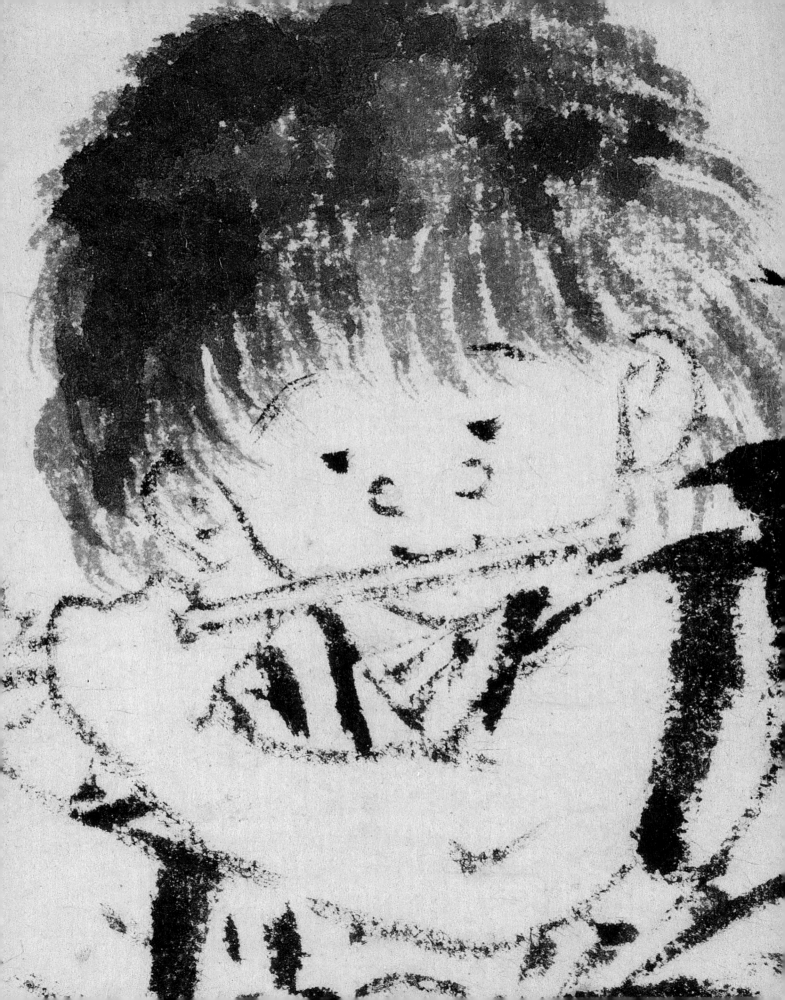

c h a p t e r

DRAWING

PRELIMINARY *Sketch*

- ❏ Some drawings have been created by dragging pieces of burnt wood across a surface.

- ❏ The lead pencil came into use during the 1500s.

- ❏ An early form of pen—the quill—was plucked from a live bird.

- ❏ Some ancient peoples obtained ink from squid and octopi.

- ❏ The original *cartoons* were full-scale preliminary drawings done on paper for projects such as fresco paintings, stained glass, or tapestries.

The first sketch was probably an accident. Perhaps some Stone Age human idly ran a twig through soft clay and was astounded to find an impression of this gesture in the ground. Perhaps this individual then made such impressions as signs for family members (as in an arrow pointing "that-a-way") and to record experiences, such as the hunt for a beast or a gathering around a fire. Similarly, a child may learn to trace a shell fragment through damp sand at the shore's edge. Soon the child is drawing sketches of geometric shapes, animals, toys, and people. Michelangelo was engaging in an essentially similar act when he sketched his models from life—albeit with a bit more skill and flair.

In this chapter we discuss drawing, the most basic of the two-dimensional artforms. In the next two chapters we will discuss two other forms of two-dimensional art—painting and printmaking. We shall see how people over the centuries have used a variety of materials, frequently from surprising sources, to express themselves through two-dimensional artforms.

In its broadest definition, **drawing** is the result of an implement running over a surface and leaving some trace of the gesture. But as we shall discover, the art of drawing goes far beyond this simple description.

The surface, or **support,** onto which an image is sketched is usually, although not always, two-dimensional. Most often the support is **monochromatic** paper or parchment, although drawings can be found on a variety of surfaces. The implements can range from charcoal (which is burnt wood) to bristle brushes dipped in ink. Most drawings, by virtue of the implements, consist of black and tones of gray. But many full-color drawings have also been created with colored chalks, pastels, and wax crayons.

Some drawings are predominantly **linear,** others are constructed solely by tonal contrasts. The quality of line and the nature of shading are affected by the texture of the support. We shall see how the artist capitalizes on the idiosyncratic characteristics of the implements and support to capture a desired expression in the drawing.

CATEGORIES OF DRAWING

Drawing is basic to the visual arts. For centuries, painters and sculptors have made countless preparatory sketches for their major projects, working out difficulties on paper before approaching the more permanent medium of paint or bronze. Architects proceed in the same fashion, outlining buildings in detail before breaking ground. Drawing has also served artists as a kind of shorthand method for recording ideas.

But drawing does not serve only a utilitarian purpose. In most cases, drawing is the most direct route from mind to support. Many artists enjoy the sheer spontaneity of drawing, tracing a pencil or piece of chalk across a sheet of paper to capture directly their thoughts or to record the slightest movement of their hand.

Many drawings, by contrast, stand as complete works of art. Thus, drawings may be said to fall into at least three categories:

1. Sketches that record an idea or provide information about something the artist has seen.

2. Plans or preparatory studies for other projects such as buildings, sculptures, crafts, paintings, plays, and films.

3. Fully developed and self-sufficient works of art.

MATERIALS

Over the millennia methods of drawing have become increasingly sophisticated and materials more varied and standardized. It would seem that we have come a long way from our prehistoric ancestors' use of twigs, hollow reeds, and lumps of clay. Drawing materials can be divided into two major groups: *dry media* and *fluid media.*

DRY MEDIA

The **dry media** used in drawing include silverpoint, pencil, charcoal, chalk, pastel, and wax crayon.

SILVERPOINT **Silverpoint** is one of the oldest drawing media. It was used widely from the late Middle Ages to the early 1500s. Silverpoint drawings are

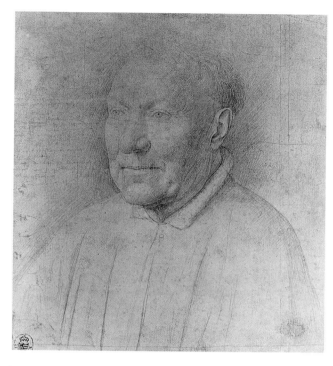

look like, and the lines must be accurate and confidently drawn. The fifteenth-century portrait, *Cardinal Niccolo Albergati* created by the Flemish artist Jan van Eyck (Fig. 3–1), illustrates both the characteristic delicacy and necessary precision of the silverpoint medium. The portrait is a cool, somewhat detached record of the cardinal's facial features rendered with the utmost clarity and control. Yet, although the drawing appears to be flawless in execution, upon close inspection you will notice that what seems to be a single, firmly drawn line defining the contour of the face (particularly around the chin) is actually composed of a number of lines that are "ghosts" of one another. These lines betray van Eyck's efforts to find the most accurately descriptive line.

In light of all the complications and limitations inherent in the silverpoint medium, you might wonder, "Why bother?" And, in fact, few artists do today.

PENCIL   Silverpoint was largely replaced by the lead **pencil,** which came into use during the 1500s. Medieval monks, like the ancient Egyptians, ruled lines with metallic lead. Pencils as we know them began to be mass produced in the late eighteenth century.

A pencil is composed of a thin rod of **graphite** encased within wood or paper. The graphite is ground to dust and mixed with clay, and the mixture is baked to harden the clay. The relative hardness or softness of the implement depends on the quantity of clay present in the mixture. The more clay, the harder the pencil.

Pencil is capable of producing a wide range of effects. Lines drawn with hard pencil can be thin and light in tone; those rendered in soft pencil can be thick and dark. The sharp point of the pencil will create a firm, fine line suitable for meticulous detail. Softer areas of tone can be achieved through a buildup of parallel lines, smudging, or stroking the support with the side of the lead tip.

As seen in the contemporaneous, though contrasting, works of Giorgio de Chirico and Umberto Boccioni, pencil can be manipulated to create dramatically different effects that complement the subject. Chirico's

created by dragging a silver-tipped implement over a surface that has been coated with a **ground** of bone dust or chalk mixed with gum, water, and **pigment.** This ground is sufficiently coarse to allow small flecks of silver from the instrument to adhere to the prepared surface as it is drawn across. These bits of metal form the lines of the drawing; they are barely visible at the start but eventually oxidize, becoming tarnished or darkened and making the image more visible. Each silverpoint line darkens to the same unvarying tone. If the artist desires to make one area of the drawing appear darker than others, it is necessary to build up a series of close, parallel, **cross-hatched** lines in that area to give the impression of deepened tone. Because they lack sharp tonal contrasts, the resultant drawings are extremely delicate in appearance.

The technique of working in silverpoint is itself delicate. The medium allows for little or no correction. Thus, the artist is not in a position to experiment or think at any length while proceeding. There must be a fairly concrete notion of what the final product will

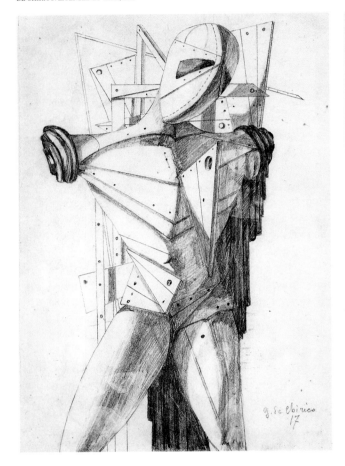

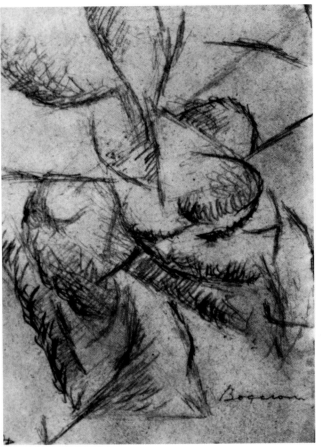

mannequin (Fig. 3–2) is a controlled construction of wood pieces that have been fitted together to the likenesses of muscles, ligaments, and tendons. The precision of the construction is communicated through the fine lines of a hard pencil point.

Boccioni's drawing (Fig. 3–3), on the other hand, is a free expression of dynamic movement. The highly abstracted male figure seems to whirl as it strides forcefully to the left. The contours of the figure are not sure and clear, but rather are composed of smaller, darker, and more agitated lines that underscore the energy of motion. A restlessness in the image is communicated through the irregularity of the line. Boccioni was not interested in creating a photographic likeness of his figure. Rather, he used his medium to render the distorted impression of a figure moving rapidly through space. Chirico, by contrast, used pencil in a more static and controlled manner to present us with a factual duplication of his bizarre inanimate object.

CHARCOAL   Like pencil, **charcoal** has a long history as a drawing implement. Used by our primitive ancestors to create images on cave walls, these initially crumbly pieces of burnt wood or bone now take the form of prepared sticks that are formed by the controlled charring of special hard woods. Charcoal sticks are available in a number of textures that vary from hard to soft. The sticks may be sharpened with sandpaper to form fine and clear lines, or may be dragged flat across the surface to form diffuse areas of varied tone. Like pencil, charcoal may also be smudged or rubbed to create a hazy effect.

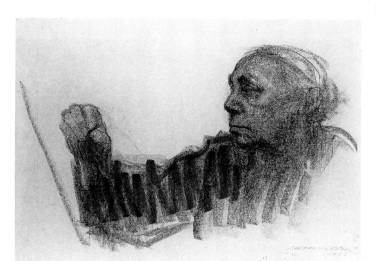

3–5 HUNG LIU
*BRANCHES: THREE
GENERATIONS OF THE WONG
FAMILY* (1988). CHARCOAL
AND OIL ON CANVAS. 1ST
PANEL 60 × 90″, 2ND PANEL
96 × 72″, 3RD PANEL 60 × 90″.

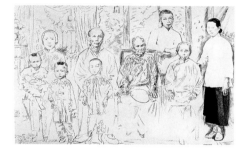

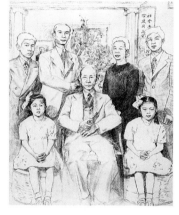

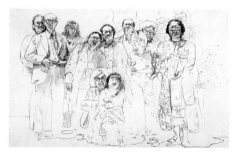

When charcoal is dragged across a surface, bits of the material adhere to that surface, just as in the case of silverpoint and pencil. But charcoal particles rub off more easily, and thus the completed drawing must be sprayed with a solution of thinned varnish to keep them affixed. Also, because of the way in which the charcoal is dispersed over a surface, the nature of the support is evident in each stroke. Coarsely textured paper will yield a grainy image, whereas smooth paper will provide a clear, almost pencil-like line.

A self-portrait of the German Expressionist Käthe Kollwitz (Fig. 3–4) reveals the character of the charcoal medium. Delicate lines of sharpened charcoal drawn over broader areas of subtle shading enunciate the two main points of interest: the artist's face and her hand. Between these two points—that of intellect and that of skill—runs a surge of energy described by aggressive, jagged strokes overlaying the lightly sketched contour of her forearm. Charcoal can be descriptive or expressive, depending on its method of application.

Values in the drawing range from hints of white at her knuckles, cheekbone, and hair to the deepest blacks of the palm of her hand, eyes, and lip area. The finer lines override the texture of the paper, whereas the shaded areas, particularly around the neck and chest, reveal the faint white lines and tiny flecks of pulp that are visual remnants of the paper-making process.

A more monumental portrait in charcoal and oil on canvas reveals the range of the medium, its delicacy, and its forcefulness. Hung Liu, a contemporary Chinese-American artist, captures the lives of three generations with her triptych of black and white "snapshot" images entitled *Branches: Three Generations of the Wong Family* (Fig. 3–5). The first panel records the root family in China; the second features the family after its immigration to the United States, now grown larger by a generation. The third panel is a portrait of a family much expanded: The grandparents, still central to the portrait and the family, have now aged; their children have married non-Asians, and their grandchildren represent a cross between eastern and western cultures. As the family grows more complex, so too does the rendition as we move from left to right. Yet the simplicity of the black lines in contrast to the white ground force the viewer to concentrate on the subjects themselves.

CHALK AND PASTEL   The effects of charcoal, **chalk,** and **pastel** as they are drawn against the paper surface are very similar, though the compositions of the media

3–6 MICHELANGELO
STUDIES FOR THE LIBYAN SIBYL (1510–11). RED CHALK.
11⅜ × 8⅜″.
THE METROPOLITAN MUSEUM OF ART, N.Y. PURCHASE, 1924, JOSEPH PULITZER BEQUEST (24.197.2).

3–7 JEAN-BAPTISTE CARPEAUX
PORTRAIT OF A WOMAN (1874). BLACK CHALK HEIGHTENED
WITH WHITE, ON BUFF PAPER. 7⅞ × 5⅞″.
STERLING AND FRANCINE CLARK ART INSTITUTE, WILLIAMSTOWN, MASS.

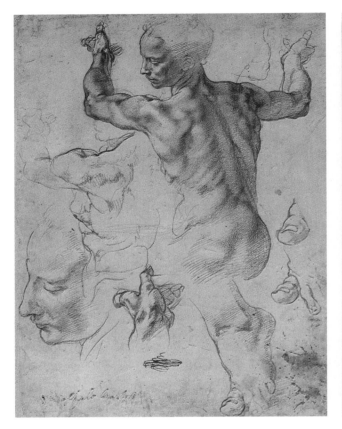

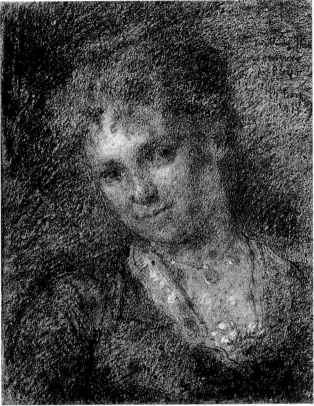

differ. Chalk and pastel consist of pigment and a **binder,** such as **gum arabic,** shaped into workable sticks.

Chalks are available in a number of colors, some of which occur in nature. **Ocher,** for example, derives its dark yellow tint from iron oxide in some clays. **Umber** acquires its characteristic yellowish or reddish brown color from earth containing oxides of manganese and iron. Other popular "organic," or "earth," colors include white, black, and a red called **sanguine.**

Michelangelo used red chalk in a sketch for the Sistine Chapel (see Chapter 13), in which he attempted to work out certain aspects of the figure of the Libyan Sibyl (Fig. 3–6). Quick, sketchy notations of the model's profile, feet, and toes lead to a detailed torso rendered with confident lines and precisely defined tonal areas built up from hatching. The exactness of muscular detail and emphasis on the edges of the body provide insight into the concerns of an artist whose forte was sculpture.

In contrast to Michelangelo's essentially linear approach to his medium, the *Portrait of a Woman* (Fig. 3–7) by the nineteenth-century French painter Jean-Baptiste Carpeaux appears to materialize from the background through subtle tonal contrasts. Whereas Michelangelo emphasized the edges of his model, Carpeaux was more interested in the subtle roundness of his model's form. Carpeaux capitalized on the effect of soft chalk drawn across a coarsely textured paper to create a hazy atmosphere that envelops the sitter.

Pastels consist of ground chalk mixed with powdered pigments and a binder. Whereas chalk drawings can be traced to prehistoric times, pastels did not come into wide use until the 1400s. They were introduced to France only in the 1700s, but within a century pastels captured the imagination of many important painters. Their wide range of brilliant colors offered a painter's palette for use in the more spontaneous medium of drawing.

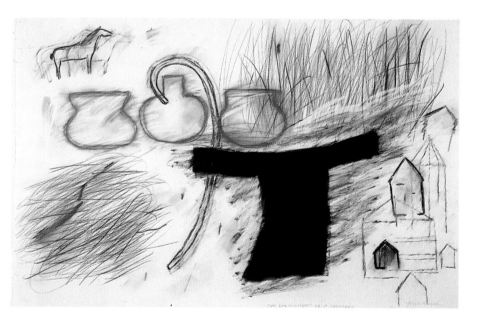

One of the masters of pastel drawing was the nineteenth-century French painter and sculptor Edgar Degas. The directness and spontaneity of the medium was well suited to some of his favorite subjects: ballet dancers in motion, horses racing toward a finish line, and women caught unaware in the midst of commonplace activities. Degas's *Woman at Her Toilette* (Fig. 3–8) is a veritable explosion of glowing color. The pastels are manipulated in countless ways to create a host of different effects. The contours of the figure are boldly sketched, whereas the flesh is composed of more erratic lines that create a sense of roundness through a spectrum of color. Degas scratched the pastels over the surface to form sharp lines or dragged them flatly to create more free-flowing strokes. At times the colors were left pure and intense, and at other times subtle harmonies were rendered through blending or smudging.

Jaune Quick-to-See Smith's *The Environment: Be a Shepherd* (Fig. 3–9) is an effective combination of drawing media: charcoal, colored chalk, and pastel. The earth tones of sepia, brown, greens, and greys evoke the desert southwest and enhance the imagery of a Native American narrative. The upper right and lower left bear charcoal sketches of a horse and a rural church; they are overworked, leaving ghost-like images of themselves reverberating in space. In the center, a shepherd's (priest's?) robe hovers with arms outstretched, like a spectre admonishing the abusers of the environment. Throughout the drawing, contrasting images that refer to intertwined cultural legacies are held together with tenuous, grass-like strokes. The media and the sketchy manner in which they are handled effectively creates the feeling of a "mental sketchbook"—fleeting memories sparked by incongruous objects.

3–9 JAUNE QUICK-TO-SEE SMITH
THE ENVIRONMENT: BE A SHEPHERD (1989). CHARCOAL,
COLORED CHALK, AND PASTEL. 47 × 31¼".

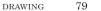

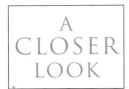

A
CLOSER
LOOK

LIFE, DEATH,
AND DWELLING
IN THE
DEEP SOUTH

Some years ago, African-American sculptor Beverly Buchanan came to know Ms. Mary Lou Furcron. Both artists, one might say. Both the builders of structures. Both nurturing, creative, and colorful. Ever since this meeting, Buchanan's life and art have revolved around the art and life of the southern shack-dweller.

It's an existence unto itself, as the photographs indicate (Fig. 3–10). Ms. Furcron's shack reflects her life, and her life reflects the shack in which she lived. She devoted a part of each day to maintaining the structure, replacing rotted posts with new logs; using bark, lathing, and other odd materials to repair the siding. The shack stood as an organic and ever-evolving structure—an extension of Ms. Furcron herself. As the shack required her constant attention for its survival, her move to a nursing home brought its rapid disrepair. Just one month after Ms. Furcron's departure, the shack was unrecognizable as its former self.

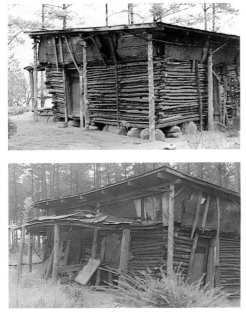

Buchanan's art, in sculpture, and especially in drawing, reflects a structural approach to the creation of the shack image. As Ms. Furcron built with the recycled remnants of nature and human existence, so does Beverly Buchanan. Her mixed-media shacks are created from old pieces of wood, metal, and found objects (*Hometown—Shotgun Shack,* 1992; Fig. 3–11). Her oil pastel drawing *Henriette's Yard* (Fig. 3–12) is vigorously and lovingly constructed of a myriad of vibrant strokes. These strokes at once serve as the building blocks of the shack image and the very stuff that reduces the structure to an almost indecipherable explosion of color. The precarious balance of the shacks in relation to one another, and the uncertain ground in which they stand, further symbolize the precious and fragile nature of the shack dwelling, and human existence.

3–10 PHOTOGRAPHS OF MS. MARY LOU FURCRON'S HOME. TOP PHOTO SHOWS THE SHACK WHILE MS. FURCRON WAS LIVING IN IT AND TENDING TO IT. PHOTO UNDERNEATH SHOWS THE SHACK JUST ONE MONTH AFTER HER PLACEMENT IN A NURSING HOME.
PHOTOGRAPHS COURTESY OF STEINBAUM KRAUSS GALLERY, N.Y.

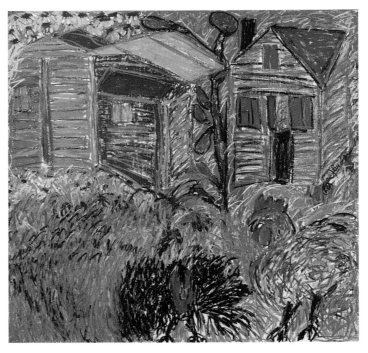

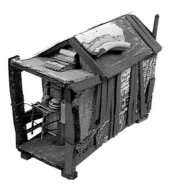

3–11 BEVERLY BUCHANAN
HOMETOWN—SHOTGUN SHACK (1992).
WOOD, MIXED MEDIA. 12 × 9¼ × 15″.
COURTESY OF STEINBAUM KRAUSS GALLERY, N.Y.

3–12 BEVERLY BUCHANAN
HENRIETTE'S YARD (1995). OIL PASTEL ON PAPER. 60 × 60″.
COLLECTION OF LOIS FICHNER-RATHUS AND SPENCER RATHUS. PHOTO COURTESY OF STEINBAUM KRAUSS GALLERY, N.Y.

3–13 GEORGES SEURAT
CAFÉ CONCERT (C. 1887–88). CONTE CRAYON WITH WHITE HEIGHTENING ON INGRES PAPER. 12 × 9¼″.
MUSEUM OF ART, RHODE ISLAND SCHOOL OF DESIGN, PROVIDENCE. GIFT OF MRS. MURRAY S. DANFORTH.

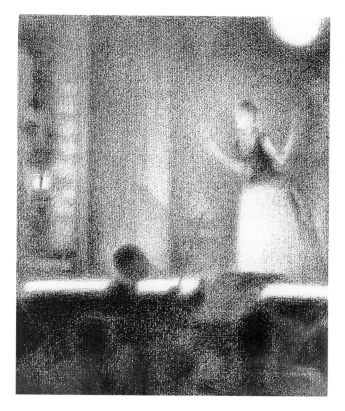

CRAYON Strictly defined, the term **crayon** includes any drawing material in stick form. Thus, charcoal, chalk, and pastels are crayons, as are the wax implements you used on walls, floors, and occasionally coloring books when you were a child. One of the most popular commercially manufactured crayons for artists is the **conte crayon.** Its effects on paper are similar to those of chalk and pastel, although its harder texture makes possible a greater clarity.

Conte crayon was one of the favorite media of the nineteenth-century French painter Georges Seurat. By working the crayon over a highly textured surface, he was able to emulate the fine points of paint he used to describe forms in his canvas works (see Chapter 15). Seurat's *Café Concert* (Fig. 3–13) is built up almost solely through contrasts of tone. Deep, velvety blacks absorb the almost invisible heads of the musicians in the orchestra pit, while a glaring strip of untouched white paper seems to illuminate the stage. The even application of crayon to coarse paper creates diffuse light that accurately conveys the atmosphere of a small café.

Wax crayons, like pastels, combine ground pigment with a binder—in this case, wax. Wax crayon moves easily over a support to form lines that have a characteristic sheen. These lines are less apt to smudge than charcoal, chalk, and pastels.

FLUID MEDIA

The primary **fluid medium** used in drawing is ink, and the instruments used to carry the medium are pen and brush. Appearing in Egyptian **papyrus** drawings and ancient Chinese scrolls, ink has a history that stretches back thousands of years. Some ancient peoples made ink from the dyes of plants, squid, and octopus. By the second century CE, blue-black inks were being derived from galls found on oak trees. The oldest known type of ink is India or China ink, which is used in oriental **calligraphy** to this day. It is a solution of carbon black and water, and it is permanent and rich black in color.

As with the dry media, dramatically different effects can be achieved with fluid media through a variety of techniques. For example, the artist may alter the composition of the medium by diluting it with water to achieve lighter tones, or may vary the widths of brushes and pen points to achieve lines of different character.

PEN AND INK Pens also have been used since ancient times. The earliest ones were hollow reeds that were slit at the ends to allow a controlled flow of ink. **Quills** plucked from live birds became popular writing instruments during the Middle Ages. These were replaced in the nineteenth century by the mass-produced metal **nib,** which is slipped into a wooden **stylus.** These are the pens that many artists use today.

Pen and ink are used to create drawings that are essentially linear, although the nature of the line can vary considerably according to the type of instrument employed. A fine, rigid nib will provide a clear, precise line that is uniform in thickness. Lines created by a more flexible quill tip, in contrast, will vary in width according to the amount of pressure the artist's hand exerts.

PEN AND WASH Fine, clear lines of pure ink are often combined in drawings with **wash**—diluted ink that is applied with a brush. Wash provides a tonal emphasis absent in pen-and-ink drawings. In Giovanni Battista

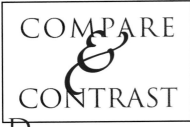

COMPARE & CONTRAST

DÜRER'S *SKETCHES OF ANIMALS AND LANDSCAPES* WITH DELACROIX'S *TWO STUDIES OF A LIONESS*

The narrative versus expressive properties of the pen-and-ink technique are well illustrated by contrasting the drawings of the German Renaissance artist Albrecht Dürer (Fig. 3–14) and the nineteenth-century French painter Eugène Delacroix (Fig. 3–15). The purpose of Dürer's drawing was to describe accurately for his fellow artists and other curious parties the exotic animals he had seen during a visit to a Brussels zoo in 1521. In the absence of photography, Dürer's task was to provide as honest a record of these creatures as his skill would allow. How does Dürer's use of line define the animals' essential characteristics, from attitude to overall shape to distinguishing markings?

Dürer's comrades would have learned little about the likeness of lions had they been looking at Eugène Delacroix's drawing. However, might they have come away with a better understanding of the power and personality of these felines? Why? Discuss the ways in which the styles of the artists differ. (Hint: Dürer's is painstakingly descriptive, whereas Delacroix's is free and expressive.) Note that in the Delacroix rendition, vigorous lines describe the animal's ferocity as she readies to spring and pounce. Curving, calligraphic strokes envelop her nonthreatening form in sleep. The lines themselves exude a certain emotion in their varying thicknesses, densities, and values.

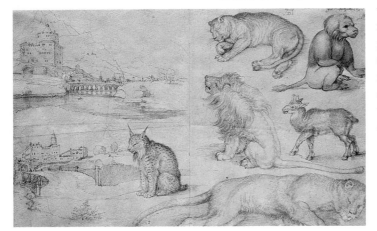

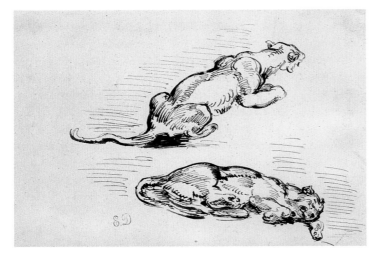

3–14 ALBRECHT DÜRER
SKETCHES OF ANIMALS AND LANDSCAPES (1521). PEN AND BLACK INK; BLUE, GRAY, AND ROSE WASH. $10^{7}/_{16} \times 15^{5}/_{8}''$.
© STERLING AND FRANCINE CLARK ART INSTITUTE, WILLIAMSTOWN, MASS.

3–15 EUGÈNE DELACROIX
TWO STUDIES OF A LIONESS (C. 1850–60). PEN AND DARK BROWN INK. $5^{3}/_{16} \times 7^{5}/_{8}''$.
© STERLING AND FRANCINE CLARK ART INSTITUTE, WILLIAMSTOWN, MASS.

IN GENESIS, ABRAHAM HAD A CHILD BY HIS WIFE'S SERVANT, HAGAR. IN JEALOUSY, SARAH BANISHED HAGAR AND THE CHILD, ISHMAEL, TO THE WILDERNESS WHERE THEY WERE RESCUED BY AN ANGEL.

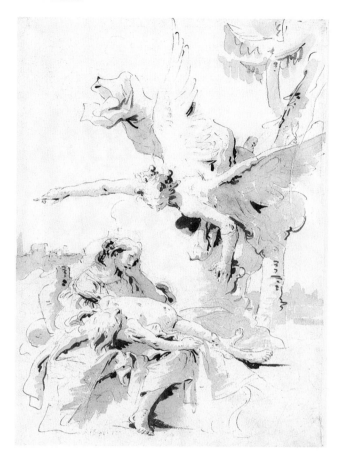

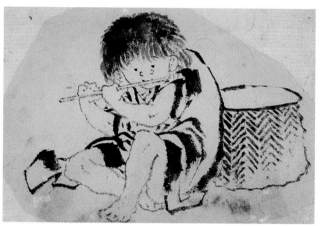

3–16 GIOVANNI BATTISTA TIEPOLO
HAGAR AND ISHMAEL IN THE WILDERNESS (C. 1725–35). PEN, BRUSH AND BROWN INK, AND WASH, OVER SKETCH IN BLACK CHALK. 16½ × 11⅛".
© STERLING AND FRANCINE CLARK ART INSTITUTE, WILLIAMSTOWN, MASS.

3–17 KATSUSHIKA HOKUSAI (1760–1849)
BOY PLAYING FLUTE. INK AND BRUSH ON PAPER. 4½ × 6¼".
COURTESY OF FREER GALLERY OF ART, SMITHSONIAN INSTITUTION, WASHINGTON, D.C.

Japanese artists are masters of the brush-and-ink medium. They have used it for centuries for every type of calligraphy, ranging from works of art to everyday writing. Their facility with the technique is most evident in seemingly casual sketches such as those done in the late eighteenth and early nineteenth centuries by Japanese artist Katsushika Hokusai (Fig. 3–17). Longer, flowing lines range from thick and dark to thin and faint, capturing, respectively, the heavy folds of the boy's clothing and the pale flesh of his youthful limbs. Short, brisk strokes humorously describe the similarity between the hemp of the woven basket and the youngster's disheveled hair. There is an extraordinary simplicity to the drawing attributable to the surety and ease with which Hokusai handles his medium.

Tiepolo's eighteenth-century drawing (Fig. 3–16), the contours of the biblical figures are described in pen and ink, but their volume derives from a clever use of wash. An illusion of three-dimensionality is created by pulling the white of the untouched paper forward to function as form and enchancing it with contrasting areas of light and dark wash. The gestural vitality of the pen lines and the generous swaths of watery ink accentuate the composition's dynamic movement.

BRUSH AND INK   Brushes are extremely versatile drawing implements. They are available in a wide variety of materials, textures, and shapes that afford many different effects. The nature of a line in brush and ink will depend on whether the brush is bristle or nylon, thin or thick, pointed or flat-tipped. Likewise, characteristics of the support—texture, absorbency, and the like—will influence the character of the completed drawing. Brush and ink touched to silk leaves an impression quite different from that produced by brush and ink touched to paper.

BRUSH AND WASH   The medium of brush and wash is even more versatile than that of brush and ink. While it can duplicate the linearity of brush-and-ink drawings, it can also be used to create images solely through tonal contrasts. The ink can be diluted to varying degrees to provide a wide tonal range. Different effects can be achieved either by adding water directly to the ink, or by moistening the support before drawing.

It is again surprising to note how adaptable the drawing media can be to different artistic styles or

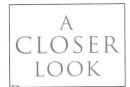

A
CLOSER
LOOK

PAPER DOLLS
FOR A
POST-COLUMBIAN
WORLD

Mark Twain once wrote that the ink with which history has been written is fluid prejudice. Most of us are just beginning to understand that there are two sides to every historical event, and that any accurate examination of history must include the view of the vanquished, the story of the minority group, a look at the peripheral events that are part of the human story.

Native American artist Jaune Quick-to-See Smith has challenged our perception of Columbus's expedition to the New World by sardonically focusing on its destructive aftermath. She offers us her pen and pastel version of paper dolls, a familiar childhood pastime, which in her hands assumes all sorts of political connotations. Our Native American couple are called Barbie and Ken Plenty Horses (Fig. 3–18). Their clothing ensembles include some "ethnic-wear" (politically correct) amidst a priest's robe, maid's uniform, saloon-keeper's costume, and alternate sheaths of skin infested with smallpox. Is this what has become of the Native American population in the name of Western "civilization"?

3–18 JAUNE QUICK-TO-SEE SMITH
PAPER DOLLS FOR A POST-COLUMBIAN WORLD WITH ENSEMBLES CONTRIBUTED BY THE U.S. GOVERNMENT (1991). PASTEL AND PEN ON PAPER. 40 × 29″.

COLLECTION DR. AND MRS. HAROLD STEINBAUM. COURTESY STEINBAUM KRAUSS GALLERY, N.Y.

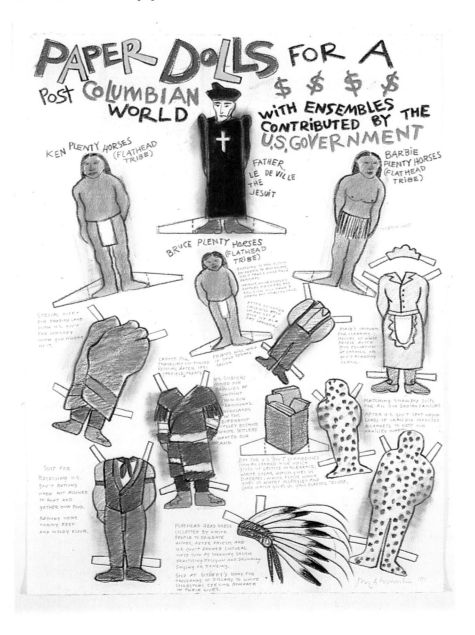

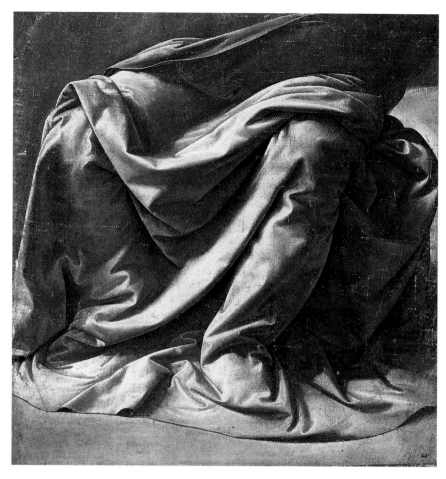

surfaces and crevices. The voluminous folds are realized through a meticulous study of tonal contrasts.

The shape of Claude's landscape also relies on tonal variations rather than line, but here the similarity ends. Leonardo's drawing is descriptive, and almost photographic in its realism. Lorrain's work is suggestive—a quick rendition of the artist's visual impression of the landscape. Whereas Leonardo worked his wash over linen, Claude worked on damp paper. By touching a brush dipped in ink to the wet surface, Claude made his forms dissolve into the surrounding field and lose their distinct contours. Broadly brushed liquid formations constructed of varying tones yield the impression of groves of trees on the bank of a body of water that leads to distant mountains. These nondescript areas of diffuse wash were here and there given more definition through bolder lines and brush strokes applied after the paper was dry. Claude used brush and wash to define space; Leonardo used it to reveal form.

CARTOONS

The word **cartoon** derives from the Italian *cartone,* meaning paper. Originally cartoons were full-scale preliminary drawings done on paper for projects such as fresco paintings, stained glass, or tapestries. The meaning of cartoon was expanded to include humorous and satirical drawings when a parody of fresco cartoons submitted for decoration of the Houses of Parliament appeared in an English magazine in 1843. Regardless of their targets, all modern cartoons rely on **caricature,** the gross exaggeration and distortion of natural features to ridicule a social or political target.

Honoré Daumier is perhaps the only famous painter to devote so great a part of his production—some 4,000 works—to cartoons. Known for his riveting images of social and moral injustices in nineteenth-century France, he also created caricatures in which he displayed a sharp,

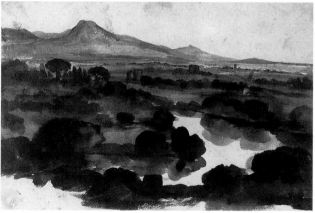

subjects. Consider the drawings by the Italian Renaissance master Leonardo da Vinci (Fig. 3–19) and the seventeenth-century French painter Claude Lorrain (Fig. 3–20). Even upon close inspection, one would not guess that both works were created in the same medium, despite their tonal emphasis. Leonardo captured the intricacies of drapery as it falls over the human form, dramatically lit to provide harsh contrasts between

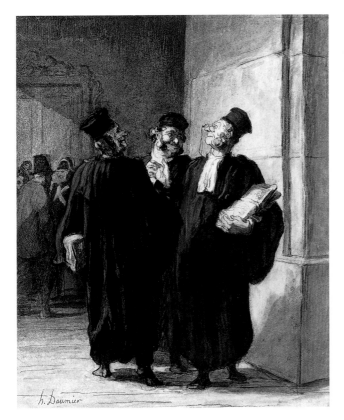

3–21 HONORÉ DAUMIER
THREE LAWYERS (C. 1855). PEN AND BLACK INK, BLACK CHALK,
BRUSH AND BLACK AND BLUE-BLACK INK, GRAY AND BEIGE
WASH, AND WHITE GOUACHE. 12¹⁵⁄₁₆ × 9¾".
STERLING AND FRANCINE CLARK ART INSTITUTE, WILLIAMSTOWN, MASS.

3–22 DRAWING BY MODELL; © 1983 THE NEW YORKER
MAGAZINE, INC.

NEW APPROACHES TO DRAWING

Thus far we have examined traditional drawing media used by artists over many centuries. Keeping in mind, however, our all-encompassing definition of a drawing, it is not surprising that today "anything goes."

It is not unusual to find drawings that are not "drawn" at all. In Figure 3–23, for example, Jackson Pollock, an American artist working in the years surrounding World War II, dripped and whipped an enamel-like paint onto paper surfaces to record his spontaneous gestures. Other artists have used airbrushes to spray a fine mist of ink onto their supports.

The surfaces on which drawings are made are also no longer sacred. They may be punctured or slashed; they may be littered with foreign matter such as string, sand, or pieces of paper. If the paper is handmade by the artist, its texture can be radically manipulated while the pulp is wet.

Contemporary artist Chris Craig does not limit herself to traditional flat pieces of paper as the supports for her drawings. In *#239* (Fig. 3–24), Craig folds her paper support and draws geometric shapes across the folds in pencil, crayons, charcoal, pastels, or acrylic paint. Acrylic paint, when used, might be spattered or dripped. The paper is then flattened so that the shapes she has drawn become fragments. She continues some of the fragmented lines, in this way completing new shapes, while others are left as they are. The paper is folded again, but sometimes along new lines. In these ways Craig's work takes on an element of accident or chance. On the wall, such drawings have the effect of three-dimensional reliefs. Given their monumental scale, the viewer who walks in front of them has the sense of shifting topography.

Art has always hinged on exploration. Although the new materials and techniques in use today might have shocked him, the inventive Leonardo da Vinci would have delighted in their unorthodoxy and their limitless possibilities.

And so drawings show surprising versatility in terms of their intended purposes, their media, and their techniques of execution. In the next chapter we shall see that paintings show similar versatility.

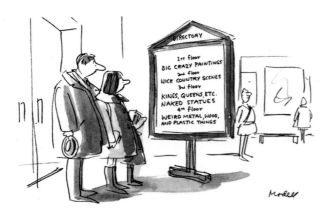

sardonic wit. Daumier's *Three Lawyers* (Fig. 3–21) is a taunting illustration of what he perceived to be the grossly overstated importance of this professional group. Each lawyer strains to raise his nose and eyebrows higher than those of his comrades, effectively communicating his self-adulation. The absurd superficiality of the trio's conversation is communicated by their attempts to strike a meaningful pose in their clownlike embodiments.

Of course, all cartoons need not have deep-rooted messages. Cartoons can also just be fun, as is the Modell cartoon (Fig. 3–22) published in *The New Yorker* magazine. One could seek to find in the drawing a "message" about the way in which the general public tends to categorize works of art, but to do so might be "reaching."

3–23 JACKSON POLLOCK
UNTITLED (1950). PENCIL, DUCO ON PAPER. 22 × 59⅜″.

GRAPHISCHE SAMMLUNG STAATSGALERIE, STUTTGART. © 1998 POLLACK-KRASNER FOUNDATION/
ARTISTS RIGHTS SOCIETY (ARS), N.Y.

3–24 CHRIS CRAIG
#239 (1987). MIXED MEDIA ON PAPER. 26 × 100″.
COURTESY OF THE ARTIST.

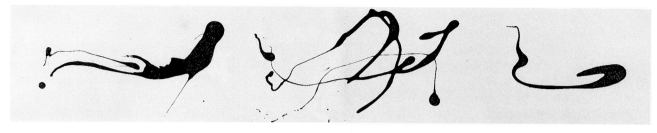

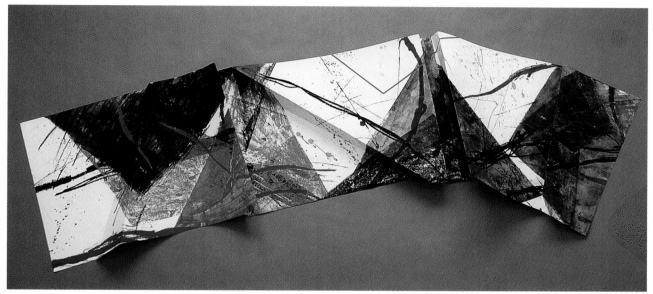

key terms

Drawing	Ground	Binder	Calligraphy
Support	Pigment	Gum arabic	Quill
Dry Media	Crosshatching	Ocher	Nib
Fluid Media	Pencil	Umber	Stylus
Monochromatic	Graphite	Sanguine	Wash
Linear	Charcoal	Crayon	Cartoon
Dry Media	Chalk	Conte crayon	Caricature
Silverpoint	Pastel	Papyrus	

artists

Jan van Eyck	Edgar Degas	Katsushika Hokusai
Giorgio de Chirico	Jaune Quick-to-See Smith	Leonardo da Vinci
Umberto Boccioni	Beverly Buchanan	Claude Lorrain
Käthe Kollwitz	Georges Seurat	Honoré Daumier
Hung Liu	Albrecht Dürer	Modell
Michelangelo	Eugène Delacroix	Jackson Pollock
Jean-Baptiste Carpeaux	Giovanni Battista Tiepolo	Chris Craig

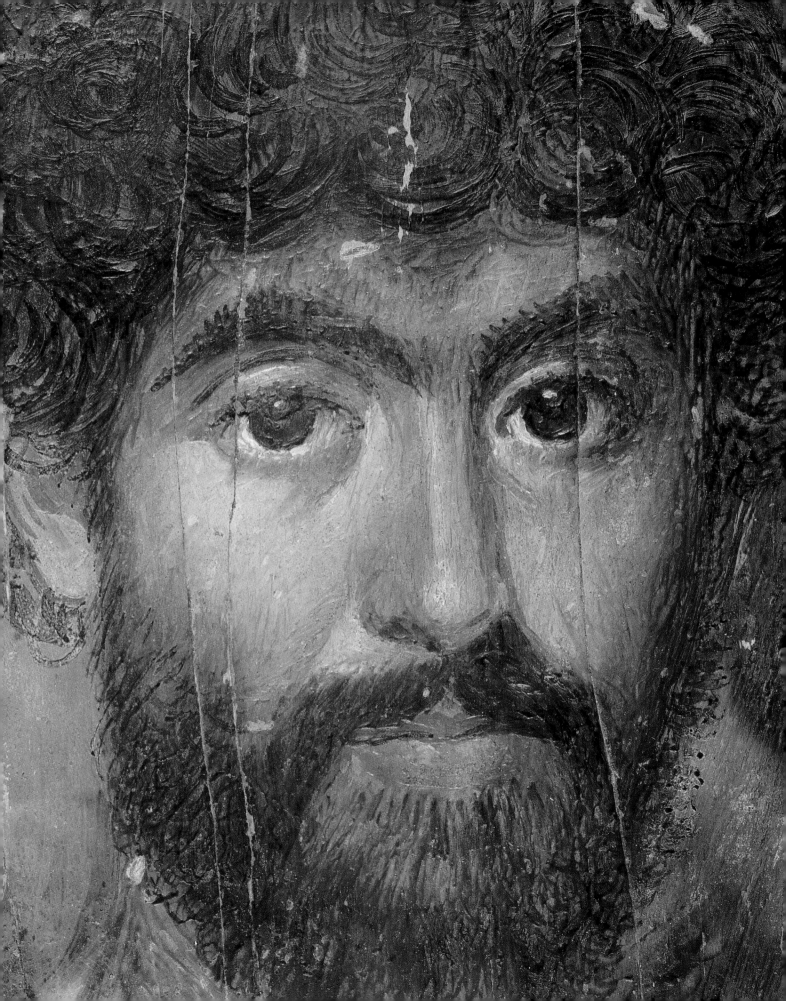

c h a p t e r

PAINTING

PRELIMINARY Sketch

- ❏ The pigments in paint are derived from chemicals found in plant and animal life, clay, soil, and sand.

- ❏ Materials such as plaster, wax, oil, acrylic, water, and gum have been used to hold pigment together.

- ❏ The ancient Egyptians and Greeks painted their sculptures so that they would look more lifelike.

- ❏ One type of paint uses the chicken egg as a major ingredient.

- ❏ The first oil paintings were made on wood panels.

- ❏ Spray painting has been used by both Paleolithic cave artists and contemporary graffiti artists.

Mummy Portrait of a Man (detail). See Figure 4–2.

The line between drawing and painting is sometimes blurred. The art historian will speak of linear aspects in painting or painterly qualities in drawing. At times the materials used in the two media will overlap. Jackson Pollock, for example, used enamel paint in his gestural paper drawings, as was noted in Chapter 3 (see Fig. 3–23). **Painting** is generally defined as the application of pigment to a surface. Yet we have already seen the use of pigment in pastel drawings.

Paint can be applied to a number of surfaces. It has been used throughout history to decorate pottery, enhance sculpture, and embellish architecture. In this section we shall explain the composition of paint and explore painting in works created on two-dimensional supports.

PAINT

To most of us, paint is synonymous with color. The color in a paint derives from its pigment. The pigment in powdered form is mixed with a binding agent, or **vehicle,** and a solvent, or **medium,** to form **paint—** the liquid material that imparts color to a surface.

Pigments are available in a wide chromatic range. Their color is derived from chemicals and minerals found in plant and animal life, clay, soil, and sand.

Different vehicles are employed in different painting media. The main criterion for a successful vehicle is that it hold the pigments together. Lime plaster, wax, egg, oil, acrylic plastic, water, and gum arabic are commonly used vehicles. Unfortunately, most vehicles are subject to long-term problems such as cracking, yellowing, or discoloration.

The task of a medium is to provide fluency to the paint, so that the color may be readily dispersed over the surface. Water or turpentine are frequently used as thinning agents for this purpose.

TYPES OF PAINTING

A variety of supports and tools have been used throughout the history of art to create paintings. We shall discuss the characteristics of several types of painting.

FRESCO

Fresco is the art of painting on plaster. **Buon fresco,** or true fresco, is executed on damp, lime plaster; **fresco secco** is painting on dry plaster. In buon fresco, the pigments are mixed only with water, and the lime of the plaster wall acts as a binder. As the wall dries, the painted image on it becomes permanent. In fresco secco—a less popular and less permanent method— pigments are combined with a vehicle of glue that affixes the color to the dry wall.

Fresco painters encounter a number of problems. Since in true fresco the paint must be applied to fresh, damp plaster, the artist cannot bite off more than it is possible to chew—or paint—in one day. For this reason, large fresco paintings are composed of small sections, each of which has been painted in a day. The artist tries to arrange the sections so that the joints will not be obvious, but sometimes it is not possible to do so. In a fourteenth-century fresco painting by the Italian master Giotto (Fig. 4–1), these joints are clearly evident, particularly in the sky, where the artist was not able to complete the vast expanse of blue all at once. It is not surprising that sixteenth-century art historian Giorgio Vasari wrote that of all the methods painters employ, fresco painting "is the most masterly and beautiful, because it consists in doing in a single day that which, in other methods, may be retouched day after day, over the work already done."

Another problem: although fresco paintings can be brilliant in color, some pigments will not form chemical bonds with lime. Thus, these pigments are not suitable for the medium. Artists in Giotto's era, for example, encountered a great deal of difficulty with the color blue. Such lime resistance limits the artist's palette and can make tonal transitions difficult.

Leonardo da Vinci, in his famous *The Last Supper* (Fig. 13–18), attempted to meet these nuisances head on, only to suffer disastrous consequences. The experimental materials and methods he employed to achieve superior results were unsuccessful. He lived to see his masterpiece disintegrate beyond repair.

Despite these problems, fresco painting enjoyed immense popularity from prehistoric times until its full flowering in the Renaissance. Although it fell out of favor for several centuries thereafter, the art of fresco was revived by Mexican muralists after World War I.

4–1 GIOTTO
LAMENTATION (C. 1305). FRESCO. 7′7″ × 7′9″.
ARENA CHAPEL, PADUA, ITALY.

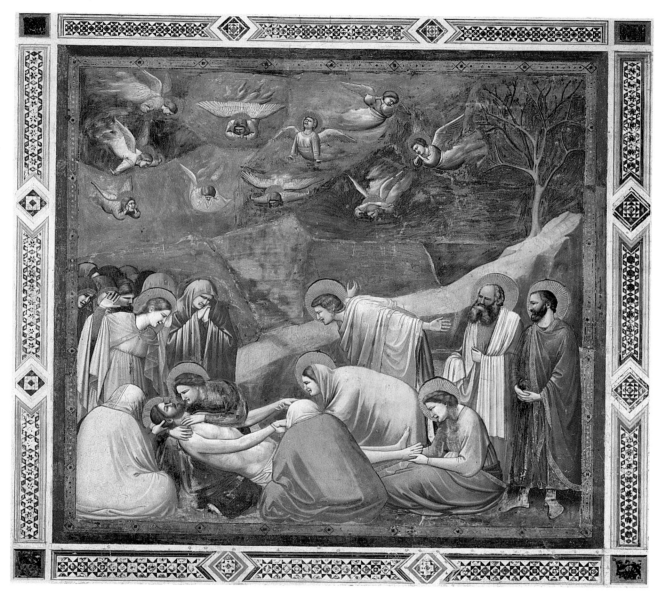

4–2 *MUMMY PORTRAIT OF A MAN*
(EGYPTO-ROMAN) (FAIYUM, C. 160–179).
ENCAUSTIC ON WOOD. 14 × 8″.

ALBRIGHT-KNOX ART GALLERY, BUFFALO, N.Y. CHARLES CLIFTON FUND, 1938.

4–3 KAY WALKINGSTICK
SOLSTICE (1982). ACRYLIC AND WAX ON CANVAS. 48 × 48 × 3½″.

COLLECTION OF THE ARTIST.

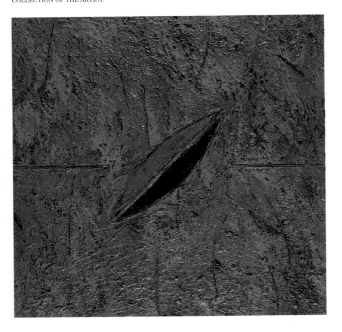

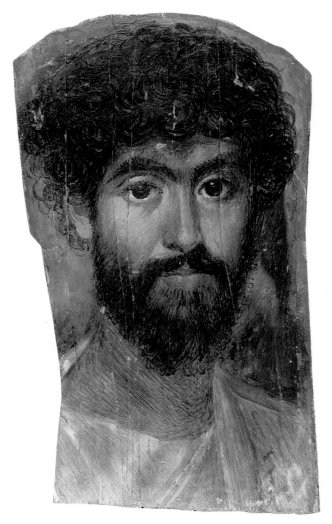

ENCAUSTIC

One of the earliest methods of applying color to a surface was **encaustic.** It consists of pigment in a wax vehicle that has been heated to a liquid state. The ancient Egyptians and Greeks tinted their sculptures with encaustic to grant them a lifelike appearance. The Romans applied encaustic to walls, using hot irons. Often, as in the Egyptian *Mummy Portrait of a Man* (Fig. 4–2) dating back to the second century CE, the medium was applied to small, portable wooden panels covered with cloth. As evidenced by the startling realism and freshness of the portrait, encaustic is an extremely durable medium whose colors remain vibrant and whose surface maintains a hard luster.

But encaustic is a difficult medium to manipulate: one must keep the molten wax at a constant temperature. For this reason, it has been used only by a handful of contemporary artists.

Native American painter Kay Walkingstick derives a certain plasticity from her very different use of acrylic and wax on canvas (Fig. 4–3). In *Solstice,* two flattened arcs of sharply contrasting hues are about to merge in a viscous sea of mauve and purple. The canoe-like image, while common to Native American symbolism, can also be viewed as an abstraction signifying the shifting of seasons from autumn to winter—a kind of quiet cosmological passage. Walkingstick builds her textural surface through successive layers of colored wax, gouging the field here and there with lines that reveal the palette of the lower layers. It is at once an image of power and of solitude.

TEMPERA

Tempera, like encaustic, was popular for centuries, but its traditional composition—ground pigments mixed with a vehicle of egg yolk or whole eggs thinned with water—is rarely used today. Tempera now describes a medium in which pigment can be mixed with an emulsion of milk, different types of glues or gums, and even the juices and saps of plants and trees. The use of tempera dates back

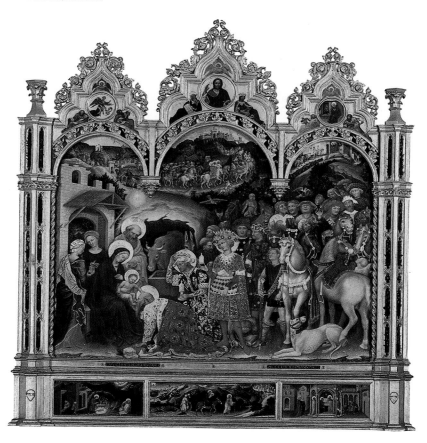

to the Greeks and Romans. Tempera was the exclusive painting medium of artists during the Middle Ages. Not until the invention of oil paint in Northern Europe in the 1300s did tempera fall out of favor.

Tempera offered many advantages. It was an extremely durable medium if applied to a properly prepared surface. Pure and brilliant colors were attainable. Colors did not become compromised by gradual oxidation. Also, the consistency and fluidity of the mixture allowed for a great deal of precision. Tempera, unlike oil paint, however, dries quickly and is difficult to rework. Also, unlike oils, it cannot provide subtle gradations of tone.

Tempera can be applied to wood or canvas panels, although the latter did not come into wide use until the 1500s. Both types of supports were prepared by covering the surface with a **ground.** The ground was generally a combination of powdered chalk or plaster and animal glue called **gesso.** The gesso ground provided a smooth, glistening white surface on which to apply color.

All that is desirable in the tempera medium can be found in Figure 4–4, the panel painting by the fifteenth-century Italian artist Gentile da Fabriano. Combined with the technique of **gilding**—the application of thinly hammered sheets of gold to the panel surface—the luminous reds and blues and pearly grays of the tempera paint provide a sumptuous display. The fine details of the ornate costumes testify to the precision made possible by egg tempera.

Several contemporary artists, such as the American Andrew Wyeth, have also been enticed by the exactness and intricacies made possible by tempera. Suited to a methodical and painstaking approach to painting, this medium of the old masters yields unparalleled displays of contrasting textures and sharp-focused realism, as shown in Figure 4–5.

Contemporary painting techniques often incorporate a variety of media, as we shall see throughout the

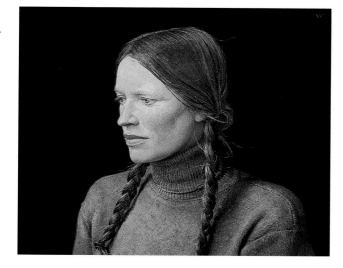

4–5 ANDREW WYETH
BRAIDS (1979). TEMPERA. 16½ × 20½″.

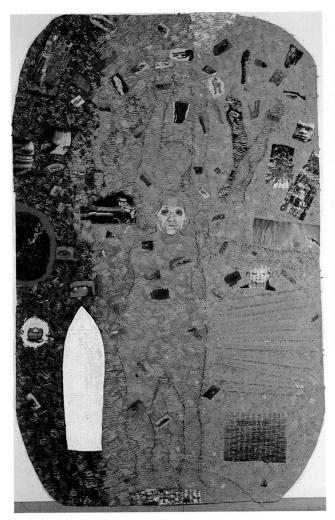

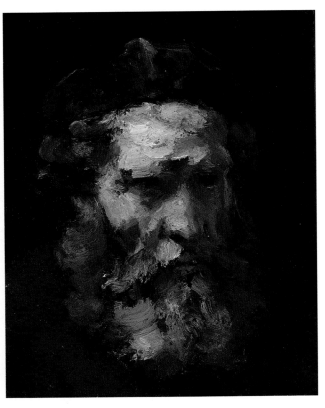

text. The base media for Howardena Pindell's *Autobiography: Water / Ancestors, Middle Passage / Family Ghosts* (Fig. 4–6) are tempera and acrylic, but the work, on sewn canvas, also incorporates an array of techniques and substances—markers, oil stick, paper, phototransfer, and vinyl tape. The detail achieved is quite remarkable. The artist seems to float in a shimmering pool of shallow water, while all around her images and objects of memory seem to enter and exit her consciousness. Included among them are the prominent white shape of an African slave ship, a reference to Pindell's African ancestry, and the whitened face of the artist's portrait that may have been influenced by Michael Jackson's "Thriller" makeup. The work resembles as much a weaving as a painting, further reflecting the tapestry-like nature of human recollection.

OIL

The transition from egg tempera to **oil paint** was gradual. For many years following the introduction of the oil medium, artists used it only to apply a finishing coat of glazes to an underpainting of tempera. **Glazing,** or the application of multiple layers of transparent films of paint to a surface, afforded subtle tonal variations and imparted a warm atmosphere not possible with tempera alone. Oil paints have been in wide use since the fifteenth century.

Oil paint consists of ground pigments combined with a linseed oil vehicle and turpentine medium or thinner. Oil paint is naturally slow in drying, but drying can be facilitated with various agents added to the basic mixture.

Oil painting's broad range of capabilities makes it a favorite among artists. It can be applied with any number of brushes or painting knives. Colors can be blended easily, offering a palette of almost limitless range. Slow drying facilitates the reworking of problem areas. When it is finely applied, oil paint can capture the most intricate detail. When it is broadly brushed, it can render diaphanous fields of pulsating color. Oil paint can be diluted to barely tinted film to achieve subtle flesh tones, or it can be applied in thick **impastos** that physically construct an image, as in Rembrandt's *Head of St. Matthew* (Fig. 4–7).

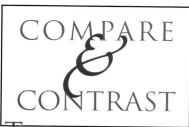

COMPARE & CONTRAST

THE *GEORGE WASHINGTONS* OF STUART AND LICHTENSTEIN

The versatility of oil paint is seen in portraits of George Washington by two American artists who worked centuries apart. Gilbert Stuart's familiar eighteenth-century portrait (Fig. 4–8) provides us with our stereotypical image of Washington. The work was left unfinished; much of the composition still reveals the reflective gesso ground. How did Stuart create a realistic likeness with his brushwork and **modeling?** The illusion of three-dimensionality is provided by the graceful play of light across the surfaces of Washington's face. Some features are sharply defined, others cast into shadow. Although this image is second nature to us, we can still notice the sensitivity with which Stuart portrayed his famous sitter. What do the delicate treatment of the pensive eyes and the firm outline of the determined jaw tell us about the personality traits of the wise and aging leader?

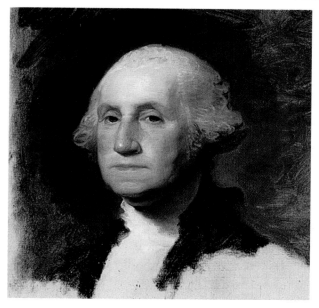

Roy Lichtenstein's contemporary portrait (Fig. 4–9), by contrast, is an image of glamour and success. What gives us this impression? A younger, debonair Washington is presented as if on a campaign poster, or as a comic-strip hero with a chiseled profile akin to that of Dick Tracy. The eyes are alert and enthralling; the chin is jaunty and confident. How does Lichtenstein capitalize on oil paint's clarity and precision? Sharp contrasts, crisp lines, and dot patterning such as that found in comic strips deprive the painting of any subtlety or atmosphere. The rich modeling that imparted a sense of roundness to Stuart's figure is replaced by stylized shadows that sit flatly on the canvas. Lichtenstein forsakes the psychological portrait in favor of billboard advertising. This is a Washington who has suffered visual saturation by the contemporary media; the physical characteristics tell us nothing of the human being to whom they refer.

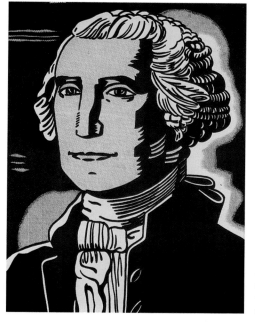

4–8 GILBERT STUART
GEORGE WASHINGTON (DETAIL/UNFINISHED PORTRAIT) (1796). OIL ON CANVAS. 39⅝ × 34½″ (ENTIRE WORK).
THE NATIONAL PORTRAIT GALLERY, SMITHSONIAN INSTITUTION, WASHINGTON, D.C.

4–9 ROY LICHTENSTEIN
GEORGE WASHINGTON (1962). OIL ON CANVAS. 51 × 38″.
© ROY LICHTENSTEIN.

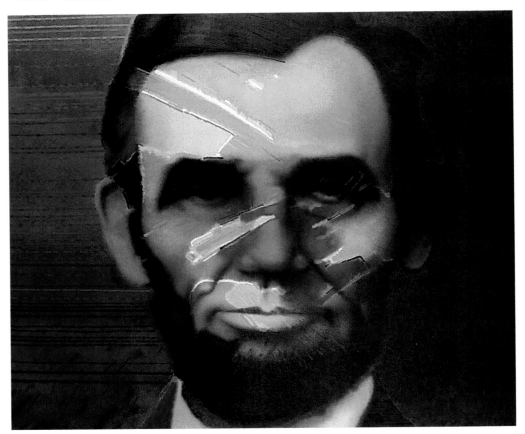

The first oil paintings were executed on wood panels, and then a gradual shift was made to canvas supports. Like wood panels, the canvas surface is covered with a gesso ground prior to painting. The pliability of fabric stretched over a wooden framework renders the working surface more receptive to the pressure of the artist's implement. The light weight of canvas also allows for larger compositions than were possible on wooden panels.

Contemporary artist Ed Paschke's oil painting of Abraham Lincoln (*Anesthesio*, Figure 4–10) brings new life to a hackneyed image by traversing it with abstract patches of neon-like color. The effect is not unlike that attained by a teenager who defaces a poster of a presidential candidate with spray paint, or it could almost be a face on a video screen with electronic color bleeding through irrelevantly on the image. In either case, environmental "noise" obscures the target. Ironically, the need to work to see through the obfuscating patches of color renders the image of the president more tantalizing.

ACRYLIC

Acrylic paint offers many of the advantages of oil paint, but "without the mess." Acrylic paint is a mixture of pigment and a plastic vehicle that can be thinned (and washed off brushes and hands) with water. Unlike linseed oil, the synthetic resin of the binder dries colorless and does not gradually compromise the brilliance of the colors. Also, unlike oil paint, acrylic can be used on a variety of surfaces that need no special preparation. Acrylic paint is flexible and fast drying, and, as it is water soluble, it requires no flammable substances for use or cleanup.

One of the few effects of oil paint that cannot be duplicated in acrylic is delicate nuance of colors. Like

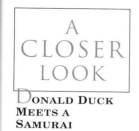
The acrylic paintings of Japanese American Roger Shimomura blend Western Pop Art with traditional Japanese imagery as found in *ukiyo-e* prints. As a child during World War II, Shimomura was interned with his parents and grandparents in Idaho. At the same time, ironically, his uncle served with the valiant 442nd division of Japanese Americans. Shimomura remembers statements made by white Americans about Japanese Americans during this deeply disturbing period. For example, Idaho's attorney general remarked, "We want to keep this a white man's country."

Shimomura's *Untitled* (Fig. 4–11) is at first glance an amusing clash of American and Japanese pop cultures. American cartoon characters like Donald Duck, Pinocchio, Dick Tracy, and the combination Batman-Superman vie for space on the crowded canvas with Japanese Samurai warriors and a contemporary Japanese. The battle of imagery East and West may reflect the tensions within the artist regarding his ancestral roots and his chosen country. In this type of work, Shimomura's conflict occurs among Eastern and Western stereotypes and myths, not flesh-and-blood people.

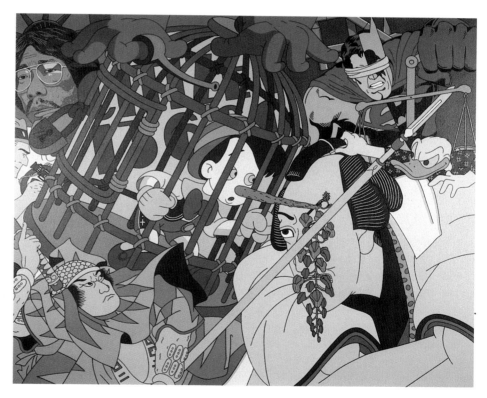

4–11 ROGER SHIMOMURA
UNTITLED (1984). ACRYLIC
ON CANVAS. 60 × 72".
COURTESY OF THE ARTIST AND STEINBAUM
KRAUSS GALLERY, N.Y.

MOUNT ST. HELENS ERUPTED ON MAY 18, 1980, IN ONE OF THE LARGEST VOLCANIC EXPLOSIONS IN AMERICAN HISTORY.

4–12 HELEN OJI
Mount St. Helens (1980). Acrylic, Rhoplex, glitter on paper. 60 × 72″.
COLLECTION HOME INSURANCE CO., N.Y.

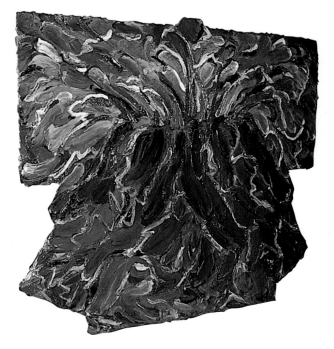

4–13 DAVID HOCKNEY
Punchinello with Block, from Ravel's *L'Enfant et les Sortilèges* (1980). Gouache on paper. 14 × 17″.
© DAVID HOCKNEY.

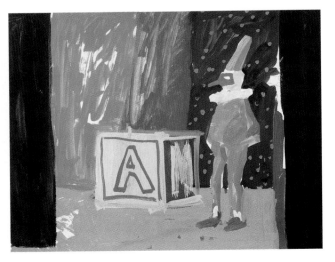

oil, however, acrylic paint can be used thinly or thickly; it can be applied in transparent films or opaque impastos, as in Helen Oji's *Mount St. Helen's* (Fig. 4–12). The artist fills the shaped canvas with an explosion of color and texture that simulates the unbridled power of one of the world's few active volcanoes. This image, which gave rise to a whole series on these natural wonders, serves, from another perspective, as "textile" ornamentation for a Japanese kimono. Canvases shaped in this garment design first preoccupied Oji in an earlier series, and here the reference to her Japanese heritage (her parents were interned during World War II, while she grew up in California) and the volcano image may symbolize a convergence of cultures from both sides of the Pacific.

WATERCOLOR

The term **watercolor** originally defined any painting medium that employed water as a solvent. Thus, fresco and egg tempera have been called watercolor processes. But today watercolor refers to a specific technique called **aquarelle,** in which transparent films of paint are applied to a white, absorbent surface. Contemporary watercolors are composed of pigments and a gum arabic vehicle, thinned, of course, with a medium of water.

Variations of the watercolor medium have been employed for centuries. Ancient Egyptian artists used a form of watercolor in their paintings. Watercolor was also used extensively for manuscript illumination during the Middle Ages, as we shall see in Chapter 12. **Gouache,** or watercolor mixed with a high concentration of vehicle and an opaque ingredient such as chalk, was the principle painting medium during the Byzantine and Romanesque eras of Christian art. This variation has enjoyed popularity across time and a myriad of styles, and is used to great effect by many contemporary artists, such as David Hockney (Fig. 4–13).

Transparent watercolor, however, did not appear until the fifteenth century with Albrecht Dürer. It is a difficult medium to manipulate, despite its simple components. Tints are achieved by diluting the colors with various quantities of water. White, then, does not exist; white must be derived by allowing the white of the paper to "shine" through the color of the composition, or by leaving areas of the paper exposed. To achieve the latter effect, all areas of whiteness must be mapped out with precision before the first stroke of color is applied.

With oil paint and acrylic, the artist sometimes overpaints areas of the canvas in order to make corrections or to blend colors. With transparent watercolors, overpainting obscures the underlying layers of color.

4–14 ALBRECHT DÜRER
THE GREAT PIECE OF TURF (1503). WATERCOLOR. 16¼ × 12⅜".
GRAPHISCHE SAMMLUNG ALBERTINA COLLECTION, VIENNA.

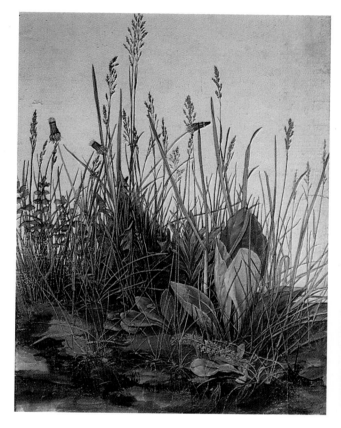

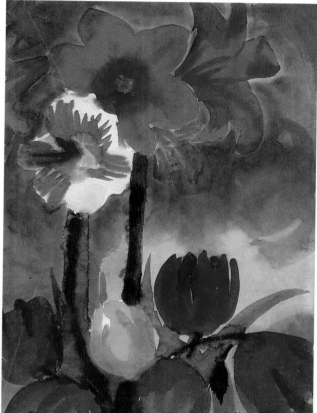

For this reason, corrections are virtually impossible, and so the artist must have the ability to plan ahead, as well as a sure hand and a stout heart. When used skillfully, watercolor has an unparalleled freshness and delicacy. The colors are pure and brilliant, and the range of effects surprisingly broad.

Dürer used transparent watercolor only briefly, although ingeniously. His virtuoso handling of the medium can be seen in small nature studies such as *The Great Piece of Turf* (Fig. 4–14), which belie the difficulties of the medium. Confident strokes of color precisely define leaves, flowers, and individual blades of grass. Washes are kept to a minimum; the painting emphasizes form over color, line over tonal patterns.

The broader appeal of watercolor, however, is not to be found in its capability of rendering meticulous detail. When the medium came into wide use during the sixteenth century, it was seen as having other, very different advantages. The fluidity of watercolor was conducive to

rapid sketches and preparatory studies. Simple materials allowed for portability. Artists were able to cart their materials to any location, indoors or outdoors, and to register spontaneously their impressions of a host of subjects.

Of course, watercolor is also used for paintings that stand as completed statements. Artists such as the German Expressionist Emil Nolde (see Fig. 4–15) were enticed by the transparency of tinted washes. Such washes permitted a delicate fusion of colors. As with the drawing medium of brush and wash, the effect is atmospheric. The edges of the forms are softened; they seem to diffuse into one another or the surrounding field. Unlike Dürer, who used watercolor in a descriptive, linear manner, Nolde creates his explosions of blossoms through delicately balanced patches of bold color and diaphanous washes. The composition is brightened by the white of the paper, which is brought forward to create forms as assertive as those in color.

4–16 CRASH (JOHN MATOS)
ARCADIA REVISITED (1988). SPRAY PAINT ON CANVAS. 96¼ × 68″.
COURTESY OF THE ARTIST.

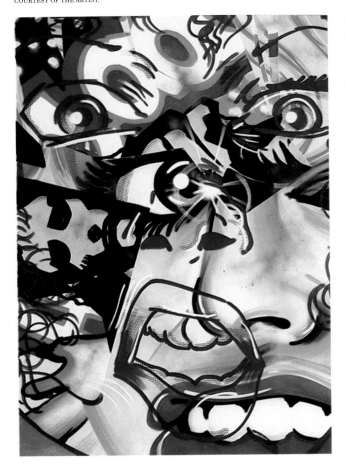

mune. Some are more likely to call this defacing public property rather than creating works of art, but how do we describe the elaborate urban "landscapes" that might cover the outside of an entire subway car, filling the space with a masterful composition of shapes, lines, textures, and colors? On the street, they are called master works, and their artists are indeed legendary.

Some graffiti writers have "ascended" to the art gallery scene, exchanging their steel "canvases" for some of fabric and their high-speed exhibition spaces for high-brow gallery walls. One such artist, "Crash" (or John Matos), created a parody of his own subway style in a complex canvas work called *Arcadia Revisited* (Fig. 4–16). All the tools and techniques of his trade—commercial cans of spray paint, the Benday dots of comic-strip fame, the sharp lines of the tag writer's logos, the diffuse spray technique that adds dimensionality to an array of otherwise flat objects—are used to describe a violent clash of cultural icons that are fragmented, superimposed, and barely contained within the confines of the canvas.

COMBINING PAINTING WITH OTHER MATERIALS

Contemporary painters have in many cases combined traditional painting techniques with other materials, or they have painted on nontraditional supports, stretching the definition of what has usually been considered painting. For example, in *The Bed* (Fig. 17–13), **Pop artist** Robert Rauschenberg splashed and brushed paint on a quilt and pillow, which he then hung on a wall like a canvas work and labeled a "combine painting." The **Synthetic Cubists** of the early twentieth century, Picasso and Braque, were the first to incorporate pieces of newsprint, wallpaper, labels from wine bottles, and oilcloth into their paintings. These works were called *papiers collés* and have come to be called **collages**.

Contemporary artist Miriam Schapiro is best known for her paint and fabric constructions which she has labeled "femmage," to express what she sees as their unification of feminine imagery and materials with the medium of collage. In *Maid of Honour* (Fig. 4–17), Schapiro combines bits of intricately patterned

SPRAY PAINT

One can consider that spray painting has had a rather long history. The subtle coloration marking different species of animals on the walls of Paleolithic caves was probably achieved by blowing pigments onto a surface through hollowed-out reeds. Why are they there: Decoration? Ritual? History? Oddly enough, these questions can be asked of the contemporary graffiti artist and the thousands upon thousands of writings that range in definition from "tags" to "master" works. Why do they do it? Is it art? Urban ritual? Will it speak in history to trials of inner-city living?

Everyone has seen graffiti, but the complexity of the work and the social atmosphere from which it is derived may not be common knowledge. Stylized signatures, or "tags," can be seen everywhere; it seems as though no urban surface—interior or exterior—is im-

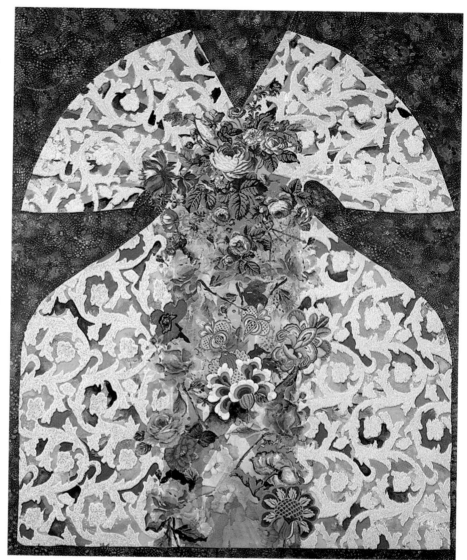

fabric with acrylic pigments on a traditional canvas support to construct a highly decorative garment that is presented as a work of art. The painting is a celebration of women's experiences with sewing, quilting, needlework, and decoration.

The two-dimensional media we have discussed in Chapters 3 and 4, drawing and painting, create unique works whose availability to the general public is usually limited to photographic renditions in books such as this. Even the intrepid museum goer usually visits only a small number of collections. So let us now turn our attention to the two-dimensional medium that has allowed millions of people to own original works by masters—printmaking.

key terms

Painting	Fresco secco	Gilding	Acrylic paint
Vehicle	Encaustic	Oil paint	Watercolor
Medium	Tempera	Glazing	Aquarelle
Paint	Ground	Impasto	Gouache
Buon fresco	Gesso	Modeling	Collage

artists

Giotto	Gilbert Stuart	Albrecht Dürer
Kay Walkingstick	Roy Lichtenstein	Emil Nolde
Gentile da Fabriano	Ed Paschke	Crash (John Matos)
Andrew Wyeth	Helen Oji	Miriam Schapiro
Howardena Pindell	Roger Shimomura	
Rembrandt van Rijn	David Hockney	

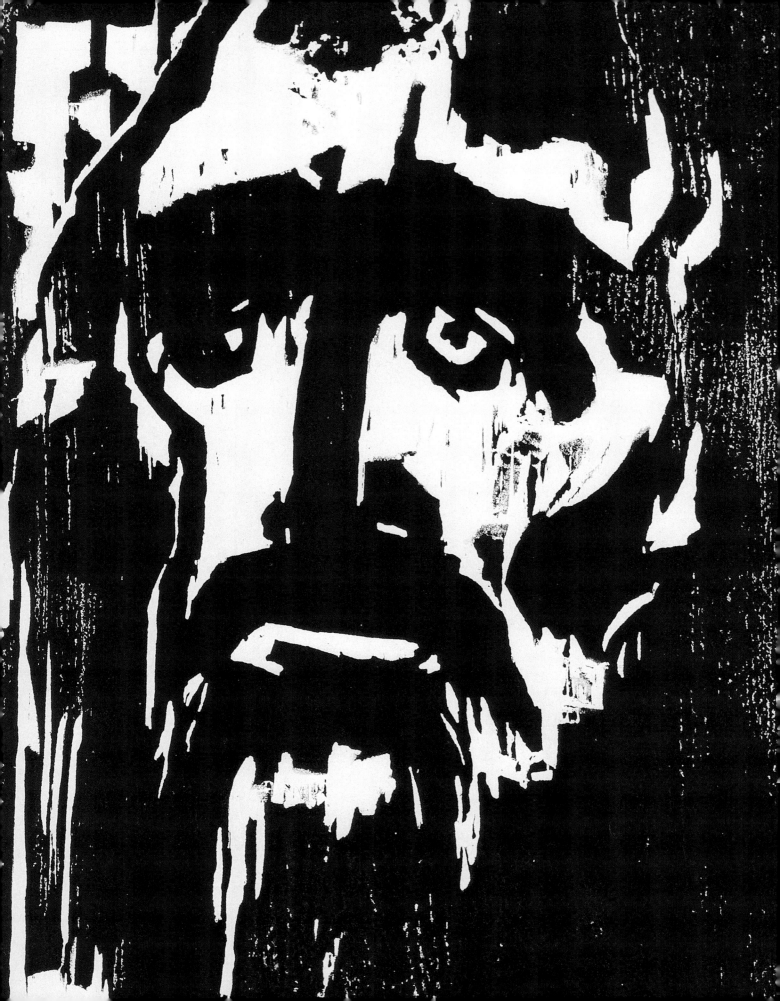

PRINTMAKING

P R E L I M I N A R Y
Sketch

- ❏ Prints have been made with tools ranging from metal gougers to acid to greasy crayons.

- ❏ The ancient Romans made identification "cards" by using woodcuts to stamp out symbols or letters.

- ❏ To make woodcuts, it may take master woodcarvers many months to transfer images that have been drawn on paper onto wood blocks.

- ❏ One form of printmaking—serigraphy—is used for making labels for cans of food as well as works of art.

- ❏ One printmaking process, the monotype, yields but a single image, and like a drawing or painting, is a unique work of art.

Emil Nolde, *The Prophet* (detail). See Figure 5–3.

The value of drawings and paintings lies, in part, in their uniqueness. Hours, weeks, sometimes years are expended in the creation of these one-of-a-kind works. Printmaking permits the reproduction of these coveted works, and also the production of many copies of original prints. Printmaking is an important artistic medium for at least two reasons. First, it allows persons to study great works of art from a distance. Second, since prints are less expensive than unique works by the same artist, they make it possible for the general public, and not just the wealthy few, to own original works. With prints, art has become accessible. Like some drawings, however, prints not only serve a functional purpose, they also may be great works of art in themselves.

METHODS OF PRINTMAKING

The printmaking process begins with a design or image made in or on a surface by hitting or pressing with a tool. The image is then transferred to paper or a similar material. The transferred image is called the **print.** The working surface, or **matrix,** varies according to the printmaking technique. Matrices include wood blocks, metal plates, stone slabs, and silk screens. There are special tools for working with each kind of matrix, but the images in printmaking are usually rendered in ink.

Printmaking processes are divided into four major categories: relief, intaglio, lithography, and serigraphy (Fig. 5–1). We shall examine a variety of techniques within each of them. Finally, we will consider the monotype and the combining of printmaking media with other media.

RELIEF

In **relief printing,** the matrix is carved with knives or gouges. Areas that are not meant to be printed are cut below the surface of the matrix (see Fig. 5–1A), and areas that form the image and are meant to be printed are left raised. Ink is then applied to the raised surfaces, often from a roller. The matrix is pressed against a sheet of paper, and the image is transferred. The transferred image is the print. Relief printing includes woodcut and wood engraving.

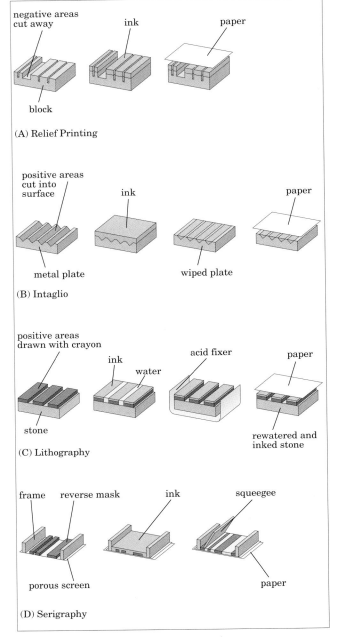

(A) Relief Printing

(B) Intaglio

(C) Lithography

(D) Serigraphy

WOODCUT

Woodcut is the oldest form of printmaking. The ancient Chinese stamped patterns onto textiles and paper using carved wood blocks. The Romans used woodcuts to stamp symbols or letters on surfaces for purposes of identification. During the 1400s in Europe, woodcuts provided multiple copies of religious images for worshippers. After the invention of the printing press, woodcut assumed an important role in book illustration.

Woodcuts are made by cutting along the grain of the flat surface of a wooden board with a knife. Different types of wood and different gouging tools yield various effects.

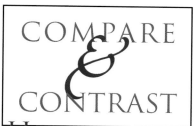

HIROSHIGE'S *RAIN SHOWER ON OHASHI BRIDGE* WITH NOLDE'S *THE PROPHET*

As is seen in a print by the nineteenth-century Japanese artist Ando Hiroshige (Fig. 5–2), the finest details can be achieved with a close-grained wood and a tightly controlled manipulation of carving tools. Clean-cut, uniform lines define the steady rain and the individuals who tread, huddled against the downpour, across a wooden footbridge.

The slow, meticulous process by which Hiroshige achieved his sharply defined images could not seem farther removed from Emil Nolde's energetic, almost violent, approach in *The Prophet* (Fig. 5–3). Nolde created his primitive image by using a broadly grained, splintering block of wood, yielding sharply contrasting areas of black and white. The downward pull of the imagery, suggested by vertical gouges parallel to the wood grain, contributes to the drama of the print.

How does the emotional impact of these two works differ? Consider the use of line, shape, and color.

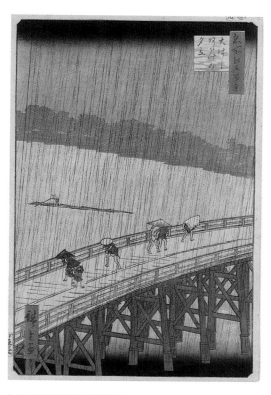

5–2 ANDO HIROSHIGE
RAIN SHOWER ON OHASHI BRIDGE (1857). COLOR WOOD BLOCK ON PAPER. 13⅞ × 9⅛″.
THE CLEVELAND MUSEUM OF ART. GIFT OF J. J. WADE, 21.318.

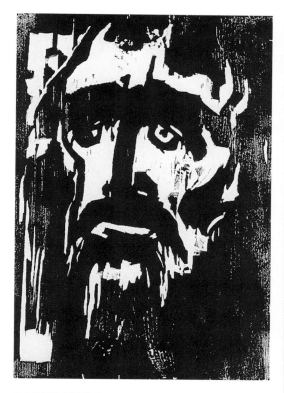

5–3 EMIL NOLDE
THE PROPHET (1912). WOODCUT. 12¾ × 9″.
© 1997 NATIONAL GALLERY OF ART, WASHINGTON, D.C. ROSENWALD COLLECTION.

5–4 HIROSHI MURATA
Momigi No Niwa (1981). WOOD BLOCK PRINT PRINTED IN
TRADITIONAL *UKIYO-E* TECHNIQUE. 18¼ × 26½″.
COURTESY OF THE ARTIST.

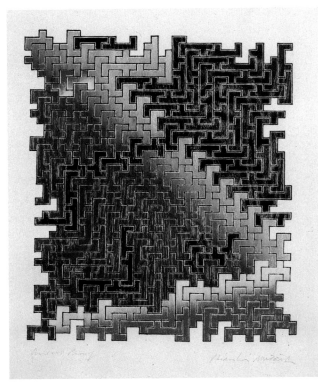

5–5 BURIN.

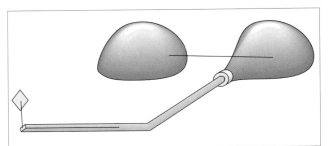

This oldest of the printmaking techniques has been
revived by a number of contemporary artists, such as
the Japanese American Hiroshi Murata. For *Momigi No
Niwa* (Fig. 5–4), which means "Maple in the Garden,"
Murata drew the imagery on rice paper and commissioned a Japanese master woodcarver to transfer the
work onto a wood block. It took the woodcarver approximately three months to carve the matrix, which was
then inked in several colors and printed. The meticulous,
mazelike design is a stable counterpoint to the diffuse
colors that spread across the paper. Despite the mechanical nature of the grid, the overall atmospheric effect
produced by the broad color fields emerging and dissolving into haze is not unlike that found in some Far Eastern
landscapes, such as those shown in Chapter 18.

WOOD ENGRAVING

The technique of **wood engraving** and its effects differ
significantly from those of woodcuts. Whereas in woodcuts the flat surface of boards is used, in wood engraving many thin layers of wood are **laminated.** Then the

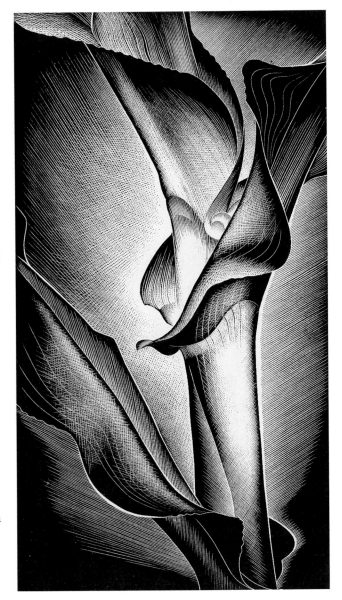

5–6 PAUL LANDACRE
GROWING CORN (1940). WOOD ENGRAVING. 8½ × 4¼″.
LIBRARY OF CONGRESS, WASHINGTON, D.C.

ends of these sections are planed flat, yielding a hard, nondirectional surface. In contrast to the softer matrix used for the woodcut, the matrix for the wood engraving makes it relatively easy to work lines in varying directions. These lines are **incised** or engraved with tools such as a **burin** or **graver** (Fig. 5–5) instead of being cut with knives and gouges. The lines can be extremely fine and are often used in close alignment to give the illusion of tonal gradations. This process was used to illustrate newspapers, such as *Harper's Weekly,* during the nineteenth century.

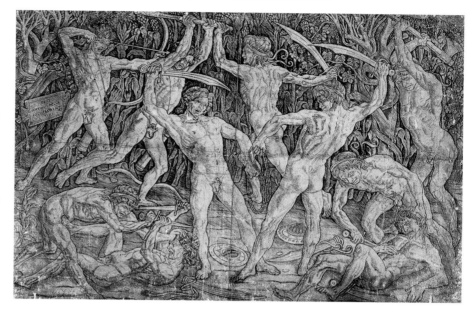

The razor-sharp tips of engraving implements and the hardness of the end-grain blocks make possible the exacting precision found in wood engravings such as that by Paul Landacre (Fig. 5–6), a famous twentieth-century American printmaker. Tight, threadlike parallel and crosshatched lines comprise the tonal areas that define the form. The rhythmic, flowing lines of the seedling's unfurling leaves contrast dramatically with the fine, prickly lines that emanate like rays from the young corn plant. The print is a display of technical prowess in a most demanding and painstaking medium.

INTAGLIO

The popularity of relief printing declined with the introduction of the **intaglio** process. Intaglio prints are created by using metal plates into which lines have been incised. The plates are covered with ink, which is forced into the linear depressions, and then the surface is carefully wiped. The cut depressions retain the ink, while the flat surfaces are clean. Paper is laid atop the plate, and then paper and plate are passed through a printing press, forcing the paper into the incised lines to pick up the ink and thereby accept the image. In a reversal of the relief process, then, intaglio prints are

derived from designs or images that lie *below* the surface of the matrix (see Fig. 5–1B).

Intaglio printing encompasses many different media, the most common of which are engraving, drypoint, etching, and mezzotint and aquatint. Some artists have used these techniques recently in interesting variations or combinations and have pioneered approaches using modern equipment such as the camera and computer.

ENGRAVING

Although **engraving** has been used to decorate metal surfaces such as bronze mirrors or gold and silver drinking vessels since ancient times, the earliest engravings printed on paper did not appear until the fifteenth century. In engraving, the artist creates clean-cut lines on a plate of copper, zinc, or steel, forcing the sharpened point of a burin across the surface with the heel of the hand. Because the lines are transferred to paper under very high pressure, they not only reveal the ink from the grooves, but themselves have a ridgelike texture that can be felt by running a finger across the print.

An early and famous engraving came from the hand of the fifteenth-century Italian painter Antonio Pollaiuolo (Fig. 5–7). Deep lines that hold a greater amount of ink define the contours of the ten fighting figures. As did Landacre, Pollaiuolo used parallel groupings of

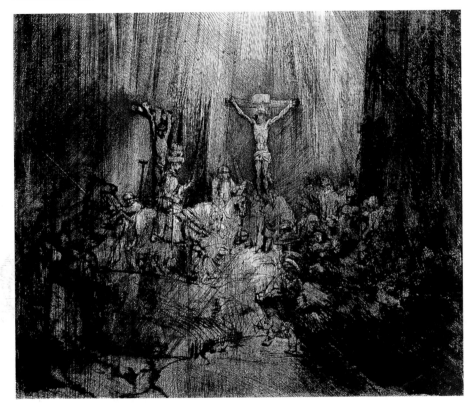

ness of the drypoint line to enhance the sense of chaos attending the crucifixion and the darkness of the encroaching storm. Lines fall like black curtains enshrouding the crowd, while rays of bright light illuminate the figure of Jesus and splash down onto the spectators.

ETCHING

Although they are both intaglio processes, **etching** differs from engraving in the way the lines are cut into the matrix. With engraving, the depth of the line corresponds to the amount of force used to push or draw an implement over the surface. With etching, minimal pressure is exerted to determine the depth of line. A chemical process does the work.

In etching, the metal plate is covered with a liquid, acid-resistant ground consisting of wax or resin. When the ground has hardened, the image is drawn upon it with a fine needle. Little pressure is exerted to expose the ground; the plate itself is not scratched. When the drawing is completed, the matrix is slipped into an acid bath which immediately begins to eat away, or etch, the exposed areas of the plate. This etching process yields the sunken line that holds the ink. The artist leaves the plate in the acid solution just long enough to achieve the desired depth of line. If a variety of tones is desired, the artist may pull the plate out of the acid solution after a while, cover lines of sufficient depth with the acid-resistant ground, and replace the plate in the bath for further etching of the remaining exposed lines. The longer the plate remains in the acid solution, the deeper the etching. Deeper crevices hold more ink, and for this reason they print darker lines.

Etching is a versatile medium, capable of many types of lines and effects. The modern French painter

thinner and thus lighter lines to render the tonal gradations that define the exaggerated musculature. The detail of the print is described with the utmost precision, revealing the artist's painstaking mastery of the burin.

DRYPOINT

Drypoint is engraving with a simple twist. In drypoint a needle is dragged across the surface, and a metal burr, or rough edge, is left in its wake to one side of the furrow. The burr retains particles of ink, creating a softened rather than crisp line when printed. The burr sits above the surface of the matrix and therefore is fragile. After many printings, it will break down, resulting in a line that simply looks engraved.

The characteristic velvety appearance of drypoint lines is seen in Rembrandt's *Christ Crucified Between the Two Thieves* (Fig. 5–8). The more distinct lines were rendered with a burin, whereas the softer lines were created with a drypoint needle. Rembrandt used the blurri-

Henri Matisse used but a few dozen uniformly etched lines to describe the essential features of a woman, *Loulou in a Flowered Hat* (Fig. 5–9). The extraordinarily simple yet complete image attests to the delicacy that can be achieved with etching.

Whereas Matisse's figure takes shape through the careful placement of line, the subject of the etching (Fig. 5–10) by Giovanni Domenico Tiepolo (who was the son of Giovanni Battista Tiepolo) exists by virtue of textural and tonal contrasts. This eighteenth-century Italian artist used a variety of wavy and curving lines to differentiate skin from cloth, fur from hair, figure from ground. Lines are spaced to provide a range of tones from the sharp white of the paper to the rich black of the man's clothing. The overall texture creates a hazy atmosphere that caresses the pensive figure.

MEZZOTINT AND AQUATINT

Engraving, drypoint, and etching are essentially linear media. With these techniques, designs or images are created by cutting lines into a plate. The illusion of tonal gradations is achieved by altering the number and concentration of lines. Some time in the mid-seventeenth century the Dutchman Ludwig von Siegen developed a technique whereby broad tonal areas could be achieved by nonlinear engraving; that is, engraving that does *not* depend on line. The medium was called **mezzotint,** from the Italian word meaning "halftint."

With mezzotint engraving, the entire metal plate is worked over with a curved, multitoothed implement called a **hatcher.** The hatcher is "rocked" back and forth over the surface, producing thousands of tiny pits that will hold ink. If printed at this point, the plate would yield an all over consistent, velvety black print. But the mezzotint engraver uses this evenly pitted surface as a point of departure. The artist creates an image by gradually scraping and burnishing the areas of the plate that are meant to be lighter. These areas will hold less ink and therefore will produce lighter tones. The more persistent the scraping, the shallower the pits and the lighter the tone. A broad range of tones is achieved as the artist works from the rich black of the rocked surface to the highly polished pitless areas that will

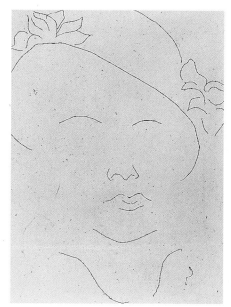

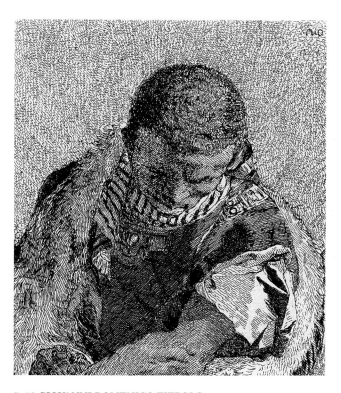

5–10 GIOVANNI DOMENICO TIEPOLO
A NEGRO (1770). ETCHING, 2ND STATE.
COURTESY MUSEUM OF FINE ARTS, BOSTON. GEORGE R. NUTTER FUND.

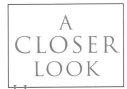

A
CLOSER
LOOK

**HUNG LIU:
CHINESE
TRADITIONS
UNBOUND**

In many ways, Hung Liu epitomizes the concerns and preoccupations of the Chinese artists whose life experiences during that country's Cultural Revolution have shaped their art, indeed their very existence. In 1984, Hung Liu arrived in the United States, in her words, "Five-thousand-year-old culture on my back. Late-twentieth-century world in my face. . . . My Alien number is 28333359." In her home country, for four years, she was forced to work in the fields. In her chosen country, she is now a professor at Mills College and has had one-woman shows in New York, San Francisco, and Texas. Her art is one that focuses on what she has called "the peculiar ironies which result when ancient Chinese images are 'reprocessed' within contemporary Western materials, processes, and modes of display."

Figure 5–11 shows an untitled mixed-media print, whose main image consists of a photo-etching onto which are affixed small rectangular wooden blocks—Mahjong pieces—bearing the "high-fashion" portraits of Chinese women. The inspiration for this print, and full oil paintings on the same theme, came from a series of photographs of turn-of-the-century Chinese prostitutes that Hung Liu discovered on a recent return trip to China. When the Communist Revolution took hold and all able-bodied individuals were forced into labor, these women were forced into prostitution because the traditions of oppression that led to the practice of binding their feet made them unfit for physical toil. They could barely walk.

Hung Liu feels the need to make known the pain, suffering, and degradation of generations of women before her. "Although I do not have bound feet, the invisible spiritual burdens fall heavy on me. . . . I communicate with the characters in my paintings, prostitutes—these completely subjugated people—with reverence, sympathy, and awe. They had no real names. Probably no children. I want to make up stories for them. Who were they? Did they leave any trace in history?"

In Hung Liu's work we come to understand a piece of history. We are challenged to reflect, as she does, upon human rights and freedoms, spiritual and physical oppression, political expression, and silenced voices.

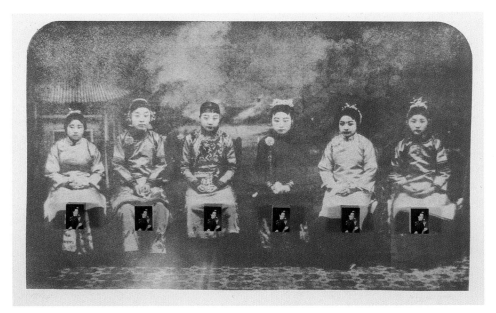

5–11 HUNG LIU
UNTITLED (1992). PHOTO-ETCHING, MIXED MEDIA. 33 × 22½″.
COLLECTION OF LOIS FICHNER-RATHUS. PHOTO COURTESY OF STEINBAUM KRAUSS GALLERY, N.Y.

5–12 PABLO PICASSO
THE PAINTER AND HIS MODEL (1964). ETCHING AND AQUATINT. 12⅝ × 18½″.
COURTESY MUSEUM OF FINE ARTS, BOSTON. LEE M. FRIEDMAN FUND. © 1998 ESTATE OF PABLO PICASSO/ARTISTS RIGHTS SOCIETY
(ARS), N.Y.

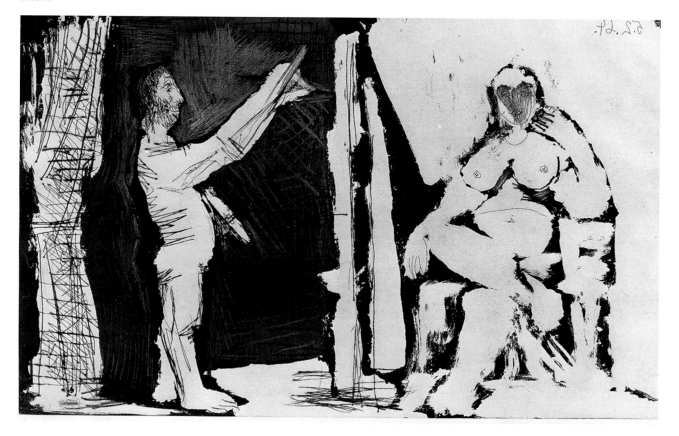

yield bright whites. Mezzotint is a rarely used, painstaking, and time-consuming procedure.

The subtle tonal gradations achieved by the mezzotint process can be duplicated with a much easier and quicker etching technique called **aquatint.** In aquatint a metal plate is evenly covered with a fine powder of acid-resistant resin. The plate is then heated, causing the resin to melt and adhere to the surface. As in line etching, the matrix is placed in an acid bath, where its uncovered surfaces are eaten away by the solution. The depth of tone is controlled by removing the plate from the acid and covering the pits that have been sufficiently etched.

Aquatint is often used in conjunction with line etching and is frequently manipulated to resemble tones produced by wash drawings. In *The Painter and His Model* (Fig. 5–12), Pablo Picasso brought the forms out of void space by defining their limits with dynamic

patches of aquatint. These tonal areas resemble swaths of ink typical of wash drawings. Descriptive details of the figures are rendered in fine or ragged lines, etched to varying depths.

OTHER ETCHING TECHNIQUES
Different effects may also be achieved in etching by using grounds of different substances. **Soft-ground etching,** for example, employs a ground of softened wax and can be used to render the effects of crayon or pencil drawings. In a technique called **lift-ground,** the artist creates the illusion of a brush-and-ink drawing by actually brushing a solution of sugar and water onto a resincoated plate. When the plate is slipped into the acid bath, the sugar dissolves, lifting the brushed image off the plate to expose the metal beneath. As in all etching media, these exposed areas accept the ink.

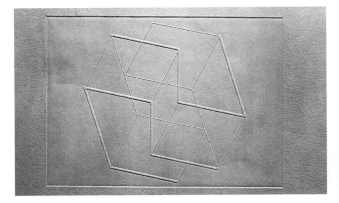

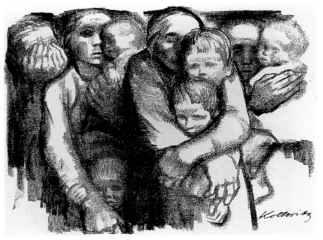

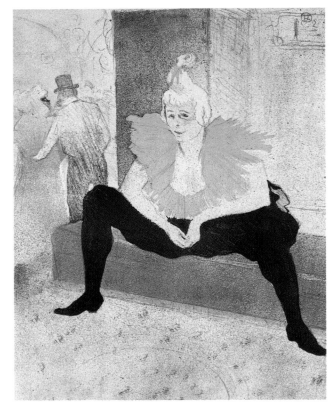

5–14 HENRI DE TOULOUSE-LAUTREC

Given that the printing process implies the use of ink to produce an image, can we have prints without ink? The answer is yes—with the medium called **gauffrage,** or inkless intaglio. Joseph Albers, a twentieth-century American abstract artist, created *Solo V,* the geometric image shown in Figure 5–13, by etching the lines of his design to two different depths. Furrows in the plate appear as raised surfaces when printed. We seem to feel the image with our eyes, as light plays across the surface of the paper to enhance its legibility. Perceptual shifts

occur as the viewer focuses now on the thick, now on the thin lines. In trying to puzzle out the logic of the form, the viewer soon discovers that Albers has offered a frustrating illustration of "impossible perspective."

LITHOGRAPHY

Lithography was invented at the dawn of the nineteenth century by the German playwright Aloys Senefelder. Unlike relief and intaglio printing, which rely on cuts in a matrix surface to produce an image, the lithography matrix is flat. Lithography is a surface or **planographic** printing process (Fig. 5–1C).

In lithography, the artist draws an image with a greasy crayon directly on a flat stone slab. Bavarian limestone is considered the best material for the slab. Sometimes a specially sensitized metal plate is used, but a metal surface will not produce the often-desired grainy appearance in the print. Small particles of crayon adhere to the granular texture of the stone matrix. After the design is complete, a solution of nitric acid is applied as a fixative. The entire surface of the matrix is then dampened with water. The untouched areas of the surface accept the water, but the waxy crayon marks repel it.

A roller is then used to cover the stone with an oily ink. This ink adheres to the crayon drawing but repels the water. When paper is pressed to the stone surface, the ink on the crayon is transferred to the paper, revealing the image.

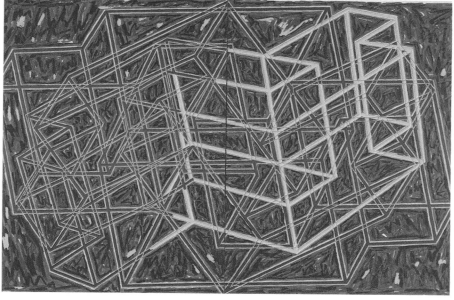

Different lithographic methods yield different results. Black crayon on grainy stone can look quite like the crayon drawing it is. Color lithographs employing brush techniques can be mistaken for paintings. Henri de Toulouse-Lautrec, a nineteenth-century French painter and lithographer, was well versed in the medium's flexibility, as is evident in his portrait of a clowness (Fig. 5–14). The outlines of the figures were drawn with a crayon, and the broad areas of her tights and ruffled collar were brushed in with liquid crayon. The overall spray effect that dapples the surface of the print was probably achieved by his scraping a fingernail along a stiff brush loaded with the liquid substance.

The impact of Käthe Kollwitz's lithograph *The Mothers* (Fig. 5–15), which highlights the plight of lower-class German mothers left alone to fend for their children after World War I, could not be further removed from that of *The Seated Clowness.* The high contrast of the black and white and the coarse quality of the wax crayon yield a sense of desperation suggestive of a newspaper documentary photograph. All the imagery is thrust toward the picture plane, as in high relief. The harsh contours of protective shoulders, arms, and hands contrast with the more delicately rendered faces and heads of the children—all contributing to the poignancy of the work.

Some artists have experimented with commercial lithography techniques similar to those used in the production of books and magazines. Hiroshi Murata's *Hinode* (Fig. 5–16), which means "Sunrise," employs what is known as *offset lithography.* The image is hand-drawn by the artist on mylar (a kind of polyester made in thin, silver-colored sheets and used for videotapes), but the principle of the technique—that water repels grease—is identical to the lithography method in which stones are used. The imagery in *Hinode* is a three-dimensional grid reminiscent of a steel-cage structure. The imagery seems to be ascending and revolving in space, like a human-made celestial body.

The sturdiness of the metallic projections provides an ironic contemporary structure for the intangible diffusion of light into space.

SERIGRAPHY

In **serigraphy** or silkscreen printing, stencils are used to create the design or image. Unlike the case with other graphic processes, these images can be rendered in paint as well as ink.

One serigraphic process begins with a screen constructed of a piece of silk, nylon, or fine metal mesh stretched on a frame. A stencil with a cutout design is then affixed to the screen, and paper or canvas is placed beneath (Fig. 5–1D). The artist forces paint or ink through the open areas of the stencil with a flat, rubber-bladed implement called a **squeegee,** similar to those used in washing windows. The image on the support corresponds to the shape cut out of the stencil. Several stencils may be used to apply different colors to the same print.

Images can also be "painted" on a screen with use of a varnishlike substance that prevents paint or ink from passing through the mesh. This technique allows for more gestural images than cutout stencils would provide. Recently a serigraphic process called *photo silkscreen* has been developed; it allows the artist to create photographic images on a screen covered with a light-sensitive gel.

Serigraphy was first developed as a commercial medium and is still used as such to create anything from posters to labels on cans of food. The American

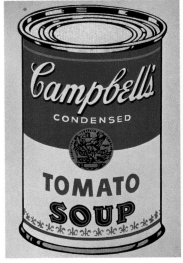

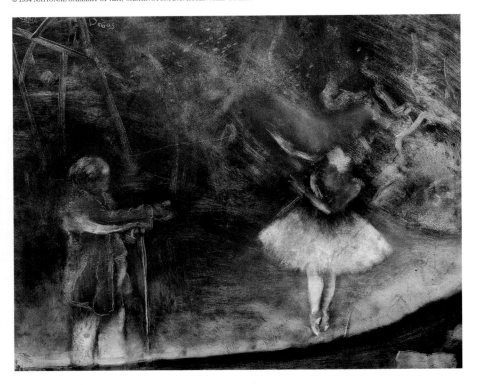

Pop Artist Andy Warhol raised the commercial aspects of serigraphy to the level of fine art in many of his silkscreen prints of the 1960s, such as *Campbell's Soup Can* (Fig. 5–17). These faithful renditions of everyday items satirize the mass media's bombardment of the consumer with advertising. They also happen to be amusing.

MONOTYPE

Monotype is a printmaking process, but it overlaps the other two-dimensional media of drawing and painting. Like drawing and painting, monotype yields but a single image, and like them, therefore, it is a unique work of art.

In monotype, drawing or painting is created with oil paint or watercolor on a nonabsorbent surface of any material. Brushes are used, but sometimes fine detail is rendered by scratching paint off the plate with sharp implements. A piece of paper is then laid on the surface and the image is transferred by hand rubbing the back of the paper or passing the matrix and paper through a press. The result, as can be seen in a monotype by Edgar Degas (Fig. 5–18), has all the spontaneity of a drawing and the lushness of a painting.

COMBINING PRINTMAKING MEDIA WITH OTHER MEDIA

Sometimes printmaking techniques can be combined, and other media can be employed collaterally, to achieve dramatic effects. An example is found in the contemporary Frank Stella print, *The Butcher Came and Slew the Ox* (Fig. 5–19), in which the artist combines lithography, linoleum-block printing, serigraphy, and other printmaking techniques. Stella also used collage and hand-colored segments of the print. In pure printmaking the artist tends to be removed from the completed work; the print is frequently made by a technician in a graphics studio, rather than by the artist. Hand coloring allowed Stella to add his personal, gestural signature to the work. *The Butcher Came and Slew the Ox* is one of a series of twelve prints based on illustrations for a children's Passover song executed by an early twentieth-century Russian artist.

In Chapters 6 and 7 we turn our attention to sculpture and architecture. In drawing, painting, and printmaking, artists have frequently attempted to create the illusion of three-dimensionality. We shall see some of the opportunities and problems that attend actual artistic expression in three dimensions.

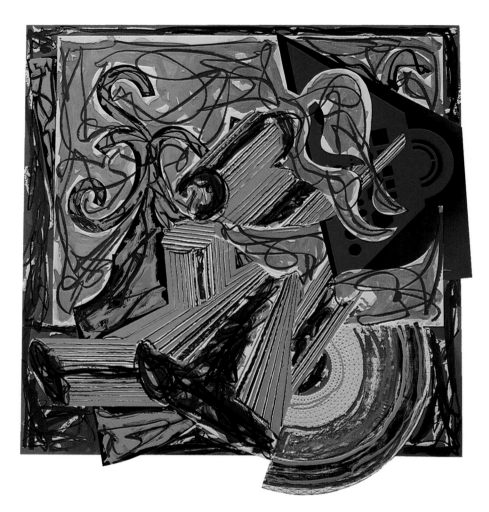

5–19 FRANK STELLA
*THE BUTCHER CAME AND
SLEW THE OX* (1984). No. 8
FROM A SERIES OF 12
"ILLUSTRATIONS AFTER
EL LISSITZKY'S *HAD GADYA*."
HAND-COLORED AND
COLLAGED WITH
LITHOGRAPHIC, LINOLEUM
BLOCK, AND SILKSCREEN
PRINTINGS. 56⅞ × 53⅜"
OVERALL SHEET.

key terms

Print	Incise	Mezzotint	Planographic
Printmaking	Burin	Hatcher	Serigraphy
Matrix	Graver	Aquatint	Squeegee
Relief printing	Intaglio	Soft-ground etching	Monotype
Woodcut	Engraving	Lift-ground etching	
Wood engraving	Drypoint	Gauffrage	
Laminate	Etching	Lithography	

artists

Ando Hiroshige	Henri Matisse	Käthe Kollwitz
Emil Nolde	Giovanni Domenico Tiepolo	Andy Warhol
Hiroshi Murata	Hung Liu	Edgar Degas
Paul Landacre	Pablo Picasso	Frank Stella
Antonio Pollaiuolo	Josef Albers	
Rembrandt van Rijn	Henri de Toulouse-Lautrec	

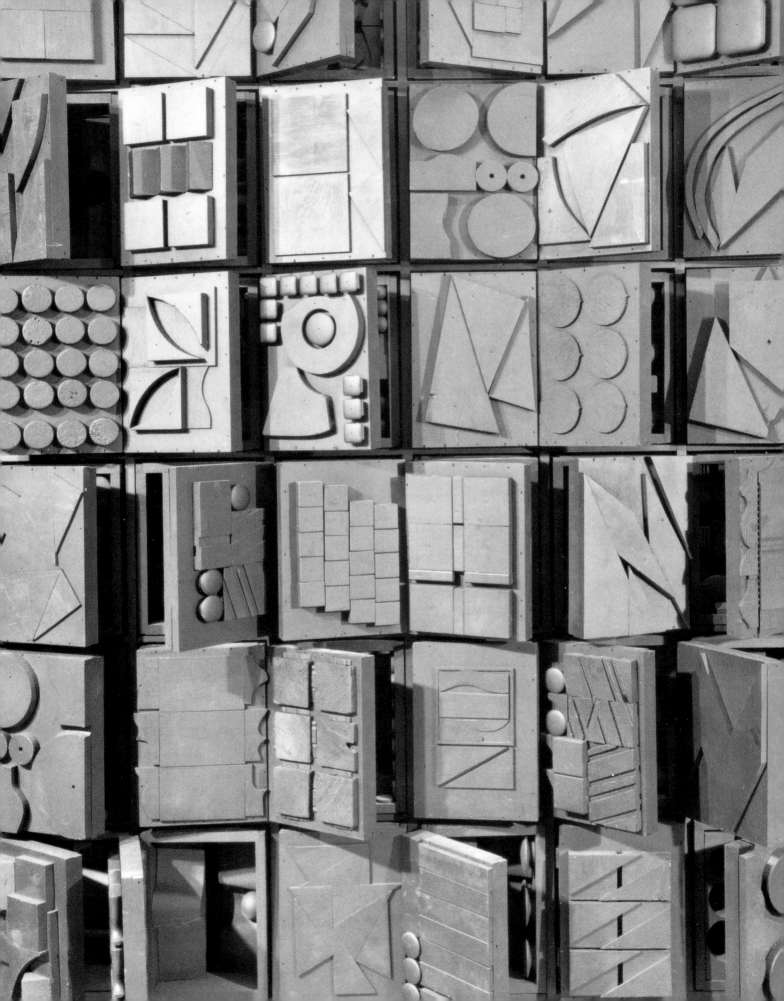

chapter

SCULPTURE

PRELIMINARY *Sketch*

- ❏ Michelangelo believed that the sculptor "liberated" forms that already existed within blocks of stone.

- ❏ George Segal creates sculpture through a process that involves placing models in plaster casts of the sort used for setting broken limbs.

- ❏ Contemporary sculptor Duane Hanson clothed his statues in trappings such as Hawaiian shirts and Bermuda shorts.

- ❏ John De Andrea simulates skin through the use of materials such as polyester and vinyl, and then adds real hair to the skin surfaces.

- ❏ Contemporary artists have made sculptures by assembling pieces of discarded objects and debris found in junkyards.

- ❏ Marcel Duchamp elevated objects such as bottle racks and urinals to works of art by placing them on pedestals.

- ❏ A sculpture of nylon and steel ran 24½ miles from the Pacific Ocean across two counties of Northern California.

Louise Nevelson, *Black Secret Wall* (detail). See Figure 6–22.

What is a stone? To a farmer it is an obstacle to be dug up and carted from the field. To a Roman warrior it was a powerful missile. To an architect it is a block, among many, to be assembled into a home or a bridge. But to a sculptor it is the repository of playful inner forms yearning for release. What is a steel girder? To an architect it is part of the skeleton of a skyscraper. To a sculptor it is the backbone of a fantastic animal or machine that never was, except in the imagination.

Stone, metal, wood, clay, plastics, light, and earth—these are some of the materials and elements that we have carved, modeled, assembled, and toyed with to create images of ourselves and to express our inmost fears and fantasies. Each of them affords the artist certain opportunities and limitations for self-expression. In this chapter we will see how they have been used in sculpture to grant three-dimensional reality to ideas. In the next chapter we will see how architects have used them to create aesthetic structures that protect us from the elements and provide settings for communal and intimate activities.

According to the Greek myth, Pygmalion, the king of Cyprus, fell in love with the idealized statue of a woman. Aphrodite, goddess of love, heard his prayers and brought the statue to life. In one version of the myth, the statue becomes the goddess herself. In still another, Pygmalion was the sculptor who created the statue. In this myth we find the elements of the human longing for perfection. We glimpse the emotionality that sculptors can pour into their works.

Sculpture is the art of carving, casting, modeling, or assembling materials into three-dimensional figures or forms. Within this broad definition, architecture could be seen as a type of sculpture. But architecture serves the utilitarian purpose of providing housing and other structures for work and play, whereas sculptures need serve no practical purpose at all.

It could be argued that sculpture is more capable of grasping the senses than do the two-dimensional art forms of drawing, painting, and printmaking. We view two-dimensional works from vantage points to the front of the support. We might move closer or farther away, or squat or stand on tiptoe to gain new

perspective, but the work itself, even if thickly laden with impasto, is essentially flat. **Relief sculptures** are similar to two-dimensional works in that their three-dimensional forms are raised from a flat background. In low-relief, or **bas-relief,** especially, the forms project only slightly from the background; in **high-relief,** figures project by at least half their natural depth.

But **free-standing sculptures** have fronts, sides, backs, and tops. They invite the viewer to walk around them. In some cases viewers may climb on them, walk through them, or, as in the case of a Calder **mobile,** look up at them from beneath. As we move about a sculpture, we are impressed by new revelations. The spaces or voids in and around the work may take on as much meaning as the sculpted forms themselves.

Two-dimensional art forms are not meant to be touched, but much of the pleasure of appreciating a sculpture derives from imagining what it would be like to run one's hands over sensuous curving surfaces of cool marble or hand-rubbed walnut. In many cases we may be prevented by ropes and guards—or by self-control—from touching sculptures, but many are made purposefully to be caressed. Some fool the eye, such as the "leather" jacket modeled from clay (see Fig. 9–2), or the fish skeleton carved from wood (Fig. 6–16).

Recently developed forms of sculpture may interact with the viewer in other ways. The viewer may become involved in watching a kinetic sculpture run full cycle, or in trying to decipher just what the cycle is. Some kinetic sculptures and light sculptures may also be literally turned on and off, sometimes by the viewer.

Sculpture is a highly familiar medium. For thousands of years we have used sculpture to portray our visions of the gods, saints, and devils. Religious people in earlier times and even now believe that their gods actually dwell within the stone they chisel or the wood they carve. We have carved and modeled the animals and plants of field and forest. We have exalted our heroes and leaders and commemorated our achievements and catastrophes, in stone and other

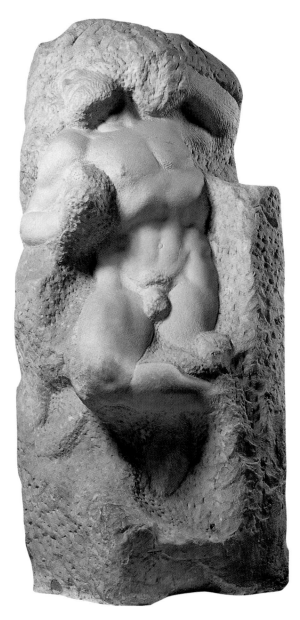

materials. The size of a sculpture has often been commensurate with the power ascribed to the hero or with the magnitude of the event. In addition to serving community and religious functions, sculptures are decorative. They adorn public buildings and parks. They sit on pedestals in walkways and stand in fountains, impervious to the spray, or perhaps contributing to the pool from the mouth or nether parts. Sculptures, of course, also serve as vehicles to express an artist's ideas and feelings.

In our discussion of sculpture we will first distinguish between subtractive and additive sculpture and describe the techniques of each. Then we will examine the characteristics of a number of works that have been rendered in the traditional materials such as stone, wood, clay, and metal. Finally we will explore several modern materials and methods, ranging from new metals and found objects to kinetic sculpture, light sculpture, and earthworks.

TYPES OF SUBTRACTIVE AND ADDITIVE SCULPTURE

Sculptural processes are either subtractive or additive. In a **subtractive process,** such as carving, unwanted material is removed. In the **additive processes** of modeling, casting, and constructing, material is added, assembled, or built up to reach its final form.

CARVING

In **carving** the sculptor begins with a block of material and cuts portions of it away until the desired form is created. Carving could be considered the most demanding type of sculpture because the sculptor, like the fresco painter, must have a clear conception of the final product at the outset. The material chosen—stone, wood, ivory—strongly influences the mechanics of the carving process and determines the type of creation that will emerge.

Michelangelo believed that the sculptor liberated forms that already existed within blocks of stone. *The Cross-Legged Captive* (Fig. 6–1) is one of a series

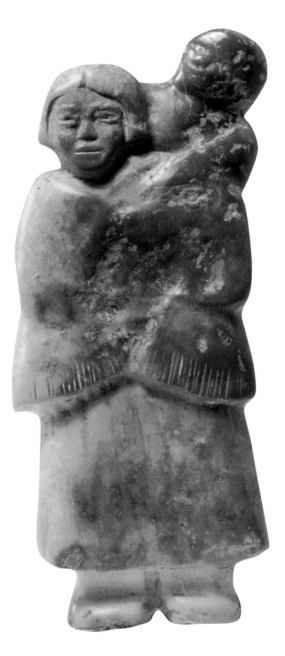

6–2 LEEKYA
Woman Carrying a Child
(1930). Green Nevada
turquoise. 4″ high, 2″ wide,
1″ deep.
COLLECTION OF THE HEARD MUSEUM,
PHOENIX, ARIZONA. PHOTOGRAPH
COURTESY OF THE HEARD MUSEUM.

of unfinished Michelangelo statues in which the figures remain partly embedded in marble. In its unfinished state, the tension and twisting in the torso almost cause us to experience the struggle of the slave to free himself fully from the marble and, symbolically, from his masters. Despite the massiveness of the musculature, the roughness of the finish imparts a curious softness and humanity to the figure, which further increase our empathy. In viewing this sculpture, it's as if we await the emergence of perfection from the imperfect—from the coarse and irregular block of stone. It is Michaelangelo's genius that allows the figure to transcend its humble origins.

A quite different conception of the figure in relation to the material from which it is carved is seen in the work of the Zuni artist, Leekya. Working with Green Nevada turquoise, the artist chisels the broad features of a woman carrying a child (Fig. 6–2), subtracting as little of the material as possible. Rather than working around, or against the imperfections of the stone, Leekya capitalizes on the stone's natural distortions to capture the details of the face, hair, and clothing.

MODELING

In **modeling** a pliable material such as clay or wax is shaped into a three-dimensional form. The artist may manipulate the material by hand and use a variety of tools. Unlike carving, in which the artist must begin with a clear concept of the result, in modeling the artist may work and rework the material until pleasing forms begin to emerge.

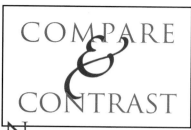
Twentieth-century sculptor Reuben Nakian created realistic **figurative** forms until the early 1940s. His **terra-cotta** *Europa and the Bull with Cupid* (Fig. 6–3) is an example of a later work in which he portrayed mythical subjects, frequently of seduction, in twisting diagonals. How do the pressing, kneading, and gouging of clay lend the fleeing female form its loose, abstract quality? How do these techniques contribute to the motion and emotion of the piece?

How does a comparison of Nakian's *Europa* with Roberta Laidman's *Anthony* (Fig. 6–4) illustrate the versatility of clay? In Nakian's work the pressure from the artist's thumbs and fingers is clearly visible, serving as a personal signature, or imprint on the material. The gestural, upward motion of the kneading lends a soaring lightness to the otherwise cumbersome forms. In sharp contrast to this technique, Laidman rolls her material into slabs and builds the image from sheets of clay. The result is a smooth, stonelike surface.

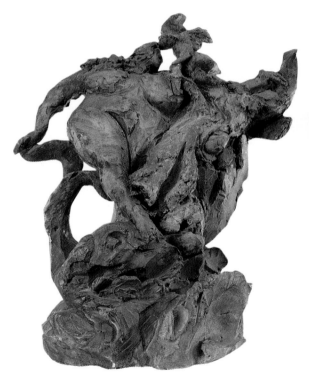

6–3 REUBEN NAKIAN
EUROPA AND THE BULL WITH CUPID (1947–48). TERRA COTTA, PAINTED. 26½ × 24¾ × 21".
HIRSHHORN MUSEUM AND SCULPTURE GARDEN, SMITHSONIAN INSTITUTION, WASHINGTON, D.C.

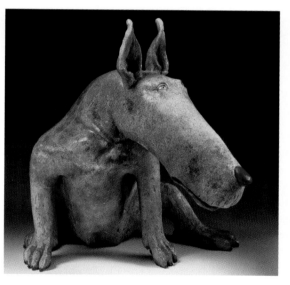

6–4 ROBERTA LAIDMAN
ANTHONY (1992). SLAB-BUILT CERAMIC.
19 × 17 × 20".
COURTESY OF THE ARTIST.

6–6 THE LOST-WAX TECHNIQUE.

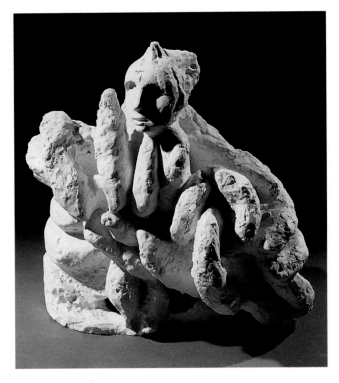

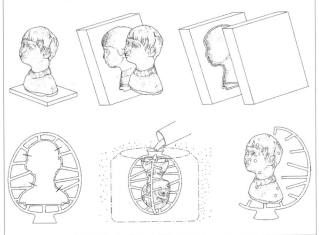

materials are also appropriate. Once the mold has been
made, the casting may be duplicated a number of times.

THE LOST-WAX TECHNIQUE   Bronze casting is usually
accomplished by means of the **lost-wax technique**
(Fig. 6–6), which has changed little over the centuries. In
this technique, an original model is usually sculpted from
clay, and a mold of it is made, usually from sectioned
plaster or flexible gelatin. Molten wax is then brushed or
poured into the mold to make a hollow wax model. If the
wax has been brushed onto the inner surface of the mold,
it will form a hollow shell. If the wax is to be poured, a
solid core can first be placed into the mold and the liquid
wax poured around the core. After the wax hardens, the
mold is removed, and the wax model stands as a hollow
replica of the clay. The hollow wax model is placed upside down in a container, and wax rods called **gates** are
connected to it. Then a sandy mixture of silica, clay, and
plaster is poured into and around the wax model, filling
the shell and the container. The mixture hardens into a
fire-resistant mold, or **investiture.** Thus the process
uses two models and two molds: models of clay and wax,
and molds of plaster or gelatin and of the silica mixture.

The silica mold, or investiture, is turned over and
placed in a **kiln.** As the investiture becomes heated, the
wax turns molten once more and runs out. Hence the
term *lost-wax technique.* The investiture is turned over
again while it is still hot, and molten bronze is poured
in. As the metal flows into the mold, air escapes

CASTING

The transition from modeling to casting can be easily
seen in Louise Bourgeois's *Portrait of Robert* (Fig. 6–5).
Here the artist has expressionistically modeled a pliable
material and converted the work to the more permanent
bronze medium through a casting process. The white
patina she has applied to finish the sculpture curiously
subverts the material's typical sheen and grants the
work a claylike appearance—the very material with
which the artist started.

In the **casting** process, a liquid material is poured
into a **mold.** The liquid hardens into the shape of the
mold and is then removed. In casting, an original model,
made of a material such as wax, clay, or even styroform,
can be translated into a more durable material such as
bronze. The mold is like a photographic negative, but one
of form and not of color; the interior surfaces of the mold
carry the reversed impressions of the model's exterior.

Any material that hardens can be used for casting.
Bronze has been used most frequently because of its
appealing surface and color characteristics, but concrete,
plaster, liquid plastics, clay diluted with water, and other

6–7 EDGAR DEGAS
THE LITTLE DANCER, 14 YEARS OLD
(1880–81). BRONZE. HEIGHT: 39″.
STERLING AND FRANCINE CLARK ART INSTITUTE, WILLIAMSTOWN, MASS.

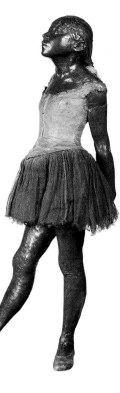

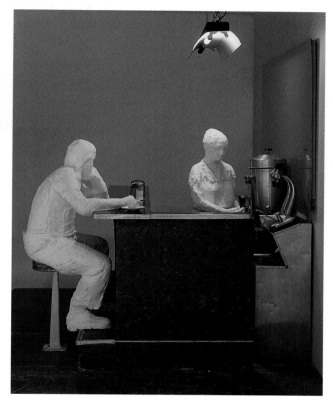

6–8 GEORGE SEGAL
THE DINER (1964–66). PLASTER, WOOD, CHROME, MASONITE, FLUORESCENT LAMP, AND FORMICA. 8′6″ × 9′ × 7′3″.
COLLECTION WALKER ART CENTER, MINNEAPOLIS. GIFT OF THE T.B. WALKER FOUNDATION, 1966.
© GEORGE SEGAL/LICENSED BY VAGA, N.Y.

through the gates so that no air pockets are left within. The bronze is given time to harden. Then the investiture and core are removed, leaving the bronze sculpture with strange projections where the molten metal had flowed up through the gates as it filled the mold. The projections are removed, and the surface of the bronze is **burnished** or treated chemically to take on the texture and color desired by the sculptor, as we shall see.

A statue by the French Impressionist Edgar Degas has an interesting history and metamorphosis from wax to bronze. As Degas grew blind, he turned to sculpture so that he could work out anatomical problems through the sense of touch. With one exception, his wax or clay experiments were left crumbling in his studio or discarded, although the intact figures were cast as a limited edition of bronze sculptures after his death. The exception was *The Little Dancer* (Fig. 6–7), which he showed as a wax model at the 1881 Impressionist exhibition and later cast in bronze. This diminutive painted wax figure startled the public and critics alike with its innovative sculptural realism: it sported real hair, a satin hair ribbon, a canvas bodice, and a tulle skirt. The styles of hair and clothing make the fourteen-year-old ballerina very much a product of her time and place.

The realism of *The Little Dancer* seems to have inspired a number of contemporary sculptors, such as Duane Hanson, who models and colors the new plastic media to create the illusion of actual flesh. Just as Degas clothed *The Little Dancer,* Hanson clothes his statues in trappings such as Hawaiian shirts to make them the products of their time and place. So that no mistake is possible—and no possibility for sardonic commentary overlooked—Hanson also bestows omnipresent twentieth-century props upon them such as shopping bags, cameras, and sunglasses (see Fig. 17–28).

CASTING OF HUMAN MODELS   *The Diner* (Fig. 6–8) by contemporary sculptor George Segal is an intriguing variation of the casting process. Segal produces ghostlike replicas of dehumanized people by means of plaster casts. "Plaster," notes Segal, "is an incredible recorder of what is there, more effective to me than the movie camera." Segal's methodology combines casting and modeling. Friends and colleagues leave impressions of parts of their bodies in quick-drying plaster casts, whose surfaces are molded and kneaded by the artist's hand as they sit. These sections are then assembled and adjusted into whole figures. Segal's figures are literally and figuratively shells. In unimaginable aloneness, his apparitions occupy an urban landscape of buses, gas stations, and other machinelike settings that take no heed of personal needs, aspirations, or—indeed—creativity. The amorphousness of the surface textures is not unlike that of the Nakian sculpture, placing the figures further into what Segal apparently sees as the limbo of contemporary life.

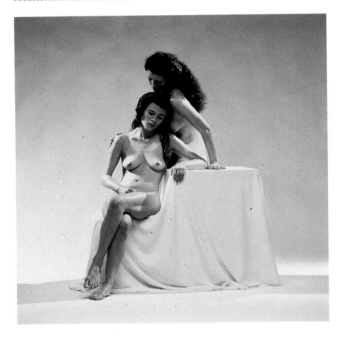

John De Andrea (Fig. 6–9) also casts from molds made of the human figure, but his surfaces are given their haunting illusionism through the use of materials such as polyester, resin, fiberglass, and vinyl. The "skin" of his mannequinlike figures is painted in oil with utmost delicacy and subtle nuance. By adding hair to the skin surfaces, the illusion of human flesh is complete; viewers standing just inches away from the sculpture will testify that they've seen a chest rise and fall in shallow breaths. Unlike Segal's work, which incorporates elaborate settings with actual objects to suggest a reality in which ghostlike figures sit frozen in time, De Andrea's settings are simple and the figures intended to give flesh-and-blood substance to the artist's notion of ideal beauty.

CONSTRUCTION

In construction, or **constructed sculpture,** forms are built from materials such as wood, paper and string, sheet metal, and wire. As we shall see in works by Picasso, Louise Nevelson, and other artists later in the chapter, traditional carving, modeling, and casting are abandoned in favor of techniques such as pasting and welding.

TYPES OF MATERIALS

Sculptors have probably employed every material known to humankind in their works. Different materials tend to be worked in different ways, and they can also create very different effects. In this section we will explore the varieties of ways in which sculptors have worked with the traditional materials of stone, wood, clay, and metal. In the section on modern and contemporary materials and methods, we shall see how sculptors have worked with nontraditional materials, such as plastic and light.

STONE SCULPTURE

Stone is an extremely hard, durable material that may be carved, scraped, drilled, and polished. The durability that makes stone so appropriate for monuments and statues that are meant to communicate with future generations also makes working with stone a tedious process. The granite used by ancient Egyptians was extremely resistant to detailed carving. This is one reason that Egyptian stone figures are simplified and resemble the shape of the quarried blocks. The Greeks used their abundant white marble to embody the idealized human form in action and in repose. However, they painted their marble statues, suggesting that they valued the material more for its durability than for its color or texture.

The hand tools used with stone—such as the chisel, mallet, and **rasp**—have not changed much over the centuries. But contemporary sculptors do not find working with stone to be quite so laborious since they can use power tools for chipping away large areas of unwanted material and for polishing the finished piece.

The Stone Age *"Venus" of Willendorf* (Fig. 10–2) has endured for perhaps 25,000 years. The same stone that lent such durability to this rotund fertility figure apparently pressed the technological limits of the sculptor. There are clues that the artist found the stone medium arduous. As with ancient Egyptian sculpture, the shape of the figurine probably adheres closely to that of the block or large pebble from which it was carved. The rough finish further suggests the primitive nature of the artist's flint tools.

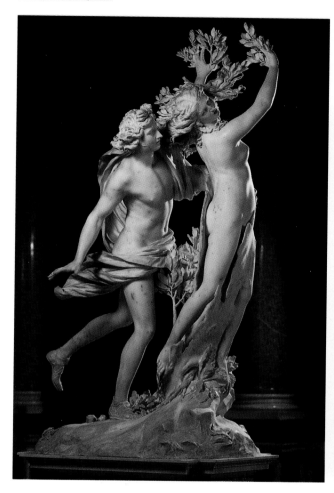

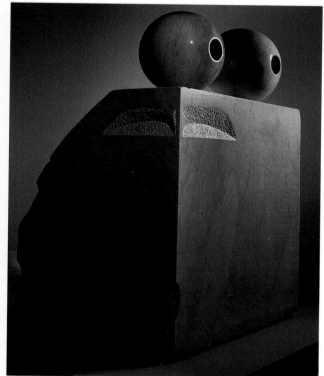

It is a leap from the stone art of the Stone Age to the sculpture of, say, Michelangelo in *The Cross-Legged Captive* (Fig. 6–1) or the *David* (Fig. 13–28). The *Captive,* interestingly, like the *Venus,* does not stray far from the shape of the block or precariously extend its limbs. But except for the eternal nature of the *David,* the statue belies the nature of the material. The furrowed brow, the taut muscles, the veins in the hand—all breathe life into the work.

The *Apollo and Daphne* (Fig. 6–10) of the Italian Baroque sculptor and architect Gianlorenzo Bernini shows us more of the potential of marble. Note how marble can capture the softness and sensuousness of flesh and the textures of hair, leaves, and bark. Observe the hundreds of slender projections and imagine the intricacy of cutting away the obstinate stone to reveal them. Bernini's work portrays the fleeting moment of myth when Daphne, fleeing the lithe god Apollo, futilely calls to her father for rescue but instead is transformed into a laurel tree. The sculpture is suffused with sweeping motion and conveys the antagonistic emotions of passion and terror.

In his *David* (see Fig. 14–6), Bernini portrays the moment in which the youth is twisting in preparation to fire the sling. David bites his marble lips; the muscles and veins of the left arm reflect the tightening of the hand; even his marble toes grip the rock beneath. When we view this sculpture, perhaps our own muscles tighten in empathy.

In *Eyes* (Fig. 6–11), contemporary sculptor Louise Bourgeois explores the relationships among a group of abstracted individuals by clustering carved marble units of varying sizes. The shapes are neither male nor female; the projections and rounded forms exude an androgynous life force. The marble medium lends these abstracted life forms an essential endurance that seems to underlie the conflicting motives for affiliation and individuation. Although Bourgeois could be thought of as remaining close to the shapes of the marble blocks that compose her work, the polish of the surfaces and the precise variations on a theme show that the blockiness of the units stems completely from aesthetic choice and not from the difficulties of working the medium.

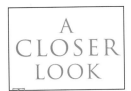
When we view the expanses of the Washington Mall, we are awed by the grand obelisk that is the Washington Monument. We are comforted by the stately columns and familiar shapes of the Lincoln and Jefferson Memorials. But many of us do not know how to respond to the two 200-foot-long black granite walls that form a V as they recede into the ground. There is no label—only the names of 58,000 victims chiseled into its silent walls:

As we descend along the path that hugs the harsh black granite, we enter the very earth that, in another place, has accepted the bodies of our sons and daughters. Each name is carved not only in the stone, but by virtue of its highly polished surface, in our own reflection, in our physical substance. We are not observers, we are participants. We touch, we write [letters to our loved ones], we leave parts of ourselves behind. This is a woman's vision—to commune, to interact, to collaborate with the piece to fulfill its expressive potential. . . .

Maya Ying Lin has foregone the [format of the triumphal monument]. She has given us [the earth mother] Gaea, who, pierced by the ebony scar of suffering death, takes back her children, as she has done since the dawn of humanity.[1]

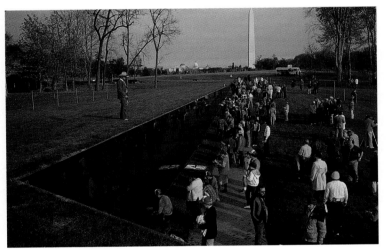

6–12 MAYA YING LIN
*VIETNAM MEMORIAL,
WASHINGTON, D.C.*
(1982). POLISHED BLACK
GRANITE. LENGTH: 492′.

This is Maya Ying Lin's Vietnam Memorial (Fig. 6–12), completed in 1982 on a two-acre site on the Mall. In order to read the names, we must descend gradually into earth, then just as gradually work our way back up. This progress is perhaps symbolic of the nation's involvement in Vietnam. As did the war it commemorates, the eloquently simple design of the memorial also stirs controversy.

This dignified understatement in stone has offended many who would have preferred a more traditional memorial. One conservative magazine branded the design a conspiracy to dishonor the dead. Architecture critic Paul Gapp of *The Chicago Tribune* argued that "The so-called memorial is bizarre . . . neither a building nor sculpture." One Vietnam veteran had called for a statue of an officer offering a fallen soldier to heaven. The public expects a certain heroicism in its monuments to commemorate those fallen in battle. Lin's work is antiheroic and antitriumphal. While most war monuments speak of giving up our loved ones to a cause, her monument speaks only of giving up our loved ones.

How did the Vietnam Memorial come to be so uniquely designed? It was picked from 1,421 entries in a national competition. The designer, Maya Ying Lin, is a Chinese-American woman who was all of twenty-two years old at the time she submitted her entry. A native of Ohio, Lin had just been graduated from Yale University, where she had majored in architecture. Lin recognized that a monumental sculpture or another grand building would have been intrusive in the heart of Washington. Her design meets the competition criteria of being "neither too commanding nor too deferential," and is yet another expression of the versatility of stone.

[1]Lois Fichner-Rathus, "A Woman's Vision of the War." *The New York Times,* August 18, 1991, p. H6.

6–13 *PORO SECRET SOCIETY MASK (KAGLE)* (LIBERIAN, DAN TRIBE). WOOD. 9″ HIGH.
YALE UNIVERSITY ART GALLERY, NEW HAVEN, CONN. GIFT OF MR. AND MRS. JAMES M. OSBORN.

WOOD SCULPTURE

Wood, like stone, may be carved, scraped, drilled, and polished. But unlike stone, wood may also be permanently molded and bent. Under heat, in fact, plywood can be bent to take on any shape. Wood, like stone, varies in hardness and grain, but it is more readily carved than stone.

Although wooden objects may last for many hundreds of years, wood does not possess the durability of stone and tends to warp and crack. But wood appeals to sculptors because of its grain, color, and workability. Wood is warm to the touch, whereas stone is cold. When polished, wood is sensuous. Wood's **tensile strength** exceeds that of stone, so that projecting wooden parts are less likely than their stone counterparts to break off. In recent years, wood has also become commonly used in assemblages.

The capacity of wood to yield beautiful, rough-hewn beauty is shown in the mask called *Kagle* (Fig. 6–13), by a sculptor of the African Dan people. The Dan of Sierra Leone, the Ivory Coast, and Liberia have carved masks for use in rituals and celebrations. Some Dan masks are polished and refined; others are intentionally crude. *Kagle* is a powerful work of thrusting and receding planes. The abstracted, geometric voids are as commanding as the wooden form itself. Such a mask is believed to endow its wearer with the powers of the bush spirits and is an essential element in the garb of tribal law-enforcement officers.

British sculptor Barbara Hepworth's abstraction, *Two Figures* (Fig. 6–14) is carved from elmwood. Like Henry Moore (see Fig. 17–25), Hepworth pierces solid masses to give contour to negative shapes. The concavities, which are painted white, and the voids in her carved figures have as much "shape-meaning"—to use Moore's term—as the solids. The viewer feels the urge to identify each form as male or female, but the sculptural "evidence" is too scant to allow such classification. At first glance it might seem that a similar artistic effect could have been achieved by carving these figures from marble, but the wood grain imparts a warmth to the surface that would not have been attained in marble, and the painting of the concavities lends them a "durability" and hardness not found in the outer sur-

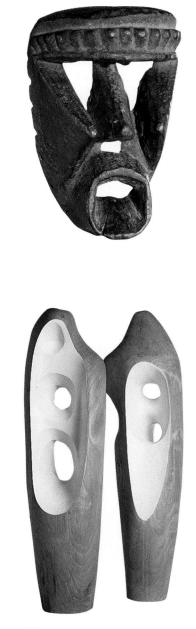

6–14 BARBARA HEPWORTH
TWO FIGURES (1947–48). ELMWOOD AND WHITE PAINT. 38 × 17″.
UNIVERSITY GALLERY, UNIVERSITY OF MINNESOTA, MINNEAPOLIS. JOHN ROOD SCULPTURE COLLECTION.

6–15 PO SHUN LEONG
FIGURE (1993). MAHOGANY WITH HIDDEN DRAWERS. 50″ HIGH.
COURTESY OF THE ARTIST.

6–16 FUMIO YOSHIMURA
DOG SNAPPER (1981). LINDEN WOOD. 21 × 40 × 12″.
COURTESY OF NANCY HOFFMAN GALLERY, N.Y.

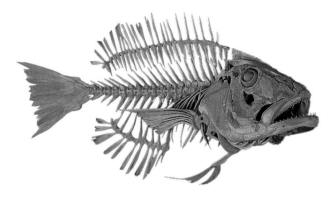

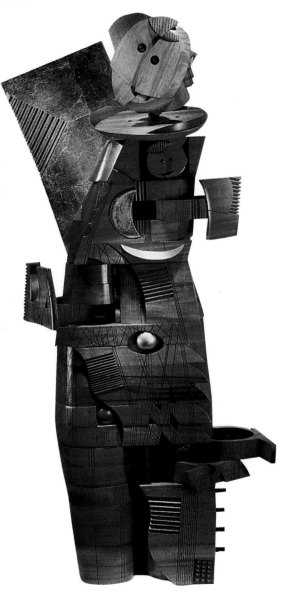

face. Ironically, the voids attain more visual solidity than the outer surfaces.

There is an implied massiveness to both the Kagle mask and Hepworth's *Two Figures*. But wood can also be used to create figures and forms of great complexity, delicacy and intricacy. The rich mahogany surfaces of Po Shun Leong's *Figure* (Fig. 6–15) have been polished, carved, striated, and gouged. There is a restlessness to the patterns which, coupled with a host of hidden drawers punctuating the form—some open, some closed—create a sense of constant motion. *Dog Snapper* (Fig. 6–16), by Japanese-born Fumio Yoshimura, is a **trompe l'oeil** sculpture whose multiple projections seem to be of natural bone, not wood. The lightness of the work would not have been attainable in stone, although the piece could have been carved from ivory. The sculptor's knowledge of the material is part and parcel of the creative process: a stone sculptor would not be likely to consider a fish skeleton as a suitable subject.

CLAY SCULPTURE

Clay is more pliable than stone or wood. The modeling of clay is personal and direct; the fingerprints of the sculptor may be found in the material. Children, like sculptors, enjoy the feel of clay and the smell of clay.

Unfortunately, clay has little strength, and it is not usually considered a permanent material, even though an *armature* may be used to prevent clay figures from sagging. Because of its weakness, clay is frequently used to make three-dimensional sketches, or models,

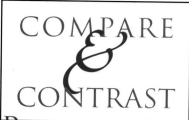

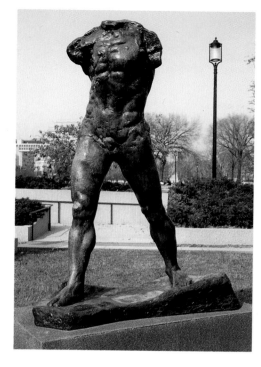

6–17 AUGUSTE RODIN
THE WALKING MAN (1905) (CAST 1962). BRONZE. 83 × 61 × 28″.

HIRSHHORN MUSEUM AND SCULPTURE GARDEN, SMITHSONIAN INSTITUTION, WASHINGTON, D.C. GIFT OF JOSEPH H. HIRSHHORN, 1966.

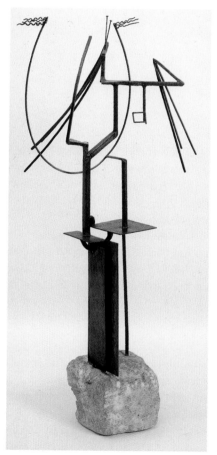

6–18 JULIO GONZALEZ
WOMAN COMBING HER HAIR (C. 1930–33). IRON. 57″ HIGH.

MODERNA MUSEET, STOCKHOLM.

Compare and contrast the materials and styles of Rodin (Fig. 6–17) and Gonzalez (Fig. 6–18). Rodin's *The Walking Man* is hollow, yet it retains the solid, massive appearance of the clay from which it was modeled—as well as the imprints of Rodin's fingers and tools. It speaks of the personal, gestural touches with which the sculptor can caress the most pliable materials, yet it has the strength, durability, and patina of bronze.

Gonzalez's work is not about constructed form. Form is evoked by lines that both embrace space and intersect it. It seems as though the artist is drawing in the air with steel. The only massive element in the composition is the stone base, which seems to anchor the piece.

Which one of the works is realistic? Which is representational? Abstract? Nonobjective? Why or why not? Which is open form? Closed form? How does each artist manipulate his materials to create or evoke form? How do the artists penetrate or envelop the surrounding space in their compositions?

for sculptures that are to be executed in more durable materials. As was noted earlier, clay models may be translated into bronze figures. In *ceramics,* clay is fired in a kiln at high temperatures so that it becomes hardened and nonporous. Before firing, clay can also be coated, or *glazed,* with substances that provide the ceramic object with a glassy monochromatic or polychromatic surface.

METAL SCULPTURE

Metal has been used by sculptors for thousands of years. Metals have been cast, **extruded, forged, stamped,** drilled, filed, and burnished. The familiar process of producing cast bronze sculptures has changed little over the centuries. But in recent years artists have also assembled **direct-metal sculptures** by welding, riveting, and soldering. Modern adhesives have also made it possible to glue sections of metal together into three-dimensional constructions.

Different metals have different properties. Bronze has been the most popular casting material because of its pleasing surface and color characteristics. Bronze surfaces can be made dull or glossy. Chemical treatments can produce colors ranging from greenish-blacks to golden or deep browns. Because of oxidation, bronze and copper surfaces age to form rich green or greenish-blue **patinas.**

The French artist Auguste Rodin is considered by many to be the greatest sculptor of the nineteenth century. Nevertheless, Rodin's *The Walking Man* (see "Compare and Contrast" feature on page 129) and similar sculptural fragments were not well received in his day, since they have an unfinished look. They were not incomplete, of course. Instead, they reflected Rodin's obsession with the correct rendition of anatomical parts.

MODERN AND CONTEMPORARY MATERIALS AND METHODS

Throughout history sculptors have searched for new forms of expression. They have been quick to experiment with the new materials and approaches that have been

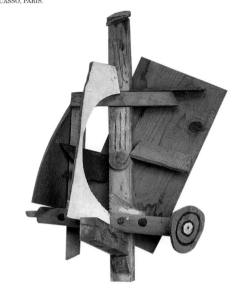

6–19 PABLO PICASSO
MANDOLIN AND CLARINET (1913). WOOD CONSTRUCTION AND PAINT. (©) 1998 ESTATE OF PABLO PICASSO/ARTISTS RIGHTS SOCIETY (ARS), NEW YORK.
MUSÉE PICASSO, PARIS.

made possible by advancing technology. During the twentieth century, technological changes have overleaped themselves, giving rise to new materials, such as plastics and fluorescent lights, and to new ways of working traditional materials.

In this section we will explore a number of new materials and approaches, including constructed sculpture, mixed media, and earthworks. Though the search for novelty has been exhausting, this list is by no means exhaustive.

CONSTRUCTED SCULPTURE

In constructed sculpture the artist builds or constructs the sculpture from materials such as cardboard, celluloid, translucent plastic, sheet metal, or wire, frequently creating forms that are lighter than those made from carving stone, modeling clay, or casting metal. Picasso inspired a movement in this direction with works such as *Mandolin and Clarinet* (Fig. 6–19). As critic Robert Hughes remarked, such works were "everything that statues had not been: not monolithic, but open, not cast or carved, but assembled from flat planes."[2] In spirit

[2]Robert Hughes, "The Liberty of Thought Itself," *Time Magazine*, September 1, 1986, p. 87.

6–20 CLAES OLDENBURG
SOFT TOILET (1966). VINYL FILLED WITH KAPOK PAINTED WITH
LIQUITEX, AND WOOD. 52 × 32 × 30″.

6–21 NIKI DE SAINT-PHALLE
NANA (C. 1965). MIXED MEDIA. 52 × 38 × 30″.

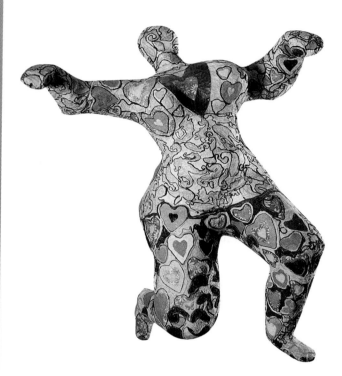

constructed sculptures. Gabo's translucent elements
transform masses into planes that frame geometric
voids. "Mass" is created in the mind of the viewer by
the empty volumes.

Pop artist Claes Oldenburg's *Soft Toilet* (Fig. 6–20)
is constructed of vinyl, kapok, cloth, and Plexiglass.
Our sensibilities are challenged in a lighthearted
work: A familiar object which we know to be hard and
cold and unmovable is rendered soft, supple, and
pliable—and certainly unusable. Similarly, Niki de
Saint-Phalle's *Nana* (Fig. 6–21) defies our senses, and
gravity itself. It seems to float on air like an alien
moon-walker, or perhaps a Thanksgiving Day Parade
balloon. The monstrous female, constructed of a
chicken-wire frame covered with fabric and gaily
painted with bright colors and bold patterns, is the
embodiment of unbridled spirit.

and style, reliefs from this era were very close to
Picasso's paintings. But the unorthodox materials—
wood, sheet metal, wire, found objects—challenged all
traditions in art-making. Sculpture would never be
the same.

A Russian visitor to Picasso's Paris studio, Vladimir
Tatlin, is credited with having realized the three-
dimensional potential of constructed sculpture, which
was then further developed in Russia by the brothers
Antoine Pevsner and Naum Gabo. Naum Gabo's
Column (Fig. 16–19) epitomizes the ascendance of form
and space over mass that is characteristic of many

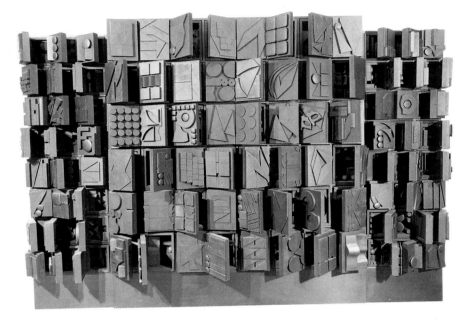

6–22 LOUISE NEVELSON
Black Secret Wall (1970). Black wood. $100 \times 139 \times 7''$.
PHOTOGRAPH COURTESY OF PACE WILDENSTEIN GALLERY, N.Y.

ASSEMBLAGE

Assemblage is a form of constructed sculpture in which preexisting, or found, objects, recognizable in form, are integrated by the sculptor into novel combinations that take on a life and meaning of their own. American artist Louise Nevelson's *Black Secret Wall* (Fig. 6–22), like many other of her wooden sculptures, is a compartmentalized assemblage of rough-cut geometric shapes painted black. Similar assemblages include banal objects such as bowling pins, chair slats, and barrel staves and may be painted white or gold as well as black.

Why walls? Here is Nevelson's explanation:

"I attribute the walls to this: I had loads . . . and loads of creative energy. . . . So I began to stack my sculptures into an environment. . . . I think there is something in the consciousness of the creative person that adds up, and the multiple image that I give, say, in an enormous wall gives me so much satisfaction."[3]

The overall effect of Nevelson's collections is one of nostalgia and mystery. They suggest the pieces of the personal and collective past, of lonely introspective journeys among the cobwebs of Victorian attics—of childhoods that never were. Perhaps they are the very symbol of consciousness, for what is the function of intellect if not to impose order on the bits and pieces of experience?

Assemblages by Richard Stankiewicz, such as *Figure* (Fig. 6–23), weld battered scraps of metal and rusted machine parts into oddly graceful structures of iron and steel. The artist's hand breathes a new vitality into discarded mechanical equipment. The work could not have been created by traditional means, nor would it have been conceived by a sculptor who used such means: the thousands of projections would have been unthinkable in stone, and one cannot imagine what would have inspired a wooden carving in this form. In *Figure* Stankiewicz seems neither worshipful of nor horrified by the machine age and its dehumanizing aspects. His objects seem silently to assert that things as we know them disintegrate with time and that their elements take on new form.

In sharp contrast to the machine-wrought debris of Stankiewicz's *Figure,* nature is the point of departure for Betye Saar's *Ancestral Spirit Chair* (Fig. 6–24). In a work that was influenced by Saar's African ancestry and tribal beliefs concerning ancestor worship, the artist combines remnants of nature with common objects of human existence. The chair is constructed of tree branches that have been sawed, shaped, or left in their natural state, reaching skyward like fingers on a hand. These "fingertips" are capped by a collection of glass saltshakers, and other found objects make their appearance here and there. The chair's surface is adorned with rhythmic white markings suggesting the body painting common to some African tribes. It is a curious piece: inviting, yet seeming to welcome only those who belong.

[3]Louise Nevelson, *Louise Nevelson: Atmospheres and Environments* (New York: C. N. Potter in association with the Whitney Museum of American Art, 1980), p. 77.

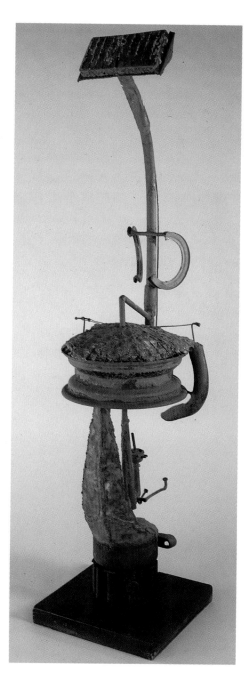

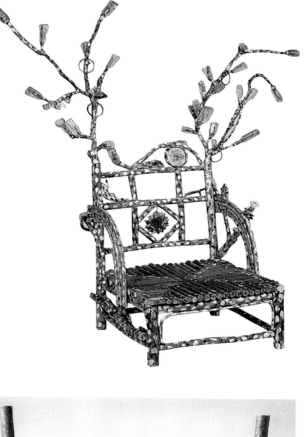

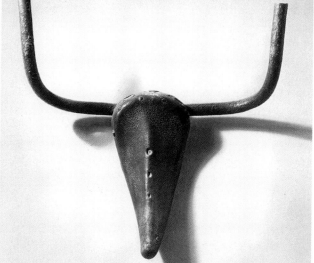

Perhaps the best-known assemblage is Picasso's *Bull's Head* (Fig. 6–25). Consisting of the seat and handlebars of an old bicycle, the work possesses a rakish vitality. It is immediately and whimsically recognizable as animal—so much so that on first impression, its mundane origins are obscured.

READY-MADES

The assemblages of Nevelson, Stankiewicz, and Picasso are constructed from found objects. Early in this century Marcel Duchamp declared that found objects, or **ready-mades,** such as bottle racks and urinals, could be literally elevated as works of art by being placed

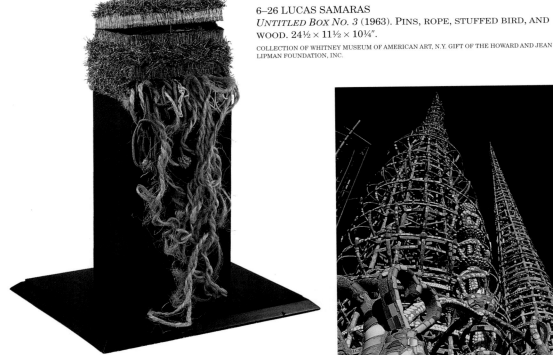

6–26 LUCAS SAMARAS
UNTITLED BOX NO. 3 (1963). PINS, ROPE, STUFFED BIRD, AND
WOOD. 24½ × 11½ × 10¼″.
COLLECTION OF WHITNEY MUSEUM OF AMERICAN ART, N.Y. GIFT OF THE HOWARD AND JEAN
LIPMAN FOUNDATION, INC.

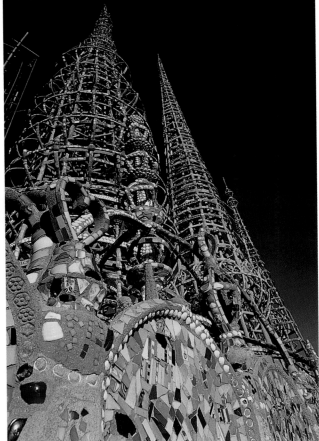

6–27 SIMON RODIA
SIMON RODIA TOWERS IN WATTS (1921–54). CEMENT WITH
VARIOUS OBJECTS. 98′ HIGH.
CULTURAL AFFAIRS DEPARTMENT, LOS ANGELES.

on pedestals—literally or figuratively. No assembly required. The urinal in Figure 1–34 could be turned on its back, to put the object in a new context, and given the title *Fountain*. These adjustments were said by the artist to invest the object with a new *idea*. Duchamp argued that the dimension of taste, good or bad, was irrelevant. The function of the ready-made—not that it needed one—was to prompt the spectator to think, and to think again.

Duchamp recognized that artists could take advantage of the concept of the ready-made object and substitute cleverness for solid work should the "making" of ready-mades become a habit. For this reason Duchamp advised that artists elevate common objects to the realm of art only a few times each year.

MIXED MEDIA

In **mixed-media** constructions and assemblages, sculptors use materials and ready-made or found objects that are not normally the elements of a work of art. Contemporary painters also sometimes "mix" their media by attaching objects to their canvases. Robert Rauschenberg, discussed in Chapter 17, has attached ladders, chairs, and electric fans to his paintings and run paint over these objects as if they were continuations of the canvas. What do we call the result—painting or sculpture?

Greek-born contemporary artist Lucas Samaras has constructed boxes with knives, razor blades, and other menacing objects that are frequently accompanied by delicate shells, pieces of colored glass, and mysterious and sensuous items of personal import. *Untitled Box No. 3* (Fig. 6–26) is constructed from wood, pins, rope, and a stuffed bird. The viewer is drawn masochistically to touch such frightening sculptures, to test their eroticism and their danger.

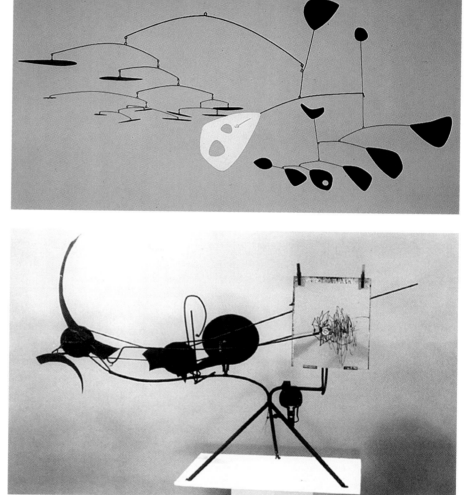

The sculptural environment known as the *Simon Rodia Towers in Watts* (Fig. 6–27) was constructed by an Italian-born tile setter who immigrated to Watts, a poor neighborhood in Los Angeles. Rodia's whimsical towers are built sturdily enough—of cement on steel frames, the tallest one rising nearly 100 feet. As a mixed-media assemblage, the towers are coated with debris such as mirror fragments, broken dishes, shards of glass and ceramic tile, and shells. The result is a lacy forest of spires that glisten with magical patterns of contrasting and harmonious colors. The towers took thirty-three years to erect and were built by Rodia's own hands. Rodia, by the way, knew nearly nothing of the world of art.

KINETIC SCULPTURE

Sculptors have always been concerned with the portrayal of movement, but **kinetic sculptures** actually do move. Movement may be caused by the wind, magnetic fields, jets of water, electric motors, variations in the intensity of light, or the active manipulation of the observer. During the 1930s the American sculptor Alexander Calder was one of the early pioneers of the first form of art that made motion as basic an element as shape or color—the mobile. As in *Zarabanda* (Fig. 6–28), carefully balanced weights are suspended on wires such that the gentlest current of air sets them moving in prescribed orbits. The weights themselves are colorfully reminiscent of animals, fish, leaves, and petals.

Among the kinetic sculptures are the intendedly absurd machines of Swiss-French sculptor Jean Tinguely.

6–29 JEAN TINGUELY
META-MATIC NO.9 (1954). MOTORIZED KINETIC SCULPTURE. 35½″ HIGH.
MUSEUM OF FINE ARTS, HOUSTON. GIFT OF D. AND J. DE MENIL. © 1998 ARTISTS RIGHTS SOCIETY (ARS), N.Y./ADAGP, PARIS.

Some of Tinguely's machines, such as the scorpionlike *Meta-matic No. 9* (Fig. 6–29), were constructed to create art. In this case, ballpoint pens—one of our less aesthetic contemporary expressive media—were affixed to agitated arms that moved about at random within certain limits. There are, of course, multiple layers of satire. The age of the machine, the conveyor belt, the automatized contraption, even the works of the artist's contemporaries fall prey to Tinguely's commentary.

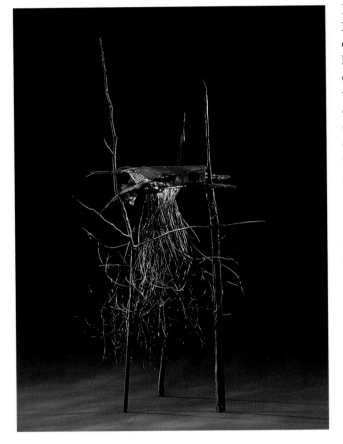

LIGHT SCULPTURE

Natural light has always been an important element in
defining sculpture, but only in the twentieth century
have sculptors experimented with the addition of artificial light to their compositions. The effects can be as
varied as light itself—from works inspired by floures-
cent commercial lighting to the mystical glow shown in
Charles Kumnick's *Spirit Hut* (Fig. 6–30). Here a
combination of metal, wood, and electrical components
take on the quality of an ancestral hut that glows from
a central hearth.

EARTHWORKS

In **earthworks,** or Land Art, large amounts of earth or
land are shaped into a sculpture. In a sense, earthworks
are nothing new. Native American sand paintings, Zen
rock gardens, Stonehenge, and contour farming provide
ample precedent. But in their contemporary form,
earthworks originated in the 1960s as something of a
literal return to nature. As expressed by land artist
Robert Smithson, "Instead of putting a work of art on
some land, some land is put into the work of art."
Perhaps earthworks were a reaction against some of
the highly industrialized, unnatural materials that had
found their way into sculpture throughout the earlier
years of the century. Earthworks are also likely to appeal
to the human desire to give shape to rude matter on a
grand scale.

Contemporary earthworks include great trenches
and drawings in the desert, collections of rocks,
shoveled rings in ice and snow, and installations of
masses of earth on the urban gallery floor. Smithson's
Spiral Jetty (Fig. 6–31) in Utah's Great Salt Lake is
composed of earth and related natural materials.
Observers may try to find microscopic and macroscopic
symbolism in the jetty: its shape might suggest the
spiraling strands of the DNA that composes our basic
genetic material, as well as the shape of galaxies. The
mass of the jetty stands somewhere between these
extremes and also forms a relationship between earth
and water.

In the next chapter we will turn our attention to
the shaping of materials into structures that house our
work, our play, our family life, our worship, and our
sleep—architecture.

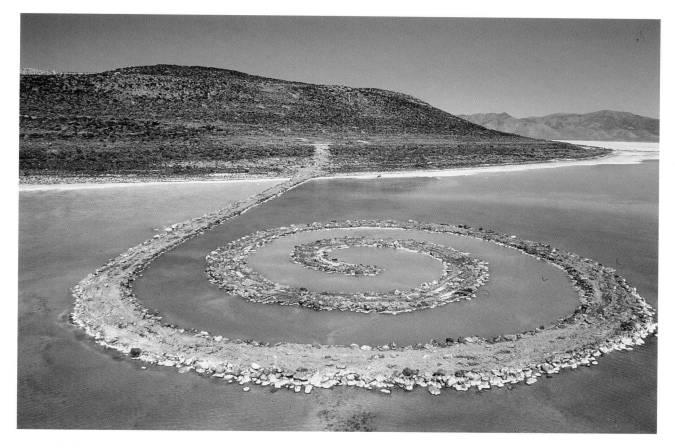

6–31 ROBERT SMITHSON
Spiral Jetty, Great Salt
Lake, Utah (1970). Black
rocks, salt, earth, water,
algae. Length: 1,500′.
Width: 15′.

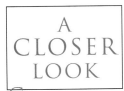
In September 1976 *Running Fence, Sonoma and Marin Counties, California, 1972–76* (Fig. 6–32), perhaps the best known collaborative work of Christo and Jeanne-Claude, was completed in northern California. The fence, 24½ miles of shimmering white nylon slung between steel posts, ran from the sea at Bodega Bay across the hills and dales of Sonoma and Marin counties.

Running Fence was a spectacular work and, to some, a spectacle. At dawn and at dusk the nylon took on a purple cast. In the brilliant sun, black clung to the inner shadows. Blues and browns reflected sky and earth. All this required 240,000 square yards of nylon, 2,050 posts, 300 workers, countless hooks, and miles and miles of wire. The Herculean effort was dismantled in two weeks. It had run its course.

The Christos finance their environmental sculptures by selling project drawings and studies. The cost of *Running Fence* was more than $3 million, much of it for legal fees to combat suits brought by concerned environmentalists. In 1981, the artists failed to convince the city of New York to grant permission to construct thousands of 15-foot-high steel gates holding saffron-colored fabric across Central Park—a chain that would have linked disparate ethnic and socioeconomic segments of the metropolis. The artists are presently working on this project.

Other cities have been more open to concepts of Christo and Jeanne-Claude. In 1983 the artists surrounded 11 small islands in Miami's Biscayne Bay in floating pink fabric. From the air the islands were transformed into colorful lily pads. After two weeks the surrounded islands, like the California landscape before them, were removed. "Art must disappear," noted Christo and Jeanne-Claude. "Art doesn't last forever." But perhaps the photographic record of their works will last as long as sculptures carved from marble.

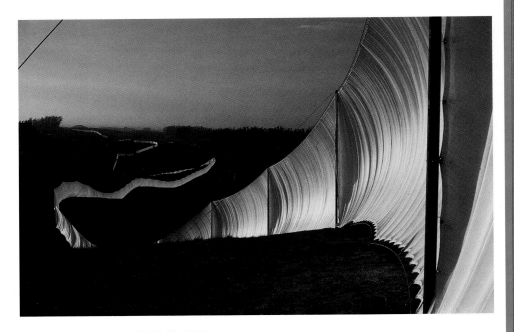

6–32 CHRISTO AND JEANNE-CLAUDE
RUNNING FENCE (1972–76). NYLON FABRIC AND STEEL POLES. HEIGHT: 18′; LENGTH: 24½ MILES.
INSTALLED IN SONOMA AND MARIN COUNTIES, CALIFORNIA, FOR TWO WEEKS, FALL, 1976. © CHRISTO 1976. PHOTO: JEANNE-CLAUDE.

key terms

Sculpture	Carving	Investiture	Stamp
Relief sculpture	Modeling	Kiln	Direct-metal sculpture
Bas-relief	Figurative	Burnish	Patina
High-relief	Terra-cotta	Constructed sculpture	Assemblage
Free-standing sculpture	Casting	Rasp	Ready-made
Mobile	Mold	Tensile strength	Mixed media
Subtractive process	Lost-wax technique	Extrude	Kinetic sculpture
Additive process	Gates	Forge	Earthwork

artists

Michelangelo	Barbara Hepworth	Betye Saar
Leekya	Po Shun Leong	Lucas Samaras
Reuben Nakian	Fumio Yoshimura	Simon Rodia
Roberta Laidman	Auguste Rodin	Alexander Calder
Louise Bourgeois	Julio Gonzalez	Jean Tinguely
Edgar Degas	Pablo Picasso	Charles Kumnick
George Segal	Claes Oldenburg	Robert Smithson
John de Andrea	Niki de Saint-Phalle	Christo and Jeanne-Claude
Gianlorenzo Bernini	Louise Nevelson	
Maya Ying Lin	Richard Stankiewicz	

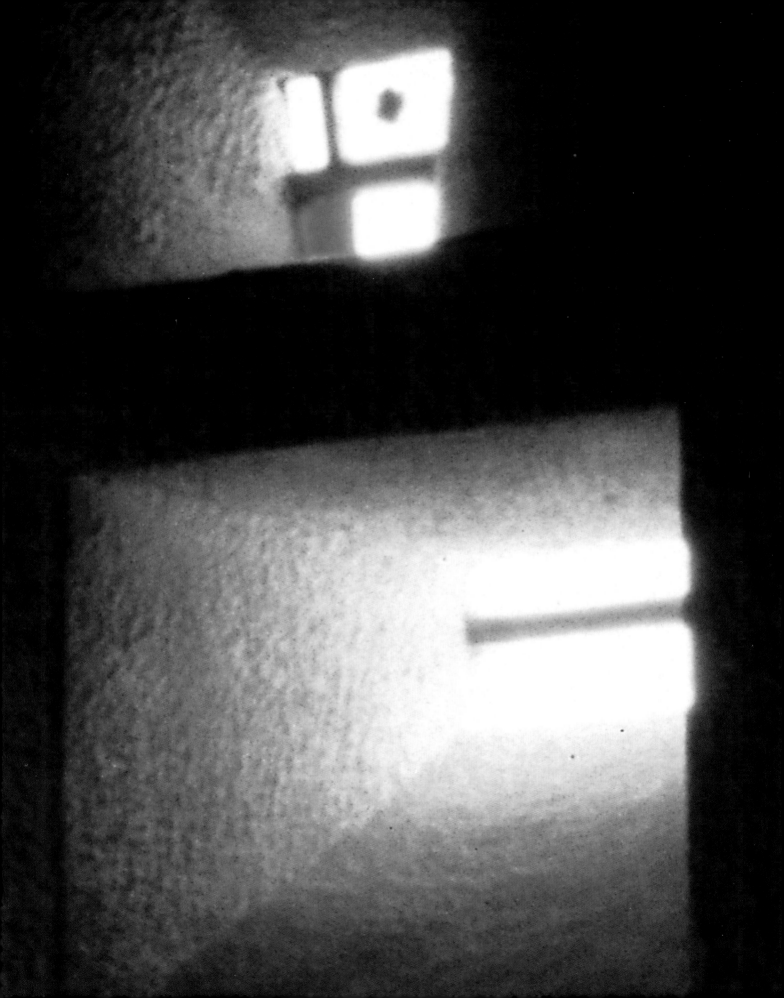

ARCHITECTURE

P R E L I M I N A R Y
Sketch

- Buildings have been fashioned from materials ranging from steel and wood to clay and ice.

- The ancient fortress of Machu Picchu was erected without benefit of mortar, yet its granite walls are pieced together so perfectly that not even a knife blade can pass between the blocks.

- The Romans constructed arches with two-ton blocks that have stood for 2,000 years and are held together only by the force of gravity.

- In many of the great cathedrals of Europe, the brute weight of the massive stones above worshippers' heads is transferred to buttresses that are positioned outside the buildings.

- Buckminster Fuller proposed that the center of Manhattan should be enclosed in a weather-controlled transparent dome two miles in diameter.

- Most houses in the United States are constructed by means of "balloon framing."

- In the mid-nineteenth century, Sir Joseph Paxton created his huge plate-glass-paneled Crystal Palace by emulating the design of a leaf.

- The Eiffel Tower was prefabricated in a factory.

Le Corbusier, *Chapel of Notre-Dame-du-Haut* (detail). See Figure 7–23.

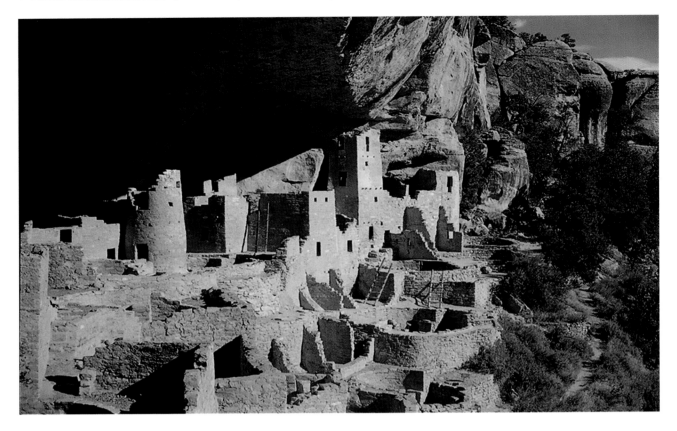

Early humans found their shelters—the mouth of a yawning cave, the underside of a ledge, the boughs of an overspreading tree. But for thousands of years we having been building shelters and fashioning them to our needs. Before we became capable of transporting bulky materials over vast distances, we had to rely on local possibilities. Native Americans have constructed huts from sticks and bark and conical tepees from animal skins and wooden poles. They have carved their way into the sides of cliffs. African villagers have woven sticks and grass into walls and plastered them with mud; their geometrically pure cone roofs sit atop cylindrical bases. Desert peoples have learned to dry clay in the sun in the form of bricks. From ice the Eskimo has fashioned the dome-shaped igloo.

Architecture is the art and science of designing buildings, bridges, and other structures to help us meet our personal and communal needs. Of all the arts, architecture probably has the greatest impact on our daily lives. For most of us, architecture determines the quality of the environments in which we work, play, meditate, and rest.

Architecture is also a vehicle for artistic expression in three dimensions. More than any other art form, architecture is experienced from within as well as without, and at great length. If sculptures have fronts,

backs, sides, tops, and bottoms, buildings have **facades,** foundations, roofs, and a variety of interior spaces that must be planned. If some sculptures are kinetic and some are composed of light sources, buildings may contain complex systems for heating, cooling, lighting, and inner transportation.

Architects, like sculptors, must work within the limits of their materials and the technology of the day. In addition to understanding enough of engineering to determine how materials may be used efficiently to span and enclose sometimes vast spaces, architects must work with other professionals and with contractors who design and install elements of the **service systems** of their buildings.

In a sense the architect is not only an artist but a mediator—a compromiser. The architect mediates between the needs of the client and the properties and aesthetic possibilities of the site. (Today's technology permits the erection of twenty-story-high, twenty-feet-wide "sliver skyscrapers" on expensive, narrow urban sites, but at what aesthetic cost to a neighborhood of row houses?) The architect balances aesthetics and the building codes of the community. (Since the 1930s architects in New York City have had to comply with the so-called set-back law and step back or contour their high-rises back from the street in order to let the sun shine in on an environment that seemed in danger of devolving into a maze of blackened canyons.) Climate, site, materials, building codes, clients, contractors, service systems, and the amount of money available—these are just some of the variables that the architect must employ or contend with, to create an aesthetically pleasing, functional structure.

In this section we will explore traditional and modern ways in which architects have come to terms with these variables. We will survey the traditional materials and methods associated with building in stone and wood. Then we will examine a number of modern and contemporary architectural materials and methods, including those associated with cast iron and steel cage construction, use of reinforced concrete, and steel cable.

STONE ARCHITECTURE

As a building material, stone is massive and virtually indestructible. Contemporary woodframe homes frequently sport stone fireplaces, perhaps as a symbol of permanence and strength as well as of warmth. The Native American cliff dwellings at Mesa Verde, Colorado, (Fig. 7–1) could be considered something of an "earthwork high relief." The cliff itself becomes the back wall or "support" of more than 100 rectangular apartments. Circular, underground **kivas** served as community centers. Construction with stone, **adobe,** and timber creates a mixed media functional fantasy. Early man also assembled stone temples and memorials.

POST-AND-LINTEL CONSTRUCTION

The prehistoric Stonehenge (see Fig. 10–4) probably served religious or astronomical purposes. Its orientation toward the sun and its layout in concentric circles is suggestive of the amphitheaters and temples to follow. Stonehenge is an early example of **post-and-lintel** construction (Fig. 7–2a). Two stones were set upright as supports and a third was placed across them, creating an opening beneath. How the massive blocks of Stonehenge were transported and erected remains a mystery.

Early stone structures were erected without benefit of mortar. Their **dry masonry** relied on masterly carving of blocks, strategic placement, and sheer weight for

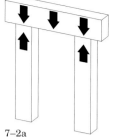

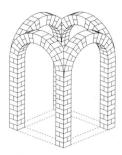

7–2a
post-and-lintel construction

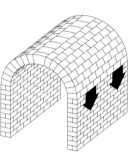

7–2b
rounded arches
enclosing square bay

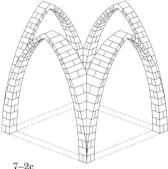

7–2c
pointed arches enclosing
rectangular bay

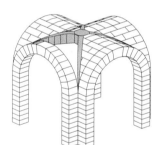

7–2d
tunnel or barrel vault

7–2e
groin vault

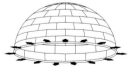

7–2f
groin vault showing ribs
that carry greatest loads

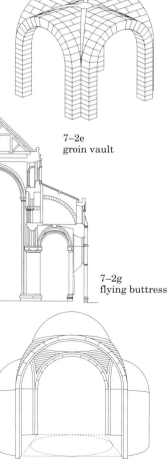

7–2g
flying buttress

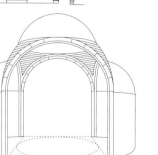

7–2i
pendentives

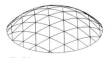

7–2h
dome

7–2j
geodesic dome

7–3 WALLS OF FORTRESS OF MACHU PICCHU, URUBAMBA VALLEY, PERU (INCAN, 1490–1530).

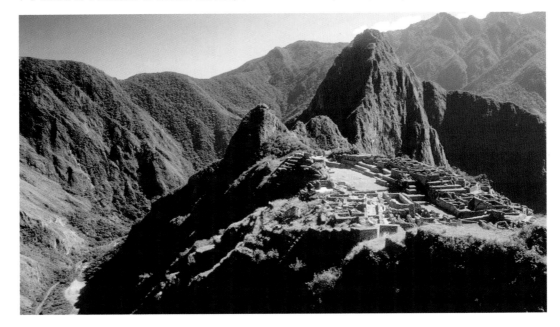

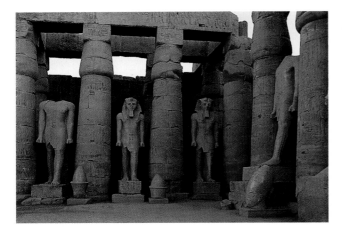

7–4 TEMPLE OF AMEN-RE, KARNAK (EGYPTIAN, XVIII DYNASTY, 1570–1342 BCE).

durability. Consider the imposing ruin of the fortress of Machu Picchu, perched high above the Urubamba River in the Peruvian Andes. Its beautiful granite walls (Fig. 7–3), constructed by the Incas, are pieced together so perfectly that not even a knife blade can pass between the blocks. The faces of the great Pyramids of Egypt (see Fig. 10–13) are assembled as miraculously, perhaps even more so considering the greater mass of the blocks.

Stone became the favored material for the public buildings of the Egyptians and the Greeks. The Egyptian Temple of Amen-Re at Karnak (Fig. 7–4) and the Parthenon (Fig. 11–9) of the Classical period of Greece begin to speak of the elegance as well as the massiveness that can be fashioned from stone. The Temple of Amen-Re is of post-and-lintel construction, but the paintings, relief sculptures, and overall smoothness of the columns belie their function as bearers of stress. The virtual forest of columns was a structural necessity because of the weight of the massive stone lintels. The Parthenon is also of post-and-lintel construction. Consistent with the Greeks' emphasis on the functional purpose of columns, the surfaces of the marble shafts are free from ornamentation. The Parthenon, which may be the most studied and surveyed building in the world, is discussed at length in Chapter 11.

ARCHES

Architects of stone also use **arches** to span distances (see Figs. 7–2b and c). Arches have many functions, including supporting other structures, such as roofs, and serving as actual and symbolic gateways. An Arch of Triumph, as in the city of Paris, provides a visual focus for the return of the conquering hero. Eero Saarinen's

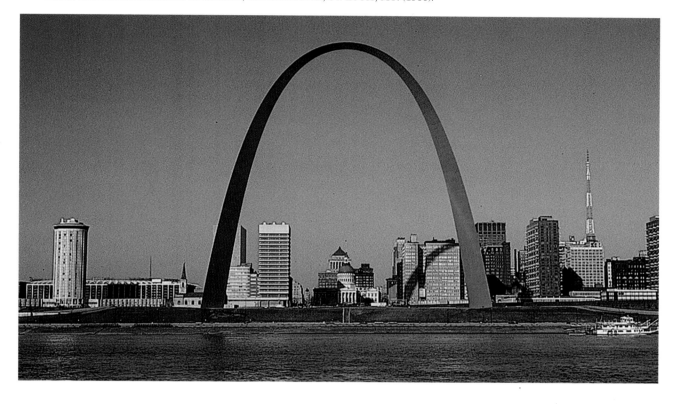

Gateway Arch (Fig. 7–5), completed in St. Louis in 1965, stands 630 feet tall at the center and commemorates the westward push of the United States after the Louisiana Purchase of 1803. The Pont du Gard (see Fig. 11–22) near Nîmes, France, employs the arch in a bridge that is part of an **aqueduct** system. It is a marvel of Roman engineering. Early masonry arches were fashioned from **bricks;** each limestone block of the Pont du Gard weighs up to 2 tons, and they were assembled without benefit of mortar. The bridge stands and functions today, two millennia after its creation.

In most arches wedge-shaped blocks of stone, called **voussoirs,** are gradually placed in position ascending a wooden scaffold called a **centering.** When the center or **keystone** is set in place, the weight of the blocks is all at once transmitted in an arc laterally and downward, and the centering can be removed. The pull of gravity on each block serves as "cement"; that is, the blocks fall into one another so that the very weight that had made their erection a marvel now prevents them from budging. The **compressive strength** of stone allows the builder to

place additional weight above the arch. The Pont du Gard consists of three **tiers** of arches, 161 feet high.

VAULTS

An extended arch is called a **vault.** A tunnel or **barrel vault** (see Fig. 7–2d) simply places arches behind one another until a desired depth is reached. In this way impressive spaces may be roofed and tunnels may be constructed. Unfortunately, the spaces enclosed by barrel vaults are dark, since piercing them to let in natural light would compromise their strength. The communication of stresses from one arch to another also requires that the centering for each arch be kept in place until the entire vault is completed.

Roman engineers are credited with the creation of the **groin vault,** which overcame limitations of the barrel vault, as early as the third century A.D. Groin vaults are constructed by placing barrel vaults at right angles to cover a square space (see Fig. 7–2e). In this way the load of the intersecting vaults is transmitted to the corners, necessitating **buttressing** at these points

7–6 BUCKMINSTER FULLER
UNITED STATES PAVILION, EXPO 67, MONTREAL (1976).

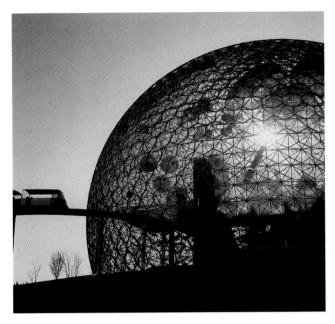

but allowing the sides of the square to be open. The square space enclosed by the groin vault is called a **bay.** Architects could now construct huge buildings by assembling any number of bays. Since the stresses from one groin vault are not transmitted to a large degree to its neighbors, the centering used for one vault can be removed and reused while the building is under construction.

The greatest loads in the groin vault are thrust onto the four arches that comprise the sides and the two arches that run diagonally across them. If the capacity of these diagonals is increased to carry a load, by means of **ribs** added to the vault (see Fig. 7–2f), the remainder of the roof can be fashioned from stone **webbing** or other materials much lighter in weight. A true stone skeleton is created.

Note from Figure 7–2b that rounded arches can enclose only square bays. One could not use rounded arches in rectangular bays because the longer walls would have higher arches. Architects over the centuries solved the rectangular bay problem in a number of ingenious ways. The most important of these is found in Gothic architecture, discussed in Chapter 12, which uses ribbed vaults and pointed arches. Pointed arches can be constructed to uniform heights even when the

sides of the enclosed space are unequal (see Fig. 7–2c). Gothic architecture also employed the so-called **flying buttress** (Fig. 7–2g), a masonry strut that transmits part of the load of a vault to a buttress positioned outside a building.

Most of the great cathedrals of Europe achieve their vast open interiors through the use of vaults. Massive stone rests benignly above the heads of worshippers and tourists alike, transmitting its brute load laterally and downward. The Ottonian St. Michael's (see Fig. 12–15), built in Germany between 1001 and 1031, uses barrel vaulting. Its bays are square, and its walls are blank and massive. The Romanesque St. Sernin (see Fig. 12–17), built in France between about 1080 and 1120, uses round arches and square bays. The walls are heavy and blunt, with the main masses subdivided by buttresses. St. Étienne (Fig. 12–19), completed between 1115 and 1120, has high rising vaults—some of the earliest to show true ribs—that permit light to enter through a **clerestory.** Stone became a fully elegant structural skeleton in the great Gothic cathedrals such as those at Laon (see Figs. 12–25 and 12–26) and Chartres (see Fig. 12–28) and in the Notre Dame of Paris (see Fig. 12–27). Lacy buttressing and ample **fenestration** lend these massive buildings an airy lightness that seems consonant with their mission of directing upward the focus of human awareness.

DOMES

Domes are hemispherical forms that are rounded when viewed from beneath (see Fig. 7–2h). Like vaults, domes are extensions of the principle of the arch and are capable of enclosing vast reaches of space. (Buckminster Fuller, who designed the American Pavilion seen in Fig. 7–6 for the 1967 World's Fair in Montreal, proposed that the center of Manhattan should be enclosed in a weather-controlled transparent dome two miles in diameter.) Stresses from the top of the dome are transmitted in all directions to the points at which the circular base meets the foundation, walls, or other structures beneath.

The dome of the Buddhist temple or Stupa of Sanchi, India, completed in the first century CE, rises 50 feet above the ground and causes the worshipper to contemplate the dwelling place of the gods. It was constructed from stones placed in gradually diminishing concentric circles. Visitors find the domed interior of the

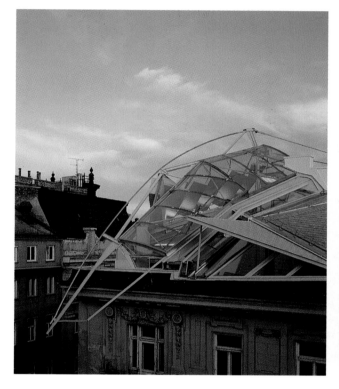

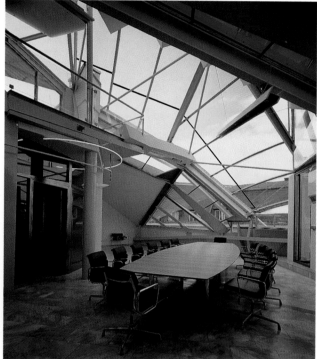

Pantheon of Rome (see Fig. 11–26), completed during the second century CE, breathtaking. Like the dome of the Stupa, the rounded inner surface of the Pantheon, 144 feet in diameter, symbolizes the heavens.

The dome of the vast Hagia Sophia (see Fig. 12–7) in Constantinople is 108 feet in diameter. Its architects, building during the sixth century CE, used four triangular surfaces called **pendentives** (see Fig. 7–2i) to support the dome on a square base. Pendentives transfer the load from the base of the dome to the **piers** at the corners of the square beneath.

Stone today is rarely used as a structural material. It is expensive to quarry and transport, and it is too massive to handle readily at the site. Metals are lighter and have greater tensile strength, and so they are suitable as the skeletons or reinforcers for most of today's larger structures. Still, buildings with steel skeletons are frequently dressed with thin facades or **veneers** of costly marble, limestone, and other types of stone. Residents of New York State were scandalized during the 1960s to learn that the public coffers had funded the

purchase of marble worth several years' production of the entire state of Vermont in order to cloak the steel monoliths of the capital's office mall with dignity. On a smaller scale, many tract homes are granted decorative patches of stone across the front facade and slabs of slate are frequently used to provide minimum-care surfaces for entry halls or patios in private homes.

It even seems that the creative solution to additions and renovation of older buildings is now more likely to consist of combinations of industrial materials with traditional ones. The Vienna law office (Figs. 7–7 and 7–8) designed by the architecture collaborative, Coop Himmelblau ("blue sky cooperative") sports a rooftop addition that is a bold and unusual counterpoint to the existing stone architecture, with its decorative carvings that characterize turn-of-the-century European facades. The new roof structure runs absolutely counter to the notion that additions ought to be synchronized with the existing structure, or at least appear to be consonant with the era in which the building was erected. Wolf D. Prix, one of the architects, says of his iconoclas-

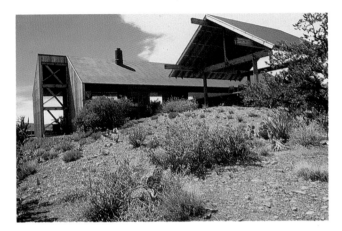

tic work that it conjures "wings" instead of columns and the "long, thin legs of architecture." Critics have called it "part praying mantis and part steel helmet"; it is nothing if not a courageous and thought-provoking compromise between sculpture and architecture. And if its exterior poses a shock to the aesthetic sense, its interior offers a chance to soar above the rooftops of Vienna—endless space, air, and light.

WOOD ARCHITECTURE

Wood is as beautiful and versatile a material for building as it is for sculpture. It is abundant and, as many advertisements have proclaimed, a renewable resource. It is relatively light in weight and is capable of being worked on the site with readily portable hand tools. Its variety of colors and grains as well as its capacity to accept paint or to weather charmingly when left in its natural state make wood a ubiquitous material. Wood, like stone, can be used as a structural element or as a facade. In many structures it is used as both.

Wood also has its drawbacks. It warps and cracks. It rots. It is also highly flammable and stirs the appetite of termites and other devouring insects. However, modern technology has enhanced the stability and strength of wood as a building material. Chemical treatments decrease wood's vulnerability to rotting from moisture.

Plywood, which is built up from sheets of wood glued together, is unlikely to warp and is frequently used as an underlayer in the exterior walls of small buildings and homes. Laminated wood beams possess great strength and are also unlikely to become distorted in shape from exposure to changing temperatures and levels of humidity.

Architect Paul Schweikher's contemporary northern Arizona home (Fig. 7–9) is a Japanese-inspired clean design of glass and wood in which sturdy but graceful fir timbers provide both a structural system and a primary source of decoration. The cedar **siding** exudes both warmth and crisp elegance. Timbers and siding are integrated into the surrounding red rock country by means of a crushed red sandstone driveway, a rock path bordered in red gravel, and a floor throughout of 4- by 8-inch **quarry tile.** There are times during the day when the light is such that the huge panels of glass seem to melt away, and the house is very much one with the butte on top of which it sits.

POST-AND-BEAM CONSTRUCTION
Schweikher's house is of **post-and-beam** construction (Fig. 7–10a), which is similar to post-and-lintel construction; vertical and horizontal timbers are cut and pieced together with wooden pegs. The beams span openings for windows, doors, and interior spaces, and they can also support posts for another story or roof trusses.

TRUSSES
Trusses are lengths of wood, iron, or steel pieced together in triangular shapes of the sort shown in Figure 7–10b in order to expand the abilities of these materials to span distances. Trusses acquire their strength from the fact that the sides of a triangle, once joined, cannot be forced out of shape. In many buildings, roof trusses are exposed and become elements of the design.

BALLOON FRAMING
Balloon framing (Fig. 7–10c), a product of the industrial revolution, dates back to the turn of the century. In balloon framing, factory-cut studs, including the famil-

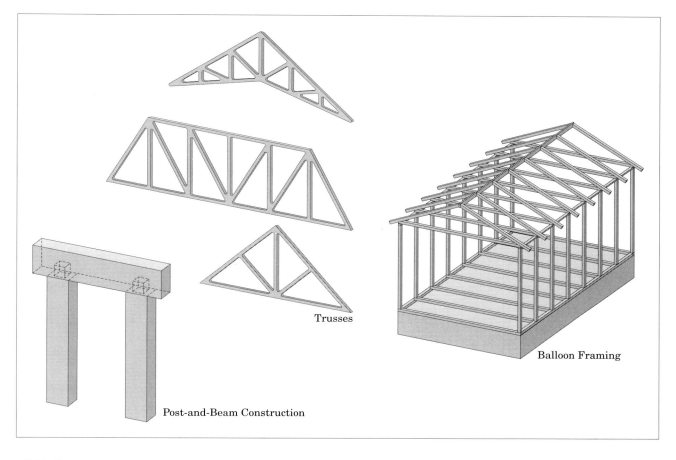

Trusses

Post-and-Beam Construction

Balloon Framing

7–10a POST-AND-BEAM CONSTRUCTION.
7–10b TRUSSES.
7–10c BALLOON FRAMING.

iar two-by-four, are mass-produced and assembled at the site by thousands of factory-produced metal nails. Several light, easily handled pieces of wood replace the heavy timber of post-and-beam construction. Entire walls are framed in place or on their sides and then raised into place by a crew of carpenters. The multiple pieces and geometric patterns of balloon framing give it a sturdiness that rivals that of the post and beam, permitting the support of slate or tile roofs, but the term *balloon* was originally a derisive term: Inveterate users of post and beam were skeptical that the frail-looking wooden pieces could provide a rugged building.

Balloon framing, of course, has now been used on millions of smaller buildings, not only homes. Sidings for balloon-framed homes have ranged from **clapboard** to asbestos shingle, brick and stone veneer, and aluminum. Roofs have ranged from asphalt or cedar shingle to tile and slate. These materials vary in cost, and each has certain aesthetic possibilities and practical advantages. Aluminum, for example, is lightweight, durable, and maintenance-free. However, when aluminum siding is shaped like clapboard and given a bogus grain, the intended trompe l'oeil effect usually fails and can create something of an aesthetic embarrassment.

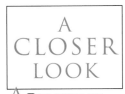

The controversy hit long before the first bulldozers. In 1983, President François Mitterrand of France used his authority to engage the Chinese-born American I. M. Pei as architect for the much-needed renovation of the Louvre; and when Pei's sleekly contemporary design emerged, it generated public outrage on both political and cultural grounds (Fig. 7–11).

Pei designed a network of underground rooms and walkways beneath the Cour Napoleon, the courtyard between the museum's two wings. The added space serves as a public entryway and reception area and houses facilities—conference rooms, storage areas, restaurants, information booths, and the like—that the museum had always lacked. Digging began in 1985; the new space opened in the fall of 1988. The focus of longstanding complaint is a mammoth pyramid—61 feet high at the apex, 108 feet wide at the base, and comprised of 105 tons of glass. It shelters the underground addition and stands in modern juxtaposition to the Palais du Louvre, whose first wing was erected by Francois I in 1527.

Mitterand, who unveiled the pyramid in an official ceremony, was attacked by those who object to a foreigner's interfering with the design of a French cultural landmark. He has been accused of defacing the nation's cultural heritage in order to leave his own personal mark. And the pyramid itself has been criticized as inappropriate, out of sync with the French spirit in general, and the Louvre's architecture in particular. Of course, in 1889, when the Eiffel Tower was erected for the Paris exposition, no one was crazy about it either. As for the pyramid, opinion polls indicate that Parisians have come around.

[1]Copyright © 1988, 1994 by The New York Times Company. Reprinted by permission.

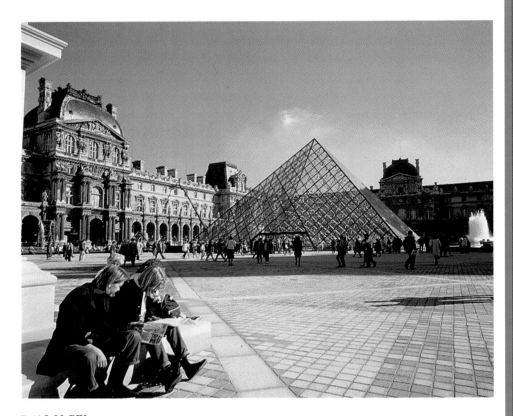

7–11 I. M. PEI
PYRAMID CONSTRUCTED AT THE LOUVRE, PARIS (1988).
COURTESY PEI COBB FREED AND PARTNERS.

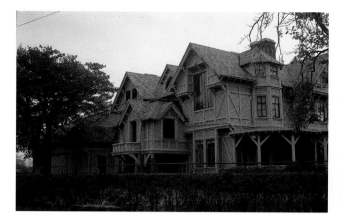

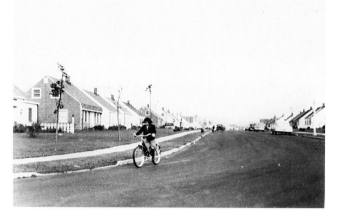

7–13 Cape Cod style houses built by Levitt & Sons, N.Y. (c. 1947–51).

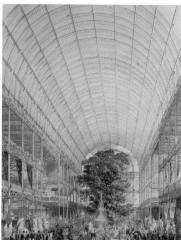

7–14 Engraving of Sir Joseph Paxton's Crystal Palace, London (1851).
Victoria and Albert Museum, London.

Two other faces of wood are observable in American architect Richard Morris Hunt's Griswold House (Fig. 7–12), built at Newport, Rhode Island, in 1862–1863 in the *Stick style,* and in the Cape Cod style home in Levittown, Long Island, a suburb of New York City (Fig. 7–13). The Griswold House shows the fanciful possibilities in wood. The Stick style sported a skeletal treatment of exteriors that remind one of an assemblage of matchsticks, open interiors, and a curious interplay of voids and solids and horizontal and vertical lines. Shapes proliferate in this short-lived movement. Turrets and gables and dormers poke the roof in every direction. Trellised porches reinforce a certain wooden laciness. One cannot imagine the Griswold House constructed in any material but wood.

The house at Levittown is more than a home; it is a socio-aesthetic comment on the need for mass suburban housing that impacted so many metropolitan regions during the marriage and baby boom that followed World War II. This house and 17,000 others almost exactly like it were built, with few exceptions, on 60- by 100-foot lots that had been carved out from potato fields. In what was to become neighborhood after neighborhood,

bulldozers smoothed already flat terrain and concrete slabs were poured. Balloon frames were erected, sided, and roofed. Trees were planted; grass was sown. The houses had an eat-in kitchen, living room, two tiny bedrooms, one bath on the first floor, and an expansion attic. Despite the tedium of the repetition, the original Levittown house achieved a sort of architectural integrity, providing living space, the pride of ownership, and an inoffensive facade for a modest price. Driving through Levittown today, it seems that every occupant thrust random additions in random directions as the family grew, despite the limitations of the lots. The trees only partly obscure the results.

CAST-IRON ARCHITECTURE

Nineteenth-century industrialization also introduced **cast iron** as a building material. It was one of a number of structural materials that would change the face of architecture. Cast iron was a welcome alternative to stone and wood. Like stone, iron has great strength, is heavy, and has a certain brittleness, yet it was the first material to allow the erection of tall buildings with relatively slender walls. Slender iron beams and bolted trusses are also capable of spanning vast interior spaces, freeing them from the forests of columns that are required in stone.

At the mid-nineteenth-century Great Exhibition held in Hyde Park, London, Sir Joseph Paxton's Crystal Palace (Fig. 7–14) covered seventeen acres. Like subsequent iron buildings, the Crystal Palace was **prefabricated.** Iron parts were cast at the factory, not the site.

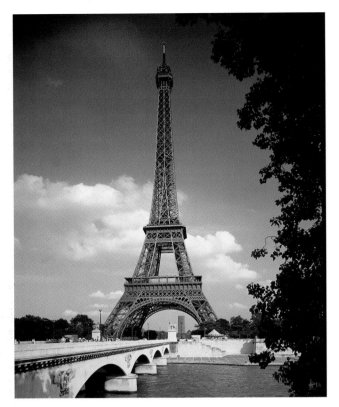

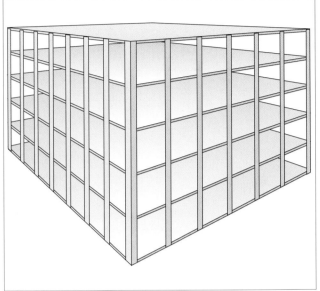

7–16 STEEL-CAGE CONSTRUCTION.

The new railroads facilitated their transportation, and it was a simple matter to bolt them together at the Exhibition. It was also a relatively simple matter to dismantle the structure and reconstruct it at another site. The iron skeleton, with its myriad arches and trusses, was an integral part of the design. The huge plate-glass-paneled walls bore no weight. Paxton asserted that "nature" had been his "engineer," explaining that he merely copied the system of longitudinal and transverse supports that one finds in a leaf. Earlier architects were also familiar with the structure of the leaf, but they did not have structural materials at hand that would permit them to build, much less conceptualize, such an expression of natural design.

The Crystal Palace was moved after the Exhibition, and until heavily damaged by fire, it served as a museum and concert hall. It was demolished in 1941 during World War II, after it was discovered that it was being used as a landmark by German pilots on bombing runs.

The Eiffel Tower (Fig. 7–15) was built in Paris in 1889 for another industrial exhibition. At the time, Gustave Eiffel was castigated by critics for building an open structure lacking the standard masonry facade. Today the Parisian symbol is so familiar that one cannot visualize it without its magnificent exposed iron trusses. The pieces of the 1,000-foot-tall tower were prefabricated, and the tower was assembled at the site in seventeen months by only 150 workers.

Structures such as these encouraged steel-cage construction and the development of the skyscraper.

STEEL-CAGE ARCHITECTURE

Steel is a strong metal of iron alloyed with small amounts of carbon and a variety of other metals. Steel is harder than iron, and more rust- and fire-resistant. It is more expensive than other structural materials, but its great strength permits it to be used in relatively small quantities. Light, narrow, prefabricated I-beams have great tensile strength. They resist bending in any direction and are riveted or welded together into skeletal forms called **steel cages** at the site (Fig. 7–16). Facades and inner walls are hung from the skeleton and frequently contribute more mass to the building than does the skeleton itself.

The Wainwright Building (Fig. 7–17), erected in 1890, is an early example of steel-cage construction. Architect Louis Sullivan, one of the fathers of modern American architecture, emphasized the verticality of the structure by running **pilasters** between the windows through the upper stories. Many skyscrapers run pilasters up their entire facades. Sullivan also empha-

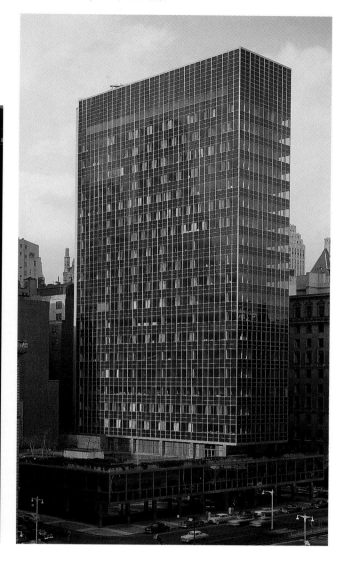

7–17 LOUIS SULLIVAN
WAINWRIGHT BUILDING, ST. LOUIS, MISSOURI (1890).

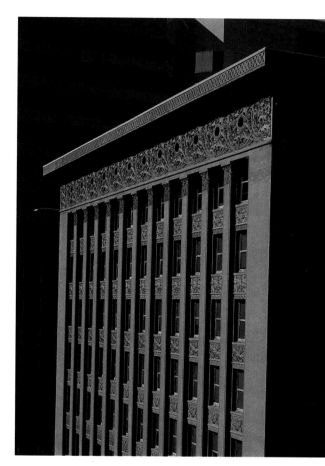

sized the horizontal features of the Wainwright Building. Ornamented horizontal bands separate most of the windows, and a severe decorated **cornice** crowns the structure. Sullivan's motto was "form follows function," and the rigid horizontal and vertical processions of the elements of the facade suggest the regularity of the rectangular spaces within. Sullivan's early "skyscraper"—in function, in structure, and in simplified form—was a precursor of the twentieth-century behemoths to follow.

One of these behemoths is New York City's Modernist Lever House (Fig. 7–18). Lever House was designed by Gordon Bunshaft of Skidmore, Owings, and Merrill, a firm that quickly became known for its "minimalist" rectangular solids with their "curtain walls" of glass. The nation was excited about the clean, austere look of Lever House, and about its donation of open plaza space to the city. The plaza prevents the shaft from

overwhelming its site. The evening light angles down across the plaza and illuminates the avenue beneath.

By the mid-1970s, the clean Modernist look of buildings such as Lever House was overwhelming the urban cityscape. A few buildings of the kind—even a few dozen buildings of the kind—would have been most welcome, but now architectural critics were arguing that a national proliferation of steel-cage rectangular solids was threatening to bury the nation's cities in boredom. Said John Perrault in 1979, "We are sick to death of cold plazas and 'curtain wall' skyscrapers."

The critics were heard. By the end of the 1970s, a new steel-cage monster was being bred throughout the land—one that utilized contemporary technology but drew freely from past styles of ornamentation. These structures, which are Postmodernist, disdain the formal simplicity and immaculate finish of Modernist structures and make a more democratic appeal to the person in the street.

7–19 BURGEE ARCHITECTS with PHILIP JOHNSON
Sony Building, N.Y. (1984). (Formerly AT&T building).

7–20 MICHAEL GRAVES
Humana Building, Louisville, Kentucky (1986).

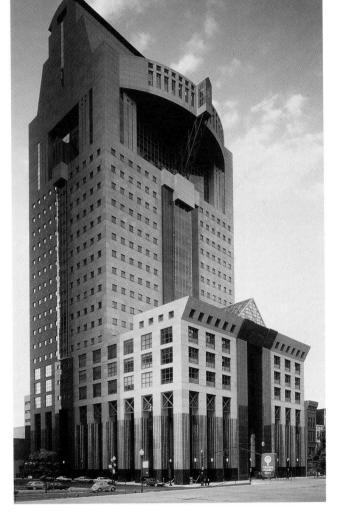

Philip Johnson designed New York's AT&T Building (Fig. 7–19), which was subsequently sold to SONY. Like many other Postmodernist structures, it is something of an architectural assemblage. Pop elements from the history of architecture are wedded to the familiar cage of steel. High atop the sweeping pink stone facade sits a Classical broken pediment, a fragment from the architectural past. How do we characterize the building: bold? brilliant? bastardized? beautiful? ugly? nonconformist? provocative? ludicrous? It is all of that. In my opinion it is also fun to look at—a feeling quite at odds with my first impression.

If the AT&T (SONY) Building is a steel-cage structure with a Chippendale hat, Michael Graves's steel-cage Humana Building (Fig. 7–20) is reminiscent of a Sphinx or of an Egyptian pharaoh seated on a throne. A high vaulted glass entryway dissolves the heavy "legs" which, left and right, look something like a pair of unwilling Wainwright Buildings. The alternation of expanses of glass with small windows punched through stone suggests that the overriding rule is that rules are made to be broken.

A more surprising, and unusual, example of steel-cage architecture is found in Mies van der Rohe's Farnsworth House (Fig. 7–21). The rhythmic procession of white steel columns suspend it above the Illinois countryside. In its perfect technological elegance, it is in many ways visually remote from its site. Why steel?

7–21 MIES VAN DER ROHE
FARNSWORTH HOUSE, FOX RIVER, PLANO, ILLINOIS (1950).

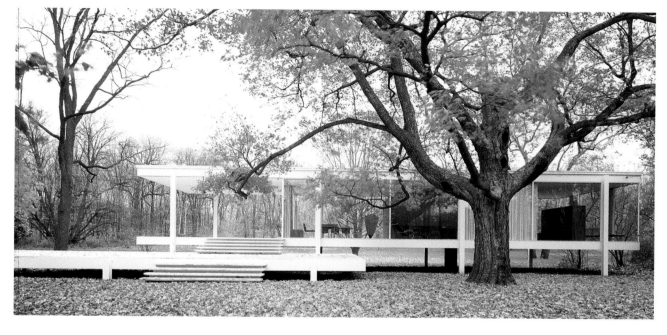

Less expensive wood could have supported this house of one story and short spans, and wood might have appeared more natural on this sylvan site. The architect's choices, of course, may be read as a symbol of our contemporary remoteness from our feral past. If so, the architect seems to believe that the powerful technology that has freed us is to the good, for the house is as beautiful as it is austere in ornamentation. The Farnsworth House has platforms, steps, and a glass curtain wall that allows the environment to flow through. The steps and platforms provide access to a less well-ordered world below.

REINFORCED CONCRETE ARCHITECTURE

Although cement was first produced in the early 1800s, the use of **reinforced concrete** is said to have begun with a French gardener, Jacques Monier, who proposed strengthening concrete flower pots with a wire mesh in the 1860s. In reinforced or **ferroconcrete,** steel rods and/or steel mesh are inserted at the points of greatest stress into concrete slabs before they harden. In the resultant slab, stresses are shared by the materials.

Ferroconcrete has many of the advantages of stone and steel, without some of the disadvantages. The steel rods increase the tensile strength of concrete, making it less susceptible to tearing or pulling apart at stress points. The concrete, in turn, prevents the steel from rusting. Reinforced concrete can span greater distances than stone, and it supports more weight than steel. Perhaps the most dramatic advantage of reinforced concrete is its capacity to take on natural curved shapes that would be unthinkable in steel or concrete alone. Curved slabs take on the forms of eggshells, bubbles, seashells, and other organic shapes that are naturally engineered for the even spreading of stress throughout their surfaces, and are, hence, enduring.

Reinforced concrete, more than other materials, has freed the architect to think freely and sculpturally. There are limits to what ferroconcrete can do, however; initial spatial concepts are frequently somewhat refined by computer-aided calculations of marginally more efficient shapes for distributing stress. Still, it would not be far from the mark to say that buildings of almost any shape and reasonable size are possible today, if one is willing to pay for them. The architects of ferroconcrete have achieved a number of buildings that would have astounded the ancient stone builders—and perhaps Joseph Paxton.

7–22 LE CORBUSIER
CHAPEL OF NOTRE-DAME-DU-HAUT, RONCHAMP, FRANCE
(1950–54).
© 1998 ARTISTS RIGHTS SOCIETY (ARS), N.Y./ADAGP, PARIS, FLC.

7–24 EERO SAARINEN
TWA TERMINAL, JOHN F. KENNEDY INTERNATIONAL AIRPORT,
N.Y. (1962).

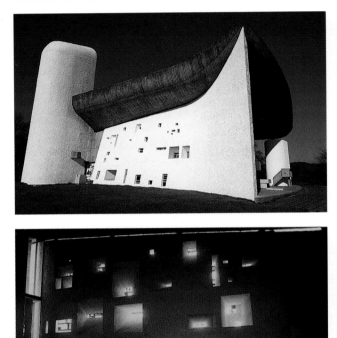

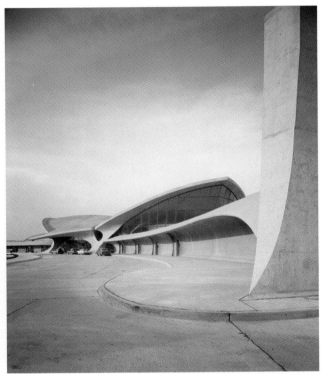

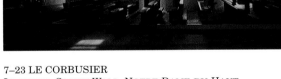

7–23 LE CORBUSIER
INTERIOR, SOUTH WALL, NOTRE-DAME-DU-HAUT.
© 1998 ARTISTS RIGHTS SOCIETY (ARS), N.Y./ADAGP, PARIS/FLC.

Le Corbusier's chapel of Notre-Dame-du-Haut
(Figs. 7–22 and 7–23) is an example of what has been
referred to as the "new brutalism," deriving from the
French *brut,* meaning rough, uncut, or raw. The steel
web is spun and the concrete is cast in place, leaving
the marks of the wooden forms on its surface. The white
walls, dark roof, and white towers are "decorated" only
by the texture of the curving reinforced concrete slabs.
In places the walls are incredibly thick. Windows of various shapes and sizes expand from small slits and rectangles to form mysterious light tunnels; they not so
much light the interior as draw the observer outward.
The massive voids of the window apertures recall the
huge stone blocks of prehistoric religious structures.

Eero Saarinen's TWA Terminal (Figs. 7–24 and
7–25) at Kennedy Airport in New York is a more dramatic example of the capacity of reinforced concrete to
span distances with curving organic forms. Saarinen
sought a unique design that would symbolize flight and
achieve an identity among the boring boxy designs of
the other terminals. He succeeded. The wing-shaped
ferroconcrete roof structure seems to belong to some fos-
silized prehistoric bird trapped in midflight. Free-form
arches and vaults span biomorphic interior spaces, so
that the sensitive traveler seems to be passing through
the maw of the beast—a part of some ancient ritual that
commemorates the passage from ground to air.

Frank Lloyd Wright's Kaufmann House (Fig. 7–26),
which has also become known as "Fallingwater," shows
a very different application of reinforced concrete. Here
cantilevered decks of reinforced concrete rush outward
into the surrounding landscape from the building's central core, intersecting in strata that lie parallel to the
natural rock formations. Wright's naturalistic style integrates his building with its site. In the Kaufmann
House, reinforced concrete and stone walls complement
the sturdy rock of the Pennsylvania countryside.

7–25 EERO SAARINEN
INTERIOR OF TWA TERMINAL, JOHN F. KENNEDY
INTERNATIONAL AIRPORT, N.Y. (1962).

7–26 FRANK LLOYD WRIGHT
KAUFMANN HOUSE, BEAR RUN, PA. (1936).

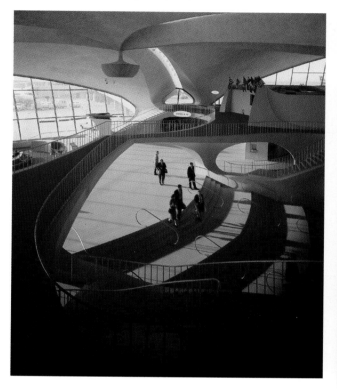

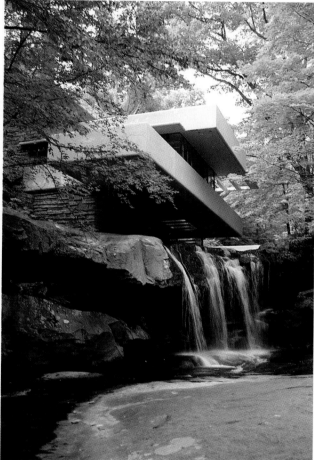

For Wright, modern materials did not warrant austerity; geometry did not preclude organic integration with the site. A small waterfall seems mysteriously to originate beneath the broad white planes of a deck. The irregularity of the structural components—concrete, cut stone, natural stone, and machine-planed surfaces—complements the irregularity of the wooded site. The Kaufmann House, naturalistic, might have always been there. It is right. The Farnsworth House, while not "wrong," is a technological surprise on its landscape.

Israeli architect Moshe Safdie's *Habitat* (Fig. 7–27) is another expression of the versatility of concrete. Habitat was erected for EXPO 67 in Montreal as one solution to the housing problems of the future. Rugged, prefabricated units were stacked like blocks about a common utility core at the site, so that the roof of one unit would provide a private deck for another. Only a couple of Safdie-style "apartment houses" have been erected since, one in Israel and one in Puerto Rico, so today Safdie's beautiful sculptural assemblage evokes more nostalgia than hope for the future. Its unique brand of rugged, blocky excitement is rarely found in mass housing, and this is our loss.

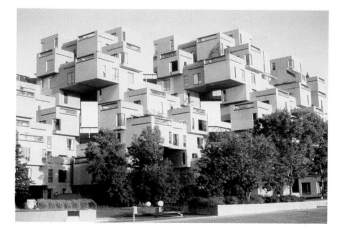

7–27 MOSHE SAFDIE
HABITAT, EXPO 67, MONTREAL (1967).

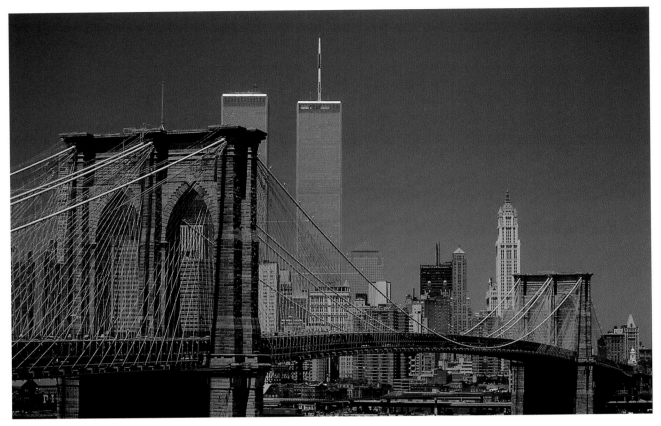

OTHER ARCHITECTURAL METHODS

STEEL-CABLE ARCHITECTURE

The notion of suspending bridges from cables is not new. Wood-and-rope suspension bridges have been built in Asia for thousands of years. Iron suspension bridges such as the Menai Straits Bridge in Wales and the Clifton Bridge near Bristol, England, were erected during the early part of the nineteenth century. But in the Brooklyn Bridge (Fig. 7–28), completed in 1883, John Roebling exploited the great tensile strength of steel to span New York's East River with **steel cable.** In such a cable, many parallel wires share the stress. Steel cable is also flexible, allowing the roadway beneath to sway, within limits, in response to changing weather and traffic conditions.

Roebling used massive vaulted piers of stone masonry to support parabolic webs of steel, which are rendered lacy by the juxtaposition. In many more recent suspension bridges, steel cable spans more than a mile, and in bridges like the Golden Gate, the George Washington, and the Verrazano Narrows, the effect is aesthetically stirring.

Steel cable has also been used to span great spaces and support the roof structures in buildings such as Eero Saarinen's Terminal for the Dulles Airport in Washington, D.C., Pier Luigi Nervi's paper mill at Mantua, Italy, and numerous exhibition halls that have had the appearance of circus tents. In Nervi's mill (Fig. 7–29), biomorphic **pylons** strut above and support the roof of an otherwise purposefully dull rectangular enclosure, freeing the interior from columns.

SHELL ARCHITECTURE

Modern materials and methods of engineering have made it possible to enclose spaces with relatively inexpensive shell structures. Masonry domes have been replaced by lightweight shells that are frequently flatter and certainly capable of spanning greater spaces. Shells have been constructed from reinforced concrete, wood, steel, aluminum, and even plastics and paper. The concept of shell architecture is as old as the canvas tent and as new as the Geodesic dome (Fig. 7–6) designed by Buckminster Fuller for the American Pavilion at EXPO 67 in Montreal. In a number of sports arenas, fabric roofs are held up by keeping the air pressure inside the building slightly greater than that outside. Like balloons, these roof structures are literally inflated.

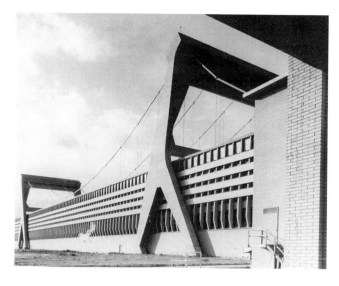

7–30 GENESIS I
FIBERGLASS DOMES TO HOUSE THE HOMELESS, LOS ANGELES.

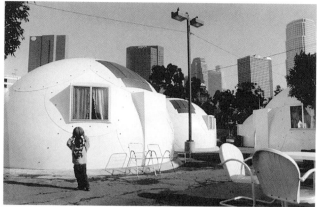

Fuller's shell is an assemblage of lightweight metal trusses into a three-quarter sphere that is 250 feet in diameter. Looking more closely, one sees that the trusses compose six-sided units that give the organic impression of a honeycomb. Light floods the climate-controlled enclosure, creating an environment for any variety of human activity—and any form of additional construction—within. Such domes can be covered with many sorts of weatherproofing, from lightweight metals and fabric to translucent and transparent plastics and glass. Here the engineering requirements clearly create the architectural design.

The dome design not only suggests a vastness of space or the heavens, as it does in Islamic architecture. It can also on a smaller scale suggest closeness, protectiveness, and a kind of reverting to the primordial hearth, as in neolithic dwellings. And so perhaps the design of fiberglass dwellings for the homeless (Fig. 7–30) is appropriate for it conjures up links to shelters of the past. These structures were erected along the Los Angeles Harbor Freeway to help homeless people turn their lives around by providing temporary stability. Yet they also appear to be the stuff of science fiction—so many lunar outposts.

CONTEMPORARY MUSEUMS: FUNCTIONS AND FORMS

Some of the more fascinating expressions of contemporary architecture are found in our museums. Museums are rather special works. Not only do they house many of our most important artworks, but they also frequently occupy prominent sites in major cities. And so their architects, cognizant of their functions and sites, see them as special design challenges and opportunities.

It is of interest that museums as we know them have existed for only about two centuries. Prior to that time works of art and other valuables were collected into treasure chambers, essentially for purposes of hoarding. Treasure chambers belonged to the ruling families of Europe, such as the Medicis, the Hapsburgs, and a few others, and were open only to a select few. But as the numbers of the educated expanded, and as a revolutionary democratic spirit swept much of Europe and the American colonies in the latter part of the eighteenth century, museums were constructed that could accommodate the general public.

Museums today serve several functions. They still "hoard" valuables, in the sense of collecting them and preserving them, but they also show their treasures to the general public, who visit in large numbers. Thus, they have large exhibition areas throughout which people must be able to circulate in comfort and relative freedom. Other public areas of the museum may include study rooms or a library, and meeting rooms or an auditorium. Most museums have shops or bookstores, and large museums also have dining facilities. In nonpublic areas of the museum, the director plans budgets and the acquisitioning and deacquisitioning of works of art. Curators catalog collections and plan exhibitions. Conservators preserve and restore older or damaged works. Educators, office workers, guards, and others carry out other functions.

7–31 FRANK LLOYD WRIGHT
THE SOLOMON R. GUGGENHEIM MUSEUM, N.Y. (1957–59).

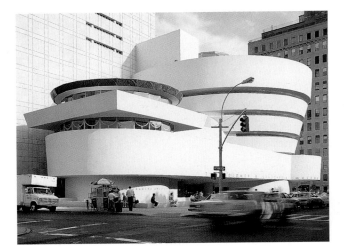

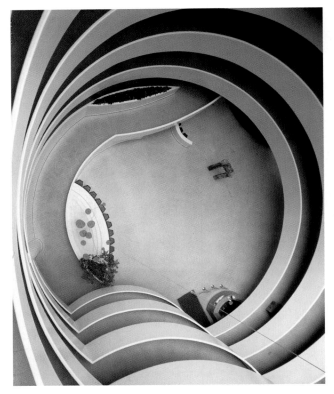

7–32 FRANK LLOYD WRIGHT
INTERIOR VIEW OF THE GUGGENHEIM MUSEUM.
DAVID HEALD. THE SOLOMON R. GUGGENHEIM FOUNDATION, N.Y.

7–33 KEVIN ROCHE, JOHN DINKERLOO, AND ASSOCIATES.
THE OAKLAND MUSEUM, OAKLAND, CALIFORNIA (1961).

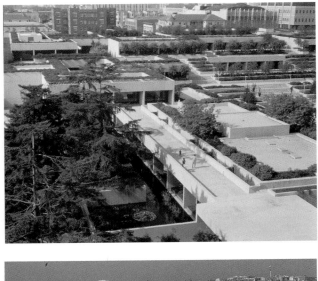

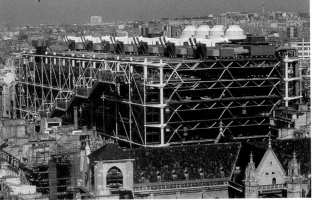

7–34 RICHARD ROGERS AND RENZO PIANO
GEORGES POMPIDOU NATIONAL CENTER OF ART AND CULTURE, PARIS (1971–78).

Frank Lloyd Wright's Solomon R. Guggenheim Museum (Figs. 7–31 and 7–32), which may be changing its name to honor a new contributor, sits across Fifth Avenue from Central Park, about ten blocks uptown from the Metropolitan Museum of Art. Its main exhibition hall is devoted to transient shows. Visitors are brought to the top of the **rotunda** by elevator and then walk down a continuous spiral gallery. Works of art are placed against the outside wall of the gallery. Visitors can peer out across the rotunda from any level, up at the glass dome, or down at exhibits that are out in the center court. The permanent collection and office and service areas are housed in rooms adjacent to the rotunda. From the outside, space flows across Fifth Avenue from the park and freely around the sculptured forms of the museum. The park is mirrored in entry-level expanses of plate glass and hanging plants within. From the interior, the openness of the rotunda and the detailing of the glass dome are stunning. If they have a fault, it is that they vie for attention with the works they exhibit.

Given the exhibition space of the Oakland Museum (Fig. 7–33), designed by Kevin Roche and John Dinkerloo,

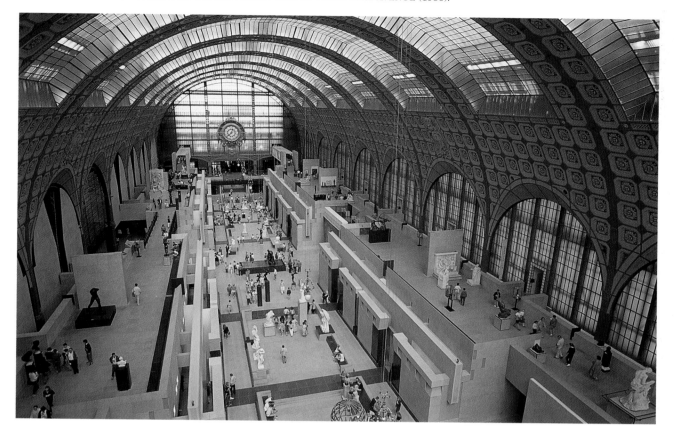

it could have been a monumental feature of the urban
landscape. Instead, the architects decided to provide
Oakland with an unexpected, terraced garden. The
roofs of one level serve as green terraces for the next.
Rather than another huge building, Oakland possesses
formal clusters of greened environments. The overall effect is one of a hilly park, which is perfectly integrated
with California's geology.

In Paris, the Georges Pompidou National Center
of Art and Culture (Fig. 7–34), designed by Richard
Rogers and Renzo Piano, is very different from the
Greek-inspired Classicism of a more familiar Parisian
jewel—the Louvre. Given its trussed steel-cage structure, it could have been just another Minimalist cube,
but the architects decided to form it much like an
animal wearing its organs outside rather than under
the skin. Service ducts, a huge escalator, and stacks
that remind one of an ocean liner serve as the building's
external ornamentation. Contemporary service
systems provide the subjects for a Pop reworking of a
Modernist theme. As if their presence were not clear
enough, the systems are boldly painted in primary
colors and white. It could, of course, be remarked that
by placing these services outside the skin, the
architects further freed interior spaces for unobstructed
circulation and visual continuity. Perhaps. But the

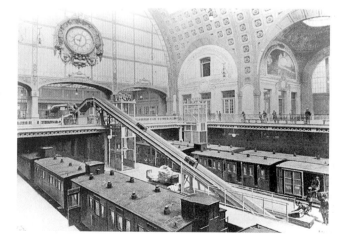

7–36 HAGENBECK L'ILUSTRATION, GARE D'ORSAY, FORMER
RAILROAD STATION, PARIS.

Pompidou Center is also a humorous assemblage, in the
best sense of the word.

The Musée d'Orsay (Figs. 7–35 and 7–36) is another
Parisian innovation. Prior to its opening in 1986, it had
been the old Gare d'Orsay, the grandest railway station
in the city. Italian architect Gae Aulenti was given the
task of resurrecting a live museum from the dead station.
In its new incarnation, the familiar floriated clock still
tells time and punctuates the imposing barrel vault

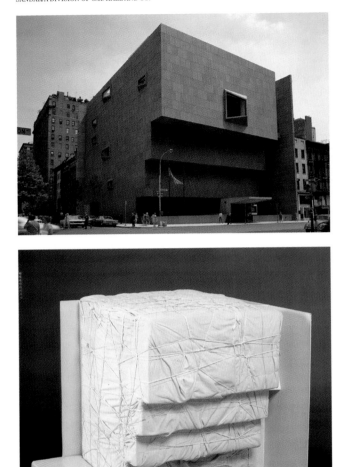

that rises a hundred feet from the floor and stretches 150 yards from end to end. Natural light still filters through this secular cathedral with its elliptical side vaults that, like the rose window of Notre Dame, look upon the Seine. Where steam locomotives once lumbered through, there is now a "sculpture avenue." Manets, Courbets, Rodins, and other works from the second half of the nineteenth century and the first decade of the twentieth populate byways where passengers once rushed. The Musée d'Orsay does many, many things. It preserves the architectural past while preserving the paintings and sculptures of the previous century. It also displays—both itself and its contents. If there is a fault, it is the same fault as that of the Guggenheim: the building competes for attention with the objects it houses. In the context of the achievement of the Musée d'Orsay, art critic Robert Hughes wrote: "A hundred years ago you had brilliant painters and dumb museums; today the reverse." Let us accept Hughes's enthusiasm for the museum but leave judgment of contemporary painters to future generations.

Marcel Breuer's Whitney Museum of American Art (Fig. 7–37) is a top-heavy work in reinforced concrete. The massiveness of the upper floors seems a cocky human thrust against the inevitability of gravity as well as a matter-of-fact statement of contemporary engineering. The few windows emphasize the fact that it is the exhibits of the inner space, rather than of the outer space, that are to be the focus of attention. The windows are similar to the light tunnels of Le Corbusier's Notre-Dame-du-Haut (Figs. 7–22 and 7–23) and seem to serve a similar purpose as focal points for meditation.

It seems appropriate to wrap up this chapter with the wrapping of the Whitney by Christo and Jeanne-Claude. (Fig. 7–38). The public and critics alike have burned several years' worth of the world supply of midnight oil in attempting to decipher the artists' cryptic messages. An acquaintance once insisted that by wrapping such massive elements of landscape and cityscape, the artists were fulfilling an unconscious urge to demonstrate that they could control them—which shows, perhaps, that we project our own needs into the intrigues of others very well.

Where do we go from here? The rest is wrapped— or rapt.

key terms

Architecture
Facade
Service systems
Kiva
Adobe
Post-and-lintel
  construction
Dry masonry
Arch
Aqueduct
Brick
Voussoir
Centering

Keystone
Compressive strength
Tier
Vault
Barrel vault
Groin vault
Buttress
Bay
Rib
Webbing
Flying buttress
Clerestory
Fenestration

Dome
Pendentives
Pier
Veneer
Plywood
Siding
Quarry tile
Post-and-beam
  construction
Truss
Balloon framing
Clapboard
Cast iron

Prefabricate
Steel
Steel cage
Pilaster
Cornice
Reinforced concrete
Ferroconcrete
Steel cable
Pylon
Rotunda

artists

Eero Saarinen
Buckminster Fuller
Wolf D. Prix
Helmut Swiczinsky
Paul Schweikher
Richard M. Hunt
I. M. Pei
Sir Joseph Paxton
Gustave Eiffel

Louis Sullivan
Gordon Bunshaft
Burgee Architects
Philip Johnson
Michael Graves
Mies van der Rohe
Le Corbusier
Frank Lloyd Wright
Moshe Safdie

John A. Roebling
Pier Luigi Nervi
Kevin Roche
John Dinkerloo
Richard Rogers
Renzo Piano
Gae Aulenti
Marcel Breuer
Christo and Jeanne-Claude

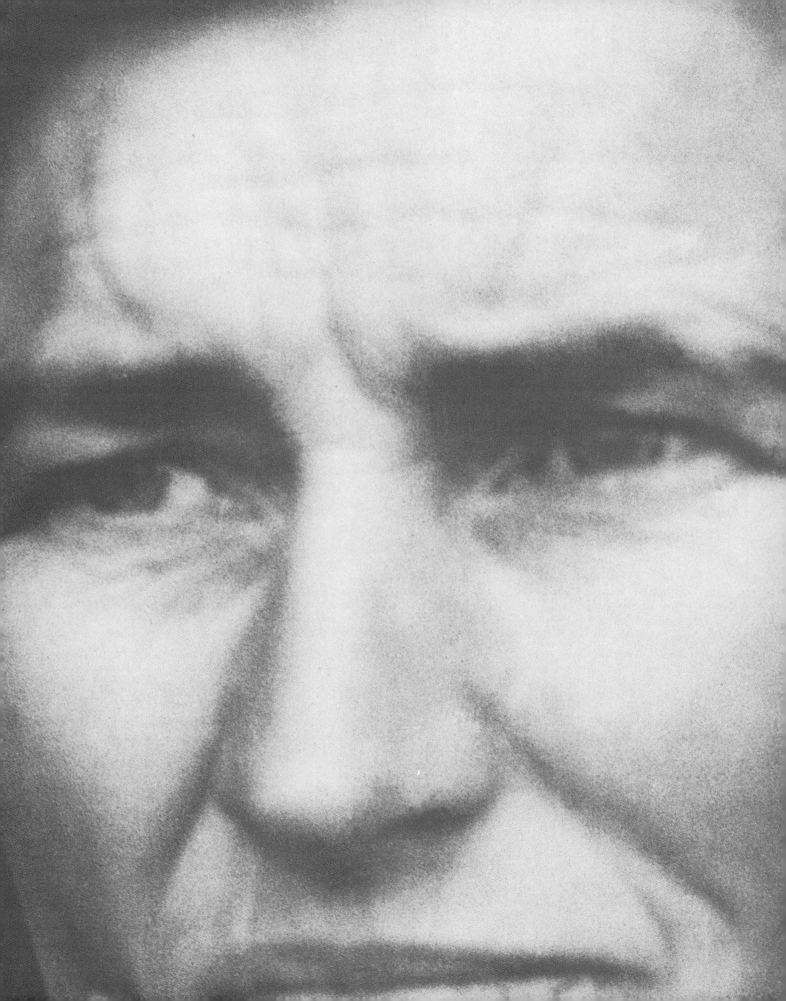

chapter

CAMERA ARTS

PRELIMINARY *Sketch*

- The basic principles of photography have been known for over 400 years.

- The first photographic plate had to be exposed to light for eight hours in order to register an image.

- It can be difficult or impossible to distinguish between images or real events and computer-generated images.

- The photographer Alfred Stieglitz was also the proprietor of a New York art gallery that featured abstract painters.

- Photographers of the U.S. Civil War carried their equipment in horse-drawn wagons referred to by the soldiers as "Whatsits."

- The motion picture camera and projector were perfected by the inventor of the light bulb.

Dorothea Lange, *Migrant Mother* (detail). See Figure 8–14.

Photography has or will eventually negate much of painting—for which the painter should be deeply grateful; relieving him, as it were, from certain public demands (such as) representation, objective seeing.

—Edward Weston

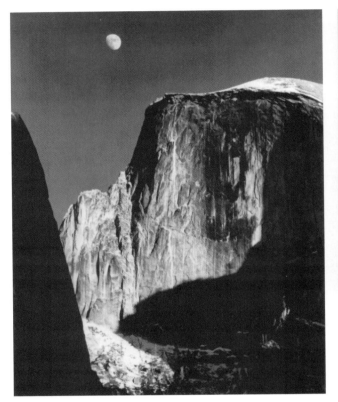

8–1 ANSEL ADAMS
MOON AND HALF DOME, YOSEMITE NATIONAL PARK, CALIFORNIA (1960).
© THE ANSEL ADAMS PUBLISHING RIGHTS TRUST.

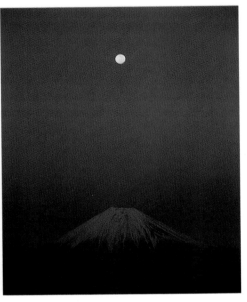

8–2 SHIRO SHIRAHATA
MOON OVER FUJI (1972).

Technology has revolutionized the visual arts. For thousands of years one of the central goals of art has been to imitate nature as exactly as possible. Today, any one of us can point a camera at a person or an object and capture a realistic image. Many cameras no longer even require that we place the subject in proper focus, or that we regulate the amount of light so as not to overexpose or underexpose the subject. Technology can do all these things for us.

Similarly, the art of the stage was once unavailable to all but those who lived in the great urban centers. Now and then a traveling troupe of actors might come by, or local groups might put on a show of sorts, but most people had little or no idea of the ways in which drama, opera, the dance, and other performing arts could affect their lives. The advent of motion pictures or **cinematography** suddenly brought a flood of new

imagery into local theaters, and a new form of communal activity was born. People from every station of life could flock to the movie theater on the weekend. Over time, cinematography evolved into an art form independent of its beginnings as a mirror of the stage.

More recently, video has brought this imagery into the home, where people can watch everything from the performing arts to sporting events in privacy and from the vantage points of several cameras. Technology has also given rise to the computer as a creative video-mediated tool. With the aid of artificial intelligence, we can instantly view models of objects from all sides. We can be led to feel as though we are sweeping in on our solar system from the black reaches of space, then flying down to the surface of our planet and landing where the programmer would set us down. Millions of children spend hours playing video games like *Tetris* that challenge them to rotate plummeting polygons to construct a solid wall, or games like *Mario Bros.* that require them to evade or blast a host of enemies before their computer-drawn heroes and heroines are sent into an abyss. Artists create computer-generated images purely for their own sake. Computer graphics is a medium full of potential. From illustrations of blue jeans

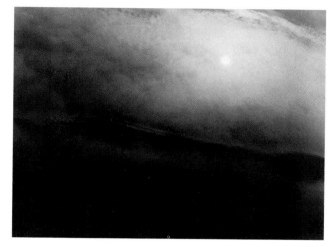

that rocket through space, to snappy graphics that entitle sporting events, to computer art for art's sake, the products of this technology punctuate our daily lives. CD-ROMs, "multimedia"-equipped computers, and "morphing" software that can blend one shape or face into another are bringing a "virtual reality" into our lives that is in some ways more alluring than (forgive me) "real reality."

In this chapter we discuss photography, cinematography, and video. Many years ago it might have been daring to assert that these media were forms of art, but today most critics will agree that these media have given rise to unique possibilities for artistic expression.

PHOTOGRAPHY

Photography is a science and an art. The word *photography* is derived from Greek roots meaning "to write with light." The scientific aspects of photography concern the ways in which images of objects are made on a **photosensitive** surface, like film, by light that passes through a **lens.** Chemical changes occur in the film so that the images are recorded. This much—the creation of an objective image of the light that has passed through the lens—is mechanical.

It would be grossly inaccurate, however, to think of the *art* of photography as mechanical. Photographers make artistic choices, from the most mundane to the most sophisticated. They decide which films and lenses to use, which photographs they will retain or discard. They manipulate lighting conditions or printing processes to achieve dazzling or dreamy effects. Always, but always, they are in search of subjects—ordinary, extraordinary, universal, personal.

Photography is truly an art of the hand, head, and heart. The photographer must understand films and grasp skills related to using the camera and, in most cases, to developing **prints.** The photographer must also have the intellect and the passion to search for and to see what is important in things—what is beautiful, harmonious, universal, and worth recording.

Photography is a matter of selection and interpretation. Similar subjects seen through the eyes of different photographers will yield wildly different results. In

Ansel Adams's *Moon and Half Dome, Yosemite National Park* (Fig. 8–1), majestic cliffs leap into a deep, cold sky. From our earthbound vantage point, the perfect order of the desolate, spherical moon contrasts with the coarseness of the living rock. Yet we know that its geometric polish is an illusion wrought by distance—the moon's surface is just as rough and chaotic. Adams's composition is as much about shape and texture as it is a photograph of a feature of the California landscape. Distance and scale come sharply into focus: This is a story of man dwarfed by nature and nature dwarfed by the stars.

In *Moon Over Fuji* (Fig. 8–2), photographer Shiro Shirahata renders Japan's extinct volcano with the etherealness and serenity of a Japanese scroll painting. The blackened peak recedes, deathlike, into the slate blue surroundings, while the most piercing of moons hovers above, seemingly full of life. The vast space that separates the upper and lower portions of the narrow photograph is pregnant with suggestions of the relationships between the heavens and the earth.

Alfred Stieglitz, the American photographer who photographed *The Steerage* (Fig. 1–25), was also the proprietor of a successful New York gallery featuring budding abstract painters. His experiments with abstraction in photography and his belief that the medium should serve as an outlet for the emotional inner life of the artist led to pioneer works such as *Equivalent* (Fig. 8–3). One of many cloud studies, the work is at once romantic and evocative of unseen forces; simultaneously figurative and abstract.

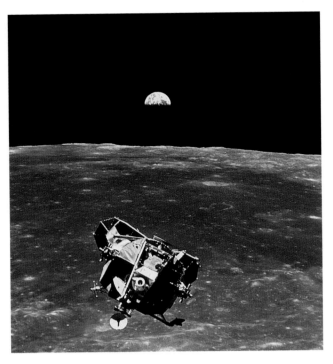

8–5 THE CAMERA AND THE HUMAN EYE COMPARED.

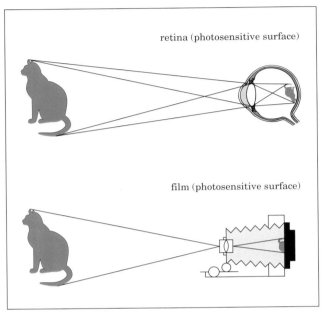

In the 1930's, when Stieglitz's photograph was taken, the stuff of which *Earthrise* (Fig. 8–4) is made would have been only fantasy. In this NASA photograph, taken during the first landing on the moon, the sharp lights and darks of the lunar landing module are silhouetted against the grays of the softly textured moon and balanced by the high-contrast values of black space and the arc of Earth above. The distance of the home planet lends it an abstract, geometric appearance. Out here, in space, the heavy landing module is very much closer and, despite its mechanical grotesqueness, it looks, frankly, much more like home.

Thus the mood, stylistic inclinations, cultural biases, and technical preferences of the artist-photographer influence the nature of the creative product. As observers, we are as enriched by the diversity of this medium as by any other of the visual arts media.

Let us now consider two of the technical aspects of photography: cameras and films. Then we chronicle the history of photography.

CAMERAS

Cameras may look very different from each other and boast a variety of equipment, but they all possess certain basic features. As you can see in Figure 8–5, the camera is similar to the human eye. In both cases, light enters a narrow opening and is projected onto a photosensitive surface.

The amount of light that enters the eye is determined by the size of the *pupil,* which is an opening in the muscle called the *iris;* the size of the pupil responds automatically to the amount of light that strikes the eye. The amount of light that enters a camera is determined by the size of the opening, or **aperture,** in the **shutter.** The aperture opening can be adjusted manually or, in advanced cameras, automatically. The size of the aperture, or opening, is the so-called **stop.** The smaller the F-stop, the larger the opening. The shutter can also be made to remain open to light for various amounts of time, ranging from a few thousandths of a second—in which case **candid** shots of fast action may be taken—to a second or more.

When the light enters the eye, the *lens* keeps it in focus by responding automatically to its distance from the object. The light is then projected onto the retina, which consists of cells that are sensitive to light and dark and to color. Nerves transmit visual sensations of objects from the retina to the brain.

In the same way, the camera lens focuses light onto **film,** which is photosensitive, like the retina. A camera lens can be focused manually or automatically. Many photographers purposely take pictures that are out of focus, for their soft, blurred effects. **Telephoto** lenses magnify faraway objects and tend to collapse the spaces between distant objects that recede from us. **Wide-angle** lenses allow a broad view of objects within a confined area.

8–6 THE CAMERA OBSCURA.

INTERNATIONAL MUSEUM OF PHOTOGRAPHY. COURTESY OF THE GEORGE EASTMAN HOUSE, ROCHESTER, N.Y.

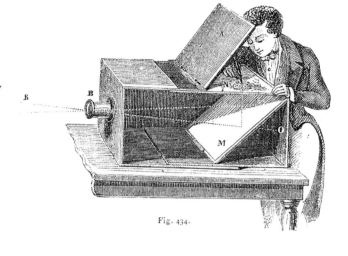

Fig. 434.

In their early days, cameras tended to be large and were placed on mounts. Today's cameras are usually small and held by hand. *The Steerage* was shot with an early hand-held camera. Many contemporary cameras contain angled mirrors that allow the photographer to see directly through the lens and thereby to be precisely aware of the image that is being projected onto the film.

FILMS

Contemporary black-and-white films are very thin, yet they contain several layers, most of which form a protective coat and backing for the photosensitive layer. The "active" layer contains an **emulsion** of small particles of a photosensitive silver salt (usually silver halide) that are suspended in gelatin.

After the film is exposed to light and treated chemically, it becomes a **negative,** in which metallic silver is formed from the crystals of silver halide. In this negative, areas of dark and light are reversed. Since the negatives are transparent, light passes through them to a print surface which becomes the final photograph, or print. Here the areas of light and dark are reversed again, now matching the shading of the original subject. Prints are also usually made significantly larger than the negative.

Black-and-white films differ in color sensitivity (the ability to show colors like red and green as different shades), in contrast (the tendency to show gradations of gray as well as black and white), in graininess (the textural quality, as reflective of the size of the silver halide crystals), and in speed (the amount of exposure time necessary to record an image). Photographers select films that will heighten the effects they seek to portray.

Color film is more complex than black-and-white film, but similar in principle. Color film also contains several layers, some of which are protective and provide backing. There are two basic kinds of color film: **color reversal film** and **color negative film.** Both types of color film contain three light-sensitive layers.

Prints are made directly from *color reversal film.* Therefore, each of the photosensitive layers corresponds to one of the *primary colors* in additive color mixtures: blue, green, or red. When color reversal film is exposed to light and treated chemically, mixtures of the primary colors emerge, yielding a full-color image of the photographic subject.

Negatives are made from *color negative film.* Therefore, each photosensitive layer corresponds to the *complement* of the primary color it represents. (See Chapter 2 for an explanation of additive color mixtures and primary and complementary colors.)

Color films, like black-and-white films, differ in color sensitivity, contrast, graininess, and speed. But color films also differ in their appropriateness for natural (daylight) or artificial (indoor) lighting conditions.

A HISTORY OF PHOTOGRAPHY

The cameras and films just described are rather recent inventions. Photography has a long and fascinating history. Although true photography does not appear much before the mid-nineteenth century, some of its principles can be traced back another three hundred years, to the *camera obscura.*

THE CAMERA OBSCURA   The **camera obscura**—literally, the covered-over or darkened room—was used by Renaissance artists to help them accurately portray depth, or perspective, on two-dimensional surfaces. The camera obscura can be a box, as shown in Figure 8–6, or an actual room with a small hole that admits light through one wall. The beam of light projects the outside scene upside down on a surface within the box. The artist then simply traces the scene, as shown, to achieve a proper perspective—to truly imitate nature.

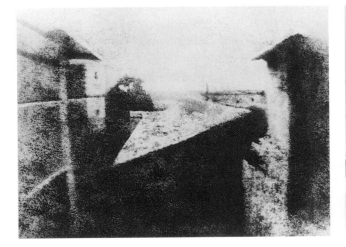

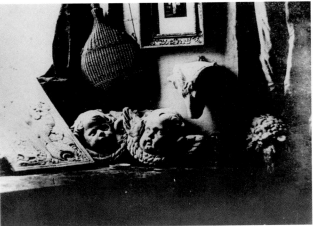

DEVELOPMENT OF PHOTOSENSITIVE SURFACES   The camera obscura could only temporarily focus an image on a surface while a person labored to copy it by tracing. The next developments in photography concerned the search for photosensitive surfaces that could permanently affix images. These developments came by bits and pieces.

In 1727 the German physicist Heinrich Schulze discovered that silver salts had light-sensitive qualities, but he never tried to record natural images. In 1802 Thomas Wedgwood, son of the well-known English potter, reported his discovery that paper soaked in silver nitrate did take on projected images as a chemical reaction to light. Unfortunately, the images were not permanent.

HELIOGRAPHY   In 1826 the Frenchman Joseph-Nicéphore Niepce invented **heliography. Bitumen,** or asphalt residue, was placed on a pewter plate to create a photosensitive surface. The bitumen was soluble in **lavender oil** if kept in the dark, but insoluble if struck by light. Niepce used a device based on the concept of the camera obscura to expose the plate to the view from his window for eight hours, and then he washed the plate in lavender oil. The pewter showed through where there had been little or no light, creating the image of the darker areas of the scene. The bitumen remained where the light had struck, however, leaving lighter values. The resultant heliograph (Fig. 8–7) was quite blurred, but it was an unmistakable image of Niepce's view.

THE DAGUERREOTYPE   The **daguerreotype** resulted from a partnership formed in 1829 between Niepce and another Frenchman, Louis-Jacques-Mandé Daguerre. The daguerreotype used a thin sheet of silver-plated copper. The plate was chemically treated, placed in a camera obscura, and exposed to a narrow beam of light. After exposure, the plate was treated chemically again.

Figure 8–8 shows the first successful daguerreotype, taken in 1837. Remarkably clear images could be recorded by this process. In this work, called *The Artist's Studio,* Daguerre, a landscape painter, sensitively assembled deeply textured objects and sculptures. The contrasting light and dark values help create an illusion of depth.

There were drawbacks to the daguerreotype. It had to be exposed for from five to forty minutes, requiring long sittings (Fig. 8–9). The recorded image was reversed, left to right, and was so delicate that it had to be sealed behind glass to remain fixed. Also, the plate that was exposed to light became the actual daguerreotype. There was no negative, and consequently, copies could not be made. However, some refinements of the process did come rapidly. Within ten years the exposure time had been reduced to about thirty to sixty seconds, and the process had become so inexpensive that families could purchase two portraits for a quarter. Daguerreotype studios opened all across Europe and the United States, and families began to collect the rigid, stylized pictures that now seem to reflect days gone by.

8–9 HONORÉ DAUMIER
PHOTOGRAPHIE. NOUVEAU PROCÉDÉ (1856). LITHOGRAPH.

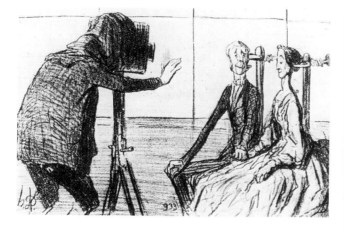

8–10 WILLIAM HENRY FOX TALBOT
BOTANICAL SPECIMEN (1839). PHOTOGENIC DRAWING.
ROYAL PHOTOGRAPHIC SOCIETY, BATH, ENGLAND.

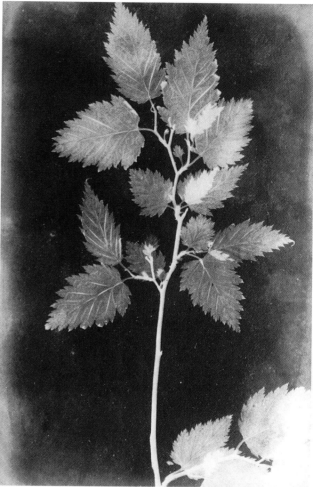

THE NEGATIVE   The negative was invented in 1839 by British scientist William Henry Fox Talbot. Talbot found that sensitized paper, coated with emulsions, could be substituted for the copper plate of the daguerreotype. He would place an object, like a sprig of a plant, on the paper and expose the arrangement to light. The paper was darkened by the exposure in all areas, except for those covered by the object. Translucent areas, allowing some passage of light, resulted in a range of greys. Talbot's first so-called "photogenic drawings" (Fig. 8–10), created by this process, seem eerie, though lyrically beautiful. The delicacy of the image underscores the impracticality of the process: How on earth would you "photograph" an elephant?

As with the daguerreotype, this process produced completed photographs in which the left and right of the image were reversed. In Talbot's "photogenic drawings," the light and dark values of the image were also inverted. Talbot improved on his early experiments with his development of the **contact print**. He placed the negative in contact with a second sheet of sensitized paper and exposed them both to light. The resultant print was a "positive," with left and right, and light and dark, again as in the original subject. Many prints could be made from the negative. Unfortunately, the prints were not as sharp as daguerreotypes, because they incorporated the texture of the paper on which they were captured. Subsequent advances led to methods in which pictures with the clarity of daguerreotypes could be printed from black and white as well as color negatives.

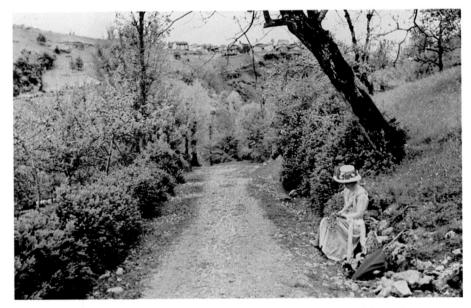

Photography improved rapidly for the next fifty or sixty years—faster emulsions, glass plate negatives, better camera lenses—and photographs became more and more available to the general public. The next major step in the history of photography came with the introduction by Louis Lumière of the "auto-chrome" color process in 1907. Autochromes were glass plates coated with three layers of dyed potato starch that served as color filters. A layer of silver bromide emulsion covered the starch. When the autochrome was developed, it yielded a positive color transparency. Lumière's autochrome photographs, such as *Young Lady with an Umbrella* (Fig. 8–11) are akin to paintings by Postimpressionist artist Georges Seurat (see page 392), an avid student of color theory, as well as to works by other photographers in the pictorial style. Autochrome technology was not replaced until 1932, when Kodak began to produce color film that applied the same principles to more advanced materials.

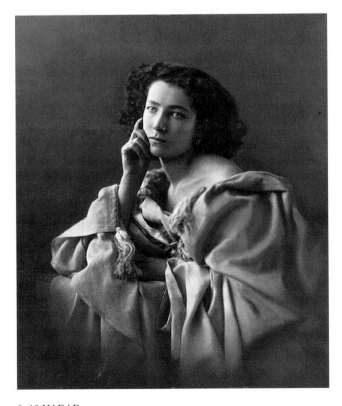

PORTRAITS   By the 1850s, photographic technology and the demands of a growing middle class in the wake of the American and French revolutions came together to create a burgeoning business in portrait photography. Having a likeness of oneself was formerly reserved for the wealthy, who could afford to commission painters to do the job. Photography became the democratic equalizer. The rich, the famous, and the average bourgeois citizen could now become memorable, could now make their presence known long after they were gone.

Photographic studios spread like wildfire, and many photographers, such as Julia Margaret Cameron and Gaspard Felix Tournachon—called "Nadar"—vied for famous clientele. Figure 8–12 is Nadar's 1859 portrait of the actress Sarah Bernhardt. It was printed

THE U.S. CIVIL WAR BROUGHT DEATH TO MORE AMERICANS THAN ANY OTHER WARS, INCLUDING WORLD WARS I AND II.

8–13 ALEXANDER GARDNER
HOME OF A REBEL SHARPSHOOTER, GETTYSBURG (JULY 1863). WET-PLATE PHOTOGRAPH.
COURTESY OF THE CHICAGO HISTORICAL SOCIETY.

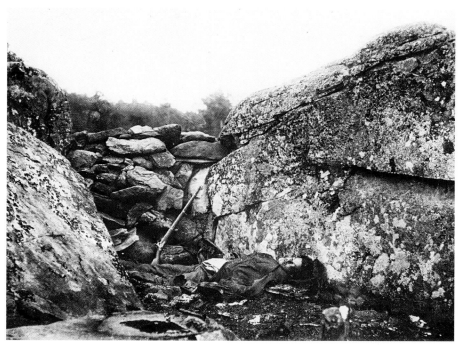

from a glass plate, which could be used several times to create sharp copies. Early portrait photographers like Nadar imitated both nature and the arts, using costumes and props that recall romantic paintings or sculpted busts caressed by flowing drapery. The photograph is soft and smoothly textured, with middle-range values predominating; Bernhardt is sensitively portrayed— pensive and brooding, but not downcast.

Cameron's impressive portfolio included portraits of Charles Dickens, Lord Tennyson, and Henry Wadsworth Longfellow.

THE ADVENT OF PHOTOJOURNALISM   Prior to the nineteenth century there were few illustrations in newspapers and magazines. Those that did appear were usually in the form of engravings or drawings. Photography revolutionized the capacity of the news media to bring realistic representations of important events before the eyes of the public. Pioneers such as Matthew Brady and Alexander Gardner first used the camera to record major historical events such as the U.S. Civil War. The photographers and their crews trudged along the roads alongside the soldiers, horses drawing their equipment behind them in wagons referred to by the soldiers as "Whatsits."

Equipment available to Brady and Gardner did not allow them to capture candid scenes, and so there is no direct record of the bloody to and fro of the battle lines, no photographic record of each lunge and parry. Instead, they brought home photographs of officers and of life in the camps along the lines. Although battle scenes themselves would not hold still for his cameras, the litter of death and devastation caused by the war and pictured in Gardner's *Home of a Rebel Sharpshooter, Gettysburg* (Fig. 8–13) most certainly did.

Despite their novelty and their accuracy, not many works of such graphic nature were sold. There are at least three reasons for this tempered success. First, the state of the art of photography made the photographs high-priced. Second, methods for reproducing photographs on newsprint were not invented until about 1900; therefore, the works of the photojournalists were usually rendered as drawings, and the drawings translated into woodcuts, before they appeared in the papers. Third, the American public might not have been ready to face the brutal realities they portrayed. In a similar vein, social commentators have suggested that the will of many Americans to persist in the Vietnam War was sapped by the incessant barrage of televised war imagery. Conversely, during the Gulf War, the virtual simultaneity of the actual events and video coverage of allied technical performance (watching smart bombs drop hundreds of feet and find their way into the front door of an ammunitions hold), probably contributed to the popular support of the invasion. One wonders whether that support may have been compromised if the camera's focus had been on the death and dying in the trenches.

8–14 DOROTHEA LANGE
MIGRANT MOTHER, NIPOMO, CALIFORNIA (1936).
GELATIN-SILVER PRINT, 12½ × 9⅞″.
© THE DOROTHEA LANGE COLLECTION, THE OAKLAND MUSEUM. GIFT OF PAUL S. TAYLOR.

8–15 ROBERT CAPA
DEATH OF A LOYALIST SOLDIER (SEPTEMBER 5, 1936).

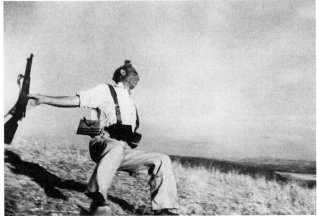

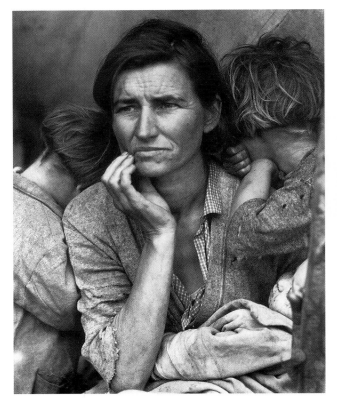

PHOTOJOURNALISM DURING THE DEPRESSION AND THE WAR YEARS

Documentary photography records the social scene of our time. It mirrors the present and documents for the future. Its focus is man in his relation to mankind. It records his customs at work, at war, at play, . . . It portrays his institutions. . . . It shows not merely their facades, but seeks to reveal the manner in which they function, absorb the life, hold the loyalty, and influence the behavior of human beings.
—Dorothea Lange

During the Great Depression, the conscience of the nation was stirred by the work of many photographers hired by the Farm Security Administration. Dorothea Lange and Walker Evans, among others, portrayed the lifestyles of migrant farm workers and sharecroppers.

Lange's *Migrant Mother* (Fig. 8–14) is an heart-rending record of a 32-year-old woman who is out of work but who cannot move on because the tires have been sold from the family car to purchase food for her seven children. The etching in the forehead is an eloquent expression of the mother's thoughts, the lines at the outer edges of her eyes tell the story of a woman who has aged beyond her years. Lange crops her photograph close to her subjects; they fill the print from edge to edge, forcing us to confront them, rather than allowing us to seek comfort in a corner of the print not consigned to such an overt display of human misery. The migrant mother and her children, who turn away from the camera and heighten the futility of their plight, are as much constrained by the camera's viewfinder as they are by their circumstances.

In the very year that Lange photographed the migrant mother, Robert Capa's fearless coverage of the Spanish Civil War resulted in such incredible photographs as *Death of a Loyalist Soldier* (Fig. 8–15). In contrast to Lange's claustrophobic, central focus composition, the vastness of space and asymmetry in Capa's work make the observer feel that there is no place to hide. Indeed, the "soldier," in ordinary street clothes save his weapon and ammunition, seems isolated and easy to pick off. Capa recorded the exact moment of the bullet's contact; we witness the instant and violent end of a human life.

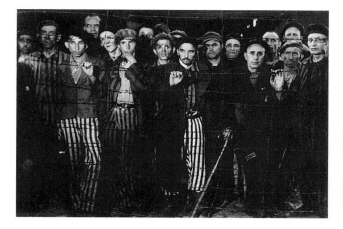

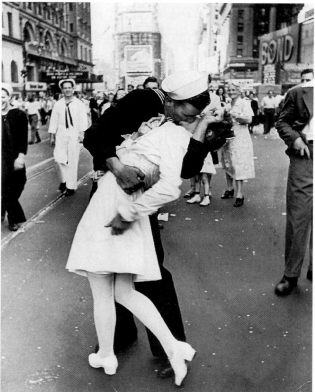

During the early 1940s, photographers such as Margaret Bourke-White carried their hand-held cameras into combat and captured tragic images of the butchery in Europe and in the Pacific. In 1929 Bourke-White became a staff photographer for *Fortune,* a new magazine published by Henry Luce. When Luce founded *Life* in 1936, Bourke-White became one of its original staff photographers. Like Dorothea Lange, she recorded the poverty of the Great Depression, but in the 1940s she travelled abroad to become one of the first female war photojournalists. As World War II was drawing to an end in Europe, Bourke-White arrived at the Nazi concentration camp of Buchenwald in time for its liberation by General Patton. Her photograph, *The Living Dead of Buchenwald, April 1945* (Fig. 8–16), published in *Life* in 1945, has become a classic image of the Holocaust, the Nazi effort to annihilate the Jewish people. The indifferent countenance of each survivor expresses, paradoxically, all that he has witnessed and endured. In her book *Dear Fatherland, Rest Quietly,* Bourke-White put into words her own reactions to Buchenwald. In doing so, she showed how artistic creation, an intensely emotional experience, can also have the effect of objectifying the subject of creation:

> *I kept telling myself that I would believe the indescribably horrible sight in the courtyard before me only when I had a chance to look at my own photographs. Using the camera was almost a relief; it*

interposed a slight barrier between myself and the white horror in front of me . . . it made me ashamed to be a member of the human race.[1]

V-J Day: Sailor Kissing Girl (Fig. 8–17), by Alfred Eisenstaedt, one of the original *Life* staff photographers, speaks of a very different aspect of the war experience—the sense of abandon and relief with which its end was met. For all its spontaneity, it is a stunning composition of high contrast figures surrounded by a range of middle values and an occasional splash of black or white. The sailor and the nurse are united in a simple C-curve; her right leg lifts off the ground and her left arm falls out of focus in the energy of the moment. *V-J Day* is clearly a record of its time and place, but it also captures the essential quality of celebration.

[1]Margaret Bourke-White, *Dear Fatherland, Rest Quietly* (New York: Simon and Schuster, 1946), p. 73.

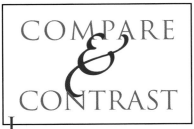

COMPARE
&
CONTRAST

JIMINEZ'S *BORDER CROSSING* WITH HALL'S *THE BORDER*

The immigration "problem" is captured from differing perspectives in the contrasts between Luis Jiminez's *Border Crossing* (Fig. 8–18) and Douglas Kent Hall's *The Border—Jailers, Agua Prieta* (Fig. 8–19). What is the political message inherent in each of the works? How do the contrasting styles and media support the political message? What is our perception of the human beings central to both works? Can you guess the artists' opinions on illegal immigration?

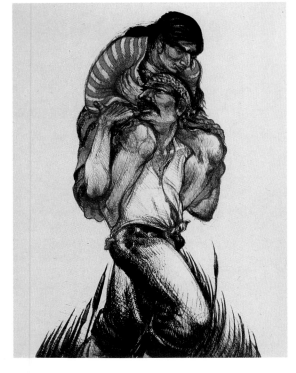

8–18 LUIS JIMINEZ
BORDER CROSSING (1987).
COLOR LITHOGRAPH.
39½ × 29½".

COURTESY OF LEWALLEN GALLERY,
SANTA FE. © 1998 LUIS JIMINEZ/ARTISTS
RIGHTS SOCIETY (ARS), N.Y.

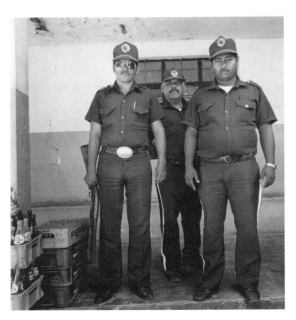

8–19 DOUGLAS KENT HALL
*THE BORDER—JAILERS,
AGUA PRIETA* (1985).
SILVER GELATIN PRINT.

COURTESY OF THE ARTIST.

Future Expectations (c. 1915). Gelatin silver print.

8–20 Edward Steichen
The Flatiron Building—Evening (1906).
The Library of Congress.

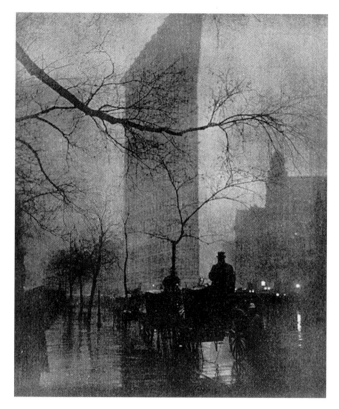

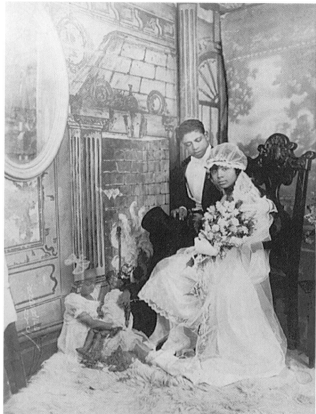

PHOTOGRAPHY AS AN ART FORM   Toward the end of the nineteenth century and in the early part of this century, photographers began to be aware of the full potential of their medium as an art form. Edward Weston, Paul Strand, Edward Steichen, and others argued that photographers must not attempt to imitate painting but must find modes of expression that are truer to their medium. Synergistically, painters were free to move toward abstraction, since the "obligation" to faithfully record nature was now assumed by the photographer. Why, after all, do what a camera can do better? In 1902 Alfred Stieglitz founded the Photo-Secession, a group dedicated to advancing photography as a separate art form. Stieglitz himself enjoyed taking pictures under adverse weather conditions and at odd times of day to show the versatility of his medium and the diversity of his expression.

Edward Steichen's *The Flatiron Building—Evening* (Fig. 8–20) is among the foremost early examples of the photograph as work of art. It is an exquisitely sensitive nocturne of haunting shapes looming in a rain-soaked atmosphere. The branch in the foreground provides the viewer with a psychological vantage point as it cuts across the composition like a bolt of lightning, or an artery pulsing with life. The values are predominantly middle grays, although here and there, beaconlike, streetlamps sparkle in the distance. The infinite gradations of gray in the cast-iron skyscraper after which the picture is named, and in the surrounding structures, yield an immeasurable softness. Although much is present that we cannot readily see, there is nothing gloomy or frightening about the scene. Rather it seems pregnant with wonderful things that will happen as the rain stops and the century progresses.

It was not long before artists began to manipulate their medium so that they, too, could venture beyond mere imitation. The first steps were tentative, building on the familiar and the readily acceptable. Photographer James Van Der Zee, known for his visual narrative of life in New York's Harlem, experimented with painted backgrounds and double-exposed images in otherwise traditional portraits. *Future Expectations* (Fig. 8–21) is both a visual record of a young couple on their wedding day and a symbol of their hopes and anticipations—a comfortable home with a blazing hearth, and beautiful children, secure in their love.

EDWIN H. LAND FOUNDED THE POLAROID CORPORATION IN 1937, WHEN HE ADAPTED POLARIZED MATERIALS FOR SUNGLASSES. TEN YEARS LATER, HE DEVELOPED A SINGLE PHOTOGRAPHIC PROCESS THAT ENABLED PHOTOS TO BE DEVELOPED IN 60 SECONDS.

8–22 SANDY SKOGLUND
RADIOACTIVE CATS (1980). CIBACHROME. 30 × 40″.
COLLECTION OF THE ARTIST.

8–23 WILLIAM WEGMAN
BLUE PERIOD (1981). COLOR POLAROID PHOTOGRAPH.
COURTESY HOLLY SOLOMON GALLERY, N.Y.

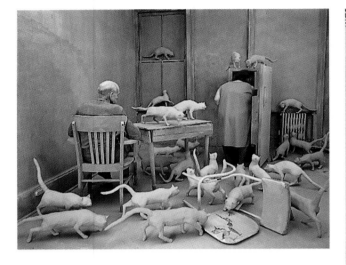

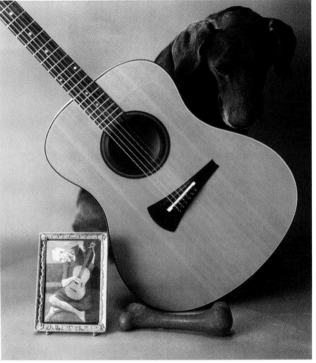

In the realm of photography and fantasy, we may take a quantum leap to the present day, when technology is such that the only impediment to the most innovative results is the artist's ability to fathom the unfathomable. In what sharp contrast to Van Der Zee's interior stands Sandy Skoglund's *Radioactive Cats* (Fig. 8–22)! Hopes and expectations for the "good life" fade into the dullness of grey, as a phlegmatic elderly couple live out their colorless lives. Yet sparks of life and humor permeate the deadly pallor of their environment—in the form of neon green cats. Skoglund sculpted the plaster cats herself and painted the room grey, controlling every aspect of the set before she shot the scene. Yet it is the photograph itself which stands as the completed work of art.

From cats to dogs. . . . Artist-photographer William Wegman happened upon his most famous subject when his Weimeraner puppy virtually insisted on performing before his lights. Man Ray, named by Wegman after the Surrealist photographer, posed willingly in hundreds of staged sets that range from the credible to the farcical. *Blue Period* (Fig. 8–23) is a spoof on Pablo Picasso's painting, *Old Guitarist* (see page 414) enframed in a souvenir version in the left lower foreground. In both works a guitar cuts diagonally across the composition, adding the only contrasting color to the otherwise monochromatic blue background. The heads of the old man and of Man Ray hang, melancholy, over the soulful

instrument. As Picasso gave the old man's flesh a bluish cast, so did Wegman tint the Weimeraner's muzzle. In Wegman's photograph, however, we find the piece de resistance—an object laden with profound meaning for the guitarist's stand-in: a blue rubber bone.

In contemporary photography, artists have often used themselves as subjects. Sculptor-photographer Lucas Samaras, known for his forbidding treasure boxes (see page 134), also did a series of "autopolaroids" that act out voyeuristic scenes based on famous works of art and "photo-transformations" in which he mutated his portrait into grossly distorted and horrific masks. Cindy Sherman also uses herself as subject, but her transformation comes by way of the persona she adopts for any given work. She recalls a mundane, early inspiration for her approach:

I had all this makeup. I just wanted to see how transformed I could look. It was like painting in a way.[2]

[2]Cindy Sherman, in Gerald Marzorati, "Imitation of Life," *Artnews 82* (September 1983): 84–85.

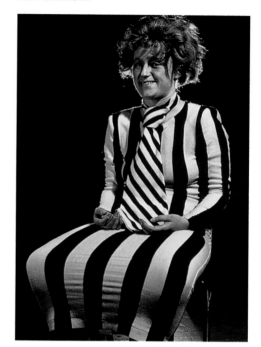

Soon she set herself before eleborate backdrops, costumed in a limitless wardrobe. Dress designers began to ask her to use their haute couture in her photographs, and works such as *Untitled* (Fig. 8–24) were actually shot as part of an advertising assignment for French *Vogue.* The result is less a sales device than a harsh view of the fashion industry. Sherman appears as a disheveled model with a troubling expression. Something here is very wrong. Regimented stripes go awry as the fabric of her dress is stretched taut across her thighs and knees. Her hands rest oddly in her lap, fingertips red with what seems to be blood. And then there is the smile—an unsettling leer implying madness.

Skoglund, Wegman, and Sherman are photographers who work, by their own admission, as painters. Similarly, many twentieth-century painters have used the camera to enhance their pictorial compositions. One of the most famous of these is Robert Rauschenberg, who came of age as an artist during the Pop Art movement of the sixties. Rauschenberg used found objects as unconventional supports for his gestural brushwork (see Fig. 17–13) and in 1962 began to print images with the photo-silkscreen technique. He recalls,

> I was bombarded with TV sets and magazines, by the refuse, by the excess of the world . . . I thought that if I could paint or make an honest work, it should incorporate all of these elements, which were and are a reality.[3]

In *Retroactive I* (Fig. 8–25), Rauschenberg used photo processes to create stencil screens from existing images, and printed these images directly onto the canvas. This fragmentary approach to subject matter, so suitable to the photographic medium, can also be seen in the work of Andy Warhol (see Chapters 1 and 17).

Whereas Rauschenberg composed his paintings of a variety of often unrelated images, painter David Hockney has used photography to construct unified compositions whose sum total of parts has a far greater impact than the whole. In the process of photographing a subject like

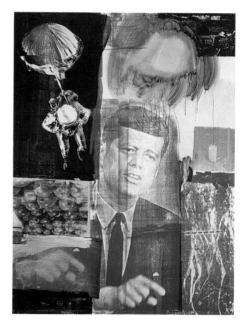

8–25 ROBERT
RAUSCHENBERG
RETROACTIVE I (1964).
SILKSCREEN.
WADSWORTH ATHENEUM,
HARTFORD/LICENSED BY VAGA, N.Y.

[3]Robert Hughes, *The Shock of the New,* (NY: Knopf) 1980, p. 345.

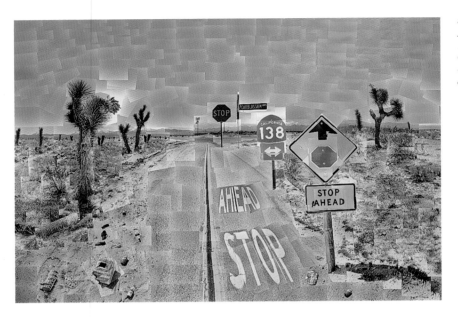

Pearblossom Highway 11–18th April 1986 #2 (Fig. 8–26), Hockney fragments the panorama, only to rebuild it in his studio. It is almost as if he were reconstructing the scene as most of us do from fragmented memories. The result is a shimmering mosaic that elevates the commonplace to the level of fine art.

Evolving technology has made it possible for photographers to achieve dazzling images such as the one in Harold Edgerton's *Fan and Flame Vortices* (Fig. 8–27). Edgerton is an electrical engineer who invented the strobe light, a device which emits brief and brilliant flashes of light that seem to slow or stop the action of people or objects in motion. *Fan and Flame Vortices* is a high-speed photograph of a metal fan blade rotating at 3,600 revolutions per minute through the flame emitted by an alcohol burner. Changes in the density of the air and other gases are responsible for the fluctuating colors. Edgerton, like many other contemporary photographers, has used technological innovations to transform some of the mundane objects of the real world into vibrant abstract images.

NEW DEVELOPMENTS IN PHOTOGRAPHY Technical advances in photography press on unrestrained. For example, the **stereoscopy** of the nineteenth century,

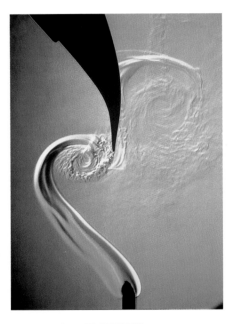

8–27 HAROLD EDGERTON
FAN AND FLAME VORTICES (1973). DYE
TRANSFER PRINT. 13 × 20″.
© 1973 KIM VANDIVER & HAROLD EDGERTON. COURTESY OF PALM
PRESS, INC.

which rendered the illusion of a three-dimensional image, has given way to the **holography** of today and a variety of other experimental techniques that may soon provide us with more realistic three-dimensional images.

Photographers today can also create and store **digitized images**. Light enters the lens of the digital camera, and is encoded as digital information by the camera. The information can be transferred to storage devices such as diskettes, hard drives, and CDs (compacts disks). The images can then be displayed on electronic devices such as computer monitors and TV sets or printed on paper or other vehicles.

It remains to be seen whether further technical refinements will meaningfully increase the range of experiences that may be communicated by photography.

Photographs have the capacity to stir us; because of their size our relationship to them is intimate. At times they speak frankly to us, sometimes at times they leave much to the imagination. As frozen moments in time, we can only wonder about what had gone before and what came after. This capacity to stir us is intensified, expanded, and altered in the art of cinematography. A large screen, movement, and—since the 1930s—sound, capture the visual and auditory senses of the audience like no other medium.

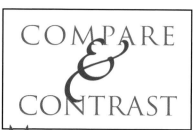
MAREY'S
*CHRONOPHOTOGRAPH
OF THE FLIGHT
OF A BIRD*
WITH
BALLA'S *SWIFTS:
PATHS OF
MOVEMENT +
DYNAMIC
SEQUENCES*

In the twentieth century, painters have frequently made use of the medium of photography, either as a point of departure for their work, as a creative tool, or as an end product in and of itself. How, in his painting, has Balla taken advantage of contemporary experiments in photography? What did Marey record in his photograph (Fig. 8–28)? How are the works similar? What is the real subject of Balla's composition (Fig. 8–29)?

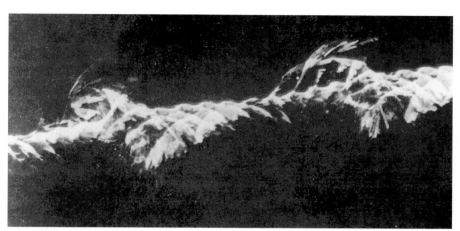

8–28 ÉTIENNE-JULES MAREY
*CHRONOPHOTOGRAPH OF THE
FLIGHT OF A BIRD* (1887).
ARCHIVES DE CINEMATHÈQUE FRANÇAISE, PARIS.

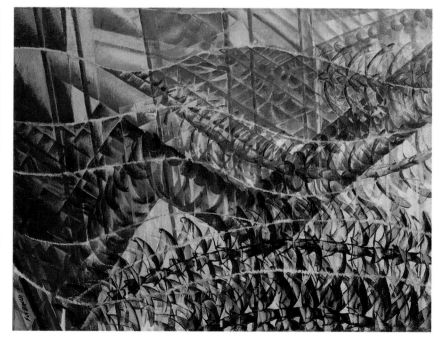

8–29 GIACOMO BALLA
*SWIFTS: PATHS OF
MOVEMENT + DYNAMIC
SEQUENCES* (1913).
OIL ON CANVAS.
THE MUSEUM OF MODERN ART, N.Y.
© GIACOMO BALLA/LICENSED BY VAGA, N.Y.

CINEMATOGRAPHY

I can make an audience laugh, scream with terror, smile, believe in legends, become indignant, take offense, become enthusiastic, lower itself or yawn with boredom. I am, then, either a deceiver or—when the audience is aware of the fraud—an illusionist. I am able to mystify, and I have at my disposal the most precious and the most astounding device [the motion picture camera] that has ever, since history began, been put into the hands of the juggler.
—Ingmar Bergman[4]

The magic of cinematography—the art of making motion pictures—envelops our senses. Some members of the audience demand to be so encompassed that they sit in the front row, with the screen looming above them like a tidal wave. What associations does cinematography evoke for you? The big screen? The silver screen? The drive-in, with long lines for hot dogs and french fries? Speakers blasting from the walls? Popcorn? Ushers complaining about bringing drinks to the seats? Gum sticking to your shoe? Teenagers laughing, shouting, and necking? All these are part of Americana. Couples not only have "our song"; they often have "our movie"—what they saw on one of their first dates, what spoke to them deeply in their emotional vulnerability.

VARIETIES OF CINEMATOGRAPHIC TECHNIQUES

Despite their power to move us, motion pictures, or "movies," do not really move themselves. The illusion of movement is created by **stroboscopic motion,** which is the presentation of a rapid progression of images of stationary objects. The audience is shown 16 to 24 pictures or frames per second, like those shown in the series of Muybridge photographs (Fig. 2–47). Each picture or frame differs slightly from that preceding it. Showing them in rapid succession creates the illusion of movement. (Children similarly draw series of shapes or figures along the outer margins of books, then flip the pages to create the illusion of movement.)

[4]Andrew Sariff, Ed., *Interviews with Film Directors,* trans. Alice Turner (New York: Avon Books, 1969), p. 35.

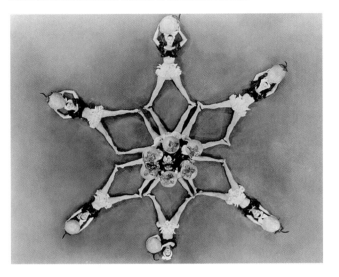

At a rate of 22 or 24 frames per second, the "motion" in a film seems smooth and natural. At fewer than 16 or so frames per second, it is choppy. For that reason, **slow motion** is achieved by filming 100 or more frames per second. When they are played back at 22 or 24 frames per second, movement appears to be very slow yet smooth and natural.

Eadward Muybridge's *Galloping Horse* sequence was shot in 1878 by 24 cameras placed along a racetrack and was made possible by new fast-acting photosensitive plates. (If these plates had been developed fifteen years earlier, Brady could have bequeathed us a photographic record of Civil War battle scenes.) Muybridge had been commissioned to settle a bet as to whether racehorses ever had all hooves off the ground at once. He found that they did, but also that they never assumed the "rocking-horse" position in which the front and back legs are simultaneously extended.

Muybridge is generally credited with performing the first successful experiments in cinematography. He fashioned a device that could photograph a rapid sequence of images, and he invented the **zoogyroscope,** which projected these images onto a screen.

The motion picture camera and projector were perfected by the inventor of the light bulb, Thomas Edison, toward the end of the nineteenth century. In 1893 the photographer Alexander Black made a motion picture of the President of the United States. In 1894

Thomas Edison's assistant Fred Ott was immortalized on film in the act of sneezing. Out of these inauspicious beginnings, a new medium for the visual arts was suddenly born.

Within a few short years, commercial movie houses sprang up across the nation and motion picture productions were distributed for public consumption. Sound was added to visual sensations by means of a **sound track,** and a number of silent film stars with noncompelling voices fell by the wayside.

Additional innovations have had a checkered history. There have been expansions to wider and wider screens, including Cinemascope, Cinerama, Panavision, and films that are projected completely around the audience on a 360-degree strip wall or on the inner surface of a hemispherical dome. Stereophonic sound has been introduced. Three-dimensional (3-D) movies requiring special eyeglasses have been made. Today the stereophonic sound, color, and reasonably wide screens remain in common use. But what photographers have noted about the role of photographic equipment seems also to apply to cinematography: the vision or creativity of the cinematographer is more important than technical advances.

Let us now consider a number of cinematographic techniques more closely: use of the fixed camera, the moving camera, editing, color, animation, and special effects.

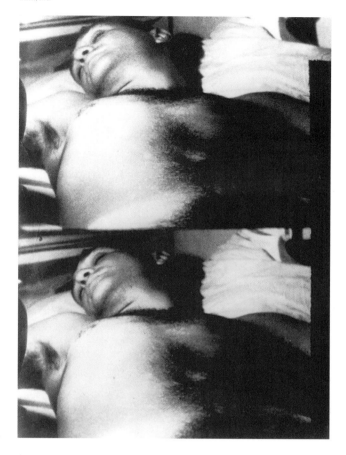

FIXED CAMERAS AND STAGED PRODUCTIONS   With a stage play, the audience is fixed and must observe from a single vantage point. Similarly, many early motion pictures used a single camera that was more or less fixed in place. Actors came on stage and exited before them.

Much of the Busby Berkeley musicals of the 1930s (Fig. 8–30) was shot on indoor stages that pretended to be nothing but stages. The motion picture had not yet broken free from the stage that had preceded it. Many directors used cinematography to bring the stages of the great urban centers to small cities and rural towns. We can note that the musicals of the 1930s were everything that the photographs of Dorothea Lange and the other Depression photographers were not: they were bubbly, frivolous, light, even saucy. Some musicals of the 1930s showed apple-cheeked "kids" getting their break on the Great White Way. Others portrayed the imaginary

shenanigans of the wealthy few in an innocent era when Hollywood believed that they would offer amusement and inspiration to destitute audiences, rather than stir feelings of social conflict through depiction of conspicuous consumption and frivolity.

Although produced relatively infrequently today, lengthy, fixed-camera "motion pictures" like that of a sleeping man (Fig. 8–31) and the Empire State Building by Pop artist Andy Warhol still appear. *Sleep* recorded the tosses, turns, and snores of one man during about eight hours of nocturnal activity. *Empire State Building* documented the changing play of light across the skyscraper over the course of a day. Some critics hailed the return of the early days of the fixed camera to the 1960s. Warhol himself suggested that these motion pictures were intended as a new form of environmental art, to be played on a wall at a cocktail party while people toyed with drinks and conversation.

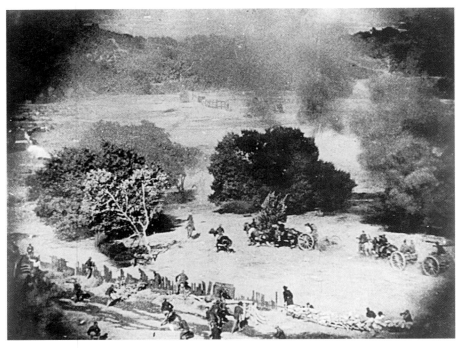

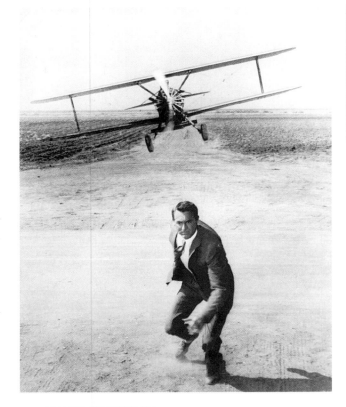

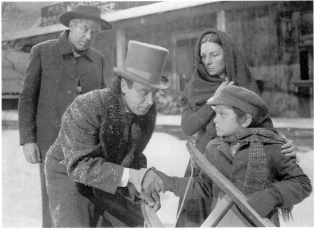

THE MOBILE CAMERA   Film critics usually argue that
motion pictures should tell their stories in ways that
are inimitable through any other medium. One way is
through the mobile camera. Film pioneer D. W. Griffith
is credited with making the camera mobile. He attached
motion-picture cameras to rapidly moving vehicles
and used them to **pan** across expanses of scenery and
action, as in the battle scenes in his *Birth of a Nation*
(Fig. 8–32). Today it is not unusual for cameras to be
placed aboard rapidly moving vehicles and also to **zoom**
in on and away from their targets.

8–35 FILM STILL FROM *GONE WITH THE WIND.* (1939)

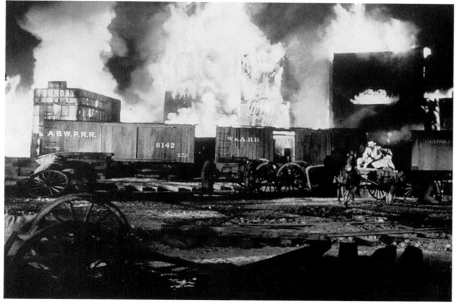

EDITING Griffith is also credited with making many advances in film **editing.** Editing is the separating and assembling, sometimes called "patching and pasting," of sequences of film. Editing helps make stories coherent and heightens dramatic impact.

In **narrative editing** multiple cameras are used during the progress of the same scene or story location. Then shots are selected from various vantage points and projected in sequence. **Close-ups** may be interspersed with **longshots,** providing the audience with abundant perspectives on the action while advancing the story. Close-ups usually better communicate the emotional responses of the actors, while longshots describe the setting, as in Alfred Hitchcock's thriller, *North by Northwest* (Fig. 8–33).

In **parallel editing,** the story shifts back and forth from one event or scene to another. Scenes of one segment of a battlefield may be interspersed with events taking place on another or back home, collapsing space. Time may also be collapsed through parallel editing, with the cinematographer shifting back and forth between past, present, and future.

In the **flashback,** one form of parallel editing, the storyline is interrupted by the portrayal or narration of an earlier episode, often through the implied fantasies of an actor or actress. Orson Welles's *Citizen Kane* (Fig. 8–34) innovated the use of the flashback. The flashback usually gives current action more meaning. In the **flashforward,** editing permits the audience glimpses of the future. The flashforward is frequently used at the beginning of dramatic television shows to capture the interest of the viewer who may be switching channels.

Motion pictures may proceed from one scene to another by means of **fading.** The current scene becomes gradually dimmer, or *fades out.* The subsequent scene then grows progressively brighter, or *fades in.* In the more rapid, current technique of the **dissolve,** the subsequent scene becomes brighter while the current scene fades out, so that the first scene seems to dissolve into the second.

In **montage,** a sequence of abruptly alternating images or scenes conveys associated ideas or the passage of time. Images can suddenly flash into focus or whirl about for impact, as in a series of newspaper headlines meant to show the progress of the actors over time.

COLOR Color came into use in the 1930s. One early color film, *The Wizard of Oz,* depicted the farm world of Kansas in black and white and the imaginary Oz in glorious, often expressionistic color. Madonna sort of reverses the pattern in *Truth or Dare,* where her stage performances (fantasy?) are in color and her (real?) backstage life is in black and white. Yet interestingly, this pattern is now frequently reversed in music videos, where fantasy is often portrayed in black and white and reality in (everyday, natural?) color.

The screen version of Margaret Mitchell's *Gone with the Wind* (Fig. 8–35) was one of the first color epics or "spectaculars." It remains one of the highest-grossing works of all film eras. In addition to the sweeping

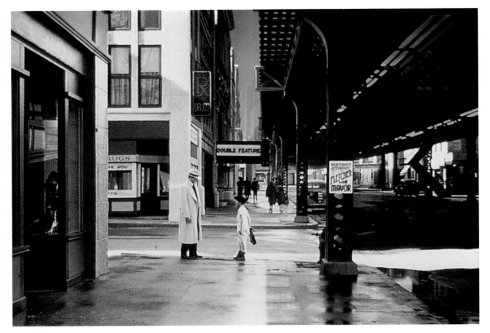

panoramas of the Civil War battlefield wounded and
the burning of Atlanta, *Gone with the Wind* included
close-ups of the passion and fire communicated by
Clark Gable as Rhett Butler and Vivian Leigh as
Scarlett O'Hara.

Color in motion pictures, as in paintings and photographs, is commonly used to provide the work with a
natural appearance. Color can also be expressionistically
varied, however, to create emotional responses, a sense
of time or place, or, as in the case of *Dick Tracy*
(Fig. 8–36), to give the work the feel of another time
and another medium. The cinematographers of *Dick
Tracy* used a limited palette to conform to the comic
strip as it appeared in the Sunday "funnies" of the
Fabulous Fifties. (The "dailies" were typically black
and white.)

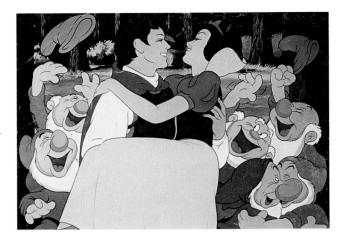

ANIMATION **Animation** is the creation of a motion
picture by photographing a series of drawings, each of
which shows a stage of movement that differs slightly
from the one preceding it. As a result, projecting the
frames in rapid sequence creates the illusion of movement. The first cartoons were in black and white and
employed a great deal of repetition.

During the 1930s Walt Disney's studios began
to produce full-color stories and images that still
possess parts of the topography of our minds. With
every rerelease, *Snow White* (Fig. 8–37) mesmerizes
young audiences of yet another generation. Disney
characters such as Mickey Mouse, Donald Duck,
Bambi, Pinocchio, the Little Mermaid, and the Genie

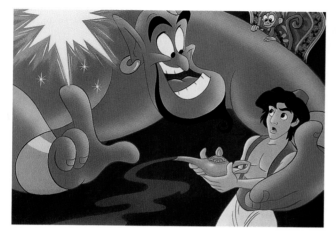

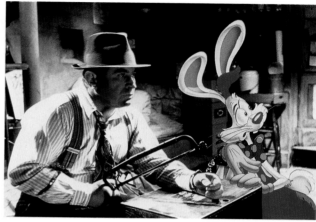

in the film *Aladdin* (Fig. 8–38) have become part of our national folklore.

Numerous attempts have been made to incorporate people and cartoon figures and landscapes. In one effort, Dick van Dyke danced with cartoon penguins in the Walt Disney film, *Mary Poppins*. In a most ambitious effort, Walt Disney's *Who Framed Roger Rabbit?* (Fig. 8–39), people interact with "Toons." Special effects were also used that allowed people to bounce around in cartoon fashion. One of the intriguing aspects of the film was the alternating depiction of "Toons" against real backdrops, and people against cartoon backdrops.

SPECIAL EFFECTS   Filmmakers also use a wide range of so-called special effects to create their magic. At the simple end of things, ketchup on a shirt may simulate blood, and a series of tiny explosions from capsules planted in the ground may simulate automatic-weapon fire. Models may be used to create movie behemoths (King Kong, the dinosaurs in *Jurassic Park*, aliens, and the like), vehicles such as star ships (as in *Star Wars*) and submarines (as in *Hunt for Red October*), and elaborated humans (as in *Beetlejuice* and *TRON*). The herd of galloping dinosaurs in *Jurassic Park* was made possible by computer animation. Some of the models for the dinosaurs that were shown in close-ups contained dozens of motors so that body parts would move realistically (Fig. 8–40).

We have focused on technique, but technique gives cinematographers the opportunity to express a variety of themes.

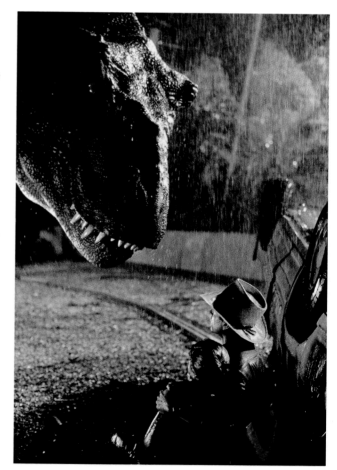

8–40 STEPHEN SPIELBERG
FILM STILL FROM *JURASSIC PARK*.

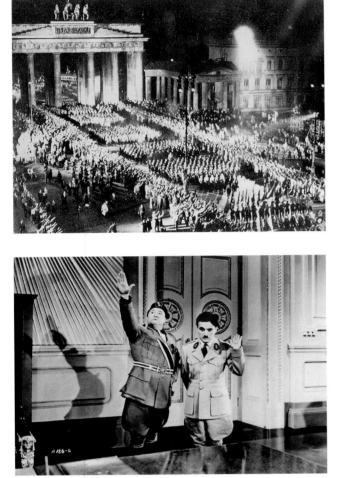

VARIETIES OF CINEMATOGRAPHIC EXPERIENCE

No discussion of cinematography can hope to recount adequately the richness of the motion picture experience. Broadly speaking, motion pictures are visual experiences that entertain or move us; as, for example, in novels, we identify with characters and become wrapped up in plots. Like other artists, cinematographers make us laugh (consider the great films of the Marx Brothers and Laurel and Hardy), create propaganda, satire, social commentary, fantasy, and symbolism, and express artistic theories and reflect artistic styles. Let us consider some of these more closely.

PROPAGANDA   While there are some early (and choppy) film records of World War I, cinematography was ready for World War II. In fact, while many American actors were embattled in Europe and the Pacific, future resident Ronald Reagan was making films for the United States that depicted the valor of the Allied soldiers and the malevolence of the enemy.

Our adversaries were active as well. Prior to the war, in fact, German director Leni Riefenstahl made what is considered one of the greatest (though also most pernicious) propaganda films of all time, *Triumph of the Will* (Fig. 8–41). Riefenstahl transformed the people and events of an historic event, the 1935 Nürnberg Congress, into abstract, symbolic patterns through the juxtaposition of longshots and close-ups, and aerial and ground-level views. Her montage of people, monuments, and flag-bedecked buildings unified flesh and stone into a hymn to Nazism. The United States, England, Canada, and some other nations paid a backhanded compliment to the power of *Triumph of the Will* by banning it.

SATIRE   Satire is the flip side of propaganda. While Riefenstahl glorified national socialism in Germany, American filmmakers derided it. In one cartoon, for example, Daffy Duck clubs a realistic-looking, speechifying Adolph Hitler over the head with a mallet. Hitler dissolves into tears and calls for his mommy. British-American filmmaker Charlie Chaplin added to the derision of the führer in *The Great Dictator* (Fig. 8–42). The film and television series *M*A*S*H* are set during the Korean War, but they satirize military procedures and authoritarianism through the ages.

SOCIAL COMMENTARY Filmmakers, like documentary photographers, have made their social comments. *The Grapes of Wrath* (Fig. 8–43), based on the John Steinbeck novel, depicts one family's struggle for survival during the Great Depression, when the banks failed and the Midwest farm basket of the United States turned into the Dust Bowl. Like a Dorothea Lange photograph, the camera comes in to record hopelessness and despair. Cinematographers have commented on everything from *Divorce, American Style* to *The Killing Fields* of Southeast Asia to the excesses of *Wall Street* in the 1980s.

FANTASY Nor are fantasy and flights of fancy limited to paintings, drawings, and the written word. In the experimental films of Robert Wiene and Salvador Dalí and Luis Buñuel, events are not confined to the material world as it is; they occupy and express the inmost images of the cinematographer. The sets for Wiene's *The Cabinet of Doctor Caligari* (Fig. 8–44) were created by three painters who employed Expressionist devices such as angular, distorted planes and sheer perspectives. The hallucinatory backdrop removes the protagonist, a carnival hypnotist who causes a sleepwalker to murder people who displease him, from the realm of reality. The muddy line between the authentic and the fantastic is further obscured by the film's ending, in which the hypnotist becomes a mental patient telling an imaginary tale. (It is akin to the ravings of the mad Salieri, who, through flashbacks, recounts his actual and fantasized interactions with Mozart in the film *Amadeus*.)

8–43 FILM STILL FROM *THE GRAPES OF WRATH*.

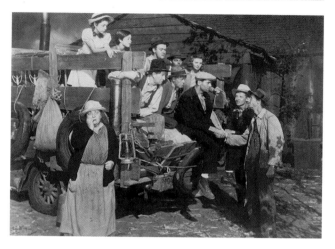

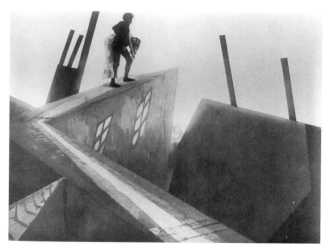

8–44 ROBERT WIENE
FILM STILL FROM *THE CABINET OF DOCTOR CALIGARI* (1919).

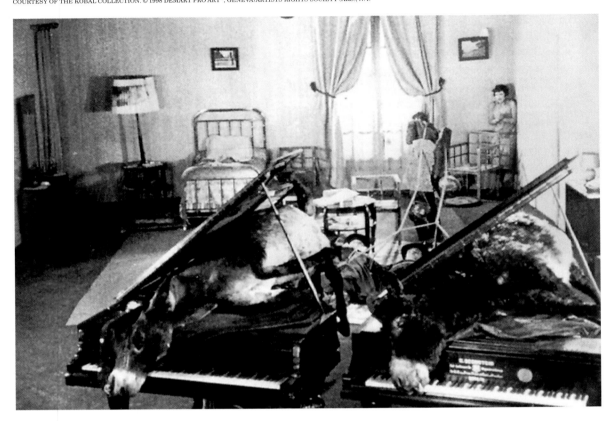

Caligari has a story, albeit an unusual one, but Dalí and Buñuel's surrealistic *Un Chien Andalou* (Fig. 8–45) has a script (if you can call it a script) without order or meaning in the traditional sense. In the shocking opening scene, normal vision is annulled by the slicing of an eyeball. The audience is then propelled through a series of disconnected, dreamlike scenes.

SYMBOLISM   In writing about *Un Chien Andalou,* Buñuel[5] claimed that his aims were to evoke instinctive reactions of attraction and repulsion in the audience, but that nothing in the film *symbolized* anything. Fantastic cinematographers often portray their depths of mind literally. They create on the screen the images that dwell deep within. Other cinematographers, like Ingmar Bergman, do frequently express aspects of the inner world through symbols.

Since the 1950s, filmgoers have been struck by Bergman's mostly black-and-white films (Fig. 8–46). As in so much other art, nature serves as counterpoint to the vicissitudes of the human spirit in Bergman's films. The Swedish summers are short and precious. The bleak winters seem, to Bergman, to be the enduring fact of life. Against their backdrop, he portrays modern alienation from comforting religion and tradition. Bergman's films have ranged from jocular comedies to unrelieved dark dramas, and his bewitching screen images have brought together Nordic mythology and themes of love, death, and ultimate aloneness.

Now let us turn our attention to video, which has been responsible for a number of art forms, including television. This is one visual medium that is found in almost every American home.

[5]Luis Buñuel, "Notes on the Making of *Un Chien Andalou*." In *Art in Cinema,* a symposium held at the San Francisco Museum of Art (reprinted, New York: Arno Press, 1968).

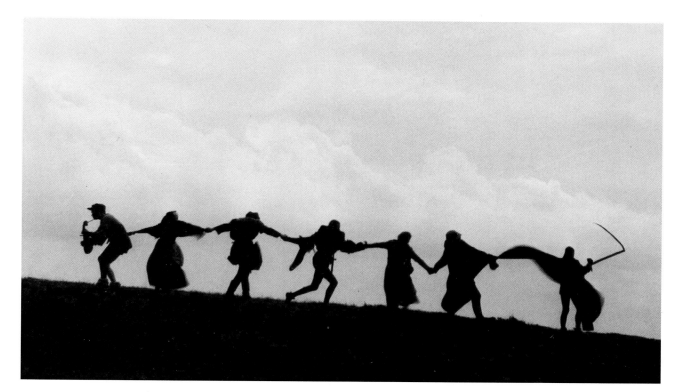

8–46 INGMAR BERGMAN
FILM STILL FROM *THE
SEVENTH SEAL* (1956).
COURTESY OF THE KOBAL COLLECTION.

VIDEO

Video is a rather new term on the art scene. It refers not only to commercial television, public television, and cable programming, but also to experimental video, computer graphics, and mixed-media works that incorporate video monitors. Many of the techniques of television are a derivation and extension of those of cinematography. Television executives broadcast motion pictures into homes and produce their own dramas. Television, like cinematography, uses the camera, and all the techniques of cinematography—methods of editing, and so on—apply to television.

TELEVISION

In its brief half-century, television has radically altered American life (consider the advent of the TV dinner)—and perhaps changed the habits of much of the world. Children spend as many hours in front of "the tube" as they do in school. Congressional committees debate the impact of televised violence. Millions over the decades have stayed at home to watch TV—from *I Love Lucy* to *The Cosby Show.* The 1950s series *The Honeymooners* (Fig. 8–47) immortalized a hot-tempered, bumbling, yet well-intentioned and devoted working-class husband. The nation waited one long summer in the 1980s to find out "Who Shot J.R.?" on *Dallas*—one of the first season-ending "cliff-hangers." Cable and public television bring us programs tailored for smaller audiences—ballets, operas, plays, serious talk shows, shows on science, educational programs such as *Sesame Street,* and experimental video productions.

Television is intimate. In contrast to the movie theater with its throngs, television is most often watched in the home, frequently by lone viewers. For many people, television is an indispensable companion.

Television affords us access to the best seats in the "house." For sporting events, it gives us better seats than we could hope for in the ballpark. If we turn away for a moment and miss an important play, we need not be concerned; we are soon barraged by instant replays from several angles. "Live" coverage of major events enabled hundreds of millions to witness Neil Armstrong's first steps on the moon. Many millions watched in horror the "live" assassination of President Kennedy, the

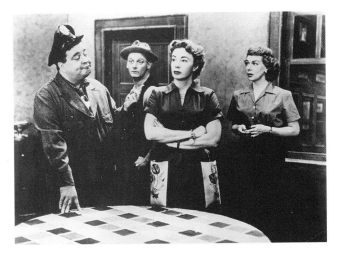

subsequent killing of Lee Harvey Oswald, and the shooting of President Reagan. Many, similarly, saw the explosion of the Challenger space shuttle "live," and many viewers became addicted to the Persian Gulf War (journalists came to call them "gulf potatoes")—the nation's first real video war—which began with Cable News Network's "live" description of fighter-bombers over Baghdad in January 1991. Viewers were fascinated by the police chase of O. J. Simpson's Ford Bronco on the L.A. Freeways, as captured live by helicoptors. They also became addicted to Simpson's murder trial, and, when it was over, there were reports of depression among inveterate viewers.

HOW TELEVISION WORKS   The sights and sounds that are recorded by the television camera are transformed into electronic codes or messages. These messages are broadcast or transmitted through the air and received by antennae, or they are transmitted into the home by means of a cable; when the cable is underground, the picture is relatively free of the distortions that can be produced by inclement weather.

The television set reconstructs these electronic messages into visual images and sounds. The picture actually consists of hundreds of lines that run across the screen. The greater the number of lines, the higher the **resolution**—that is, the sharper the picture. The impression of a single picture is built up from light and

8–48 MADONNA IN PERFORMANCE.

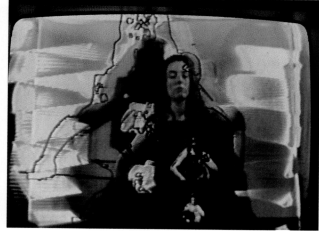

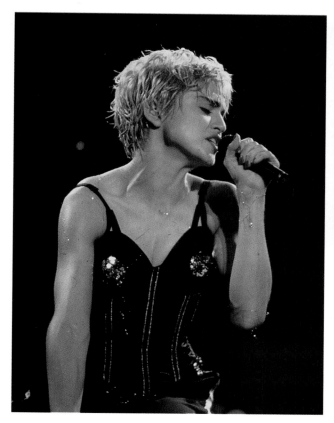

dark areas along these lines. Color television is made possible by the exciting of various particles within the screen that glow either blue, green, or red. The wide range of hues we see is created by additive color mixtures.

MUSIC VIDEOS

Some cable channels, such as MTV, program a succession of music videos, a medium that became popular in the 1980s. They essentially provide visual imagery for popular songs, but now have become a sophisticated artform in themselves. Some—the less creative—are records of concerts; others involve elaborate narratives, something like pop opera. Music videos tend to last but a few minutes, yet some cram every imaginable cinematographic technique into that time period: narrative and parallel editing (often with peripatetic short scenes and oblique camera angles); color and black and white

(frequently in the same video); cartoons and real people (again, often in the same video); and a host of special effects.

Madonna (Fig. 8–48) has become a concert and music video superstar who combines rock-'n'-roll rhythms with song, modern dance, and an eccentric sexuality. It is difficult to say whether music videos reflect or help make the times. Perhaps they do both. (Adolescents have survived everything else over the generations; why not this?)

VIDEO ART

Video is most often used to transmit some other event to viewers—news, sporting events, staged events, and films. Korean-born Nam June Paik and a number of others, however, have experimented with video as their medium in the direct creation of works of art. Paik refers to his approach as **video art,** in order to distinguish it from the commercial efforts of the television establishment.

Paik's *Global Groove* (Fig. 8–49) flashes fragmented segments of Japanese Pepsi commercials, Korean drummers, a videotaped theater group, poet Allen Ginsberg reading from his work, women tap dancers, and a musical piece in which a cellist draws her bow across a man's back. The stream of consciousness is somewhat surrealistic, but the imagery provides a reasonably recognizable pastiche of television worldwide.

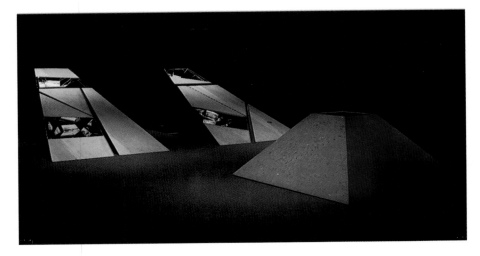

8–50 SHIGEKO KUBOTA
THREE MOUNTAINS
(1976–79). 4-CHANNEL VIDEO
INSTALLATION WITH
3 MOUNTAINS, CONSTRUCTED
OF PLYWOOD AND PLASTIC
MIRRORS, CONTAINING
7 MONITORS;
MOUNTAIN I: 38 × 17″
AT TOP AND 59 × 59″ AT BASE;
MOUNTAINS II AND III:
67 × 21″ AT TOP AND
100 × 60″ AT BASE; 4 COLOR
VIDEOTAPES, EACH 30 MIN.
COLLECTION OF THE ARTIST; COURTESY,
ELECTRONIC ARTS INTERMIX, N.Y.

experience of the open western landscape. Video monitors are installed in a plywood base—the cut-outs lined with mirrors. The mixed-media work confronts the viewer with multiple images of the Grand Canyon, as seen from a helicopter; a drive along Echo Cliff, Arizona; a Taos, New Mexico, sunset; and a Teton sunset. Kubota commented:

> My mountains exist in fractured and extended time and space. My vanishing point is reversed, located behind your brain. Then, distorted by mirrors and angles, it vanishes in many points at once. Lines of perspective stretch on and on, crossing at steep angles, sharp, like cold thin mountain air.[6]

How better to depart the chapter than with a video work entitled *Perfect Leader* (Fig. 8–51)? Max Almy's visionary tale "tunes in" to some wry social commentary through lavish special effects, including a television set in a man's forehead. Technology, once our servant, ultimately renders us unrecognizable? After the man with the set and a woman forsake the twentieth century, a voice-over explains their departure: The woman left because she had no particular belief in the future and wanted to take a look for herself. The man's migration was somewhat less philosophically inspired, however: "He left because there was nothing good on television." Amen.

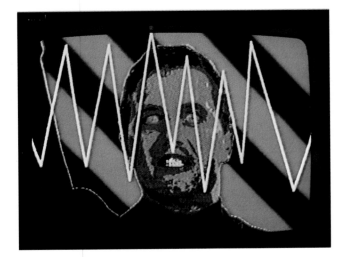

8–51 MAX ALMY
PERFECT LEADER (1983). VIDEOTAPE STILL.
COURTESY ELECTRONIC ARTS INTERMIX, N.Y.

WOMEN AND VIDEO ART   Video has been a particularly fertile medium for women artists—perhaps in part because it is a nontraditional medium and one which has not been dominated by male artists and critics. Perhaps too, women have been drawn to video because it lends itself to narrative, or storytelling—a tradition attributed to women, who for generations have kept stories alive in their families.

In *Three Mountains* (Fig. 8–50), Japanese artist Shigeko Kubota incorporates video into a pyramidal sculptural piece, a combination intended to recreate the

[6]Shigeko Kubota, *Video Sculptures* (Berlin: Daadgalerie; Essen: Museum Folkwang; Zurich: Kunsthaus, 1982), p. 37.

key terms

Cinematography
Photography
Photosensitive
Lens
Prints
Aperture
Shutter
Stop
Candid
Film
Telephoto lens
Wide-angle lens

Emulsion
A negative
Color reversal film
Color negative film
Camera obscura
Heliography
Bitumen
Lavender oil
Daguerreotype
Contact print
Stereoscopy
Holography

Digitized images
Stroboscopic motion
Slow motion
Zoogyroscope
Sound track
Pan
Zoom
Film editing
Narrative editing
Close-ups
Longshots
Parallel editing

Flashback
Flashforward
Fading
Dissolve
Montage
Panorama
Animation
Video
Resolution
Video art

artists

Ansel Adams
Shiro Shirahata
Alfred Stieglitz
Joseph Nicéphore Niepce
Louis-Jacques-Mandé Daguerre
Honoré Daumier
William Henry Fox Talbot
Louis Lumière
Nadar
Alexander Gardner
Dorothea Lange
Robert Capa
Margaret Bourke-White
Alfred Eisenstaedt

Luis Jiminez
Douglas Kent Hall
Edward Steichen
James van der Zee
Sandy Skoglund
William Wegman
Cindy Sherman
Robert Rauschenberg
David Hockney
Harold Edgerton
Étienne-Jules Marey
Giacomo Balla
Busby Berkeley
Andy Warhol

D. W. Griffith
Alfred Hitchcock
Orson Welles
Stephen Spielberg
Leni Riefenstahl
Robert Wiene
Salvador Dali
Luis Buñuel
Ingmar Bergman
Nam June Paik
Shigeko Kubota
Max Almy

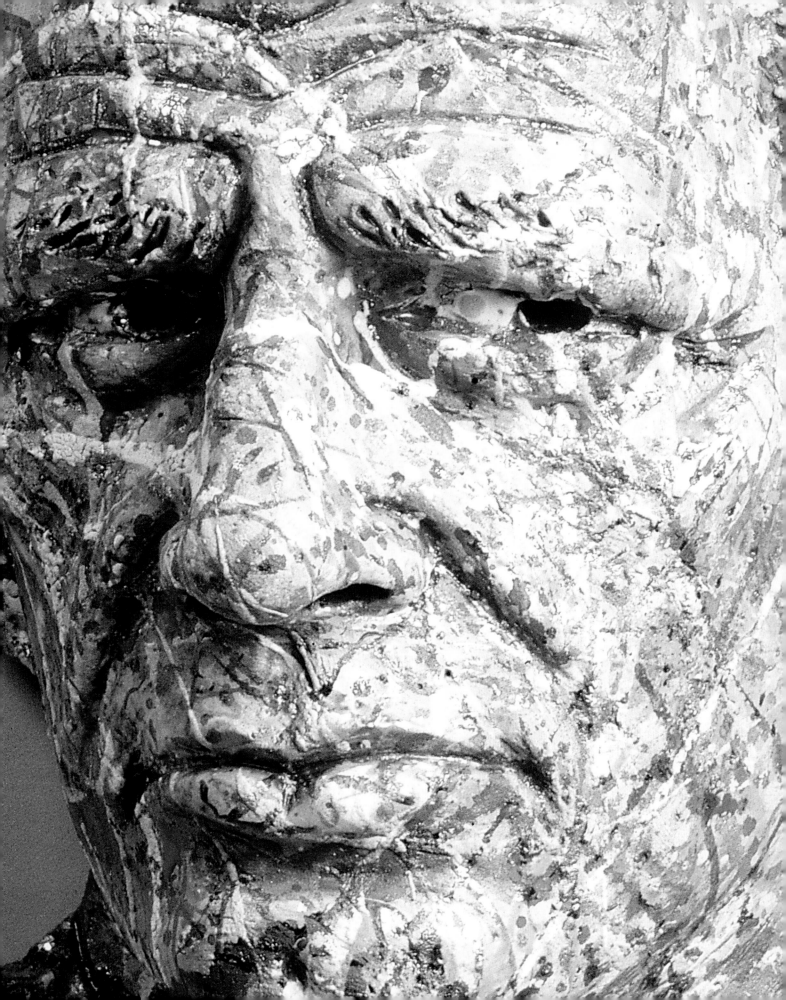

CRAFT AND DESIGN

P R E L I M I N A R Y
Sketch

- Greek philosophers such as Plato believed that artisans were more important than artists because, for example, the carpenter makes that which the painter can only imitate.

- The potter's wheel has been in use for some 6,000 years.

- Ceramic tiles are used to protect space shuttles from the heat of reentry into the Earth's atmosphere.

- Glass is made from sand.

- Many Persian carpets have been woven with as many as 1,000 hand-tied wool knots to the square inch.

- Medieval weavers, like fresco painters, worked from patterns called *cartoons*.

- People experience strong social pressure to conform their clothing to that worn by the groups with which they identify.

- During some historic periods, the clothing of men has been more flamboyant and colorful than that of women.

- The Museum of Modern Art displays superior industrial designs including teapots, electric coffeemakers, and the Movado watch.

Robert Arneson, *Jackson Pollock* (detail). See Figure 9–7.

9–1 EUPHRONIOS and EUXITHEOS
CALYX KRATER (1ST QUARTER OF 5TH
CENTURY BCE). CERAMIC. HEIGHT: 18″;
DIAMETER: 21 11/16″.

THE METROPOLITAN MUSEUM OF ART, N.Y. BEQUEST OF JOSEPH H.
DURKEE, GIFT OF DARIUS OGDEN MILLS, AND GIFT OF C. RUXTON
LOVE, BY EXCHANGE, (1972.11.10)

An Attic vase, a Navajo rug, Tiffany glass, a Chippendale desk—Which is art? Which is craft? Art critics and historians once had easy answers to these questions. Now, however, the perception of the relationship among functional objects, craft materials and techniques, and works of fine art has changed. Consider this story concerning one of the Metropolitan Museum of Art's most precious acquisitions, as retold by art critic Arthur C. Danto:[1]

According to Thomas Hoving, the director of the museum at the time of the purchase, the vase in Figure 9–1 is "the single most perfect work of art [he] ever encountered. . . an object of total adoration." In his memoirs, Hoving further described his feelings upon his first encounter with the piece: "the first thought that came to mind was that I was gazing not at a vase, but at a painting." The director was obviously swept off his feet by this masterpiece of Greek art—a terra cotta vessel painted with the scene of the *Dead Sarpedon Carried by Thanatos and Hypnos* and signed by both the potter and the painter. But why did Hoving diminish the significance of the potter's craft by essentially dismissing the pot as a mere support for an extraordinary painting? Danto suggests that Hoving's reaction is indicative of an artworld prejudice of sorts—one that attaches less importance to functional objects and decoration of any kind. He warns that "the painting [on the vase] is there to decorate an object of conspicuous utility" and cannot be considered without reference to the vase itself. In fact, doing so precludes any real understanding of the work in the historical and artistic context in which it was created.

What purpose does this esoteric argument have for us who, as students, are trying to understand art? Simply this: The distinction between fine art and functional object is linked to the historical and cultural context in which a work was created. As Danto pointed out, the Greek philosophers praised craftspersons as somewhere between artists and philosophers, but held the view that no one was lower than the artist. Danto paraphrases Plato in *The Republic*: "The carpenter knows how to fashion in real life what the painter can merely imitate; therefore . . . artists have no real knowledge at all, trafficking only in the outward appearance of things."[2] Over 2000 years later, a French philosopher would declare that "Only what serves no purpose is truly beautiful."[3]

Today, many painters are turning their talent to utilitarian objects or creating paintings with techniques traditional to craft. Ceramic artists are creating works of sculpture and sculptors are finding innovative ways to manipulate clay, wood, and metal. The glassmaker's art has reached new heights of experimentation, while employing centuries-old techniques. For many artists, the distinction between art and craft is an artificial and limiting one. Any and all options should be exercised in pursuit of artistic expression. And the aesthetic and artistic merit of any creative work ought to be recognized.

In this chapter we shall discuss a variety of media and categories of artistic expression. We shall consider the materials traditional to craft—clay, glass, fiber, metal, and wood—using historical and contemporary works as evidence of the broad technical and stylistic ranges of the media. We shall also examine different aspects of design—graphic design, clothing design, industrial, interior, and urban design. These have been included in this chapter because, in the area of design, the distinction between art for art's sake and art for utility's sake is sometimes also blurred.

CERAMICS

Ceramics refers to the art or process of making objects of baked clay. Ceramics includes many objects ranging from the familiar pots and bowls that comprise **pottery** to building bricks and the extremely hard tiles that protect the surface of the space shuttles from the intense heat of atmospheric reentry.

[1]Arthur C. Danto, "Fine Art and the Functional Object," *Glass,* No. 51, Spring 1993, pp. 24–29.

[2]Ibid.

[3]Théophile Gautier, Preface to his novel *Mademoiselle de Maupin,* 1835.

9–2 MARILYN LEVINE
JOHN'S JACKET (1981). CERAMIC, ZIPPER, AND METAL
FASTENERS. 36 × 23½ × 7″.
COURTESY OF THE ARTIST.

9–3 THE HANDS OF THE POTTER.
CONRAD KNOWLES FORMING A TRAY AND A BOWL FOR HIS
COLLECTION OF ARTFUL POTTERY.

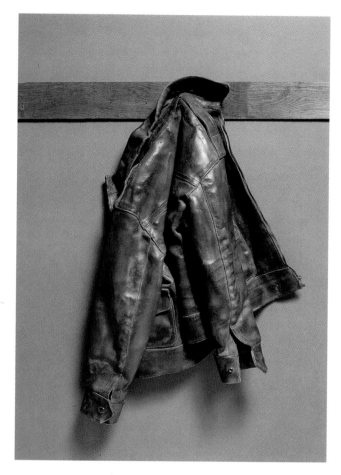

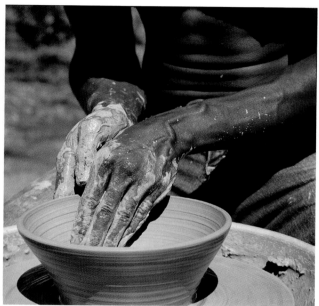

METHODS OF WORKING WITH CLAY

Ceramics is a venerable craft that was highly refined in the ancient lands of the Middle East and in China. For thousands of years people have modeled, pinched, and patted various types of wet clay into useful vessels and allowed them to dry or bake in the sun, creating hard, durable containers. They have rolled clay into rope shapes, which they coiled around an open space. They have rolled out slabs of clay like dough, cut them into pieces, fastened them together, and smoothed them with simple tools, as Native Americans still do today.

They discovered that if they allowed clay vessels to dry, then fired them in a type of oven called a **kiln,** or over coals, they became waterproof and yet more durable.

Marilyn Levine's mostly clay *John's Jacket* (Fig. 9–2) shows the whimsical use of materials that

sometimes defines the aesthetic of the craftsperson. In galleries we circle suspiciously around works such as these. We are drawn to test out our visual sensations by touching them, and perhaps we are simultaneously amused by and annoyed at the craftsperson who would push our senses to the limit. Perhaps we are also on the lookout for gallery employees who might frown on our using our hands to test what we sense with our eyes, and for fellow patrons who might doubt our intelligence or criticize our quest for tactile sensation. Ultimately the combination of the phony and the real shock the sense of touch. Levine's jacket is, in reality, composed of rolled-out slabs of clay that have the look of leather, while the work also contains stitching and real metal snaps and a zipper. The shifting back and forth between illusion and reality functions as a metaphor for what arts and crafts are all about: in so many instances they transform the world that they represent.

THE POTTER'S WHEEL

The potter's wheel (Fig. 9–3) was first used in the Middle East about 4000 BCE and seems to have come into common use a thousand years later. A pot can be **thrown** quite rapidly and effortlessly on a wheel once the techniques have been mastered, in contrast to the more laborious and time-consuming process of building a pot

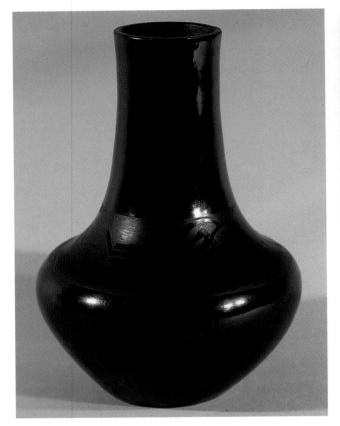

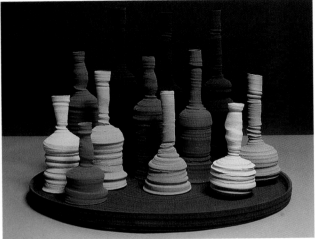

by **coiling.** In coiling, ropes of clay are fashioned, then stacked upon one another. The walls of the pot are then scraped to a smooth finish and molded to the desired vessel shape. The walls of a wheel-thrown pot tend to be thinner and more uniform in thickness than coiled pots, and the outer and inner surfaces smoother. This does not suggest, however, that coiled pots in the hands of some craftspersons do not approach a wheel-thrown pot in their accomplishment. For example, Native American tribes of the southwestern United States have never used the potter's wheel and yet their hand-built pots can be as thin-walled and symmetrical as their wheel-thrown counterparts. A wonderful example of coiling can be found in works by the famous Native American potter Martha Martinez. Her black-on-black vessels (Fig. 9–4), adorned with stylized natural forms, flowers, and animals are among the finest works of the Pueblo people.

Anyone who has been a student in a ceramics class appreciates the difficulty experienced in mastering the potter's wheel. The body movement, rhythm of the wheel, placement, and force of the fingers must come together like a smoothly choreographed dance. The goal, generally, is to achieve perfect symmetry and a smooth contour. How ironic, then, are the works of James Makins (Fig. 9–5), which, when seen alone, may look like the failed efforts of "frustrated student, Ceramics 101." These objects—vases? vessels? bottles?—are, in effect, records of variations in mental concentration, hand pressure, wheel speed, and glaze experimentation. Set on trays as they are, they suggest ritual or domestic objects, or to some, figures on a stage. The entire composition—incidentally, an exceptional example of variety within unity—appears foremost as a sculpture, probably because these bottles seem far from utilitarian.

GLAZING

Variation in color and texture is secured by the choice of clay and by **glazing.** The earliest known glaze dates from about 3000 BCE and is found on tile from the tomb of the Egyptian King Menes.

Glazes, which contain finely ground minerals, are used in liquid form. They are brushed, sprayed, or poured on ceramics after a preliminary **bisque firing** removes all water. During the second firing, the glaze

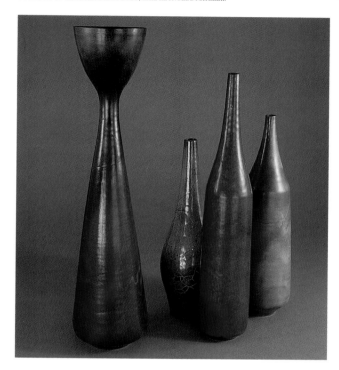

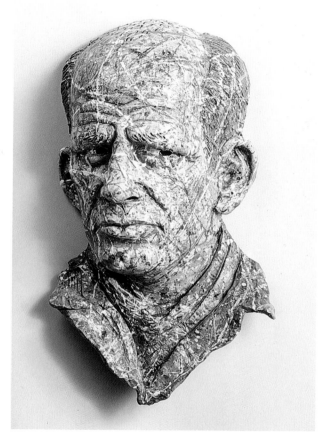

becomes glasslike, or **vitrifies,** fusing with the clay.
It gives the clay a glassy, nonporous surface coating
that can be shiny or dull, depending on its composition.
Glazing can create intricate, glossy patterns across
otherwise uniform and dull surfaces.

Contrast the simple, pure forms of the vases by
Gertrud and Otto Natzler (Fig. 9–6) with the unrefined
forms of James Makins. The deep but mellow glazes of
the Natzler pieces are modulated by light to impart a
glowing intensity, in contrast to the opaque and un-
modulated glazes of Makins. In both groups, the glazes
complement the potters' techniques. The graceful
contours of the Natzler vases would lose their sensuality and delicacy with the bold colors and matte finish
of the Makins piece, and the spontaneity, brusqueness,
and uniqueness of those lilting bottles would be lost if
they were to be enshrouded in a uniform, pearlescent
glaze.

Robert Arneson's *Jackson Pollock* (Fig. 9–7) provides a very different example of a glazed ceramic
work and illustrates how blurred the line between

craft and fine art can be. Arneson's figures are purposefully unrefined, intentionally flawed, mirroring
the ceramic artist's view of human nature as imperfect.
The subject of the work, Jackson Pollock, was an
Abstract Expressionist who became renowned for his
drip paintings (see Chapter 17). Arneson's clay portrait unifies the artist and his works by providing the
illusion of overall dripping and splattering on the bust.

TYPES OF CERAMICS

Ceramic objects and **wares** are classified according to
the type of clay and the temperature at which they are
fired.

Earthenware derives its name from the fact that
it is usually red or tan in color. It is made from coarse
clay or shale clay and is usually fired at 1,000 to 2,000
degrees Fahrenheit. It is somewhat porous and is used

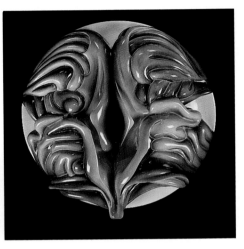

9–8 MANGBETU PORTRAIT BOTTLE (ZAIRE, 19TH–20TH
CENTURIES). TERRA COTTA. HEIGHT: 11⅜".

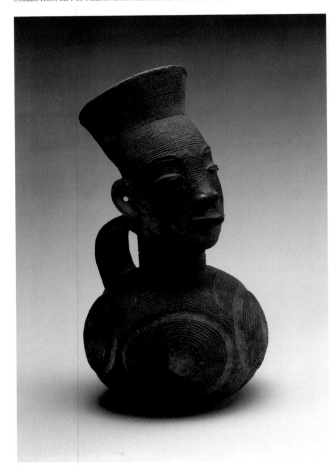

for common bricks and coarse pottery. The Mangbetu
bottle from Zaire (Fig. 9–8) is made from **terra-cotta,**
a heavy clay earthenware product fired at a higher
temperature of about 2,070 to 2,320 degrees F. The head
is an effigy or portrait of a Mangbetu citizen. Note that
the textural decoration is reminiscent of a basket weave.
It was probably fired in the open, on a bed of straw and
twigs.

Stoneware is usually gray but may be tan or reddish. It is fired at from about 2,300 to 2,700 degrees F.
It is slightly porous or fully nonporous and is used for
most dinnerware and much ceramic sculpture.

Porcelain is hard, nonporous, and usually white or
gray in color. It is made from fine, white kaolin clay and
contains other minerals such as feldspar, quartz, and
flint in various proportions. It is usually fired at 2,400 to
2,500 degrees F., and it is used for fine dinnerware.
Chinese porcelain, or **china,** is white and fired at low
porcelain temperatures. It is glasslike or *vitreous,* nonporous, and may be translucent. It makes a characteristic ringing sound when struck with a fingernail. Porcelain
has been used by various cultures for vases and dinnerware for thousands of years. Like other kinds of wares,
it has also provided a vehicle for artistic expression.

The thirty-nine porcelain plates from Judy Chicago's
The Dinner Party have quite a different look. Chicago's
feminist work consists of a table in the shape of an
equilateral triangle with thirteen place settings along
each 48-foot-long side. Each setting symbolizes the life

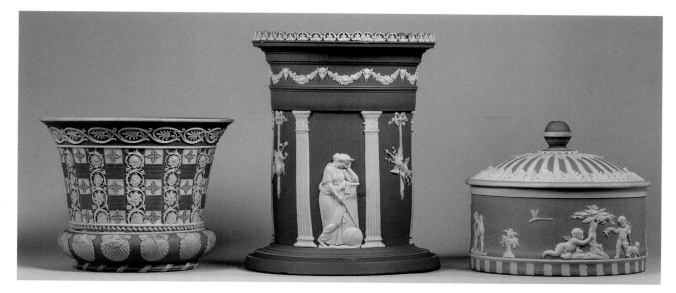

9–10 JOSIAH WEDGWOOD
FLOWERPOT, VASE, AND BOX WITH COVER (C. 1780–1800).
COURTESY OF THE METROPOLITAN MUSEUM OF ART, N.Y., ROGERS FUND, 1909 (09.194.7–.9).

and achievements of a great woman, such as Queen Elizabeth I, suffragette Susan B. Anthony, poet Emily Dickinson, and American artist Georgia O'Keeffe (Fig. 9–9). The equilateral triangle symbolizes equality, and the patterns on the plates are frequently suggestive of female genitalia. O'Keeffe's plate exudes an organic power and permanence, inspired by botany and by O'Keeffe's own work. Many of Georgia O'Keeffe's gigantic paintings of flowers, such as the one shown in Figure 16–17, are also often reminiscent of female sex organs.

Jasper, or jasperware, is a type of porcelain developed by the Englishman Josiah Wedgwood in the second half of the eighteenth century. It is characterized by a dull surface, usually in green or blue, and white raised designs (Fig. 9–10). The raised patterns usually show Greek themes or draped figures in graceful robes.

Because of its expense, families are more likely to buy a few pieces of Wedgwood for decoration than they are to buy sets for table use. Most tableware is mass-produced, machine-made stoneware or porcelain. Much is relatively plain and unadorned or has simple lines that accent the shapes of the pieces. Other tableware in daily use has printed designs that range from users' first names to landscapes to animals and Pop art types

of images. Tableware varies widely in price and aesthetic value.

One of the fascinating features of clay is its versatility. Clay can be used to form the refined vessels of the Natzlers and the crude, slablike structures of both primitive and contemporary workers. It is said that one test of the integrity of a work is its trueness to its material. In the case of ceramics, however, one would be hard pressed to point to any one of the products of clay as representative of its "true" face.

GLASS

Glass, like ceramics, has had a long history and has been used to create fine art and functional objects. The Roman historian Pliny the Elder traced the beginnings of glassmaking (albeit accidental) to an account of Phoenician sailors preparing a meal on a beach. They set their pots on lumps of *natron*—an alkali they had on deck to embalm the dead—lit a fire and, when the hot natron mixed with the sand of the beach, molten glass flowed. In fact, glass predates the Phoenicians and the Romans and the tale as recounted by Pliny probably has some gaps. But the truth is that the recipe for glass is

9–11 HEAD OF AMENHOTEP II.
EGYPTIAN, NEW KINGDOM, 18TH DYNASTY (C. 1400 BCE).
BRIGHT BLUE GLASS COVERED WITH TAN WEATHERING; CAST.
HEIGHT 1⁹⁄₁₆″ (4 CM).
THE CORNING MUSEUM OF GLASS.

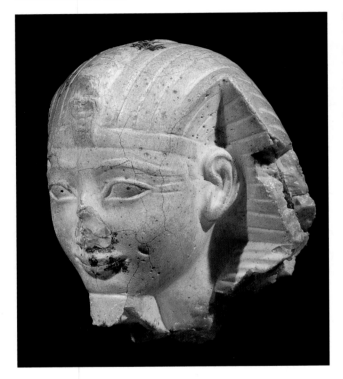

fine filaments. It can be woven into yarn for textiles, used in woolly masses for insulation, and pressed and molded into a plastic material that is tough enough to be used for the body of an automobile. About 4,000 years ago the Egyptians modeled small bottles and jars from molten glass. Contemporary machine-made glassware is usually pressed. Molten glass is poured into molds and then forced into shape by a plunger. The plate glass that is used for windows and mirrors is made by passing rollers over molten glass as it cools.

The earliest glass works come from Mesopotamia and date as far back as 2500 BCE. They consist mostly of beads and small objects, but more sophisticated works of glass also have an ancient history. The glass head of an Egyptian king (Fig. 9–11), for example, was probably cast in a mold some 3,400 years ago. It is quite small—under two inches high—and was no doubt part of a complete figure. Though the detail of this fragment is remarkably preserved, the color of the glass has faded from what is thought to have been a bright blue.

The head of Amenhotep was cast in a mold, an early form of glassmaking. While this technique continued to be used, some one thousand years later other methods were pioneered. Hot glass was shaped around a core of clay and dung, for example, to create objects that could hold liquids and ointments. At this time, as we can imagine, glass was not commonplace; it was available only to the privileged classes.

Just as the potter's wheel transformed the making of clay vessels both in terms of quality and quantity, so did the technique of **glass blowing** change the nature of glass production. This technique was developed by the Romans (Fig. 9–12) who created pieces of all shapes, sizes, colors, and functions, making glass containers commonplace. In this method, a hollow tube or blowpipe is dipped into molten glass and then removed. Air is blown through the tube, causing the hot glass to form a spherical bubble (Fig. 9–13) whose contours are shaped through rolling and pulling with various tools. The process is usually quite rapid, but the glass can be reheated if it must be worked extensively.

Once the desired shape has been achieved, the surface of glass can be decorated by cutting or **engraving** planes that reflect light in certain patterns, by etching, or by printing.

quite simple; as researchers[4] have found in trying to replay the sailor's experience, it could happen! The result may not have been that wondrous substance— transparent or translucent—that has the power to transform light into an ephemeral, jewel-like palette. But it was surely glass.

TECHNIQUES OF WORKING GLASS

Glass is generally made from molten sand, or **silica,** mixed with minerals such as lead, copper, cobalt, cadmium, lime, soda, or potash. Certain combinations of minerals afford the glass a rich quality as found in the stained-glass windows of the great cathedrals and in the more recent stained-glass works of Henri Matisse and Marc Chagall.

Like ceramics, glass is versatile. Molten glass can be modeled, pressed, rolled, blown, and even spun into threads. **Fiberglass** is glass that has been spun into

[4]William S. Ellis, "Glass: Capturing the Dance of Light," *National Geographic,* Vol. 184, No. 6, December 1993, pp. 37–69.

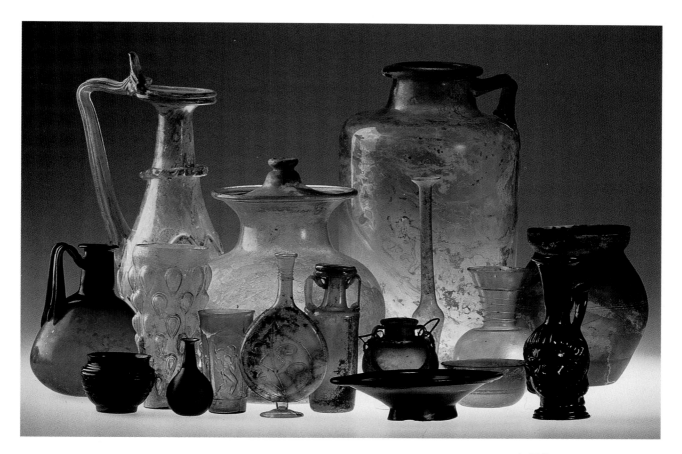

9–12 ROMAN GLASSWARE
(MOSTLY 1ST–4TH
CENTURIES).
THE CORNING MUSEUM OF GLASS.

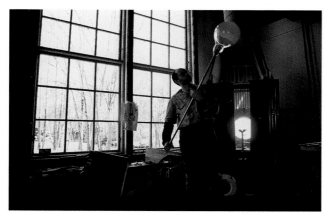

9–13 GLASS-BLOWING.
MASTER GLASS BLOWER
JAN-ERIK RIZMAN IN
HIS STUDIO.

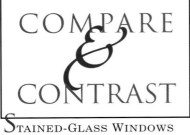

COMPARE & CONTRAST

In the early twelfth century, a man named Abbot Suger equated the filtered, colored light pouring through stained-glass windows with the divine presence. From that point forward, it can be argued that no art form was more significant to Christian art and architecture than stained glass. The art form reached its height during the Gothic era when, because of advanced techniques in building, large areas of wall could be given over to glass. From the beginnings in the choir of St. Denis to the ultimate realization in the apse of St. Chappelle, the result was mystical and mesmerizing. Stained-glass windows not only flood solid stone cathedrals with light; they also illuminate the great narratives of Christian belief and offer historical insights into daily Medieval life.

The *Tree of Jesse* (genealogy of Christ) (Fig. 9–14) is one of a series of windows in the west facade wall of Chartres Cathedral. This majestic window, like the others, consists of hundreds of pieces of tinted glass that are bound together by strips of lead. The fine details, such as the hair, eyes, and folds of drapery, were painted or drawn on the glass surfaces.

Matisse's contemporary stained-glass windows for the Chapel of the Rosary of the Dominican Nuns (Fig. 9–15) are assembled in much the same way as the Gothic windows, but lightness and gaiety are accomplished through juxtaposition of broad areas of pure tone. In this way, the colors achieve maximum intensity and create form rather than decorate form.

Which of the stained-glass windows do you believe is likely to lend a more spiritual experience? Why?

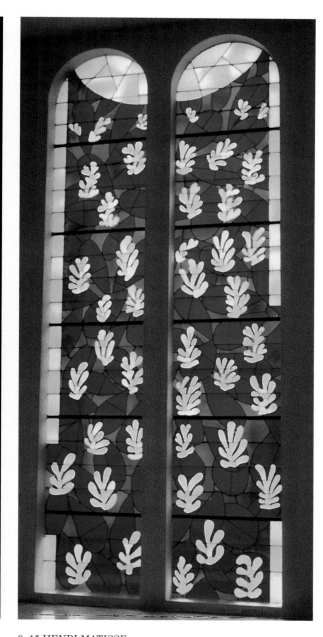

9–14 *Tree of Jesse.*
Stained-glass window,
Chartres Cathedral,
west facade (13th
century).

9–15 Henri Matisse
Stained-glass windows,
Chapel of the Rosary of
the Dominican Nuns,
Vence, France (c. 1951).

9–16 PORTLAND VASE (ROMAN, 3RD CENTURY).
CAMEO-CUT GLASS.
BRITISH MUSEUM, LONDON.

9–17 LOUIS COMFORT TIFFANY
SIX PIECES OF GLASSWARE IN ART NOUVEAU STYLE MADE BY
THE TIFFANY STUDIOS. GLASS, FAVRILE. LEFT TO RIGHT:
8 9/16″ HIGH; 18 11/15″ HIGH; 7 5/8″ HIGH; 16 1/4″ HIGH; 4 1/2″ HIGH.
THE METROPOLITAN MUSEUM OF ART, N.Y. (96.17.42; 51.121.9; 51.121.17–.18; 55.213.22; 55.213.28).

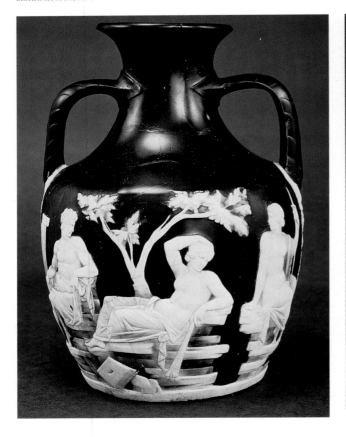

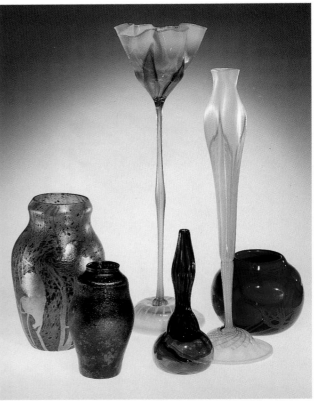

EXAMPLES OF GLASSWARE

One of the earliest and best-known pieces of glassware is the Roman Portland Vase (Fig. 9–16), which survives from the third century CE. The refinement of the piece testifies to the long tradition of glassmaking in Rome even before that time. The Portland Vase was created in three steps. The underlying form was blown from dark-blue glass. Next a coating of semi-opaque white glass was added to the surface of the basic blue form. Finally, the white glass was carved away to provide the bas-relief of figures and vegetation that circumscribe the vase. The relief consists of many subtle gradations. Where it is thinnest, the blue from beneath shows through to provide a shaded quality. Imagine the patience of the cameo cutter who meticulously chipped glass away from glass, leaving unscratched the brittle blue surface that serves as background for the figures.

In various eras, different world centers became renowned for glassmaking. For example, during the Middle Ages, Venetian glass became known for its lightness and delicacy.

Eighteenth-century Stiegel glass, made in Pennsylvania, became known for its use of flint (lead oxide) to achieve hardness and brightness. So-called **flint glass** is used for lenses of optical instruments and for crystal. Nineteenth-century Sandwich glass—from the town of Sandwich, Massachusetts—was pressed into molds to take on the appearance of a cut pattern. Ornamental Sandwich glass pieces in the shapes of cats, dogs, hens, and ducks became common home decorations.

During the second half of the nineteenth century, Louis Comfort Tiffany designed some of the most handsome **Art Nouveau** interiors. His glassware (Fig. 9–17) attains a similar marriage of simplicity and exotic refinement. Graceful botanical forms swell and become attenuated. The translucent or iridescent glass is decorated by spiral shapes, swirling lines, and floating forms that seem naturally to grow out of the glassblowing

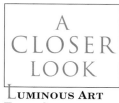
It's not the subway station to heaven, but the Matissean blues of the stained-glass triptych recently installed at a station in the Bronx may make many commuters think they've entered one.

"When I saw it at the station, I thought of an explosion of jazz," said Benoit Gilsoul, who with Helmut Schardt transformed a maquette by the late Romare Bearden into an artwork as luminous and calming as the sunlit windows of a church.

The work, *City of Light* (Fig. 9–18), is at the elevated IRT station for the No. 6 train, at East Tremont Avenue and Williamsbridge Road. It was commissioned by the Metropolitan Transportation Authority through its Arts for Transit program.

City of Light, illuminated by both the sun and artificial lighting, depicts an image of a city, including a skyline and a subway. But unlike its real counterpart, the tiny train in the work seems to travel quietly through the blue metropolis.

Bearden, who died in 1988 at 75, painted images of life in Harlem and rural America. He also lived in Paris in the jazz-heady Latin Quarter.

The 9-by-6-foot work, made of heavy glass from West Virginia, cost $45,000 to fabricate.

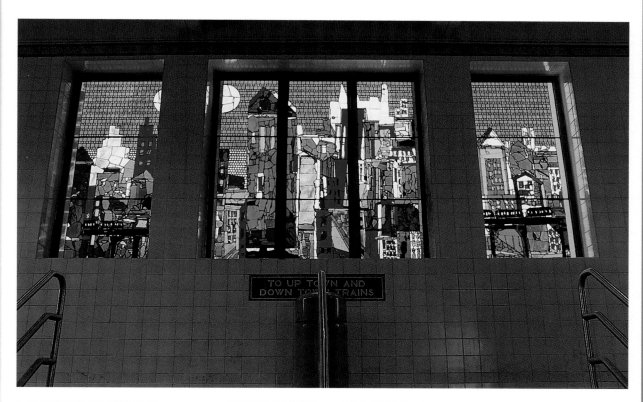

9–18 ROMARE BEARDEN. FABRICATED BY BENOIT GILSOUL AND HELMUT SCHARDT.
CITY OF LIGHT (1994). STAINED-GLASS TRIPTYCH. 9′6″ × 20′.

INSTALLED WESTCHESTER SQUARE SUBWAY STATION, BRONX, N.Y. COMMISSIONED BY METROPOLITAN
TRANSPORTATION AUTHORITY/ARTS FOR TRANSIT AND OWNED BY MTA N.Y.C. TRANSIT.

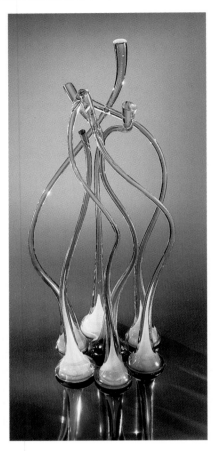

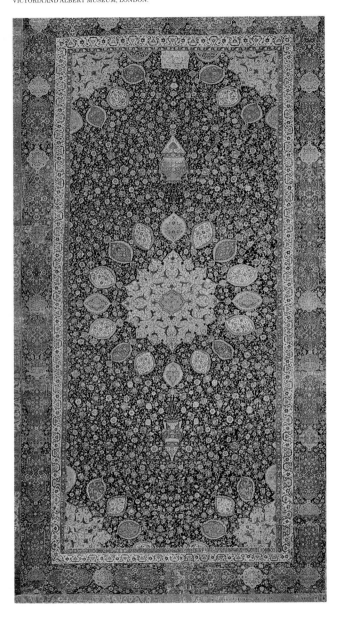

process. They keep faith with the Art Nouveau creed that decoration should be a natural expression of the manufacturing process. Tiffany also fashioned many fine candlesticks, lamps, and lighting fixtures from bronze showing the same botanical whimsy he expressed in his glassware.

Harvey K. Littleton's contemporary *Implied Movement* (Fig. 9–19), like Tiffany's glassware, shows bulbous organic forms that become attenuated toward the tips. Littleton's work, moreover, could be either botanical or zoological, depending perhaps on whether the viewer perceives the "implied movement" to stem from fluctuations in air or under water, or from the movement of abstract limbs. Also, whereas Tiffany's works, despite our reluctance to "use" them, do function as vessels, Littleton's graceful forms speak more of art for art's sake.

FIBER ARTS

Fibers are slender, threadlike structures that are derived from animals (for example, wool or silk), vegetable (cotton or linen), or synthetic (rayon, nylon, or fiberglass) sources. The fiber arts refer to a number of disciplines in which fibers are combined to make

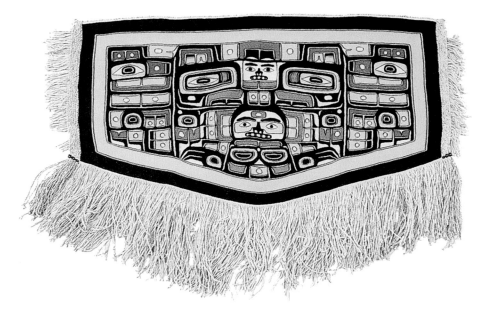

functional or decorative objects or works of art. They include, but are not limited to, weaving, embroidery, crochet, and macrame.

WEAVING

Weaving was known to the Egyptians, who placed patterned fabrics before the thrones of the pharaohs 5,000 years ago. Only royalty could tread on certain fabrics. According to ancient Greek legend, King Agamemnon showed excessive pride by walking upon purple fabrics that were intended for the gods.

The **weaving** of fabric or cloth is accomplished by interfacing horizontal and vertical threads. The lengthwise fibers are called the **warp,** and the crosswise threads are called the **weft** or **woof.** The material and type of weave determine the weight and quality of the cloth. Wool, for example, makes soft, resilient cloth that is easy to dye. Nylon is strong, more durable than wool, moth-proof, resistant to mildew and mold, nonallergenic, and easy to dye.

There are a number of types of weaves. The **plain weave** found in burlap, muslin, and cotton broadcloth is the strongest and simplest: the woof thread passes above one warp fiber and beneath the next. In the **satin weave,** woof threads pass above and beneath several warp threads. Warp and woof form broken diagonal patterns

in the **twill weave. In pile weaving,** which is found in carpeting and in velvet, loops or knots are tied; when the knotting is done, the ends are cut or sheared to create an even surface. In sixteenth-century Persia, where carpet weaving reached an artistic peak, pile patterns often had as many as 1,000 knots to the square inch.

The Persian rug shown in Figure 9–20 was woven in the seventeenth century. Like others of its kind, it portrays the old Islamic concept of Paradise as a garden. Here a light-colored tree and an assortment of other plants grow on a claret red background. The date palm, the iris, a symbolic tree of life, hyacinths, and tulips were frequently depicted on such rugs.

Weaving is typically carried out by the hand **loom** or a power loom, although some weavings, like the Alaskan Chilkat blanket (Fig. 9–21), were woven by Native American women without benefit of a loom. Chilkat women achieved a very fine texture with a thread made from a core of a strand of cedar bark covered with the wool from a mountain goat. Clan members used blankets such as these on important occasions to show off the family crest. Here a strikingly patterned animal occupies the center of a field of eyes, heads, and mysterious symbols.

Traditional weaving techniques may surface in innovative ways in the hands of contemporary artists.

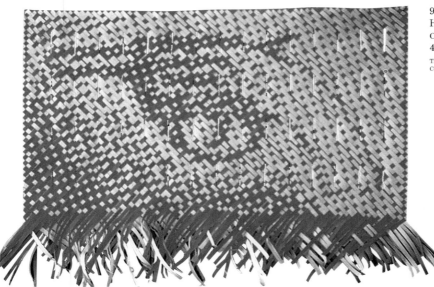

9–22 ED ROSSBACH
HANDGUN (1975). PLAITED
CONSTRUCTION PAPER.
40 × 54".

THE COLLECTION OF CRAFT ALLIANCE.
COURTESY OF THE ARTIST.

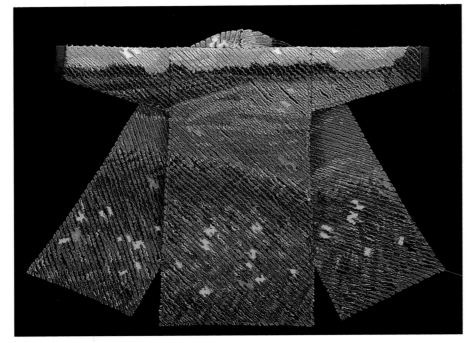

9–23 TIM HARDING
COAT (1987). DYED, LAYERED,
QUILTED, SLASHED AND
FRAYED COTTONS.
54 × 70 × 3".

COURTESY OF JULIE ARTISAN'S GALLERY,
N.Y. AND THE ARTIST.

Ed Rossbach's wall hanging (Fig. 9–22) which, in overall shape, is not unlike the Chilkat blanket, is worlds apart in its choice of materials and its strong political message. Rossbach plaits construction paper in such a manner that his image emerges subtly from an overall mottled background.

A tightly woven tapestry of the quality of the Unicorn Tapestries (see Fig. 1–5) could take years to complete on a hand loom. Medieval weavers worked from patterns called "cartoons," such as those used in fresco painting (see p. 85). Cartoons were as large as the final product and enabled the weaver to incorporate hundreds of colors into intricate scenes. The first power looms were adapted

to carpet weaving in England and France in the late 1830s, and the textile industry experienced rapid growth throughout Europe and America soon afterward. It is the power loom that has placed wall-to-wall pile carpeting within the reach of the middle class.

APPLYING DESIGNS TO FABRICS

The surfaces of fabrics can be enhanced by printing, embroidery, tie-dyeing, or batik. Hand printing has been known since ancient times, and Oriental traders brought the practice to Europe. A design was stamped on a fabric with a carved wooden block that had been inked. Contemporary machine printing uses inked

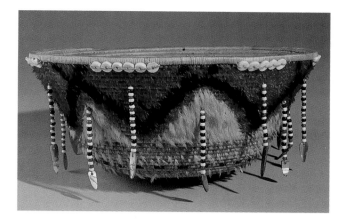

rollers in the place of blocks, and fabrics can be printed at astonishingly rapid rates. In **embroidery,** the design is made by needlework.

Tie-dyeing and batik both involve dyeing fabrics. In **tie-dyeing,** designs are created by sewing or tying folds in the cloth to prevent the dye from coloring certain sections of fabric. In **batik,** applications of wax prevent the dye from coloring sections of fabric that are to be kept light-colored or white. A series of dye baths and waxings can be used to create subtly deeper colors.

Tim Harding's textile works, such as *Coat* (Fig. 9–23), consist of many layers of hand-dyed cotton cloth that have been quilted or sewn together. He then slashes through one or more of the quilted sections with a knife, revealing the colors of dyed cloth beneath the surface. After the garment is washed, the edges of these slashed lines fray or curl back so that the underlayers are revealed. The result is a highly textured textile relief that is at once crisp and weathered in appearance. Harding's garments range from shimmery waves of color with subtle variations of tone to intricate landscape designs with a strong suggestion of topographical variations.

OTHER FIBER ARTS

There are a number of other fiber arts, including but not limited to basketry and stitchery or embroidery.

In *basketry,* or basket weaving, fibers are also woven together in various patterns. The delightful Pomo gift basket (Fig. 9–24) was woven from grass and glass beads. Triangles of warm primary red leap out from a backdrop of cool primary blue and pale straw. These Native Americans from California made extremely fine basketry, with as many as sixty stitches to the inch. Barks, roots, and other fibers supplemented grass, and precious feathers and shells were sometimes employed in the design.

Needlework is practiced here and there today, but during the nineteenth century American women embroidered many pillows, **samplers,** and furniture covers. A few women stitched ambitious artistic works.

Joan Livingstone creates fiber sculptures from resin-impregnated sewn felt. They are at once abstract and organic, reminiscent of fruits, pods (Fig. 9–25), or flaring blossoms. She assembles her sculptures from pieces of industrial felt, which—when soaked by resins—give the smooth sculptural surfaces the character of animal hide. Livingstone's work is another example of craft techniques used in the service of fine art.

METALWORK AND JEWELRY

The refining and working of metals has been known for thousands of years. Iron and its alloys have been used to fashion horseshoes and arrowheads and, more recently (see Chapter 7), the skeletons of skyscrapers. **Stainless steel** is used in kitchen utensils and furniture. Lightweight aluminum is used in cookware and in aircraft. Bronze is the favorite metal of sculptors. **Brass** is seen everywhere from andirons to candlesticks to beds.

Silver and gold have been prized for millennia for their rarity and their appealing colors and textures. They are used in jewelry, fine tableware, ritual vessels, and sacred objects. In jewelry these precious metals often serve as settings for equally precious gems or polished stones, or their surfaces can be **enameled** by melting powdered glass on them. These metals even find use as currency; in times of political chaos, gold and

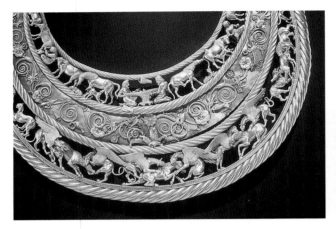

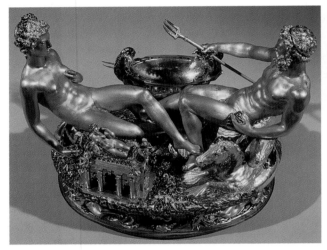

9–27 BENVENUTO CELLINI
SALTCELLAR OF FRANCIS I (1539–43). GOLD AND ENAMEL.
10⅛″ HIGH; 13¹⁄₁₆″ LONG.
KUNSTHISTORISCHES MUSEUM, VIENNA.

9–28 JOHN CONEY
MONTEITH BOWL (C. 1700–10). SILVER. 10¾″ HIGH.
YALE UNIVERSITY ART GALLERY, NEW HAVEN, CONN. MABEL BRADY GARVAN COLLECTION.

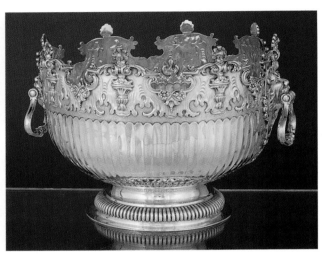

silver are sought even as the value of paper money
drops off to nothing. Threads of gold and silver find
their way onto precious china and into the garments
and vestments of clergy and kings. Gold leaf adorns
books, paintings, and picture frames.

Metals can be hammered into shape, **embossed**
with raised designs, and cast according to procedures
described for bronze in Chapter 6. Each form of working
metal has its own tradition and its advantages and
disadvantages.

Some of the finest gold jewelry was wrought by
ancient Greek goldsmiths. The pectoral piece shown in
Figure 9–26 was meant to be worn across the breast of
some nomadic chieftain from southern Russia, and,
probably, buried with him. Fortunately, it was not.
People and animals are depicted with a realism that
renders the fanciful **griffins** in the lower register as

believable as the horses, dogs, and grasshoppers found
elsewhere in the piece. The figures are balanced by the
refined scrollwork in the central register, and all are
contained by the magnificent coils.

The Renaissance sculptor and goldsmith Benvenuto
Cellini created a gold and enamel saltcellar (Fig. 9–27)
for the French King Francis I that shows the refinement
of his art. Its allegorical significance is merely an excuse
for displaying the skill of Cellini's craft. Salt, drawn
from the sea, is housed in a boat-shaped salt container
and watched over by a figure of Neptune. The pepper,
drawn from the earth, is contained in a miniature
triumphal arch and guarded by a female personification
of Earth. Figures on the base represent the seasons and
the segments of the day—all on a piece 13 inches long.
Unfortunately, the saltcellar is Cellini's sole major work
in gold that survives.

The large silver punch bowl shown in Figure 9–28,
like the Cellini saltcellar, is an emblem of the conspicuous
consumption of the very wealthy. It may represent the
most embellished work of Boston silversmith John Coney.
The **gadrooning** of the base balances the **fluting** of the
swelling upper body. The elaborate **corbels** of the rim
are decorated with intricate patterns of leaves and
flowers and balanced by swiveling handles that are
attached to the bowl at lions' heads with open mouths.
Wine glasses and ladles can be hung from the notched
rim and chilled by the ice water inside.

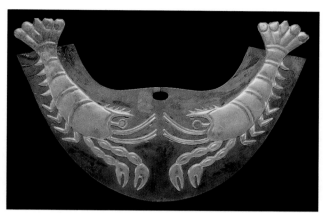

9–29 RACHELLE THIEWES
EAR WRAPPINGS, SILVER (1981).
COURTESY ADAIR MARGO GALLERY, EL PASO, TEXAS.

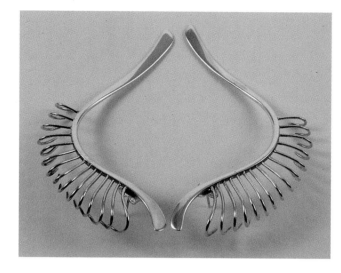

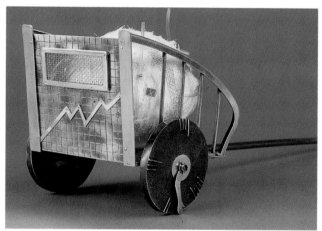

9–31 KIFF SLEMMONS
TRANSPORT (1990). STERLING SILVER, ALUMINUM, GAUZE, MESH,
TAPE, TUBING, PEARLS. 5 × 14 × 4½".
COURTESY OF THE ARTIST. PHOTO BY ROD SLEMMONS.

Few Americans have owned elaborate punch bowls
of precious metal, but American homes have been the
settings for ornate and sometimes whimsical work
wrought from more common metals. Doorknobs, handles, bolts and locks, key plates, andirons, stair rails,
gates, and fences have all received embellishment.
Weather vanes have been enhanced with fish and fowl,
animals, and the initials of the owner.

Jewelry usually serves decorative functions, and
finger rings can also offer information about the
wearer's marital status or alma mater. Bracelets may
carry "charms" that commemorate special occasions.
Rachel Thiewes's contemporary jewelry is fabricated
from wire or sheets of metal with traditional metal-
smithing techniques like soldering, forming, and fitting.
Her lyrical ear wrappings (Fig. 9–29), made from silver
and gold, have an organic quality, as of ribs arching
away from a curved spinal cord. The "spines" follow the
outer edges of the ears while the "ribs" embrace the
upper lobe.

Body ornament, ever-growing in popularity to this
day, spans history and geography. Consider the nose
ornament from Peru in Figure 9–30. It seems a more
literal representation of Thiewes's arachnidlike abstractions. The piece is fashioned of gold, silver, and turquoise
inlay, and is a characteristic example of the ancient
Peruvian facility in handling complex metal techniques.
Much of the jewelry available for us to see today has

been unearthed from tombs of the very wealthy among
Peruvian society. The images and their symbolism
remain mostly undeciphered, but archaeologists have
nonetheless constructed a view of these people from
such artifacts.

We close our section on metalwork with a miniature
sculpture that again bridges the supposed gulf between
fine art and the functional object. Kiff Slemmons's
Transport (Fig. 9–31) was constructed for the *Artworks
for AIDS* exhibition that was held in Seattle in 1990. It
is a miniature two-wheeled cart that refers to the history of mass deaths. Throughout the ages, such carts
have been used in cities to truck away the victims of
epidemics. The wheels of the cart are clocks with human
hands, seeming to tick away as the number of deaths
due to AIDS mounts. Hospital waste and a stylized
"progress" chart with an alarming indicator of the rising
toll of the epidemic complete the political message.

9–32 MELVYN FIRMAGER
UNTITLED (1993, DESTROYED IN 1994 LOS ANGELES
EARTHQUAKE). EUCALYPTUS GUNNII. 13½″ HIGH, 8″ IN
DIAMETER.
PHOTO COURTESY DEL MANO GALLERY, LOS ANGELES.

9–33 MICHELLE HOLZAPFEL
OAK LEAF VASE (1991). MAPLE BURL, TURNED AND CARVED.
14 × 10 × 10″.
COURTESY PETER JOSEPH GALLERY, N.Y.

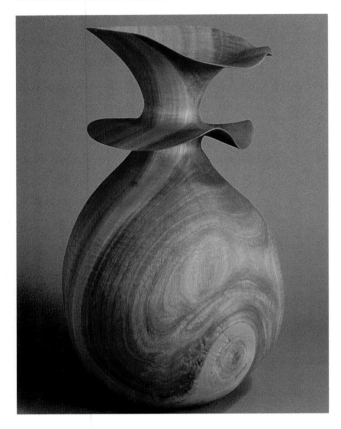

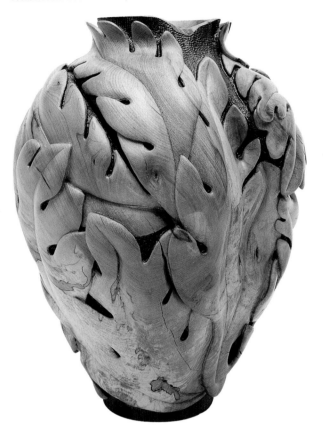

WOOD

Some relatively sophisticated technology is require to
convert glass, metal, and clay into something of use.
Wood, however, has only to be cut and carved to form a
functional object.

　　Three wood vases hint at the versatility of the
medium. The soft, flowing contours of Melvyn Firmager's
vase (Fig. 9–32) highlight the swirling grain patterns of
the wood, which almost take on the character of glazing
on a ceramic vase. Michelle Holzapfel's *Oak Leaf Vase*
(Fig. 9–33) is a combination of turned and carved maple
burl. Her vase is barely hollow. It is not about containing space. Rather it is intended as a sculpture of a vessel than a vessel itself.[6] The simple roundness, highly
polished surface, and inherent grain patterns in David
Ellsworth's vase (Fig. 9–34) create the illusion of stone.

[6]Deborah Krasner, "Michelle Holzapfel: Sacred Elements of Domestic Ritual,"
American Craft, June/July 1993, pp. 48–50.

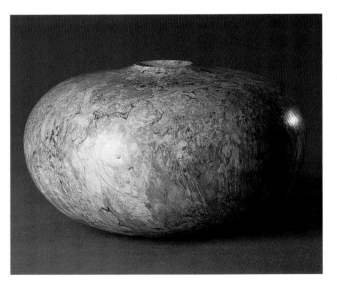

9–34 DAVID ELLSWORTH
VESSEL (1992). NORWAY MAPLE BURL. 4″ HIGH × 7″ DIAMETER.
COURTESY OF THE ARTIST.

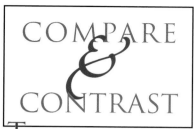

COMPARE & CONTRAST

The Chippendale
Card Table
with
The Osgood Shell Desk

Some of the most intricate examples of woodworking are to be found in the annals of furniture history. From meticulous carving to complex patterns of inlaid woods, these functional objects have graced palaces, mansions, and, today, museums.

One of the most famous examples of English and American furniture style is the Chippendale (Fig. 9–35) of the Middle Georgian period (1750–1770). This card table was commissioned by a Philadelphia merchant in 1759. Upon his death it was valued at 50 cents, but in the 1990s was put up for auction at Sotheby's with an estimated value of $1 million. The contemporary elliptical shell desk by Jere Osgood (Fig. 9–36) is very different in conception. The "ornamentation" of the piece is derived from featuring the highly polished wood grain rather than elaborate carving. Whether this piece will be valued at $1 million 200 years from now is an open question. However, one thing is certain: today it sells for more than 50 cents.

Which piece of furniture is more appealing to the eye? Why? Which would you prefer to touch, to run your hands over? Why?

9–35 GARVAN CARVER
CHIPPENDALE CARD TABLE (1759).
CARVED FROM MAHOGANY, WITH
BRASS.
COURTESY, THE CHIPSTONE FOUNDATION; PHOTO: GAVIN ASHWORTH.

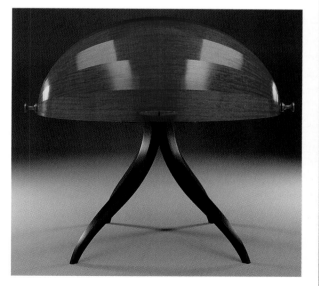

9–36 JERE OSGOOD
ELLIPTICAL SHELL DESK (1993).
BUBINGA, WENGE, BIRD'S-EYE
MAPLE, LEATHER.
48¼" HIGH × 53½" WIDE × 38½" DEEP.
COURTESY OF PRITAM & EAMES, EAST HAMPTON, N.Y.

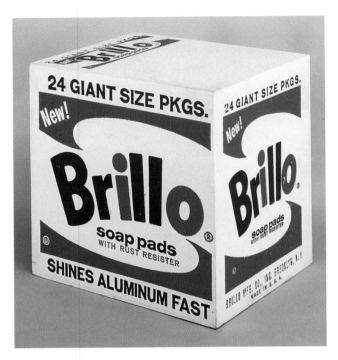

9–37 ANDY WARHOL
BRILLO (1964). SILKSCREEN INK ON WOOD. 17 × 17 × 13″.
© 1995 THE ANDY WARHOL FOUNDATION FOR THE VISUAL ARTS/ARTISTS RIGHTS SOCIETY (ARS), N.Y.

DESIGN

> *Successful designs . . . stand out because . . .*
> *they raise the human spirit and make life a*
> *little easier.*
> —Wolf Von Eckardt

In this section we will discuss the design disciplines that raise the quality of life. They touch us in every advertisement we see, everything we wear, every product we use, every interior in which we live, work, and play, and every town and city.

GRAPHIC DESIGN

Graphic design refers to visual arts in which designs or patterns are made for commercial purposes. Examples of graphic design include postage stamps, greeting cards, book designs, advertising brochures, newspaper and magazine ads, billboards, product packages, posters, signs, trademarks, and **logos.** Frequently, graphic products include written copy that is set in type. **Typography** refers to the related art or process of setting and arranging type for printing. Once graphic products, including type, have been designed, they are usually mass produced by one of the types of printing discussed in Chapter 5, through use of blocks, plates, or screens.

PACKAGE DESIGN   The packaging of products is a delicate affair. Not only must packages catch consumers' eyes as they wander down the aisles of supermarkets, they must also communicate something about the nature and quality of the contents. Manufacturers must state their case quickly, for people may glance at their packages for only a fraction of a second. In order to achieve this end, some packages have simple contemporary designs. Others hark back to "the old days."

The familiarity of many product packages has provided a fertile inspiration for **Pop art.** Much of the work of Andy Warhol and other Pop artists depicts the designs of these packages. Warhol is perhaps best known for his series of silkscreens of Campbell's Soup cans (Fig. 5–17), but he has also produced multiple images of Coca-Cola bottles (Fig. 17–15) and oversized assemblages of Brillo boxes made from acrylic silkscreen on wood (Fig. 9–37). Manufacturers use the same silkscreen process for printing many of their packages.

POSTERS

Posters are relatively large printed sheets of paper, usually illustrated, that publicize or advertise products or events. Posters from art galleries frequently show a single work of art from a current exhibition and contain some explanatory copy. Since they are usually attractive and inexpensive, college students tend to use them for wall decorations.

Jules Cheret's poster art was intended to advertise the shows at the Parisian Folies Bergères and other establishments. As is suggested in his color lithograph poster of Loïe Fuller (Fig. 9–38), Cheret's poster art

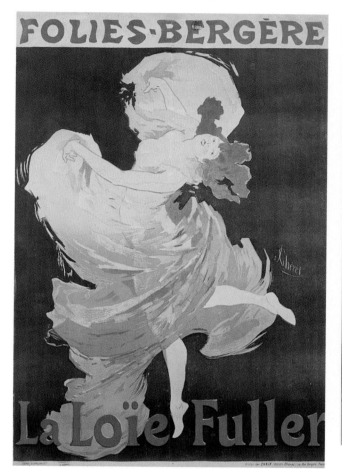

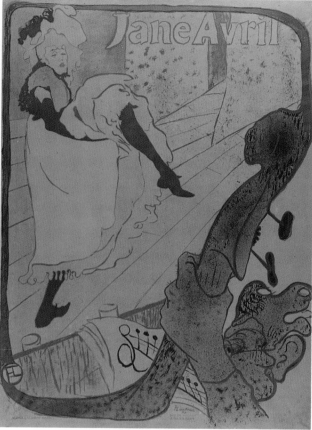

came to do more than gather audiences; it also contributed to the Art Nouveau movement and to the flat, serpentine rendering of line found in Postimpressionist art. Cheret's poster is a joyous and provocative depiction of the female form in motion. The dancer's flowing costume provides abstract lines suggestive of movement as well as the decency of drapery.

Perhaps with the exception of the shapely turn of calf, the color lithograph poster of cabaret dancer Jane Avril (Fig. 9–39) by the French Postimpressionist Henri de Toulouse-Lautrec is a more abstract and vibrant crowd puller. Toulouse-Lautrec dwelled in nighttime Paris—its cafés, music halls, night clubs, and brothels.

The oblique perspective and bold patterns of line in his poster were probably influenced by Japanese prints. The high contrast in values may reflect the glare of artificial lighting and suggests a potent juxtaposition of textures. The dramatic silhouetting and bold outlining provided by dancer and violin add an abstract quality that speaks of a direct titillation of the senses.

The Cheret and Toulouse-Lautrec posters capture in a single image the spirit and personality of the establishments they advertise. Contemporary artists who make posters for motion pictures, rock concerts, and museum exhibitions face the same challenge and opportunity.

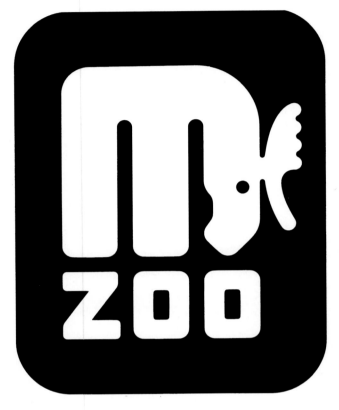

LOGOS

The logo of a company or an organization is extremely important. It communicates an instant impression of the company character, and it becomes part of the company identity. The next time you are watching television, note the CBS eye and the NBC peacock. Observe company logos in magazine ads and on buildings. Note the emblem of the company of your automobile. All of them are carefully planned to deliver a specific visual message.

The Minnesota Zoo logo (Fig. 9–40), designed by Lance Wyman, Ltd., is a refreshing, clean graphic design of white set against a backdrop of blue. With a few whimsical strokes, the "M" is transformed into a moose. The assertive yet gentle and charming sign telegraphs the fact that the zoo has the world's premier collection of this north-country mammal. The Microsoft Windows logo (Fig. 9–41) is a colorful, lyrical pennant shape that suggests the nature of the software program—that it permits people to sort of hop (or "click" their way?) from application to application.

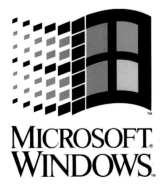

CLOTHING DESIGN

There is a saying that "Clothing makes the man"—or woman. It would be more accurate, perhaps, to say that clothing helps create a first impression of men and women. Psychologists have found, for example, that hitchhikers wearing neatly pressed suits are more likely to be offered rides than the same individuals in shabby dress.

By and large we tend to gravitate toward those who dress like us, and not to socialize with those whose dress is very different. We experience powerful social pressure to conform our clothing to that worn by the groups with which we identify. Rising businessmen and businesswomen wear suits, or comparably tailored clothing, while many students would not be caught in anything other than jeans. When people seem indifferent to what they wear, we tend to assume, correctly or incorrectly, that they are indifferent about the ways in which they behave.

Clothing, like architecture, protects us from the elements, and like architecture, clothing also serves many

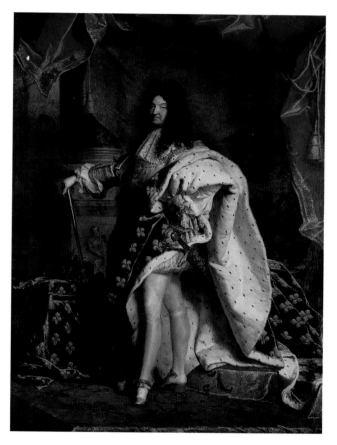

9–42 HYACINTHE RIGAUD
LOUIS XIV (1701). OIL ON CANVAS. 9′1″ × 6′3″.
LOUVRE MUSEUM, PARIS.

other purposes. Clothing is a reflection of the modesty of an age: it indicates what may or may not be revealed at the office, at the beach, or in the bedroom. Clothing is an expression of personality, mood, taste, socioeconomic status, aesthetic preferences, and even, to some degree, political attitudes. Clothing can be a sign of one's occupation or activities. The military, the police, Boy and Girl Scouts, and nurses all wear uniforms that say something about what they do.

The apparel of *Giovanni Arnolfini and His Bride* (Fig. 13–3) contributes to the sanctity of the occasion. The shoes have been removed to show that the room is a sacred place. The heads of bride and groom are both covered, as the Bible proclaims that they must be before God. The extensive draping of bride and groom emphasizes the spiritual as opposed to the carnal meaning of the sacraments of marriage.

FASHION AND FAD IN CLOTHING DESIGN   The garments with which Arnolfini and his bride are draped are not the invention of the painter Jan van Eyck; they reflect the fashions of northern Europe in the fifteenth century. Arnolfini's overgarment is lavish in its use of fur, and his high-crowned hat is made from beaver fur, a costly, rare status symbol. His pointed shoes are conservative in style, as would befit a wealthy man. The bride's kerchief is edged with a wealth of ruffles. Her neckline is flat. Round, vertical pleats distribute the fashionable fullness of her hoop skirt. (She is not yet in a "family way.")

Styles come and go. Hemlines rise and fall, ties narrow and widen, and so do lapels. One year bell-bottom jeans are in style; the next year "everyone" is wearing straight legs. A new style can seem atrocious at first glance, and we may wonder how the trailblazers can wear it. But then, as time passes, we often see the new "look" as the normal state of affairs. There may be no limit to the diversity of styles that look right once we have become habituated to them.

Today women's dress tends to be somewhat more colorful and flamboyant than men's, but it was not always so. Note Hyacinthe Rigaud's painting of *Louis XIV* (Fig. 9–42), the "sun king." The fleur-de-lis design of the cape, the ermine lining, and the stockings might today

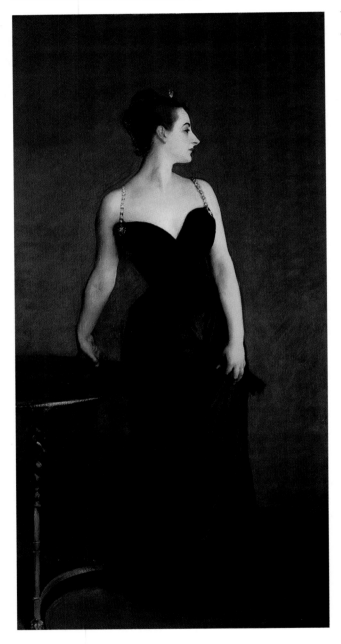

be considered appropriate for society women, but certainly not for men. Yet there was nothing effeminate about the king's dress; in his day such finery, along with elaborate wigs, was the norm for men of high station.

Since the reign of Louis XIV, the world has tended to look to Paris as the center of **haute couture,** or high fashion, to see, for example, what the French designers would do about hemlines or shoulder pads this year. What designers do in a given year is also to some degree expressed in concurrent developments in the visual arts and crafts.

John Singer Sargent's portrait of *Madame X* (Fig. 9–43), painted toward the end of the nineteenth century, shows how simple lines can enhance the female form. The color of the dress contrasts sharply with the alabaster skin of the model, Madame Pierre Gautreau, and Madame Gautreau, along with her family, is said to have been outraged by the decolletage. While her dress is hardly shocking by today's standards, it highlights how clothing designers have been assigned the challenge of simultaneously draping and enticing.

Only the very few could afford to dress like Madame Gautreau. Today, as well, very few can afford "originals" by noted designers. But the changes in haute couture frequently trickle down to the masses. France now has lost something of its unique position in the fashion world. New York, London, Tokyo, and a few other cities are also considered fashion centers, and their designers make major contributions to the new looks.

Since the nineteenth century, blue jeans have been mass produced and, because of their durability, comfort, and affordability, have been worn by many laborers. Figure 9–44 suggests the current chic and popularity of designer jeans. While standard jeans sell for from $15 to $30 or so, designer jeans sell for about $50 to $100 or more, increasing their acceptability as general leisure wear among today's relatively affluent members of the middle class. Of course, designer jeans usually have more tightly woven denim, better fits, higher-quality stitching, and a bit more flair in the detailing—but part of the price clearly goes for the right to identify one's backside with the logo of the designer.

INDUSTRIAL DESIGN

Industrial design refers to the planning and artistic enhancement of industrial products ranging from space shuttles and automobiles to coffeemakers, typewriters, and microcomputers. To a large degree, functional and mechanical problems have been the responsibility of engineers. Designers then embellish the mechanical necessities as best they can by creating attractive skins or housing for them.

FORM AND FUNCTION   Consider the forms of the lunar landing module shown in the photograph *Earthrise* (Fig. 8–4) and the space shuttle. The forms of each were determined largely by their functions. The lunar landing module needed only to travel from outer space down to the lunar surface and then back from the Moon to an orbiting spacecraft. It never navigated through an atmosphere, and so it did not need to be aerodynamic; it could afford its odd shape and many protrusions. The space shuttle, on the other hand, must glide from outer space down to the surface of the Earth. To a large degree, its shape is designed mathematically so that the atmosphere will provide a maximum of lift to the underside of its bulky body. The instrument panels in both spacecrafts were designed by experts in human psychology and engineering. They had to be placed in strategic locations and differentiated from one another. In order not to hamper the work of pilots and navigators, their forms had to suggest their functions.

In most cases, designers have a larger influence on the final appearance of a product than they did with the lunar landing module and the space shuttle. The factors that usually enter into an industrial design include utility (that is, in what form is the equipment easiest to use?), cost, and aesthetic considerations. The aesthetic appeal of an industrial product not only provides a sense of satisfaction for the designer and the manufacturer, it also affects sales.

New York's Museum of Modern Art has an extensive collection of superior industrial designs. It includes teapots (Fig. 9–45), Olivetti typewriters, Breuer and Barcelona chairs, electric coffeemakers, the Movado

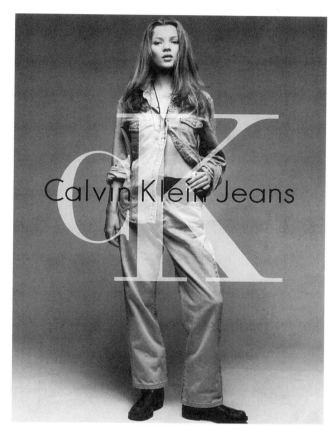

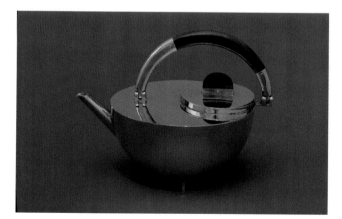

9–45 MARIANNE BRANDT
TEAPOT (1924). NICKEL SILVER, EBONY. 7″ HIGH.
THE MUSEUM OF MODERN ART, N.Y. PHYLLIS B. LAMBERT FUND.

9–46 NATHAN GEORGE HORWITT
Watch Face (1947). Diameter 1⅜″. Specially designed face
without numerals, silver hands and single silver dot
indicating position of number twelve.
THE MUSEUM OF MODERN ART, N.Y. GIFT OF THE DESIGNER.

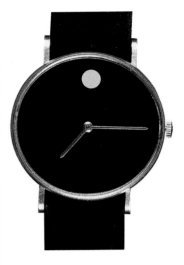

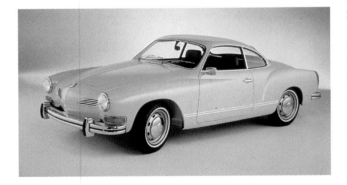

9–47 1972 VW KHARMANN GHIA
COURTESY OF VOLKSWAGEN OF AMERICA, INC. ENGLEWOOD CLIFFS, N.J.

watch (Fig. 9–46), and the Volkswagen sports car the Kharmann Ghia (Fig. 9–47). The design of the minimalist Movado watch is pure, elegant, and efficient. At the time of the Kharmann Ghia's appearance in the 1950s, it was one of a very few automobiles that could boast efficient use of space and gasoline as well as a unique and, to some degree, aerodynamic, sculpted body. In more recent years, the Mazda Miata, the Lexus, and the Porsche have been applauded by industrial designers for their engineering and appearance.

INTERIOR DESIGN

Interior design is the organization and furnishing of interior spaces to serve human needs in the home, at places of business, and in other enclosed areas. The fine interior designer has spatial relations ability, knowledge of architecture, awareness of the elements of art, a sense of composition, knowledge of the history and periods of furniture and the fiber arts, the skill to use contemporary materials, and an understanding of the human needs of everyday living.

A fine interior design is expressive of the personalities of its inhabitants. The designer must use lighting, structural materials, fabrics, and colors that set certain moods and are consistent with the lifestyles of the clients. Good interior design is also true to the architecture of the building. This does not mean that a contemporary building must have contemporary furniture, but it does mean that the relationship between a building and its furnishings cannot look arbitrary.

EXAMPLES OF INTERIORS   The largely Neoclassic interior from the period of Louis XVI (Fig. 9–48) shows furnishings with light and delicate proportions. The straight line predominates over the free curve of the earlier Rococo period in the **dentil molding** that projects from the **cornice,** the rectangular paneling of the walls, the mantle of the fireplace, the backs of armchairs, and the shape of the desk. The intricately ornate console table beneath the mirror is a frivolous remnant from the reign of Louis XV, but good taste does not require that we discard our favorite pieces when styles change.

The room has a free flow of space around the central area, which is defined by the desk and elegant chandelier. The mirror between the windows balances the mirror over the mantel. Cornice and moldings, area rug, windows, wall panels, **wainscoting,** and door decorations all fortify the rhythmic Neoclassic repetition of the rectangle.

The Peacock Room (Fig. 9–49), decorated by American artist James McNeill Whistler, exudes an organic quality that contrasts with the Neoclassic geometry of the Grand Salon. The lamps, for example, are the blossoms on stems that grow down from the ceiling.

9–48 Grand Salon of the Hôtel de Tessé, Paris (1768–72).
Painted and gilded oak, with 4 plaster overdoor reliefs. 16′ high; 33′7½″ long; 29′ 6½″ wide.
The Metropolitan Museum of Art, N.Y. Gift of Mrs. Herbert N. Straus, 1942 (42. 203.1).

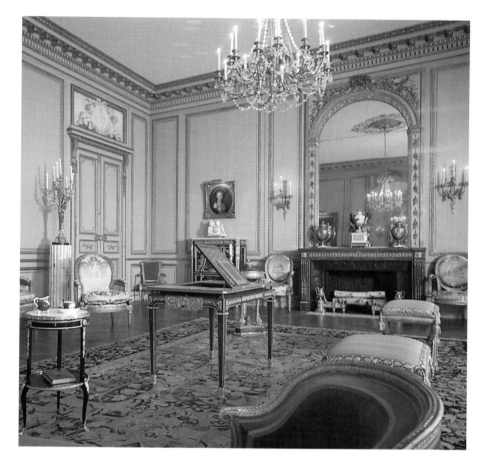

9–49 James A. McNeill Whistler
The Peacock Room, home of F. R. Leyland. (1876–77). *Harmony in Blue and Gold.* Oil, color, and gold on leather and wood. Approx. 13.8′ × 32.8′ × 19.7′.
Courtesy of the Freer Gallery of Art, Smithsonian Institute, Washington, D.C. (04.61)

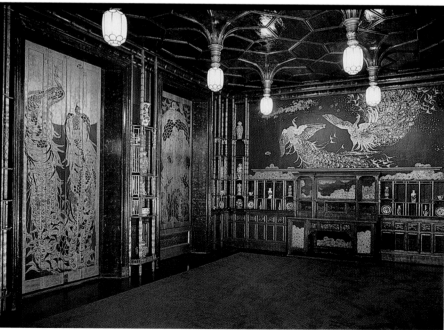

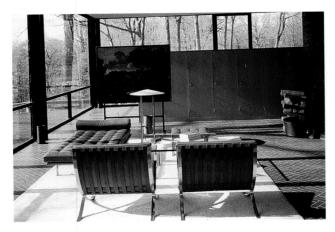

Intended as a showcase for the owner's collection of Japanese porcelain, the room shows Japanese and English Tudor influences. Whistler's painted blue and gold peacocks were intended to heighten the Japanese atmosphere of the design.

The contemporary interior of Philip Johnson's Glass House (Fig. 9–50), like the Grand Salon, shows a predominance of classical straight lines and is fully consistent with the severe horizontals and verticals of the house itself. The furniture was designed by fellow architect Mies van der Rohe and includes the latter's Barcelona chair. (Johnson and Mies would later collaborate on the Seagram Building.) Space flows without obstruction from the bucolic Connecticut setting through the house. A formal island for conversation is defined by the area rug. A theme of machined flawlessness replaces the sense of hand-crafted perfection that pervaded the Louis XVI interior. Like the chandelier and Rococo table in the Neoclassic room, the organic sculpture and the plant serve as counterpoint to the unrelieved rectangularity of ceiling, walls, furnishings, and floor. Each room possesses an elegant unity that expresses a major aesthetic of its times.

STAGE DESIGN

Many artists over time have turned their talents to stage design. Creating sets for ballets and dramatic performances has literally and figuratively added a new dimension to their work. In 1917, Pablo Picasso collaborated with the writer Jean Cocteau, the composer Erik Satie, and the choreographer Leonide Massine on a ballet called *Parade* for Sergei Diaghilev's Russian Ballet

Company. The Russian constructivist artist, Naum Gabo, also worked with Diaghilev in the 1920s. The painters Edvard Munch, Raoul Dufy, Salvador Dalí, and Marie Laurencin were similarly drawn to stage design. In 1929, the architect Walter Gropius, a major figure in Germany's Bauhaus school, developed designs for what he called "Total Theater." His concept of an entirely flexible combination of performance and audience spaces are still influential today.

Contemporary painter David Hockney thus takes his place in a long line of artists who have translated their painting skills and styles to the stage. His set design for the opera *Die Frau ohne Schatten* in Covent Garden, England (Fig. 9–51), represents, for us, a brilliant combination of line, shape, light, and color. In Hockney's words, it was a "visual extravaganza" that the opera itself demanded. To describe the wilds of nature, from landscape to forest, Hockney's compositions included a range of elements—from linear tendrils to bold silhouetted shapes. The extreme color saturation and the glowing light transport the viewer to other worlds. With the addition of costume designs coordinated to the sets, the composition is ever-changing, a ceaselessly evolving work of art.

While these examples illustrate the adaptability of the fine artist's productions to the arena of performing arts, stage design in general has nurtured its own creative talent. Anyone who has recently been to the theater has noticed that simple descriptive sets have given way to an array of special effects that hold their own against those of the cinema. While stage designers here and there will still work with spare or realistic sets, the overwhelming tendency in contemporary theater is to make the leap from stage design to what critic Vincent Canby has called "stage illusion."[7] The collapse of the chandelier over the heads of the orchestra patrons in *Phantom of the Opera*, the helicopter landing in *Miss Saigon*, or the paratrooper sequence in *Tommy*—in which actors seem to jump from a very high platform (or airplane) (Fig. 9–52) through a stage trap door the size of a manhole—are but a few current examples of "sleight of hand" that can take your breath away. Canby has said that "For better or worse, we are in the Age of

[7]Vincent Canby, "Is Broadway Fogbound in a Special-Effects Age?" *The New York Times,* January 16, 1994, pp. H1, H5.

9–51 DAVID HOCKNEY
PRODUCTION SHOT FROM *DIE FRAU OHNE SCHATTEN,* ROYAL OPERA HOUSE,
COVENT GARDEN, 1992.
COURTESY OF THE PERFORMING ARTS LIBRARY, LONDON.

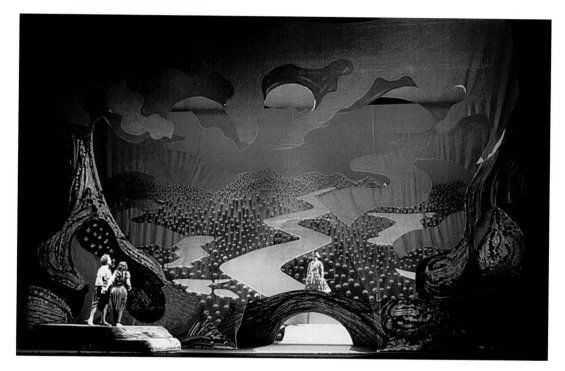

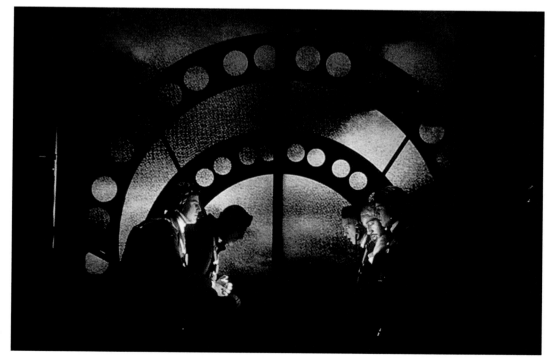

9–52 PARATROOPERS IN THE BROADWAY MUSICAL *TOMMY* (1993).
COURTESY OF JOAN MARCUS/BYRAN BROWN.

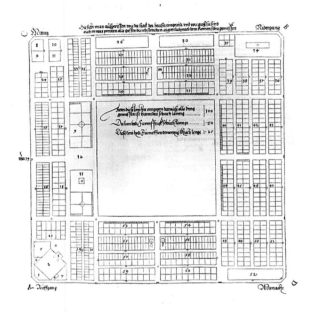

has said that "For better or worse, we are in the Age of Scenery and Set Decoration . . . when each succeeding show must somehow up the ante and be more eye-popping that the one before."[8] He defines this stage illusion as the triumph of theatrical craft that liberates the imagination in a way that even the most dramatic special effects in film do not: "Here is the art of the production designer, and of all those associates who make happen things that shouldn't be able to happen, at least in a live theatrical performance." And today, the seeming ever-presence of stage fog goes a long way toward keeping alive the mystery as to how it's all done.

URBAN DESIGN

Perhaps it is in urban design that our desire for order and harmony achieves its most majestic expression. Throughout history most towns and cities have more or less sprung up. They have pushed back the countryside in all directions, as necessary, with little evidence of an overall guiding concept. As a result, the masses of great buildings sometimes press against other masses of great buildings, and transportation becomes a worrisome afterthought. The Rome of the early republic, for example, was an impoverished seat of empire, little more than a disordered assemblage of seven villages on seven hills. Later, the downtown area was a jumble of narrow streets winding through mud-brick buildings. Not until the first century BCE were the major building programs undertaken by Sulla and then the Caesars.

THE RECTANGULAR PLAN   The new towns of the Roman empire were laid out largely on a rectangular grid. This pattern was common among centrist states, where bits of land were parceled out to the subjects of mighty rulers. The gridiron was also found to be a useful basis for design by the ancient Greeks and the colonial Americans.

The rectangular plan shown in Figure 9–53 was designed by Albrecht Dürer. It is a city-fortress with a central square intended for public gatherings and for the housing of the ruler and his court. It serves not to meet social needs, but to answer the military question of how a prince or duke can construct satellite towns to protect the heart of his domain.

[8]Ibid.

9–54 PLAN FOR PALMA NUOVA.
FROM *PAOLO SOLERI, ARCOLOGY: THE CITY IN THE IMAGE OF MAN.*
© 1969 BY M.I.T., CAMBRIDGE, MASS. REPRODUCED BY PERMISSION OF M.I.T. PRESS.

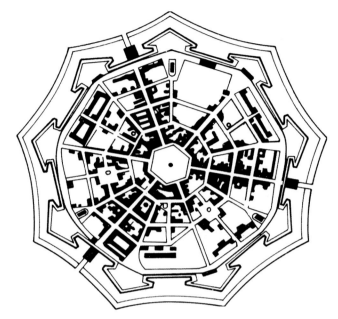

9–55 PIERRE-CHARLES L'ENFANT
PLAN FOR WASHINGTON, D.C. (1792).

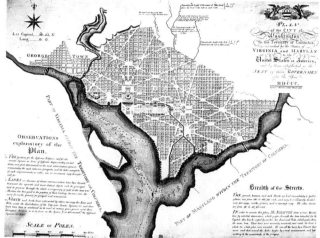

THE CIRCULAR PLAN   Many cities of the Near and Middle East, like Baghdad, have a circular tradition in urban design, which may reflect the old belief that they were the hubs of the universe. The throne room of the palace in eighth-century Baghdad was at the center of the circle. The "palace"—including attendant buildings, a game preserve, and pavilions set in perfumed gardens—was more than a mile in diameter, and the remainder of the population occupied a relatively narrow ring around the palace. But the population eventually exploded in several outward directions. Members of the court began to construct other palaces in the suburbs, creating a sort of cluster of intersecting circles.

The late sixteenth-century plan for Palma Nuova (Fig. 9–54), a Venetian outpost village, is another example of the city-fortress. The city center is a hexagon in which troops can be gathered. Radiating streets permit rapid deployment to any part of the city wall.

PARIS   Much of Paris is centered around the Place de la Concorde, a square that was constructed along the Seine River during the eighteenth century. From the center of the Place de la Concorde, one can look in any direction and find major monuments. To the west, along the Champs-Élysees, is the Place de l'Étoile, in which is set the Arc de Triomphe, built by Napoleon to celebrate his victorious armies. And from the Place de l'Étoile again radiate many streets.

WASHINGTON, D.C.   Few urban designs are as simple and rich as Pierre-Charles L'Enfant's plan for Washington, D.C. (Fig. 9–55). The city is cradled between two branches of the Potomac River, yielding an uneven overall diamond shape. Within the diamond a rectangular grid of streets that run east-west and north-south is laid down. Near the center of the diamond, with its west edge at the river, an enormous mall or green space is set aside. At the east end of the mall is the Capitol Building. To the north, at its west end, is the President's house (which is now the White House). Broad boulevards radiate from the Capitol and from the White House, cutting across the gridiron. One radiating boulevard runs directly between the Capitol and the White House, and other boulevards parallel it.

The design is a worthy composition in which the masses of the Capitol Building and White House balance one another, and the rhythms of the gridiron pattern and radiating boulevards provide contrast and unity. The mall provides an open central gathering place reminiscent of the central polygons of the Renaissance city-fortresses.

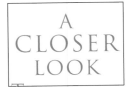
In the center of the "asphalt jungle" of Manhattan lies Central Park—a rectangular strip of grass, trees, hills, and lakes some 2½ miles long and almost a mile wide (Fig. 9–56). A jewel of landscape architecture and urban design, it forms the geographical and spiritual heart of Manhattan. Joggers run around the reservoir, children sail boats in a pond, animals stretch and growl in the zoo, and lovers meander along its paths. New Yorkers pay premium rents to have a view of the park.

According to a book review that appeared in *The New York Times,* Frederick Law Olmsted was "an authentic American genius." His major contribution to the quality of American life lay in a series of urban parks that he designed to provide city dwellers with a "sense of enlarged freedom" and a "common, constant pleasure."

Olmsted's parks are verdant, living works of art. Each one achieves uniqueness and unity by being designed according to one theme or motif. Of their composition, Olmsted wrote that all are "framed upon a single noble motive, to which design of all its parts, in some more or less subtle way, shall be confluent and helpful."

A central theme and major innovation in Manhattan's Central Park is its transportation system. Multiple roadways meander above and below one another so that through-traffic, pedestrian walkways, and bridle paths can all function simultaneously. Forty-six bridges and arches contribute to the harmonious functioning of the transportation system. So that monotony could be avoided, each is different.

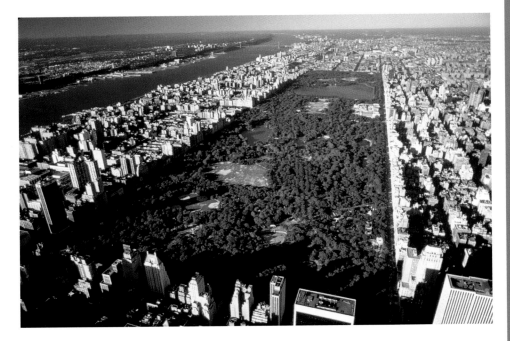

9–56 FREDERICK LAW OLMSTED
CENTRAL PARK,
NEW YORK CITY (C. 1858).

key terms

Ceramics
Pottery
Kiln
Throwing (a pot)
Coiling
Glazing
Bisque firing
Vitrify
Wares
Earthenware
Terra-cotta
Stoneware
Porcelain

China
Jasper
Silica
Fiberglass
Glass blowing
Engraving
Flint glass
Art Nouveau
Fibers
Weaving
Warp
Weft
Woof

Plain weave
Satin weave
Twill weave
Pile weaving
Loom
Embroidery
Tie-dyeing
Batik
Sampler
Stainless steel
Brass
Enamel
Emboss

Griffin
Gadrooning
Fluting
Corbel
Graphic design
Logo
Typography
Haute couture
Industrial design
Interior design
Dentil molding
Cornice
Wainscoting

artists

Euphronios
Euxitheos
Marilyn Levine
Martha Martinez
James Makins
Gertrud and Otto Natzler
Robert Arneson
Judy Chicago
Josiah Wedgwood
Henri Matisse
Benoit Gilsoul
Helmut Schardt
Romare Bearden
Louis Comfort Tiffany

Harvey K. Littleton
Ed Rossbach
Tim Harding
Joan Livingstone
Benvenuto Cellini
John Coney
Rachelle Thiewes
Kiff Slemmons
Melvyn Firmager
Michelle Holzapfel
David Ellsworth
Garvan Carver
Jere Osgood
Andy Warhol

Jules Cheret
Henri de Toulouse-Lautrec
Lance Wyman
Hyacinthe Rigaud
John Singer Sargent
Marianne Brandt
Nathan George Horwitt
James A. McNeill Whistler
Philip Johnson
Mies van der Rohe
David Hockney
Albrecht Dürer
Pierre-Charles L'Enfant
Frederick Law Olmsted

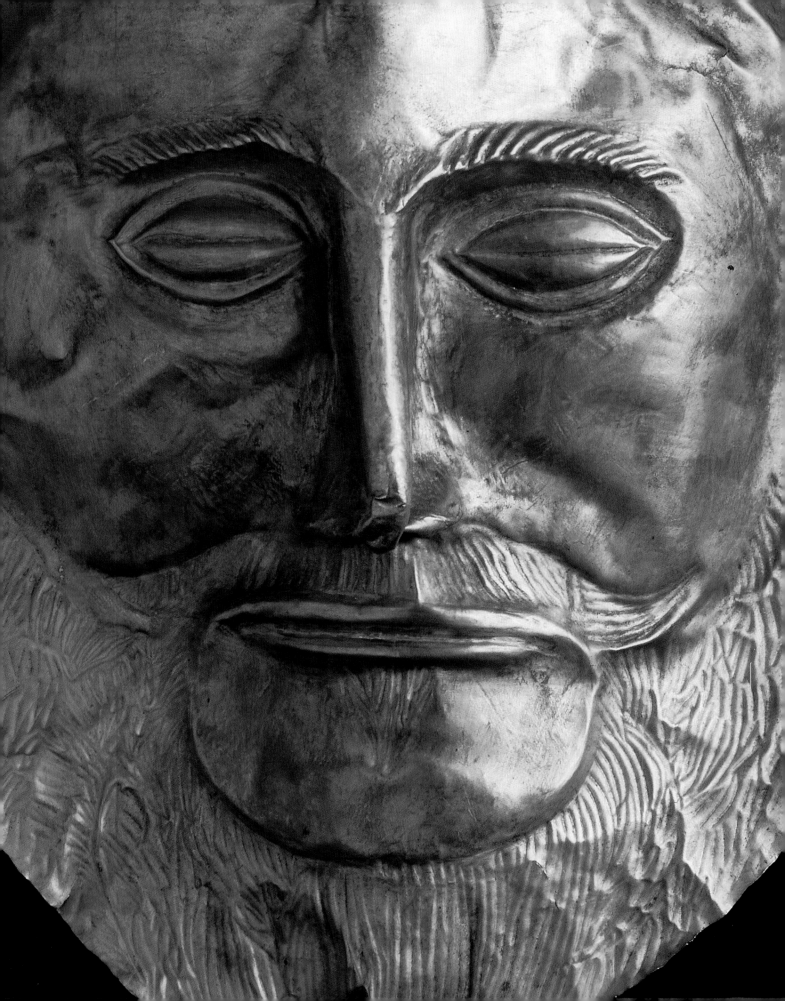

chapter

THE ART OF THE ANCIENTS

P R E L I M I N A R Y
Sketch

- Links between religion and art were forged as early as the Stone Age.

- Prehistoric cave paintings were discovered by young boys chasing after a dog.

- Stone Age artists used foreshortening and contrasts of light and shadow to create the illusion of three-dimensional forms.

- The purpose of Stonehenge remains a mystery.

- The date when an ancient work of art was created can be determined by measuring the deterioration of a form of carbon in nearby garbage.

- The ziggurat at Babylon was named the "Tower of Babel" by the Hebrews, who disapproved of its construction because of the belief that people should not be so proud as to try to reach their God.

- Egyptian life and culture could not have existed without the Nile River, which was therefore perceived as a god.

- The largest Egyptian pyramid has nearly 2⅓ million blocks of stone, each of which weighs about 2½ tons.

- The richest finds of ancient Egypt have come from the tomb of an 18-year-old boy.

- A nineteenth-century archaeologist used geographical "directions" found in Greek epics to locate ancient Aegean civilizations.

Funeral Mask (detail). See Figure 10–25.

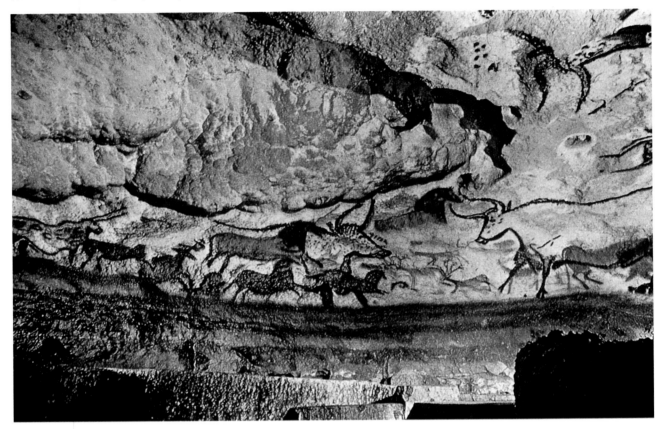

The phrase "Stone Age" often conjures up an image of men and women dressed in skins, huddling before a fire in a cave, while the world around them—the elements and the animals—threatens their survival. We do not generally envision prehistoric humankind as intelligent and reflective, as having needs beyond food, shelter, and reproduction. Somehow we never imagine these people as performing religious rituals or as creating works of art. Yet these aspects of life were perhaps as essential to their survival as warmth, nourishment, and offspring.

As the Stone Age progressed from the Paleolithic to the Neolithic periods, people began to lead more stable lives. They settled in villages and shifted from hunting wild animals to herding domesticated animals and farming. They also fashioned tools of stone and bone and created pottery and woven textiles. Most important for our purposes, they became image makers, capturing forms and figures on cave walls with the use of primitive artistic implements.

Stone Age people were preoccupied with protecting themselves from intimidating or unknown forces. To this purpose they created shelters and tools and even images. It is possible, for example, that Stone Age artists tried to ensure the successful capture of prey by first "capturing" it in wall painting. They also tried to ensure their own continuation by carving small fertility goddesses.

Images, symbols, supernatural forces—these were but a few of the concerns of prehistoric and ancient artists. Stone Age people were the first to forge links between religion and life, life and art, and art and religion.

PREHISTORIC ART

Prehistoric art is divided into three phases that correspond to the cultural periods of the Stone Age: **Upper Paleolithic** (the late years of the Old Stone Age), **Mesolithic** (Middle Stone Age), and **Neolithic** (New

Stone Age). These periods span roughly the years 14,000 to 2000 BCE.

Works of art from the Stone Age include cave paintings, reliefs, and sculpture of stone, ivory, and bone. The subjects consist mainly of animals, although some highly abstracted human figures have been found. There is no surviving architecture as such. Many Stone Age dwellings consisted of caves and rock shelters. Some impressive "architectural" monuments such as Stonehenge exist, but their function remains a mystery.

10-2 VENUS OF WILLENDORF (UPPER PALEOLITHIC, C. 15,000–10,000 BCE). STONE. HEIGHT: 4⅜". NATURHISTORISCHES MUSEUM, VIENNA.

UPPER PALEOLITHIC ART

Upper Paleolithic art is the art of the last ice age, during which time glaciers covered large areas of northern Europe and North America. As the climate got colder, people retreated into the protective warmth of caves, and it is here that we find their first attempts at artistic creation.

The great cave paintings of the Stone Age were discovered by accident in northern Spain and south-western France. At Lascaux, France (see Map 1, p. 237), two boys whose dog chased a ball into a hole followed the animal and discovered beautiful paintings of bison, horses, and cattle that are estimated to be over 15,000 years old. At first, because of the crispness and realistic detail of the paintings, they were thought to be forgeries. But in time, geological methods proved their authenticity.

One of the most splendid examples of Stone Age painting, the so-called Hall of Bulls (Fig. 10–1), is found in a cave at Lascaux. Here, superimposed upon one another, are realistic images of horses, bulls, and reindeer that appear to be stampeding in all directions. With one glance, we can understand the early skepticism concerning their authenticity. So fresh, lively, and purely sketched are the forms that they seem to have been rendered yesterday!

In their attempt at **naturalism,** the artists captured the images of the beasts by first confidently outlining the contours of their bodies. They then filled in these dark outlines with details and colored them with shades of ocher and red. The artists seem to have used a variety of techniques ranging from drawing with chunks of raw pigment to applying pigment with fingers and sticks. They also seem to have used an early "spray painting" technique in which dried, ground pigments were blown through a hollowed-out bone or reed. Although the tools were primitive, the techniques and results were not. They used foreshortening and contrasts of light and shadow to create the illusion of three-dimensional forms. They strove to achieve a most convincing likeness of the animal.

Why did prehistoric people sketch these forms? Did they create these murals out of a desire to delight the eye, or did they have other reasons? We cannot know for certain. However, it is unlikely that the paintings were merely ornamental, because they were confined to the deepest recesses of the cave, far from the areas that were inhabited, and were not easily reached. Also, the figures were painted atop one another with no apparent regard for composition. It is believed that successive artists added to the drawings, respecting the sacredness of the figures that already existed. It is further believed that the paintings covered the walls and ceilings of a kind of inner sanctuary where religious rituals concerning the capture of prey were performed. Some have suggested that by "capturing" these animals in art, Stone Age hunters believed that they would be guaranteed success in capturing them in life.

The prehistoric artist also may have attempted to "capture" fertility by creating small sculptures of nude women called **Venuses** by archaeologists. The most famous of these is the "Venus" of Willendorf (Fig. 10–2). The tiny figurine is carved of stone and is just over 4 inches high. As with all sculptures of this type, the female form is highly abstracted, and the emphasis is placed on the anatomical parts associated with fertility: the breasts, swollen abdomen, and enlarged hips. Other parts of the body are subordinated to those related to reproduction.

Thus, the artistic endeavors of the Stone Age during the Upper Paleolithic period reflected a concern with survival. People created their images, and perhaps their religion, as a way of coping with these concerns.

10–3 Ritual Dance (c. 10,000 bce).
Rock engraving. Cave of Addaura,
Monte Pellegrino (Palermo).
soprintendenza beni culturali ambrentali, palermo.

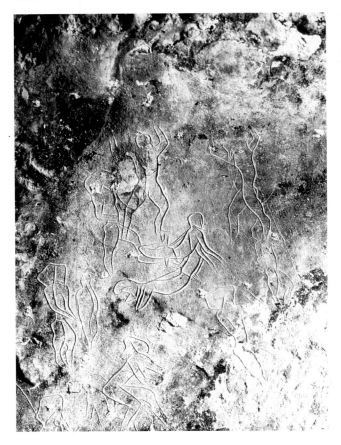

Mesolithic Art

The Middle Stone Age began with the final retreat of the glaciers. The climate became milder and people began to adjust to the new ecological conditions by experimenting with different food-gathering techniques. They established fishing settlements along river banks and lived in rock shelters. In the realm of art, a dramatic change took place. Whereas Paleolithic artists emphasized animal forms, Mesolithic artists concentrated on the human figure.

The human figure was abstracted, and the subjects ranged from warriors to ceremonial dancers. Of the many wall paintings and stone carvings that survive, perhaps none is more appealing to the modern eye than the Ritual Dance (Fig. 10–3). Fluid yet concise outlines describe the frenzied movement of human figures dancing and diving in the presence of animals. These simple and expressive contours call to mind the languid nudes

of twentieth-century artists such as Henri Matisse (Fig. 2–52). Whatever the function of a Mesolithic work such as this might have been, it is clear that human beings were beginning to assert their identities as a more self-sufficient species.

Neolithic Art

During the New Stone Age, life became more stable and predictable. People domesticated plants and animals, relinquishing hunting weapons for plows. Toward the end of the Neolithic period, in some areas crops such as maize, squash, and beans were cultivated, metal implements were fashioned, and writing appeared. About 4000 bce, huge architectural monuments were erected.

The most famous of these monuments is Stonehenge (Fig. 10–4) in southern England. It consists of two concentric rings of stones surrounding others placed in a horseshoe shape. Some of these stones are quite large and weigh several tons. They are called **megaliths,** from the Greek meaning "large stones." The purpose of Stonehenge remains a mystery, although over the years many theories have been advanced to explain it. At one time it was widely believed to have been a druid temple. Lately, some astronomers have suggested that the monument served as a complex calendar that charted the movements of the sun and moon, as well as eclipses. This theory, too, has been contested, but archaeologists seem to agree that the structure had some type of religious function.

The Neolithic period probably began about 8000 bce and spread throughout the world's major river valleys between 6000 and 2000 bce—the Nile in Egypt, the Tigris and Euphrates in Mesopotamia, the Indus in India, and the Yellow in China. In the next section, we examine the birth of the great Mesopotamian civilizations.

ART OF THE ANCIENT NEAR EAST

Historic (as opposed to prehistoric) societies are marked by a written language, advanced social organization, and developments in the areas of government, science, and art. They are also often linked with the development of agriculture. Historic civilizations began toward the end of the Neolithic period. In this section we will discuss the art of the Mesopotamian civilizations of

10–4 STONEHENGE, SALISBURY PLAIN, WILTSHIRE, ENGLAND (NEOLITHIC, C. 1800–1400 BCE). DIAMETER OF CIRCLE: 97′; HEIGHT OF STONES ABOVE GROUND: 13½′.

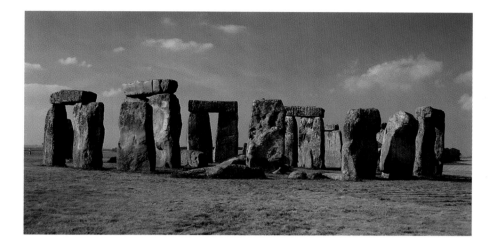

Sumer, Akkad, Babylonia, Assyria, and Persia. We will begin with Sumer, which flourished in the river valley of the Tigris and Euphrates at about 3000 BCE.

SUMER

The Tigris and Euphrates rivers flow through what is now Syria and Iraq, join in their southernmost section, and empty into the Persian Gulf (Map 2). The major civilizations of ancient Mesopotamia lay along one or the other of these rivers, and the first to rise to prominence was Sumer.

Sumer was located in the Euphrates River valley in southern Mesopotamia. The origin of its people is unknown, although they may have come from Iran or India. The earliest Sumerian villages date back to prehistoric times. By about 3000 BCE, however, there was a thriving agricultural civilization in Sumer. The Sumerians constructed sophisticated irrigation systems, controlled river flooding, and worked with metals such as copper, silver, and gold. They had a government based on independently ruled city-states, and they developed a system of writing called **cuneiform,** from the Latin *cuneus*, meaning "wedge": the characters in cuneiform writing are wedge-shaped.

Excavations at major Sumerian cities have revealed sculpture, craft art, and monumental architecture that seems to have been created for worship. Thus the Sumerian people may have been among the first to establish a formal religion.

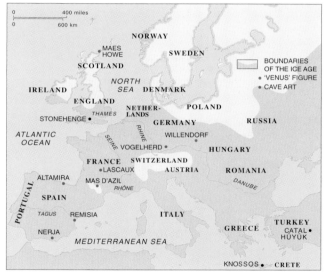

MAP 1 PREHISTORIC EUROPE.

One of the most impressive testimonies to the Sumerian's religion-oriented society is the **ziggurat,** a form of temple also found in the Babylonian and Assyrian civilizations of later years. The ziggurat was the focal point of the Sumerian city, towering high above the fields and dwellings. It was a multilevel structure consisting of a core of sun-baked brick faced with fired brick, sometimes of bright colors. Access to the shrine, which sat atop the ziggurat, was gained by a series of ramps leading from one level to the next, or, in some instances, by a spiral ramp that rose continuously from ground to summit.

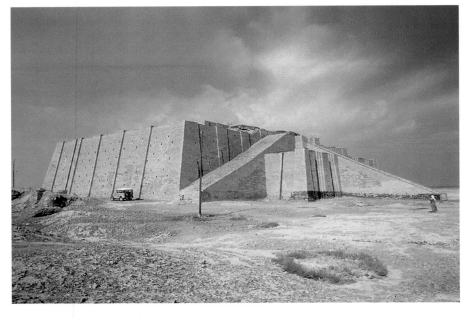

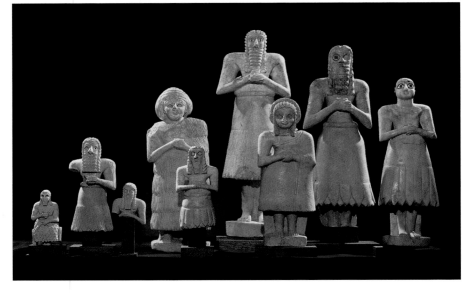

The Sumerian gods were primarily deifications of nature. Anu was the god of the sky; Abu, the god of vegetation. Votive sculptures found in the sanctuary of Abu also indicate the Sumerians' preoccupation with religion. A group of these sculptures from Tel Asmar (Fig. 10–6) show interesting characteristics. The cylindrical figures wear skirtlike garments, some of whose hems were adorned with feathers. They all stand erect with hands folded over their chests, as if in prayer. The men are distinguished by stylized beards and long, patterned hair. All the figures stare forward with wide eyes that have been inlaid with shell and black limestone, rendering the figures hauntingly realistic despite their strong stylization. The largest figure may represent a king, since it is common to find representations of kings and queens of ancient Near Eastern civilizations towering over their accompanying figures.

These Sumerian statuettes are sculpted from marble, but clay was the most readily available material. It is believed that the Sumerians traded crops for metal, wood, and stone so that they could create works

The Ziggurat at Ur (Fig. 10–5) is a splendid example of this type of architecture. The base alone is some 50 feet high. Some ziggurats, such as the one erected in Babylon, reached a height of almost 300 feet. It was the ziggurat at Babylon that was named the "Tower of Babel" by the Hebrews, who scorned its construction on the basis that people should never be so proud as to try to reach their God.

of art from these materials as well. Because of the abundance of clay, however, the Sumerians were expert ceramicists and their buildings were constructed of mud brick.

The Sumerian repertory of subjects included fantastic creatures such as music-making animals, bearded bulls, and composite man-beasts with bull heads or scorpion bodies. These were rendered in lavishly decorated objects of hammered gold inlaid with lapis lazuli. These art works were found in the Sumerian royal courts. Their function, too, is believed to have been religious. Perhaps they represented struggles between known and unknown forces.

For a long time the Sumerians were the principle force in Mesopotamia, but they were not alone. Semitic peoples to the north became increasingly strong, and eventually they established an empire that ruled all of Mesopotamia and assimilated the Sumerian culture.

Akkad

Akkad, located north of Sumer, centered around the valley of the Tigris River. Its government, too, was based on independent city-states which, along with those of Sumer, eventually came under the influence of the Akkadian ruler Sargon. It was under Sargon and his successors that the civilization of Akkad flourished.

Akkadian art exhibits distinct differences from that of Sumer. It commemorates rulers and warriors instead of offering homage to the gods. It is an art of violence instead of prayer. Also, although artistic conventions are present, they are coupled with a naturalism that was absent from Sumerian art.

Of the little extant Akkadian art, the **Stele** of Naram Sin (Fig. 10–7) shines as one of the most significant works. This relief sculpture commemorates the military exploits of Sargon's grandson and successor, Naram Sin. The king, represented somewhat larger in scale than the other figures, ascends a mountain, trampling his enemies underfoot. He is accompanied by a group of marching soldiers, spears erect, whose positions contrast strongly with those of the fallen enemy. One wrestles to pull a spear out of his neck, another pleads for mercy, another falls head first off the mountain. The chaos on the right side of the composition is opposed by the rigid advancement on the left. All takes place under the watchful celestial bodies of Ishtar and Shamash, the gods of fertility and justice.

The king and his men are represented in a **conceptual manner.** That is, the artist rendered the human body in all of its parts as they are known to be, not as they appear at any given moment to the human eye. This method resulted in figures that are a combination of frontal and profile views. **Naturalism** was reserved for

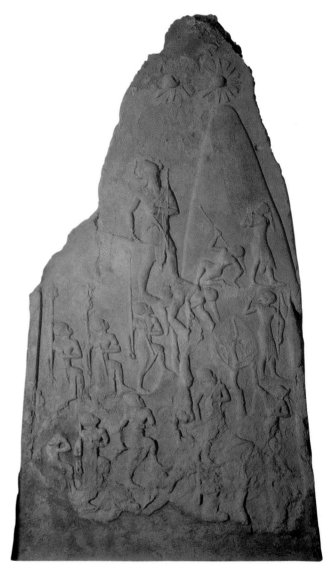

the enemy, whose figures fall in a variety of contorted positions. It may be that the convention of conceptual representation was maintained as a sign of respect. On the other hand, the conceptual manner complements the upright positions of the victorious, while the naturalism echoes the disintegration of the enemy camp.

The Akkadian Empire eventually declined, for reasons that are not clear. Historians have traditionally attributed its collapse to the invasion of tribes of barbarians. However, recent archaeological research has led to the theory that it was not human violence that put an end to Akkadian supremacy but rather a severe and unrelenting drought that gripped the region for 300 years. With the end of the drought it seems that the Sumerians regained power for a while, but they too were eventually overtaken by fierce warring tribes. Mesopotamia remained in a state of chaos until the rise of Babylon under the great lawmaker and ruler, Hammurabi.

BABYLONIA

During the eighteenth century BCE the Babylonian Empire, under Hammurabi, rose to power and dominated Mesopotamia. Hammurabi's major contribution to civilization was the codification of Mesopotamian laws. Laws had become cloudy and conflicting after the division of Mesopotamia into independent cities.

This law code was inscribed on the Stele of Hammurabi (Fig. 10–8), a relief sculpture of **basalt** that also contains the figures of Hammurabi and Shamash, the god who was believed to have inspired him to the task. The representation of the figures is similar to that reserved for important personages—a combination of frontal and profile views. Shamash is seated on a stylized mountain. His legs and face are shown in profile, while his torso faces front. He gestures toward Hammurabi with a staff that symbolizes his divine power. Hammurabi is also depicted in combined profile and frontal views, although the artist has turned his figure toward us in an attempt at a more naturalistic stance. Draped from shoulder to feet, Hammurabi's figure is columnar, bearing similarity to the cylindrical votive figures of Sumeria's Tel Asmar. Note that at this time the artist conceptualizes the god in human form, not as the composite beast of Sumerian art or the abstracted celestial sphere of the Akkadian period.

After the death of Hammurabi, Mesopotamia was torn apart by invasions. It eventually came under the influence of the Assyrians, a warring people to the north who had had their eyes on the region for hundreds of years.

ASSYRIA

The ancient empire of Assyria developed along the upper Tigris River. For centuries the Assyrians fought with their neighbors, earning a deserved reputation as

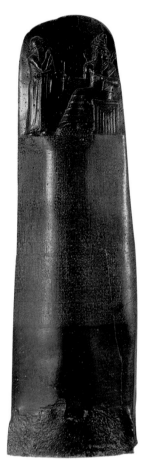

10–8 STELE INSCRIBED WITH THE LAW CODE OF HAMMURABI, AT SUSA (BABYLONIAN, C. 1760 BCE). DIORITE. HEIGHT: 25½".
LOUVRE MUSEUM, PARIS.

a fierce, bloodthirsty people. They eventually prevailed, and from about 900 to 600 BCE they controlled all of Mesopotamia.

The Assyrians owed much to the Babylonians, having been influenced by their art, culture, and religion. Unlike Babylonia, Assyria was an empire built wholly on military endeavors. Because the Assyrians were obsessed with war and conquering, they began to be undermined by economic problems. They spent too much money on military campaigns and eventually depleted their resources. They ignored agriculture and wound up having to import most of their food. Their preoccupation with violence instead of production eventually led to their demise.

Assyrian art became distinct from Babylonian art in about 1500 BCE. The most common art form in Assyria was carved stone relief depicting scenes of war and hunting. The figures were carved in great detail, and many representations of animals like horses and lions are to be found. The Assyrians commemorated the activities of their kings, such as royal hunting expeditions, in relief sculptures. One of the most touching and

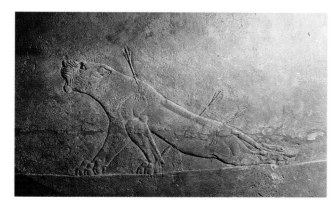

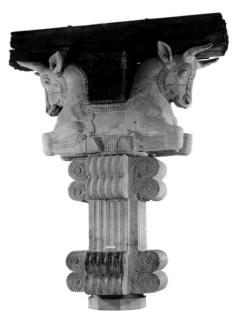

sensitive works of ancient art records such an event. It is ironic that it should come from a culture considered to be insensitive and merciless. The Dying Lioness (Fig. 10–9) is a limestone relief that depicts the carnage resulting from a king's sport. A naturalistically portrayed lioness, bleeding profusely from arrow wounds, emits a pathetic, helpless roar as she drags her hindquarters, paralyzed in the assault. The musculature is clearly defined, and the details are extremely realistic. This is quite different from the way in which kings and other human figures were depicted. In these there is an adherence to convention; the forms are rigid and highly stylized.

PERSIA

At about the time that the Assyrians were beginning to develop a unique artistic style, another culture was gaining strength just east of Mesopotamia in what is now Iran. It consisted of nomadic warring tribes. By the ninth century bce the mighty Assyrians had become embroiled in battle with them. By the sixth century bce the Persian Empire, under King Cyrus, had grown very strong. It eventually conquered great nations such as Egypt and succumbed to defeat only at the hands of the Greeks at the moment when victory seemed to be within its grasp.

The art of Persia consists of sprawling palaces of grand dimensions and sculpture that is almost totally abstract in its simplicity of design. Favorite subjects included animal forms, such as birds and **ibexes,** translated into decorative column **capitals** or elegant vessels

of precious metals. A capital from the Royal Audience Hall of the palace of King Artaxerxes II (Fig. 10–10) illustrates the Persian combination of decorative motifs and stylization. The upper part of the capital consists of beautifully carved back-to-back bulls sharing hindquarters. They rest on intricately carved **volutes** that resemble fronds of vegetation. This stylization leads to the perception of the animals as abstract patterns rather than naturalistic forms and is characteristic of Persian art in general.

In 525 bce Persia conquered the kingdom of Egypt. But as in Mesopotamia, civilization in Egypt had begun some 3,000 years earlier. In the next section we will trace its art from the early post-Neolithic period to the reign of the boy-king Tut in the fourteenth century bce.

EGYPTIAN ART

The lush land that lay between the Tigris and Euphrates rivers, providing sustenance for the Mesopotamian civilizations, is called the **Fertile Crescent.** Its counterpart in Egypt, called the **Fertile Ribbon,** hugs the banks of the great Nile River which flows north from Africa and empties into the Mediterranean Sea

MAP 2 THE ANCIENT NEAR EAST.

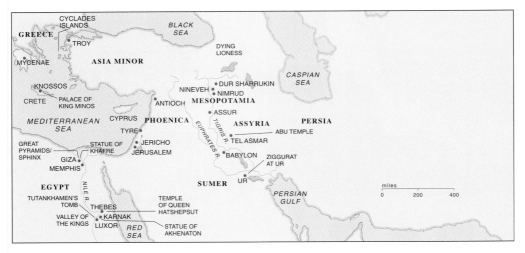

(see Map 2, above). Like the rivers of the Fertile Crescent, the Nile was an indispensable part of Egyptian life. Without it, Egyptian life would not have existed. For this reason, it also had spiritual significance; the Nile was perceived as a god.

Like Sumerian art, Egyptian art was religious. There are three aspects of Egyptian art and life that stand as unique: their link to *religion*, their link to *death,* and their ongoing use of strict *conventionalism* in the arts that affords a sense of permanence.

The art and culture of Egypt are divided into three periods. The Old Kingdom dates from 2680 to 2258 BCE, the Middle Kingdom from 2000 to 1786 BCE, and the New Kingdom from 1570 to 1342 BCE. Art styles proceed from the Old to the New Kingdom with very few variations. The exception to this trend took place between 1372 and 1350 BCE, during the Amarna Revolution under the leadership of the pharaoh Akhenaton. We will begin our exploration of Egyptian art with the Old Kingdom.

OLD KINGDOM

Egyptian religion was bound closely to the afterlife. Happiness in the afterlife was believed to be ensured through the continuation of certain aspects of earthly life. Thus tombs were decorated with everyday objects and scenes depicting common earthly activities. Sculptures of the deceased were placed in the tombs, along with likenesses of the people who surrounded them in life.

In the years prior to the dawn of the Old Kingdom, art consisted of funerary offerings of one type or another including small sculpted figures, carvings of ivory, pottery, and slate palettes used for cosmetics. Toward the end of this period, called the Predynastic period, large limestone sculptures for which Egypt became famous began to be created.

SCULPTURE   Old Kingdom art brought forth a manner of representation that would last thousands of years. It is characterized by a conceptual approach to the rendering of the human figure that we encountered in Mesopotamian relief sculpture. In Egyptian art, the head, pelvis, and legs are presented in profile while the upper torso and eye are shown in a frontal view. The figures tend to be flat, with no sense of three-dimensionality, and they are placed in space with no use of perspective. Thus, no attempt was made to give the illusion of forms moving within three-dimensional space. Relief sculpture was carved very low with a great deal of **incised** detail. Sculpture in the round closely adhered to the block form. Color was applied at times but was not used widely because of the relative impermanence of the material. These characteristics were duplicated, with few exceptions, by artists during all of the periods of Egyptian art. There are instances in

10–11 NARMER PALETTE, FRONT (*RIGHT*) AND BACK (*LEFT*) VIEWS (EGYPTIAN, OLD KINGDOM, C. 3200 BCE). SLATE. HEIGHT: 25″.
EGYPTIAN MUSEUM, CAIRO.

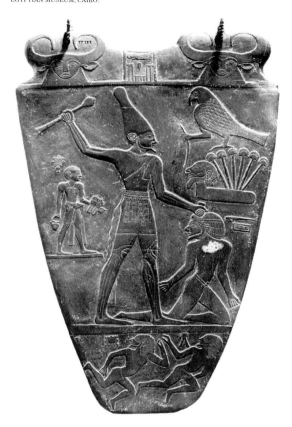 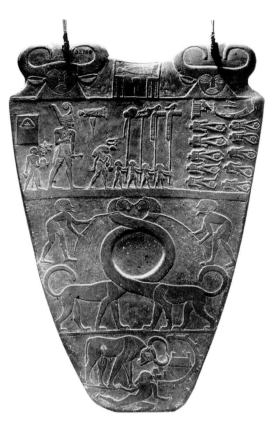

which a certain naturalism was sought, but the artist rarely strayed from the inherited stylistic conventions. Art historian Erwin Panofsky has stated that this Egyptian method of working clearly reflects their artistic intention, "directed not toward the variable, but toward the constant, not toward the symbolization of the vital present, but toward the realization of a timeless eternity."

One of the most important sculptures from the Old Kingdom period, the Narmer Palette (Fig. 10–11), illustrates these conventions. The Narmer Palette is an example of a type of **cosmetic palette** found in the Predynastic period, but it symbolizes much more. It commemorates the unification of Upper Egypt and Lower Egypt, an event that Egyptians saw as marking the beginning of their civilization.

The back of the palette depicts King Narmer in the crown of Upper Egypt (a bowling pin shape) clubbing the head of his enemy. He stands on a horizontal band representing the ground. Beneath his feet, on the lowest

part of the palette, lie two dead enemy warriors. To the king's right is a hawk perched on stylized papyrus plants that seem to grow out of the "back" of a strange object with a man's head. The hawk, a symbol for the Egyptian sky god, stands on this symbol of Lower Egypt. Thus, the gods appear to be sanctioning Narmer's takeover of Lower Egypt. The topmost part of the palette is sculpted with two bull-shaped heads with human features, representing the goddess Hathor, who traditionally symbolized love and joy.

The king is depicted in the typical conventional manner. His head, hips, and legs are sculpted in low relief and rendered in profile. The musculature is defined in incised lines that appear as stylized patterns. His eye and upper torso are shown in full frontal view. He is shown as larger than the people surrounding him, a symbol of his elevated position. The artist has disregarded naturalism and has instead created a kind of timeless rendition of his subject.

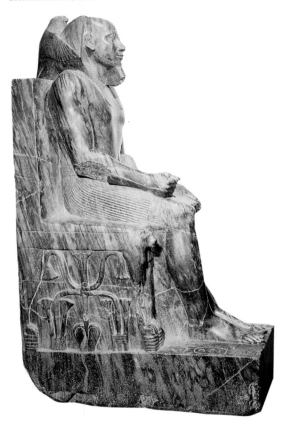

Tomb sculpture included large-scale figures in the round carved in very hard materials to ensure permanence. These figures consisted of conventionally represented stylized bodies with portrait heads rendered in an **idealistic** manner. The touch of realism in the faces reflects the function of the sculptures. They were created as images in which the spirit of the deceased could reside if **mummification** failed to provide a sanctuary. The figures are called **Ka figures;** the Ka was the soul thought to inhabit the body after death.

The statue of Khafre (Fig. 10–12), an Old Kingdom pharaoh, is typical of Ka figures. Carved in diorite, a gray-green rock, it shows the pharaoh seated on a throne ornamented with lotus blossoms and papyrus. He sits rigidly, and his frontal gaze is reminiscent of the staring eyes of the Mesopotamian votive figures. He is shown with the conventional attributes of the pharaoh: a finely pleated kilt, a linen headdress gracing the shoulders, and a long thin beard, a part of which has broken off. The sun god **Horus,** represented again as a hawk, sits behind his head. The artist confined his figure to the block of stone from which it was carved instead of allowing it to stand freely in space. The legs and torso are molded to the throne, and the arms and fists remain close to the body. There is a solidity to the figure that echoes its conception as the permanent and enduring resting place for the Ka.

The representation of the body is stylized according to a specific **canon of proportions** relating different anatomical parts to one another. The forms rely on predetermined rules and not on optical fact. Yet a touch of naturalism is present in the facial features, which are rendered with some degree of truth to reality. This naturalism is intermittent in Egyptian art, but more prevalent in the art of the Middle Kingdom and the Amarna period.

ARCHITECTURE   The most spectacular remains of Old Kingdom Egypt, and the most famous, are the Great Pyramids at Giza (Fig. 10–13). Constructed as tombs, they provided a resting place for the pharaoh, underscored his status as a deity, and lived after him as a monument to his accomplishments. They stand today as haunting images of a civilization long gone, isolated as coarse jewels in an arid wasteland.

The front of the palette is divided into horizontal segments, or **registers,** into which have been placed many figures. The depressed section of the palette held eye paint, and it is emphasized by the entwined necks of lionlike figures being tamed by two men carved in low relief. The top register depicts King Narmer once again, in the process of reviewing the captured and deceased enemy. He is now shown wearing the crown of Lower Egypt and holding the instruments that symbolize his power. To his right are stacks of decapitated bodies. This is not the first time that we have seen a sculpted monument to a royal conquest, complete with gory details. We witnessed it in the Akkadian victory Stele of Naram Sin (Fig. 10–7). In both works the kings are shown in commanding positions, larger than the surrounding figures, but in the Narmer Palette the king is also depicted as a god. This concept of the ruler of Egypt, along with the strict conventions of his representation, would last some 3,000 years.

The Pyramids are massive. The largest has a base that is about 775 feet on a side and is 450 feet high. It is constructed of limestone blocks that weigh about 2½ tons each—2,300,000 of them! The massive stones were dragged by slaves up ramps. Thousands of slaves from captive civilizations engaged in this great labor for many generations. Among them, according to the Old Testament, were the Hebrews, who were eventually led out of bondage by Moses. Interestingly, there is no Egyptian record of the bondage or exodus of the Hebrews. After the stones were placed in position, the exterior slopes of the Pyramids were surfaced with white limestone.

The interiors of the Pyramids consist of a network of chambers, galleries, and airshafts. One of the problems with the Pyramids was that grave robbers found them as impressive as did the pharaohs, and wasted no time in plundering the tombs. During the Middle Kingdom, the Egyptians designed more inconspicuous and less easily penetrated dwelling places for their spirits.

MIDDLE KINGDOM

The Middle Kingdom witnessed a change in the political hierarchy of Egypt, as the pharaohs began to be threatened by powerful landowners. During the early years of the Middle Kingdom, the development of art was stunted by internal strife. Egypt was finally brought back on track, reorganized, and reunited under King Mentuhotep, and art began to flourish once again.

Middle Kingdom art carried the Old Kingdom style forward, although there was some experimentation outside of the mainstream of strict conventionalism. We find this experimentation in extremely sensitive portrait sculptures and freely drawn fresco paintings.

A striking aspect of Middle Kingdom architecture were the rock-cut tombs, which may have been built in an attempt to prevent robberies. They were carved out of the **living rock,** and their entranceways were marked by columned **porticoes** of post-and-lintel construction. These porticoes led to a columned entrance hall, followed by a chamber along the same axis. The walls of the hall and tomb chamber were richly decorated with relief sculpture and painting, much of which had a sense of liveliness not found in Old Kingdom art.

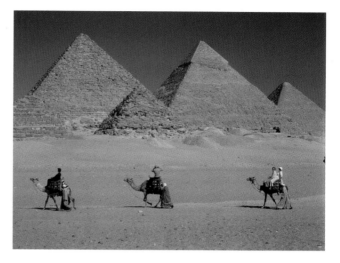

10–13 GREAT PYRAMIDS AT GIZA (EGYPTIAN, OLD KINGDOM, C. 2570–2500 BCE).

NEW KINGDOM

The Middle Kingdom also collapsed, and Egypt fell under the rule of an Asiatic tribe called the Hyskos. They introduced to Egypt Bronze Age weapons, as well as the horse. Eventually the Hyskos were overthrown by the Egyptians, and the New Kingdom was launched. It proved to be one of the most vital periods in Egyptian history, marked by expansionism, increased wealth, and economic and political stability.

The art of the New Kingdom combined characteristics of the Old and Middle Kingdom periods. The monumental forms of the earliest centuries were coupled with the freedom of expression of the Middle Kingdom years. As was the case throughout Egyptian art, a certain vitality appeared in the two-dimensional works. Sculpture in the round retained its concentration on solidity and permanence with few stylistic changes.

Egyptian society embraced a death cult, and some of its most significant monuments continued to be linked with death or worship of the dead. During the New Kingdom period, a new architectural form was created—the **mortuary temple.** Mortuary temples were carved out of the living rock, as were the rock-cut tombs of the Middle Kingdom, but their function was quite different. They did not house the mummified remains of the pharaohs but rather served as their place for worship during life, and a place at which they could be worshipped after death.

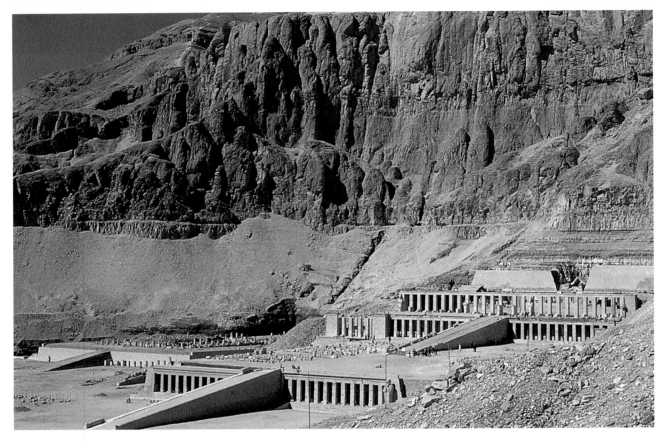

One of the most impressive mortuary temples of the New Kingdom is that of a female pharaoh, Queen Hatshepsut (Fig. 10–14). The temple backs into imposing cliffs and is divided into three terraces, which are approached by long ramps that rise from the floor of the valley to the top of pillared **colonnades.** Although the terraces are now as barren as the surrounding country, during Hatshepsut's time they were covered with exotic vegetation. The interior of the temple was just as lavishly decorated, with some 200 large sculptures as well as painted relief carvings.

As the civilization of Egypt became more advanced and powerful, there was a tendency to build and sculpt on a monumental scale. Statues and temples reached gigantic proportions. The delicacy and refinement of earlier Egyptian art fell by the wayside in favor of works that reflected the inflated Egyptian ego. Throughout the New Kingdom period, conventionalism was, for the most part, maintained. During the reign of Akhenaton, however, Egypt was offered a brief respite from stylistic rigidity.

THE AMARNA REVOLUTION: THE REIGN OF AKHENATON AND NEFERTITI

During the fourteenth century BCE a king by the name of Amenhotep IV rose to power. His reign marked a revolution in both religion and the arts. Amenhotep IV, named for the god Amen, changed his name to Akhenaton in honor of the sun god, Aton, and he declared that Aton was the only god. In his monotheistic fury, Akhenaton spent his life tearing down monuments to the old gods and erecting new ones to Aton.

The art of Akhenaton's reign, or that of the *Amarna period* (so named because the pharaoh moved the capital of Egypt to Tel el-Amarna), was as revolutionary as his approach to religion. The wedge-shaped stylizations

The great pyramids of Giza are generally thought of as some of the most glorious monuments of Western civilization. Few of us stop to think that they were produced on a continent that figures most prominently in our histories of non-Western art—Africa. Connections between the ancient Egyptians and indigenous African peoples have often been cited by art historians, among others, seeking to explain the combinations of facial features in some Egyptian sculptures. It is clear that some of the individuals portrayed have African bone structure and features common to the peoples of Africa. There is a growing consensus that ancient Egyptian society was racially pluralistic.

Lorraine O'Grady, a contemporary African-American artist, has similarly considered the resemblances between her family members and portraits of ancient Egyptian women. In works such as *Sisters #II: Nefertiti's Daughter Merytaten; Devonia's Daughter Candace* (Fig. 10–15), she has juxtaposed ancient and contemporary family portraits to draw on "the deep historic black substratum that bridges the mulatto cultures of ancient Egypt and contemporary America."

O'Grady seems to suggest that when African Americans consider their cultural heritage, they can draw on a varied background—one that includes the works found throughout the Nile River valley as well as the works found in other parts of the African continent.

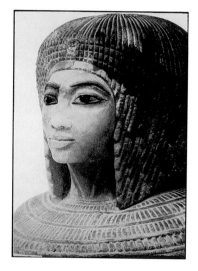 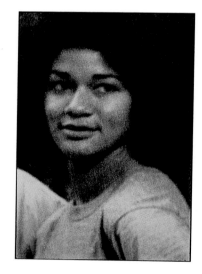

10–15 LORRAINE O'GRADY
SISTERS #II: NEFERTITI'S DAUGHTER MERYTATEN;
DEVONIA'S DAUGHTER CANDACE (1988).
CIBACHROMES PHOTOGRAPHS. 26⅞ BY 38⅜".
COURTESY OF THE ARTIST.

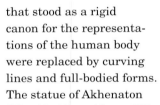

10–16 PILLAR STATUE OF
AKHENATON FROM TEMPLE OF
AMEN-RE, KARNAK (EGYPTIAN,
NEW KINGDOM, C. 1356 BCE).
SANDSTONE, PAINTED.
EGYPTIAN MUSEUM, CAIRO.

that stood as a rigid
canon for the representa-
tions of the human body
were replaced by curving
lines and full-bodied forms.
The statue of Akhenaton
(Fig. 10–16) could not differ more from its precedents
in the Old and Middle Kingdoms. The fluid contours
of the body contrast strongly with those in earlier
sculptures of pharaohs, as do the elongated jaw, thick
lips, and thick-lidded eyes. These characteristics
suggest that the artist was attempting to create a
naturalistic likeness of the pharaoh, "warts and all,"
as the saying goes.

Aside from its being at odds stylistically with other
Egyptian sculptures, the very concept of the work is different. Throughout the previous centuries, adherence to
a stylistic formality had been maintained, especially in
the sculptures of revered pharaohs. If naturalism was
present at all, it was reserved for lesser works depicting
lesser figures. During the Amarna period it was used in
monumental statues depicting members of the royal
family as well.

One of the most beautiful and famous works of art
from this period is the bust of Akhenaton's wife, Queen
Nefertiti (Fig. 10–17). The classic profile reiterates the
linear patterns found in the pharaoh's sculpture. An almost top-heavy crowned head extends gracefully on a
long and sensuous neck. The naturalism of the work is
enhanced by the paint that is applied to the limestone.

The naturalism characteristic of the works of the
Amarna period was short-lived. Just as Akhenaton
destroyed the images and shrines of gods favored by
earlier pharaohs, so did his successors destroy his
temples to Aton. With Akhenaton's death came the
death of monotheism—for the time being. Some have
suggested that Akhenaton's loyalty to a single god may
have set a monotheistic example for other religions.

Akhenaton's immediate successor was Tutankhamen—the famed King Tut. Called the boy-king, Tut died
at about the age of 18. His tomb was not discovered
until 1922, when British archaeologists unearthed a
treasure trove of gold artworks, many inlaid with semiprecious stones. One of these works is an inlaid gold
throne **embossed** with the figures of the young
pharaoh and his wife (Fig. 10–18). Seated on a throne,
Tutankhamen is being attended by his wife under the
rays of the god Amen. In this work, we observe some
residual stylistic effects of the Amarna period. Tut's
body consists of curvilinear forms not unlike those of
the statue of Akhenaton. There is also an emotional
naturalism in the tender contact between the boy and
his queen.

After Akhenaton's death, Egypt returned to normal.
That is, the worship of Amen was resumed and art
reverted to the rigid stylization typical of earlier
dynasties. The divergence that had taken place with
Akhenaton and been carried forward briefly by his
successor soon disappeared. Instead, the permanence
that was so valued by this people endured for another
1,000 years virtually unchanged despite the kingdom's
gradual decline.

AEGEAN ART

The Tigris and Euphrates valleys and the Nile River
banks provided the climate and conditions for the survival of Mesopotamia and Egypt. Other ancient civilizations also flourished because of their geography. Those
of the Aegean—Crete in particular—developed and
thrived because of their island location. As maritime
powers, they maintained contact with distant cultures
with whom they traded—including those of Egypt and
Asia Minor.

10–17 Bust of Queen Nefertiti (Egyptian, New Kingdom, c. 1344 bce). Limestone. Height: c. 20″.
Agyptisches Museum State Museums, West Berlin.

10–18 Tutankhamen's Throne (detail—back) (Egyptian, New Kingdom, c. 1340 bce). Wood covered with gold leaf, with inlays of silver, colored glass, and carnelian. Width of back: 21″.
Egyptian Museum, Cairo.

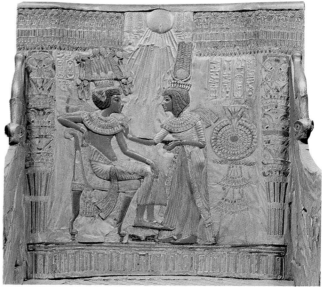

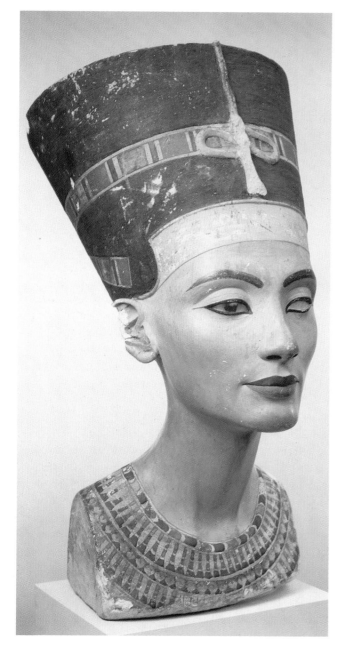

Up until about CE 1870, some Aegean civilizations were thought not to have existed. Although they had been sung by the Greek master of the epic, Homer, their strange names were attributed to an overactive imagination. But during the last decades of the nineteenth century, a German archaeologist, Heinrich Schliemann, followed the very words of Homer and unearthed some of the ancient sites, including Mycenae, on the mainland of Greece (Map 3, p. 250). Following in Schliemann's footsteps, Sir Arthur Evans excavated on the island of Crete and uncovered remains of the Minoan civilization cited by Homer. These cultures and that of the Cyclades Islands in the Aegean comprise the Bronze Age civilizations of **pre-Hellenic** Greece.

THE CYCLADES

The Cyclades Islands are part of an archipelago in the Aegean Sea off the southeast coast of mainland Greece. They are six in number and include Melos, the site where the famed Venus de Milo (see Fig. 11–17) was found; and Paros, one of the chief quarry locations for marble used in ancient Greece. The Cycladic culture flourished on these six islands during the Early Bronze Age, from roughly 2500 to 2000 BCE.

The art that survives has been culled mostly from tombs and includes pottery and small marble figurines. Most of these figures represent fertility goddesses and appear as pared-down geometric versions of the

MAP 3 GREECE, FIFTH CENTURY BCE.

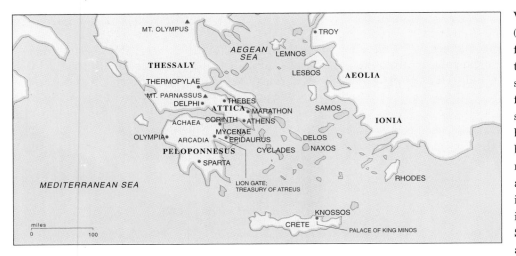

Venus of Willendorf (Fig. 10–2). The fertility figure in Figure 10–19 is typical of these little sculptures. Note the flattened oval head, the square torso with the bare suggestion of breasts, the arms folded rigidly across the abdomen, and the incised outlines suggesting the pubic region. Some male figures have also been found, most represented as musicians playing highly abstracted instruments. All of these figures are believed to have had a religious function, or at least to have been linked with certain rituals surrounding death.

The Cycladic culture seems to have ended at the same time that the great civilization of Crete was developing. The latter was one of the most remarkable cultures to thrive in the ancient world.

CRETE

The civilization that developed on the island of Crete is called the Minoan civilization, named after the legendary king of Crete, Minos. The myths surrounding Minoan life are many, but the most famous is that of the minotaur of King Minos, a cruel beast that was half-man and half-bull and that often devoured Greek boys and girls. The youths were supposedly placed within a complex **labyrinth** that the minotaur roamed and were forced to try to escape a certain death.

Although Homeric reports such as these were deemed to be myth, the actuality of the Minoan civilization was not. Sir Arthur Evans's excavations revealed Crete to be a bustling culture with exciting artistic and architectural remains. Evans divided the history of Minoan civilization into three parts: the Early Minoan period, known as the pre-Palace period, from which survive some small sculptures and pottery; the Middle Minoan period, or the period of the Old Palaces, which began around 2000 BCE and ended three centuries later with what was probably a devastating earthquake; and

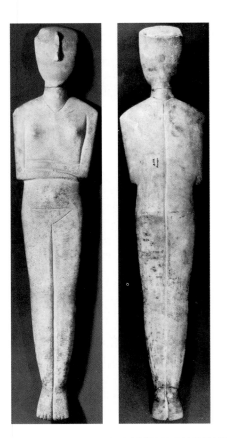

10–19 CYCLADIC IDOL, FROM AMORGOS (FRONT AND BACK VIEWS) (C. 2500–1100 BCE). MARBLE. HEIGHT: 30″.
ASHMOLEAN MUSEUM, OXFORD, ENGLAND.

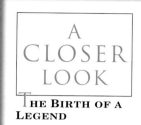
The legend of King Minos and his minotaur is a very familiar one. The creature—half-man, half-beast—was confined to a labyrinth and every nine years was fed with the blood of young Athenians. Theseus, the son of Aegeus, King of Athens, eventually entered the labyrinth and slew the minotaur.

However preposterous, there are often kernels of truth in legends. What truth might serve as the origin of the legend of the minotaur? Does it hark back to times of human sacrifice? Does the minotaur represent a real bull rather than a legendary creature, or a Minoan king in a bull's mask? Were the victims aspirants to the bull ring?

Perhaps a clue is found in the so-called Toreador Fresco (Fig. 10–20) from the palace at Knossos. A bull leaps through space with front and hind legs splayed as a trio of acrobats performs daring feats. One acrobat takes the bull by the horns, a second flips over the animal's back, and a third lands safely with the flourish of a successful gymnast.

What are they doing? Why are they doing it? Although the work is referred to as the Toreador fresco, it is pretty much agreed that this is not at all a bull-fight but something more along the lines of a bull *dance*. Perhaps the dance is part of a ceremony or religious ritual, particularly because the bull was commonly worshipped in ancient Crete.

Did visitors to Crete witness such a bull dance ritual? Was their tale distorted into the legend of the minotaur with its retelling? Is this Minos's bull? Are these the children who might have been "devoured" by the beast? Was the notorious labyrinth of Greek myth actually the palace of Knossos, with its *mazelike* floorplan?

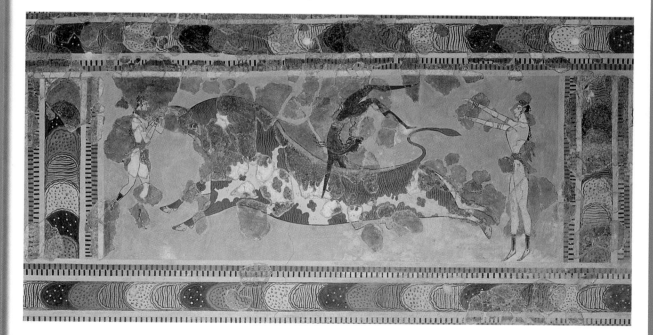

10–20 *TOREADOR FRESCO* FROM THE PALACE AT KNOSSOS
(MIDDLE MINOAN, C. 1500 BCE). HEIGHT: APPROXIMATELY 24½″.
ARCHAEOLOGICAL MUSEUM, HERAKLION, CRETE.

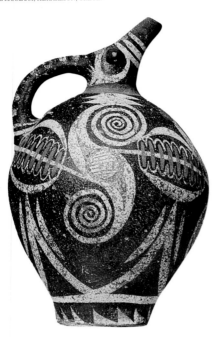

the Late Minoan period, during which these palaces were reconstructed, beginning in the sixteenth century BCE and probably ending in about 1400 BCE. It was at that time that the stronghold of Western civilization shifted from the Aegean to the Greek mainland. We shall focus on the Middle and Late Minoan periods.

THE MIDDLE MINOAN PERIOD   During the Middle Minoan period, the great palaces, including the most famous one at Knossos, were constructed. A form of writing based on **pictographs,** called Linear A, was developed. Refined articles of ivory, metal, and pottery were also produced.

Some of the finest ceramics of the ancient world prior to the Greek civilization were created on Crete. They were largely due to the development of the potter's wheel, which enabled artists to execute wares that were more uniform in shape and had thinner, more delicate walls. They were gaily decorated with abstract motifs inspired by the local vegetation and marine life.

Many of the vessels have been found in a cave at Kamares and thus have been called Kamares ware. A Kamares pitcher (Fig. 10–21) is an example of this type of pottery. The pitcher is a full-bodied vessel of elegant contours and impeccable symmetry, due, in part, to the

throwing process. Characteristic of Kamares ware of this period is the painted decoration of light patterns on a dark black ground, dotted with bolder tones of red and yellow. The patterns portray no particular plant life, although the swirling forms, tight spirals, and broadly brushed "leaves" or "stems" have a definite organic quality. More important than the individual patterns, however, is the way the painter allows the voluminous forms to embrace and echo the swelling portions of the pitcher. The most dynamic shapes are distributed at the widest part, or shoulder, of the vessel. This freedom of expression reflected the Minoan attitude toward life, which was much more passionate and free-spirited than that of Egypt.

Unlike those of Mesopotamia and Egypt, Minoan architectural projects did not consist of tombs, mortuary temples, or shrines. Instead, the Minoans constructed lavish palaces for their kings and the royal entourage. Not much is known of the old palaces, except for those that were subsequently built on their ruins. We will examine the architecture of the principal palace at Knossos, erected first during the Middle Minoan period, in our discussion of Late Minoan art.

THE LATE MINOAN PERIOD   Toward the end of the Middle Minoan period, the palace at Knossos was reduced to rubble either by an earthquake or by invaders. About a century after its destruction, however, it was rebuilt on a grander scale. Also during the Late Minoan period, a type of writing called Linear B was developed. This system, finally deciphered in 1953, turned out to be an early form of Greek. The script, found on clay tablets, perhaps indicates the presence of a Greek-speaking people—the Mycenaeans—on Crete during this period.

The most spectacular of the restored palaces on Crete is that at Knossos. It was so large and sprawling that one can easily understand how the myth of the minotaur arose. The adjective "labyrinthine" certainly describes it. A large variety of rooms were set off major corridors and arranged about a large central court. The rooms included the king's and queen's bedrooms, a throne room, reception rooms, servants' quarters, and many other spaces including rows of **magazines,** or storage areas, where large vessels of grain and wine

10–22 QUEEN'S BEDROOM IN PALACE AT KNOSSOS (LATE MINOAN, C. 1500 BCE).

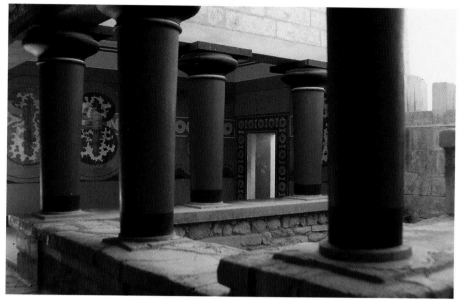

were embedded in the earth for safekeeping. The palace was three stories high, and the upper floors were reached by well-lit stairways. Beneath the palace were the makings of an impressive water supply system of terra-cotta pipes that would have provided running water for bathrooms.

Some of the most interesting decorative aspects of the palace at Knossos—seen in the queen's bedroom (Fig. 10–22)—are its unique columns and its vibrant fresco paintings. The columns, carved of stone, are narrower at the base than at the top. This proportion is the reverse of that of the standard columns found in Mesopotamia, Egypt, and later, in Greece. The columns are crowned by cushion-shaped capitals that loom large over the curious stem of the column shaft, often painted bright red or blue.

The rooms were also adorned with painted panels of plant and animal life. Stylized **rosettes** accent doorways, while delicately painted dolphins swim across the surface of the wall, giving one the impression of looking into a vast aquarium. This fascination with marine life that we also see in Minoan pottery of the late period is no doubt due to the fact that, as an island, Crete was surrounded by water and was an impressive maritime power.

The palace at Knossos, and all the other palaces on Crete, were again destroyed sometime in the fifteenth century BCE. At this point the Mycenaeans of the Greek mainland may have moved in and occupied the island. However, their stay was short-lived. Knossos, and the Minoan civilization, had been finally destroyed by the year 1200 BCE.

MYCENAE

Although the origins of the Mycenaean people are in doubt, we know that they came to the Greek mainland as early as 2000 BCE. They were a Greek-speaking people who were sophisticated in the forging of weapons. They were also versatile potters and architects. The Minoans clearly influenced Mycenaean art and culture, even though by about 1600 BCE Mycenae was by far the more powerful of the two civilizations. Mycenaeans occupied Crete after the palaces were destroyed. The peak of Mycenaean supremacy lasted about two centuries, from 1400 to 1200 BCE. At the end of that period, invaders from the north—the fierce and undaunted Dorians—gained control of mainland Greece. They intermingled with the Mycenaeans to form the beginnings of the peoples of ancient Greece.

Lacking the natural defense of a surrounding sea that was to Crete's advantage, the Mycenaeans were constantly facing threats from land invaders. They met these threats with strong fortifications, such as the citadels in the major cities of Mycenae and Tiryns. Much of the architecture and art of the Mycenaean civilization reflects the preoccupation with arms.

ARCHITECTURE   As concerned as the Mycenaeans were with matters of protection, they had not lost their aesthetic sense. Citadels were ornamented with frescoes and sculpture, some of which served as architectural decoration. One of the most famous carved pieces from

10–23 LION GATE AT MYCENAE (C. 1300 BCE). HEIGHT OF SCULPTURE ABOVE LINTEL, 9′6½″.

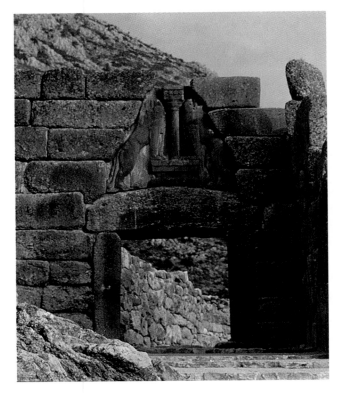

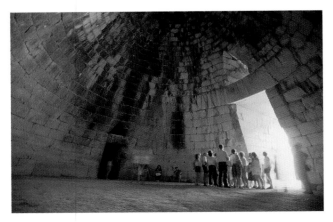

10–24 THE TREASURY OF ATREUS (MYCENAEAN, C. 1300–1250 BCE).

this civilization is the Lion Gate at Mycenae (Fig. 10–23). This gate served as one of the entranceways to the citadel. The actual gateway consists of two massive vertical pillars on which rests a heavy lintel—another example of post-and-lintel construction. Additional large stones were piled horizontally above the lintel and beveled to form an open triangular area; they thus decreased the load to be born by the lintel. Within this triangular space was placed a thick slab sculpted with lions flanking a column that can be recognized as Minoan in style. The heads of the beasts, now gone, were carved of separate pieces of stone and fit into place. Although the animal figures are not intact, their prominent and realistic musculature, carved in high relief, is an awesome sight, one that was sure to give an intruder pause.

Another contribution of the Mycenaean architect was the **tholos,** or beehive tomb. During the early phases of the Mycenaean civilization, members of the royal family were buried in so-called **shaft graves.** These were no more than pits in the ground, lined with stones. The only evidence of their existence was a *stele,* a type of headstone, set above the entrance to the grave. As time went on, however, the tombs became more ambitious.

The Treasury of Atreus (Fig. 10–24), a tholos tomb so named by Schliemann because he believed it to have been the tomb of the mythological ancient Greek king Atreus, is typical of such constructions. The Treasury consists of two parts: the *dromos,* or narrow passageway leading to the tomb proper; and the *tholos,* or beehive-shaped tomb chamber. The latter's circular walls consist of hundreds of stones laid atop one another in concentric rings of diminishing size. The Treasury rose to a height of some 40 feet and enclosed a vast amount of space, an architectural feat not to be duplicated until the domed ceilings of ancient Rome were constructed.

GOLD WORK   Homer's favorite epithet for Mycenae was "rich in gold." To be sure, the Mycenaeans apparently had an insatiable desire to have gold and to work with it. This was verified by the shaft grave excavations that were carried out by Schliemann. The tholos tombs were quickly plundered after their construction, suffering the hazards of being ostentatious, much as was the case

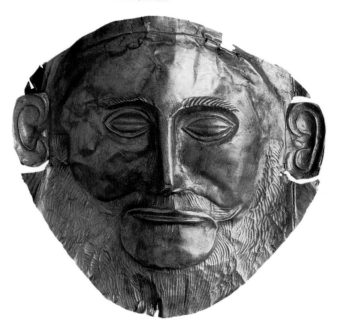

10–25 Funeral mask from the royal tombs at Mycenae (c. 1500 BCE). Beaten gold. Height: 12″.
NATIONAL ARCHAEOLOGICAL MUSEUM, ATHENS.

with the Pyramids. But a wealth of treasures was still found by Schliemann in the shaft graves. One such find is a gold death mask (Fig. 10–25). Masks such as these were created from thin, hammered sheets of gold laid over the faces of the deceased. Some elements of the face were stylized, such as the ears, eyebrows, and coffee-beanlike eyes, while other features were more naturalistically rendered. Much other craft art was found, including weapons such as inlaid daggers, and spectacular gold vessels.

But even the cyclopian walls of the Mycenaean citadels could not ward off enemies for long. After roughly 1200 BCE, the Mycenaean civilization collapsed at the hands of better-equipped warriors—the Dorians. The period following the Dorian invasions of the Greek mainland witnessed no significant developments in art and architecture. But the peoples of this area formed the seeds of one of the world's most influential and magnificent civilizations—that of ancient Greece.

key terms

Upper Paleolithic	Stele	Idealistic	Colonnade
Mesolithic	Conceptual manner	Mummification	Pre-Hellenic
Neolithic	Capital	Ka figures	Pictograph
Naturalism	Volute	Horus	Tholos
Megaliths	Fertile Crescent	Canon of proportions	Shaft graves
Cuneiform	Fertile Ribbon	Portico	
Ziggurat	Incise	Mortuary temple	

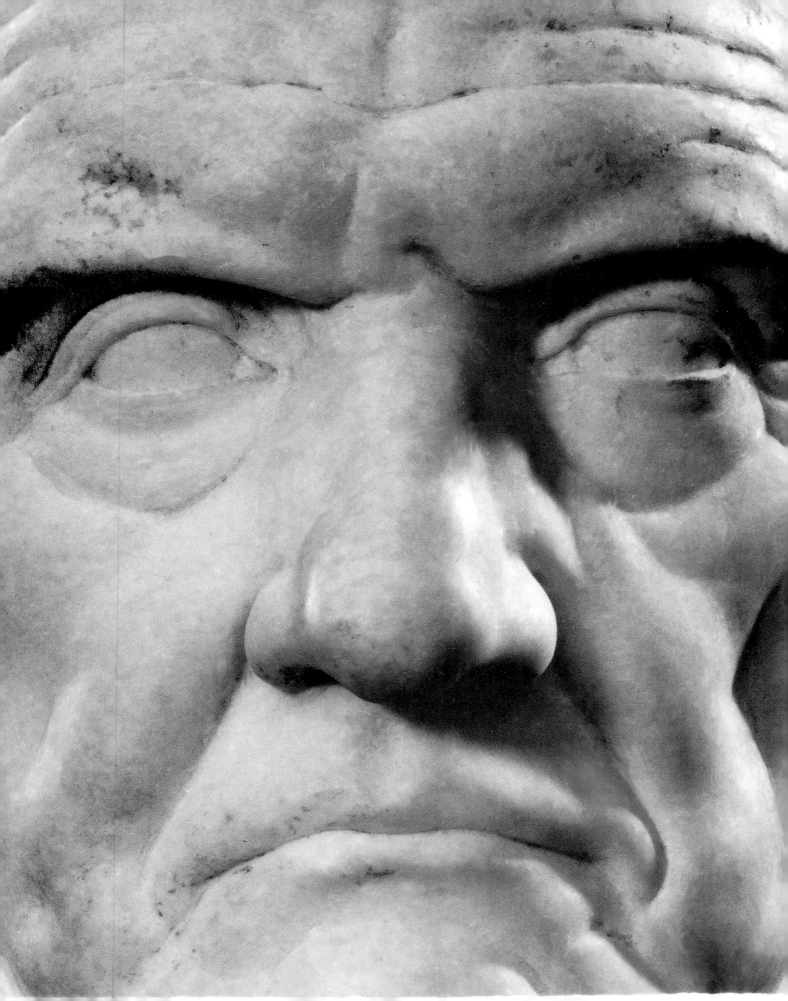

c h a p t e r

CLASSICAL ART: GREECE AND ROME

- The greatest achievements in Greek art, literature, philosophy, and drama were made within a span of only eighty years.

- Although ancient Greece was conquered and absorbed by Rome, Greek culture lived on through its influence on Roman culture.

- The Greeks sought perfection through both physical and intellectual development—that is, a sound mind in a sound body (*mens sana in corpore sano*).

- The Parthenon once contained a 40-foot-high statue of Athena made of ivory and gold.

- The Parthenon remained intact for 2,000 years until it was gutted by bombs when it was being used as an ammunition dump.

- The Greek sculptor Polykleitos developed the canon of proportions we still use to teach figure drawing today.

- The Romans kept wax death masks of their loved ones in the way we keep photographs today.

- The Colosseum in Rome was the site of a naval battle.

- A sculpture of Marcus Aurelius survived because of a case of mistaken identity.

Bust of a Roman. (detail). See Figure 11–19.

. . . the glory that was Greece
And the grandeur that was Rome.

—*Edgar Allan Poe*

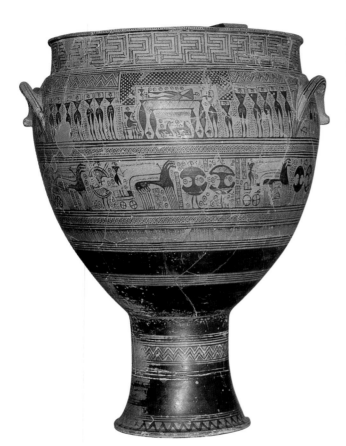

11–1 DIPYLON VASE WITH FUNERY SCENE
(GREEK, 8TH CENTURY BCE).
TERRA COTTA. HEIGHT: 42⅝″.
THE METROPOLITAN MUSEUM OF ART, N.Y. ROGERS FUND 1914 (14.130.14).

No other culture has had as far-reaching or lasting an influence on art and civilization as that of ancient Greece. It has been said that "nothing moves in the world which is not Greek in origin." To this day, Greece's influence can be felt in science, mathematics, law, politics, and art. Unlike some other cultures which flourished, died, and left barely an imprint on the pages of history, that of Greece has asserted itself time and again over the 3,000 years since its birth. During the fifteenth century, there was a revival of Greek art and culture called the Renaissance, and on the eve of the French Revolution of 1789, artists of the Neoclassical period again turned to the style and subjects of ancient Greece. Our forefathers looked

to Greek architectural styles for the buildings of our nation's capital, and nearly every small town in America has a bank, post office, or library constructed in the Greek Revival style.

Despite its cultural and artistic achievements, ancient Greece was conquered and absorbed by Rome—one of history's strongest and largest empires. Although Greece's political power waned, its influence as a culture did not. It was assimilated by the admiring Romans. The spirit of **Hellenism** lived on in the glorious days of the Roman Empire.

In contrast to the Greeks' intellectual and creative achievements, the Romans' cultural contributions lay in the areas of building, city planning, government, and law. Although sometimes thought of as uncultured and crude, the Romans civilized much of the ancient world following military campaigns that are still studied in military academies.

Despite its awesome might, the Roman Empire also fell. It was replaced by a force whose ideals differed greatly and whose kingdom was not of this world—Christianity. In this chapter we shall examine the artistic legacy of Greece and Rome. This legacy—called **Classical art**—has influenced almost all of Western art, from Early Christian mosaics to contemporary Manhattan skyscrapers.

GREECE

The most important concerns of the ancient Greeks were man, reason, and nature, and these concerns formulated their attitude toward life. The Greeks considered themselves (that is, men and not women or slaves) to be the center of the universe—the "measure of all things." This concept is called **humanism.** The value put on the individual led to the development of democracy as a system of government among independent city-states throughout Greece. It was also the responsibility of the individual to reach his or her full potential. Much emphasis was placed on the notion of a "sound body"; physical fitness was of utmost importance. The Greeks also recognized the power of the intellect. Their love of reason and admiration for intellectual pursuits led to the development of **rationalism,** a philosophy in which knowledge is assumed to come from reason alone, without input from the senses. Perfection for the Greeks was the achievement of a sound mind in a sound body (*mens sana in corpore sano*). This is not to say that the Greeks were wholly without emotion—on the contrary, they were vital and passionate—but the Greeks sought a balance between elements: mind and body, emotion and intellect.

The Greeks had a profound love and respect for nature and viewed human beings as a reflection of its perfect order. In art, this concern manifested itself in a **naturalism,** or truth to reality, based on a keen observation of nature. But the Greeks were also lovers of beauty. Thus, although they based their representation of the human body on observation, they could not resist perfecting it. The representation of forms according to an accepted notion of beauty or perfection is called **idealism,** and in the realm of art idealism ruled the Greek mind.

Ancient Greece has given us such names as Aeschylus, Aristophanes, and Sophocles in the world of drama; Homer and Hesiod in the art of poetry; Aristotle, Socrates, and Plato in the field of philosophy; and Archimedes and Euclid in the realms of science and mathematics. It has also given us gods such as Zeus and Apollo and heroes such as Achilles and Odysseus. Even more astonishing is the fact that Greece gave us these figures and achieved its accomplishments during a very short period of its history. Although ancient Greek culture spans almost 1,000 years, her "Golden Age," or period of greatest achievement, lasted no more than eighty years.

As with many civilizations, the development of Greece occurred over a cycle of birth, maturation, perfection, and decline. These points in the cycle correspond to the four periods of Greek art that we will examine in this chapter: Geometric, Archaic, Classical, and Hellenistic.

GEOMETRIC PERIOD

The **Geometric period** spanned approximately two centuries, from about 900 to 700 BCE. During this time, a series of invasions took place, resulting in a decline of the arts. Art will flourish during times of peace, but during a period of war there is little time and money

available for it. This period is called Geometric because during this time geometric patterns predominated in art. As in Egyptian art, the representation of the human figure was conceptual rather than optical. When the human figure was present, it was usually reduced to a combination of geometric forms such as circles and triangles. This style changed in later years as Greek artists began to rely more heavily on the observation of nature.

The Dipylon Vase (Fig. 11–1) is a fine example of the Geometric style. The vase takes its name from the site at which it was found—the Dipylon Cemetery in Athens. Except for two distinct bands, the entire body of the Dipylon Vase is decorated with geometric motifs, some of which may have been inspired by the patterns of woven baskets. The painting is meticulous and the forms are rigidly rendered. The subject of the vase is a funeral procession, which is depicted in the wider bands of the broadest part of the vessel. Highly abstracted female figures with wedge-shaped torsos and profile legs march along with the rigidity of the geometric patterns. In the center there is a bier on which rests the horizontal figure of the deceased. The band below features figures of warriors with apple-core shields and teams of chariots. The deceased was likely a Greek soldier.

These geometric elements can also be seen in small bronze sculptures of the period, but the stylistic development is most evident in the art of vase painting.

ARCHAIC PERIOD

The **Archaic period** spanned roughly the years from 660 to 480 BCE, but the change from the Geometric style to the Archaic style in art was gradual. As Greece expanded its trade with Eastern countries, it was influenced by their art. Flowing forms and fantastic animals inspired by Mesopotamia appeared on Greek pottery. There was a growing emphasis on the human figure, which supplanted geometric motifs.

VASE PAINTING
During the Archaic period, Eastern patterns and forms gradually disappeared. During the Geometric period the human figure was subordinated to decorative motifs, but in the Archaic period it became the preferred

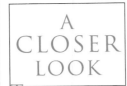
THE WOMEN
WEAVERS OF
ANCIENT GREECE

There are no names of important women artists recorded in ancient Greece. Yet there is plenty of evidence that women did have outlets for creative expression in the media of pottery, basketry, and, particularly, weaving. It was typical for wealthy women as well as for common women and slaves to weave either as a pastime or to earn a living. Athena, the most important female god in the Greek pantheon, was the patron goddess of weavers and potters.

Stories of women weaving come down to us from Homer in *The Iliad* and *The Odyssey*. Helen of Troy weaves in *The Iliad*. In *The Odyssey,* the saga of the wanderings of Odysseus throughout the Mediterranean following the sacking of Troy, Odysseus's wife, Penelope, ruled Ithaca in her husband's absence and was beset by offers of marriage from many suitors who wished her to accept her husband's absence as evidence of his death. Penelope evaded the suitors through a deception that involved weaving. She promised to marry one of them when she had finished a shroud for Odysseus's father, Laertes. Penelope spent her days weaving the shroud and her nights unraveling it.

The importance of the craft is suggested in a black-figure vase attributed to the Amasis Painter (Fig. 11–2). A large central panel on the body of the vessel contains the images of women working on looms and attending to other tasks in the production of cloth. Some art historians have suggested an even more widespread influence of women's weaving by connecting the patterns of geometric vase painting (Fig. 11–1) with those of Dorian wool fabrics.

The tradition of weaving is thus an early one, but it is one that continues throughout the centuries. In the Middle Ages, for example, noblewomen, nuns, and commoners alike were taught the skills of weaving and embroidery. The most remarkable tapestries of this era were certainly created by women. In our time, artists like Faith Ringgold (Fig. 1–26) and Miriam Schapiro (Fig. 4–17) have explored the expressive possibilities of traditional needlework in their work.

11–2 ATTRIBUTED TO
THE AMASIS PAINTER
ATTIC LEKYTHOS. WOMEN
WORKING WOOL ON A LOOM
(GREEK, C. 540 BCE).
TERRA COTTA. HEIGHT: 6¾″.
SAID TO HAVE BEEN FOUND
IN ATTICA.
THE METROPOLITAN MUSEUM OF ART, N.Y.
FLETCHER FUND, 1931 (31.11.10).

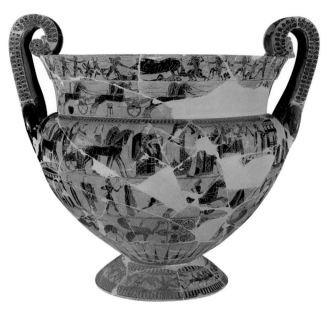

subject. In the François Vase (Fig. 11–3), for example, geometric patterns are restricted to a few areas. The entire body of the vessel, a **volute krater,** is divided into six wide bands featuring the exploits of Greek heroes like Achilles. Even though the drawing is meticulous and somewhat stilted, the figures of men and animals have been given substance, and an attempt at naturalistic gestures has been made. Unlike the figures of the Dipylon Vase, those of the François Vase are not static. In fact, the movement of the battling humans and the prancing horses is quite lively. This energetic mood is enhanced by the spring forms of the volute handles.

The François Vase is one of the finest examples we have of Archaic vase painting. No doubt, those who made it were also proud of their work, since the vessel is signed by both the potter and the painter. The vase is an example of the **black-figure painting technique.** Vases of this kind consist of black figures on a reddish background. This color combination was achieved through a three-stage firing process in the kiln. The decoration was applied to the clay pot using a brush and a **slip,** a liquid of sifted clay. The first stage of the firing process was called the **oxidizing phase** because oxygen was allowed into the kiln. Firing under these conditions turned both the pot and the slip decoration red. In the second phase of firing, called the **reducing phase,** oxygen was eliminated from the kiln, and the vase and the slip both turned black. In the third and final phase, called a **reoxidizing phase,** oxygen was again introduced into the kiln. The coarser material of the pot turned red, while the fine clay of the slip remained black. The result was a vase with black figures silhouetted against a red ground. The finer details of the figures were incised with sharp instruments that scraped away portions of the black to expose the red clay underneath. In addition, the vases were painted with touches of red and purple pigment to highlight the forms. Although this technique was fairly versatile, Greek artists did not care for the heavy quality of the black forms. Around 530 BCE, a reversal of the black-figure process was developed, enabling painters to create lighter, more realistic red forms on a black ground.

ARCHITECTURE

Some of the greatest accomplishments of the Greeks can be witnessed in their architecture. Although their personal dwellings were simple, the dwellings for their gods were fantastic monuments. During the Archaic period, an architectural format was developed that provided the basis for temple architecture throughout the history of ancient Greece. It consisted essentially of a central room (derived in shape from the Mycenaean **megaron**) surrounded by a single or double row of columns. This central room, called the **cella,** usually housed the cult statue of the god or goddess to whom the temple was dedicated. The overall shape of the temple was rectangular, and it had a pitched roof.

There were three styles, or orders, in Greek architecture: the **Doric, Ionic,** and **Corinthian.** The Doric order, which originated on the Greek mainland, was the earliest, simplest, and most commonly used. The more ornate Ionic order was introduced by architects from Asia Minor and was generally reserved for smaller temples. The Corinthian order was by far the most intricate of the three and was used later in less significant buildings, but it was the favorite order of Roman architects,

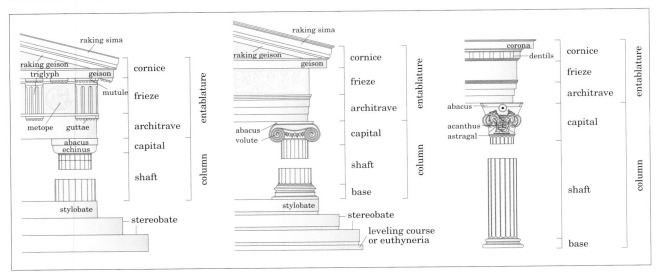

who adopted it in the second century BCE. Figure 11–4 compares the Doric, Ionic, and Corinthian orders and illustrates the basic parts of the temple facade. The major weight-bearing elements of the temple are the columns. These cylindrical vertical forms are composed of drums stacked on top of one another and fitted with dowels. They help support the roof structure from either a platform (the **stylobate**) or a base. The main body, or shaft, of the column is crowned by a **capital** that marks a transition from the shaft to a horizontal member (the **entablature**) that directly bears the weight of the roof. In the Doric order, the capital is simple and cushionlike. In the Ionic order it consists of a scroll or volute similar to those seen on the François Vase (Fig. 11–3). The Corinthian capital is by far the most elaborate, consisting of an all-around carving of overlapping acanthus leaves. The columns directly support the entablature, which is divided into three parts: the **architrave, frieze,** and **cornice.** The architrave of the Doric order is a solid undecorated horizontal band, while those of the Ionic and Corinthian orders are subdivided into three narrower horizontal bands. The frieze, which sits directly above the architrave, contains some sculptural decoration. The Doric frieze is divided vertically into compartments called **triglyphs** and **metopes.** The triglyphs were

sculpted panels consisting of clusters of three vertical elements. These alternate with panels that were filled with sculpted figures. The Ionic and Corinthian friezes, by contrast, were sculpted with a continuous band of figures or—particularly in the Corinthian order— repetitive patterns. The absence of compartments freed sculptors from having to work within a square format. Consequently the decoration flows more freely. The topmost element of the entablature is called a cornice. In all three orders, it consists of a projecting horizontal band. The entablature is crowned by a **pediment,** a triangular member formed by the slope of the roof lines at the short ends of the temple. This space was also ornamented with figures sculpted to fit within the triangular shape.

Although the Doric order originated in the Archaic period, it attained perfection in the buildings of the Classical period. The Corinthian order, although developed by the Greeks, was used more universally by the Romans who came after them.

SCULPTURE

In the Archaic period, sculpture emerged as a principal art form. In addition to sculptural decoration for buildings, free-standing, life-size, and larger-than-life-size statues were executed. Such monumental sculpture was

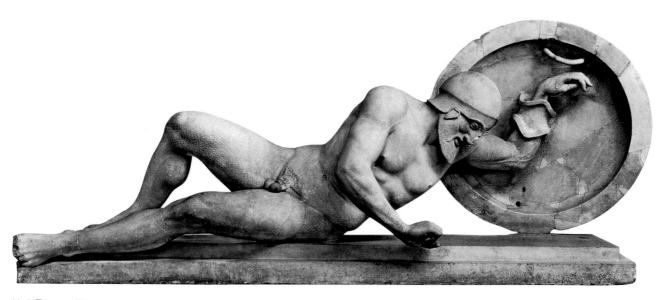

11–5 *FALLEN WARRIOR* FROM TEMPLE OF APHAIA AT AEGINA, GREECE. MARBLE. LENGTH: 6′.
STAATLICHE ANTIKENSAMMLUNGEN UND GLYPTOTHEK, MUNICH.

probably inspired by Egyptian figures that Greek travelers would have seen during the early Archaic period.

ARCHITECTURAL SCULPTURE   In Greek temples, the nonstructural members of the building were often ornamented with sculpture. These included the frieze and pediment. Because early Archaic sculptors were forced to work within relatively tight spaces, the figures from this period are often cramped and cumbersome. However, toward the end of the Archaic period artists compensated for the irregularity of the spaces by arranging figures in poses that corresponded to the peculiarities of the architectural element. For example, the *Fallen Warrior* (Fig. 11–5) from the Temple of Aphaia at Aegina, was sculpted for one of the sharp angles of its triangular pediment. The warrior's feet would have been wedged into the left corner of the pediment, and his body would have fanned out toward the shield, corresponding to the dimensions of the angle. As in vase painting of the period, the figure is based somewhat on the observation of nature. However, at this early date, stylizations remain as artists were following certain conventions for the representation of

the human body. These conventions are most obvious in the sculpting of the warrior's head. He has thick-lidded eyes, overdefined lips that purse in an artificial "smile," and an unnaturally pointed beard. Some of the lines of musculature are also stylized, indicating an obsession with anatomical patterns instead of adherence to optical fact. Yet for its conventional representation, the work reveals a marvelous attention to detail. It is, after all, a pitiful sight. The warrior, wounded in battle, crashes down upon the field with his shield in hand. He struggles to lift himself with his right arm, but to no avail. The hopelessness of the situation is echoed in the helplessness of the left arm, which remains trapped in the grasp of the cumbersome shield. It hangs there useless, the band of the shield restricting its flow of blood. It is an emotionally wrenching scene, and yet the emotion comes from the viewer and not from the warrior. The expression on his face is not consonant with his plight. It remains masklike, bound to the restraining conventions of the Archaic style.

FREE-STANDING SCULPTURE   The *Fallen Warrior* from Aegina was created during the last years of the Archaic period, but the history of Archaic Greek sculpture began

11–6 KOUROS FIGURE (GREEK, ARCHAIC, C. 600 BCE). MARBLE.
HEIGHT: 6′1½″.
THE METROPOLITAN MUSEUM OF ART, N.Y., FLETCHER FUND, 1932 (32.11.1).

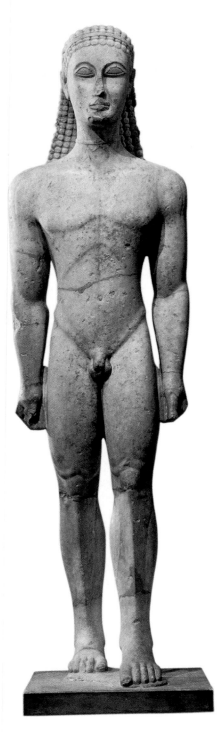

more than a century earlier. About 600 BCE, large free-standing sculpture began to appear. Some of the earliest of these are the so-called **kouros** figures, which are statues of young men, thought to have been dedicated to a god. Figure 11–6 is typical of these figures. The shape of the body adheres essentially to the block of marble from which it was carved. The arms lie close to the body, the fists are clenched tightly, and one leg advances only slightly. The musculature is full and thick, and parts of the anatomy are emphasized by harsh, patterned lines. The kneecaps, groin muscles, rib cage, and pectoral muscles are all flexed unrealistically. The head has also been treated according to the artistic conventions of the day. The hair is stylized and intricate in pattern. The eyes are thick-lidded and stare directly forward. The youth has very high cheekbones and clearly defined lips that appear to curl upward in a smile. This facial expression is seen in most sculpture of the Archaic period. It is believed to have been a convention rather than an actual smile that the sculptor was trying to render. Thus it is called the "archaic smile."

The function of these figures is unclear, although they may have been executed to commemorate the subject's accomplishments. In its stately repose and grand presence, the figure might impress us as a god, rather than a mortal. In looking at this kouros figure, one is reminded of the oft-repeated statement, "The Greeks made their gods into men and their men into gods."

The female counterpart to the kouros is the **kore** figure. Unlike the kouros, the kore is clothed and often embellished with intricate carved detail. The *Peplos Kore* (Fig. 11–7), so named because the garment the model wears is a **peplos,** or heavy woolen wrap, is one of the most enchanting images in Greek art, partly because touches of paint remain on the sculpture, giving it a lifelike gaze and sensitive expression. We tend to think of Greek architecture and sculpture as pristine and glistening in their pure white surfaces. Yet, most sculpture was painted, some in gaudy colors. Architectural sculpture combined red, blue, yellow, green, black, and sometimes gold pigments. None of this painted decoration remains on temple sculpture. However, statues and wooden panels were painted with **encaustic,** a more durable and permanent medium.

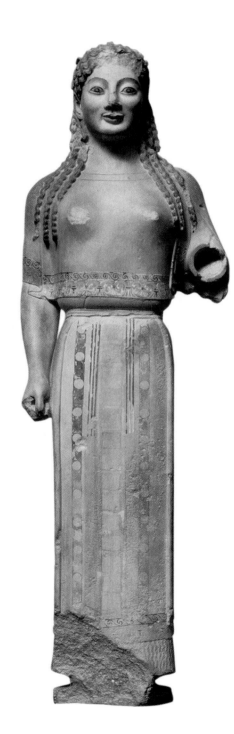

Much of the beauty of the *Peplos Kore* lies in its simplicity. The woman's body is composed of graceful columnar lines echoed in the delicate play of the long braids that grace her shoulders. As is the case in the kouros figures, she remains close to the shape of the marble block. Her right arm, in fact, is attached to her side at the fist. The left arm, now missing, extended outward and probably held a symbolic offering. Although the function of the kore figures is also unknown, some have interpreted them as votive sculptures because many have been found among the ruins of temples.

These architectural and free-standing sculptures were all made of marble. Although expensive, marble was readily available. Some of the finest in the world came from areas immediately around Athens.

The Archaic period was an era of great productivity for the Greeks, but it ended with the invasion of the Persians. After a series of battles, the Persians went for the heart of the Athenian people. In 480 BCE they sacked the **Acropolis,** the sacred hill above the city that was the site of the Athenians' temples. It was a devastating blow, but one from which the proud and enduring Greeks would recover.

EARLY CLASSICAL ART

The change from Archaic to Classical art coincided with the Greek victory over the Persians in a naval battle at Salamis in 480 BCE. The Greek mood was elevated after this feat, and a new sense of unity among the city-states prevailed, propelling the country into what would be called its "Golden Age." Athens, the site of the Acropolis, became the center for all important postwar activity and was especially significant for the development of the arts. The art of the early phase of the Classical period, which lasted some thirty years, is marked by a power and austerity that reflected the Greek character responsible for the defeat of the Persians. Although it indicates great strides from the Archaic style, some of the rigidity of the earlier period remains. The Early Classical style is therefore sometimes referred to as the Severe style.

TRADITION MAINTAINS THAT THE FIRST OLYMPIC GAMES WERE HELD AT THE GREEK
SANCTUARIES OF DELPHI AND OLYMPIA IN 776 BCE.

11–8 MYRON
DISCOBOLUS (DISCUS THROWER) (C. 450 BCE). ROMAN MARBLE
COPY AFTER BRONZE ORIGINAL. LIFE-SIZE.
PALAZZO VECCHIO, FLORENCE.

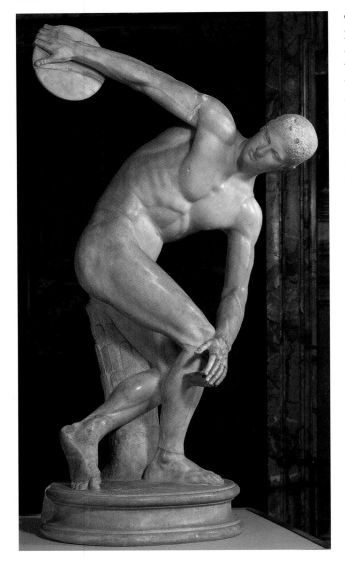

discus throw. The figure, shown as a young man in his prime, is caught by the artist at the moment when the arm stops its swing backward and prepares to sling forward to release the discus. The athlete's muscles are tensed as he reaches for the strength to release the object. His torso intersects the arc shape of his extended arms, resembling an arrow pulled taut on a bow. It is an image of pent-up energy that the artist will not allow to escape. As in most of Greek Classical art, there is a balance between motion and stability, between emotion and restraint.

CLASSICAL ART

Greek sculpture and architecture reached a height of perfection during the Classical period. Greece embarked upon a period of peace—albeit short-lived—and turned its attention to rebuilding its monuments and advancing art, drama, and music. The dominating force behind these accomplishments in Athens was the dynamic statesman Pericles. His reputation was recounted centuries after his death by the Greek historian Plutarch:

> . . . the works of Pericles are . . . admired—though built in a short time they have lasted for a long time. For, in its beauty, each work was, even at that time, ancient, and yet, in its perfection, each looks even at the present time as if it were fresh and newly built. Thus there is a certain bloom of newness in each work and an appearance of being untouched by the wear of time. It is as if some ever-flowering life and unaging spirit had been infused into the creation of these works.

SCULPTURE

The most significant development in Early Classical art was the introduction of implied movement in figure sculpture. This went hand in hand with the artist's keener observation of nature. One of the most widely copied works of this period, which encompasses these new elements, is the *Discobolos* (Fig. 11–8), or *Discus Thrower,* by Myron. Like most Greek monumental sculpture, it survives only in a Roman copy. The life-size statue depicts an event from the Olympic games—the

ARCHITECTURE

After the Persians destroyed the Acropolis, the Athenians refused to rebuild their shrines with the fallen stones that the enemy had touched. What followed, then, was a massive building campaign under the direction of Pericles. Work began first on the temple that was sacred to the goddess **Athena,** protector of Athens and its people. This temple, the Parthenon (Fig. 11–9), became one of the most influential buildings in the history of architecture.

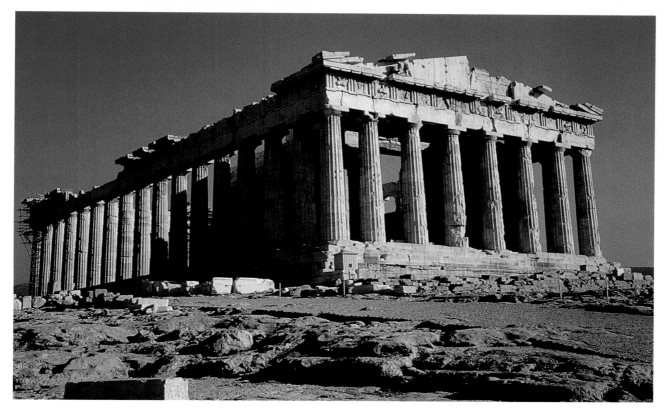

Constructed by the architects Ictinos and Callicrates, the Parthenon stands as the most accomplished representative of the Doric order. A single row of Doric columns, now gracefully proportioned, surrounds a two-roomed cella that housed a treasury and a 40-foot-high statue of Athena made of ivory and gold. At first glance, the architecture appears austere, with its rigid progression of vertical elements crowned by the strong horizontal of its entablature. Yet few of the building's lines are strictly vertical or horizontal. For example, the stylobate, or top step of the platform from which the columns rise, is not straight, but curves downward toward the ends. This convex shape is echoed in the entablature. The columns are not exactly vertical, but rather tilt inward. They are not evenly spaced; the intervals between the corner columns are narrower. The shafts of the columns themselves also differ from one another. The corner columns have a wider diameter, for example. In addition, the shaft of each column swells in diameter as it rises from the base, narrowing once again before reaching the capital. This swelling is called **entasis**.

The reasons for these variations are unknown, although there have been several hypotheses. Errors in construction can be discounted because these variations can be found in other temples. Some art historians have suggested that the change from straight to curved lines is functional. A convex stylobate, for example, might make drainage easier. Others have suggested that the variations are meant to compensate for perceptual distortions on the part of the viewer that would make straight lines look curved from a distance. Regardless of the actual motive, we can assume that the designers of the Parthenon were after an integrated and organic look to their building. The wide base and relatively narrower roof give the appearance of a structure that is anchored firmly to the ground, yet growing dramatically from it. While it has a grandeur based on a kind of austerity, it also has a lively plasticity. It appears as if the Greeks conceived their architecture as large, free-standing sculpture.

11–10 *The Three Goddesses*, from east pediment of the Parthenon (c. 438–431 BCE). Marble. Height of center figure: 4'7".
BRITISH MUSEUM, LONDON.

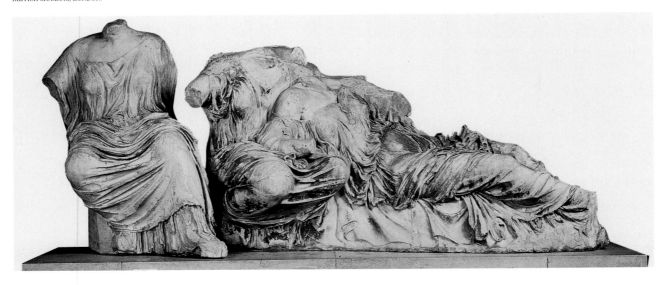

The subsequent history of the Parthenon is both interesting and alarming. In the sixth century CE it was converted into a Christian church, and afterward it was used as an Islamic mosque. The Parthenon survived more or less intact until the seventeenth century, when the Turks used it as an ammunition dump in their war against the Venetians. Venetian rockets hit the bull's eye, and the center portion of the temple was blown out in the explosion. The cella still lies in ruins, although fortunately the exterior columns and entablatures were not beyond repair.

SCULPTURE

ARCHITECTURAL SCULPTURE The sculptor Phidias was commissioned by Pericles to oversee the entire sculptural program of the Parthenon. Although he was involved in creating the cult statue and thus had no time to carve the architectural sculpture, his assistants followed his style closely. The Phidian style is characterized by a lightness of touch, attention to realistic detail, contrast of textures, and fluidity and spontaneity of movement.

As was the case with other Doric temples, the sculpted surfaces of the Parthenon were confined to the friezes and the pediments. The subjects of the frieze panels consisted of battles between the Lapiths and the Centaurs, the Greeks and the Amazons, and the Gods and the Giants. In addition, the Parthenon had a continuous Ionic frieze atop the cella wall. This was carved with scenes from the Panathenaic procession, an event that took place every four years when the peplos of the statue of Athena was changed. The pediments depicted the Birth of Athena and the Contest between Athena and Poseidon for the city of Athens.

The *Three Goddesses* (Fig. 11–10), a figural group from the corner of the east pediment, is typical of the Phidian style. The bodies of the goddesses are weighty and substantial. Their positions are naturalistic and their gestures fluid, despite the fact that limbs and heads are broken off. The draperies hang over the bodies in a realistic fashion, and there is a marvelous contrast of textures between the heavier garments that wrap around the legs and the more diaphanous fabric covering the upper torsos. The thinner drapery clings to the body as if it were wet, revealing the shapely figures of the goddesses. The intricate play of the linear folds renders a tactile quality not seen in art before this time. The lines both gently envelop the individual figures and integrate them in a dynamically flowing composition. Phidias has indeed come a long way from the Archaic artist for whom the contours of the pediment were all but an insurmountable problem.

Some of the Parthenon sculptures were taken down by Lord Elgin (Thomas Bruce) between 1801 and 1803 while he was British ambassador to Constantinople. He sold them to his government, and they are now on view in the British Museum.

FREE-STANDING SCULPTURE   Some of the greatest free-standing sculpture of the Classical period was created by a rival of Phidias named Polykleitos. His favorite medium was bronze and his preferred subject athletes. As with most Greek sculpture, we know his work only from marble Roman copies of the bronze originals.

Polykleitos's work differed markedly from that of Phidias. Whereas the Parthenon sculptor emphasized the reality of appearances and aimed to delight the senses through textural contrasts, Polykleitos's statues were based upon reason and intellect. Rather than mimicking nature, he tried to perfect nature by developing a **canon of proportions** from which he would derive his "ideal" figures.

Polykleitos's most famous sculpture is the *Doryphoros* (Fig. 11–11), or *Spearbearer.* The artist has "idealized" the athletic figure—that is, made it more perfect and beautiful—by imposing on it a set of laws relating part to part (for example, the entire body is equal in height to eight heads). Although some of Phidias's spontaneity is lost, the result is an almost godlike image of grandeur and strength. One of the most significant elements of Polykleitos's style is the principle of **weight shift.** The athlete rests his weight on the right leg, which is planted firmly on the ground. It forms a strong vertical that is accented by the vertical of the relaxed arm. These are counterbalanced by a relaxed left leg bent at the knee, and a tensed left arm bent at the elbow. Tension and relaxation of limbs are balanced across the body *diagonally*; the relaxed arm opposes the relaxed leg, and the tensed arm is opposite the tensed, weight-bearing leg. The weight-shift principle lends naturalism to the figure. Rather than facing forward in a rigid pose, such as that of the kouros figures, the *Doryphoros* stands comfortably at rest. Yet typical of the Polykleitan working method, this appearance of naturalism was derived from a careful balancing of opposing anatomical parts.

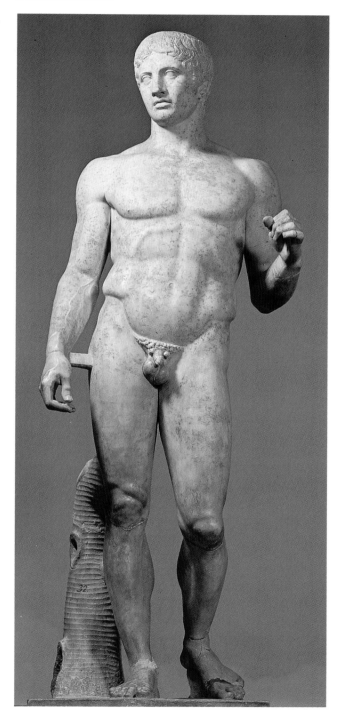

11–12 "NIOBID PAINTER"
ARGONAUT KRATER. ATTIC
RED-FIGURE KRATER
DEPICTING DEATH OF
NIOBIDES. (GREEK,
C. 460 BCE). CERAMIC.
HEIGHT: 24¼".
LOUVRE MUSEUM, PARIS.

VASE PAINTING

The principle of weight shift and the naturalistic use of im plied movement can be seen in Classical vase painting as well. The Argonaut Krater (Fig. 11–12), a red-figure vase decorated by the Niobid Painter, incorporates these elements while devoting significantly more space on the body of the vessel to the human figure. In the Dipylon Vase, the human figure was confined to a single band, whereas the François Vase devoted all of its horizontal bands to the figure (see Figs. 11–1 and 11–3). On later vases, the bands are eliminated and the broad field of the vessel is given over to the human figure in a variety of positions. Yet up until the Classical period, all heads on the vase were arranged on one level. The Niobid Painter, by contrast, attempted to create a three-dimensional space by crudely outlining a foreground, middleground, and background. This was a noble attempt at naturalism, based on optical percep-tion; but it failed because the artist neglected to reduce the size of the figures he placed in the background. The ability to arrange figures in space convincingly would come later with the development of perspective.

Vase painting was not the only two-dimensional art form in ancient Greece. There was also mural painting, none of which has survived. It is believed, however, that the Romans copied Greek mural painting, as they did sculpture, and it is thus possible to learn what Greek painting looked like by examining surviving Roman wall painting (see Fig. 11–21).

LATE CLASSICAL ART

SCULPTURE

The Late Classical period brought a more humanistic and naturalistic style, with emphasis on the expression of emotion. In addition, the stocky muscularity of the Polykleitan ideal was replaced by a more languid sensu-ality and gracefulness. One of the major proponents of this new style was Praxiteles. His works show a lively spirit that was lacking in some of the more austere sculptures of the Classical period.

The *Hermes and Dionysos* of Praxiteles (Fig. 11–13), interest ingly, is the only undisputed original work we have of the Greek masters of the Classical era. Unlike most of the other sculptors, who seem to have favored bronze, Praxiteles excelled in carving. His ability to translate harsh marble surfaces into subtly modeled flesh was unsurpassed. We need only compare his figural group with the *Doryphoros* to witness the changes that had taken place since the Classical period. The *Hermes* is delicately carved and realistic in its muscular emphasis, suggesting a keen observation of nature rather than sculpting according to a rigid canon. The messenger-god holds the infant Dio-nysos, the god of wine, in his left arm, which is propped up by a tree trunk covered with a drape. His right arm is broken above the elbow but reaches out in front of him. It has been suggested that Hermes once held a bunch of grapes toward which the infant was reaching.

Praxiteles's ability to depict variations in texture is fascinating. Note, for example, the difference between the solid muscularity of Hermes and the soft, chubby body of the infant Dionysos, the rough treatment of Hermes's hair contrasted with the ivory smoothness of his skin, and the deeply carved and billowing drapery against the solidity of the body. This realism is enhanced by the use of a double weight-shift principle. Hermes shifts his weight from the right leg to the left arm, rest-ing it on the tree. The resultant stance is known as an **S-curve,** because the contours of the body form an S-shape around an imaginary vertical axis.

Perhaps most remarkable is the emotional content of the sculpture. The aloof quality of Classical statuary is replaced with a touching scene between the two gods. Hermes's facial expression as he teases the child is one of pride and amusement. Dionysos, on the other hand, exhibits typical infant behavior—he is all hands and reaching impatiently for something to eat. There still remains a certain balance to the movement and to the emotion, but it is definitely on the wane. In the Hel-lenistic period, that time-honored balance will no longer be sought, and the emotionalism present in Praxiteles's sculpture will reach new peaks.

11–13 PRAXITELES
HERMES AND DIONYSOS (C. 330–320 BCE). MARBLE. HEIGHT: 7'1".
MUSEUM, OLYMPIA, GREECE.

11–14 LYSIPPOS
APOXYOMENOS (C. 330 BCE). ROMAN MARBLE COPY AFTER A
BRONZE ORIGINAL. HEIGHT: 6'6¾".

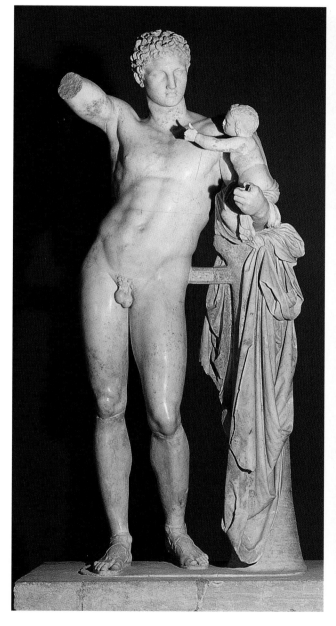

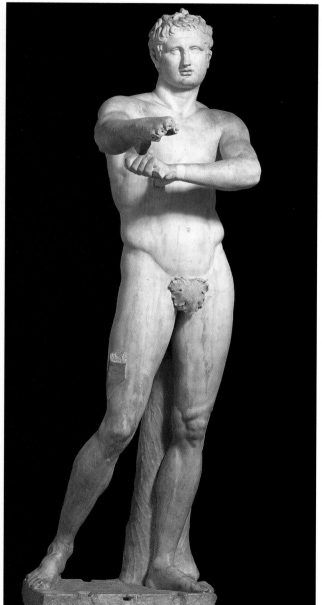

The most important and innovative sculptor to follow Praxiteles was Lysippos. He introduced a new canon of proportions that resulted in more slender and graceful figures, departing from the stockiness of Polykleitos and assuming the fluidity of Praxiteles. Most important, however, was his new concept of the motion of a figure in space. All of the sculptures that we have seen so far have had a two-dimensional perspective. That is, the whole of the work can be viewed from a single point before the sculpture. This is not the case in works such as the *Apoxyomenos* (Fig. 11–14) by Lysippos. The figure's arms envelop the surrounding space. The athlete is scraping oil from his body, after which he will bathe. This stance forces the viewer to

IN 214 BCE CONSTRUCTION WAS BEGUN ON THE GREAT WALL OF
CHINA.

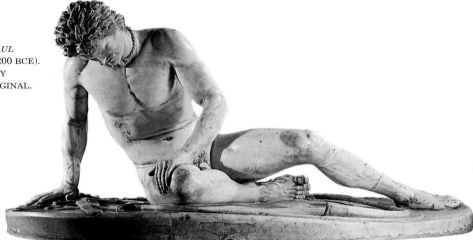

11–15 *The Dying Gaul*
(Hellenistic, 240–200 bce).
Roman marble copy
after a bronze original.
Life-size.
Capitoline Museum, Rome.

walk around the sculpture to appreciate its details.
Rather than adhering to a single plane, as even the
S-curve figure of *Hermes* does, the *Apoxyomenos* seems
to spiral around a vertical axis.

Lysippos's reputation was almost unsurpassed.
In fact, so highly thought of was his work that Alexander the Great, the Macedonian king who spread Greek
culture throughout the Near East, chose him as his
court sculptor. It is said that Lysippos was the only
sculptor permitted to execute portraits of Alexander.
Years after the *Apoxyomenos* was created, it was still
seen as a magnificent work of art. Pliny, a Roman
writer on the arts, recounted an amusing story about
the sculpture:

> *Lysippos made more statues than any other artist,*
> *being, as we said, very prolific in the art; among*
> *them was a youth scraping himself with a strigil,*
> *which Marcus Agrippa dedicated in front of his*
> *baths and which the Emperor Tiberius was*
> *astonishingly fond of. [Tiberius] was, in fact, unable*
> *to restrain himself in this case . . . and had it moved*
> *to his own bedroom, substituting another statue in*
> *its place. When, however, the indignation of the*
> *Roman people was so great that it demanded, by*
> *an uproar . . . that the Apoxyomenos be replaced,*
> *the Emperor, although he had fallen in love with it,*
> *put it back.*[1]

[1] J. J. Pollitt, *The Art of Greece 1400–31 B.C.: Sources and Documents* (Englewood
Cliffs, N.J.: Prentice-Hall, 1965), p. 144.

HELLENISTIC ART

Greece entered the Hellenistic period under the reign
of Alexander the Great. His father had conquered the
democratic city-states, and Alexander had been raised
amid the art and culture of Greece. When he ascended
the throne, he conquered Persia, Egypt, and the entire
Near East, bringing with him his beloved Greek culture, or Hellenism. With the vastness of Alexander's
empire, the significance of Athens as an artistic and cultural center waned.

Hellenistic art is characterized by excessive, almost
theatrical emotion and the use of illusionistic effects
to heighten realism. In three-dimensional art, the space
surrounding the figures is treated as an extension of
the viewer's space, at times narrowing the fine line
between art and reality.

Sculpture

The Dying Gaul (Fig. 11–15) illustrates the Hellenistic
artist's preoccupation with high drama and unleashed
passion. Unlike the *Fallen Warrior* (Fig. 11–5), in which
the viewer has to extract the emotion by piecing together scattered realistic details, *The Dying Gaul* presents all of the elements that communicate the pathos
of the work. Bleeding from a large wound in his side,
the fallen barbarian attempts to sustain his weight on a
weakened right arm. His head, with expressionistically
rendered disheveled hair, hangs down, appearing to

MAP 4   THE ROMAN EMPIRE IN 2ND CENTURY CE.

lean on his shoulder. He has lost his battle and is now about to lose his life. Strength seems to drain out of his body and into the ground, even as we watch. Our perspective is that of a theatergoer; the Gaul seems to be sitting on a stage. Although the artist intended to evoke pity and emotion from the viewer, the melo-dramatic pose of the figure and his position on a stagelike platform detach the viewer from the event. We tend to see the scene as well-acted drama rather than cruel reality.

In 146 BCE, the Romans sacked Corinth, a Greek city on the Pelop-ponesus, after which Greek power waned. Both the territory and the culture of Greece were assimilated by the powerful and growing Roman state. In the next section, we shall examine the art of the Etruscans, a civilization on the Italian peninsula that predated that of the Romans.

THE ETRUSCANS

The center of power of the Roman state was the penin-sula of Italy, but the Romans did not gain supremacy over this area until the fourth century BCE, when they began to conquer the **Etruscans.** The Italian peninsula was inhabited by many peoples, but the Etruscan civi-lization was the most significant one before that of an-cient Rome. The Etruscans had a long and interesting history, dating back to around 700 BCE, the period of transition from the Geometric to the Archaic period in Greece. They were not **indigenous** peoples, but rather are believed to have come from Asia Minor. This link may explain some similarities between Etruscan art and culture and that of Eastern countries.

Etruria and Greece had some things in common. The Italian civilization, for example, was a great sea power. Etruria was also divided into independent city-states. They even borrowed motifs and styles from the art of Greece. There is one more similarity between the two civilizations: Etruria also fell prey to the Romans.

They were no match for Roman organization, especially since neighboring city-states never came to each other's aid in a time of crisis. By 88 BCE, the Romans had van-quished the last of the Etruscans.

ARCHITECTURE

The only "architecture" that survives from the Etruscan civilization is tombs, the interiors of which were con-structed to resemble those of domestic dwellings. The walls were covered with hundreds of everyday items carved in low relief, including such things as kitchen utensils and weapons. The Etruscans apparently wanted to duplicate their earthly environments for "use" in the afterlife.

SCULPTURE

Much sculpture of bronze and clay has survived from these Etruscan tombs, and we have learned a great deal about the Etruscan people from these finds. For exam-ple, even though no architecture survives, we know what the exterior of domestic dwellings looked like from the clay models of homes that served as **cinerary urns.** We have also been able to gain insight into the person-alities of the Etruscan people through their figural sculpture, particularly that which topped the lids of their **sarcophagis.**

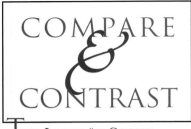

COMPARE & CONTRAST

THE *LAOCOÖN GROUP*
WITH
APHRODITE OF MELOS

The theatricality of Hellenistic art can be seen in one of the most elaborate figural groups in Greek art. The *Laocoön Group* (Fig. 11–16) depicts the gruesome death of the Trojan priest Laocoön and his two sons, who were strangled by sea serpents. The slithery creatures were ordered to attack, some say by Poseidon, to punish Laocoön for having warned his people of the Trojan Horse.

Hellenistic artists were often drawn to subjects with inherent drama. They focused not on a balance between emotion and restraint, but portrayed human excess. In what way does the *Laocoön Group* mark a departure from the classical ideal of balance and moderation? What details of the composition best communicate Laocoön's terrible plight and that of his sons?

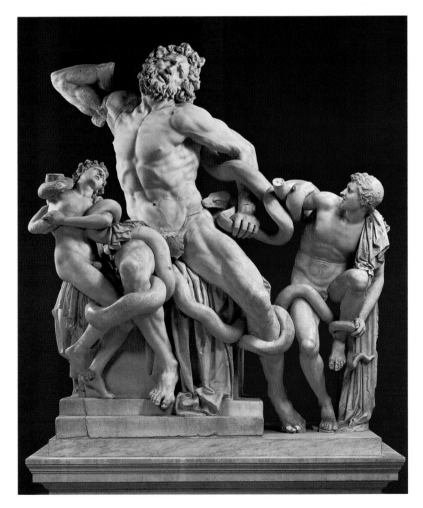

11–16 AGESANDAR,
ATHENODOROS AND
POLYDOROS OF RHODES
LAOCOÖN GROUP
(HELLENISTIC
1ST CENTURY BCE).
MARBLE. HEIGHT: 8′.
VATICAN MUSEUMS, ROME.

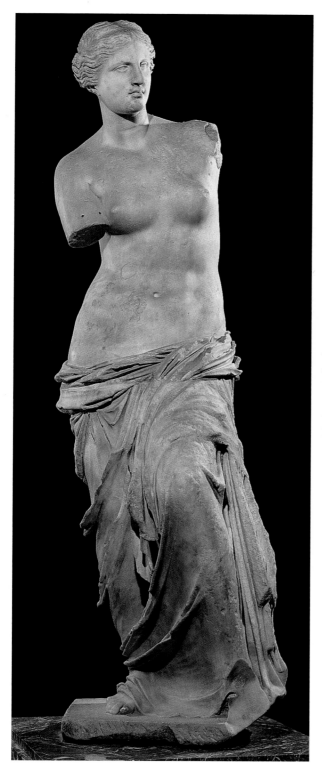

The snakes bind the figures not only physically, but compositionally as well. Explain how. (Hint: They pull together the priest and his sons, who otherwise thrust away from the center of the pyramidal composition.) How does the artist control the potentially runaway action? How do alternating thrusts and constraints heighten the tension and illustrate the mortals' futile attempts to battle the gods?

In the midst of this theatricality, there was another trend in Hellenistic art that reflected the simplicity and idealism of the Classical period. The harsh realism and passionate emotion of the Hellenistic artist could not be farther in spirit from the serene and idealized form of the *Aphrodite of Melos* (Fig. 11–17), often called the *Venus de Milo*. In what ways is the *Aphrodite of Melos* closer in style to Classical figures than to the Hellenistic sculptures in this section? What in particular does the *Aphrodite* owe to the works of Praxiteles?

11–17 *APHRODITE OF MELOS* (*VENUS DE MILO*) (HELLENISTIC, 2ND CENTURY BCE). MARBLE. LARGER THAN LIFE-SIZE.
LOUVRE MUSEUM, PARIS.

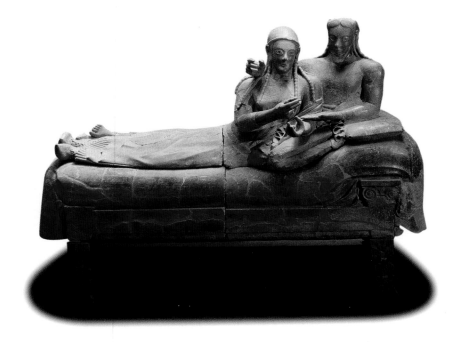

The Sarcophagus from Cerveteri (Fig. 11–18) is a translation into terra cotta of the banquet scenes of which the Etruscans were so fond. A man and wife are represented reclining on a lounge and appear to be enjoying some banquet entertainment. Their gestures are sprightly and naturalistic, even though their facial features and hair are rigidly stylized. These stylizations, especially the thick-lidded eyes, resemble Greek sculpture of the Archaic period and were most likely influenced by it. However, the serenity and severity of Archaic Greek art are absent. The Etruscans appear to be as relaxed, happy, and fun-loving in death as they were in life.

ROME

In about 500 BCE the Roman Republic was established, and it would last some four centuries. The Roman arm of strength reached into northern Italy, conquering the Etruscans, who were probably responsible for having civilized Rome in the first place. Eventually it stretched in all directions, gaining supremacy over Greece, Western Europe, North Africa, and parts of the Near East. No

longer was this the republican city of Rome flexing its muscles—this was the Roman Empire.

Roman art combined native talent, needs, and styles with other artistic sources, particularly those of Greece. The art that followed the absorption of Greece into the Roman Empire is thus often called Greco-Roman. It was fashionable for Romans to own—or at the very least, have copies of—Greek works of art. This tendency gave the Romans a reputation as mere imitators of Greek art, and inferior imitators at that. However, Roman art has been reexamined recently for its own merits, and they are many. A marvelous, unabashed eclecticism pervaded much of Roman art, resulting in vigorous and sometimes unpredictable combinations of motifs. The Romans were also fond of a harsh, almost trompe l'oeil, realism in their portrait sculpture, which we have not seen prior to their time. They were also master builders who created some of the grandest monuments in the history of architecture.

THE REPUBLICAN PERIOD

The ancient city of Rome was built on seven hills to the east of the Tiber River, and served as the central Italian base from which the Romans would come to control most of the known world in the West. Their illustrious beginnings are traced to the **Republican period,** which followed upon the heels of their final victories over the Etruscans and lasted until the death of Julius Caesar in 44 BCE. The Roman system of government during this time was based on two parties, although the distribution of power was not equitable. The **patricians** ruled the country and could be likened to an aristocratic class. They came from important Roman families and later were characterized as nobility. The majority of the Roman population, however, belonged to the **plebeian** class. Members of this class were common folk and

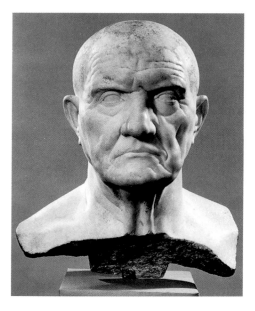

11–19 *BUST OF A ROMAN* (REPUBLICAN PERIOD, 1ST CENTURY BCE). MARBLE. HEIGHT: 14⅜″.
THE METROPOLITAN MUSEUM OF ART, N.Y., ROGERS FUND, 1912 (12.233).

11–20 TEMPLE OF FORTUNA VIRILIS, ROME (ROME, REPUBLICAN PERIOD, LATE 2ND CENTURY BCE).

had less say in running the government. They were, however, permitted to elect their patrician representatives. It was during the Republican period that the famed Roman senate became the governing body of Rome. The rulings of the senate were responsible for the numerous Roman conquests that would expand its borders into a seemingly boundless empire.

By virtue of its construction, however, the Republic was doomed to crumble. It was never a true democracy. The patricians became richer and more powerful as a result of the plundering of vanquished nations. The lower classes, on the other hand, demanded more and more privileges and resented the wealth and influence of the aristocracy.

After a series of successful military campaigns and the quelling of internal strife in the Republic, Julius Caesar emerged as dictator of the Roman Empire. Under Caesar important territories were accumulated, and Roman culture reached a peak of refinement. The language of Greece, its literature, and its religion were adopted along with its artistic styles.

On March 15 (the ides of March) in 44 BCE, Julius Caesar was assassinated by members of the Senate. With his death came the absolute end of the Roman Republic and the beginnings of the Roman Empire under his successor, Augustus.

SCULPTURE

Although much Roman art is derived in style from that of Greece, its portrait sculpture originated in a tradition that was wholly Italian. It is in this sculpture that we witness Rome's unique contribution to the arts—that of **realism.**

It was customary for Romans to make wax death masks of their loved ones and to keep them around the house, as we do photographs. At times, the wax masks were translated into a more permanent medium such as bronze or terra cotta. The process of making a death mask produced intricately detailed images that recorded every ripple and crevice of the face. As these sculptures were made from the actual faces and heads of the subjects, their realism is unsurpassed. The *Head of a Roman* (Fig. 11–19) records the facial features of an old man, from his bald head and protruding ears to his furrowed brow and almost cavernous cheeks. No attempt has been made by the artist to idealize the figure. Nor does one get the sense, on the other hand, that the artist emphasized the hideousness of the character. Rather, it serves more as an unimpassioned and uninvolved record of the existence of one man.

ARCHITECTURE

Rome's greatest contribution lay in architecture, although the most significant buildings, monuments, and civic structures were constructed during the Empire period. Architecture of the Republican period can be stylistically linked to both Greek and Etruscan precedents, as can be seen in the Temple of Fortuna Virilis (Fig. 11–20). From the Greeks, the Romans adopted the Ionic order and post-and-lintel construction. From the Etruscans,

11–21 *Ulysses in the Land of the Lestrygonians,* from a Roman patrician house (50–40 BCE). Fresco. Height 60″.
VATICAN LIBRARY, ROME.

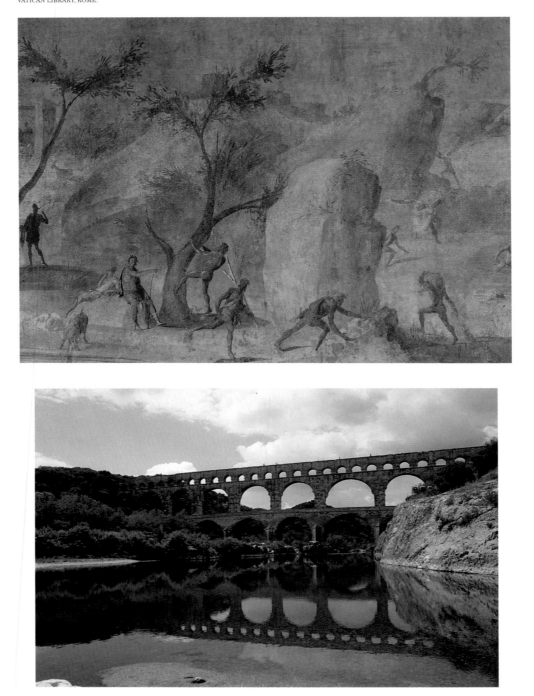

11–22 Pont du Gard, Nîmes, France (Early Empire, c. 14). Length: 900′. Height: 160′.

they adopted the podium on which the temple stands, as well as the general plan of a wide cella extending to the side columns and a free portico in front. But there are Roman innovations as well. The column shafts, for example, are **monolithic** instead of being composed of drums stacked one atop the other. The columns along the sides of the temple are not free-standing but rather are engaged. Also, the Ionic frieze has no relief sculpture. The most marked difference between the temples of Greece and of Rome is the feeling that the Romans did not treat their buildings as sculpture. Instead, they designed them straightforwardly, with an eye toward function rather than aesthetics.

PAINTING

The walls of Roman domestic dwellings were profusely decorated with frescoes and mosaics, some of which have survived the ravages of time. These murals are significant in themselves, but they also provide a missing stylistic link in the artistic remains of Greece. That country, you will recall, was prolific in mural painting, but none of it has survived.

Roman wall painting passed through several phases, beginning in about 200 BCE and ending with the destruction of Pompeii by the eruption of Mount Vesuvius in 79 CE. The phases have been divided into four overlapping styles.

Ulysses in the Land of the Lestrygonians (Fig. 11–21) is an example of the **Architectural style.** Works in this style give the illusion of an opening of space away from the plane of the wall, as if the viewer were looking through a window. In a loosely sketched and liberally painted landscape, the artist recounts a scene from the Odyssey, in which Ulysses's men were devoured by a race of giant cannibals. The figures rush through the landscape in a variety of poses and gestures, their forms defined by contrasts of light and shade. They are portrayed convincingly in three-dimensional space through the use of **herringbone perspective,** a system whereby **orthogonals** vanish to a specific point along a vertical line that divides the canvas. It is believed that Greek wall painting was similar to the Roman Architectural Style.

With the death of Julius Caesar, a dictator, Rome entered its **Empire period** under the rule of Octavian Caesar—later called Augustus. This period marks the beginning of the Roman Empire, Roman rule by emperor, and the Pax Romana, a 200-year period of peace.

THE EARLY EMPIRE

With the birth of the empire there emerged a desire to glorify the power of Rome by erecting splendid buildings and civic monuments. It was believed that art should be created in the service of the state. Although Roman expansionism left a wake of death and destruction, it was responsible for the construction of cities and the provision of basic human services in the conquered areas.

To their subject peoples, the Roman conquerors gave the benefits of urban planning, including apartment buildings, roads, and bridges. They also provided police and fire protection, water systems, sanitation, and food. They even built recreation facilities for the inhabitants, including gymnasiums, public baths, and theaters. Thus, even in defeat, many peoples reaped benefits because of the Roman desire to glorify the empire through visible contributions.

ARCHITECTURE

Although the Romans adopted structural systems and certain motifs from Greek architecture, they introduced several innovations in building design. The most significant of these was the arch, and, after the second century, the use of concrete to replace cut stone. The combination of these two elements resulted in domed and vaulted structures (see Chapter 7) which were not part of the Greek repertory.

One of the most outstanding of the Romans' civic projects is the **aqueduct,** which carried water over long distances. The Pont du Gard (Fig. 11–22) in southern France carried water over 30 miles and furnished each recipient with some 100 gallons per day. Constructed of three levels of arches, the largest of which spans about 82 feet, the aqueduct is some 900 feet long and 160 feet high. It had to slope down gradually over the long distance in order for gravity to carry the flow of water from the source.

Although the aqueduct's reason for existence is purely functional, the Roman architect did not neglect design. The Pont du Gard has long been admired for

11–23 COLOSSEUM, ROME (ROMAN, EARLY EMPIRE, 80).
CONCRETE (ORIGINALLY FACED WITH MARBLE). HEIGHT: 160′;
DIAMETER: 620′ AND 513′.

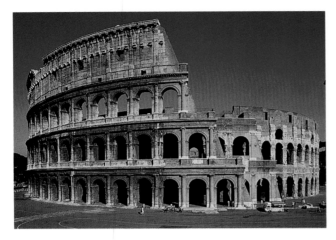

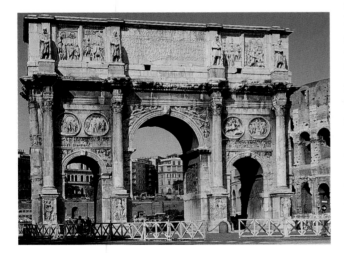

11–24 ARCH OF CONSTANTINE, ROME (312–315).

both its simplicity and its grandeur. The two lower tiers of wide arches, for example, anchor the weighty structure to the earth, while the quickened pace of the smaller arches complements the rush of water along the top level. Not only is there a concern in such civic projects for function and form, but in works such as the Pont du Gard, the form *follows* the function.

THE COLOSSEUM One of the most impressive and famous remains of ancient Rome is the Colosseum (Fig. 11–23). Dedicated in 80 CE, the structure consists of two back-to-back **amphitheaters** forming an oval arena, around which are tiers of marble seats. This vast "stadium" was the site of entertainment for as many as 50,000 spectators, who were shielded from the blazing Italian sun by canopies stretched over the top of the structure. The events ranged from grueling battles between gladiators to sadistic contests between men and beasts. On opening day, the arena was flooded for a mock sea battle that included some 3,000 "sailors." The Colosseum stood for Rome at its worst, but it also represented Rome at its best.

Even in its present condition, having suffered years of pillaging and several earthquakes, the Colosseum is a spectacular sight. The structure is composed of three tiers of arches separated by engaged columns. (This combination of arch and column can also be seen in another type of Roman architectural monument—the triumphal arch [Fig. 11–24]). The Colosseum's lowest level, whose arches provided easy access and exit for the spectators, is punctuated by Doric columns. This order is the weightiest in appearance of the three and thus visually anchors the structure to the ground. The second level utilizes the Ionic order, and the third level the Corinthian. This combination produces a sense of lightness as one proceeds from the bottom to the top tier. Thick entablatures rest atop the rings of columns, firmly delineating the stories. The topmost level is almost all solid masonry, except for a few regularly spaced rectangular openings. It is ornamented with Corinthian pilasters and is crowned by a heavy cornice.

The exterior was composed of masonry blocks held in place by metal dowels. These dowels were removed over the years when metal became scarce, and thus gravity is all that remains to keep the structure intact.

11–25 THE PANTHEON, ROME
(ROMAN, EARLY EMPIRE, 117–125).

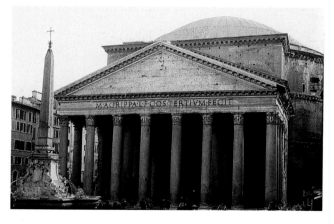

THE PANTHEON   The Roman engineering genius can be seen most clearly in the Pantheon (Fig. 11–25), a brick and concrete structure originally erected to house sculptures of the Roman gods. Although the building no longer contains these statues, its function remains religious. Since the year 609 CE, it has been a Christian church.

The Pantheon's design combines the simple geometric elements of a circle and a rectangle. The entrance consists of a rectangular portico, complete with Corinthian columns and pediment. The main body of the building, to which the portico is attached, is circular. It is 144 feet in diameter and is crowned by a dome equal in height to the diameter. Supporting the massive dome are 20-foot-thick walls pierced with deep niches, which in turn are vaulted in order to accept the downward thrust of the dome and distribute its weight to the solid wall. These deep niches alternate with shallow niches, in which sculptures were placed (Fig. 11–26).

The dome itself consists of a rather thin concrete shell that thickens toward the base. The interior of the dome is **coffered,** or carved with recessed squares that physically and visually lighten the structure. The ceiling was once painted blue, with a gilded bronze rosette in the center of each square. The sole source of light in the Pantheon is the **oculus,** a circular opening in the top of the dome, 30 feet in diameter and open to the sky.

The interior was lavishly decorated with marble slabs and granite columns that glistened in the spotlight of the sun as it filtered through the opening, moving its focus at different times of the day.

It has been said that Roman architecture differs from other ancient architecture in that it emphasizes space rather than solids. Instead of constructing buildings from a variety of forms, the Romans conceptualized a certain space and then proceeded to enframe it. Their methods of harnessing this space were unique in the ancient world and served as a vital precedent for future architecture.

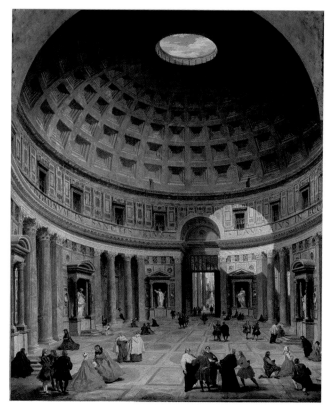

11–26 GIOVANNI PAOLO PANNINI
INTERIOR OF THE PANTHEON, ROME (C. 1734–35). OIL ON CANVAS. 50½ × 39″.

SCULPTURE

During the empire period, Roman sculpture took on a different flavor. The pure realism of the Republican period portrait busts was joined to Greek idealism. The

11–27 *AUGUSTUS OF PRIMAPORTA* (ROMAN, C. 20 BCE). MARBLE. HEIGHT: 6′8″.

VATICAN MUSEUMS, ROME.

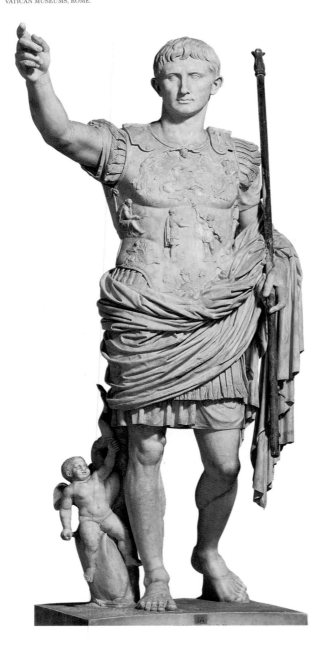

11–28 *IMPERIAL PROCESSION*, FROM THE *ARA PACIS* FRIEZE. MARBLE RELIEF.

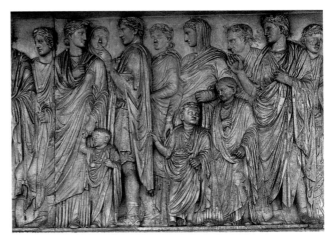

result, evident in *Augustus of Primaporta* (Fig. 11–27), was often a curious juxtaposition of individualized heads with idealized, anatomically perfect bodies in classical poses. The head of Augustus is somewhat idealized and serene, but his unique facial features are recognizable as those that appeared on empire coins. Augustus adopts an authoritative pose not unlike that of Polykleitos's *Doryphoros* (Fig. 11–11). Attired in military parade armor, he proclaims a diplomatic victory to the masses. His officer's cloak is draped about his hips and his ceremonial armor is embellished with reliefs that portray both historic events and allegorical figures.

As the first emperor, Augustus was determined to construct monuments reflecting the glory, power, and influence of Rome on the Western world. One of the most famous of these monuments is the *Ara Pacis,* or Altar of Peace, created to celebrate the empire-wide peace that Augustus was able to achieve. The *Ara Pacis* is composed of four walls surrounding a sacrificial altar. These walls are adorned with relief sculptures of figures and delicately carved floral decoration. Panels such as *The Imperial Procession* (Fig. 11–28) exhibit, once again, a blend of Greek and Roman devices. The right- to-left procession of individuals, unified by the flowing lines of their drapery, clearly refers to the frieze sculptures of the Parthenon. Yet the sculpture differs from its Greek prototype in several respects: The individuals are rendered in portrait likenesses; the relief commemorates a specific event with specific persons present; and these figures are set within a shallow, though very convincing, three-dimensional space. By working in high and low relief, the artist creates the sense of a crowd; fully three rows of people are compressed into this space. They actively turn, gesture, and seem to converse. Despite a noble grandness which gives the panel an idealistic cast, the participants in the procession look and act like real people.

As time went on, the Roman desire to accurately record a person's features gave way to a more introspective portrayal of the personality of the sitter. Although portrait busts remained a favorite format for Roman sculptors, their repertory also included relief sculpture, full-length statuary, and a new design—the **equestrian portrait.**

The bronze sculpture of Marcus Aurelius (Fig. 11–29) depicts the emperor on a sprightly horse, as if caught in the action of gesturing to his troops or recognizing the applause of his people. The sculpture combines the Roman love of realism with the later concern for psychologically penetrating portraits. The commanding presence of the horse is rendered through pronounced musculature, a confident and lively stride, and a vivacious head with snarling mouth, flared nostrils, and protruding veins. In contrast to this image of brute strength is a rather serene image of imperial authority. Marcus Aurelius, clothed in flowing robes, sits erectly on his horse and gestures rather passively. His facial expression is calm and reserved, reflecting his adherence to **Stoic** philosophy. Stoicism advocated an indifference to emotion and things of this world, maintaining that virtue was the most important goal in life.

The equestrian portrait of Marcus Aurelius survives because of a case of mistaken identity. During the Middle Ages, objects of all kinds were melted down because of a severe shortage of metals, and ancient sculptures that portrayed pagan idols were not spared. This statue of Marcus Aurelius was saved because it was mistakenly believed to be a portrait of Constantine, the first Roman emperor to recognize Christianity. The death of Marcus Aurelius brings us to the last years of the empire period, which were riddled with internal strife. The days of the great Roman Empire were numbered.

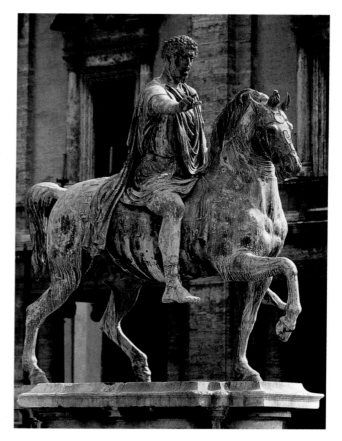

THE LATE EMPIRE

During its late years, the Roman Empire was torn from within. A series of emperors seized the reigns of power only to meet violent deaths, some at the hands of their own soldiers. By the end of the third century, the situation was so unwieldy that the empire was divided into eastern and western sections, with separate rulers for each. When Constantine ascended the throne, he returned to the one-ruler system, but the damage had already been done—the empire had become divided against itself. Constantine then dealt the empire its final blow by dividing its territory among his sons and moving the capital to Constantinople (present-day Istanbul). Thus imperial power was shifted to the eastern empire, leaving Rome and the western empire vulnerable. These were decisions from which the empire would never recover.

11–30 BASILICA OF MAXENTIUS AND CONSTANTINE, ROME (ROMAN, LATE EMPIRE, C. 310–320). 300 × 215′.

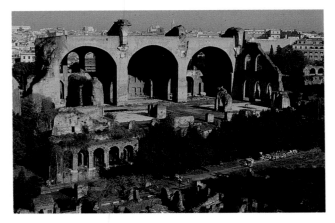

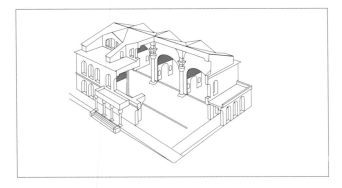

11–31 RECONSTRUCTION OF BASILICA OF MAXENTIUS AND CONSTANTINE, ROME.

11–32 HEAD OF CONSTANTINE THE GREAT (ROMAN, LATE EMPIRE, EARLY 4TH CENTURY). CAPITOLINE MUSEUM, ROME.

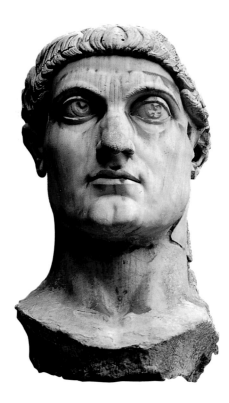

ARCHITECTURE

Although the empire was crumbling around him, Constantine continued to erect monuments to glorify it. Before moving to the East, he completed a basilica begun by his predecessor Maxentius (Fig. 11–30) that bespoke the grandeur that had been Rome. In ancient Rome, basilicas were large public meeting halls that were usually built around or near the **forums.** The basilica of Maxentius and Constantine was a huge structure, measuring some 300 by 215 feet. It was divided into three rectangular sections, or aisles, the center one reaching a height of 114 feet (Fig. 11–31). The central aisle, called a **nave,** was covered by a **groin vault,** a ceiling structure very popular in buildings of such a vast scale. Little remains of the basilica today, but it survived long enough to set a precedent for Christian

church architecture. It would serve as the basic plan for basilicas and cathedrals for centuries to come.

SCULPTURE

Some 300 years before Constantine's reign, a new force began to gnaw at the frayed edges of the Roman Empire— Christianity. It is said that a man called Jesus was put to death for his beliefs, as well as his disregard for Roman authority, and after him, his followers were persecuted by the Romans for the same reasons. The slaying stopped when Constantine proclaimed tolerance of Christianity. This series of events influenced artistic styles, as can be seen in the Head of Constantine (Fig. 11–32). The literalness and materialism of Roman art and life gave way to a new spirituality and otherworldliness in art. The Head of Constantine was part of a mammoth sculpture of the emperor, consisting of a wooden torso covered with bronze and a head and limbs sculpted from marble. The head is 8½ feet high and weighs over 8 tons. The realism and idealism that we have witnessed in Roman sculpture is replaced by an almost archaic rendition of the emperor, complete with an austere expression and thick-lidded, wide-staring eyes. The artist now elaborates the pensive, passive rigidity of form that we sensed in the portrait of Marcus Aurelius. Constantine's face seems both resigned to the fall of his empire and reflective of the Christian emphasis on a kingdom that is not of this world.

key terms

Hellenism
Classical art
Humanism
Rationalism
Naturalism
Idealism
Geometric period
Archaic period
Volute krater
Black-figure painting
  technique
Slip
Oxidizing phase
Reducing phase

Reoxidizing phase
Megaron
Cella
Doric order
Ionic order
Corinthian order
Stylobate
Capital
Entablature
Architrave
Frieze
Cornice
Triglyphs
Metopes

Pediment
Kouros
Kore
Peplos
Encaustic
Acropolis
Athena
Entasis
Canon of proportions
Weight-shift principle
S-curve
Etruscans
Cinerary urns
Sarcophagus

Republican period
Patrician
Plebeian
Monolithic
Herringbone perspective
Orthogonals
Empire period
Aqueduct
Amphitheater
Coffer
Oculus
Equestrian portrait
Forum
Nave

artists

The Amasis Painter
Kleitias
Myron
Ictinos
Kallicrates

Polykleitos
The Niobid Painter
Praxiteles
Lysippos
Agesander

Athenodoros
Polydoros of Rhodes
Giovanni Paolo Pannini

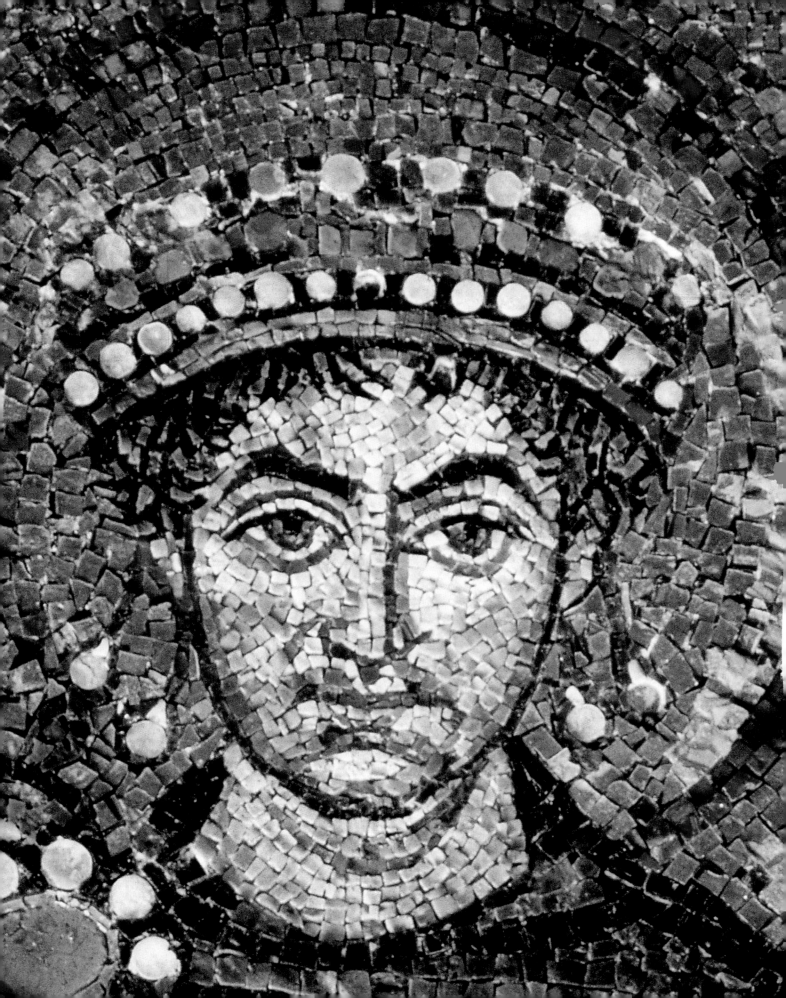

chapter 12

CHRISTIAN ART: FROM CATACOMBS TO CATHEDRALS

PRELIMINARY Sketch

- ❏ Approximately 6 million bodies were buried beneath the streets of Rome between the second and fourth centuries CE.

- ❏ The Romans saw the early Christians as members of a religious cult who refused to acknowledge the emperor as a god.

- ❏ Early Christians carved out underground chapels as places of secret worship.

- ❏ The capital of the Western Roman Empire was moved from Rome to Ravenna in an effort to escape barbarians.

- ❏ The Roman-built Hagia Sophia has served at one time or other as an Eastern Orthodox church, an Islamic mosque, and a museum.

- ❏ "Barbarians" were indirectly responsible for the construction of our most magnificent cathedrals.

- ❏ During the Middle Ages, the only place one could get a decent education was in a monastery.

- ❏ Some of the greatest monuments of Western civilization were created by people who remain nameless.

Justinian and Attendants (detail). See Figure 12–6.

THE USE OF PARCHMENT—ANIMAL SKIN PREPARED FOR WRITING—LED, IN THE FOURTH
CENTURY, TO THE ADOPTION OF THE CODEX, OR BOOK.

12–1 CATACOMB DI PRISCILLA.

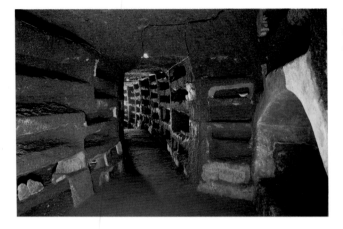

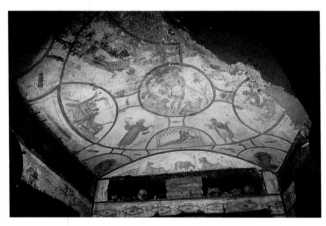

12–2 *THE GOOD SHEPHERD* IN THE CATACOMB OF STS. PIETRO
AND MARCELLINO, ROME (EARLY CHRISTIAN, EARLY 4TH
CENTURY).

FRESCO PONTIFICA COMMISSIONE DI ARCHITETTURA SACRA, VATICAN CITY.

It has been said that the glorious Roman Empire fell to
its knees before one mortal man. Of this man we have
little factual information, although his life is said to be
documented by his followers in the New Testament of
the Bible. The month, date, and year of his birth are
unknown, although they are stated to be December 25,
1 CE. He was a Jew named Jesus, whose followers
considered him to be the fulfillment of the biblical
messianic prophecy. To the Romans, this was blasphemy,
and for this and other crimes, Jesus was put to death
when he was in his thirties. After his death, he became
known as *Jesus Christ* (*Christ* is synonymous with
Messiah).

We cannot attribute the fall of the Roman Empire
solely to Jesus or to his followers, the Christians. The
empire had been having its own problems, both internal
and external. It would also be hard to believe that the
organizational abilities and influence of the mighty
Roman Empire could have succumbed to a handful of
religious believers. Still the power of spirituality over
materialism—and, in this case, of Christianity over
worship of the oppressive Caesars—should not be
underestimated.

This chapter examines the way in which Christians
attempted—through the arts—to glorify Jesus in a
period that spans ten centuries or more.

EARLY CHRISTIAN ART

Christianity flowered among the ruins of the Roman
Empire, even if it did not cause the empire to collapse.
Over many centuries Christianity, too, had its internal
and external problems, but unlike the Roman Empire,
it has survived. In fact, the concept of survival is central
to the understanding of Christianity and its art during
the first centuries after the death of Jesus.

To be a Christian before Emperor Constantine's
proclamation of religious tolerance, one had to endure
persecution. Under the emperors Nero, Trajan, and
Domitian, Christians were slain for their beliefs. The
Romans saw the Christians as mad cult members and
barbaric subversives who refused to acknowledge the
emperor as a god.

In the third century CE, two things happened:
First, Emperor Constantine declared in the Edict of
Milan that Christianity would be tolerated. Later, he
proclaimed Christianity to be the religion of the
Roman Empire. Early Christian art, then, can be
divided into two phases: The Period of Persecution,
before Constantine's proclamation, and then the
Period of Recognition.

THE PERIOD OF PERSECUTION

During the Period of Persecution, Christians worshipped
in secret, using private homes as well as chapels in
catacombs. The catacombs were secret burial places
for Christians beneath city streets. A huge network of

288   CHRISTIAN ART: FROM CATACOMBS TO CATHEDRALS

galleries and burial chambers which accommodated almost 6 million bodies existed beneath the city of Rome (Fig. 12–1). The galleries were carved out of porous stone, and the walls housed niches into which the bodies were placed. Sometimes small chapels were carved out of the gallery walls, and here early Christians worshipped and prayed for the dead. These chapels were very simple, although sometimes they were decorated with frescoes, as in the painted ceiling of the catacomb of Saints Pietro and Marcellino (Fig. 12–2).

The semicircular vault of the chapel was decorated with a cross inscribed in a circle, the symbols for the Christian faith and eternity. The arms of the cross radiate from a central circle in which Jesus is shown as the Good Shepherd, and terminate in **lunettes** depicting scenes from the story of Jonah. Between the lunettes stand figures with arms outstretched in an attitude of prayer. These figures are called **orans,** from the Latin *orare*, meaning "to pray." The style of this fresco is reminiscent of the Classical vase and wall painting of Greece and Rome. The poses are realistic, the proportions are Classical, and the drapery falls over the body naturally. The early Christians shared the art and culture of Rome, if not its religion. Therefore, there were bound to be similarities in style.

Not all catacomb frescoes were as finished as the one of Saints Pietro and Marcellino. The lighting was poor in the catacombs, and the artists probably wanted to get the work done quickly to avoid having to breathe in the stench of decaying flesh any longer than necessary. It was also unusual to populate such "illicit" frescoes with human figures. Not only was the Christians' place of worship secret, the representation of their Savior, Jesus, was often just as mysterious. Perhaps for safety's sake, they adopted symbols that were already present in Roman art for their own purposes. For example, the fish was used to symbolize Jesus, and grapes to represent the promise of salvation through the blood Jesus had shed. This use of symbols, perhaps at first a survival tactic (Romans might not suspect their meaning), would be of central importance to Christian art over the centuries. The study and interpretation of symbols is called **iconology,** and a work of art's symbolic meaning is called its **iconography.** Both words derive from the Greek *eikōn*, meaning "image."

12–3 PLAN AND SECTION OF OLD ST. PETER'S IN ROME (EARLY CHRISTIAN, FIRST HALF OF 4TH CENTURY CE).

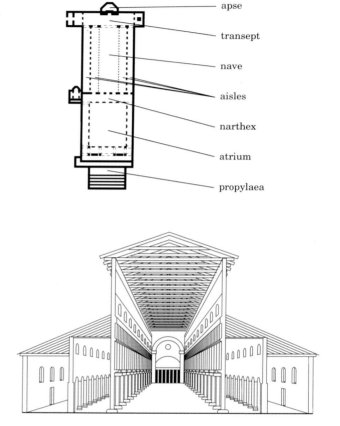

THE PERIOD OF RECOGNITION

After Constantine adopted Christianity as the faith of the Roman Empire, life for the Christians improved considerably. No longer were they forced to keep their worship secret. Consequently, they poured their energies into constructing houses of worship. It is not surprising that the Christians turned to what they already knew for building models—the basilicas of Rome.

One of the first and most important buildings to be erected during the Early Christian period was the first St. Peter's Cathedral in Rome. The architects of the church, called Old St. Peter's, drew on basilican plans and derived a plan for a Christian cathedral that functioned for centuries to come. The plan of Old St. Peter's (Fig. 12–3) consisted of seven parts. Unlike the Roman

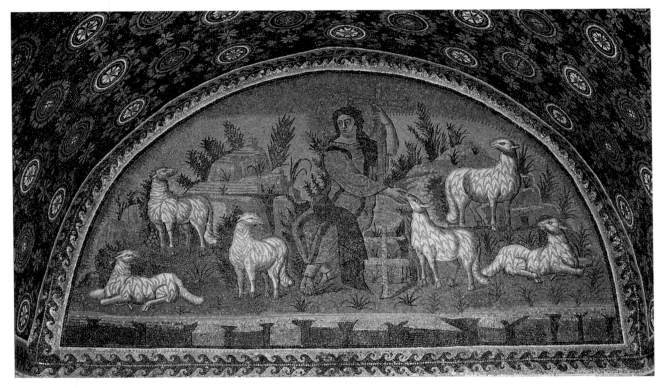

basilica, it was entered from one of the short sides, through a kind of gateway called the **propylaeum.** Passing through this gateway, the worshipper entered a large courtyard, or **atrium,** which was open to the sky. Although these two elements were present in the plan of Old St. Peter's, and appeared occasionally in subsequent churches, they were not carried forward into later buildings with any regularity. Such was not the case with the remainder of the plan. The worshipper gained access to the heart of the basilica through the **narthex,** a portal or series of portals leading to the interior. The long central aisle of the church was called the **nave,** and it was usually flanked by side aisles. As a worshipper walked away from the narthex and up the nave, he or she encountered the **altar** sitting in the **apse.** The apse was generally found at the easternmost end of the structure and was preceded by the **transept,** a kind of crossing arm that intersected the nave and side aisles and was parallel to the narthex. The transept often extended its "arms" beyond the boundaries of the side

aisles, resembling a cross in structure. Because of its heritage, this plan is often called a **Latin Cross plan;** it is also referred to as a **longitudinal plan.**

The longitudinal plan was most prominent in Western Europe. Small circular buildings with **central plans** were popular in the East but were used only in ancillary buildings in the West.

Old St. Peter's was decorated lavishly with inlaid marble and **mosaics,** none of which survive. The art of mosaic was adopted from the Romans and comprised most of the ornamentation of Early Christian churches. Many of the mosaics were Classical in style. The mosaic of *Christ as the Good Shepherd* (Fig. 12–4) from the Mausoleum of Galla Placidia, for example, is reminiscent of Pompeian wall paintings. The figure of Jesus is seated in a well-defined landscape, amidst a flock of sheep. The figures have substance and are rendered three-dimensional through the use of light and shade. The poses are complex, and the gestures and drapery are naturalistic.

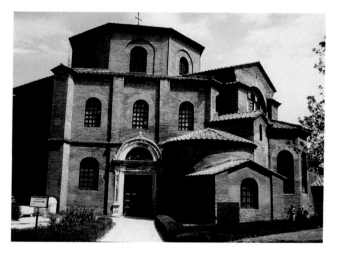

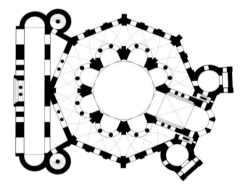

Artists of the Period of Recognition also **illuminated manuscripts** and created some sculpture and small carvings. Their style, like that of the mosaics, can best be described as Late Roman.

BYZANTINE ART

The term **Byzantine** comes from the town of ancient Byzantium, the site of Constantine's capital, Constantinople. The art called "Byzantine" was produced after the Early Christian era in Byzantium, but also in Ravenna, Venice, Sicily, Greece, Russia, and other Eastern countries. We may describe the difference between Early Christian and Byzantine art as a transfer from an earthbound realism to a more spiritual, otherworldly style. Byzantine figures appear to be weightless; they stand in an indeterminate space. Byzantine art also uses more symbolism and is far more decorative in detail.

San Vitale, Ravenna

The city of Ravenna, on the Adriatic coast of Italy, was initially settled by the ruler of the Western Roman Empire who was trying to escape barbarians by moving his capital from Rome. As it turned out, the move was timely; eight years later, Rome was sacked. The early history of Ravenna was riddled with strife, its leadership changing hands often. It was not until the age of the emperor Justinian that Ravenna attained some stability and that the arts began to flourish.

During Justinian's reign, the church of San Vitale (Fig. 12–5), one of the most elaborately decorated buildings in the Byzantine style, was erected. The church has a central plan. Its perimeter is an octagon. Although the narthex is placed slightly askew, the rest of the plan is highly symmetrical. A dome, also octagonal, rises above the church, supported by eight massive piers. Between the piers are semicircular niches that extend into a surrounding aisle, or **ambulatory,** like petals of a flower. The "stem" of this flower is a sanctuary that intersects the ambulatory. At the end of this sanctuary is

the apse, which in the Byzantine church is often **polygonal.** Unlike the rigid axial alignment of the Latin Cross structures that follow the basilican plan, San Vitale has an organic quality. Soft, curving forms press into the spaces of the church and are countered by geometric shapes that seem to complement their decorativeness rather than restrain it. The space flows freely, and yet the disparate forms are unified.

This vital, organic quality can also be seen in the interior decoration of the church. Columns are crowned by highly decorative capitals carved with complex, interlacing designs. Decorative mosaic borders, organic in inspiration, form repetitive abstract patterns.

This abstracted, patternlike treatment of forms can also be seen in the representation of human figures in

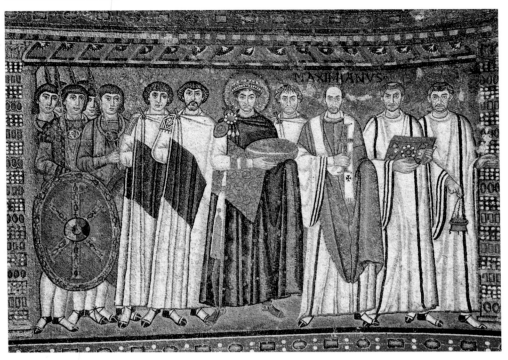

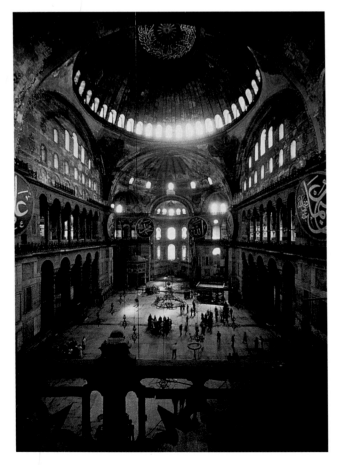

12–7 INTERIOR OF CHURCH OF HAGIA SOPHIA, ISTANBUL
(BYZANTINE, 532–537).

San Vitale's mosaics. *Justinian and Attendants*
(Fig. 12–6), an apse mosaic, represents the Byzantine
style at its peak of perfection in this medium. The
mosaic commemorates Justinian's victory over the
Goths and proclaims him as ruler of Ravenna and the
western half of the empire. His title is symbolically
sanctioned by the presence of military and religious
figures in his entourage. The figures form a strong
horizontal band that marches friezelike across the
viewer's space. Although they are placed in groups,
some slightly in front of others, the heads form a single
line. The heavily draped bodies seem to have no substance. The costumes seem to hang on invisible frames.
Thickly lidded eyes stare outward, and gestures are unnatural. Space is suggested by a goldish background
and a green, grassy band below the figures' feet, but the
placement of the images within this space is uncertain.
Notice how the feet hover above the earth. They have
nothing to do with the support of these weightless bodies. These characteristics contrast strongly with the
Classicism of Early Christian art and with mosaics such
as the *Christ as the Good Shepherd* (Fig. 12–4).

HAGIA SOPHIA, CONSTANTINOPLE
Even though Ravenna was the capital of the western
empire, its emperor's most important public building
was erected in Constantinople. Constantine moved the
capital of the Roman Empire to the ancient city of
Byzantium and renamed it after himself. After his

additions
to original
structure

entrance

entrance

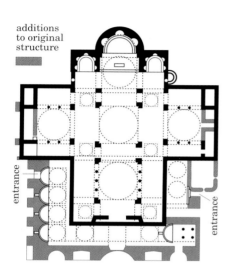

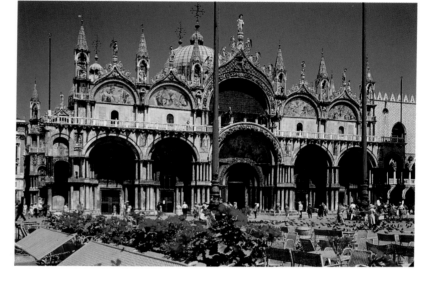

death, the empire was divided into eastern and western halves, and the eastern faction remained in Constantinople. It is in this Turkish city—present-day Istanbul—that Justinian built his Church of the Holy Wisdom, or Hagia Sophia (Fig. 12–7). It is a fantastic structure that has served at one time or other in its history as an **Eastern Orthodox** church, an Islamic mosque, and a museum. The most striking aspects of Hagia Sophia are its overall dimensions and the size of its dome. Its floor plan is approximately 240 by 270 feet (Constantine's basilica in Rome was 300 by 215). The dome is about 108 feet across and rises almost 180 feet above the church floor (the dome of the Pantheon, by contrast, rose to a mere 144 feet). Thus its grandiose proportions put Hagia Sophia in the same league with the great architectural monuments of Roman times. To create their dome, the architects Anthemius of Tralles and Isidorus of Miletus used **pendentive** construction (see Chapter 7). Although massive, the dome appears to be light and graceful due to the placement of a ring of arched windows at its base. The light filtering through these windows sometimes gives the impression that the dome is actually hovering on a ring of light, further emphasizing the building's spaciousness.

Like most Byzantine churches, the exterior of Hagia Sophia is very plain. The towering **minarets**

that grace the corners of the structure are later additions. This plainness contrasts strongly with the interior wall surfaces, which are decorated lavishly with marble inlays and mosaics.

Later Byzantine Art

Byzantine architecture continued to flourish until about the twelfth century, varying between the central and longitudinal plans described above. One interesting variation was the **Greek Cross plan** used in such buildings as St. Mark's Cathedral in Venice (Fig. 12–8). In this plan, the "arms" of the cross are equal in length, and the focus of the interior is usually a dome that rises above the intersection of these elements. The long nave of the Latin Cross plan is eliminated.

EARLY MEDIEVAL ART

The 1,000 years that span 400 and 1400 CE have been called the Middle Ages or the **Dark Ages.** Some historians consider this millennium a holding pattern between the era of Classical Rome and the rebirth of its art and culture in the Renaissance of the fifteenth century. Some viewed these 1,000 years as a time when the light of Classicism was temporarily extinguished. The negative attitude toward the people and art of the Middle

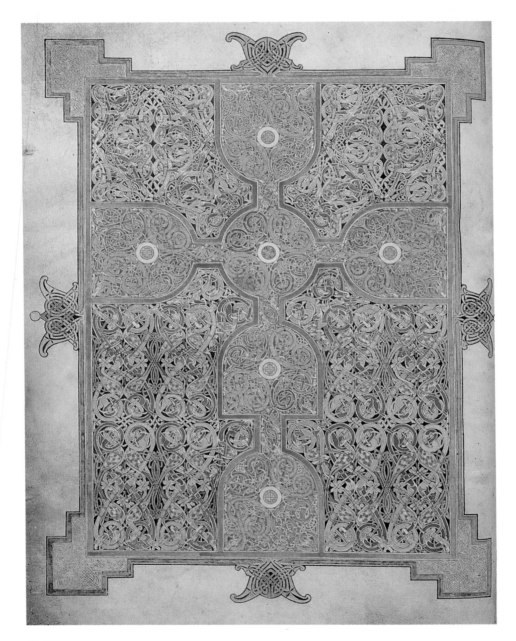

12–9 Page from the
Lindisfarne Gospels
(Early Medieval, c. 700).
Illuminated manuscript.
13½ × 9¾″.

Ages has recently shifted as awareness of their contributions to economics, religion, scholarship, architecture, and the fine arts has increased. Many works of art from the Early Middle Ages exhibit characteristics similar to those that appear in the small carvings and metalwork of the barbarian tribes who migrated across Eurasia for centuries. An illuminated page from the Book of Lindisfarne (Fig. 12–9) depicts a cross inscribed with incessantly meandering scrolls of many colors. Surrounding the cross are repetitive linear patterns that can be decoded as fantastic snakes consuming themselves. This patterning represents the barbarian obsession with fantastic human-animal forms.

During the barbarian period of migrations, these forms graced many objects—from ship prows to body ornamentation. The same types of forms and patterns that describe the cross page above can be seen in a gold plaque from Siberia (Fig. 12–10). It is a highly compact scene of violence and destruction in which an eagle, wolf, tiger, and colt tear at one another to the death. Yet the violent content reads second to a swirl of pleasing lines and patterns. As is often the case in barbarian art, the overall richness and complexity of the design overrides the content of the work. Such motifs became central to Western European decoration during the Early Middle Ages.

CAROLINGIAN ART

The most important name linked to medieval art during the period immediately following the migrations is that of Charlemagne (Charles the Great). This powerful ruler tried to unify the warring factions of Europe under the aegis of Christianity, and, modeling his campaign on those of Roman emperors, he succeeded in doing so. In the year 800, Charlemagne was crowned Holy Roman emperor by the pope, thus establishing a bond among the countries of Western Europe that lasted over a millennium (see Map 5, above).

The period of Charlemagne's supremacy is called the **Carolingian period**. He established his court at Aachen, a western German city on the border of present-day Belgium, and imported the most significant intellectuals and artists of Europe and the Eastern countries.

MAP 5 EUROPE, C. 800.

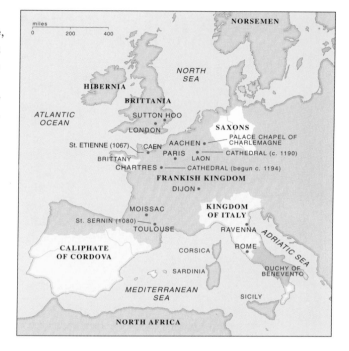

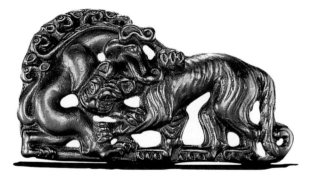

12–10 SCYTHIAN PLAQUE WITH ANIMAL INTERLACE. HORNED ANIMAL ATTACKING TIGER. GOLD. LENGTH: 6⅝".
THE STATE HERMITAGE MUSEUM, ST. PETERSBURG.

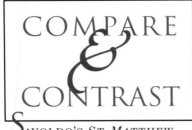
The style of Charlemagne's own gospel book, called the *Coronation Gospels* (Fig. 12–11), reflects his love of Classical art. Matthew, an evangelist who was thought to have written the first gospel, is represented as an educated Roman writer diligently at work. Only the halo surrounding his head reveals his sacred identity. He does not appear as an otherworldly weightless figure awaiting a bolt of divine inspiration. His attitude is calm, pensive, deliberate. His body has substance, it is seated firmly, and the drapery of his toga falls naturally over his limbs. The artist uses painterly strokes and contrast of light and shade to define his forms much in the way that the wall painters of ancient Rome had done (see Fig. 11–21).

Although Classicism was the preferred style of the Holy Roman emperor, it was not the only style pursued during the Carolingian period. *The Gospel Book of Archbishop Ebbo of Reims* (Fig. 12–12) was created only five to ten years after the Coronation Gospels and yet, in terms of style, it

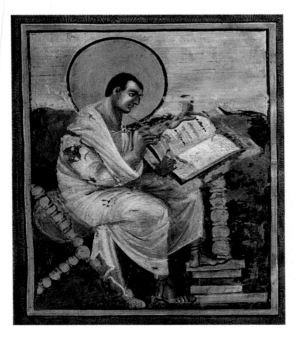

12–11 St. Matthew at work, in
Charlemagne's *Coronation Gospels*
(Carolingian, c. 795–810).
Illuminated manuscript.
Kunsthistorisches Museum, Vienna.

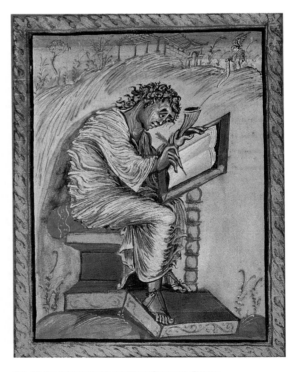

12–12 St. Matthew in *The Gospel Book
of Archbishop Ebbo of Reims*
(Carolingian, 816–841). Illuminated
manuscript.
Bibliothèque Municipale, Epernay, France.

could not be further removed. The Classical balance of emotion and restraint evident in Charlemagne's gospel book has succumbed to a display of passion and energy in Ebbo's evangelist. Both figures sit within a landscape, at work before their writing tables. Charlemagne's Matthew, however, appears to rely on his own intellect to set forth the gospels, whereas Ebbo's evangelist, scroll in hand, rushes to jot down every word being set forth by an angel of God, hovering in the upper right corner. He seems to be feverishly trying to keep up! His brow is furrowed, and his hands and feet cramp under the strain of his task.

The mood in the paintings also differs drastically. The calm Classical landscape and soft folds of Matthew's drapery create a dignified, intellectual atmosphere in the Coronation Gospels. By contrast, the restless drapery, disheveled hair, facial contortions, and heaving landscape in the Archbishop Ebbo Gospels create an air of dramatic, frantic energy. Interestingly, it is this emotionally charged style that will be most influential in Romanesque art. The naturalism of the Coronation Gospels will not appear again with any regularity until the birth of Early Renaissance art in the fourteenth century.

Savoldo's *St. Matthew* (Fig. 12–13), painted about 700 years later, is front-lit by a small flame. He leans back from his manuscript into the darkness, where an angel whispers to him. People in the background suggest that he has stolen away to a hidden chamber to seek divine inspiration.

What do the three St. Matthews suggest about each artist's views of the relationship between God and humanity? How does each artist use lighting, brushwork, and backgrounds to express his concept?

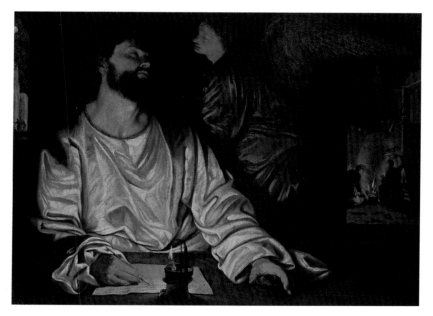

12–13 GIROLAMO SAVOLDO
ST. MATTHEW AND THE ANGEL (C. 1535).
OIL ON CANVAS. 36¾ × 49″.

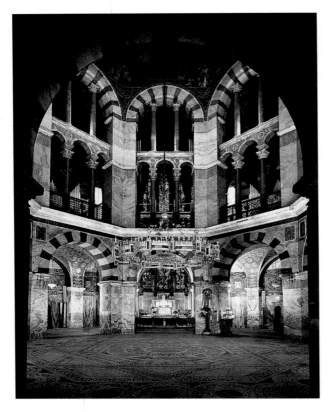

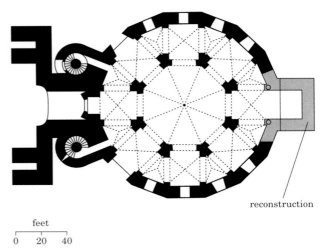

reconstruction

feet
0   20   40

THE PALATINE CHAPEL OF CHARLEMAGNE   Charlemagne constructed his **Palatine** (palace) **Chapel** with two architectural styles in mind (Fig. 12–14). He sought to emulate Roman architecture but was probably also influenced by the central plan church of San Vitale, erected under the Emperor Justinian. Like San Vitale, the Palatine Chapel is a central plan with an ambulatory and an octagonal dome. However, this is where the similarity ends. The perimeter of Charlemagne's chapel is polygonal, with almost sixteen facets instead of San Vitale's eight. There is also greater axial symmetry in the Palatine Chapel due to the logical placement of the narthex.

The interior displays differences from that of San Vitale as well. The semicircular niches that alternated with columns and pressed into the space of the Ravenna ambulatory have been eliminated at Aachen. There is more definition between the central domed area and the surrounding ambulatory. This clear articulation of parts is a hallmark of Roman design and stands in contrast to the fluid, organic character of some Byzantine architec-

ture. The walls of the Palatine Chapel are divided into three distinct levels, and each level is divided by Roman-inspired archways or series of arches. Classicizing structural elements, decorative motifs, and a general blockiness of form point to the development of **Romanesque architecture** during the eleventh century. However, even though Charlemagne chose a Classical central plan, the longitudinal plan would be preferred by the later Christian architects.

MANUSCRIPT ILLUMINATION   Charlemagne's pet project was the decipherment of the true biblical text. Over the years, illiterate scribes with illegible handwriting had gotten the text of the Bible to the point where it was barely decipherable. It was Charlemagne's love of knowledge and pursuit of truth—despite his own illiteracy—that helped keep scholarship alive during the Early Middle Ages.

OTTONIAN ART

Following Charlemagne's death, internal and external strife threatened the existence of the Holy Roman Empire. It was torn apart on several occasions, only to be consolidated time and again under various rulers. The most significant of these were three German emperors, each named Otto, who succeeded one another in what is now called the **Ottonian** period. In many respects their reigns symbolized an extension of Carolingian ideals, as is evident in the architecture and sculpture of the period.

12–15 ABBEY CHURCH OF ST. MICHAEL AT HILDESHEIM, GERMANY (RESTORED). EXTERIOR (*ABOVE LEFT*), INTERIOR (*RIGHT*), AND PLAN (*BOTTOM LEFT*)

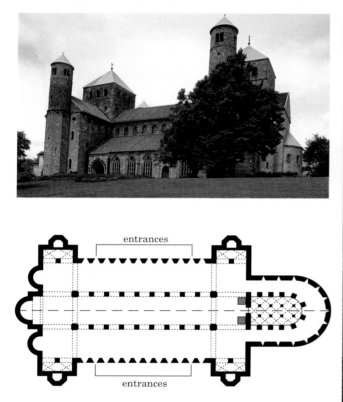

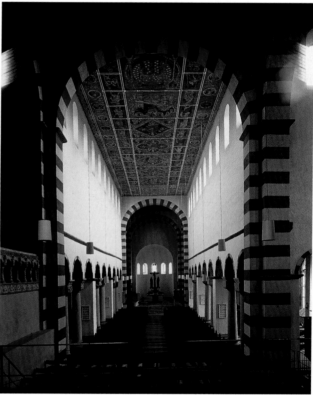

ARCHITECTURE   The most important architectural achievement of the Ottonian period was the construction of the abbey church of St. Michael in Hildesheim, Germany (Fig. 12–15). St. Michael's offers us our first glimpse of the modified Roman basilica plan that will serve as a basis for Romanesque architecture.

The abbey church does not retain the propylaeum or atrium of Old St. Peter's, and it uses the lateral entrances of Roman basilicas, but all the other elements of a typical Christian cathedral are present: the narthex, nave, two side aisles, a transept, and a much enlarged apse with an ambulatory. Most significant for the future of Romanesque and **Gothic** architecture, however, is the use of the **crossing square** to define the spaces within the rest of the church. The crossing square is formed by the intersection of the nave and the transept. In the plan of St. Michael's, for example, the nave consists of three modules that are equal in dimensions to the crossing square and marked off by square pillars. This design is an early example of what is called **square schematism,** in which the crossing square determines the dimensions of the entire structure.

St. Michael's also uses an **alternate support system** in the walls of its nave. In such a system, alternating structural elements (in this case pillars and columns) bear the weight of the walls and ultimately the load of the ceiling. The alternating elements in St. Michael's read as pillar-column-column-pillar; its alternate support system is then classified as **a-b-b-a** in terms of repetition of the supporting elements. An alternate support system of one kind or another will be a constant in Romanesque architecture.

As with Old St. Peter's, the exterior of St. Michael's reflects the character of its interior. Nave, side aisles, and other elements of the plan are clearly articulated in the blocky forms of the exterior. The exterior wall surfaces remain unadorned, as were those of the Early Christian and Byzantine churches. However, St. Michael's was the site of the recovery of the art of sculpture, which had not thrived since the fall of Rome.

12–16 *Adam and Eve Reproached by the Lord* (Ottonian, 1015). Panel of bronze doors. 23 × 43".
Abbey church of St. Michael, Hildesheim.

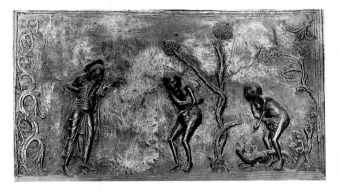

SCULPTURE *Adam and Eve Reproached by the Lord* (Fig. 12–16), a panel from the bronze doors of St. Michael's, represents the first sculpture cast in one piece during the Middle Ages. It closely resembles the manuscript illumination of the period and in mood and style is similar to the Matthew page of the Archbishop Ebbo gospels. It, too, is an emotionally charged work, in which God points his finger accusingly at the pathetic figures of Adam and Eve. They, in turn, try to deflect the blame; Adam points to Eve and Eve gestures toward Satan, who is in the guise of a fantastic dragonlike animal crouched on the ground. These are not Classical figures who bear themselves proudly under stress. Rather, they are pitiful, wasted images that cower and frantically try to escape punishment. In this work, as well as in that of the Romanesque period, God is shown as a merciless judge, and human beings as quivering creatures who must beware of God's wrath.

ROMANESQUE ART

The Romanesque style appeared in the closing decades of the eleventh century among rampant changes in all aspects of European life. Dynasties, such as those of the Carolingian and Ottonian periods, no longer existed. Individual monarchies ruled areas of Europe, rivaling one another for land and power. After the barbarians stopped invading and started settling, feudalism began to structure Europe, with monarchies at the head.

Feudalism was not the only force in medieval life of the Romanesque period. Monasticism also gained in importance. The monasteries were still the only places

12–17 Church of St. Sernin, Toulouse, France (Romanesque, c. 1080–1120).

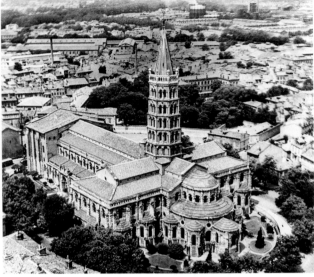

for decent education and had the added attraction of providing guarantees for eternal salvation. Salvation from the fires of hell in the afterlife was a great preoccupation of the Middle Ages and served as the common denominator among classes. Nobility, clergy, and peasantry all directed their spiritual efforts toward this goal.

Two phenomena reflect the medieval obsession with salvation in the afterlife: the Crusades and the great pilgrimages. The Crusades were holy wars waged in an effort to recover the Holy Land from the Moslems, who had taken it over in the seventh century. The pilgrimages were lengthy journeys to visit and worship at sacred shrines or the tombs of saints. Participating in the Crusades and making pilgrimages were seen as weights that would help tip the scale in one's favor on Judgment Day.

The pilgrims' need of a grand place to worship at journey's end gave impetus to church construction during the Romanesque period.

ARCHITECTURE

In the Romanesque cathedral, there is a clear articulation of parts, with the exterior forms reflecting the interior spaces. The interiors consist of five major areas, with variations on this basic plan evident in different regions of Europe. We can add two Romanesque criteria

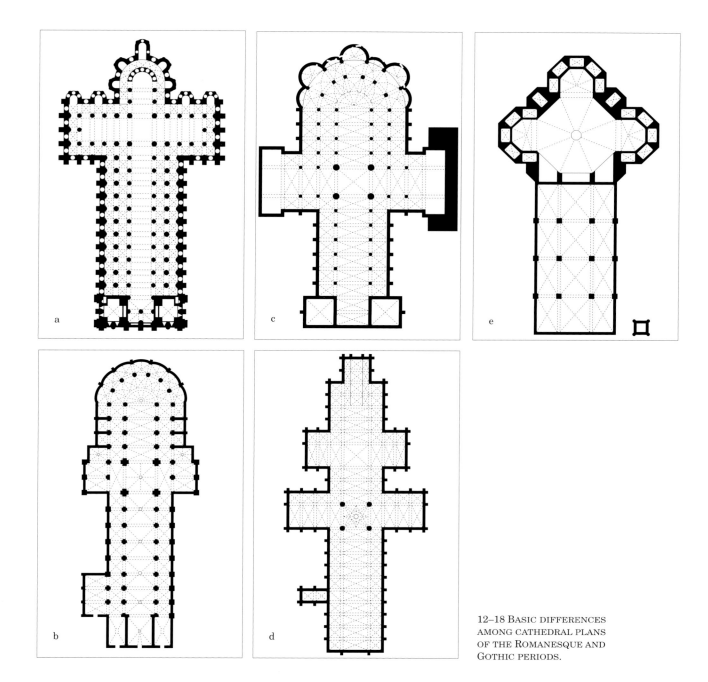

12–18 BASIC DIFFERENCES AMONG CATHEDRAL PLANS OF THE ROMANESQUE AND GOTHIC PERIODS.

to this basic format: spaciousness and fireproofing. The large crowds drawn by the pilgrimage fever required larger structures with interior spaces that would not restrict the flow of movement. After barbarian attacks left churches in flames, it was also deemed necessary to fireproof the buildings by eliminating wooden roofs and covering the structures with cut stone.

ST. SERNIN The church of St. Sernin (Fig. 12–17) in Toulouse, France, fitted all the requirements of a Romanesque cathedral. An aerial view of the exterior shows the blocky forms that outline a nave, side aisles, narthex to the west, a prominent transept crowned by a

multilevel spire above the crossing square, and an apse at the eastern end from whose ambulatory extend five **radiating chapels.** If you follow the outer aisle up from the narthex in the plan of St. Sernin (Fig. 12–18a), you notice that it continues around the outer borders of the transept arm and runs into the ambulatory around the apse. Along the eastern face of the transept, and around the ambulatory, there is a series of chapels that radiate, or extend, from the aisle. These spaces provided extra room for the crowds of pilgrims and offered free movement around the church, preventing interference with worship in the nave or the celebration of Mass in the apse. Square schematism has been employed in this

12–19 CATHEDRAL OF ST. ÉTIENNE, CAEN, FRANCE (ROMANESQUE, 1067–87).

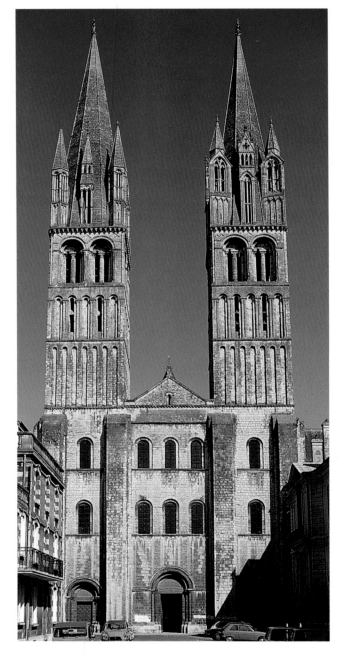

plan; each rectangular bay measures one-half of the crossing square, and the dimensions of each square in the side aisles measures one-fourth of the main module.

In St. Sernin, the shift was made from a flat wood ceiling characteristic of the Roman basilica to a stone vault that met the requirement for fireproofing. The ceiling structure, called a **barrel vault,** resembles a semicircular barrel punctuated by arches that spring from engaged columns in the nave to define each bay. The massive weight of the vault is supported partially by the nave walls and partially by the side aisles that accept a share of the downward thrust. This is some-what alleviated by the **tribune gallery,** which, in ef-fect, reduces the dropoff from the barrel vault to the lower side aisles. The tribune gallery also provided extra space for the masses of worshippers.

Because the barrel vault rests directly atop the tribune gallery, and because **fenestration** would weaken the structure of the vault, there is little light in the interior of the cathedral. Lack of light was considered a major problem, and solving it would be the primary concern of future Romanesque architects. The history of Romanesque architecture can be written as the history of vaulting techniques, and the need for light provided the incentive for their development.

ST. ÉTIENNE   The builders of the cathedral of St. Étienne in Normandy contributed significantly to the future of Romanesque and Gothic architecture in their design of its ceiling vault (Fig. 12–18b). Instead of using a barrel vault that tunnels its way from narthex to apse, they divided the nave of St. Étienne into four distinct modules that reflect the shape of the crossing square. Each of these modules in turn is divided into six parts by **ribs** that spring from engaged columns and **compound piers** in the nave walls. Some of these ribs connect the midpoints of opposing sides of the squares; they are called **transverse ribs.** Other ribs intersect the space of the module diagonally, as seen in the plan; these are called **diagonal ribs.** An **alternate a-b-a-b support system** is used, with every other engaged column sending up a supporting rib that crosses the vault as a transverse arch. These engaged columns are distinguished from other nonsupporting members by their attachment to pilasters. The vault of St. Étienne is

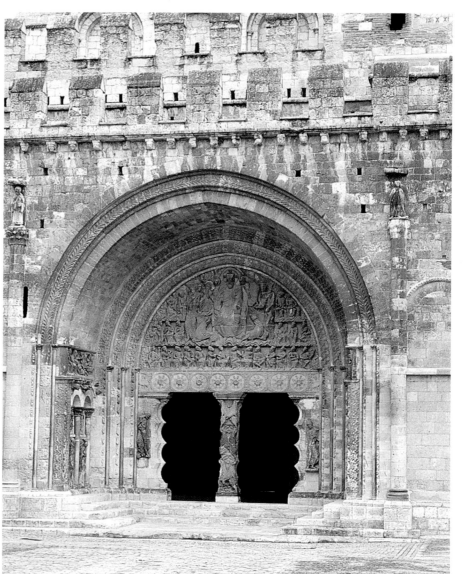

12–20 South portals of the Abbey Church of St. Pierre in Moissac, France (Romanesque, c. 1100).

one of the first true rib vaults in that the combination of diagonal and transverse ribs functions as a skeleton that bears some of the weight of the ceiling. In later buildings the role of ribs as support elements will be increased, and reliance on the massiveness of nave walls will be somewhat decreased.

Even though the nave walls of St. Étienne are still quite thick when compared with those of later Romanesque churches, the interior has a sense of lightness that does not exist in St. Sernin. The development of the rib vault made it possible to pierce the walls directly above the tribune gallery with windows. This series of windows that appears cut into the slightly domed modules of the ceiling is called a **clerestory.** The clerestory will become a standard element of the Gothic cathedral plan.

The facade of St. Étienne (Fig. 12–19) also served as a model for Gothic architecture. It is divided vertically into three sections by thick **buttresses,** reflecting the nave and side aisles of the interior, and horizontally into three bands, pierced by portals on the entrance floor and arched windows on the upper levels. Two bell towers complete the facade, each of which is also divided into three parts (the spires were later additions). This two-tower, tripartite facade will appear again and again in Gothic structures, although the walls will be pierced by more carving and fenestration, lending a lighter look. Yet the symmetry and predictability of the St. Étienne design will be maintained.

SCULPTURE

Although we occasionally find free-standing sculpture from the Romanesque and Gothic periods, it was far more common for sculpture to be restricted to architectural decoration around the portals. The decorated surfaces (Fig. 12–20) include the **tympanum,** a semicircular space above the doors to a cathedral; **archivolts,** concentric moldings reiterating the shape of the tympanum; the **lintel,** a horizontal, friezelike band on which the tympanum rests; the **trumeau,** a column or pillar

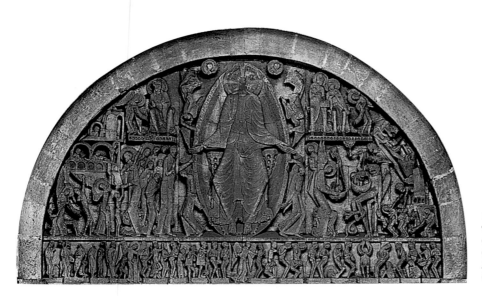

12–21 *ABOVE*: WEST TYMPANUM OF CATHEDRAL OF AUTUN IN BURGUNDY (ROMANESQUE, C. 1130). *BELOW: LAST JUDGMENT* (DETAIL).

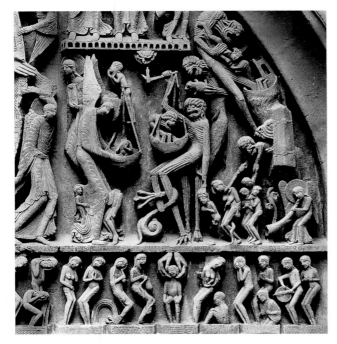

in the center of the cathedral doors; and **jambs,** technically the side posts of a doorway, but in this context the wall surfaces that abut the doorway to either side.

Some of the most important and elaborate sculptural decoration is found in cathedral tympanums, such as that of the cathedral of Autun (Fig. 12–21) in Burgundy. The tympanum was an important site for relief carvings because people who entered the church could not help but see it. In sculpting the tympanum of the cathedral of Autun, the opportunity was seized to warn the people that their earthly behavior would be judged harshly. The scene depicted is that of the Last Judgment. The tympanum rests on a lintel carved with small figures representing the dead. The archangel Michael stands in the center, dividing the horizontal

band of figures into two groups. The naked dead on the left gaze upward, hopeful of achieving eternal reward in heaven, while those to the right look downward in despair. Above the lintel, Jesus is depicted as an even-handed judge, overseeing the process of selection. To his left, tall, thin figures representing the apostles observe the scene, while some angels lift bodies into heaven. To Jesus' right, by contrast, is a gruesome event. The dead are snatched up from their graves, and their souls are being weighed on a scale by an angel on the left and a devil-serpent on the right. The devil cheats by adding a little weight, and some of his companions stand ready to grab the souls and fling them into hell.

As in the bronze doors of St. Michael's, humankind is shown as a pitiful, defenseless race, no match for the wiles of Satan. The figures crouch in terror of their surroundings, in strong contrast to the serenity of their impartial judge.

The Romanesque sculptor sought stylistic inspiration in Roman works, the small carvings of the pre-Romanesque era, and especially manuscript illumination. In the early phase of Romanesque art, naturalism was of no concern. The artist turned to art rather than to nature for models, and thus his forms are at least twice, and perhaps one hundred times, removed from the original source. It is no wonder, then, that they appear as dolls or marionettes. The figure of Jesus is squashed within a large oval, and his limbs bend in sharp angles in order to fit. Although his drapery seems to correspond to the body beneath, the folds are reduced to stylized patterns of concentric arcs that play across a relatively flat surface. Realism is not the goal. The sculptor is merely trying to convey his frightful message with the details and emotionalism that will have the most dramatic impact on the observing worshipper or penitent sinner.

MANUSCRIPT ILLUMINATION

The relationship between Romanesque sculpture and manuscript illumination can be seen in a page from The Life and Miracles of St. Audomarus (Fig. 12–22). As with the figure of Jesus in the Autun tympanum, the long and gangling limbs of the three frenzied figures are joined to the torso at odd angles. Although the drapery responds somewhat to the unnatural body movement, it is reduced to patterned folds that are also unrealistic. As with other Romanesque artists, the emotion of the scene is of primary importance, and reality fades in its wake.

Toward the end of the Romanesque period, artists paid more attention to their surroundings, and there was a significant increase in naturalism. The drapery falls softly rather than in sharp angles, and the body begins to acquire more substance. The gestures are less frantic and a balance between emotion and restraint begins to reappear. These elements reached their peak of perfection during the Gothic period and pointed to a full-scale revival of Classicism during the Renaissance of the fifteenth century.

TAPESTRY

While the tasks of copying sacred texts and illuminating their margins with decorative patterns, symbols, and thumbnail sketches were sometimes given to women, the art form remained primarily a male preserve. Not so with the medium of tapestry. In the Middle Ages, weaving and embroidery were taught to women of all social classes and walks of life. Noblewomen and nuns would find themselves weaving and decorating elaborate tapestries, clothing, and liturgical vestments, using the finest linens, wools, gold and silver thread, pearls, and other gems.

Perhaps the most famous surviving tapestry, the *Bayeux Tapestry* (Fig. 12–23), was almost certainly created by a team of women on the commission of Odo, the Bishop of Bayeux. The tapestry describes the invasion of England by William the Conqueror in a continuous narrative. Although the tapestry is less than 2 feet in height, it originally measured in excess of 230 running feet and was meant to run clockwise around the entire nave of the Cathedral of Bayeux. In this way, the narrative functioned much in the same way as the continuous narrative of the Ionic frieze of the Parthenon.

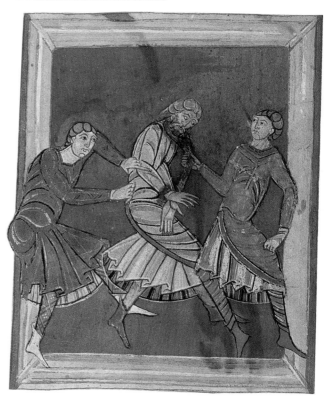

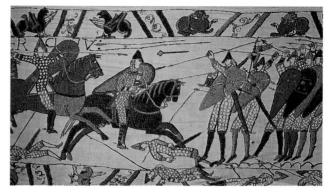

12–23 *BAYEUX TAPESTRY*, DETAIL (ROMANESQUE, C. 1073–83). WOOL EMBROIDERY ON LINEN. HEIGHT: 20″, LENGTH 230′ (DETAIL). MUSEE DE LA TAPISSERIE, BAYEUX, FRANCE.

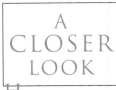
During the Middle Ages, the production and illustration of sacred books took place, for the most part, in the monastery and the abbey, with the greatest percentage of scribes and painters being men. Yet some upper-class women looking for an alternative to marriage and eager to follow these and other intellectual and aesthetic pursuits entered the contemplative life of the nunnery.

One such woman was the German abbess, Hildegarde of Bingen (1098–1179). Hildegarde was a mystic whose visions of otherworldly phenomena began during childhood and led to a life of scholarship illucidating her extraordinary experiences. She wrote books on medicine and history, composed music, debated political and religious issues, and designed illustrations to accompany written records of her visions. Hildegarde also devised a secret language. Her most valuable work is the *Liber Scivias*, a text built around images of light and darkness. Sun, stars, moon, and flaming orbs struggle against dragons, demons, and other denizens of darkness.

Figure 12–24 is a twelfth-century copy of Hildegarde's *Vision of the Ball of Fire*, an illustration no doubt designed by the abbess and most likely executed by her nuns. An elaborately patterned orb floats in the center of a simpler rectangular frame. Its central symbols are surrounded by a field of star-flowers spreading outward toward a wreath of flames. Here and there one can spot demons spewing forth fire. The neatness of the execution bears similarity to the fine needlepoint and embroidery techniques characteristic of medieval tapestries. Here follows Hildegarde's vision on which the painting was based:

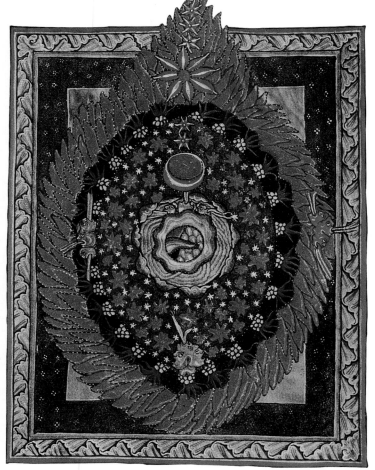

Then I saw a huge image, round and shadowy. It was pointed at the top, like an egg. . . . Its outermost layer was of bright fire. Within lay a dark membrane. Suspended in the bright flames was a burning ball of fire, so large that the entire image received its light. Three more lights burned in a row above it. They gave it support through their glow, so that the light would never be extinguished.

12–24 HILDEGARDE OF BINGEN
VISION OF THE BALL OF FIRE
ILLUMINATION FROM
THE LIBER SCIVIAS
(12TH CENTURY).
RUPERTBERG, GERMANY (ORIGINAL DESTROYED).

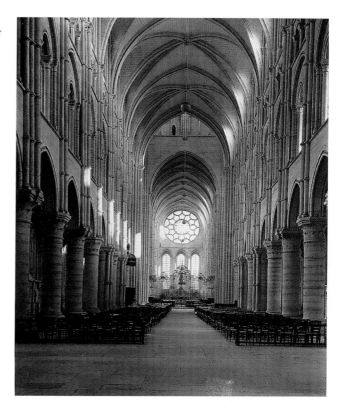

GOTHIC ART

Art and architecture of the twelfth and thirteenth centuries is called Gothic. The term *Gothic* originated among historians who believed that the Goths were responsible for the style of this period. Because critics believed that the Gothic style only further buried the light of Classicism, and because the Goths were "barbarians," "Gothic" was used in a disparaging sense. For many years, the most positive criticism of Gothic art was that it was a step forward from the Romanesque. Today such views have been abandoned. "Gothic" is no longer a term of derision, and the Romanesque and Gothic styles are seen as distinct and as responsive to the unique tempers of their times.

ARCHITECTURE

In the history of art it is rare indeed to be able to trace the development of a particular style to a single work, or the beginning of a movement to a specific date. However, it is generally agreed that the Gothic style of architecture began in 1140 with the construction of the choir of the church of St. Denis near Paris. The vaults of the choir consisted of weight-bearing ribs that formed the skeleton of the ceiling structure. The spaces between the ribs were then filled in with cut stone. At St. Denis the pointed arch is used in the structural skeleton, rather than the rounded arches of the Romanesque style. This vault construction also permitted the use of larger areas of stained glass, dissolving the massiveness of the Romanesque wall.

LAON CATHEDRAL   Although Laon Cathedral is considered an Early Gothic building, its plan resembles those of Romanesque churches. For example, the ceiling is a sexpartite rib vault supported by groups of columns in an alternate a-b-a-b rhythm (Fig. 12–25). Yet there were important innovations at Laon. The interior displays a change in wall elevation from three to four levels. A series of arches, or **triforium,** was added above the tribune gallery to pierce further the solid surfaces of the nave walls. The obsession with reducing the appearance of heaviness in the walls can also be seen on the exterior (Fig. 12–26). If we compare the facade of St. Étienne with that of Laon, we see a change from a massive,

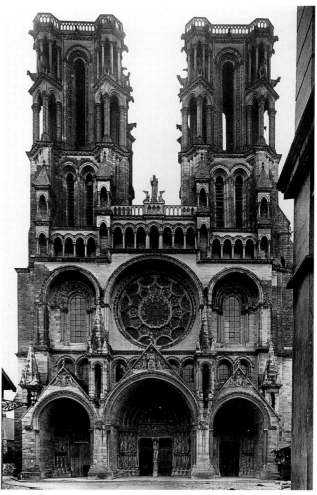

12–27 Cathedral of Notre Dame, Paris (Gothic, begun 1163, completed 1250).

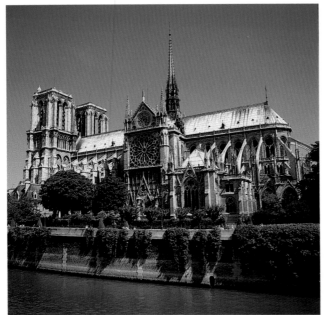

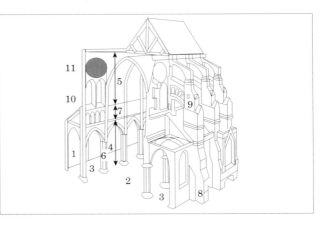

fortresslike appearance to one that seems plastic and organic. The facade of Laon Cathedral is divided into three levels, although there is less distinction between them. The portals seem to jut forward from the plane of the facade, providing a tunnel-like entrance. The stone is pierced by arched windows, arcades, and a large **rose window** in the center, and the twin bell towers seem to be constructed of voids rather than solids.

As the Gothic period progressed, all efforts were directed toward the dissolution of stone surfaces. The walls were pierced by greater expanses of glass, nave elevations became higher, and carved details became lacier. There was a mystical quality to these buildings in their seeming exemption from the laws of gravity.

NOTRE DAME   One of the most famous buildings in the history of architecture is the cathedral of Notre Dame de Paris (Fig. 12–27). Perched on the banks of the Seine, it has enchanted visitors ever since its construction. Notre Dame is a curious mixture of old and new elements. It retains a sexpartite rib vault and was originally planned to have an Early Gothic four-level wall elevation. It was begun in 1163 and was not completed until almost a century later, undergoing extensive modifications between 1225 and 1250. Some of these changes

reflected the development of the High Gothic style, including the elimination of the triforium and the use of **flying buttresses** to support the nave walls. The exterior of the building also communicates this combination of early and late styles. While the facade is far more massive than that of Laon Cathedral, the north and south elevations look light and airy due to their fenestration and the lacy buttressing.

CHARTRES CATHEDRAL   Chartres Cathedral is generally considered to be the first High Gothic church. Unlike Notre Dame, Chartres was planned to have a three-level wall elevation and flying buttresses. The three-part wall structure allowed for larger windows in the clerestory, admitting more light into the interior (Fig. 12–28). The use of large windows in the clerestory was in turn made possible by the development of the flying buttress.

In the High Gothic period there is a change from square schematism to a **rectangular bay system** (Fig. 12–18c). In the latter, each rectangular bay has its own cross rib vault, and only one side aisle square flanks each rectangular bay. Thus the need for an alternate support system is also eliminated. The interior of a High Gothic cathedral presents several dramatic vistas. There is a continuous sweep of space from the narthex to the apse along a nave that is uninterrupted by alternating supports. There is also a strong vertical thrust from floor to vaults that is enhanced by the elimination of the triforium and the increased heights of the arches in the nave arcade and clerestory windows. The solid

12–29 CATHEDRAL OF FLORENCE (GOTHIC, BEGUN 1368).

wall surfaces are further dissolved by quantities of stained glass that flood the interior with a mysterious, soft light. The architects directed all of their efforts to creating a spiritual escape to another world. They did so by defying the properties of matter, by creating the illusion of weightlessness in stone, and by capitalizing on the mesmerizing aspects of colored streams of light.

GOTHIC ARCHITECTURE OUTSIDE OF FRANCE The cathedral architecture that we have examined thus far was constructed in France, where the Gothic style flourished. Variations on the French Gothic style can also be perceived elsewhere in northern Europe, although in some English and German structures the general "blockiness" of Romanesque architecture was maintained. The plan of Salisbury Cathedral (Fig. 12–18d) in England illustrates some differences between English and French architecture of the Gothic period, as seen in the double transept and the unique square apse. The profile of Salisbury Cathedral also differs from that of a French church in that the bell towers on the western

end are level with the rest of the facade, and a tall tower rises above the crossing square. Still, the remaining characteristics of the cathedral, including the rectangular bay system, bear close relationship to the French Gothic style.

In Italy, on the other hand, there was no strict adherence to the French style, as is seen in the cathedral of Florence (Fig. 12–29). The most striking features of its exterior are the sharp, geometric patterns of green and white marble incrustation and the horizontality, or earthbound quality. These contrast with the vertical lines of the French Gothic cathedral that seem to reach for heaven. The French were obsessed with the visual disintegration of massive stone walls. The Italians, on the other hand, preserved the mural quality of the structure. In the cathedral of Florence, there are no flying buttresses. The wall elevation has been reduced to two levels, with a minimum of fenestration.

The cathedral of Florence is also different in plan (Fig. 12–18e) from French cathedrals. A huge octagonal dome overrides the structure. The nave, which seems

12–30 Jamb figures, west portals, Chartres Cathedral (Gothic, c. 1140–50).

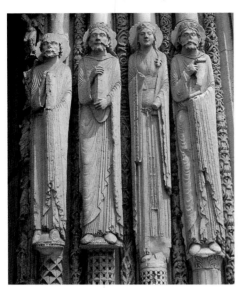

12–31 Jamb figures, west portals, Reims Cathedral (Gothic, begun 1210).

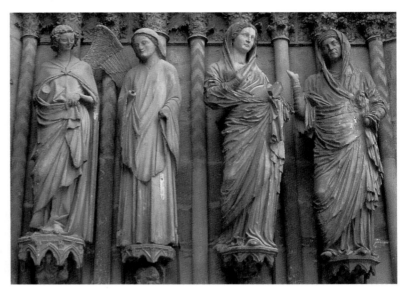

like an afterthought, consists of four large and clearly defined modules, flanked by rectangular bays in the side aisles. Finally, there is only one bell tower in the Italian cathedral, and it is detached from the facade.

Why would this Italian Gothic cathedral differ so markedly from those of the French? Given its strong roots in Classical Rome, it may be that Italy never succumbed wholeheartedly to Gothicism. It is perhaps for this reason that Italy will be the birthplace of the revival of Classicism during the Renaissance. We shall discuss the cathedral of Florence further in Chapter 13, because the designer of its dome was one of the principal architects of the Renaissance.

SCULPTURE

Sculpture during the Gothic period exhibits a great change in mood from that of the Romanesque. The iconography is one of redemption rather than damnation. The horrible scenes of Judgment Day that threatened the worshipper upon entering the cathedral have been replaced by scenes from the life of Jesus or apocalyptic visions. The Virgin Mary also assumes a primary role. Carved tympanums, whole sculptural programs, even cathedrals themselves (for example, Notre Dame, which means "Our Lady") are dedicated to her.

Gothic sculpture is still pretty much confined to decoration of cathedral portals. Every square inch of the

tympanums, lintels, and archivolts of most Gothic cathedrals is carved with a dazzling array of figures and ornamental motifs. However, some of the most advanced full-scale sculpture is to be found adorning the jambs. Early Gothic jamb figures, such as those found around the portals of Chartres Cathedral (Fig. 12–30; Chartres was rebuilt after a fire in the High Gothic style, but the portal sculpture remained intact), are rigid in their poses, confined by the columns to which they are attached. The drapery falls in predictable folds, at times stylized into patterns reminiscent of manuscript illumination. Yet there is a certain weightiness to the bodies and the elimination of the "hinged" treatment of the limbs that heralds changes from the sculpture of the Romanesque period. During the High Gothic period, these simple elements led to a naturalism not witnessed since Classical times.

The jamb figures of Reims Cathedral (Fig. 12–31) exhibit an interesting combination of styles. The individual figures were no doubt carved by different artists. The detail of the central portal of the facade illustrates two groups of figures. To the left is an Annunciation scene with the angel Gabriel and the Virgin Mary, and to the right is a Visitation scene depicting the Virgin Mary and Saint Elizabeth. All the figures are detached from columns and instead occupy the spaces between them. Although they have been carved for these specific niches and they are perched on small pedestals, they have a freedom of movement not found in the figures of the Chartres jambs.

The Virgin Mary of the Annunciation group is the least advanced in technique of the four figures. Her stance is the most rigid, and her gestures and facial expression are the most stylized. Yet her body has substance, and anatomical details are revealed beneath a drapery that responds realistically to the movement of the limbs.

The figure of Gabriel contrasts strongly in style with that of the Virgin Mary. He seems relatively tall and lanky. His head is small and delicate, and his facial features are refined. His body has a subtle sway that is accented by the flowing lines of his drapery. Stateliness and sweetness characterize this courtly style; it will be carried forward into the Early Renaissance period in the **International Gothic** style.

Yet Classicism will be the major style of the Renaissance, and in the Visitation group of the Reims portals we have a fascinating introduction to it. The weighty figures of Mary and Elizabeth are placed in a **contrapposto** stance. The folds of drapery articulate the movement of the bodies beneath with a realism that we have not seen since Classical times. Even the facial features and hair styles are reminiscent of Greek and Roman sculpture. Although we have linked the reappearance of naturalism to the Gothic artist's increased awareness of nature, we must speculate that the sculptor of the Visitation group was looking directly to Classical statues for inspiration. The similarities are too strong to be coincidental. With his small and isolated attempt to revive Classicism, this unknown artist stands as a transitional figure between the spiritualism of the medieval world and the rationalism of the Renaissance.

key terms

Catacomb
Orans
Iconology
Iconography
Propylaeum
Atrium
Narthex
Nave
Altar
Apse
Transept
Latin Cross plan
Longitudinal plan
Central plan

Mosaic
Manuscript illumination
Byzantine
Ambulatory
Pendentive
Minaret
Greek Cross plan
Carolingian period
Palatine Chapel
Romanesque
  architecture
Ottonian
Gothic
Crossing square

Square schematism
Alternate support
  system
Radiating chapels
Barrel vault
Tribune gallery
Fenestration
Ribs
Compound piers
Transverse ribs
Diagonal ribs
Alternate a-b-a-b
  support system
Clerestory

Buttress
Tympanum
Archivolts
Lintel
Trumeau
Jamb
Triforium
Rose window
Flying buttresses
Rectangular bay system
International Gothic
  style
Contrapposto

artists

Girolamo Savoldo
Anthemius of Tralles

Isidorus of Miletus

Hildegarde of Bingen

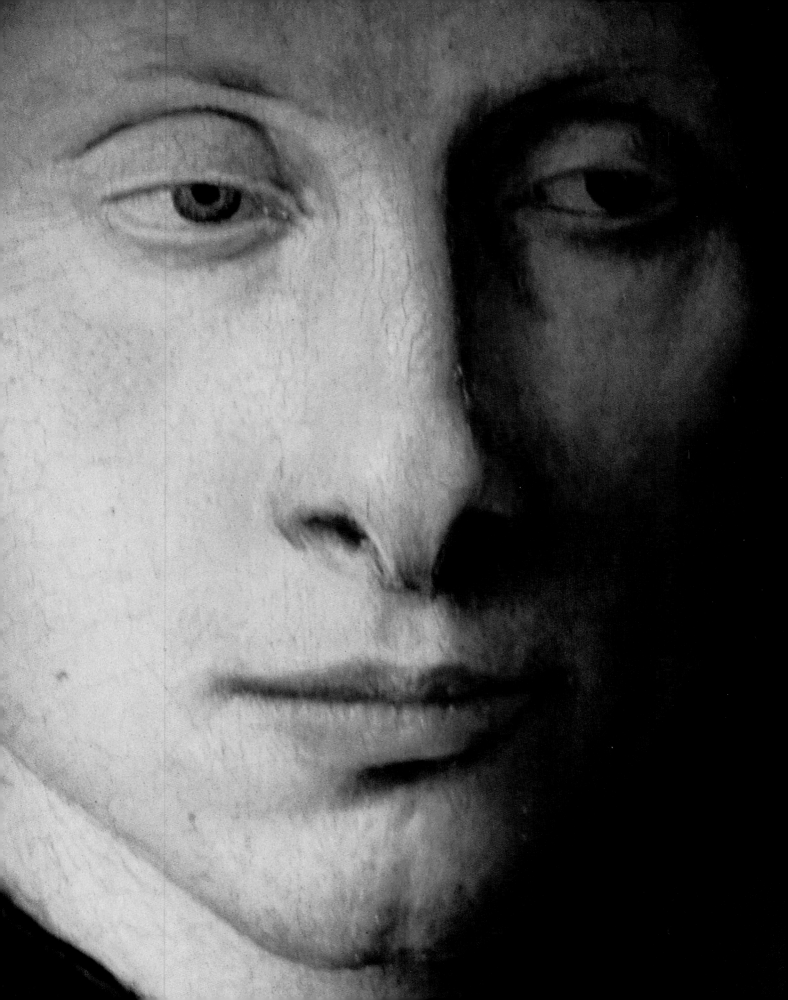

13

c h a p t e r

THE RENAISSANCE

PRELIMINARY *Sketch*

- Shakespeare was born in the year that Michelangelo died.

- The painter Robert Campin depicted the Virgin Mary as a prim and proper middle-class woman within a typical middle-class household.

- Jan van Eyck's double portrait of *Giovanni Arnolfini and His Bride* served as a record of the exchange of marriage vows.

- America was named after the cousin of the model who posed for Botticelli's *The Birth of Venus*.

- Leonardo da Vinci not only painted the definitive version of *The Last Supper*; he also drew plans for flying machines and submarines.

- Michelangelo was coerced into creating some of his most famous projects by a stubborn patron.

- The distortion of the figures in El Greco's paintings may be due to astigmatism.

While Columbus was coasting along the shores of the New World in 1492, a 17-year-old Michelangelo Buonarroti was perfecting his craft of chiseling human features from blocks of marble. In 1564, the year that Shakespeare was born, Michelangelo died.

These are but two of the marker dates of the **Renaissance.** "Renaissance" is a French word meaning "rebirth," and the Renaissance in Europe was a period of significant historical, social, and economic events. The old feudal system that had organized Europe during the Middle Ages fell to a system of government based on independent city-states with powerful kings and princes at their helms. The economic face of Europe changed, aided by an expansion of trade and commerce with Eastern countries. The cultural base of Europe shifted from Gothic France to Italy. A plague wiped out the populations of entire cities in Europe and Asia. Speculation on the world beyond, which had so preoccupied the medieval mind, was abandoned in favor of scientific observation of the world at hand. Although Copernicus proclaimed that the sun and not the earth was at the center of the solar system, humanity, and not heaven, became the center of all things.

The Renaissance spans roughly the fourteenth through the sixteenth centuries and is seen by some as the beginning of modern history. During this period we witness a revival of Classical themes in art and literature, a return to the realistic depiction of nature through keen observation, and the revitalization of the Greek philosophy of Humanism, in which human dignity, ideas, and capabilities are of central importance.

Although we can speak of a Renaissance period in England, France, and Spain, the two most significant areas of Europe for the arts were Italy in the South, and Flanders (present-day Belgium and the Netherlands) in the North (see Map 6, below). Given her Classical roots, Italy never quite succumbed to Gothicism, and readily introduced elements of Greek and Roman art into her works. But Flanders was steeped in the medieval tradition of Northern Europe and continued to concern herself with the spiritualism of the Gothic era, enriching it with a supreme realism. The difference in attitudes was summed up during the later Renaissance years by one of Italy's great artists, Michelangelo Buonarroti, not entirely without prejudice:

> *Flemish painting will, generally speaking, please the devout better than any painting in Italy, which will never cause him to shed a tear, whereas that of Flanders will cause him to shed many; . . . In Flanders they paint with a view to external exactness or such things as may cheer you and of which you cannot speak ill, as for example saints and prophets. They paint stuffs and masonry, the green grass of the fields, the shadows of trees, and rivers and bridges.*[1]

[1] Robert Goldwater and Marco Treves, eds., *Artists on Art* (New York: Pantheon Books, 1972), p. 68.

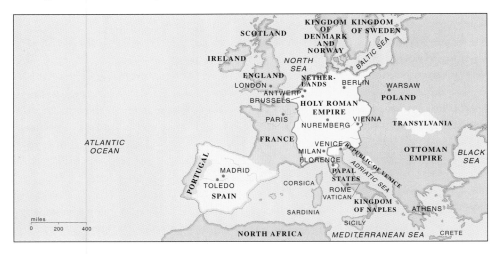

MAP 6 RENAISSANCE EUROPE, C. 16TH CENTURY.

Thus the subject matter of Northern artists remained more consistently religious, although their manner of representation was that of an exact, **trompe l'oeil** rendition of things of this world. They used the "trick-the-eye" technique to portray mystical religious phenomena in a realistic manner. The exactness of representation of which Michelangelo spoke originated in manuscript illumination, where complicated imagery was reduced to a minute scale. Since this imagery illustrated the writings, it was often laden with symbolic meaning. Symbolism was carried forth into panel paintings, where **iconography** was fused with a keen observation of nature.

FIFTEENTH-CENTURY NORTHERN PAINTING

FLEMISH PAINTING: FROM PAGE TO PANEL

A certain degree of naturalism appeared in the work of the Northern book illustrator during the Gothic period. The manuscript illuminator *illuminated* literary passages with visual imagery. As the art of manuscript illumination progressed, these thumbnail sketches were enlarged to fill greater portions of the manuscript page, eventually covering it entirely. As the text pages became less able to contain this imagery, the Northern Renaissance artist shifted to painting in tempera on wood panels.

THE LIMBOURG BROTHERS   One of the most dazzling texts available to illustrate this transfer from minute to more substantial imagery is *Les Très Riches Heures du Duc de Berry,* a Book of Hours illustrated by the Limbourg brothers (b. after 1385, d. by 1416) during the opening decades of the fifteenth century. Books of Hours were used by nobility as prayer books and included psalms and litanies to a variety of saints. As did most Books of Hours, *Les Très Riches Heures* contained calendar pages that illustrated domestic tasks and social events of the twelve months of the year. In "May" (Fig. 13–1), one of the calendar pages, we witness a parade of aristocratic gentlemen and ladies who have come in their bejeweled costumes of pastel hues to celebrate the first day of May. Complete with glittering regalia and festive song, the entourage romps through a woodland clearing on carousel-like horses. In the background looms a spectacular castle complex, the chateau of Riom. The calendar pages of *Les*

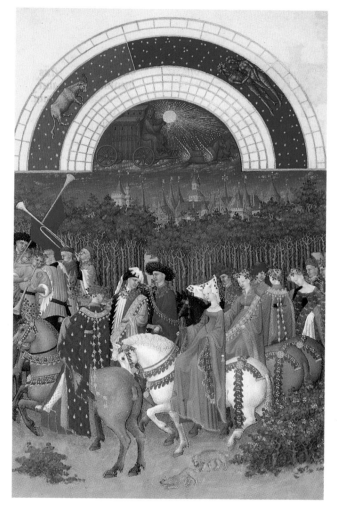

Très Riches Heures are rendered in the **International style,** a manner of painting common throughout Europe during the late fourteenth and early fifteenth centuries. This style is characterized by ornate costumes embellished with gold leaf and by subject matter literally fit for a king, including courtly scenes and splendid processions. The refinement of technique and attention to detail in these calendar pages recall earlier manuscript illumination. These qualities, and a keen observation of the human response to the environment—or in this case the merrymaking—bring to mind Michelangelo's assessment of Northern painting as obsessed with representation of the real world through the painstaking rendition of its everyday objects and occurrences.

13–2 ROBERT CAMPIN

MERODE ALTARPIECE: THE ANNUNCIATION WITH DONORS AND ST. JOSEPH (C. 1425–28).
OIL ON WOOD. CENTER: 24¼ × 24⅞"; WINGS: 25⅜ × 10⅞" EACH.
THE METROPOLITAN MUSEUM OF ART, THE CLOISTERS, NEW YORK. PURCHASE.

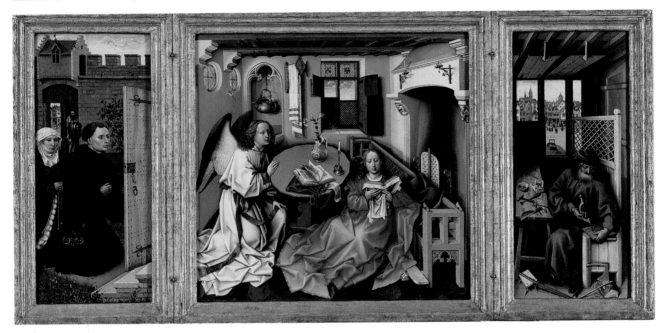

Although these calendar pages illustrated a holy book, the themes were secular. Renaissance artists tried to reconcile religious subjects with scenes and objects from everyday life, and Northern artists accomplished this by using symbolism. Artists would populate ordinary interiors with objects that might bear some spiritual significance. Many, if not most, of the commonplace items might be invested with a special religious meaning. You might ask how you, the casual observer, are supposed to decipher the cryptic meaning lurking behind an ordinary kettle. Chances are that you would be unable to do so without a specialized background. Yet you can enjoy the warm feeling of being invited into someone's home when you look at a Northern Renaissance interior, and be all the more enriched by the knowledge that there really is something more there than meets the eye.

ROBERT CAMPIN, THE MASTER OF FLÉMALLE   Attention to detail and the use of commonplace settings were carried forward in the soberly realistic religious figures painted by Robert Campin, the Master of Flémalle (c. 1378–1444). His *Merode Altarpiece* (Fig. 13–2) is a triptych whose three panels, from left to right, contain the kneeling donors of the altarpiece, an **Annunciation** scene with the Virgin Mary and the angel Gabriel, and

Joseph, the foster father of Jesus, at work in his carpentry shop. The architectural setting is a typical contemporary Flemish dwelling. The donors kneel by the doorstep in a garden thick with grass and wildflowers, each of which has special symbolic significance regarding the Virgin Mary. Although the door is ajar, it is not clear whether they are witnessing the event inside, or whether Campin has used the open door as a compositional device to lead the spectator's eye into the central panel of the triptych. In any event, we are visually and psychologically coaxed into viewing this most atypical Annunciation. Mary is depicted as a prim and proper middle-class Flemish woman surrounded by the trappings of a typical Flemish household, all rendered in exacting detail. Just as the closed outdoor garden symbolizes the holiness and purity of the Virgin Mary, the items within also possess symbolic meaning. For example, the bronze kettle hanging in the Gothic niche on the back wall symbolizes the Virgin's body—it will be the immaculate container of the redeemer of the Christian world. More obvious symbols of her purity include the spotless room and the vase of lilies on the table. In the upper left corner of the central panel a small child can be seen, bearing a cross and riding on streams of "divine light." The wooden table situated between Mary and Gabriel

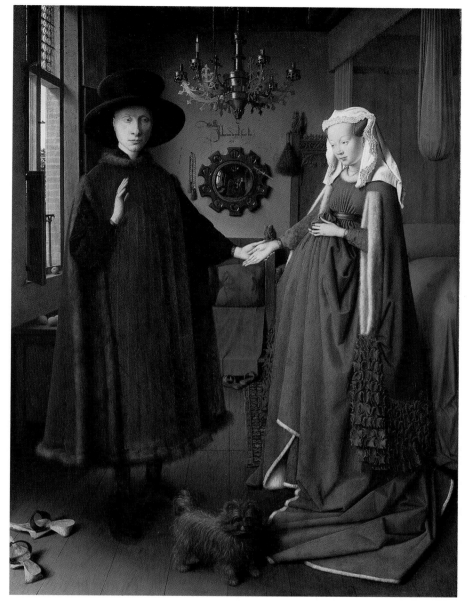

and the room divider between Mary and Joseph guarantee that the light accomplished the deed. Typically Joseph is shown as a man too old to have been the biological father of Jesus, although Campin's depiction does not quite follow this tradition. He is gray, but by no means ancient. Jesus' earthly father is busy preparing mousetraps—one on the table and one on the windowsill—commonplace objects that symbolize the belief that Christ was the bait with which Satan would be trapped. The symbolism in the altarpiece presents a fascinating web for the observer to untangle and interpret. Yet it does not overpower the hard-core realism of the ordinary people and objects. With the exceptions of the slight inconsistency of size and the tilting of planes toward the viewer, Campin offers us a continuous realism that sweeps the three panels. There is no distinction between saintly and common folk; the facial types of the heavenly beings are as individual as the portraits of the donors. Although fifteenth-century viewers would have been aware of the symbolism and the sacredness of the event, they would have also been permitted to become "a part" of the scene, so to speak, and to react to it as if the people in the painting were their peers and just happened to find themselves in extraordinary circumstances.

JAN VAN EYCK   We might say that Campin "humanized" his Mary and Joseph in the *Merode Altarpiece.* As religious subjects became more secular in nature, and the figures themselves became rendered as "human," an interest in ordinary, secular subject matter sprang up. During the fifteenth century in Northern Europe we have the development of what is known as **genre painting,** painting that depicts ordinary people engaged in run-of-the-mill activities. These paintings make little or no reference to religion; they exist almost as art for art's sake. Yet they are no less devoid of symbolism.

Giovanni Arnolfini and His Bride (Fig. 13–3) was executed by one of the most prominent and significant Flemish painters of the fifteenth century, Jan van Eyck (c. 1395–1441). This unique double portrait was commissioned by an Italian businessman working in Bruges to serve as a kind of marriage contract, or record of the couple's taking of marriage vows in the presence of two witnesses. The significance of such a document—in this case a visual one—is emphasized by the art historian, Erwin Panofsky: According to Catholic dogma, the sacrament of matrimony is "immediately accomplished by the mutual consent of the persons to be married when this consent is expressed by words and actions" in

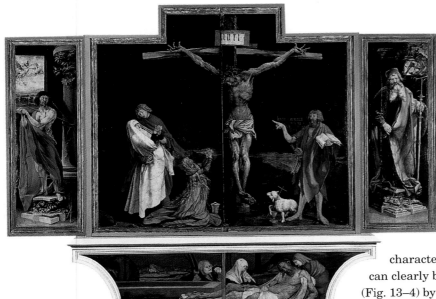

13–4 MATTHIAS GRÜNEWALD
THE CRUCIFIXION, CENTER PANEL OF THE *ISENHEIM ALTARPIECE* (EXTERIOR) (COMPLETED 1515). OIL ON PANEL. 8′10″ × 10′1″.
MUSÉE D'UNTERLINDEN, COLMAR, FRANCE.

German artists. Their work contains less symbolism and less detail than that of Flemish artists, but their message is often more powerful.

MATTHIAS GRÜNEWALD   These characteristics of German Renaissance art can clearly be seen in the *Isenheim Altarpiece* (Fig. 13–4) by Matthias Grünewald, (c. 1480–1528), painted more than three-quarters of a century after Jan van Eyck's Arnolfini portrait. The central panel of the German altarpiece is occupied by a tormented representation of the Crucifixion, one of the most dramatic in the history of art. The dead Christ is flanked by his mother, Mary, the apostle John, and Mary Magdalene to the left, and John the Baptist and a sacrificial lamb to the right. These figures exhibit a bodily tension in their arched backs, clenched hands, and rigidly pointing fingers, creating a melodramatic, anxious tone. The crucified Christ is shown with a deadly pallor. His skin appears cancerous, and his chest is sunken with his last breath. His gnarled hands reach painfully upward, stretching for salvation from the blackened sky. We do not find such impassioned portrayals outside Germany during the Renaissance.

the presence of two or three witnesses. Records of the marriage were necessary to avoid lawsuits in which "the validity of the marriage could be neither proved nor disproved for want of reliable witnesses."[2]

Once again we see the Northern artist's striking realism and fidelity to detail offering us exact records of the facial features of the wedding couple. The figures of the two witnesses are reflected in the convex mirror behind the Arnolfinis. Believe it or not, they are Jan van Eyck and his wife, a fact corroborated by the inscription above the mirror: "Jan van Eyck was here." As in most Flemish paintings, the items scattered about are invested with symbolism relevant to the occasion. The furry dog in the foreground symbolizes fidelity, and the oranges on the windowsill may symbolize victory over death. Giovanni himself has kicked off his shoes out of respect for the holiness of the ground on which this sacrament takes place. Finally, the finial on the bedpost is an image of St. Margaret, the patroness of childbirth, and around her wooden waist is slung a small whisk broom, a symbol of domesticity. It would seem that Giovanni had his bride's career all mapped out. With Jan van Eyck, Flemish painting reached the height of symbolic realism in both religious and secular subject matter. No one ever quite followed in his footsteps.

GERMAN ART

Northern Renaissance painting is not confined to the region of Flanders and, indeed, some of the most emotionally striking work of this period was created by

ALBRECHT DÜRER   We appropriately close our discussion of Northern Renaissance art with the Italianate master, Albrecht Dürer (1471–1528). His passion for the Classical in art stimulated extensive travel in Italy, where he copied the works of the Italian masters, who were also enthralled with the Classical style. The development of the printing press made it possible for him to disseminate the works of the Italian masters throughout Northern Europe.

Dürer's Adam and Eve (Fig. 13–5) conveys his admiration for the Classical style. In contrast to figures rendered by other German and Flemish artists, Dürer emphasized the idealized beauty of the human body. His Adam and Eve are not everyday figures of the sort Campin depicted in his Virgin Mary. Instead, the images arise from Greek and Roman prototypes.

[2]Erwin Panofsky, "Jan van Eyck's 'Arnolfini' Portrait," *Burlington Magazine*, LXIV (1934), 117–27.

DÜRER MADE TWO TRIPS TO ITALY DURING WHICH HE MADE DRAWINGS AFTER ANCIENT
SCULPTURE, INSPIRING FIGURES SUCH AS THOSE IN *ADAM AND EVE*.

13–5 ALBRECHT DÜRER
ADAM AND EVE (1504). ENGRAVING, 1ST STATE. 9⅞ × 7⅝″.
THE METROPOLITAN MUSEUM OF ART, NEW YORK. FLETCHER FUND, 1919 (19.73.1).

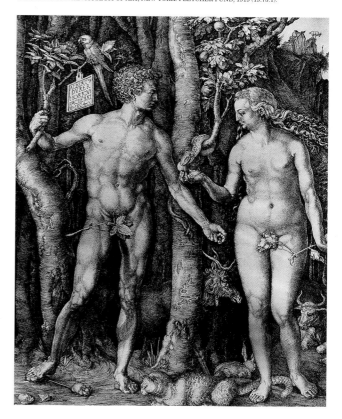

Adam's young muscular body could have been drawn from a live model or from Classical statuary. Eve represents a standard of beauty different from that of other Northern artists. The familiar slight build and refined facial features have given way to a more substantial and well-rounded woman. She is reminiscent of a fifth-century BCE Venus in her features and her pose. The symbols associated with the event—the Tree of Knowledge and the Serpent (Satan)—play a secondary role. Dürer has chosen to emphasize the profound beauty of the human body. Instead of focusing on the consequences of the event as an admonition against sin, we delight in the couple's beauty for its own sake. Indeed, this notion is central to the art of Renaissance Italy.

THE RENAISSANCE IN ITALY

THE EARLY RENAISSANCE

Not only was there a marked difference between Northern and Italian Renaissance art, but there were notable differences in the art of various sections of Italy itself. Florence and Rome witnessed a resurgence of Classicism as Roman ruins were excavated in ancient sites, hillsides, and people's backyards. In Siena, on the other hand, the International style lingered, and in Venice a Byzantine influence remained strong. There may be several reasons for this diversity, but the most obvious is that of geography. For example, while the Roman artist's stylistic roads led to that ancient city, the trade routes in the northeast brought an Eastern influence to works of art and architecture.

The Italian Renaissance took root and flourished most successfully in Florence. The development of this city's painting, sculpture, and architecture parallels that of the Renaissance in all of Italy. Throughout the Renaissance, as Florence went, so went the country.

CIMABUE AND GIOTTO

Some of the earliest changes from a medieval to a Classical style can be perceived in the painting of Florence during the late thirteenth and early fourteenth

centuries, the prime exponents being Cimabue and Giotto. So significant were these artists that Dante Alighieri, the fourteenth-century poet, mentioned both of them in his *Purgatory* of *The Divine Comedy*:

> *O gifted men, vainglorious for first place,*
> *how short a time the laurel crown stays green*
> *unless the age that follows lacks all grace!*
> *Once Cimabue thought to hold the field*
> *in painting, and now Giotto has the cry*
> *so that the other's fame, grown dim, must yield.[3]*

Who were these artists? Apparently they were rivals, although Cimabue (c. 1240–c.1302) was older than Giotto (c. 1276–c.1337) and probably had a formative influence on the latter, who would ultimately steal the limelight.

[3]From *The Divine Comedy*, by Dante Alighieri, translated by John Ciardi. Translation copyright 1954, 1957, 1959, 1960, 1961, 1965, 1967, 1970 by the Ciardi Family Publishing Trust. Reprinted by permission of W. W. Norton & Company, Inc.

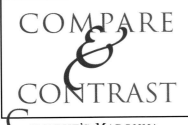

CIMABUE'S *MADONNA ENTHRONED*
WITH
GIOTTO'S *MADONNA ENTHRONED*

The similarities and differences between the works of Cimabue and Giotto can be seen in two tempera paintings on wood panels depicting the Madonna and Child enthroned. A curious combination of Late Gothic and Early Renaissance styles betrays Cimabue's composition (Fig. 13–6) as a transitional work. The massive throne of the Madonna is Roman in inspiration, with column and arch forms embellished with **intarsia.** The Madonna has a corporeal presence that sets her apart from "floating" medieval figures, but the effect is compromised by the unsureness with which she is placed on the throne. She does not sit solidly; her limbs are not firmly "planted." Rather, the legs resemble the "hinged" appendages of Romanesque figures. This characteristic placement of the knees causes the drapery to fall in predictable folds— concentric arcs reminiscent of a more stylized technique. The angels supporting the throne rise parallel to it, their glances forming an abstract zig zag pattern. The resultant lyrical arabesque, the flickering color patterns of the wings, and the lineup of unobstructed heads recall the Byzantine tradition, particularly the Ravenna mosaics (see Fig. 12–6).

Giotto's rendition of the same theme (Fig. 13–7) offers some dramatic differences. The overall impression of the *Madonna Enthroned* is one of stability and corporeality instead of instability and weightlessness. Giotto's Madonna sits firmly on her throne, the outlines of her body and drapery forming a solid triangular shape. Although the throne is lighter in appearance than Cimabue's Roman throne—and is, in fact, Gothic, with pointed arches—it too seems more firmly planted on the earth. Giotto's genius is also evident in his conception of the forms in three-dimensional space. They not only have height and width, as do those of Cimabue, but they also have depth and mass. This is particularly noticeable in the treatment of the angels. Their location in space is from front to rear, rather than atop one another as in Cimabue's composition. The halos of the foreground angels obscure the faces of the background attendants, since they have mass and occupy space.

Despite these differences between the works, what elements do they have in common? How does each artist use chiaroscuro? Which composition is more naturalistic? Why? Does one composition seem flatter or more two-dimensional? Does one seem to better replicate space or three-dimensionality?

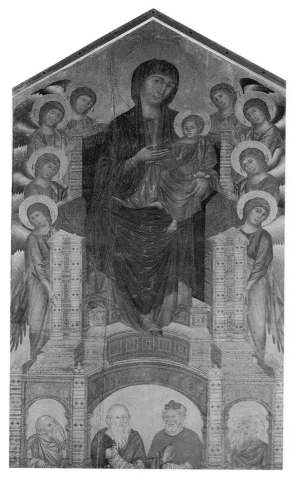

13–6 CIMABUE
Madonna Enthroned
(C. 1280–90). TEMPERA ON
WOOD PANEL. 12′7½″ × 7′4″.
UFFIZI GALLERY, FLORENCE.

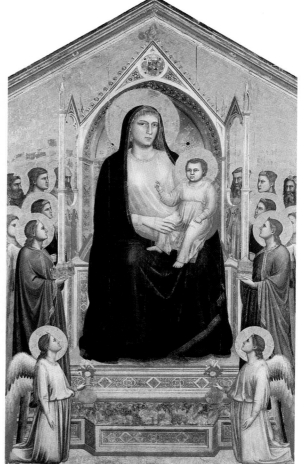

13–7 GIOTTO
Madonna Enthroned
(C. 1310). TEMPERA ON
WOOD PANEL. 10′8″ × 6′8″.
UFFIZI GALLERY, FLORENCE.

IN SEPTEMBER OF 1402, THE TROOPS OF THE DUKE OF MILAN HAD FLORENCE SURROUNDED. ALL SEEMED LOST WHEN THE DUKE DIED SUDDENLY. FLORENCE SAW ITSELF AS SAVED THROUGH DIVINE INTERVENTION, MUCH AS ISAAC HAD BEEN CENTURIES EARLIER.

13–8 FILIPPO BRUNELLESCHI
SACRIFICE OF ISAAC (1401–02). GILT BRONZE. 21 × 17½".
MUSEO NAZIONALE DEL BARGELLO, FLORENCE.

13–9 LORENZO GHIBERTI
SACRIFICE OF ISAAC (1401–2). GILT BRONZE, 21 × 17½".
MUSEO NAZIONALE DEL BARGELLO, FLORENCE.

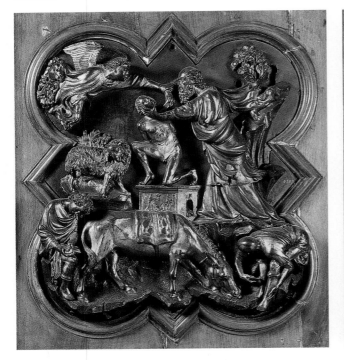

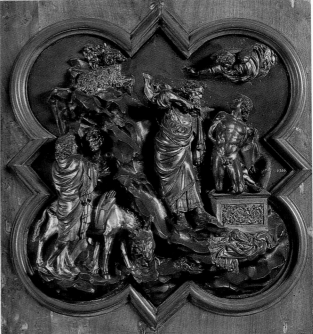

THE RENAISSANCE BEGINS, AND SO DOES THE COMPETITION

With Cimabue and Giotto we witness strides toward an art that was very different from that of the Middle Ages. But artists, like all of us, must walk before they can run, and those very "strides" that express such a stylistic advance from the "cut-out dolls" of the Ravenna mosaics and the "hinged marionettes" of the Romanesque era will look primitive in another half-century. Because the art of Cimabue and Giotto contains vestiges of Gothicism, their style is often termed proto-Renaissance. But at the dawn of the fifteenth century in Florence, the Early Renaissance began—with a competition.

Imagine workshops and artists abuzz with news of one of the hottest projects in memory up for grabs. Think of one of the most prestigious architectural sites in Florence. Savor the possibility of being known as *the* artist who had cast, in gleaming bronze, the massive doors of the Baptistery of Florence. This landmark competition was held in 1401. There were countless entries but only two panels have come down to us. The artists had been given a scene from the Old Testament to translate into bronze—the sacrifice of Isaac by his father Abraham. There were specifications, naturally, but the most obvious is the **quatrefoil** format. Within this space, a certain cast of characters was mandated, including Abraham, Isaac, an angel, and two "extras" who appear to have little or nothing to do with the scene. The event takes place out of doors, where Abraham has lured his son to the sacrificial altar on the pretense of performing a ritual animal sacrifice. When they arrive on the scene, Abraham, in an attempt to prove his love and loyalty to God, turns the blade to Isaac's throat. At this moment, an angel flies in to prevent Abraham from completing the deed.

FILIPPO BRUNELLESCHI AND LORENZO GHIBERTI

The two extant panels were executed by Filippo Brunelleschi (c. 1377–1446) and Lorenzo Ghiberti (1378–1455). The obligatory characters, bushes, animals, and altar are present in both, but the placement of these elements, the artistic style, and the emotional energy within each work differ considerably. Brunelleschi's panel (Fig. 13–8) is divided into sections by strong vertical and horizontal

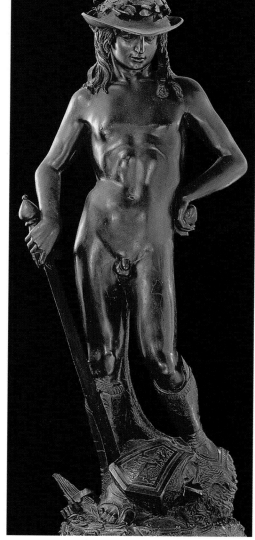

13–10 DONATELLO
DAVID (1408). BRONZE. HEIGHT: 5′2″.
MUSEO NAZIONALE DEL BARGELLO, FLORENCE.

elements, each section filled with objects and figures. In contrast to the rigidity of the format, a ferocious energy bordering on violence pervades the composition. Isaac's neck and body are distorted by his father's grasping fist, and Abraham himself lunges viciously toward his son's throat with a knife. With similar passion, an angel flies in from the left to grasp Abraham's arm. But this intense drama and seemingly boundless energy are weakened by the introduction of ancillary figures who are given more prominence than the scene requires. The donkey, for example, detracts from Isaac's plight by being placed broadside and practically dead center. Also, one is struck by the staccato movement throughout. Although this choppiness complements the anxiety in the work, it compromises the successful flow of space and tires the eye.

In Lorenzo Ghiberti's panel (Fig. 13–9), the space is divided along a diagonal rock formation that separates the main characters from the lesser ones. Space flows along this diagonal, exposing the figural group of Abraham and Isaac and embracing the shepherd boys and their donkey. The boys and donkey are appropriately subordinated to the main characters but not sidestepped stylistically. Abraham's lower body parallels the rock formation and then lunges expressively away from it in a dynamic counterthrust. Isaac, in turn, pulls firmly away from his father's forward motion. The forms move rhythmically together in a continuous flow of space. Although Ghiberti's emotion is not quite as intense as Brunelleschi's, and his portrayal of the sacrifice is not quite as graphic, the impact of Ghiberti's narrative is as strong.

It is interesting to note the inclusion of Classicizing elements in both panels. Brunelleschi, in one of his peasants, adapted the Classical sculpture of a boy removing a thorn from his foot, and Ghiberti rendered his Isaac in the manner of a fifth-century sculptor. Isaac's torso, in fact, may be the first nude in this style since Classical times.

Oh, yes—Ghiberti won the competition and Brunelleschi went home with his chisel. The latter never devoted himself to sculpture again, but went on to become the first great Renaissance architect. Ghiberti himself was not particularly modest about his triumph:

To me was conceded the palm of victory by all the experts and by all . . . who had competed with me. To me the honor was conceded universally and with no exception. To all it seemed that I had at that time surpassed the others without exception, as was recognized by a great council and an investigation of learned men . . . highly skilled from the painters and sculptors of gold, silver, and marble.[4]

DONATELLO   If Brunelleschi and Ghiberti were among the last sculptors to harbor vestiges of the International style, Donatello (c. 1386–1466), the Florentine master, was surely among the first to create sculptures that combined Classicism with realism. In his *David* (Fig. 13–10), the first life-size nude statue since Classical times, Donatello struck a balance between the two styles by presenting a very real image of an

[4]E. G. Holt, ed., *Literary Sources of Art History* (Princeton, N.J.: Princeton University Press, 1947), pp. 87–88.

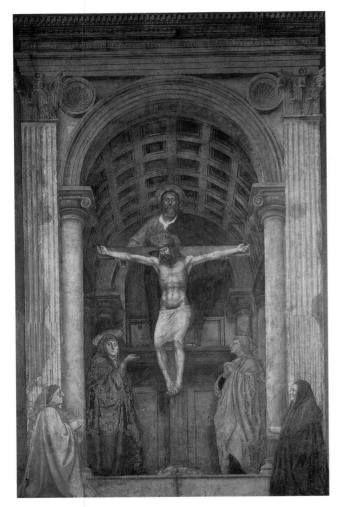

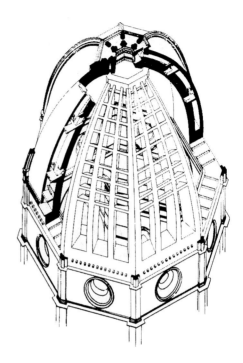

as David himself seems incredulous as he glances down toward his body. What David lacks in stature he has made up in intellect, faith, and courage. His fate was in his own hands—one of the ideals of the Renaissance man.

MASACCIO   The Early Renaissance painters shared most of the stylistic concerns of the sculptors. However, included in their attempts at realism was the added difficulty of projecting a naturalistic sense of three-dimensional space on a two-dimensional surface. In addition to copying from nature and Classical models, these painters developed rules of perspective to depict images in the round on flat walls, panels, and canvases. One of the pioneers in developing systematic laws of one-point **linear perspective** was Brunelleschi, of Baptistery Doors near-fame.

Masaccio's *Holy Trinity* (Fig. 13–11) uses these laws of perspective. In this chapel fresco, Masaccio (1401–1428) creates the illusion of an extension of the architectural space of the church by painting a **barrel-vaulted** "chapel" housing a variety of holy and common figures. God the Father supports the cross that bears his cruci-

Italian peasant boy in the guise of a Classical nude figure. David, destined to be the second king of Israel, slew the Philistine giant Goliath with a stone and a sling. Even though Donatello was inspired by Classical statuary, notice that he did not choose a Greek youth in his prime as a prototype for his David. Instead, he chose a barely developed adolescent boy, his hair still unclipped and his arms flaccid for lack of manly musculature. After decapitating Goliath, whose head lies at David's feet, his sword rests at his side—almost too heavy for him to handle. Can such a youth have accomplished such a forbidding task? Herein lies the power of Donatello's statement. We are amazed, from the appearance of this young boy, that he could have done such a deed, much

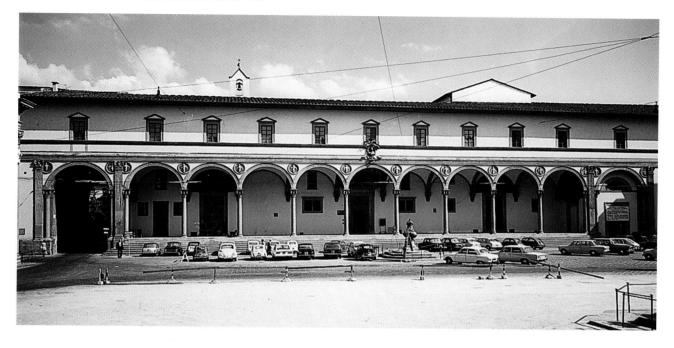

fied son while the Virgin Mary and the apostle John attend. Outside the columns and pilasters of the realistic, Roman-inspired chapel kneel the donors, who are invited to observe the scene. Aside from the trompe l'oeil rendition of the architecture, the realism in the fresco is enhanced by the donors, who are given importance equal to that of the "principal" characters, similar to Campin's treatment of the donors in the *Merode Altarpiece* (Fig. 13–2). The architecture appears to extend our physical space, and the donors appear as extensions of ourselves.

FILIPPO BRUNELLESCHI   The revival of Classicism was even more marked in the architecture of the Renaissance. Some twenty years after Brunelleschi's unsuccessful bid for the Baptistery Doors project in Florence, he was commissioned to cover the crossing square of the cathedral of Florence with a dome. Interestingly, Ghiberti worked with him at the outset but soon bowed out, and Brunelleschi was left to complete the work alone. It was quite an engineering feat, involving a double-shell dome constructed around twenty-four ribs (Fig. 13–12). Eight of these ribs rise upward to a crowning lantern on the exterior of the dome. You might wonder why Brunelleschi, whose architectural models were essentially Classical, would have constructed a somewhat pointed dome reminiscent of the Middle Ages. The fact is that the architect might have preferred a more rounded or hemispherical structure, but the engineering problem required an ogival, or pointed, section, which is inher-

ently more stable. The dome was a compromise between a somewhat Classical style and traditional Gothic building principles.

Although the cathedral dome is Brunelleschi's greatest engineering achievement, his Ospedale degli Innocenti (Hospital for Foundlings) in Florence (Fig. 13–13) is more characteristic of his architectural style. The hospital stands as another example of Brunelleschi's commitment to a highly rational expression of Classical elements. The sweeping horizontal facade is marked by a procession of round arches and slender Corinthian columns framed by substantial pilasters which visually support the simple flat entablature. The rhythm is repeated on the second floor, where a series of windows topped by pediments serve as counterpoints to the archways beneath. Although Brunelleschi was influenced by Romanesque architecture, the utter logic of the foundling hospital links it more clearly to Classical architecture than to the more recent Medieval period. Brunelleschi's clear restatement of Classical elements would influence architecture for decades to come.

RENAISSANCE ART AT MIDCENTURY AND BEYOND

ANDREA DEL VERROCCHIO   As we progress into the middle of the fifteenth century, the most important and innovative sculptor is Andrea del Verrocchio (1435–1488). An extremely versatile artist who was trained as a goldsmith, Verrocchio ran an active shop that attracted many young artists, including Leonardo

THE GUTENBERG BIBLE WAS PRODUCED IN GERMANY BETWEEN 1450 AND 1456. IT WAS THE
FIRST COMPLETE BOOK PRINTED WITH INDEPENDENT, MOVABLE TYPE.

13–14 ANDREA DEL VERROCCHIO
DAVID (C. 1470). BRONZE. HEIGHT: 49⅝″.
MUSEO NAZIONALE DEL BARGELLO, FLORENCE.

13–15 PIERO DELLA FRANCESCA
RESURRECTION (C. LATE 1450S). FRESCO.
TOWN HALL, BORGO SAN SEPOLCRO.

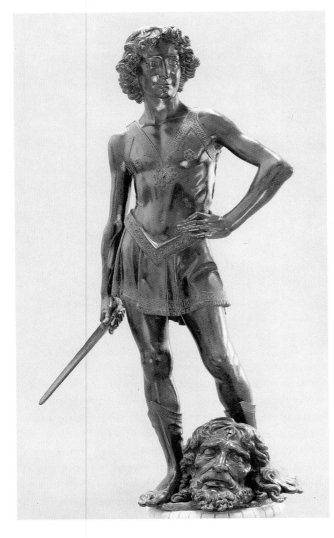

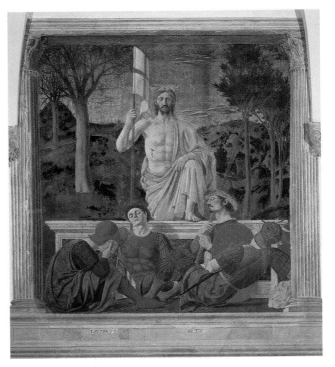

Middle Easterner. The sculptures differ considerably
also in terms of technique. Donatello's *David* is essentially a closed-form sculpture with objects and limbs
centered around an **S-curve** stance; Verrocchio's sculpture is more open, as is evidenced by the bared sword
and elbow jutting away from the central core. Donatello's graceful pose has been replaced, in the Verrocchio, by a jaunty **contrapposto** that enhances David's
image of self-confidence.

PIERO DELLA FRANCESCA   The artists of the Renaissance, along with the philosophers and scientists,
tended to share the sense of the universe as an orderly
place that was governed by natural law and capable of
being expressed in mathematical and geometric terms.
Piero della Francesca (c. 1420–1492) was trained in
mathematics and geometry and is credited with writing
the first theoretical treatise on the construction of
systematic perspective in art. Piero's art, like his
scientific thought, was based on an intensely rational
construction of forms and space.

His *Resurrection* fresco (Fig. 13–15) for the town
hall of Borgo San Sepolcro reveals the artist's obsessions

da Vinci. We see in Verrocchio's bronze *David* (Fig.
13–14), commissioned by the Medici family, a strong
contrast to Donatello's handling of the same subject.
The Medici also owned the Donatello *David,* and
Verrocchio probably wanted to outshine his predecessor.
Although both artists chose to represent David as an
adolescent, Verrocchio's hero appears somewhat older
and exudes pride and self-confidence rather than a
dreamy gaze of disbelief. Whereas Donatello reconciled
realistic elements with an almost idealized, Classically
inspired torso, Verrocchio's goal was supreme realism
in minute details, including orientalizing motifs on the
boy's doublet that would have made him look like a

THE BIRTH OF VENUS (C. 1482). OIL ON CANVAS. 5′ 8⅞″ × 9′ 1⅞″.
UFFIZI GALLERY, FLORENCE.

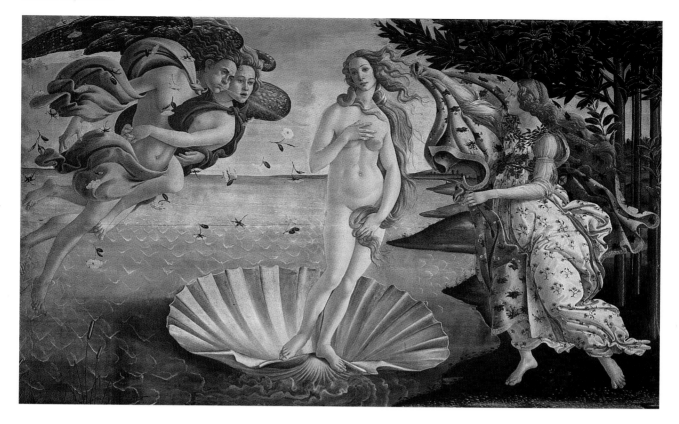

with order and geometry. Christ ascends vertical and triumphant, like a monumental column, above the "entablature" of his tomb, which serves visually as the pedestal of a statue. Christ and the other figures are constructed from the cones, cylinders, spheres, and rectangular solids that define the theoretical world of the artist. There is a tendency here toward the simplification of forms—not only of people, but also of natural features such as trees and hills. All the figures in the painting are contained within a triangle—what would become a major compositional device in Renaissance painting—with Christ at the apex. The sleeping figures and the marble sarcophagus provide a strong and stable base for the upper two-thirds of the composition. Regimented trees rise in procession behind Christ, as they never do when nature asserts its random jests; Piero's trees are swept back by the rigid cultivation of scientific perspective. They crown, as ordered, just above the crests of rounded hills. The artist of the Renaissance was not only in awe of nature, but also commanded it fully.

SANDRO BOTTICELLI During the latter years of the fifteenth century, we come upon an artistic personality whose style is somewhat in opposition to the prevailing trends. Since the time of Giotto, painters had relied on chiaroscuro, or the contrast of light and shade, to create a sense of roundness and mass in their figures and objects in an effort to render a realistic impression of three-dimensional forms in space. Sandro Botticelli (c. 1444–1510), however, constructed his compositions with line instead of tonal contrasts. His art relied primarily on drawing. Yet when it came to subject matter, his heart lay with his Renaissance peers, for, above all else, he loved to paint mythological themes. Along with other artists and men of letters, his mania for these subjects was fed and perhaps cultivated by the Medici prince Lorenzo the Magnificent, who surrounded himself with Neoplatonists, or those who followed the philosophy of Plato.

One of Botticelli's most famous paintings is *The Birth of Venus* (Fig. 13–16), or, as some art historians would have it, "Venus on the Half-Shell." The model for this Venus was Simonetta Vespucci, a cousin of Amerigo Vespucci, the navigator and explorer after whom America was named. The composition presents Venus, born of the foam of the sea, floating to the shores of her sacred island on a large scallop shell, aided in its drifting by the sweet breaths of entwined zephyrs. The nymph Pomona awaits her with an

AMERIGO VESPUCCI, AFTER WHOM AMERICA WAS NAMED, SAILED HIS VOYAGE OF DISCOVERY
BETWEEN 1499 AND 1502. HE DIED IN 1512 OF MALARIA, CONTRACTED DURING HIS TRAVELS.

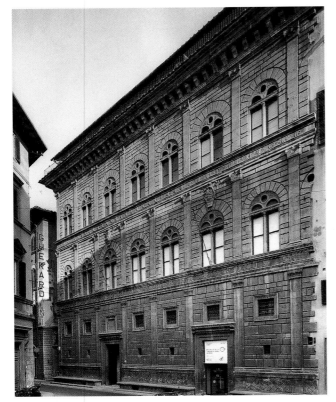

13–17 LEON BATTISTA ALBERTI
PALAZZO RUCELLAI, FLORENCE (1446–51).

ornate mantle and is herself dressed in a billowing, flowered gown. Botticelli's interest in Classicism is evident also in his choice of models for the Venus. She is a direct adaptation of an antique sculpture of this goddess in the collection of the Medici family. Notice how the graceful movement in the composition is evoked through a combination of different lines. A firm horizon line and regimented verticals in the trees contrast with the subtle curves and vigorous arabesques that caress the mythological figures. The line moves from image to image and then doubles back to lead your eye once again. Shading is confined to areas within the harsh, linear sculptural contours of the figures. Botticelli's genius lay in his ability to utilize the differing qualities of line to his advantage; with this formal element he created the most delicate of compositions.

LEON BATTISTA ALBERTI   Some of the purest examples of Renaissance Classicism lie in the buildings designed by Leon Battista Alberti (1404–1472). Alberti was among the first to study treatises written by Roman architects, the most famous of whom was Vitruvius, and he combined his Classical knowledge with innovative ideas in his grand opus, *Ten Books on Architecture*. One of his most visually satisfying buildings in the great Classical tradition is the Palazzo Rucellai (Fig. 13–17) in Florence. The building is divided by prominent horizontal string courses into three stories, crowned by a heavy cornice. Within each story are apertures enframed by pilasters of different orders. The first-floor pilasters are of the Tuscan order, which resembles the Doric order in its simplicity; the second story uses a composite capital of volutes and acanthus leaves, seen in the Ionic and Corinthian orders respectively; and the top-floor pilasters are crowned by capitals of the Corinthian order. As in the Colosseum (see Fig. 11–23), this combination of orders gives an impression of increasing lightness as we rise from the lower to the upper stories. This effect is enhanced in Alberti's building by a variation in the masonry. Although the texture remains the same, the upper stories are faced with lighter-appearing smaller blocks in greater numbers. The palazzo's design, with its clear articulation of parts, overall balance of forms, and rhythmic placement of elements in horizontals across the facade, shows a clear understanding of Classical design adapted successfully to the contemporary nobleman's needs.

THE HIGH RENAISSANCE

Demanding patrons, the high cost of materials, and a lack of money have a way of fostering crabbiness among artists as well as butchers, bakers, and candlestick makers. It can be difficult to concentrate on our endeavors when others are mistreating us.

Sometime in 1542, Pope Julius II and Michelangelo Buonarroti were in conflict, with the artist bearing the brunt of the pontiff's behavior. As if backing out of his tomb commission and refusing to pay for materials were not enough, the Pope laid the last straw by having Michelangelo thrown out of the Vatican by one of his attendants on one occasion when the artist sought to redress his grievances. Was that any way to treat a genius? The artist thought not, as he complained in a letter to one of Julius's underlings:

> . . . a man paints with his brains and not with his hands, and if he cannot have his brains clear he will come to grief. Therefore I shall be able to do nothing well until justice has been done me. . . . As soon as the Pope [carries] out his obligations towards me I [will] return, otherwise he need never expect to see me again.

> All the disagreements that arose between Pope Julius and myself were due to the jealousy of Bramante and of Raffaelo da Urbino; it was because of them that he did not proceed with the tomb, . . . and they brought this about in order that I might thereby be ruined. Yet Raffaello was quite right to be jealous of me, for all he knew of art he learned from me.[5]

[5]Robert Goldwater and Marco Treves, eds., *Artists on Art* (New York: Pantheon Books, 1972), p. 63.

Although this is only one side of the story, and Michelangelo might also have been somewhat jealous of Raffaelo (Raphael), this passage affords us a glimpse of the personality of an artist of the High Renaissance. He was independent yet indispensable—arrogant, aggressive, and competitive.

From the second half of the fifteenth century onward, a refinement of the stylistic principles and techniques associated with the Renaissance can be observed. Most of this significant, progressive work was being done in Florence, where the Medici family played an important role in supporting the arts. At the close of the decade, however, Rome was the place to be, as the popes began to assume the grand role of patron. The three artists who were most in demand—the great masters of the High Renaissance in Italy—were Leonardo da Vinci, a painter, scientist, inventor, and musician; Raphael, the Classical painter thought to have rivaled the works of the ancients; and Michelangelo, the painter, sculptor, architect, poet, and enfant terrible. Donato Bramante is deemed to have made the most significant architectural contributions of this period. These are the stars of the Renaissance, the artistic descendants of the Giottos, Donatellos, and Albertis, who, because of their earlier place in the historical sequence of artistic development, are sometimes portrayed as but steppingstones to the greatness of the sixteenth-century artists, rather than as masters in their own right.

LEONARDO DA VINCI   If the Italians of the High Renaissance could have nominated a counterpart to the Classical Greek's "four-square man," it most assuredly would have been Leonardo da Vinci (1452–1519). His capabilities in engineering, the natural sciences, music, and the arts seemed unlimited, as he excelled in everything from solving drainage problems (a project he undertook in France just before his death), to designing prototypes for airplanes and submarines, to creating some of the most memorable Renaissance paintings.

13–18 LEONARDO DA VINCI
THE LAST SUPPER (1495–98). FRESCO. 13′ 10″ × 29′ 7½″.
SANTA MARIA DELLE GRAZIE, MILAN.

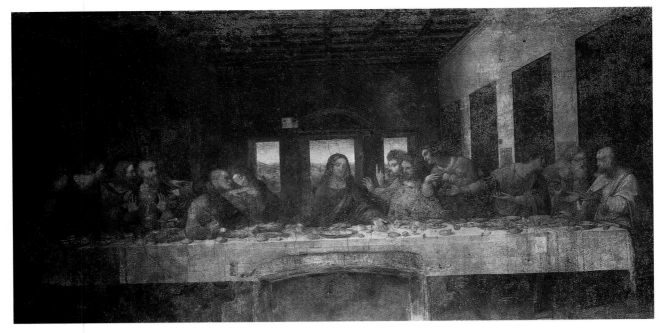

The Last Supper (Fig. 13–18), a fresco painting executed for the dining hall of a Milan monastery, stands as one of Leonardo's greatest works. The condition of the work is poor, because of Leonardo's experimental fresco technique—although the steaming of pasta for centuries on the other side of the wall may also have played a role. Nonetheless, we can still observe the Renaissance ideals of Classicism, humanism, and technical perfection, now coming to full fruition. The composition is organized through the use of one-point linear perspective. Solid volumes are constructed from a masterful contrast of light and shadow. A hairline balance is struck between emotion and restraint.

The viewer is first attracted to the central triangular form of Jesus sitting among his apostles by **orthogonals** that converge at his head. His figure is silhouetted against a triple window that symbolizes the Holy Trinity and pierces the otherwise dark back wall. One's attention is held at this center point by the Christ-figure's isolation that results from the leaning away of the apostles. Leonardo has chosen to depict the moment

when Jesus says, "One of you will betray me." The apostles reflexively fall back at this shocking statement, gesturing expressively, denying personal responsibility, and asking, "Who can this be?" The guilty one, of course, is Judas, who is shown clutching a bag of silver pieces at Jesus' left, with his elbow on the table. The two groups of apostles, who sweep dramatically away from Jesus along a horizontal line, are subdivided into four smaller groups of three that tend to moderate the rush of the eye out from the center. The viewer's eye is wafted outward and then coaxed back inward through the "parenthetic" poses of the apostles at either end. Leonardo's use of strict rules of perspective and his graceful balance of motion and restraint underscore the artistic philosophy and style of the Renaissance.

Although Leonardo does not allow excessive emotion in his *Last Supper*, the reactions of the apostles seem genuinely human. There is probably no better example of Humanism in sixteenth-century Renaissance art, however, than the subject of Virgin and Child. One of the most significant paintings to capture this spirit is

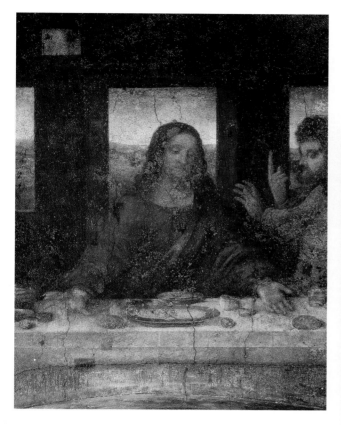

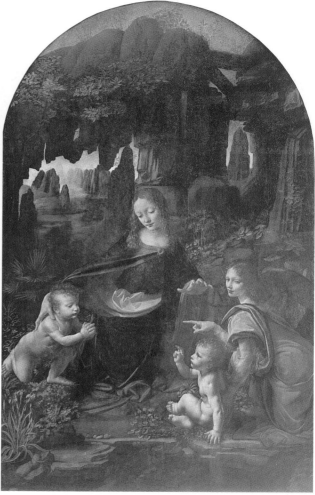

13–19 LEONARDO DA VINCI
MADONNA OF THE ROCKS (C. 1483). OIL ON PANEL,
TRANSFERRED TO CANVAS. 78½ × 48″.
LOUVRE MUSEUM, PARIS.

the *Madonna of the Rocks* (Fig. 13–19) by Leonardo.
Notice all that has changed in the representation of this
figural group during the course of the preceding century.
Mary is no longer portrayed as the queen of heaven,
enthroned and surrounded by angels in a nondescript
golden environment, but rather as a mother in the
midst of the world—in this case a grotto embellished
with luscious vegetation and beautiful rock formations.
She has been given a human portrayal. Compositionally, she forms the apex of a rather broad, stable triangle, extending her arms toward the infants Jesus and
John the Baptist. Her right arm embraces John, but
she is unable to reach the child Jesus because of the
interfering hand of an angel who sits near him. Mary's
inability to complete her embrace may symbolize her
ultimate inability to protect him from his fate. Yet the
tender human aspect of the scene stands independent
of its iconography.

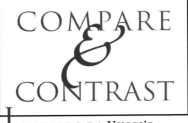

COMPARE & CONTRAST

LEONARDO DA VINCI'S
MONA LISA, MARCEL
DUCHAMP'S *L.H.O.O.Q.,*
G. ODUTOKUN'S *DIALOGUE
WITH MONA LISA,* AND SADIE
LEE'S *BONA LISA*

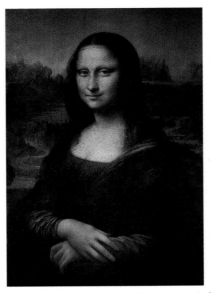

13–20 LEONARDO DA VINCI
MONA LISA (C. 1503).
OIL ON WOOD. 30 × 21″.
LOUVRE MUSEUM, PARIS.

So if somebody asked you to close your eyes and think of the most famous work of art in all of history, what would you say? Odds are that the first piece to come up on your memory-screen would be none other than the lead-off work in this exercise. Her portrait has captivated poets and lyricists, museum-goers and, yes, artists, for centuries. Simply put, her face has been everywhere. Why and how did she attain this icon status? The *Mona Lisa* (Fig. 13–20) is a portrait of a banker's wife, worked on by Leonardo for four years and, as was much of his work, left unfinished.

In its own day, though, it was quite an innovative composition. Among other things, Leonardo rejected the traditional profile portrait bust in favor of a three-quarter-turned, half-length figure. The inclusion of the hands in a natural position, for the most part uncharacteristic of earlier portraiture, was essential for Leonardo as a method of exploring and revealing the personality of the sitter: "A good painter has two chief objects to paint, man and the intention of his soul; the former is easy, the latter hard, because he has to represent it by the attitudes and movements of the limbs." A new look at portrait painting, to be sure. But there is still the matter of that enigmatic smile. And those eyes, which many have vouched, follow the viewer's movements across a room. The *Mona Lisa* is a beautiful painting, but does that account for why a visitor in search of the master-piece in Paris's Louvre Museum need only look for the one painting that cannot be viewed because of the crowd surrounding it?

The selection of images in this exercise represents but a sampling of work that attempts to come to terms with "Mona Lisa: The Icon." One of the earlier revisions of Leonardo's painting was assembled by the Dada artist,

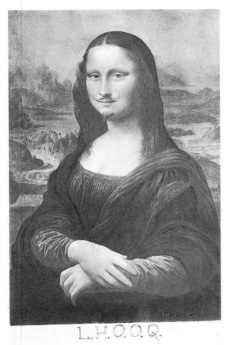

L.H.O.O.Q.

13–21 MARCEL DUCHAMP
MONA LISA (L.H.O.O.Q.) (1919)
RECTIFIED READYMADE; PENCIL ON A
REPRODUCTION. 7¾ × 4⅞″.

Marcel Duchamp (Fig. 13–21). Using a reproduction of the original work, Duchamp modified the image—graffiti-style—by pencilling in a moustache and goatee. Beneath the image of the banker's wife is Duchamp's irreverent explanation of that enigmatic smile: If you read the letters aloud with their French pronunciation, using a slurred, legato style, the sound your ears will hear is "elle a chaud au cul." (Rough translation: "She is hot in the pants.") Part of the underlying philosophy of the Dada movement was the notion that the museums of the world are filled with "dead art" that should be "destroyed." Why do you imagine Duchamp would have used the image of the *Mona Lisa* to convey something of this philosophy? Duchamp was certainly a capable enough draughtsman to have rendered his own copy of the *Mona Lisa*. Do you think he used a reproduction simply to expedite completion of the work?

The gouache composition by G. Odutokun (Fig. 13–22) is another clear illustration of the icon status of the *Mona Lisa*. In this work, cultural exchanges are explored through the interaction between images symbolic of Western and non-Western traditions. What do you think the artist aims to suggest through the title of the work? Look closely at the content of the piece. Who is painting whom, who is sculpting whom? Even though the artist seems to be portraying a cross-cultural encounter, would this work be as relevant to a contemporary European viewer as to a contemporary African viewer? What does this composition say about standards of beauty that are culturally defined?

And is the standard of beauty that the *Mona Lisa* has represented for generations one that is gender-biased as well as culturally biased? This question is posed in Sadie Lee's revision entitled *Bona Lisa* (Fig. 13–23). At first glance, the portrait seems to be a male version of Leonardo's female sitter. In reality, Lee has represented the banker's wife as a lesbian with close-cropped hair and masculine attire. Edward Lucie-Smith has interpreted this work as an "ironic comment on the popular image of a 'butch' lesbian."

From politics and protest to the protest of political correctness, each of the artists we have here observed has understood the significance of attaching their message to Leonardo's master work. What are your impressions?

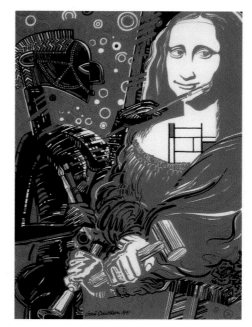

13–22 G. ODUTOKUN
DIALOGUE WITH MONA LISA (1991).
GOUACHE ON PAPER. 30 × 22″
VISUAL ARTS LIBRARY, LONDON/PRIVATE COLLECTION.

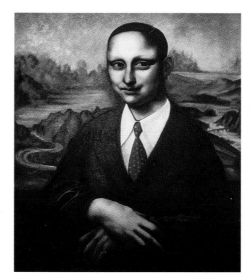

13–23 SADIE LEE
BONA LISA (1992).
OIL ON BOARD. 23 × 19″.
© VISUAL ARTS LIBRARY, LONDON.

13–24 RAPHAEL
THE SCHOOL OF ATHENS (1506). FRESCO. 26 × 18'.
STANZA DELLA SEGNATURA, VATICAN, ROME.

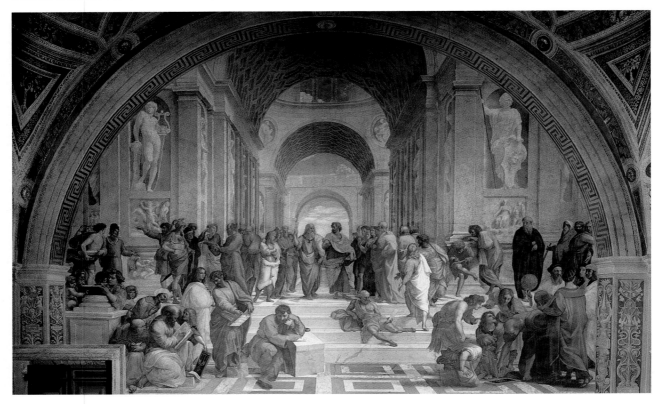

RAPHAEL SANZIO   A younger artist who assimilated the lessons offered by Leonardo, especially on the Humanistic portrayal of the Madonna, was Raphael Sanzio (1483–1520). As a matter of fact, Michelangelo was not far off base in his accusation that Raphael copied from him, for the younger artist freely adopted whatever suited his purposes. Raphael truly shone in his ability to combine the techniques of other masters with an almost instinctive feel for Classical art. He rendered countless canvases depicting the Madonna and Child along the lines of Leonardo's *Madonna of the Rocks.* Raphael was also sought after as a muralist. Some of his most impressive Classical compositions, in fact, were executed for the papal apartments in the Vatican. The commission, of course, came from Pope Julius and, to add fuel to Michelangelo's fire, was executed at the same time Michelangelo was at work on the Sistine Chapel ceiling. For the Stanza della Segnatura, the room in which the highest papal tribunal was held, Raphael painted *The School of Athens* (Fig. 13–24), one of four frescoes designed within a semicircular frame.

In a textbook exercise of one-point linear perspective, Raphael crowded a veritable "who's who" of Classical Greece convening beneath a series of barrel-vaulted archways. The figures symbolize philosophy, one of the four subjects deemed most valuable for a pope's education. (The others were law, theology, and poetry.) The members of the gathering are divided into two camps representing opposing philosophies and are led, on the right, by Aristotle and on the left, by his mentor, Plato. Corresponding to these leaders are the Platonists, whose concerns are the more lofty realm of Ideas (notice Plato pointing upward), and the Aristotelians, who are more in touch with matters of the Earth such as natural science. Some of the figures have been identified: Diogenes, the Cynic philosopher, sprawls out on the steps, and Herakleitos, a founder of Greek metaphysics, sits pensively just left of center. Of more interest is the fact that Raphael included a portrait of himself, staring out toward the viewer, in the far right foreground. He is shown in a group surrounding the geometrician Euclid. Raphael clearly saw himself as important enough to be

13–25 MICHELANGELO
THE SISTINE CHAPEL IN THE VATICAN, ROME (1508–12).
5,800 SQ. FT.
VATICAN MUSEUM, ROME

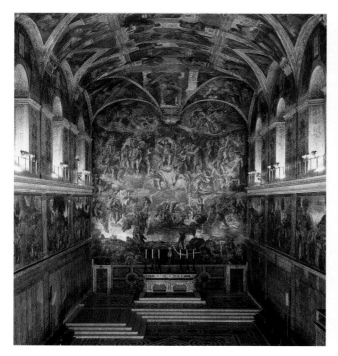

13–26 MICHELANGELO
THE CEILING OF THE SISTINE CHAPEL (1508–12). 5,800 SQ. FT.
VATICAN MUSEUM, ROME.

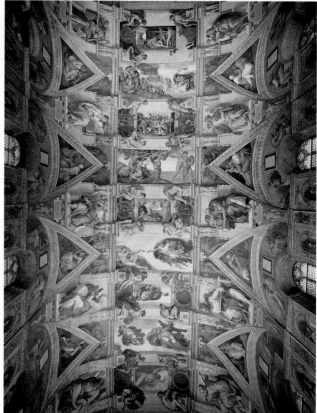

commemorated in a Vatican mural as an ally of the
Aristotelian camp.

As in *The Last Supper* by Leonardo, our attention is
drawn to the two main figures by orthogonals leading
directly to where they are silhouetted against the sky
breaking through the archways. The diagonals that lead
toward a single horizon point are balanced by strong
horizontals and verticals in the architecture and figural
groupings, lending a feeling of Classical stability and
predictability. Stylistically, as well as iconographically,
Raphael has managed to balance opposites in a perfectly graceful and logical composition.

MICHELANGELO BUONARROTI   Of the three great Renaissance masters, Michelangelo (1475–1564) is probably most familiar to us. During the 1964 World's Fair in
New York City, hundreds of thousands of culture seek-
ers and religious pilgrims were trucked along a conveyor belt for a brief glimpse of his *Pietà* at the Vatican
Pavilion. Many of us have seen the film *The Agony and
the Ecstasy,* in which Charlton Heston—who, by the
way, bears a striking resemblance to the artist—lies flat
on his back on a scaffold 70 feet off the ground painting
a ceiling for the Pope. It took Charlton Heston under an

hour and a half; Michelangelo, who was paid less,
required four years. Such is the gulf between art
and . . . art?

In any event, that famed ceiling is the vault of the
chapel of Pope Sixtus IV, known as the Sistine Chapel.
The decorative fresco cycle was commissioned by none
other than Pope Julius II, but the iconographic scheme
was Michelangelo's. The artist had agreed to the project
in order to pacify the temperamental Julius in the hope
that the pontiff would eventually allow him to complete
work on his mammoth tomb. For whatever reason, we
are indeed fortunate to have this painted work from the
sculptor's hand. After much anguish and early attempts
to populate the vault with a variety of religious figures,
Michelangelo settled on a division of the ceiling into
geometrical "frames" (Figs. 13–25 and 13–26) housing
biblical prophets, mythological soothsayers, and Old
Testament scenes from Genesis to Noah's flood.

13–27 MICHELANGELO
THE CREATION OF ADAM (DETAIL FROM CEILING OF THE SISTINE CHAPEL).
VATICAN MUSEUM, ROME.

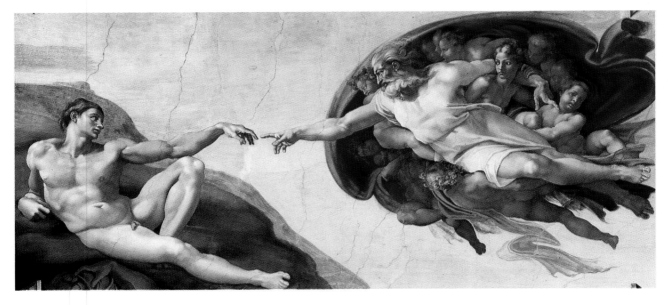

The most famous of these scenes is *The Creation of Adam* (Fig. 13–27). As Leonardo had done in *The Last Supper,* Michelangelo chose to communicate the event's most dramatic moment. Adam lies on the Earth listless for lack of a soul, while God the Father rushes toward him amidst a host of angels, who enwrap him in a billowing cloak. The contrasting figures lean toward the left, separated by an illuminated diagonal that provides a backdrop for the Creation. Amidst an atmosphere of sheer electricity, the hand of God reaches out to spark spiritual life into Adam—but does not touch him! In some of the most dramatic negative space in the history of art, Michelangelo has left it to the spectator to complete the act. In terms of style, Michelangelo integrated **chiaroscuro** with Botticelli's extensive use of line. His figures are harshly drawn and muscular with almost marblelike flesh. In translating his sculptural techniques to a two-dimensional surface, the artist has conceived his figures in the round and has used the tightest, most expeditious line and modeling possible to render them in paint.

It is clear that Michelangelo saw himself more as a sculptor than as a painter. The "sculptural" drawing and modeling in *The Creation of Adam* attest to this.

When Michelangelo painted the Sistine Chapel ceiling, he was all of 33 years old, but he began his career some twenty years earlier as an apprentice to the painter Domenico Ghirlandaio (1449–1494). His reputation as a sculptor, however, was established when, at the age of 27, he carved the 13½-foot-high *David* (Fig. 13–28) from a single piece of almost unworkable marble. Unlike the Davids of Donatello and Verrocchio, Michelangelo's hero is not shown after conquering his foe. Rather, David is portrayed as a most beautiful animal preparing to kill—not by savagery and brute force, but by intellect and skill. Upon close inspection, the tensed muscles and the furrowed brow negate the first impression that this is a figure at rest. David's sling is cast over his shoulder and the stone is grasped in the right hand, the veins prominent in anticipation of the fight. Michelangelo's *David* is part of the Classical tradition of the "ideal youth" who has just reached manhood and is capable of great physical and intellectual feats. Like Donatello's *David,* Michelangelo's sculpture is closed in form. All of the elements move tightly around a central axis. Michelangelo has been said to have sculpted by first conceptualizing the mass of the work and then carefully extracting all of the

13–28 MICHELANGELO
DAVID (1501–4). MARBLE. HEIGHT: 13½'.
ACADEMY, FLORENCE.

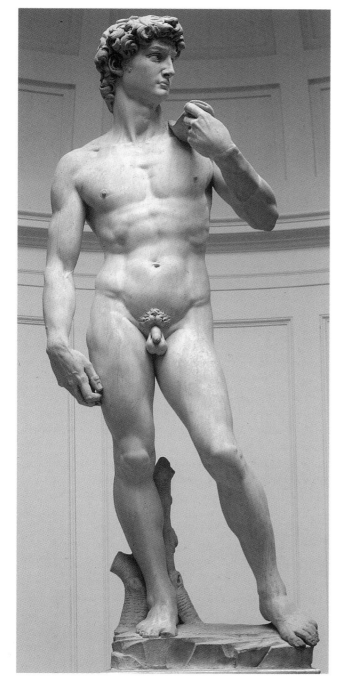

13–29 DONATO BRAMANTE
ORIGINAL PLAN FOR ST. PETER'S (1506).
VATICAN, ROME.

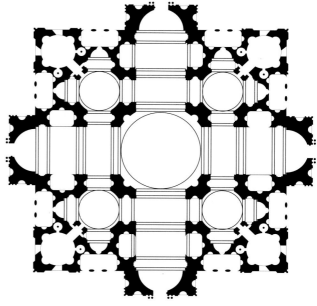

marble that was not part of the image. Indeed, in the
David, it appears that he worked from front to back
instead of from all four sides of the marble block, allowing the figure, as it were, to "step out of" the stone.
The identification of the figure with the marble block
provides a dynamic tension in Michelangelo's work,
as the forms try at once to free themselves from and
succumb to the binding dimensions.

Michelangelo's life spanned ninety years and the
entire High Renaissance. His last great undertaking
was work on St. Peter's in Rome, a building that sums
up the ideas of the Renaissance while heralding the age
of the Baroque. Many architects had worked on the
basilica, but it was left to a reluctant Michelangelo to
revise the extant plan and complete the dome. The
commission for the renovation was given initially to
Donato Bramante (1444–1514) by Pope Julius II, but
the architect died before his plans could be realized.
Bramante's plan for St. Peter's was that of a central
cross with arms of equal length ending in apses
(Fig. 13–29). The crossing square, or point where the

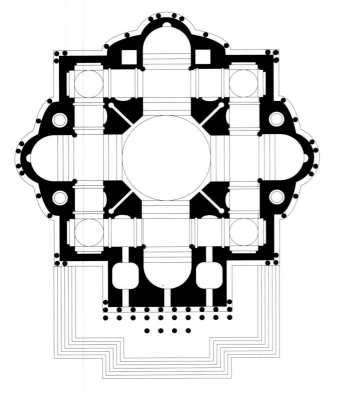

13–30 MICHELANGELO
PLAN OF ST. PETER'S (1546–64).
VATICAN, ROME.

arms intersect, was to be covered by an extremely large dome, while smaller domes covering chapels would echo along the diagonal axes of the square plan. Michelangelo used Bramante's basic plan but simplified it by inscribing the Greek Cross within a square, reducing the number of chapels to four, and relegating them to the corners of the square (Fig. 13–30). He also had plans for a majestic dome, wholly Classic in its hemispherical shape and rhythmic application of details. Michelangelo's other contribution was to have been the western portico, which, in plan, resembles the Pantheon's in relation to the main mass of the building (see Fig. 11–25). Michelangelo's plan bears no resemblance to the St. Peter's of today, which is longitudinal in plan (see Fig. 14–1). The dome was completed after Michelangelo's death by another architect, who had to resort to the ogival section of Brunelleschi's dome, and the western portico was ultimately constructed with another plan. The southern elevation of the building, however, indicates Michelangelo's intentions. Balance, unity, strength through simplicity, respect for Classicism, and an almost sculptural treatment of the architecture characterize his contribution to the development of St. Peter's. It would be taken over by master architects and sculptors of the Baroque era who would capitalize on this concept of treating architecture as sculpture on a vast scale—indeed, making it a central precept of their style. It is fitting that this painter-sculptor-architect, this "crazed" genius, paved the way for the successful fusion of these arts in the seventeenth century.

HIGH AND LATE RENAISSANCE IN VENICE

The artists who lived and worked in the city of Venice were the first in Italy to perfect the medium of oil painting that we witnessed with van Eyck in Flanders. Perhaps influenced by the mosaics in St. Mark's Cathedral, perhaps intrigued by the dazzling colors of imports from eastern countries into this maritime province, the Venetian artists sought the same clarity of hue and lushness of surface in their oil-on-canvas works. In the sixteenth century, Venice would come to figure as prominently in the arts as Florence had in the fifteenth.

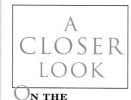

A CLOSER LOOK

ON THE MUTILATION OF MICHELANGELO'S *PIETÀS*

The art world recoiled in shock in 1972 when a crazed man viciously hacked off the Virgin's nose in Michelangelo's famed Vatican *Pietà*. Centuries earlier, around 1555, another crazed man, it is believed, hacked off Christ's leg in Michelangelo's Florence *Pietà*. The contemporary villain was apprehended and identified. The Renaissance culprit was never so much as scolded. It was Michelangelo himself.

Why would the artist mutilate his own work, especially one that obsessed him during his last years, one designed for his own tomb? There has been much speculation. The art historian Leo Steinberg believed that Michelangelo was disturbed by the possible sexual connotations associated with the leg of Jesus being slung over that of his mother. The scholar Tolnay believed that the sculpture was not disfigured at all, but rather that the leg "was originally made from a separate piece of marble." Psychiatrist Robert S. Liebert suggests that Michelangelo had committed a technical error in executing the leg and, out of disappointment, removed it, with the intention of carving another. He further posits that the notion of not carving a single sculpture from a single block of marble disturbed Michelangelo and thus, in frustration, he tried to destroy the work.[6]

Yet one piece of the puzzle has never quite been integrated into any of these explanations. Michelangelo himself, when asked why he had mutilated the work, answered that it was because his servant had nagged him to finish it. Liebert follows up this clue and links it with Michelangelo's despair over his servant's ultimate death and a fear of his own imminent death, offering a psychoanalytic interpretation of the deed. Michelangelo was very close to his servant of twenty-six years, and if, in fact, the latter had "nagged" him into completing the work before he died, then perhaps, Liebert argues, Michelangelo was afraid of creating a kind of self-fulfilling prophecy. Were Michelangelo to complete the work, the servant might actually die. The fear of his own death might also have caused him to destroy the work for the very same reason.

[6]Robert S. Liebert, "Michelangelo's Mutilation of the Florence 'Pietà':
A Psychoanalytic Inquiry," *The Art Bulletin, 59* (March 1977), 47–53.

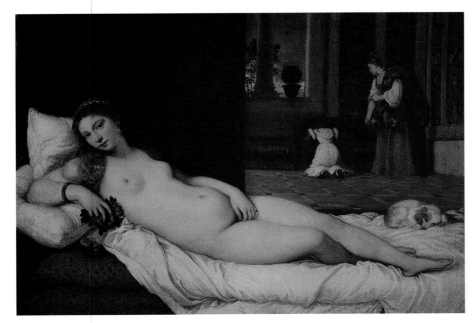

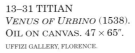

13–31 TITIAN
Venus of Urbino (1538).
Oil on canvas. 47 × 65″.
UFFIZI GALLERY, FLORENCE.

TITIAN   Although he died in 1576, almost a quarter-century before the birth of the Baroque era, the Venetian master Tiziano Vecellio (b. 1477)—called Titian—had more in common with the artists who would follow him than with his Renaissance contemporaries in Florence and Rome. Titian's pictorial method differed from those of Leonardo, Raphael, and Michelangelo in that he was foremost a painter and colorist rather than a draftsman or sculptural artist. He constructed his compositions by means of colors and strokes of paint and layers of varnish, rather than by line and chiaroscuro. A shift from painting on wood panels to painting on canvas occurred at this time, and with it a change from tempera to oil paint as the preferred medium. Oil painting served Titian well, with its versatility and lushness, its vibrant, intense hues, and its more subtle, semitransparent glazes.

Titian's *Venus of Urbino* (Fig. 13–31) is one of the most beautiful examples of the **glazing** technique. The composition was painted for the duke of Urbino, from which its title derives. Titian adopted the figure of the reclining Venus from his teacher Giorgione, and it has served as a model for many compositions since that time. In the foreground, a nude Venus pudica rests on voluptuous pillows and sumptuous sheets spread over a red brocade couch. Her golden hair, complemented by the delicate flowers she grasps loosely in her right hand, falls gently over her shoulder. A partial drape hangs in the middle ground, providing a backdrop for her upper torso and revealing a view of her boudoir. The background of the composition includes two women looking into a trunk—presumably handservants—and a more distant view of a sunset through a columned veranda. Rich, soft

tapestries contrast with the harsh Classicism of the stone columns and inlaid marble floor. Titian appears to have been interested in the interaction of colors and the contrast of textures. The creamy white sheet complements the radiant golden tones of the body of Venus, built up through countless applications of glazes over flesh-toned pigment. Her sumptuous roundness is created by extremely subtle gradations of tones in these glazes, rather than by the harshly sculptural chiaroscuro that Leonardo or Raphael might have used. The forms evolve from applications of color instead of line or shadow. Titian's virtuoso brushwork allows him to define different textures: the firm yet silken flesh, the delicate folds of drapery, the servant's heavy cloth dress, the dog's soft fur. The pictorial dominance of these colors and textures set the work apart from so many examples of Florentine and Roman painting. It appeals primarily to the senses, rather than to the intellect.

Titian's use of color as a compositional device is significant. We have already noted the drape, whose dark color forces our attention on the most important part of the composition—Venus's face and upper torso. It also blocks out the left background, encouraging viewers to narrow their focus on the vista in the right background. The forceful diagonal formed by the looming body of Venus is balanced by three elements opposite her: the little dog at her feet and the two handmaidens in the distance. They do not detract from her since they are engaged in activities that do not concern her or the spectator. The diagonal of her body is also balanced by an intersecting diagonal that can be visualized by integrating the red areas in the lower left and upper

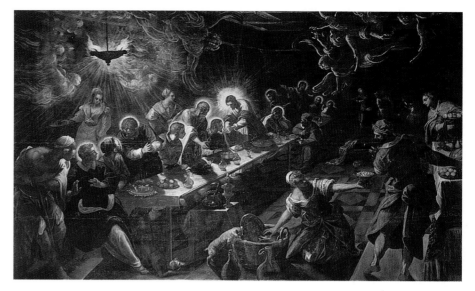

right corners. Titian thus subtly balances the composition in his placement of objects and color areas.

TINTORETTO   Perhaps no other Venetian artist anticipated the Baroque style so strongly as Jacopo Robusti, called Tintoretto, or "little dyer," after the profession of his father. Supposedly a pupil of Titian, Tintoretto (1518–1594) emulated the master's love of color, although he combined it with a more linear approach to constructing forms. This interest in draftsmanship was culled from Michelangelo, but the younger artist's compositional devices went far beyond those of the Florentine and Venetian masters. His dynamic structure and passionate application of pigment provide a sweeping, almost frantic, energy within compositions of huge dimensions.

Tintoretto's painting technique was indeed unique.[7] He arranged doll-like figures on small stages and hung his flying figures by wires in order to copy them in correct perspective for the final canvas. This he first executed on sheets of paper, which he then translated onto the much larger canvases using a grid.

Tintoretto primed the entire canvas with dark colors. Then he quickly painted in the lighter sections. Thus many of his paintings appear very dark, except for bright patches of radiant light. The artist painted extremely quickly, using broad areas of loosely swathed paint. John Ruskin, a nineteenth-century art critic, is said to have suggested that Tintoretto painted with a broom.[8] Although this is unlikely, Tintoretto had certainly come a long way from the sculptural, at times marblelike, figures of the High Renaissance and the

painstaking finish of Titian's glazed *Venus of Urbino*. This loose brushwork and dramatic white spotlighting on a dark ground anticipate the Baroque style.

The Last Supper (Fig. 13–32) seals his relationship to the later period. A comparison of this composition with Leonardo's *The Last Supper* (Fig. 13–18) will illustrate the dramatic changes that had taken place in both art and the concept of art over almost a century. The interests in motion, space, and time, the dramatic use of light, and the theatrical presentation of subject matter are all present in Tintoretto's *The Last Supper*. We are first impressed by the movement. Everything and everyone is set into motion: People lean, rise up out of their seats, stretch, and walk. Angels fly and animals dig for food. The space, sliced by a sharp, rushing diagonal that goes from lower left toward upper right, seems barely able to contain all of this commotion; but this "cluttered" effect enhances the energy of the event. Leonardo's obsession with symmetry, and his balance between emotion and restraint, yield a composition that appears static in comparison to the asymmetry and overpowering emotion in Tintoretto's canvas. Leonardo's apostles seem posed for the occasion when contrasted with Tintoretto's spontaneously gesturing figures. A particular moment is captured. We feel that if we were to look away for a fraction of a second, the figures would have changed position by the time we looked back! The timelessness of Leonardo's figural poses has given way to a seemingly temporary placement of characters. The moment that Tintoretto has chosen to depict also differs from Leonardo's. The Renaissance master chose the point at which Jesus announced that one of his apostles would betray him. Tintoretto, on the other hand, chose the moment when

---

[7]Frederick Hartt, *History of Italian Renaissance Art,* 2nd ed. (Englewood Cliffs, N.J.: Prentice-Hall, and New York: Harry N. Abrams, 1979), p. 615.

[8]Ibid.

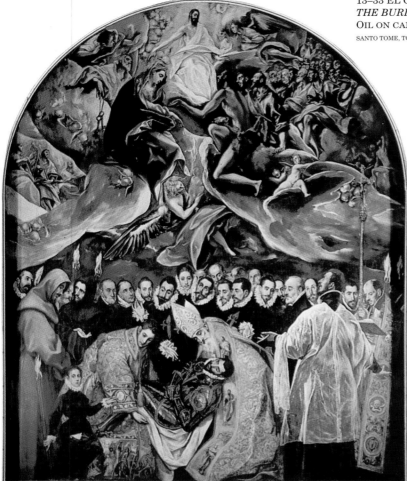

and the distortion of his figures and use of an ambiguous space speak for his interest in Mannerism, which is discussed at the end of this chapter.

These pictorial elements can clearly be seen in one of El Greco's most famous works, *The Burial of Count Orgaz* (Fig. 13–33). In this single work, El Greco combines mysticism and realism. The canvas is divided into two halves by a horizontal line of white-collared heads, separating "heaven" and "earth." The figures in the lower half of the composition are somewhat elongated, but well within the bounds of realism. The heavenly figures, by contrast, are extremely attenuated and seem to move under the influence of a sweeping, dynamic atmosphere. It has been suggested that the distorted figures in El Greco's paintings might have been the result of astigmatism in the artist's eyes, but there is no convincing proof of this. For example, at times El Greco's figures appear no more distorted than those of other Mannerists. Heaven and earth are disconnected psychologically but joined convincingly in terms of composition. At the center of the rigid, horizontal row of heads that separates the two worlds, a man's upward glance encourages the viewer to follow a path into the upper realm. This compositional device is complemented by a sweeping drape that rises into the upper half of the canvas from above his head, continuing to lead the eye between the two groups of figures, left and right, up toward the image of the resurrected Christ. El Greco's color scheme also complements the worldly and celestial habitats. The colors used in the costumes of the earthly figures are realistic and vibrantly Venetian, but the colors of the upper half of the composition are of discordant hues, highlighting the otherworldly nature of the upper canvas. The emotion is high-pitched and exaggerated by the tumultuous atmosphere. This emphasis on emotionalism links El Greco to the onset of the Baroque era. His work contains a dramatic, theatrical flair, one of the hallmarks of the seventeenth century.

Jesus shared bread, which symbolized his body as the wine stood for his blood. This moment is commemorated to this day during the celebration of Mass in the Roman Catholic faith. Leonardo chose a moment signifying death, Tintoretto a moment signifying life, depicted within an atmosphere that is teeming with life.

HIGH AND LATE RENAISSANCE OUTSIDE OF ITALY

EL GRECO The Late Renaissance outside of Italy brought us many different styles, and Spain is no exception. Spanish art polarized into two stylistic groups of religious painting: the mystical and the realistic. One painter was able to pull these opposing trends together in a unique pictorial method. El Greco (1541–1614), born Domeniko Theotokopoulos in Crete, integrated many styles in his work. As a young man he traveled to Italy, where he encountered the works of the Florentine and Roman masters, and he was for a time affiliated with Titian's workshop. The colors that El Greco incorporated in his paintings suggest a Venetian influence,

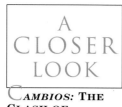

CAMBIOS: THE CLASH OF CULTURES AND THE ARTISTIC FALLOUT

In the year 1492, the King and Queen of Spain funded Columbus's trip to the New World. The day after he left Spain's shores, Jews were expelled from the country by decree. Some twenty-seven years later, the Spaniard Hernán Cortez sailed to Mexico and conquered the Aztec Empire. His campaign was brilliant; the empire fell to only 500 Spanish soldiers. The Aztec capital was vanquished in a bloody siege, and much of the Native Mexican population eventually succumbed to smallpox, a virus that the Spaniards introduced and to which the Native Mexicans had not developed immunity. The picture of Spain in the sixteenth century is one of sharp contrasts. It was a country in its "Golden Age," marked by feats of exploration and cultural masterworks and, at the same time, marked by prejudice, savage domination, and the infliction of pain.

The culture of Mexico survived, albeit in a transformed state. And the works of art that emerged during the Spanish Colonial Period in Mexico, Central America, and South America bear evidence as well of artistic transformation. These works were the subject of a 1993 exhibition at the Santa Barbara Museum of Art in California— *Cambios: The Spirit of Transformation in Spanish Colonial Art.* Cultural clash almost always leaves in its wake fascinating artistic imagery; perhaps in no other encounter of peoples has the interaction and reconciliation of disparate motifs been more well-defined than in the clash of the Spanish and Meso-American cultures.

The exhibition focused on how indigenous art forms, motifs, and techniques were integrated with European influences. In a review of the show in *Latin American Art,* Leslie Westbrook[9] noted that the exhibit illustrated the great diversity of design influences as well as the willingness of artists to combine vocabularies from different cultures and contexts to create a "new world order" on the palette, so to speak. Some examples of motifs include the Meso-American jaguar, flower-filled jars, leaf patterns, and elaborate borders (Fig. 13–34) reconciled with the lion image, a European formal symmetry, and, of course, Christian subject matter. Of special interest is a newly attributed work by Miguel Cabrera entitled *Castas (Depiction of Racial Mixtures)* (Fig. 13–35). It represents the *mestizo*— the child born of the union of a European and a Native American. These children bear the physical characteristics of the two peoples and as such symbolize the "marriage" of two cultures.

The "Cambios" exhibition brought together remnants of a sometimes cruel history, where, as the reviewer remarked, one civilization superseded and dominated another. Yet nothing directly spoke of the cruel and devastating effects of Spanish domination. Instead, a free-wheeling creativity—one of absorption, reconciliation, and ancestral legacy—dominated the show, a testimony to the resilience of the human spirit.

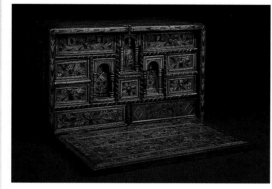

13–34 *BARGUEÑO* (18TH CENTURY). INLAID WOOD, BOLIVIA, 17¼ × 28 × 16¼″.
COLLECTION: MICHAEL HASKELL, SANTA BARBARA, CALIFORNIA.

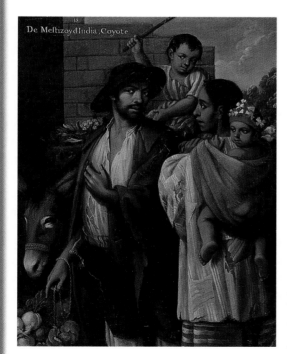

13–35 MIGUEL CABRERA
CASTAS (DEPICTION OF RACIAL MIXTURES) (1763). OIL ON CANVAS, 52 × 40½″.
PRIVATE COLLECTION.

[9]Leslie A. Westbrook (1993). "Cambios: The Spirit of Transformation in Spanish Colonial Art." *Latin American Art,* Vol. 5, No. 1, 54–57.

13–36 GIOVANNI DA BOLOGNA
THE RAPE OF THE SABINE WOMEN (COMPLETED 1583).
MARBLE. HEIGHT: 13′6″.
LOGGIA DEI LANZI, FLORENCE.

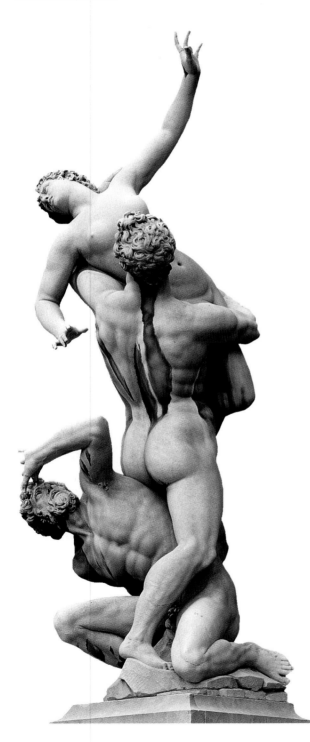

GIOVANNI DA BOLOGNA   The bodily distortion characteristic of Mannerist painting appeared in sculpture as well, although not all artists subscribed to it fully. This stylistic characteristic was not very important for the future of sculpture, but that was not the case with other innovations in sculpture of the latter sixteenth century. One of the most important artists of this time was the Flemish Giovanni da Bologna (1529–1608) (Jean de Boulogne), who preferred to imbue his name with an Italian flavor. Giovanni da Bologna was a transitional figure. His work encompassed the accomplishments of Michelangelo and anticipated the Baroque through several compositional innovations, as illustrated in *The Rape of the Sabine Women* (Fig. 13–36).

Giovanni did not utilize the weightlessness and distortion characteristic of his contemporaries in the two-dimensional arts. Rather, the solidity and muscularity of his forms hearken back to the High Renaissance. His originality lies in his compositional format. During the Renaissance, a contrapposto stance often formed what was perceived as an S-curve that followed a strong vertical axis. In most cases, the figures appeared to lie in a single plane. Thus one could comprehend the work by observing from a single point. Such is not the case in *The Rape of the Sabine Women*. Giovanni moved significantly from a two-dimensional S-curve to a three-dimensional spiral. His figures revolve around a central axis, such that their positions appear to change as the spectator moves around the work. This movement is encouraged by a series of deliberately placed diagonals in arms and legs that force the viewer to move around to take in the entire work. Limbs also begin to extend into space, suggesting quite a different concept from Michelangelo's respect for the block of marble. This minimal extension will be adopted by Baroque artists, who will also use the spiral and force their forms even farther into the surrounding space.

PIETER BRUEGEL THE ELDER   During the second half of the sixteenth century in the Netherlands, changes in the subject matter of painting were taking place that would affect the themes of artists working in Northern Europe during the Baroque period. Scenes of everyday life involving ordinary people were becoming more popular. One of the masters of this genre painting was

13–37 PIETER BRUEGEL THE ELDER
Hunters in the Snow (1565). Oil and tempera on panel. 46 × 63¾″.
KUNSTHISTORISCHES MUSEUM, VIENNA.

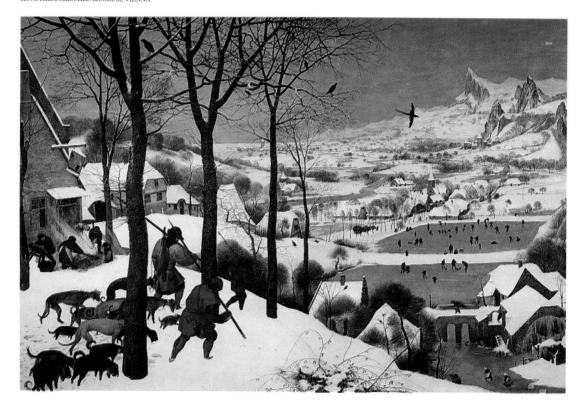

Pieter Bruegel the Elder (c. 1520–1569), whose compositions focused on human beings in relation to nature and the life and times of plain Netherlandish folk. *Hunters in the Snow* (Fig. 13–37) is a good example of Bruegel's "slice of life" canvases. It also shows an interest in landscape painting that was common among Northern European artists. Perched high above the action, the viewer observes people in the midst of their daily tasks. Hunters return from the woods accompanied by a pack of dogs. All trudge through the heavy blanket of snow while women stoke a fire and skaters glide over frozen ponds. Below and in the distance lies a peaceful landscape of snow-covered roofs, steeples, and craggy mountain tops. Regimented trees march down the hillside, while birds sit frozen in the leafless branches or fly boldly to free their icy wings. There is no hidden message here, no religious fervor, no battle between mythological giants. Human activities are presented as sincere and viable subject matter. There are few examples of such painting before this time, but genre painting

will play a principal role in the works of Netherlandish artists during the Baroque period.

MANNERISM

During the Renaissance, the rule of the day was to observe and emulate nature. Toward the end of the Renaissance and before the beginning of the seventeenth century, this rule was suspended for a while, during a period of art that historians have named Mannerism. Mannerist artists abandoned copying directly from nature and copied art instead. Works thus became "secondhand" views of nature. Line, volume, and color no longer duplicated what the eye saw but were derived instead from what other artists had already seen. Several characteristics separate Mannerist art from the art of the Renaissance and the Baroque periods: distortion and elongation of figures; flattened, almost two-dimensional space; lack of a defined focal point; and the use of discordant pastel hues.

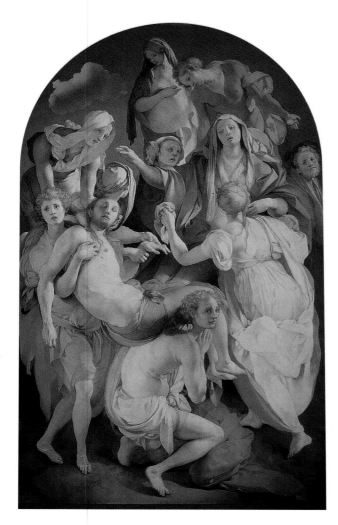

JACOPO PONTORMO   A representative of early Mannerism, Jacopo Pontormo (1494–1557) used most of its stylistic principles. In *Entombment* (Fig. 13–38), we witness a strong shift in direction from High Renaissance art, even though the painting was executed during Michelangelo's lifetime. The weighty sculptural figures of Michelangelo, Leonardo, and Raphael have given way to less substantial, almost weightless, forms that balance on thin toes and ankles. The limbs are long and slender in proportion to the torsos, and the heads are dwarfed by billowing robes. There is a certain innocent beauty in the arched eyebrows of the haunted faces and in the nervous glances that dart this way and that past the boundaries of the canvas. The figures are pressed against the picture plane, moving within a very limited space. Their weight seems to be thrust outward toward the edges of the composition and away from the almost void center. The figures' robes are composed of odd hues, departing drastically in their soft pastel tones from the vibrant primary colors of the Renaissance masters. The weightlessness, distortion, and ambiguity of space create an almost otherworldly feeling in the composition, a world in which objects and people do not come under an earthly gravitational force. The artist accepts this "strangeness" and makes no apologies for it to the viewer. The ambiguities are taken in stride. For example, note that the character in a turban behind the head of the dead Jesus does not appear to have a body—there is really no room for it in the composition. And even though a squatting figure in the center foreground appears to be balancing Christ's torso on his shoulders after having taken him down from the cross a moment before, there is no cross in sight! Pontormo seems to have been most interested in elegantly rendering the high-pitched emotion of the scene. Iconographic details and logical figural stances are irrelevant.

The artists from the second half of the sixteenth century through the beginning of the seventeenth century all broke away from the Renaissance tradition in one way or another. Some were opposed to the stylistic characteristics of the Renaissance and turned them around in an original but ultimately uninfluential style called Mannerism. Others, such as Titian and Tintoretto, emphasized the painting *process,* constructing their compositions by means of stroke and color rather than line and shadow. Still others combined an implied movement and sense of time in their compositions, foreshadowing some of the concerns of the artist in the Baroque period. The High and Late Renaissance witnessed artists of intense originality who provide a fascinating transition between the grand Renaissance and the dynamic Baroque.

key terms

Renaissance
Trompe l'oeil
Iconography
International style

Annunciation
Genre painting
Intarsia
Quatrefoil

Linear perspective
S-curve
Contrapposto
Orthogonals

Chiaroscuro
Glazing

artists

Limbourg Brothers
Robert Campin
Jan van Eyck
Matthias Grünewald
Albrecht Dürer
Cimabue
Giotto
Filippo Brunelleschi
Lorenzo Ghiberti
Donatello

Masaccio
Andrea del Verrocchio
Piero della Francesca
Sandro Botticelli
Leon Battista Alberti
Leonardo da Vinci
Marcel Duchamp
G. Odutokun
Sadie Lee
Raphael

Michelangelo
Donato Bramante
Titian
Tintoretto
El Greco
Miguel Cabrera
Giovanni da Bologna
Pieter Bruegel the Elder
Jacopo Pontormo

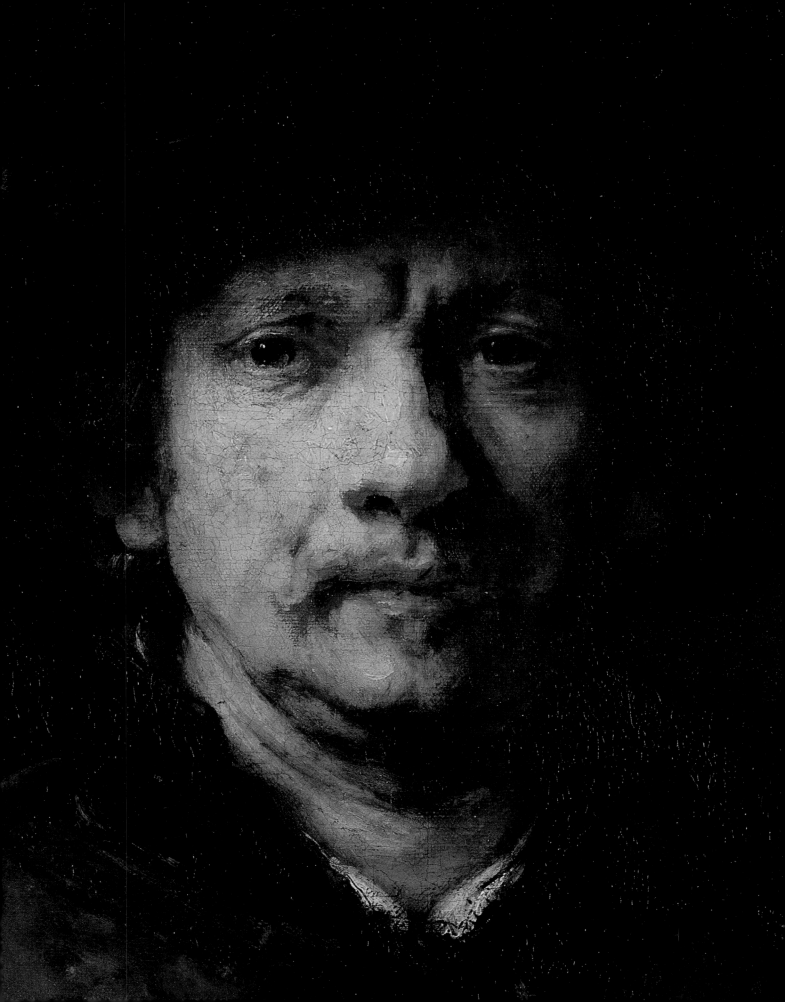

chapter 14

THE AGE OF BAROQUE

PRELIMINARY *Sketch*

❏ Motion and space were major concerns of Baroque artists, as they were of scientists of the period such as Sir Isaac Newton and Galileo.

❏ Caravaggio had a police record with offenses ranging from assault to murder.

❏ Artemisia Gentileschi's work is thought by some to be an attempt to resolve her conflict over being raped by her painting instructor.

❏ Velásquez anticipated Impressionism by two centuries in his construction of forms with a myriad of brushstrokes that capture light as it plays over different surface textures.

❏ Rembrandt's *Syndics of the Draper's Guild* inspired the trademark of Dutch Masters cigars.

❏ The internationally renowned Dutch artist Vermeer never left the town in which he was born.

Rembrandt van Rijn, *Self-Portrait* (detail). See Figure 14–17.

The Baroque period spans roughly the years from 1600 to 1750. Like the Renaissance, which preceded it, the Baroque period was an age of genius in many fields of endeavor. Sir Isaac Newton derived laws of motion and of gravity that have only recently been modified by the discoveries of Einstein. The achievements of Galileo and Kepler in astronomy brought the vast expanses of outer space into sharper focus. The Pilgrims also showed an interest in motion when, in 1620, they put to sea and landed in what is now Massachusetts. Our forefathers had a certain concern for space as well—they wanted as much as possible between themselves and their English oppressors.

The Baroque period in Europe included a number of post-Renaissance styles that do not have all that much in common. On the one hand, there was a continuation of the Classicism and naturalism of the Renaissance. On the other, a far more colorful, ornate, painterly, and dynamic style was born. If one name had to be applied to describe these different directions, it is just as well that that name is **Baroque**—for the word is believed to derive from the Portuguese *barroco,* meaning "irregularly shaped pearl." The Baroque period was indeed irregular in its stylistic tendencies, and it also gave birth to some of the most treasured gems of Western art.

Motion and *space* were major concerns of the Baroque artists, as they were of the scientists of the period. The concept of *time,* a dramatic use of *light,* and a passionate *theatricality* complete the list of the five most important characteristics of Baroque art, as we shall see throughout this chapter.

THE BAROQUE PERIOD IN ITALY

The Baroque era was born in Rome, some say in reaction to the spread of Protestantism resulting from the **Reformation.** Even though many areas of Europe were affected by the new post-Renaissance spirit, it was more alive and well and influential in Italy than elsewhere—partly because of the strengthening of the papacy in religion, politics, and patronage of the arts. During the Renaissance, the principal patron of the arts was the infamous Pope Julius II. However, during the Baroque era, a series of powerful popes—Paul V, Urban VIII, Innocent X, and Alexander VII—assumed this role. The Baroque period has been called the Age of Expansion,

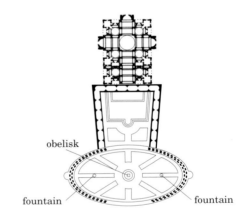

obelisk

fountain   fountain

14–1 PLAN OF ST. PETER'S CATHEDRAL, ROME (1605–13).

HAPSBURG TERRITORIES

KINGDOM
OF
DENMARK
AND
NORWAY

KINGDOM
OF SWEDEN

KINGDOM
OF
GREAT BRITTAIN
AND
IRELAND

NORTH
SEA

BALTIC SEA

KINGDOM
OF POLAND

AMSTERDAM
NETHER-
LANDS

LONDON

HOLY ROMAN
EMPIRE

VERSAILLES
PARIS
AMALIENBURG

MUNICH

KINGDOM
OF HUNGARY

SWITZ.

ATLANTIC
OCEAN

KINGDOM
OF FRANCE

VENICE

BLACK
SEA

ADRIATIC SEA

OTTOMAN
EMPIRE

KINGDOM
OF PORTUGAL

MADRID

TUSCANY

PAPAL STATES

ROME

KINGDOM
OF SPAIN

KINGDOM
OF
SARDINIA

KINGDOM
OF THE
TWO
SICILIES

miles
0   200   400

NORTH AFRICA

MEDITERRANEAN SEA

CRETE

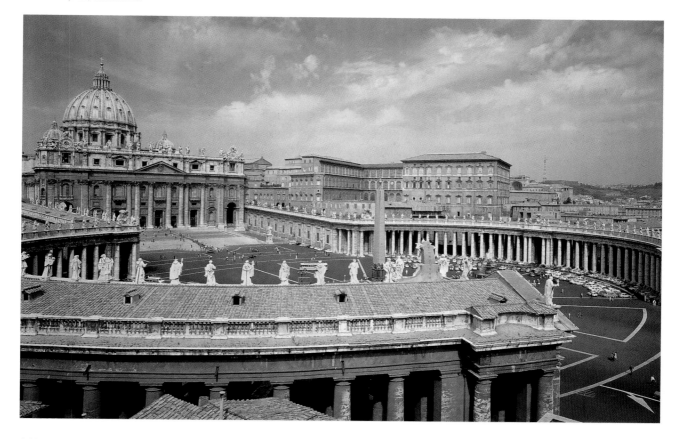

following the Renaissance Age of Discovery, and this expansion is felt keenly in the arts.

ST. PETER'S The expansion and renovation of St. Peter's Cathedral in Rome (Fig. 14–1) is an excellent project with which to begin our discussion of the Baroque in Italy, for three reasons: The building expresses the ideals of the Renaissance, stands as a hallmark of the Baroque style, and brings together work by the finest artists of both periods—Michelangelo and Bernini.

The major change in the structure of St. Peter's was from the central **Greek Cross** plans of Bramante and Michelangelo to a longitudinal **Latin Cross** plan. Thus, three bays were added to the nave between the domed crossing and the facade. The architect Carlo Maderno was responsible for this task as well as the design for the new facade, but the job of completing the project fell into the hands of the most significant sculptor of the day, Gianlorenzo Bernini.

GIANLORENZO BERNINI Gianlorenzo Bernini (1598–1680) made an extensive contribution to St. Peter's as we see it today, both to the exterior and the interior. In his design for the **piazza** of St. Peter's, visible in the aerial view (Fig. 14–2), Bernini had constructed two expansive arcades extending from the facade of the church and culminating in semicircular "arms" enclosing an oval space. This space, the piazza, was divided into trapezoidal "pie sections" in the center of which rises an Egyptian obelisk. The Classical arcades, true in details to the arts that inspired them, stretch outward into the surrounding city, as if to welcome worshippers and cradle them in spiritual comfort. The curving arms, or arcades, are composed of two double rows of columns with a path between, ending in Classical pedimented "temple fronts." In the interior of the cathedral, beneath Michelangelo's great dome, Bernini designed a bronze canopy to cover the main altar. In the apse, Bernini combined architecture, sculpture, and stained glass in a brilliantly golden display for the *Cathedra Petri,* or Throne of St. Peter. Through his many other sculptural contributions to St. Peter's, commissioned by various popes, Bernini's reputation as a master is solidified.

Bernini's *David* (see the "Compare and Contrast" feature on page 352) testifies to the artist's genius and also illustrates the dazzling characteristics of Baroque sculpture. This David is remarkably different from those of Donatello, Verrocchio, and Michelangelo. Three of the five characteristics of Baroque art are present in Bernini's sculpture: motion (in this case, implied),

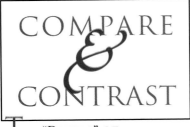
THE "DAVIDS" OF
DONATELLO, VERROCCHIO,
MICHELANGELO, AND
BERNINI

Sometime soon after the year 1430, a bronze statue of David (Fig. 14–3) stood in the courtyard of the house of the Medici. The work was commissioned of Donatello by Cosimo d'Medici himself, the founding father of the Republic of Florence. It was the first free-standing, life-sized nude since classical antiquity, poised in the same contrapposto stance as the victorious athletes of Greece and Rome. But soft, and somehow oddly unheroic. And the incongruity of the heads: David's boyish, expressionless face, framed by soft tendrils of hair and shaded by a laurel-crowned peasant's hat; Goliath's tragic, contorted expression, made sharper by the pentagonal helmet and coarse, dishevelled beard. Innocence and evil. The weak triumphing over the strong. The city of Florence triumphing over the aggressive dukes of Milan? "David" as a civic-public monument.

In the year 1469, Ser Piero from the Tuscan town of Vinci moved to Florence to become a notary. He rented a house on the Piazza San Firenze, not far from the Palazzo Vecchio. His son, who was a mere 17 years old upon their arrival, began an apprenticeship in the Florentine studio of the well-known artist, Andrea Verrocchio. At that time, Verrocchio was at work on a bronze sculpture of the young David (Fig. 14–4). Might the head of this fine piece be a portrait of the young Leonardo da Vinci?

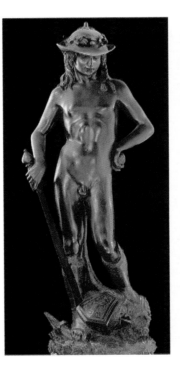

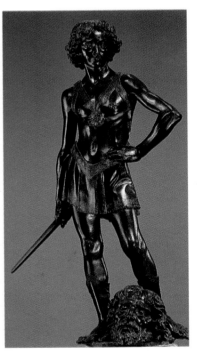

14–3 DONATELLO
DAVID (C. 1425–30). BRONZE,
HEIGHT 62¼ ".
MUSEO NAZIONALE DEL BARGELLO, FLORENCE.

14–4 ANDREA VERROCCHIO
DAVID (C. 1470). BRONZE,
HEIGHT 49⅝".
MUSEO NAZIONALE DEL BARGELLO, FLORENCE.

For many years a block of marble lay untouched, tossed aside as unusable, irretrievable evidence of a botched attempt to carve a human form. It was eighteen feet high. A young sculptor, 26 years old, riding high after the enormous success of his figure of the Virgin Mary holding the dead Christ, decided to ask for the piece. The wardens of the city in charge of such things let the artist have it. What did they have to lose? Getting anything out of it was better than nothing. So this young sculptor named Michelangelo measured and calculated. He made a wax model of David with a sling in his hand. And he worked on his David (Fig. 14–5) continuously for some three years, until, a man named Vasari tells us, he brought it to perfect completion. Without letting anyone see it.

A century later, a young sculptor, 25 years old, stares into a mirror at his steeled jaw and determined brow. A contemporary source tells us that on this day, perhaps, the mirror is being held by Cardinal Maffeo Barberini while Bernini transfers what he sees in himself to the face of his David (Fig. 14–6). Gianlorenzo Bernini: sculptor and architect, painter, dramatist, composer. Bernini, who centuries later would be called the undisputed monarch of the Roman High Baroque, identifying with David, whose adversary is seen only by him.

The great transformation in style that occurred between the Early Renaissance and the Baroque can be followed in the evolution of David. Look at them: A boy of 12, perhaps, looking down incredulously at the physical self that felled an unconquerable enemy; a boy of 14 or 15, confident and reckless, with enough adrenaline pumping to take on an army; an adolescent on the brink of adulthood, captured at that moment when, the Greeks say, sound mind and sound body are one; and another full-grown youth at the threshold of his destiny as King.

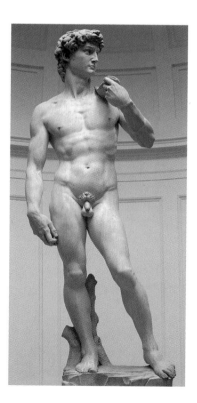 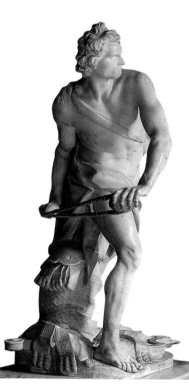

14–5 MICHELANGELO
DAVID (1501–04). MARBLE,
HEIGHT 13′5″.
GALLERIA DELL'ACCADEMIA, FLORENCE.

14–6 GIANLORENZO BERNINI
DAVID (1623). MARBLE.
HEIGHT: 6′7″.
BORGHESE GALLERY, ROME.

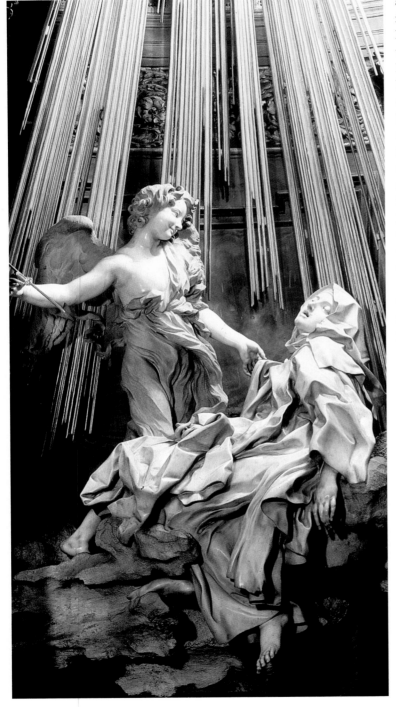

14–7 GIANLORENZO BERNINI
THE ECSTASY OF ST. THERESA (1645–52). MARBLE. HEIGHT OF GROUP: C. 11′6″.
CORNARO CHAPEL, STA. MARIA DELLA VITTORIA, ROME.

a different way of looking at space, and the introduction of the concept of time. The Davids by Donatello and Verrocchio were figures at rest after having slain their Goliaths. Michelangelo, by contrast, presented David before the encounter, with the tension and emotion evident in every vein and muscle, bound to the block of marble that had surrounded the figure. Bernini does not offer David before or after the fight, but instead *in the process* of the fight. He has introduced an element of time in his work. As in *The Last Supper* by Tintoretto, we sense that David would have used his weapon if we were to look away and then back. We, the viewers, are forced to complete the action that David has begun for us.

A new concept of space comes into play with David's positioning. No longer does the figure remain still in a Classical contrapposto stance but rather extends *into* the surrounding space away from a vertical axis. This movement outward from a central core forces the viewer to take into account both solids and voids—that is, both the form and the spaces between and surrounding the forms—in order to appreciate the complete composition. We must move around the work in order to understand it fully, and as we move, the views of the work change radically.

We may compare the difference between Michelangelo's *David* and Bernini's *David* to the difference between Classical and Hellenistic Greek sculpture. The movement out of Classical art into Hellenistic art was marked by an extension of the figure into the surrounding space, a sense of implied movement, and a large degree of theatricality. The time-honored balance between emotion and restraint coveted by the Classical Greek artist as well as the Renaissance master had given way in the Hellenistic and Baroque periods to unleashed passion.

Uncontrollable passion and theatrical drama might best describe Bernini's *The Ecstasy of St. Theresa* (Fig. 14–7), a sculptural group executed for the chapel of the Cornaro family in the church of Santa Maria della Vittoria in Rome. The sculpture commemorates a mystical event involving St. Theresa, a Carmelite nun who believed that a pain in her side was caused by an angel of God stabbing her repeatedly with a fire-tipped arrow. Her response combined pain and pleasure, as conveyed by the sculpture's submissive swoon and impassioned facial expression. Bernini summoned all of his sculptural powers to execute these figures, and combined the arts of architecture, sculpture, and painting to achieve his desired theatrical effect. Notice the way in which Bernini described vastly different textures with his sculptural tools: the roughly textured clouds, the heavy folds of St. Theresa's woolen garment, the diaphanous "wet-look" drapery of the angel. "Divine" rays of glimmering bronze shower down on the figures, as if emanating from the painted ceiling of the chapel, and are illuminated by a hidden window. Bernini enhanced this self-conscious theatrical effect by including marble sculptures in the likenesses of members of the Cornaro family in theater boxes to the left and right. They observe, gesture, and discuss the scene animatedly as would theatergoers. The fine line between the rational and the spiritual that so interested the Baroque artist was presented by Bernini in a tactile yet illusionary masterpiece of sculpture.

CARAVAGGIO   This theatrical drama and passion found its way into Baroque painting as well, and can be seen most clearly in the work of Michelangelo de Merisi, called Caravaggio (1573–1610). Unlike Bernini's somewhat idealized facial and figural types, the models for Caravaggio came literally from the streets. Whereas Bernini was comfortable in the company of popes and princes, Caravaggio was more comfortable with the dregs of humanity. In fact, he was one of them and had a police record for violent assaults. Caravaggio chose lower-class models for quite a shocking painting, *The Conversion of St. Paul* (Fig. 14–8). Paul—originally Saul—was chosen as an apostle while riding his horse.

Blinded by a bright light, he was thrown from the animal, only to hear a voice ask why he was persecuting Christians. Saul was ultimately persuaded to convert, stop the killing, and change his name. Very much in the Baroque spirit, Caravaggio has chosen the exact moment when Saul was thrown from his horse. He lies flat on his back, his arms flailing in space as he struggles with the shock of the episode as well as his resultant blindness. He looks as if he is about to be trampled by his horse, but the animal is held and calmed by the strong hands of an unknown man. The piercing light of God flashes upon an otherwise dark scene, picking out certain forms while casting others into the night. This exaggerated chiaroscuro is attributed to Caravaggio and has been called **tenebrism,** or "dark manner." Tenebrism, which usually involved one very small source of light and evoked a harsh realism or naturalism in the figures, profoundly influenced Baroque artists elsewhere in Europe, including France and Spain.

ARTEMISIA GENTILESCHI   Among the foremost of Caravaggio's contemporaries was Artemisia Gentileschi (1593–c.1652), the daughter of a successful Roman artist, who recognized her talent and sent her to study with Agostino Tassi, a well-known fresco painter. Artemisia developed a dramatic and passionate Baroque style and, after her marriage to a Florentine, brought this expressive style to her adopted city.

One of the most successful—and violent—paintings of her Florentine period is based on the Old Testament story of the heroine *Judith Decapitating Holofernes* (see the "Compare and Contrast" feature on page 358). Artemisia painted many pictures of Judith. In this painting the artist pulls no punches. There is no way for the viewer to escape the graphic violence. The forms of the figures are all placed in the foreground and dramatically lit. The head, the sword, and Judith's powerful hands meet at the center of the dynamic composition. There the arms of the three participants also interact dramatically, thrusting in different directions. Judith's arms are not the arms of a delicate damsel, but of a sturdy warrior, lending further credibility to the action in the work. All of this takes place upon the firm "pedestal" of Holofernes's bed, which ought to provide for rest, not murder.

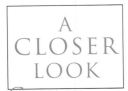

CARAVAGGIO'S POLICE BLOTTER: THE ART OF VIOLENCE

One of Caravaggio's major works is *The Conversion of St. Paul,* which captures the apostle at a moment when he renounces violence, recognizing the error of his ways. It is rather ironic that the artist's own life showed a pattern of increasing violence, such that he acquired a lengthy police record in Rome. Between 1600 and 1606 he was arrested for: attacking a man with a sword, disrespect toward a police officer, carrying weapons without a permit, breaking windows, assaulting a waiter, and wounding a man following an argument about a prostitute. He fled Rome in 1606, after killing a man during an argument about a tennis match. Exile from Rome did not quite lead to reform, however: A few years later he was forced to flee Messina after attacking a teacher who accused him of molesting schoolchildren.

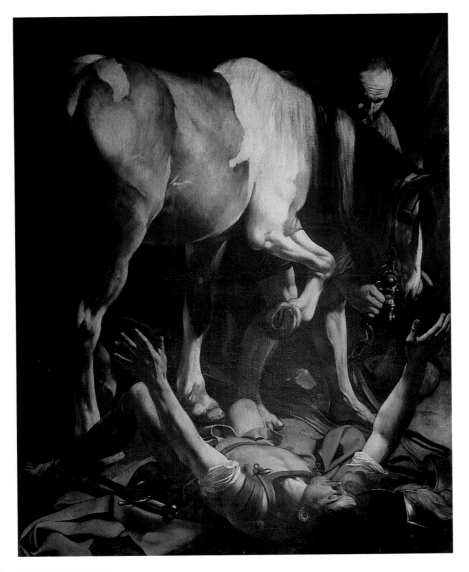

14–8 CARAVAGGIO
THE CONVERSION OF ST. PAUL (1600–1601).
OIL ON CANVAS. 90 × 69″.
SANTA MARIA DEL POPOLO, ROME.

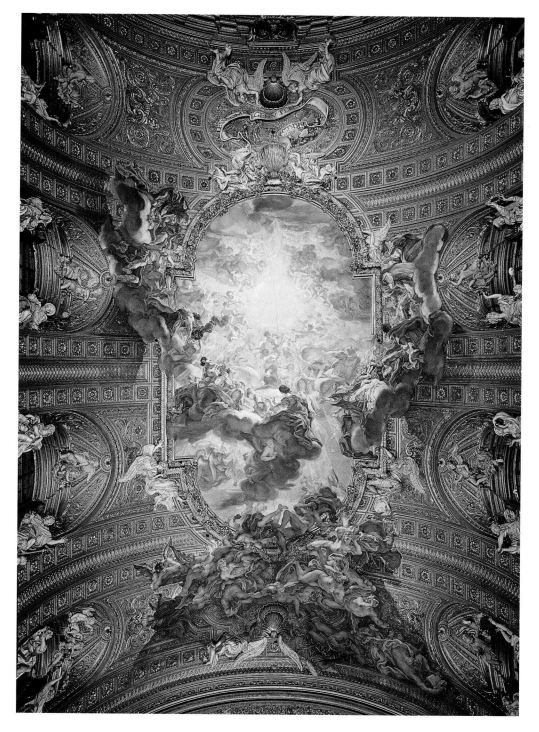

BAROQUE CEILING DECORATION   The Baroque interest in combining the arts of painting, sculpture, and architecture found its home in the naves and domes of churches and cathedrals as artists used the three media to create an unsurpassed illusionistic effect. Unlike Renaissance ceiling painting, as exemplified by Michelangelo's decoration for the Sistine Chapel, the space was not divided into "frames" with individual scenes. Rather, the Baroque artist created the illusion of a ceiling vault open to the heavens with figures flying freely in and out of the church (Fig. 14–9). Baciccio's *Triumph of the Sacred Name of Jesus* is an energetic

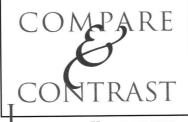

COMPARE & CONTRAST

JUDITH AND HOLOFERNES BY CARAVAGGIO, GENTILESCHI, AND DONATELLO

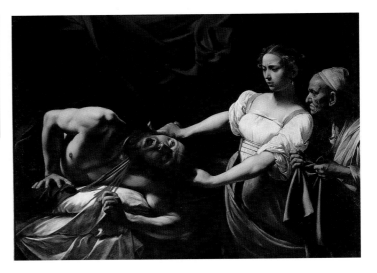

14–10 CARAVAGGIO
JUDITH AND HOLOFERNES (C. 1598). OIL ON CANVAS.
APPROX. 56¾ × 76¾".
GALLERIA NAZIONALE D'ARTE ANTICA, PALAZZO BARBERINI, ROME.

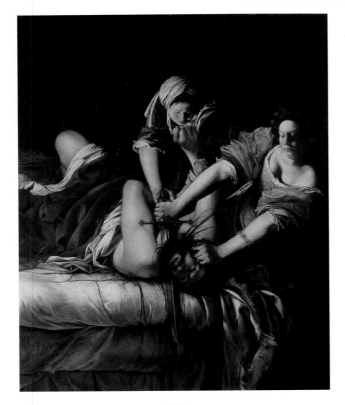

14–11 ARTEMISIA GENTILESCHI
JUDITH DECAPITATING HOLOFERNES (C. 1620). OIL ON CANVAS.
UFFIZI GALLERY, FLORENCE.

Artemesia Gentileschi once said, albeit in the context of being cheated out of a commission, "If I were a man, I can't imagine it would have turned out this way . . ." How particularly apt a statement in reference to these three works on the subject of Judith and Holofernes.

Consider first the roughly contemporary paintings by Caravaggio (Fig. 14–10) and Gentileschi (Fig. 14–11). They are prime examples of the Baroque style—vibrant palette, dramatic lighting, an impassioned subject heightened to excess by our coming face to terrified face with a man at the precise moment of his bloody execution. Who is this man? And what has led to this woman's unspeakable wrath? The paintings refer to an Old Testament story of the heroine, Judith, who rescues her people by decapitating the tyrannical Assyrian general, Holofernes. She steals into his tent under the cover of night, and pretends to respond to his seductive overtures. When he is besotted, with her and with drink, she uses his sword to cut off

358

his head. What are our impressions of Judith, and the task that befalls her, in Caravaggio's work? What are our impressions of Judith rendered by the hand of Gentileschi? Do you divine any gender differences? Caravaggio is a male artist, Gentileschi a female. Caravaggio killed a man during an argument over a tennis match. Gentileschi testified in court, and under torture, that she was raped by an artist to whom she was apprenticed. How much of the artist *is* brought to these paintings? How much, in these paintings, is unspeakable wrath?

There has been a high degree of discomfort with the subject of Judith and Holofernes, all the way around. From what we can see, contemporary Baroque commentators and current critics and historians alike don't view Caravaggio's painting or Donatello's sculpture in any context other than that of the artists' oeuvre. But one would be hard-pressed to find an analysis of Gentileschi's work—its raw power and explosive action—that doesn't also make mention of the circumstances surrounding the artist's rape. Is this context essential to understanding Gentileschi's work? Why do we obsess about it? It is not, after all, an entirely uncommon subject.

The Early Renaissance sculptor, Donatello, did a version as well (Fig. 14–12). In his work, Judith seems a triumphant crusader, entranced by courage and determination. Holofernes is in his own trance—a drunken stupor, that is. Donatello's sculpture is a far more traditional, less emotionally charged, version of the subject. Yet this sculpture proved to be problematic in its own way. The work began as a commission by the Medici family, intended to be a privately housed work. But soon after its completion in 1457, the work was moved to the very public, political center of the city of Florence—the Piazza della Signoria. There, as suggested by an inscription on its base, it assumed the symbolism of the invincibility of the Florentine republic. It even became the property of the government. What ensued, however, was what Yael Even has called "a relentless attempt all but to dispose of [the work]." Norma Broude and Mary Garrard, in an introduction to Even's essay, describe the Piazza della Signoria in Florence "as a primary site of the expression of gender ideology, pointing to the frequent relocation in the square of Donatello's *Judith and Holofernes* and its displacement by . . . statues [by other artists] in which violence is done to a woman by a man rather than to a man by a woman. [Even] suggests that a psychological as well as political need to express that radical subordination of women to men underlay the gradual suppression of Donatello's statue and the decisions to commission images glorifying Perseus' decapitation of Medusa and the rape of the Sabine women."

Let us close our discussion with another look at that "particularly apt statement" at the beginning of this exercise. . . .

14–12 DONATELLO
JUDITH AND HOLOFERNES
(1456–57). BRONZE.
PALAZZO VECCHIO, FLORENCE.

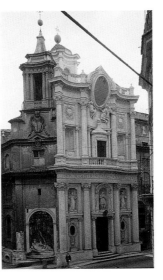

display of figures painted on plaster that spill out beyond the gilded frame of the ceiling's illusionistic opening. The trompe l'oeil effect is achieved by combining these painted figures with white stucco modeled sculptures and a gilded stucco ceiling. Attention to detail is remarkable, from the blinding light of the heavens to the deep shadows cast on the ceiling by the painted forms. Saints and angels fly upward toward the light while sinners are banished from the heavens to the floor of the church. Artists like Baciccio and their patrons spared no illusionistic device to create a total, mystical atmosphere.

FRANCESCO BORROMINI   Although it is hard to imagine an architect incorporating the Baroque elements of motion, space, and light in buildings, this was accomplished by the great seventeenth-century architect Francesco Borromini (1599–1667). His San Carlo alle Quattro Fontane (Fig. 14–13) shows that the change from Renaissance to Baroque architecture was one from the static to the organic. Borromini's facade undulates in implied movement complemented by the concave entablatures of the bell towers on the roof. Light plays across the plane of the facade, bouncing off the engaged columns while leaving the recessed areas in darkness. The stone seems to breathe because of the **plasticity** of the design and the innovative use of light and shadow. The interior is equally alive, consisting of a large oval space surrounded by rippling concave and convex walls. For the first time since we examined the Parthenon (see Fig. 11–9) do we appreciate a building first as sculpture and only second as architecture.

THE BAROQUE PERIOD OUTSIDE OF ITALY

Baroque characteristics were found in the art of other areas of Europe also. Artists of Spain and Flanders adopted the Venetian love of color, and with their application of paint in loosely brushed swaths, they created an energetic motion in their compositions. Northern artists had always been interested in realism, and during the Baroque period they carried this emphasis to an extreme and used innovative pictorial methods to that end. Paintings of everyday life and activities became the favorite subjects of Dutch artists, who followed in Bruegel's footsteps and perfected the art of genre painting. The Baroque movement also extended into France and England, but there it often manifested itself in a strict adherence to Classicism. The irregularity of styles suggested by the term "baroque" is again apparent.

SPAIN

Spain was one of the wealthiest countries in Europe during the Baroque era—partly because of the influx of riches from the New World—and the Spanish court was lavish in its support of the arts. Painters and sculptors were imported from different parts of Europe for royal commissions, and native talent was cultivated and treasured.

DIEGO VELÁSQUEZ   Born in Spain, Diego Velásquez (1599–1660) rose to the position of court painter and confidant of King Philip IV. Although Velásquez relied on Baroque techniques in his use of Venetian colors, highly contrasting lights and darks, and a deep, illusionistic space, he had contempt for the idealized images that accompanied these elements in the Italian art of the period. Like Caravaggio, Velásquez preferred to use common folk as models to assert a harsh realism in his canvases. Velásquez brought many a mythological subject down to earth by portraying ordinary facial types and naturalistic attitudes in his principal characters. Nor did he restrict this preference to paintings of the masses. Velásquez adopted the same genre format in works involving the royal family, such as the famous *Las Meninas* (Fig. 14–14). The huge canvas is crowded with figures engaged in different tasks. *Las Meninas,* "the maids in waiting," are attending the little princess Margarita, who seems dressed for a portrait-painting session. She is being entertained by the favorite members of her entourage, including two dwarfs and a family dog. We suspect that they are keeping her company while the artist, Velásquez, paints before his oversized canvas.

Is Velásquez, in fact, supposed to be painting exactly what we see before us? Some have interpreted the work in this way. Others have noted that Velásquez would not be standing behind the princess and her attendants if he were painting them. Moreover, on the back wall of his studio, we see the mirror images of the king and queen standing next to one another with a red drape falling behind. Since we do not actually see them in the flesh, we may assume that they are standing in the viewer's position, before the canvas and the artist. Is the princess being given a few finishing touches before joining her parents in a family portrait? We cannot know for sure. The reality of the scene has been left a mystery by Velásquez, just as has the identity of the gentleman observing the scene from an open door in the rear of the room. It is interesting to note the prominence of the artist in this painting of royalty. It makes us aware of his importance to the court and to the king in particular. Recall the portrait of Raphael in *The School of Athens* (see Fig. 13–24). Raphael's persona is almost furtive by comparison.

Velásquez pursued realism in technique as well as in subject matter. Building upon the Venetian method of painting, Velásquez constructed his forms from a myriad of strokes that captured the light exactly as it played over different surface textures. Upon close examination of his paintings (Fig. 14–15), we find small and

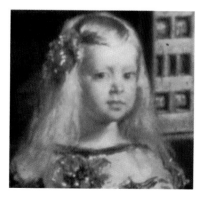

14–15 DIEGO VELÁSQUEZ
LAS MENINAS (DETAIL).

separate strokes that hover on the surface of the canvas, divorced from the very forms they are meant to describe. Yet from a few feet away, together they evoke an overall *impression* of silk or fur or flowers. This dissolution of forms into small, roughly textured brushstrokes that recreate the play of light over surfaces would be the foundation of a movement called **Impressionism** some two centuries later. In his pursuit of realism, Velásquez truly was an artist before his time.

FLANDERS

After the dust of Martin Luther's Reformation had settled, the region of Flanders was divided. The northern sections, now called the Dutch Republic (present-day Holland), accepted Protestantism, while the southern sections, still called Flanders (present-day Belgium), remained Catholic. This separation more or less dictated the subjects that artists rendered in their works. Dutch artists painted scenes of daily life, carrying forward the tradition of Bruegel, while Flemish artists continued painting the religious and mythological scenes already familiar to us from Italy and Spain.

PETER PAUL RUBENS   Even the great power and prestige held by Velásquez were exceeded by the Flemish artist Peter Paul Rubens (1577–1640). One of the most sought-after artists of his time, Rubens was an ambassador, diplomat, and court painter to dukes and kings. He ran a bustling workshop with numerous assistants to help him complete commissions. Rubens's style combined the sculptural qualities of Michelangelo's figures with the painterliness and coloration of the Venetians. He also emulated the dramatic chiaroscuro and theatrical presentation of subject matter we found in the Italian Baroque masters. Much as had Dürer, Rubens admired and adopted from his southern colleagues. Although Rubens painted portraits, religious subjects, and mythological themes, as well as scenes of adventure, his canvases were always imbued with the dynamic energy and unleashed passion we link to the Baroque era.

In *The Rape of the Daughters of Leucippus* (Fig. 14–16), Rubens recounted a tale from Greek mythology in which two mortal women were seized by the twin sons of Zeus, Castor and Pollux. The action in the composition is described by the intersection of strong diagonals and verticals that stabilize the otherwise unstable composition. Capitalizing on the Baroque "stop-action" technique, which depicts a single moment in an event, Rubens placed his struggling, massive forms within a diamond-shaped structure that rests in the foreground on a single point—the toes of a man and a woman. Visually, we grasp that all this energy cannot be supported on a single point, so we infer continuous movement. The action has been pushed up to the picture plane, where the viewer is confronted with the intense emotion and brute strength of the scene. Along with these Baroque devices, Rubens used color and texture much in the way the Venetians used it. The virile sun-tanned arms of the abductors contrast strongly with the delicately colored flesh of the women. The soft blonde braids that flow outward under the influence of all of this commotion correspond to the soft, flowing manes of the overpowering horses.

HOLLAND

The grandiose compositional schemes and themes of action executed by Rubens could not have been further removed from the concerns and sensibilities of most seventeenth-century Dutch artists. Whereas mysticism and religious naturalism flourished in Italy, Flanders, and Spain amidst the rejection of Protestantism and the invigorated revival of Catholicism, artists of the Low Countries turned to secular art, abiding by the Protestant mandate that man not create "false idols." Not only did artists turn to scenes of everyday life, but the collectors of art were themselves everyday folk. In the Dutch quest for the establishment of a middle class, aristocratic patronage was lost and artists were forced to "peddle" their wares in the free market. Landscapes, still lifes, and genre paintings were the favored canvases, and realism was the word of the day. Although the subject matter of Dutch artists differed radically from that of their colleagues elsewhere in Europe, the spirit of the Baroque, with many, if not most, of its artistic characteristics, was present in their work.

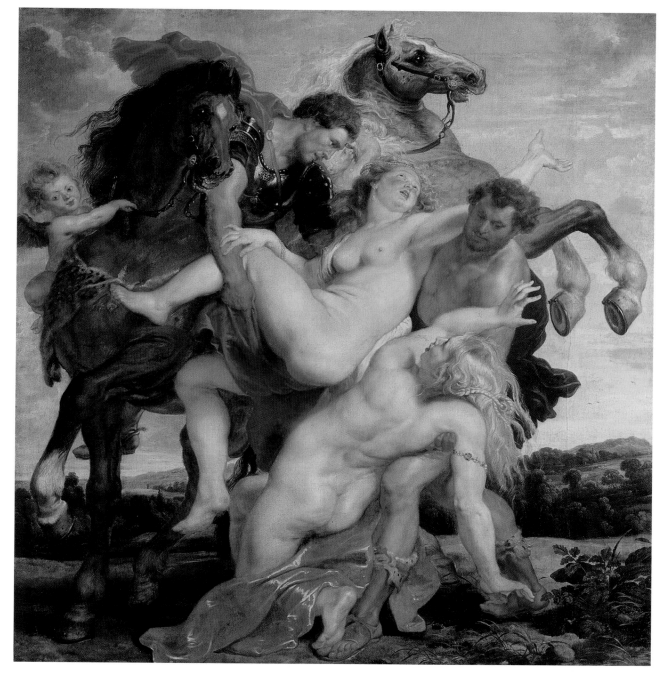

14–16 PETER PAUL RUBENS
*THE RAPE OF THE DAUGHTERS OF
LEUCIPPUS* (1617). OIL ON CANVAS.
7′3″ × 6′10″.
ALTE PINAKOTHEK, MUNICH.

14–17 REMBRANDT VAN RIJN
SELF-PORTRAIT (1652). OIL ON CANVAS. 45 × 32″.
KUNSTHISTORISCHES MUSEUM, VIENNA.

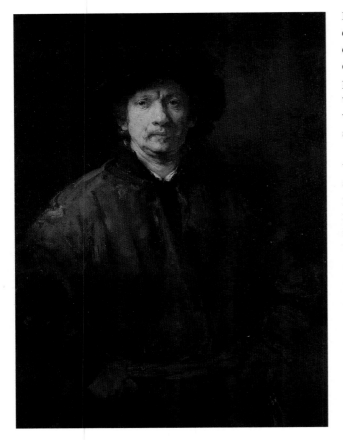

REMBRANDT VAN RIJN   The golden-toned, subtly lit canvases of Rembrandt van Rijn (1606–1669) possess a certain degree of timelessness. Rembrandt concentrates on the personality of the sitter or the psychology of a particular situation rather than on surface characteristics. This introspection is evident in all of Rembrandt's works, whether religious or secular in subject, landscapes or portraits, drawings, paintings, or prints.

Rembrandt painted a great number of self-portraits that offer us an insight into his life and personality. In a self-portrait at the age of 46 (Fig. 14–17), Rembrandt paints an image of himself as a self-confident, well-respected, and sought-after artist who stares almost impatiently out toward the viewer. It is as if he had been caught in the midst of working and will allow us only a moment. It is a powerful image, with piercing eyes, thoughtful brow, and determined jaw that betray a productive man who is more than satisfied with his position in life. All of this may seem obvious, but notice how few clues he gives us to reach these conclusions about his personality. He stands in an undefined space with no props that reveal his identity. The figure itself is cast into darkness; we can hardly discern his torso and hands resting in the sash around his waist. The penetrating light in the canvas is reserved for just a portion of the artist's face. Rembrandt gives us a minute fragment with which he beckons us to complete the whole. It is at once a mysterious and revealing portrayal that relies on a mysterious and revealing light.

Rembrandt also painted large group portraits. In his *Syndics of the Drapers' Guild* (Fig. 14–18), which you may recognize from the cover of Dutch Masters' cigar boxes, we, the viewers, become part of a scene involving Dutch businessmen. Bathed in the warm light of a fading sun that enters the room through a hidden window to the left, the men appear to be reacting to the entrance of another person. Some rise in acknowledgment. Others seem to smile. Still others gesture to a ledger as if to explain that they are gathering to "go over the books." Even though the group operates as a whole, the portraits are highly individualized and themselves complete. As in his self-portrait, Rembrandt concentrates his light on the heads of the sitters, from

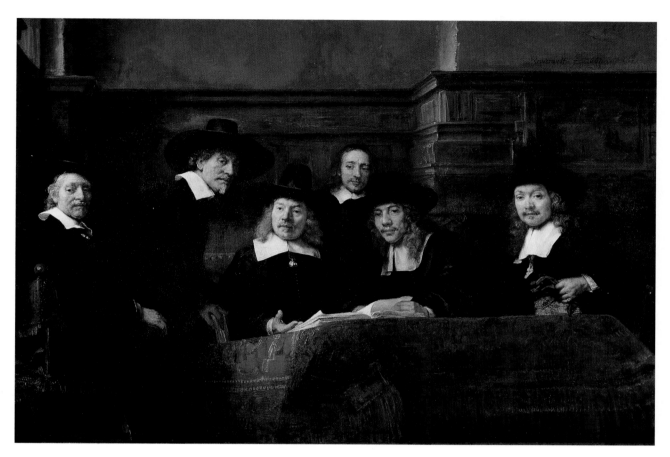

14–18 REMBRANDT VAN RIJN
SYNDICS OF THE DRAPERS' GUILD (1661–62).
OIL ON CANVAS. 72⅞ × 107⅛″.
RIJKSMUSEUM, AMSTERDAM.

which we, the viewers, gain insight into their personalities. The haziness that surrounds Rembrandt's figures is born from his brushstroke and his use of light. Rembrandt's strokes are heavily loaded with pigment and applied in thick **impasto.** As we saw in the painterly technique of Velásquez, Rembrandt's images are more easily discerned from afar than from up close. As a matter of fact, Rembrandt is reputed to have warned viewers to keep their "nose" out of his painting because the smell of paint was bad for them. We can take this to mean that the technical devices Rembrandt used to create certain illusions of realism

are all too evident from the perspective of a few inches. Above all, Rembrandt was capable of manipulating light. His is a light that alternately constructs and destructs, that alternately bathes and hides from view. It is a light that can be focused as unpredictably, and that shifts as subtly, as the light we find in nature.

Although Rembrandt was sought after as an artist for a good many years and was granted many important commissions, he fell victim to the whims of the free market. The grand master of the Dutch Baroque died at the age of 63, out of fashion and penniless.

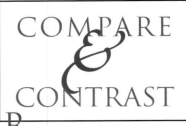
Rembrandt's *The Resurrection of Christ* (Fig. 14–19) differs vastly from the rendering of the same subject by the Renaissance artist Piero della Francesca (Fig. 14–20). Piero's vision is the model of restraint. Christ is risen, calm, and stately; the soldiers sleep; and the genetic imperatives of nature follow the precise mathematical precepts of the artist. Rembrandt's Christ is rising amidst the tumult and fury of the Baroque universe. Here, too, there is a figure triangle—but what a difference in the figures. An angel at the apex, born of an unworldly light, pulls back the lid of the sepulchre, unleashing forces that blast away the soldiers in attendance. Piero's figures seemed to pose for the rendering, whereas Rembrandt chose to capture a fleeting, dynamic moment.

Very often the style and content of a work of art complement one another. At other times, they can work against each other. Which style—Piero's or Rembrandt's—seems to be more consonant with the subject of the resurrection? Why?

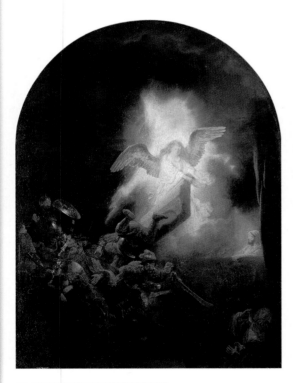

14–19 REMBRANDT VAN RIJN
RESURRECTION OF CHRIST
(C. 1635–39). OIL ON CANVAS.
91.9 × 67 CM.
ALTE PINAKOTHEK, MUNICH.

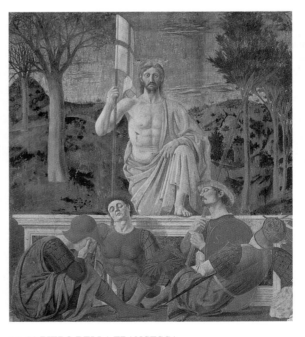

14–20 PIERO DELLA FRANCESCA
RESURRECTION (C. LATE 1450S).
FRESCO.
TOWN HALL, BORGO SAN SEPOLCRO.

14–21 JAN VERMEER
YOUNG WOMAN WITH A WATER JUG (C. 1665).
OIL ON CANVAS. 18 × 16″.
THE METROPOLITAN MUSEUM OF ART, N.Y. GIFT OF HENRY G. MARQUAND, 1889. MARQUAND
COLLECTION (89.15.21).

JAN VERMEER If there is a single artist who typifies the Dutch interest in painting scenes of daily life, the commonplace narratives of middle-class men and women, it is Jan Vermeer (1632–1675). Although he did not paint many pictures and never strayed from his native Delft, his precisely sketched and pleasantly colored compositions made him well respected and influential in later centuries.

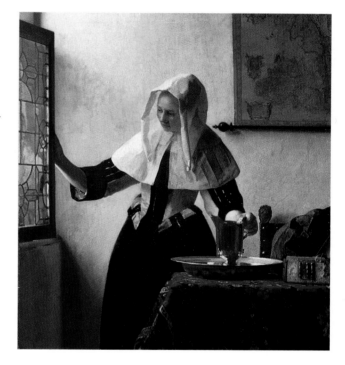

Young Woman with a Water Jug (Fig. 14–21) exemplifies Vermeer's subject matter and technique. In a tastefully underfurnished corner of a room in a typical middle-class household, a woman stands next to a rug-covered table, grasping a water jug with one hand and, with the other, opening a stained-glass window. A blue cloth has been thrown over a brass and leather chair, a curious metal box sits on the table, and a map adorns the wall. At once we are presented with opulence and simplicity. The elements in the composition are perfectly placed. One senses that their position could not be moved even a fraction of an inch without disturbing the composition. Pure colors and crisp lines grace the space in the painting rather than interrupting it. Every item in the painting is of a simple, almost timeless, form and corresponds to the timeless serenity of the porcelainlike image of the woman. Her simple dress and starched collar and bonnet epitomize grace and serenity. We might not see this as a Baroque composition if it were not for three things: a single source of light bathing the elements in the composition, the genre subject, and a bit of mystery surrounding the moment captured by Vermeer. What is the woman doing? She has opened the window and taken a jug into her hand at the same time, but we will never know for what purpose. Some have said that she may intend to water flowers at a window box. Perhaps she was in the midst of doing something else and paused to investigate a noise in the street. Vermeer gives us a curious combination of the momentary and the eternal in this almost photographic glimpse of everyday Dutch life.

FRANCE

During the Baroque period, France, under the reign of the "sun king," Louis XIV, began to replace Rome as the center of the art world. The king preferred Classicism.

Thus did the country, and painters, sculptors, and architects alike create works in this vein. Louis XIV guaranteed adherence to Classicism by forming academies of art that perpetuated this style. These academies were art schools of sorts, run by the state, whose faculties were populated by leading proponents of the Classical style.

When we examine European art during the Baroque period, we thus perceive a strong stylistic polarity. On the one hand, we have the exuberant painterliness and high drama of Rubens and Bernini, and, on the other, a reserved Classicism that hearkens back to Raphael.

NICOLAS POUSSIN The principal exponent of the Classical style in French painting was Nicolas Poussin (1594–1665). Although he was born in France, Poussin spent much of his life in Rome, where he studied the works of the Italian masters, particularly Raphael and

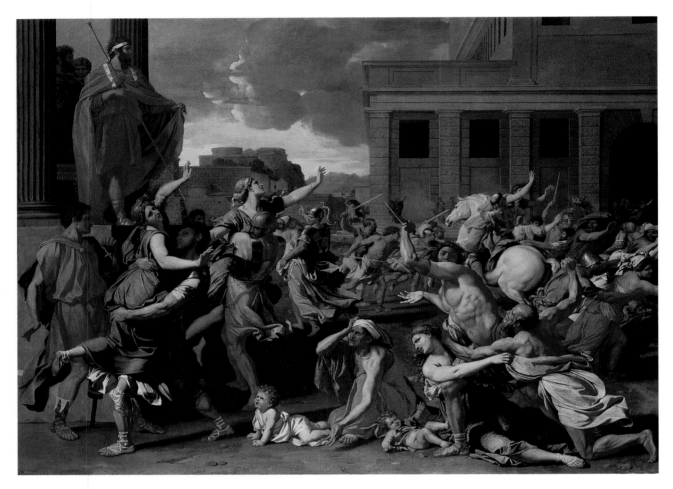

14–22 NICOLAS POUSSIN
THE RAPE OF THE SABINE WOMEN (C. 1636–37).
OIL ON CANVAS. 60⅞ × 82⅝".
THE METROPOLITAN MUSEUM OF ART, N.Y. HARRIS BRISBANE DICK FUND, 1946 (46.160).

Titian. Although his *Rape of the Sabine Women* (Fig. 14–22) was painted four years before he was summoned back to France by the king, it illustrates the Baroque Classicism that Poussin would bring to his native country. The flashy dynamism of Bernini and Rubens gives way to a more static, almost staged, motion in the work of Poussin. Harshly sculptural, Raphaelesque figures thrust in various directions, forming a complex series of intersecting diagonals and verticals. The initial impression is one of chaos, of unrestrained movement and human anguish. But as

was the case with the Classical Greek sculptors and Italian Renaissance artists, emotion is always balanced carefully with restraint. For example, the pitiful scene of the old woman in the foreground, flanked by crying children, forms part of the base of a compositional triangle that stabilizes the work and counters excessive emotion. If one draws a vertical line from the top of her head upward to the top border of the canvas, one encounters the apex of this triangle, formed by the swords of two Roman abductors. The sides of the triangle, then, are formed by the diagonally thrusting torso

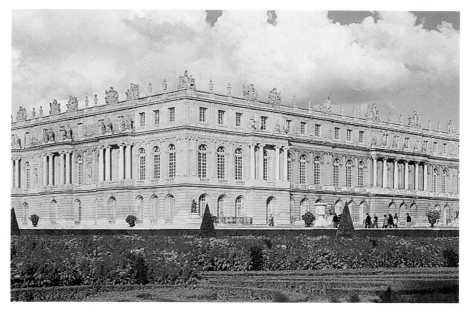

of the muscular Roman in the right foreground and the arms of the Sabine women on the left, reaching hopelessly into the sky. This compositional triangle, along with the Roman temple in the right background that prevents a radically receding space, are Renaissance techniques for structuring a balanced composition. Poussin used these, along with a stagelike, theatrical presentation of his subjects, to reconcile the divergent styles of the harsh Classical and the vibrant Baroque.

Polar opposites in style occur in other movements throughout the history of art. It will be important to remember this aspect of the Baroque, because in later centuries we will encounter the polarity again, among artists who divide themselves into the camps **Poussiniste** and **Rubeniste**.

VERSAILLES The king's taste for the Classical extended to architecture, as seen in the Palace at Versailles (Fig. 14–23). Originally the site of the king's hunting lodge, the palace and surrounding area just outside of Paris were converted by a host of artists, architects, and landscape designers into one of the grandest monuments to the French Baroque. In their tribute to Classicism, the architects Louis Le Vau (1612–1670) and Jules Hardouin-Mansart (1646–1708) divided the horizontal sweep of the facades into three stories. The structure was then divided vertically into three major sections, and these were in turn subdivided into three additional sections. The windows march along the facade in a rhythmic beat accompanied by rigid pilasters that are wedged between the strong horizontal bands that delineate the floors. A balustrade tops the palace, further emphasizing the horizontal sweep while restraining any upward movement suggested by the building's vertical members. The divisions into Classically balanced threes and the almost obsessive emphasis on the horizontal echo the buildings of

Renaissance architects. The French had come a long way from the towering spires of their glorious Gothic cathedrals!

THE ROCOCO

We have roughly dated the Baroque period from 1600 to 1750. However, art historians have recognized a more distinct style within the Baroque that began shortly after the dawn of the eighteenth century. This **Rococo** style strayed further from Classical principles than did the Baroque. It is more ornate and characterized by sweetness, gaiety, and light. The courtly pomp and reserved Classicism of Louis XIV were replaced with a more delicate and sprightly representation of the leisure activities of the upper class.

The early Rococo style appears as a refinement of the painterly Baroque in which Classical subjects are often rendered in wispy brushstrokes that rely heavily on the Venetian or Rubensian palette of luscious golds and reds. The later Rococo period, following midcentury, is more frivolous in its choice of subjects (that of love among the very rich), palette (that of the softest pastel hues), and brushwork (the most delicate and painterly strokes).

14–24 JEAN-HONORÉ FRAGONARD
HAPPY ACCIDENTS OF THE SWING (1767).
OIL ON CANVAS. 31⅞ × 25⅜".

14–25 ELISABETH VIGÉE-LEBRUN
MARIE ANTOINETTE AND HER CHILDREN (1781).
OIL ON CANVAS. 8'8" × 6'10".
PALACE OF VERSAILLES.

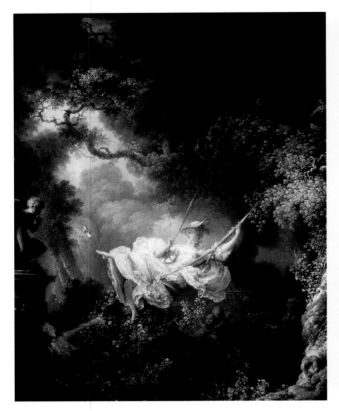

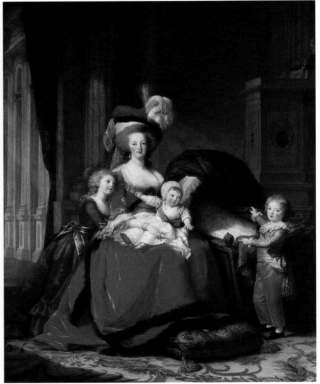

JEAN-HONORÉ FRAGONARD Jean-Honoré Fragonard
(1732–1806) is one of the finest representatives of the
Rococo style, and his painting *Happy Accidents of the
Swing* (Fig. 14–24) is a prime example of the aims and
accomplishments of the Rococo artist. In the midst of a
lush green park, whose opulent foliage was no doubt inspired by the Baroque, we are offered a glimpse of the
"love games" of the leisure class. A young, though not-
so-innocent, maiden, with petticoats billowing beneath
her sumptuous pink dress, is being swung by an unsus-
pecting bishop high over the head of her reclining gentleman friend, who seems delighted with the view. The
subjects' diminutive forms and rosy cheeks make them
doll-like, an image reinforced by the idyllic setting. This
is eighteenth-century life at its best—pampered by subtle hues, embraced by lush textures, and bathed by the
softest of lights. Unfortunately, this was all a mask for
life at its worst. As the ruling class continued to ignore
the needs of the common people, the latter were preparing to rebel.

ELISABETH VIGÉE-LEBRUN Whereas Rembrandt epitomizes the artists who achieves recognition after death,
Elisabeth Vigée-Lebrun (1755–1842) was a complete
success during her lifetime. The daughter of a portrait
painter, she received instruction and encouragement
from her father and his colleagues from an early age.
As a youngster she also studied paintings in the Louvre
and was particularly drawn to the works of Rubens. By
the time she reached her early twenties, she commanded high prices for her portraits and was made an
official portrait painter for Marie Antoinette, the
Austrian wife of Louis XVI. Neither Marie Antoinette
nor her husband survived the French Revolution, but
Vigée-Lebrun's fame spread throughout Europe, and by
the end of her career she had created some 800 paintings.

Marie Antoinette and Her Children (Fig. 14–25)
was painted nearly a decade after Vigée-Lebrun had
begun to paint the royal family. In this work she was
commissioned to counter the antimonarchist sentiments
spreading throughout the land by portraying the queen

as, first and foremost, a loving mother. True, the queen is set within the imposing Salon de la Paix at Versailles, with the famous Hall of Mirrors to the left and the royal crown atop the cabinet on the right. True, the queen's enormous hat and voluminous skirts create a richness and monumentality to which the common person could not reasonably aspire. But the triangular composition and the child on the lap are reminiscent of Renaissance images of the Madonna and child (see Chapter 13), at once creating a sympathetic portrait of a mother and her children and, subliminally, asserting their divine right. Even amid the opulence at Versailles, Marie Antoinette displays her children as her real jewels. The young dauphin to the right, set apart as the future king, points to an empty cradle that might have originally contained the queen's fourth child, an infant who died two months before the painting was scheduled for exhibition.

The French populace, of course, was not persuaded by this portrait or by other public relations efforts to paint the royal family as accessible and sympathetic. The artist, in fact, did not exhibit her painting as scheduled for fear that the public might destroy it. Two years after the painting was completed, the convulsions of the French Revolution shook Europe and the world. The royal family were imprisoned and then executed. More than the royal family had passed into history, and more than democracy was about to be born. Modern art was also to be ushered into this brave new world.

key terms

Baroque	Piazza	Rococo
Reformation	Tenebrism	

artists

Gianlorenzo Bernini	Baciccio	Jan Vermeer
Donatello	Francesco Borromini	Nicolas Poussin
Andrea Verrocchio	Diego Velásquez	Louis Le Vau
Michelangelo	Peter Paul Rubens	Jules Hardouin-Mansart
Caravaggio	Rembrandt van Rijn	Jean-Honoré Fragonard
Artemisia Gentileschi	Piero della Francesca	Elisabeth Vigée-Lebrun

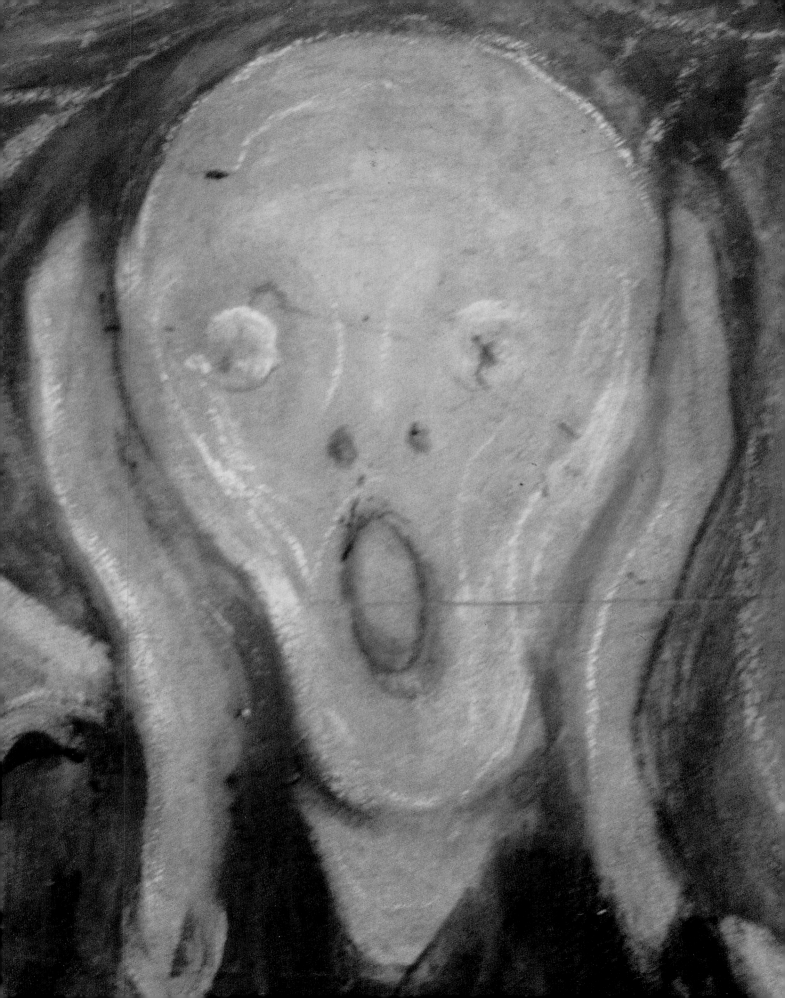

15

c h a p t e r

MODERN ART

❏ The painter Jacques-Louis David was a survivor who painted *The Oath of the Horath* for Louis XVI, then supported the French Revolution which deposed the monarch, and later painted a work that commemorated the coronation of Napoleon as emperor.

❏ The term *Impressionism* was coined by a critic who characterized works by Monet and others as mere "impressions"—quick and easy sketches—of the painter's view of the world.

❏ Paul Gauguin began his career as a stock broker and ended it as a savage.

❏ Only one of van Gogh's paintings was sold during his lifetime.

❏ The British destroyed one of their own landmarks of modern architecture during World War II because it was being used as a guidepost by enemy pilots on bombing runs.

❏ Thomas Jefferson, author of the Declaration of Independence and third President of the United States, was also a gifted Neoclassical architect.

Edvard Munch, *The Scream* (detail). See Figure 15–31.

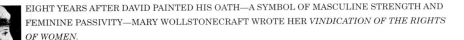

Historians of modern art have repeatedly posed the question, "When did modern art begin?" Some link the beginnings of modern painting to the French Revolution in 1789. Others have chosen 1863, the year of a landmark exhibition of "modern" painting in Paris.

Another issue of interest has been, "Just what is modern about modern art?" The artists of the mid-fifteenth century looked upon their art as modern. They chose new subjects, materials, and techniques that signaled a radical change from a medieval past. Their development of one-point linear perspective altered the face of painting completely. From our perspective, modern art begins with the changes in the representation of space introduced by artists of the late eighteenth century. Unlike the Renaissance masters, who sought to open up endless vistas within the canvas, the artists of the latter 1700s brought all of the imagery to the picture plane. The flatness or two-dimensionality of the canvas surface was asserted by the use of **planar recession** rather than **linear recession.** Not all artists of the eighteenth and nineteenth centuries abided by this novel treatment of space, but with this innovation the die was cast for the future of painting.

In short, what was *modern* about the modern art of the eighteenth century in France was its concept of space. In a very real sense, the history of modern art is the history of two differing perceptions and renderings of that space.

As we shall see in this chapter, the first period of modern art to use planar recession was *Neoclassicism.* We shall also examine its contemporaneous though often contrary movement, *Romanticism.* We shall discuss the survival of Academic painting in the nineteenth century and address the use of art for political purposes. At mid-nineteenth century we shall witness the rise of a group of **bohemian** artists, whose painting of optical impressions stood as the scandal of the age and the legacy to the future. Although we shall focus our attention on Paris and its surroundings—the center of the art world during these dynamic years—we shall glance at contemporaneous trends in Germany and in the United States.

The emphasis in this chapter will be on painting, the medium in which modernism made its greatest strides.

NEOCLASSICISM

Modern art declared its opposition to the whimsy of the late Rococo style with **Neoclassicism.** The Neoclassical style is characterized by harsh sculptural lines, a subdued palette, and, for the most part, planar instead of linear recession into space. The subject matter of Neoclassicism was inspired by the French Revolution and designed to heighten moral standards. The new morality sought to replace the corruption and decadence of Louis XVI's France. The Roman Empire was often chosen as the model to emulate. For this reason, the artists of the Napoleonic era imitated the form and content of Classical works of art. This interest in antiquity was fueled by contemporaneous archeological finds at sites such as Pompeii as well as by numerous excavations in Greece.

JACQUES-LOUIS DAVID   The sterling proponent of the Neoclassical style and official painter of the French Revolution was Jacques-Louis David (1748–1825). David literally gave postrevolutionary France a new look. He designed everything from clothing to coiffures. David also set the course for modern art with a sudden and decisive break from the ornateness and frivolity of the Rococo.

In *The Oath of the Horath* (Fig. 15–1), David portrayed a dramatic event from Roman history in order to heighten French patriotism and courage. Three brothers prepare to fight an enemy of Rome, swearing an oath to the Empire on swords upheld by their father. To the right, their mother and other relatives collapse in despair. They weep for the men's safety but are also distraught because one of the enemy men is engaged to be married to a sister of the Horath. Family is pitted against family in a conflict that no one can win. Such a subject could descend into pathos, but David controlled any tendency toward sentimentality by reviving the Classical balance of emotion and restraint. The emotionality of the theme is countered by David's cool rendition of forms. The elements of the composition further work to harness emotionalism. Harsh sculptural lines define the figures and setting. The palette is reduced to muted blues and grays, with an occasional splash of deep red. Emotional response is barely evident in the idealized Classical faces.

15–1 JACQUES-LOUIS DAVID
THE OATH OF THE HORATH (1784). OIL ON CANVAS. 14 × 11′.
LOUVRE MUSEUM, PARIS.

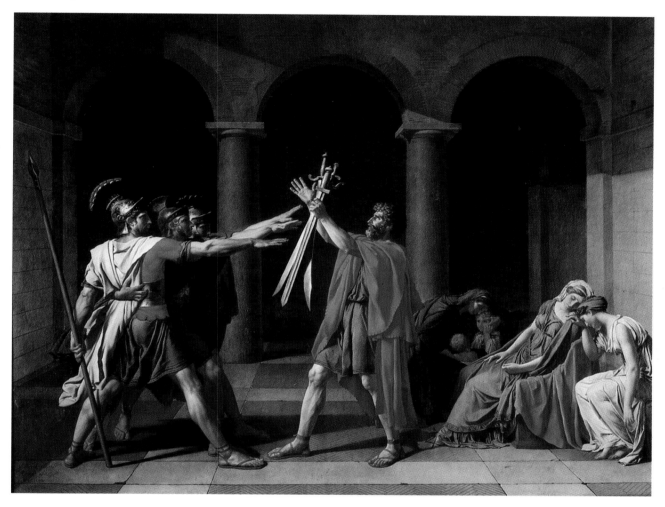

A number of Classical devices in David's compositional format also function to balance emotion and restraint. The figural groups form a rough triangle. Their apex—the clasped swords of the Horath—is the most important point of the composition. In the same way that Leonardo used three windows in his *Last Supper,* David silhouetted his dramatic moment against the central opening of three arches in the background. David further imitated Renaissance canvases by presenting cues for a linear perspective in the patterning of the floor. But unlike sixteenth-century artists, David led his orthogonals into a flattened space instead of a vanishing point on a horizon line. The closing off of this background space forces the viewer's eye to the front of the picture plane, where it encounters the action of the composition and the canvas surface itself. No longer does the artist desire to trick observers into believing they are looking through a window frame into the distance. Now the reality of the two-dimensionality of the canvas is asserted.

David was one of the leaders of the French Revolution, and his political life underwent curious turns. Although he painted *The Oath of the Horath* for Louis XVI, he supported the faction that deposed him. Later he was to find himself painting a work commemorating the coronation of Napoleon. Having struggled against the French monarchy and then living to see it restored, David chose to spend his last years in exile in Brussels.

15–2 ANGELICA KAUFFMAN
THE ARTIST IN THE CHARACTER OF DESIGN LISTENING TO THE INSPIRATION OF POETRY (1782). OIL ON CANVAS. CIRCULAR: 24″ IN DIAMETER.
THE IVEAGH BEQUEST, KENWOOD, LONDON (ENGLISH HERITAGE).

ANGELICA KAUFFMAN   Another leading neoclassical painter Angelica Kauffman (1741–1807) was an exact contemporary of David. Born in Switzerland and educated in the neoclassical circles in Rome, Kauffman was responsible for the dissemination of the style in England. She is known for her portraiture, history painting, and narrative works such as *The Artist in the Character of Design Listening to the Inspiration of Poetry* (Fig. 15–2). In this allegorical work, Kauffman paints her own features in the person of the muse of design, who is listening attentively with paper and pencil in hand to her companion muse of poetry. Poetry's idealized facial features, along with the severe architecture, classically rendered drapery, and rich palette place the work firmly in the neoclassical style.

JEAN-AUGUSTE-DOMINIQUE INGRES   David abstracted space by using planar rather than linear recession. His most prodigious student, Jean-Auguste-Dominique Ingres (1780–1867), created sensuous, though pristinely classical compositions in which line functions as an abstract element. Above all else, Ingres was a magnificent draftsman.

Ingres's work is a combination of harsh linearity and sculptural smoothness on the one hand, and delicacy and sensuality on the other. His *Grande Odalisque* portrays a Turkish harem mistress in the tradition of the great reclining Venuses of the Venetian Renaissance; yet how different it is, for example, from Titian's *Venus of Urbino!* (See the nearby "Compare and Contrast" feature.) The elongation of the former's spine, her attenuated limbs, and odd fullness of form recall the distortions and abstractions of Mannerist art. In the *Grande Odalisque,* Ingres also delights in the differing qualities of line. The articulation of heavy drapery contrasts markedly with the staccato treatment of the bed linens and the languid, sensual lines of the mistress's body. Like David's, Ingres's forms are smooth and sculptural, and his palette is muted. Ingres also flattens space in his composition by placing his imagery in the foreground, as in a relief.

THE YEAR 1826 MARKS THE COMPLETION OF *THE DEATH OF SARDANAPALUS*. IT ALSO MARKS
THE BIRTH OF THOMAS JEFFERSON IN VIRGINIA ON THE FOURTH OF JULY.

15–3 EUGÈNE DELACROIX
THE DEATH OF SARDANAPALUS (1826). OIL ON CANVAS. 12'11½" × 16'3".
LOUVRE MUSEUM, PARIS.

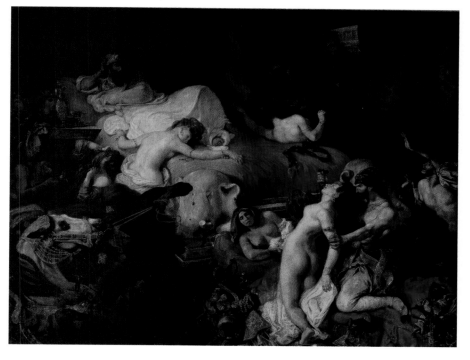

Ingres's exotic nudes were a popular type of imagery in the late eighteenth century, but such subjects were often rendered quite differently by other artists. There was a popularity of style during this period that was similar to that existing during the Baroque era. On the one hand were artists such as David and Ingres, who represented the linear style. On the other hand were artists whose works were painterly. The foremost proponents of the painterly style were Géricault and Delacroix. The linear artists, called **Poussinistes,** followed in the footsteps of Classicism with their subdued palette and emphasis on draftsmanship and sculptural forms. The painterly artists, termed the **Rubenistes,** adopted the vibrant palette and aggressive brushstroke of the Baroque artist. The two factions argued vehemently about the merits and the shortcomings of their respective styles. No artists were more deeply entrenched in this feud than the leaders of the camps, Ingres and Delacroix. Such was the state of art at the turn of the nineteenth century.

ROMANTICISM

Both Neoclassicism and **Romanticism** reflected the revolutionary spirit of the times. Neoclassicism emphasized restraint of emotion, purity of form, and subjects that inspired morality, however, whereas Romantic art sought extremes of emotion enhanced by virtuoso brushwork and a brilliant palette. As a movement, Romanticism is not as easily defined as Neoclassicism. Artists classified as Romantic differed in style. Some were mirror images of the Baroque, and others were more abstracted. Still others dedicated themselves wholeheartedly to representing the passion of the French Revolution.

EUGÈNE DELACROIX   The most famous Rubeniste—and Ingres's archrival—was Eugène Delacroix (1798–1863). Whereas Ingres believed that a painting was nothing without drawing, Delacroix advocated the spontaneity of painting directly on canvas without the tyranny of meticulous preparatory sketches. Ingres believed that color ought to be subordinated to line, but Delacroix maintained that compositions should be constructed of color. Their contrasting approaches to painting can be seen clearly in the *Odalisques* by each artist (see the nearby "Compare and Contrast" feature), fine examples of the difference between the Neoclassical and Romantic styles.

One of Delacroix's most dynamic statements of the Romantic style occurs in one of his many compositions devoted to the more exciting themes from literary history. *The Death of Sardanapalus* (Fig. 15–3), inspired by a tragedy by Byron, depicts the murder-suicide of an Assyrian king who, rather than surrender to his attackers, set fire to himself and his entourage. All of the monarch's earthly possessions, including concubines, servants, and Arabian stallions, are heaped upon his lavish gold and velvet bed, now turned funeral pyre.

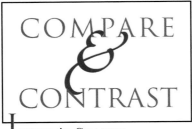

COMPARE & CONTRAST

INGRES'S *GRANDE ODALISQUE,* DELACROIX'S *ODALISQUE,* CÉZANNE'S *A MODERN OLYMPIA,* AND SYLVIA SLEIGH'S *PHILIP GOLUB RECLINING*

Compare and contrast exercises are often used to stimulate a student's powers of visual recognition and discrimination, to test the student's ability to characterize and categorize, and to force the student to think critically about the content and context of the work. If put together just right, they ought also to act as a springboard for discussion of issues that push beyond the discipline of art. Tall order? You bet! But somehow these four meet the demands.

You can write paragraphs on the stylistic differences between the *Odalisques* by Ingres (Fig. 15–4) and Delacroix (Fig. 15–5) alone. They are arch examples of the contrast between a linear and painterly approach to the same subject; they offer clear evidence of the "battle" between the Poussinistes and the Rubenistes during the Romantic period (those whose draughtsmanship was inspired by the classical baroque artist Nicolas Poussin vs. those who "went to school" on the Flemish baroque painter Peter Paul Rubens.) On the other hand, they have one very important thing in common. Both bespeak an enormous fascination with the exotic, with the "orient," with the *other;* a seemingly insatiable fascination not only with the trappings of an exotic *sens*uality—turbans, silken scarves, peacock feathers, opium pipes—but also with what was perceived as an unrestrained and exotic *sex*uality. These two works are in abundant company in nineteenth-century France. Can you do a bit of leg work and find out what circumstances (historical, political, sociological, etc.) prevailed at this moment in time that might have led to a market for such paintings? Why did these very different artists find the same subject so captivating, so fashionable?

The historian and feminist scholar of nineteenth-century art, Linda Nochlin, has suggested that such paint-

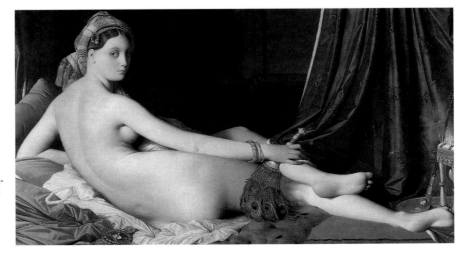

15–4 JEAN-AUGUSTE-DOMINIQUE INGRES *GRANDE ODALISQUE* (1814). OIL ON CANVAS. 35¼ × 63¾". LOUVRE MUSEUM, PARIS.

ings speak volumes about contemporary ideology and gender discourse—"the ways in which representations of women in art are founded upon and serve to reproduce indisputably accepted assumptions held by society in general, artists in particular, and some artists more than others about men's power over, superiority to, difference from, and necessary control of women, assumptions which are manifested in the visual structures as well as the thematic choices of the pictures in question." Among several that Nochlin lists are assumptions about women's weakness and passivity and sexual availability for men's needs.

The works in this feature speak to the tradition of the reclining nude in western art. In another "Compare and Contrast" exercise in the text you can see some other examples of this tradition and are asked for whose "gaze" you think they were intended. In fact, the concept of the "male gaze" has been central to feminist theory for the past decade. In a landmark article written in 1973, Laura Mulvey— a filmmaker—explained the roles of the viewer and the viewed in art, literature, and film this way: Men are in the position of looking, and women are "passive, powerless objects of their controlling gaze."

Paul Cézanne's *A Modern Olympia* (Fig. 15–6) and Sylvia Sleigh's *Philip Golub Reclining* (Fig. 15–7) seem to address the issue of the "male gaze" straight on, but in ways that could not differ more from one another. Cézanne was surely commenting on Edouard Manet's *Olympia* (Fig. 15–15), which was painted just ten years before and which made quite a splash when exhibited. What are the similarities in content, what are the differences? Note, among other things, that Cézanne has placed himself in the picture—owning up, as it were, to the male gaze. Sleigh attacks the issue head on by reversing the "power relationship" in painting. The artist is seen in the background, in mirror reflection, painting the nude torso of Philip Golub from the rear. Does the work raise questions like "Is this also what women really want to paint?" or "Is this what women want to gaze upon?" Or do you think the purpose of this painting is to call our attention to a tradition in the arts of perpetuating ideological gender attitudes?

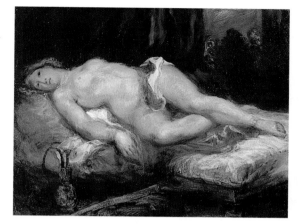

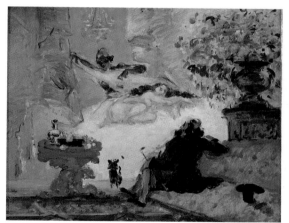

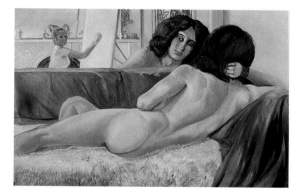

15–5 EUGÈNE DELACROIX
ODALISQUE (1845–50). OIL ON CANVAS. 14⅞ × 18¼".
FITZWILLIAM MUSEUM, CAMBRIDGE, ENGLAND. REPRODUCTION BY PERMISSION OF THE SYNDICS OF THE FITZWILLIAM MUSEUM.

15–6 PAUL CÉZANNE
A MODERN OLYMPIA (1873–74). OIL ON CANVAS. 18¼ × 21⅞".
MUSÉE D'ORSAY, PARIS.

15–7 SYLVIA SLEIGH
PHILIP GOLUB RECLINING (1971). OIL ON CANVAS. 42 × 60".
COURTESY OF THE ARTIST.

15–8 FRANCISCO GOYA
THE THIRD OF MAY, 1808 (1814–15).OIL ON CANVAS. 8′9″ × 13′4″.
PRADO, MADRID.

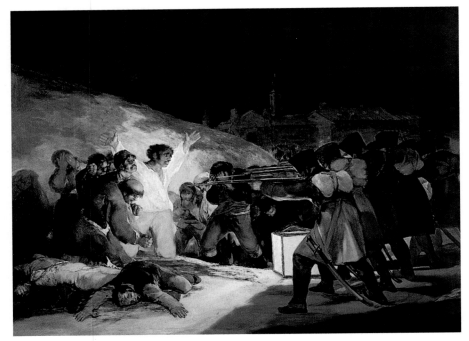

prints foreshadowed the art of the nineteenth-century **Impressionists**.

Francisco Goya (1746–1828) was born in Spain and, except for an academic excursion to Rome, spent his entire life there. He enjoyed a great reputation in his native country and was awarded many important commissions, including religious frescoes and portraits of Spanish royalty. But Goya is best known for his works with political overtones, ranging from social satire to savage condemnation of the disasters of war. One of his most famous depictions of war is *The Third of May, 1808* (Fig. 15–8).

The painting commemorates the massacre of the peasant-citizens of Madrid after the city fell to the French. Reflecting the procedures of Velásquez and Rembrandt—two Baroque masters whom Goya acknowledged as influential in the development of his style—Goya focuses the viewer's attention on a single moment in the violent episode. A Spaniard thrusts his arms upward in surrender to the bayonets of the faceless enemy. The brusqueness of the application of pigment corresponds to the harshness of the subject. The dutiful and regimented procedure of the executioners, dressed in long coats, contrasts visually and psychologically with the expressions of horror, fear, and helplessness on the faces of the ragtag peasants. The emotion is heightened by the use of acerbic tones and by a strong chiaroscuro that illuminates the pitiful victims while relegating all other details to darkness.

The chaos and terror of the event is rendered by Delacroix with all the vigor and passion of a Baroque composition. The explicit contrast between the voluptuous women and the brute strength of the king's executioners brings to mind *The Rape of the Daughters of Leucippus* by Rubens (Fig. 14–16). Arms reach helplessly in all directions and backs arch in hopeless defiance or pitiful submission before the passive Sardanapalus. Delacroix's unleashed energy and assaulting palette were strongly criticized by contemporaries who felt that there was no excuse for such a blatant depiction of violence. But his use of bold colors and freely applied pigment, along with the observations on art and nature that he recorded in his journal, were an important influence on the young artists of the nineteenth century who were destined to transform artistic tradition.

FRANCISCO GOYA   Ironically, the man considered the greatest painter of the Neoclassical and Romantic periods belonged to neither artistic group. He never visited France, the center of the art world at the time, and was virtually unknown to painters of the late eighteenth and early nineteenth centuries. Yet his paintings and

Goya devoted much of his life to the graphic representation of man's inhumanity to man. Toward the end of his life he was afflicted with deafness and plagued with bitterness and depression over the atrocities he had witnessed. These feelings were manifested in macabre paintings and lithographs which presaged the style of the great painters of the nineteenth century.

THE ACADEMY

Ingres's paintings spoke of a calm, though exotic, Classicism. Delacroix retrieved the dynamism of the Baroque. Goya swathed his canvases with the spirit of revolution. Ironically, the style of painting that had the least impact on the development of modern art was the most popular type of painting in its day. This was **Academic art**, so called because its style and subject matter were derived from conventions established by the Academie Royale de Peinture et de Sculpture in Paris.

Established in 1648, the Academy had maintained a firm grip on artistic production for over two centuries. Many artists steeped in this tradition were followers rather than innovators, and the quality of their production left something to be desired. Some, however, like David and Ingres, worked within the confines of a style acceptable to the Academy but rose above the generally rampant mediocrity.

ADOLPHE WILLIAM BOUGUEREAU   One of the more popular and accomplished Academic painters was Adolphe William Bouguereau (1825–1905). Included among his oeuvre are religious and historical paintings in a grand Classical manner, although he is most famous for his meticulously painted nudes and mythological subjects. *Nymphs and Satyr* (Fig. 15–9) is nearly photographic in its refined technique and attention to detail. Four sprightly and sensuous wood nymphs corral a satyr and pull him into the water against his will. Their innocent playfulness would have appealed to the Frenchman on the street, although the saccharine character of the subject matter and the extreme lighthandedness with which the work was painted served only as a model against which the new wave of painters rebelled.

REALISM

The "modern" painters of the nineteenth century objected to Academic art on two levels: The subject matter did not represent life as it really was, and the manner in which the subjects were rendered did not reflect reality as it was observed by the naked eye.

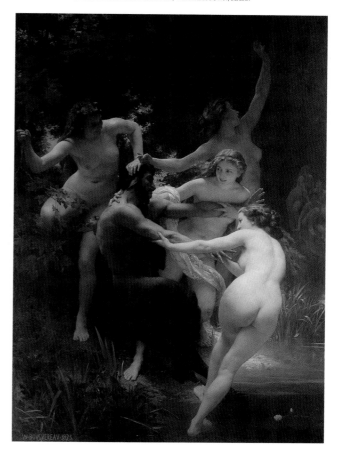

The modern artists chose to depict subjects that were evident in everyday life. The way in which they rendered these subjects also differed from that of Academic painters. They attempted to render on canvas objects as they saw them—optically—rather than as they knew them to be— conceptually. In addition, they respected the reality of the medium they worked with. Instead of using pigment merely as a tool to provide an illusion of three-dimensional reality, they emphasized the two-dimensionality of the canvas and asserted the painting process itself. The physical properties of the pigments were highlighted. Artists who took these ideas to heart were known as the **Realists.** They include Honoré Daumier and two painters whose work stands on the threshold of the Impressionist movement: Gustave Courbet and Edouard Manet.

15–10 HONORÉ DAUMIER
THE THIRD-CLASS CARRIAGE (C. 1862). OIL ON CANVAS. 25¾ × 35½".

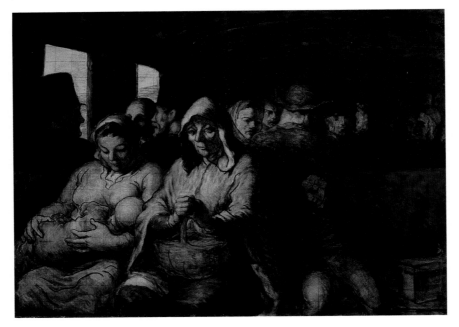

HONORÉ DAUMIER   Of all of the modern artists of the mid-nineteenth century, Honoré Daumier (1808–1879) was perhaps the most concerned with bringing to light the very real subject of the plight of the masses. Daumier worked as a caricaturist for Parisian journals, and he used his cartoons to convey his disgust with the monarchy and contemporary bourgeois society. His public ridicule of King Louis Phillipe landed him in prison for six months.

Daumier is known primarily for his lithographs, which number some 4,000, although he was also an important painter. He brought to his works on canvas the technique and style of a caricaturist. Together, they make for a powerful rendition of his realistic subjects. One of Daumier's most famous compositions is *The Third-Class Carriage* (Fig. 15–10), an illustration of a crowded third-class compartment of a French train. His caricaturist style is evident in the flowing dark outlines and exaggerated features and gestures, but it also underscores the artist's concern for the working class by advertising their ill fortune. The peasants are crowded into the car, their clothing poor and rumpled, their faces wide and expressionless. They contrast markedly with bourgeois commuters, whose felt top hats tower above

their kerchiefed heads. It is a candid-camera depiction of these people. Wrapped up in their own thoughts and disappointments, they live their quite ordinary lives from day to day, without significance and without notice.

GUSTAVE COURBET   The term "realist," when it applies to art, is synonymous with Gustave Courbet (1819–1877). Considered to be the father of the Realist movement, Courbet used the term "realism" to describe his own work and even issued a manifesto on the subject. As was the case with many artists who broke the mold of the Academic style, Courbet's painting was shunned and decried by contemporary critics. But Courbet proceeded undaunted. After his paintings were rejected by the jurors of the 1855 **salon,** he set up his own pavilion and exhibited some forty of his own paintings. Such antics, as well as his commitment to realistic subjects and vigorous application of pigment, served as a strong model for the younger painters at midcentury who were also to rebel against the established Academic tradition in art.

Paintings such as *The Stone-Breakers* (Fig. 15–11) were the objects of public derision. Courbet was moved to paint the work after seeing an old man and a young

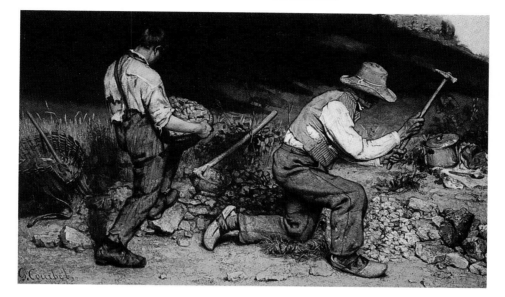

boy breaking stones on a roadside. So common a subject was deplored by contemporary critics who favored mythological or idealistic subjects. But Courbet, who was quoted as saying that he couldn't paint an angel because he had never seen one, continued in this vein despite the art world's rejection. It was not only the artist's subject matter, however, that the critics found offensive. They also spurned his painting technique. Although his choice of colors was fairly traditional—muted tones of brown and ochre—their quick application with a palette knife resulted in a coarsely textured surface that could not have been farther removed from the glossy finish of an Academic painting. Curiously, although Courbet believed that this type of painting was more realistic than that of the salons, in fact the reverse is closer to the truth. The Academic painter strove for what we would today consider to be an almost photographically exact representation of the figure, while Courbet attempted quickly to jot down his impressions of the scene in an often spontaneous flurry of strokes. (For this reason, Courbet can be said to have foreshadowed the Impressionist movement, which we shall discuss in the next section.) Despite Courbet's advocacy of hard-core realism, the observer of *The Stone-Breakers* is presented ultimately with the artist's subjective view of the world.

Courbet's painting may have laid the groundwork for Impressionism, but he himself was not to be a part of the new wave. His old age brought conservatism, and with it disapproval of the younger generation's painting techniques. One of the targets of Courbet's derision was Edouard Manet (1832–1883). According to some art historians, Manet is the artist most responsible for changing the course of the history of painting.

EDOUARD MANET What was modern about Manet's painting was his technique. Instead of beginning with a dark underpainting and building up to bright highlights—a method used since the Renaissance—Manet began with a white surface and worked to build up dark tones. This approach lent a greater luminosity to the work, one that duplicated sunlight as closely as possible. Manet also did not model his figures with a traditional chiaroscuro. Instead, he applied his pigments flatly and broadly. With these techniques he attempted to capture an impression of a fleeting moment, to duplicate on canvas what the eye would perceive within that collapsed time frame.

All too predictably, these innovations met with disapproval from critics and the public alike. Manet's subjects were found to be equally abrasive. One of his most

15–12 EDOUARD MANET
LE DÉJEUNER SUR L'HERBE (1863). OIL ON CANVAS. 7′ × 8′10″.
MUSÉE D'ORSAY, GALERIE DU JEU DE PAUME.

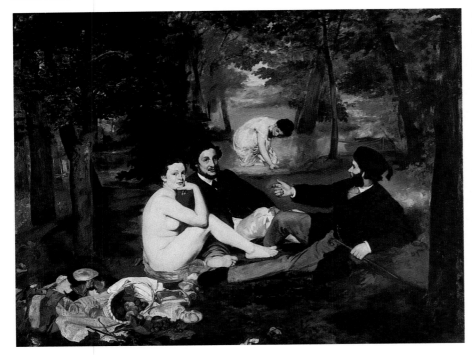

shocking paintings, *Le Déjeuner sur l'Herbe* or *Luncheon on the Grass* (Fig. 15–12), stands as a pivotal work in the rise of the Impressionist movement. Manet's luncheon takes place in a lush woodland setting. Its guests are ordinary members of the French middle class. It is culled from a tradition of Venetian Renaissance **pastoral** scenes common to the masters Giorgione and Titian. The composition is rather traditional. The figural group forms a stable pyramidal structure that is set firmly in the middle ground of the canvas. In fact, the group itself is derived from an engraving by Marcantonio Raimondi after a painting by Raphael called *The Judgment of Paris* (Fig. 15–13).

What was so alarming to the Parisian spectator, and remains so to this day, is that there is no explanation for the behavior of the picnickers. Why are the men clothed and the women undraped to varying degrees? Why are the men chatting between themselves, seemingly unaware of the women? The public was quite used to the painting of nudes, but they were not prepared to witness one of their fold—an ordinary citizen—displayed so shamefully on such a grand scale. The painting was further intolerable because the seated woman meets the viewer's stare, as if the viewer had intruded on their gathering in a voyeuristic fashion.

Viewers expecting another pastoral scene replete with nymphs and satyrs got, instead, portraits of Manet's model (Victorine Meurend), his brother, and a sculptor friend. In lieu of a highly polished Academic painting, they found a broadly brushed application of flat, barely modeled hues that sat squarely on the canvas with no regard for illusionism. With this shocking subject and unconventional technique, modernism was on its way.

Manet submitted the work to the 1863 Salon, and it was categorically rejected. He and other artists whose

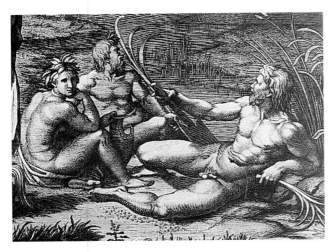

15–13 MARCANTONIO RAIMONDI
ENGRAVING AFTER RAPHAEL'S *THE JUDGMENT OF PARIS* (DETAIL) (C. 1520).
THE METROPOLITAN MUSEUM OF ART, N.Y. ROGERS FUND, 1919 (19.74.1).

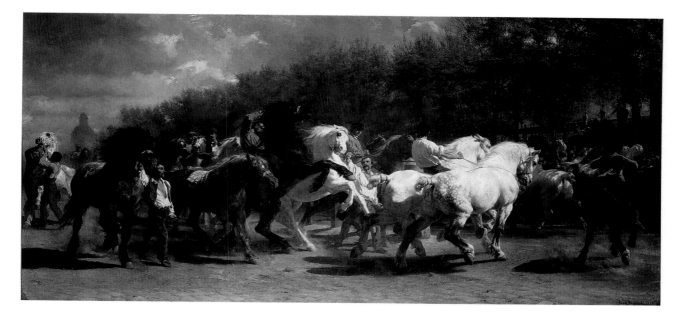

works were rejected that year rebelled so vehemently that Napoleon allowed them to exhibit their work in what was known as the **Salon des Réfusés,** or Salon of the Rejected Painters. It was one of the most important gatherings of **avant-garde** painters in the century.

Although Manet was trying to deliver a message to the art world with his *Déjeuner,* it was not his wish to be ostracized. He was just as interested as the next painter in earning recognition and acceptance. Commissions went to artists whose style was sanctioned by the academics, and painting salon pictures was, after all, a livelihood. Fortunately, Manet had the private means by which he could continue painting in the manner he desired.

Manet was perhaps the most important influence on the French Impressionist painters, a group of artists which advocated the direct painting of optical impressions. *Déjeuner* began a decade of exploration of these new ideas that culminated in the first Impressionist exhibition of 1874. Although considered by his followers to be one of the Impressionists, Manet declined to exhibit with that avant-garde group. A quarter of a century later, only seventeen years after his death, Manet's works were shown at the prestigious Louvre Museum.

ROSA BONHEUR Rosa Bonheur (1822–1899) was one of the most successful artists working in the second half of the nineteenth century. In terms of style, she is most closely related to Courbet and the other Realist painters, although for the most part she shunned human subjects in favor of animals—both domesticated and wild. She was an artist who insisted on getting close to her subject; she reveled in working "in the trenches." Bonheur was seen in men's clothing and hip boots, plodding through the bloody floors of slaughter-houses in her struggle to understand the anatomy of her subjects.

The Horse Fair (Fig. 15–14) is a panoramic scene of extraordinary power, inspired by the Parthenon's horse-men frieze. The dimensions—over twice as long as it is high—compel the viewer to perceive the work as just a small portion of a vast scene in which continuation of action beyond the left and right borders of the canvas is implied. The dramatic contrasts of light and dark underscore the struggle between man and beast, while the painterly brushwork heightens the emotional energy in the painting. *The Horse Fair* was an extremely popular work which was bought widely in engraved reproductions, cementing Bonheur's fame and popularity.

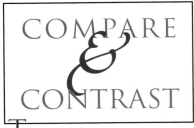

COMPARE & CONTRAST

TITIAN'S *VENUS OF URBINO,* MANET'S *OLYMPIA,* GAUGUIN'S *TE ARI VAHINE,* AND VALADON'S *THE BLUE ROOM*

"We never encounter the body unmediated by the meanings that cultures give to it." Right out of the starting gate, can you challenge yourself to support or contest this statement with reference to the four works in this exercise? The words are Gayle Rubin's, and they can be found in her essay, "Thinking Sex: Notes for a Radical Theory of the Politics of Sexuality." Which of these works, in your view, are about "thinking sex"? Which address the "politics of sexuality"?

Titian's reclining nude (Fig. 15–15) was commissioned by the Duke of Urbino for his private quarters. There is no doubt that in the sixteenth century there was a considerable market for erotic paintings. Indeed, one point of view maintains that many of the "great nudes" of western art were, in essence, created for the same purpose as the "pin-up." Yet there is also no doubt that this particular reclining nude has had an undisputed place in the canon of "great art." And this much, at least, has been reaffirmed by the reinterpretations and revisions the work has inspired into the twentieth century. One of the first artists to use Titian's *Venus* as a point of departure for his own masterpiece was Edouard Manet. In his *Olympia* (Fig. 15–16), Manet intentionally mimicked the Renaissance composition as a way of challenging the notion that modern art lacked credibility when brought face-to-face with the "Old Masters." In effect, Manet seemed to be saying, "You want a Venus? I'll give you a Venus." And just where do you find a "Venus" in nineteenth-century Paris? In the bordellos of the Parisian demimonde. What do these paintings have in common? Where do they depart? What details does Titian use to create an air of innocence and vulnerability? What details does Manet use to do just the opposite?

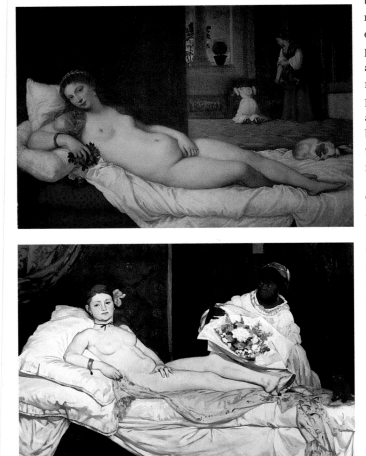

15–15 TITIAN
VENUS OF URBINO (1538). OIL ON CANVAS. 47 × 65".
UFFIZI GALLERY, FLORENCE.

15–16 EDOUARD MANET
OLYMPIA (1863). OIL ON CANVAS. 51⅜ × 74¾".
LOUVRE MUSEUM, PARIS.

Paul Gauguin, the nineteenth-century French painter who moved to Tahiti, was also inspired by the tradition of the western reclining nude in the creation of *Te Ari Vahine* or *The King's Wife* (Fig. 15–17). The artist certainly knew Manet's revision of the work; in fact,

he had a photograph of *Olympia* tacked on the wall of his hut. How does this Tahitian "Venus" fit into the mix? All three of these works have a sense of self-display. In which do the women solicit our gaze? Refuse our gaze? How do the stylistic differences influence our interpretation of the women and our relationship to them? How is the flesh modeled in each work? What overall effect is provided by the different palettes? And the $64,000 question: Are these paintings intended for the "male gaze," "the female gaze," or both?

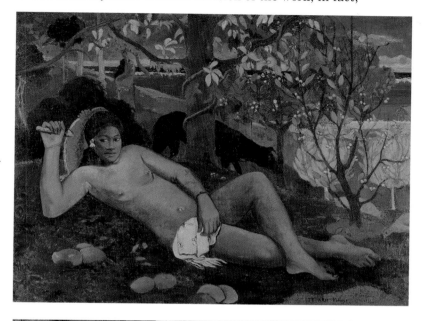

Suzanne Valadon would probably say that such an image is not one that appeals equally to men and women. More to the point, Valadon would argue that the painting of such subjects is not at all of interest to women artists. Perhaps this belief was the incentive behind her own revision of the reclining nude: *The Blue Room* (Fig. 15–18). With this work she seems to be informing the world that when women relax, they really *don't* look like the "Venuses" of Titian, or Manet, or Gauguin. Instead, they get into their loose-fitting clothes, curl up with a good book, and sometimes treat themselves to a bit of tobacco.

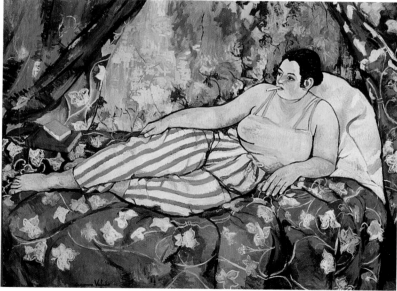

15–17 PAUL GAUGUIN
Te Ari Vahine (The King's Wife) (1896). Oil on canvas.
97 × 130 cm.
Pushkin Museum, Moscow.

15–18 SUZANNE VALADON
The Blue Room (1923). Oil on canvas. 35½ × 45⅝″.
Musée National d'Art Moderne, Paris. © 1998 Artists Rights Society (ARS), N.Y./ADAGP, Paris.

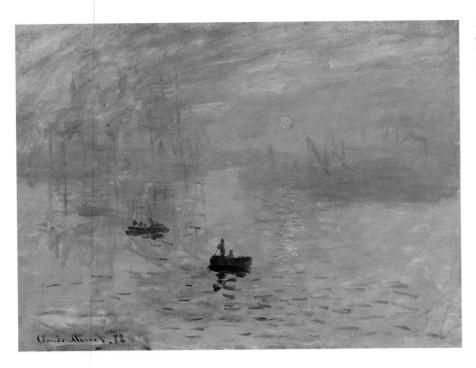

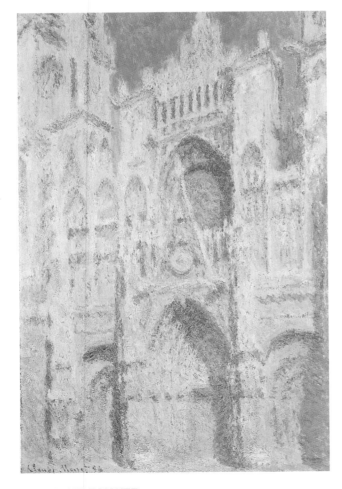

15–20 CLAUDE MONET
ROUEN CATHEDRAL (1894). OIL ON CANVAS. 39¼ × 25⅞".
THE METROPOLITAN MUSEUM OF ART, N.Y. THEODORE M. DAVIS COLLECTION, 1915 (30.95.250).

IMPRESSIONISM

While Bonheur won quick acceptance by The Academy, a group of younger artists were banding together against the French art establishment. Suffering from lack of recognition and vicious criticism, many of them lived in abject poverty for lack of commissions. Yet they stand today as some of the most significant and certainly among the most popular artists in the history of art. They were called the *Impressionists*. The very name of their movement was coined by a hostile critic and intended to malign their work. The word "impressionism" suggests a lack of realism, and realistic representation was the standard of the day.

The Impressionist artists had common philosophies about painting, although their styles differed widely. They all reacted against the constraints of the Academic style and subject matter. They advocated painting out-of-doors and chose to render subjects found in nature. They studied the dramatic effects of atmosphere and light on people and objects and, through a varied palette, attempted to duplicate these effects on canvas.

Through intensive investigation, they arrived at awareness of certain visual phenomena. When bathed in sunlight, objects are optically reduced to facets of pure color. The actual color—or local color—of these objects is altered by different lighting effects. Solids tend to dissolve into color fields. Shadows are not black or gray but a combination of colors.

15–21 PIERRE-AUGUSTE RENOIR
LE MOULIN DE LA GALETTE
(1876). OIL ON CANVAS.
51½ × 69″.
LOUVRE MUSEUM, PARIS.

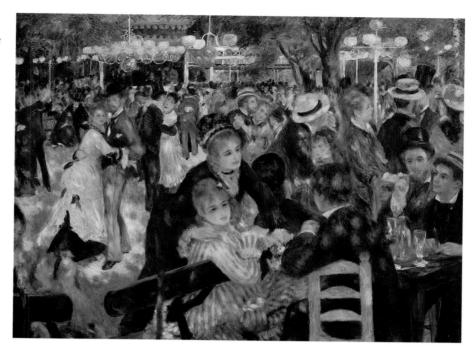

Technical discoveries accompanied these revelations. The Impressionists duplicated the glimmering effect of light bouncing off the surface of an object by applying their pigments in short, choppy strokes. They juxtaposed complementary colors such as red and green to reproduce the optical vibrations perceived when one is looking at an object in full sunlight. Toward this end they also juxtaposed primary colors such as red and yellow to produce, in the eye of the spectator, the secondary color orange. We shall discuss the work of the Impressionists Claude Monet, Pierre Auguste Renoir, Berthe Morisot, and Edgar Degas.

CLAUDE MONET   The most fervent follower of Impressionist techniques was the painter Claude Monet (1840–1926). His canvas *Sunrise* (Fig. 15–19) inspired the epithet "impressionist" when it was exhibited at the first Impressionist exhibition in 1874. Fishing vessels sail from the port of Le Havre toward the morning sun, which rises in a foggy sky to cast its copper beams on the choppy, pale blue water. The warm blanket of the atmosphere envelops the figures, their significance having paled in the wake of nature's beauty.

The dissolution of surfaces and the separation of light into its spectral components remain central to Monet's art. They are dramatically evident in a series of canvases depicting *Rouen Cathedral* (Fig. 15–20) from a variety of angles, during different seasons and times of day. The harsh stone facade of the cathedral dissolves in a bath of sunlight, its finer details obscured by the bevy of brushstrokes crowding the surface. Dark shadows have been transformed into patches of bright blue and splashes of yellow and red. With these delicate touches, Monet has recorded for us the feeling of a single moment in time. He offers us his impressions as eyewitness to a set of circumstances that will never be duplicated.

PIERRE-AUGUSTE RENOIR   Most Impressionists counted among their subject matter landscape scenes or members of the middle class enjoying leisure-time activities. Of all the Impressionists, however, Pierre-Auguste Renoir (1841–1919) was perhaps the most significant figure painter. Like his peers, Renoir was interested primarily in the effect of light as it played across the surface of objects. He illustrated his preoccupation in one of the most wonderful paintings of the Impressionist period, *Le Moulin de la Galette* (Fig. 15–21). With characteristic feathery strokes, Renoir communicated all of the charm and gaiety of an afternoon dance. Men and women caress and converse in frocks that are dappled with sunlight filtering through the trees. All of the spirit of the event is as fresh as if it were yesterday. From the billowing skirts and ruffled dresses to the rakish derbies, top hats, and skimmers, Renoir painted all the details that imprint such a scene on the mind forever.

BERTHE MORISOT   Like a number of other Impressionists, Berthe Morisot (1841–1895) exhibited at the salon early in her career, but she surrendered the safe path as an expression of her allegiance to the new. Morisot was a granddaughter of the eighteenth-century painter

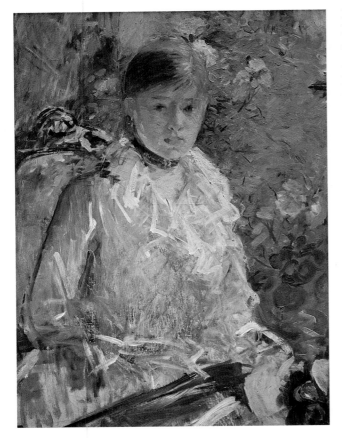

EDGAR DEGAS   We can see the vastness of the aegis of Impressionism when we look at the work of Edgar Degas (1834–1917), whose approach to painting differed considerably from that of his peers. Degas, like Morisot, had exhibited at the salon for many years before joining the movement. He was a superb draftsman who studied under Ingres. While in Italy, he copied the Renaissance masters. He was also intrigued by Japanese prints and the new art of photography.

The Impressionists, beginning with Manet, were strongly influenced by Japanese woodcuts, which were becoming readily available in Europe, and oriental motifs appeared widely in their canvases. They also adopted certain techniques of spatial organization found in Japanese prints, including the use of line to direct the viewer's eye to different sections of the work and to divide areas of the essentially flattened space (see Chapter 18). They found that the patterning and flat forms of oriental woodcuts complemented similar concerns in their own painting. Throughout the Impressionist period and even more so in the Postimpressionist period, the influence of Japanese artists remained strong.

Degas was also greatly influenced by the developing art of photography, and the camera's exclusive visual field served as a model for the way in which he framed his own paintings. *Ballet Rehearsal (Adagio)* (Fig. 15–23) contains elements of both photographs and Japanese prints. Degas draws us into the composition with an unusual and vast off-center space that curves around from the viewer's space to the background of the canvas. The diagonals of the floorboards carry our eyes briskly from outside the canvas to the points at which the groups of dancers congregate. The imagery is placed at eye level so that we feel we are part of the scene. This feeling is enhanced by the fact that our "seats" at the rehearsal are less than adequate; a spiral staircase to the left blocks our view of the ballerinas. In characteristic camera fashion, the borders of the canvas slice off the forms and figures in a seemingly arbitrary manner.

Although it appears as if Degas has failed to frame his subject correctly or has accidentally cut off the more important parts of the scene, he carefully planned the placement of his imagery. These techniques are what render his assymmetrical compositions so dynamic and, in the spirit of Impressionism, so immediate.

Jean-Honoré Fragonard (see Chapter 14) and the sister-in-law of Edouard Manet. Manet painted her quite often. In fact, Morisot is the seated figure in his *The Balcony.*

In Morisot's *Young Girl by the Window* (Fig. 15–22), surfaces dissolve into an array of loose brushstrokes, applied, it would seem, at a frantic pace. The vigor of these strokes contrasts markedly with the tranquility of the woman's face. The head is strongly modeled, and a number of structural lines, such as the back of the chair, the contour of her right arm, the blue parasol astride her lap, and the vertical edge of drapery to the right, anchor the figure in space. Yet in this as in most of Morisot's works, we are most impressed by her ingenious ability to suggest complete forms through a few well-placed strokes of pigment.

THE FIRST BALLET THAT COMBINED DANCE WITH MUSIC, STAGE
DECORATION, AND SPECIAL EFFECTS WAS PERFORMED IN FRANCE
AT THE COURT OF CATHERINE DE' MEDICI IN 1581.

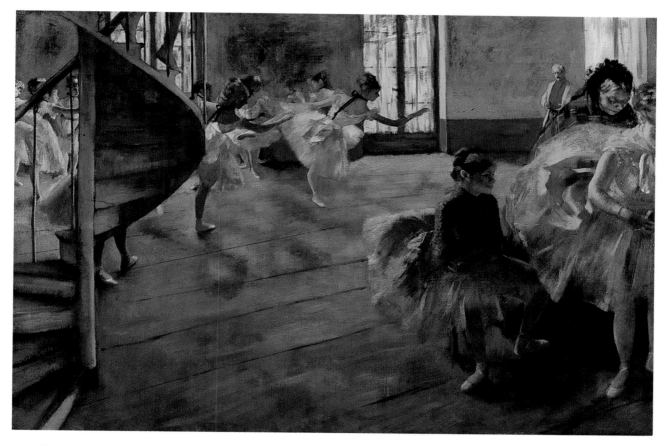

15–23 EDGAR DEGAS
THE REHEARSAL (ADAGIO) (C. 1874). OIL ON CANVAS. 26 × 39⅜".
GLASGOW MUSEUMS: THE BURRELL COLLECTION, GLASGOW 35/246.

POSTIMPRESSIONISM

The Impressionists were united in their rejection of
many of the styles and subjects of the art that preceded
them. These included Academic painting, the emotionalism of Romanticism, and even the depressing subject
matter of some of the Realist artists. During the latter
years of the nineteenth century, a group of artists that
came to be called **Postimpressionists** were also united
in their rebellion against that which came before
them—in this case, Impressionism. The Postimpressionists were drawn together by their rebellion against
what they considered an excessive concern for fleeting
impressions and a disregard for traditional compositional elements.

Although they were united in their rejection of Impressionism, their individual styles differed considerably. Postimpressionists fell into two groups that in
some ways parallel the stylistic polarities of the
Baroque period as well as the Neoclassical-Romantic period. On the one hand, the work of Georges Seurat and
Paul Cézanne had at its core a more systematic approach to compositional structure, brushwork, and
color. On the other hand, the lavishly brushed canvases
of Vincent van Gogh and Paul Gauguin coordinated line
and color with **symbolism** and emotion.

15–24 GEORGES SEURAT
A Sunday Afternoon on the Island of La Grande Jatte (1884–86).
OIL ON CANVAS. 81 × 120⅜".

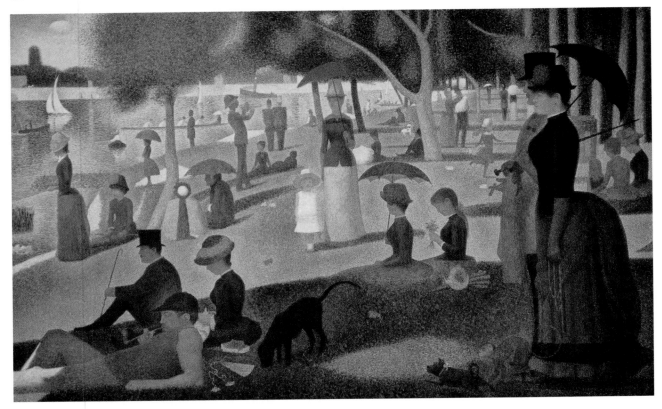

GEORGES SEURAT   At first glance, the paintings by Georges Seurat (1859–1891), such as *A Sunday Afternoon on the Island of La Grande Jatte* (Fig. 15–24), have the feeling of Impressionism "tidied up." The small brushstrokes are there, as are the juxtapositions of complementary colors. The subject matter is entirely acceptable within the framework of Impressionism. However, the spontaneity of direct painting found in Impressionism is relinquished in favor of a more tightly controlled, "scientific" approach to painting.

Seurat's technique has also been called **Pointillism,** after his application of pigment in small dabs, or points, of pure color. Upon close inspection, the painting appears to be a collection of dots of vibrant hues— complementary colors abutting one another, primary colors placed side by side. These hues intensify or blend to form yet another color in the eye of the viewer who beholds the canvas from a distance.

Seurat's meticulous color application was derived from the color theories and studies of color contrasts by the scientists Hermann von Helmholtz and Michel-Eugène Chevreul. He used these theories to restore a more intellectual approach to painting that countered nearly two decades of works that focused wholly on optical effects.

PAUL CÉZANNE   From the time of Manet, there was a movement away from a realistic representation of subjects toward one that was abstracted. Early methods of abstraction assumed different forms. Manet used a flatly painted form, Monet a disintegrating light, and Seurat a tightly painted and highly patterned composition. Paul Cézanne (1839–1906), a Postimpressionist who shared with Seurat an intellectual approach to painting, is credited with having led the revolution of abstraction in modern art from those first steps.

Cézanne's method for accomplishing this radical departure from tradition did not disregard the Old Masters. Although he allied himself originally with the Impressionists and accepted their palette and subject matter, he drew from Old Masters in the Louvre and desired somehow to reconcile their lessons with the thrust of modernism, saying, "I want to make of Impressionism something solid and lasting like the art in the museums." Cézanne's innovations include a structural use of color and brushwork that appeals to the intellect, and a solidity of composition enhanced by a fluid application of pigment that delights the senses.

Cézanne's most significant stride toward modernism, however, was a drastic collapsing of space, seen in works such as *Boy in a Red Vest* (Fig. 15–25). Here a boy stands in the shallow space between the picture plane and a background drape. The shape, color, and brushwork of his left shirtsleeve echo the folds of drapery along side of it, while in the lower left, the fabric of the boy's trousers blends imperceptibly with the surrounding elements. In the latter section, figure and ground virtually become one, canceling pictorial depth.

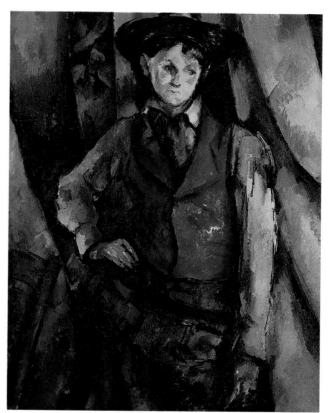

Flatness is achieved similarly in *Still Life with Basket of Apples* (Fig. 15–26). All of the imagery is forced to the picture plane; the tabletop is tilted toward us, and we simultaneously view the basket, plate, and wine bottle from front and top angles. Cézanne did not paint the still-life arrangement from one vantage point either. He moved around his subject, painting not only the objects but the relationships among them. He focused not only on solids, but on the void spaces between two objects as well. If you run your finger along the tabletop in the background of the painting, you will see that it is not possible to trace a continuous line. This discontinuity follows from Cézanne's movement around his subject. In spite of this spatial inconsistency, the overall feeling of the composition is one of completeness.

Cézanne's painting technique is also innovative. The lusciously rumpled fabric and lusciously round fruits are constructed of small patches of pigment crowded within dark outlines. The apples look as if they would roll off the table were it not for the supportive facets of the tablecloth.

Cézanne can be seen as advancing the flatness of planar recession begun by David over a century earlier. Cézanne asserted the flatness of the two-dimensional canvas by eliminating the distinction between foreground and background, and at times merging the two. This was perhaps the most significant contribution to future modern movements.

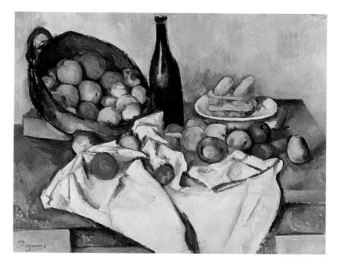

15–26 PAUL CÉZANNE
STILL LIFE WITH BASKET OF APPLES (C. 1895).
OIL ON CANVAS. 65 × 80 CM.

15–27 VINCENT VAN GOGH
THE STARRY NIGHT (1889).
OIL ON CANVAS. 29 × 36¼".
THE MUSEUM OF MODERN ART, N.Y. ACQUIRED THROUGH THE LILLIE P. BLISS BEQUEST.

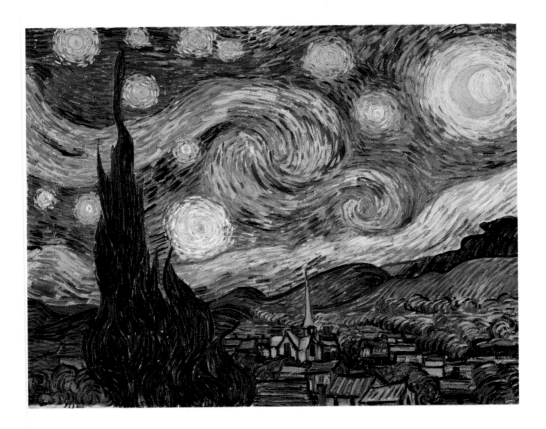

VINCENT VAN GOGH   One of the most tragic and best-known figures in the history of art is the Dutch Post impressionist Vincent van Gogh (1853–1890). We associate him with bizarre and painful acts, such as the mutilation of his ear and his suicide. With these events, as well as his tortured, eccentric painting, he typifies the impression of the mad, artistic talent. Van Gogh also epitomizes the cliché of the artist who achieves recognition only after death: Just one of his paintings was sold during his lifetime.

"Vincent," as he signed his paintings, decided to become an artist only ten years before his death. His most beloved canvases were created during his last 29 months. He began his career painting in the dark manner of the Dutch Baroque, only to adopt the Impressionist palette and brushstroke after he settled in Paris with his brother, Theo. Feeling that he was a constant burden on his brother, he left Paris for Arles, where he began to paint his most significant Postimpressionist works. Both his life and his compositions from this

period were tortured, as Vincent suffered from what may have been bouts of epilepsy and mental illness. He was eventually hospitalized in an asylum at Saint-Rémy, where he painted the famous *Starry Night* (Fig. 15–27).

In *Starry Night* an ordinary painted record of a sleepy valley town is transformed into a cosmic display of swirling fireballs that assault the night sky and command the hills and cypresses to undulate to their sweeping rhythms. Vincent's palette is laden with vibrant yellows, blues, and greens. His brushstroke is at once restrained and dynamic. His characteristic long, thin strokes define the forms but also create the emotionalism in the work. He presents his subject not as we see it but as he would like us to experience it. His is a feverish application of paint, an ecstatic kind of drawing, reflecting at the same time his joys, hopes, anxieties, and despair. Vincent wrote in a letter to his brother, Theo, "I paint as a means to make life bearable. . . . Really we can speak only through our paintings."

Two days before Christmas in the year 1888, the 35-year-old Vincent van Gogh cut off the lower half of his left ear (see Fig. 15–28). He took the ear to a brothel, asked for a prostitute by the name of Rachel, and handed it to her. "Keep this object carefully," he said.

How do we account for this extraordinary event? Over the years, many explanations have been advanced. Many of them are psychoanalytic in nature.[1] That is, they argue that van Gogh fell prey to unconscious primitive impulses.

As you consider the following suggestions, keep in mind that van Gogh's bizarre act occurred many years ago, and that we have no way today to determine which, if any, of them is accurate. Perhaps one of them cuts to the core of van Gogh's urgent needs; perhaps several of them contain a kernel of truth. But it could also be that all of them fly far from the mark. In any event, here are a number of explanations suggested in the *Journal of Personality and Social Psychology*:[2]

1. Van Gogh was frustrated by his brother's engagement and his failure to establish a close relationship with Gauguin. The aggressive impulses stemming from the frustrations were turned inward and expressed in self-mutilation.

2. Van Gogh was punishing himself for experiencing homosexual impulses toward Gauguin.

3. Van Gogh identified with his father, toward whom he felt resentment and hatred, and the cutting off of his own ear was a symbolic punishment of his father.

4. Van Gogh was influenced by the practice of awarding the bull's ear to the matador after a bullfight. In effect, he was presenting such an "award" to the lady of his choice.

5. Van Gogh was influenced by newspaper accounts of Jack the Ripper, who mutilated prostitutes. Van Gogh was imitating the "ripper," but his self-hatred led him to mutilate himself rather than others.

6. Van Gogh was seeking his brother's attention.

7. Van Gogh was seeking to earn the sympathy of substitute parents. (The mother figure would have been a model he had recently painted rocking a cradle.)

8. Van Gogh was expressing his sympathy for prostitutes, with whom he identified as social outcasts.

9. Van Gogh was symbolically emasculating himself so that his mother would not perceive him as an unlikeable "rough" boy. (Unconsciously, the prostitute was a substitute for his mother.)

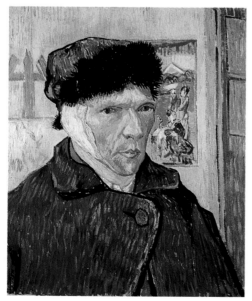

10. Van Gogh was troubled by auditory hallucinations (hearing things that were not there) as a result of his mental state. He cut off his ear to put an end to disturbing sounds.

11. In his troubled mental state, Van Gogh may have been acting out a biblical scene he had been trying to paint. According to the New Testament, Simon Peter cut off the ear of the servant Malchus to protect Christ.

12. Van Gogh was acting out the crucifixion of Jesus, with himself as victim.

[1]William McKinley Runyan, *Journal of Personality and Social Psychology*, June, 1981.

[2]Ibid.

15–28 VINCENT VAN GOGH
SELF-PORTRAIT WITH BANDAGED EAR (1889–90).
OIL ON CANVAS. 23⅝ × 9¼".
COURTAULD INSTITUTE GALLERIES, LONDON.

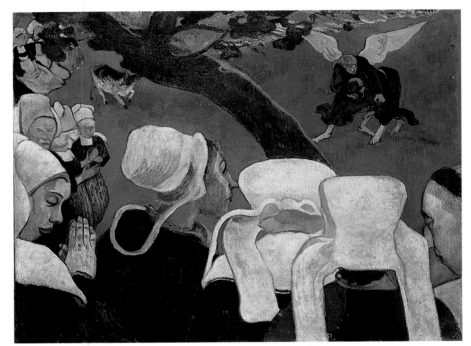

PAUL GAUGUIN Paul Gauguin (1848–1903) shared with van Gogh the desire to express his emotions on canvas. But whereas the Dutchman's brushstroke was the primary means to that end, Gauguin relied on broad areas of intense color to transpose his innermost feelings to canvas.

Gauguin, a stockbroker by profession, began his artistic career as a weekend painter. It was not until the age of 35 that he devoted himself full time to his art, leaving his wife and five children to do so. Gauguin identified early with the Impressionists, adopting their techniques and participating in their exhibitions. But Gauguin was a restless soul. Soon he decided to leave France for Panama and Martinique, primitive places where he hoped to purge the civilization from his art and life. The years until his death were spent between France and the South Seas, where he finally died of syphilis five years after he attempted to take his own life and failed.

Gauguin developed a theory of art called **Synthetism,** in which he advocated the use of broad areas of unnaturalistic color and primitive or symbolic subject matter. His *Vision After the Sermon (Jacob Wrestling with the Angel)* (Fig. 15–29), one of the first canvases to illustrate his theory, combines reality with symbolism. After hearing a sermon on the subject, a group of Breton women believed they had a vision of Jacob, ancestor of the Hebrews, wrestling with an angel. In a daring composition that cancels pictorial depth by thrusting all elements to the front of the canvas, Gauguin presented all details of the event, actual and symbolic. An animal in the upper left portion of the canvas walks near a tree that interrupts a bright vermillion field with a slashing diagonal. The Bible tells us that it was on the banks of the Jabbok River in Jordan that Jacob had wrestled with an angel. Caught, then, in a moment of religious fervor, the Breton women may have imagined the animal's four legs to have been those of the wrestling couple and the tree trunk might have been visually analogous to the river.

Gauguin's contribution to the development of modern art lay largely in his use of color. Writing on the subject, he said: "How does that tree look to you? Green? All right, then use green, the greenest on your palette. And that shadow, a little bluish? Don't be afraid. Paint it as blue as you can." He intensified the colors he observed in nature to the point where they became unnatural. He exaggerated his lines and patterns until they became abstract. These were the lessons he learned from the primitive surroundings of which he was so fond. They were his legacy to art.

HENRI DE TOULOUSE-LAUTREC Along with van Gogh, Henri de Toulouse-Lautrec (1864–1901), is one of the best-known nineteenth-century European artists—both for his art and for the troubled aspects of his personal life. Born into a noble French family, Toulouse-Lautrec broke his legs during adolescence and they failed to develop correctly. This deformity resulted in alienation

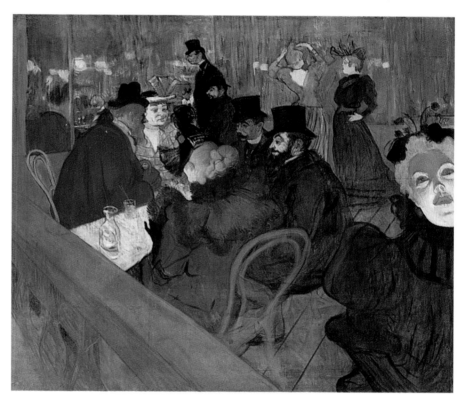

from his family. He turned to painting and took refuge in the demimonde of Paris, at one point taking up residence in a brothel. In this world of social outcasts, Toulouse-Lautrec, the dwarflike scion of a noble family, apparently felt at home.

He used his talents to portray life as it was in this cavalcade of cabarets, theaters, cafes, and bordellos—sort of seamy, but also vibrant and entertaining, and populated by real people. He made numerous posters to advertise cabaret acts (see Fig. 9–39) and numerous paintings of his world of night and artificial light. In *At the Moulin Rouge* (Fig. 15–30), we find something of the Japanese-inspired oblique perspective we found earlier in his poster work. The extension of the picture to include the balustrade on the bottom and the heavily powdered entertainer on the right is reminiscent of those "poorly cropped snapshots" of Degas, who had influenced Toulouse-Lautrec. The fabric of the entertainer's dress is constructed of fluid Impressionistic brushstrokes, as are the contents of the bottles, the lamps in the background, and the amorphous overall backdrop—lost suddenly in the unlit recesses of the Moulin Rouge. But the strong outlining, as in the entertainer's face, marks the work of a Postimpressionist. The artist's palette is limited and muted, except for a few accents as found in the hair of the woman in the center of the composition and the bright mouth of the entertainer. The entertainer's face is harshly sculpted by artificial light from beneath, rendering the shadows a grotesque but not ugly green. The green and red mouth clash, of course, since green and red are complementary colors, giving further intensity to the entertainer's masklike visage. But despite her powdered harshness, the entertainer remains human—certainly as human as her audience. Toulouse-Lautrec was accepting of all his creatures, just as he hoped that they would be accepting of him. The artist is portrayed within this work as well, his bearded profile facing left, toward the upper part of the composition, just left of center—a part of things, but not at the heart of things, certainly out of the glare of the spotlight. There, so to speak, the artist remained for many of his brief 37 years.

EXPRESSIONISM

A polarity existed in Postimpressionism that was like the polarity of the Neoclassical-Romantic period. On the one hand were artists who sought a more scientific or intellectual approach to painting. On the other were artists whose works were more emotional, expressive, and laden with symbolism. The latter trend was exemplified by van Gogh and particularly Gauguin. These artists used color and line to express inner feelings. In their vibrant palettes and bravura brushwork, van Gogh and Gauguin foreshadowed **Expressionism**.

15–31 EDVARD MUNCH
THE SCREAM (1893). CASEIN ON PAPER. 35½ × 28 2/3".
NATIONAL GALLERY, OSLO.

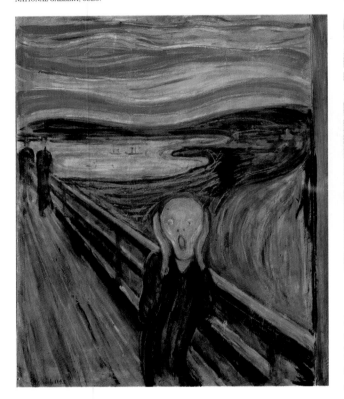

15–32 KÄTHE KOLLWITZ
THE OUTBREAK (1903). PLATE NO. 5 FROM *THE PEASANTS' WAR*.
LIBRARY OF CONGRESS, WASHINGTON, D.C.

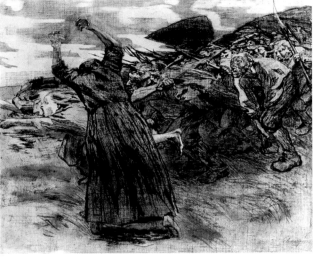

EDVARD MUNCH   The expressionistic painting of Gauguin was adopted by the Norwegian, Edvard Munch (1863–1944), who studied the Frenchman's works in Paris. Munch's early work was Impressionistic, but during the 1890s he abandoned a light palette and lively subject matter in favor of a more somber style that reflected an anguished preoccupation with fear and death.

The Scream (Fig. 15–31) is one of Munch's best-known works. It portrays the pain and isolation that became his central themes. A skeletal figure walks across a bridge toward the viewer, cupping his ears and screaming. Two figures in the background walk in the opposite direction, unaware of or uninterested in the sounds of desperation piercing the atmosphere. Munch transformed the placid landscape into one that echoes in waves the high-pitched tones that emanate from the sunken head. We are reminded of the swirling forms of van Gogh's *Starry Night,* but the intensity and horror pervading Munch's composition speaks of his view of humanity as being consumed by an increasingly dehumanized society.

KÄTHE KOLLWITZ   It is not often in the history of art that we find two artists whose backgrounds are so similar that we can control for just about every variable except for personality when comparing their work. But such is the case with Edvard Munch and Käthe Kollwitz (1867–1945). They were born and died within a few years of one another. They both lived through two World Wars; Kollwitz lost a son in World War I and a grandson in World War II. Both are expressionist artists. Yet their choice of subjects speaks of their idiosyncratic concerns. While Munch looked for symbols of isolation that would underscore his own sense of loneliness, or themes of violence and perverse sexuality that reflected his own psychological problems, Kollwitz sought universal symbols for inhumanity, injustice, and mankind's destruction of itself.

The Outbreak (Fig. 15–32), is one of a series of seven prints by Kollwitz representing the sixteenth-century Peasants' War. In this print, Black Anna, a woman who led the laborers in their struggle against their oppressors, incites an angry throng of peasants to action. Her back is toward us, her head down, as she raises her gnarled hands in inspiration. The peasants rush forward in a torrent, bodies and weapons lunging at Anna's command. Although the work records a specific historical incident, it stands as an inspiration to all those who strive for freedom against the odds. There are few more forceful images in the history of art.

15–33 JAMES ABBOTT MCNEILL WHISTLER
ARRANGEMENT IN BLACK AND GRAY: THE ARTIST'S MOTHER
(1871). OIL ON CANVAS. 57 × 64½ . (©) RMN.
LOUVRE MUSEUM, PARIS.

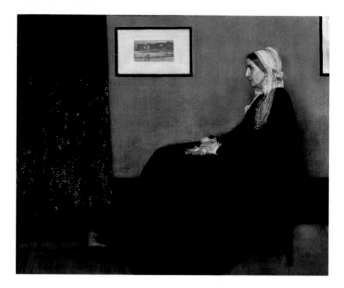

The styles of these early expressionists would be adopted in the twentieth century by younger German artists who shared their view of the world. Many revived the woodcut medium to complement their expressive subjects. This younger generation of artists worked in various styles, but collectively were known as the Expressionists. We shall examine their work in Chapter 16.

AMERICAN EXPATRIATES

Until the twentieth century, art in the United States remained fairly provincial. Striving artists of the eighteenth and nineteenth centuries would go abroad for extended pilgrimages to study the Old Masters and mingle with the avant-garde. In some cases, they emigrated to Europe permanently. These artists, among them Mary Cassatt and James Abbott McNeill Whistler, are called the American Expatriates.

MARY CASSATT   Born in Pittsburgh, Mary Cassatt (1844–1926) spent most of her life in France, where she was part of the inner circle of Impressionists. Her early career was influenced by the artists Manet and Degas, photography, and Japanese prints. Cassatt was a figure painter whose subjects centered on women and children.

A painting such as *The Boating Party* (see the nearby "Compare and Contrast" feature), with its broad areas of color, bold lines, and collapsed space, suggests Cassatt's debt to Japanese prints. These qualities of color, line, and the compressed sense of space, along with the simplified shapes of the boat and sail, construct a solid composition that differs from the atmospheric and transitory images of other Impressionists.

JAMES ABBOTT MCNEILL WHISTLER   In the same year that Monet painted his *Sunrise* and launched the movement of Impressionism, the American artist James Abbott McNeill Whistler (1834–1903) painted one of the best-known compositions in the history of art. Who among us has not seen "Whistler's Mother," whether on posters, billboards, or television commercials? *Arrangement in Black and Gray:*

The Artist's Mother (Fig. 15–33) exhibits a combination of candid realism and abstraction that indicates two strong influences on Whistler's art: Courbet and Japanese prints. Whistler's mother is silhouetted against a quiet backdrop in the right portion of the composition. The strong contours of her black dress are balanced by an oriental drape and a simple rectangular picture on the left. The subject is rendered in a harsh realism reminiscent of northern Renaissance portrait painting. However, the composition is seen first as a logical and pleasing arrangement of shapes in tones of black, gray, and white that work together in pure harmony.

AMERICANS IN AMERICA

While Whistler and Cassatt were working in Europe, several American artists of note remained at home working in the Realist tradition. This realism can be detected in figure painting and landscape painting, both of which were tinted with romanticism.

THOMAS EAKINS   The most important American portrait painter of the nineteenth century was Thomas Eakins (1844–1916). Although his early artistic training took place in the United States, his study in Paris with painters who depicted historical events provided the major influence on his work. The penetrating realism of

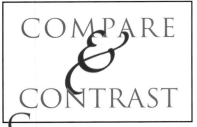

COMPARE & CONTRAST

CASSATT'S *THE BOATING PARTY* WITH MANET'S *BOATING*

Mary Cassatt painted *The Boating Party* (Fig. 15–34) twenty years after Manet's *Boating* (Fig. 15–35) and was probably inspired by the earlier work. Yet, in her version, Cassatt dramatically changes the focus from the male rower to the sensitive portrait of mother and child. How does each artist frame or draw the viewer's attention to the central characters? How would you characterize the women and the men in each of these paintings, their personalities and their relationship to one another? What does each painting seem to be saying about gender-role stereotypes? If you didn't know which of these works was painted by a man and which was painted by a woman, what would you conjecture about the authorship? Why?

15–34 MARY CASSATT
THE BOATING PARTY (1893–94).
OIL ON CANVAS. 35½ × 46⅛″.

© 1994 NATIONAL GALLERY OF ART, WASHINGTON, D.C.
CHESTER DALE COLLECTION.

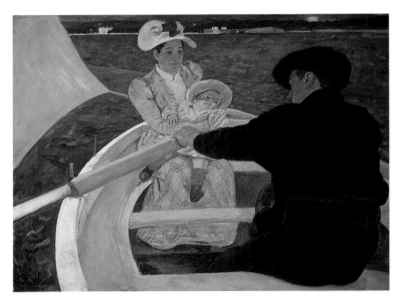

15–35 EDOUARD MANET
BOATING (1874). OIL ON
CANVAS. 38¼ × 51¼″.

METROPOLITAN MUSEUM OF ART, N.Y. BEQUEST
OF MRS. H. O. HAVEMEYER, 1929.
THE H. O. HAVEMEYER COLLECTION (29.100.115).

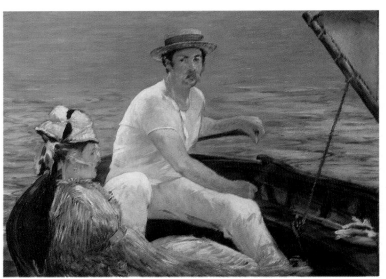

15–36 THOMAS EAKINS
THE GROSS CLINIC (1875). OIL ON CANVAS. 96 × 78″.
JEFFERSON MEDICAL COLLEGE OF THOMAS JEFFERSON UNIVERSITY, PHILADELPHIA.

15–37 THOMAS COLE
THE OXBOW (CONNECTICUT RIVER NEAR NORTHAMPTON)
(1836). OIL ON CANVAS. 51½ × 76″.
THE METROPOLITAN MUSEUM OF ART, N.Y. GIFT OF MRS. RUSSELL SAGE, 1908 (08.228).

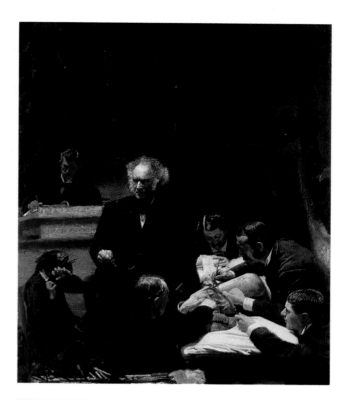

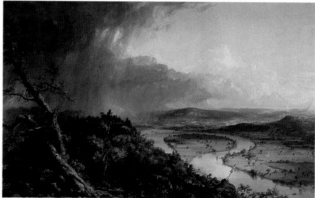

a work such as *The Gross Clinic* (Fig. 15–36) stems from Eakins's endeavors to become fully acquainted with human anatomy by working from live models and dissecting corpses. Eakins's dedication to these practices met with disapproval from his colleagues and ultimately forced his resignation from a teaching post at the Pennsylvania Academy of Art.

The Gross Clinic—no pun intended—depicts the surgeon Dr. Samuel Gross operating on a young boy at the Jefferson Medical College in Philadelphia. Eakins thrusts the brutal imagery to the foreground of the painting, spotlighting the surgical procedure and Dr. Gross's bloody scalpel while casting the observing medical students in the background into darkness. The painting was deemed so shockingly realistic that it was rejected by the jury for an exhibition. Part of the impact of the work lies in the contrast between the matter-of-fact discourse of the surgeon and the torment of the boy's mother. She sits in the lower left corner of the painting, shielding her eyes with whitened knuckles. In brush technique Eakins is close to the fluidity of Courbet, although his compositional arrangement and dramatic lighting are surely indebted to Rembrandt.

Eakins devoted his career to increasingly realistic portraits. Their haunting veracity often disappointed sitters who would have preferred more flattering renditions. The artist's passion for realism led him to use photography extensively, as a point of departure for his paintings as well as an art form in itself. Eakins's style and ideas influenced American artists of the early twentieth century who also worked in a Realist vein.

THOMAS COLE   During the nineteenth century, American artists turned, for the first time, from the tradition of portraiture to landscape painting. Inspired by French landscape painting of the Baroque period, these artists fused this style with a pride in the beauty of their native United States and a romantic vision that was embodied in the writings of James Fenimore Cooper.

One such artist was Thomas Cole (1801–1848). Although Cole was born in England, he emigrated to the United States at the age of 17. Cole was always fond of landscape painting and settled in New York, where there was a ready audience for this genre. Cole became the leader of the **Hudson River School**—a group of

artists whose favorite subjects included the scenery of the Hudson River Valley and the Catskill Mountains in New York State.

The Oxbow (Fig. 15–37) is typical of such paintings. It records a natural oxbow formation in the Connecticut River Valley. Cole combines a vast, sun-drenched space with meticulously detailed foliage and farmland. There is a contrast in moods between the lazy movement of the river, which meanders diagonally into the distance, and the more vigorous diagonal of the gnarled tree trunk in the left foreground. Half of the canvas space is devoted to the sky, whose storm clouds roll back to reveal rays of intense light. These atmospheric effects, coupled with our "crow's-nest" vantage point, magnify the awesome grandeur of nature and force us to contemplate the relative insignificance of humans.

WEAVING
TOGETHER
BIBLICAL AND
PERSONAL
STORIES

In 1859, Harriet Beecher Stowe, renowned author of *Uncle Tom's Cabin*, described the quilting bee:

The day was spent in friendly gossip as they rolled and talked and laughed. . . . One might have learned in that instructive assembly how best to keep moths out of blankets; how to make fritters of Indian corn undistinguishable from oysters; how to bring up babies by hand; how to mend a cracked teapot; how to take grease from a brocade; how to reconcile absolute decrees with free will; how to make five yards of cloth answer the purpose of six; and how to put down the Democratic party.[3]

Many years later, an author on quiltmaking quoted her great-grandmother:

My whole life is in that quilt. It scares me sometimes when I look at it. All my joys and all my sorrows are stitched into those little pieces.[4]

The art of quiltmaking was clearly not only an acceptable vehicle for women's artistic expression but also an arena for consciousness raising on the practical and political problems of the day. Beyond this, the object recorded family history, kept memory alive, and ensured the survival of the matriarch/quilter through that historical record.

Around the turn of the century, African-American quilter Harriet Powers (Fig. 15–38) created her *Bible Quilt*. Its fifteen squares of cotton appliqué weave together stories from the Bible with significant events from the family and community of the artist (Fig. 15–39). For example, reading left to right, the fourth square is a symbolic depiction of Adam and Eve in the Garden of Eden. A serpent tempts Eve beneath God's all-seeing eye and benevolent hand; simple shapes describing the sun, moon, and animals of paradise fill the remaining space. In the sixth square, Jonah is swallowed by a whale. The last square is a stylized depiction of the Crucifixion. Amidst the religious subjects are records of meaningful days. For example, the eleventh square was described by Powers as "Cold Thursday," February 10, 1895. A woman is shown frozen at a gateway while at prayer. Icicles form from the breath of a mule. All bluebirds are killed. The thirteenth square includes an "independent" hog that was said to have run 500 miles from Georgia to Virginia, and the fourteenth square depicts the creation of animals in pairs.

Unity in the quilt is created by a subtle palette of complementary hues, and by simple, cut-out shapes that define celestial orbs, biblical and familial characters, and biblical and local animals. The quilt has an arresting combination of widely known themes—as found in the readily decipherable frames that depict Adam and Eve, Jonah, Noah's Ark, and the Crucifixion—and of private events known to the artist and her family. The juxtaposition establishes an equivalence between biblical and personal stories. The work personalizes the religious events and imbues the personal and provincial events with universal meaning.

Because of the hardness of the times, the artist sold the quilt for $5.[5]

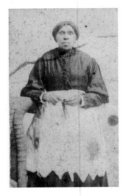

15–38 *HARRIET POWERS*
PHOTOGRAPH.
3.2 × 5.5 CM.
COURTESY MUSEUM OF FINE ARTS, BOSTON, MA.

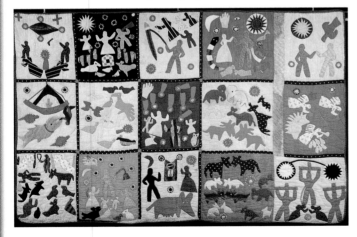

15–39 HARRIET POWERS
THE CREATION OF THE ANIMALS (1895–98). PIECED, APPLIQUÉD, AND PRINTED COTTON EMBROIDERED WITH COTTON AND METALLIC YARN. 69 × 105″.
BEQUEST OF MAXIM KAROLIK, COURTESY, MUSEUM OF FINE ARTS, BOSTON.

[3]Harriet Beecher Stowe, *The Minister's Wooing*, 1859.

[4]Marguerite Ickis, *The Standard Book of Quiltmaking and Collecting* (New York: Dover, 1960).

[5]In Mirra Bank, *Anonymous Was a Woman* (New York: St. Martin's Press, 1979), p. 118.

ART NOUVEAU

In looking at examples of French, Norwegian, and
American art of the nineteenth century, we witnessed a
collection of disparate styles that reflected the artists'
unique situations or personalities. Given the broad
range of circumstances that give rise to a work of art,
it would seem unlikely that a cross-cultural style could
ever evolve. However, at the turn of the century, or
fin de siècle, there arose a style called **Art Nouveau**
whose influence extended from Europe to the United
States. Its idiosyncratic characteristics could be found
in painting and sculpture as well as architecture,
furniture, jewelry, fashion, and glassware.

Art Nouveau is marked by a lyrical linearity, the
use of symbolism, and rich ornamentation. There is an
overriding sense of the organic in all of the arts of this
style, with many of the forms, such as those in Victor
Horta's (1861–1947) staircase (Fig. 15–40), reminiscent
of exotic plant life. Antonio Gaudi's (1852–1926) apartment house in Barcelona, Spain, (Fig. 15–41) shows an
obsessive avoidance of straight lines and flat surfaces.
The material looks as if it had grown in place, or hardened in malleable wood forms, as would cement; in
actuality, it is cut stone. The rhythmic roof is wavelike,
and the chimneys seem dispensed like shaving cream or
soft ice cream. Nor are any two rooms on a floor alike.
This multistory organic hive is clearly the antithesis of
the **steel-cage construction** that was coming into its
own at the same time.

Art Nouveau originated in England. It was part of
an arts and crafts movement that arose in rebellion
against the pretentiousness of nineteenth-century art.
Although it continued into the early years of the twentieth century, the style disappeared with the onset of
World War I. At that time art began to reflect the needs
and fears of humanity faced with self-destruction.

THE BIRTH OF MODERN SCULPTURE

Some of the most notable characteristics of modern
painting include a new found realism of subject and
technique, a more fluid, or impressionistic handling of

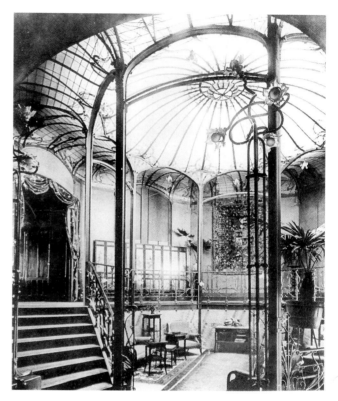

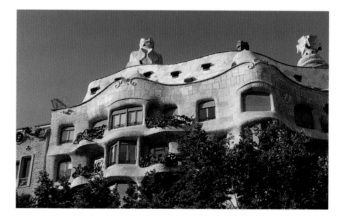

15–41 ANTONIO GAUDI
CASA MILA APARTMENT HOUSE, CATALONIA, SPAIN (1905–1907).

15–42 AUGUSTE RODIN
THE BURGHERS OF CALAIS (1886; CAST 1930S–BEFORE 1947).
BRONZE. 79⅜ × 80⅞ × 77⅛".
HIRSHHORN MUSEUM AND SCULPTURE GARDEN, SMITHSONIAN INSTITUTION, WASHINGTON, D.C. GIFT OF JOSEPH H. HIRSHHORN, 1966.

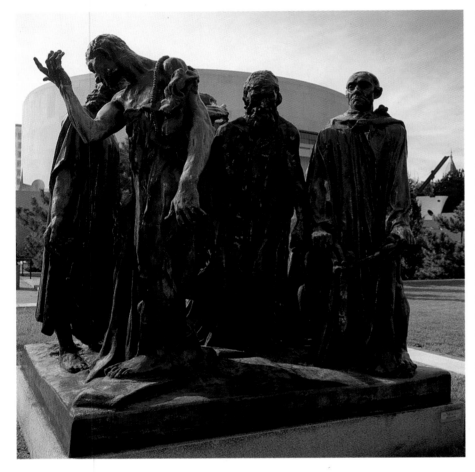

so startlingly intense that he was accused of casting the sculptures from live models (see Fig. 6–17). (It is interesting to note that casting of live models is used in the twentieth century [see Fig. 6–8] without such negative criticism).

Rodin's *The Burghers of Calais* (Fig. 15–42) represents all of the innovations of modernism thrust into three dimensions. The work commemorates an historical event in which six prominent citizens of Calais offered their lives to the conquering English so that their fellow townspeople might be spared. They present themselves in coarse robes with nooses around their necks. Their psychological states range from quiet defiance to frantic desperation. The reality of the scene is achieved in part by the odd placement of the figures. They are not a symmetrical or cohesive group. Rather, they are a scattered collection of individuals, who were meant to be seen at street level. By capturing them as they are, at a particular moment in time, Rodin ensured that spectators would partake of the tragic emotion of the scene for centuries to come.

the medium, and a new treatment of space. Nineteenth-century sculpture, for the most part, continued stylistic traditions that artists saw as complementing the inherent permanence of the medium with which they worked. It would seem that working on a large scale with materials such as marble or bronze was not well suited to the spontaneous technique that captured fleeting impressions.

One nineteenth-century artist, however, changed the course of the history of sculpture by applying to his work the very principles on which modern painting was based, including Realism, Symbolism, and Impressionism—Auguste Rodin.

AUGUSTE RODIN   Auguste Rodin (1840–1917) devoted his life almost solely to the representation of the human figure. His figures were imbued with a realism

Rodin preferred modeling soft materials to carving because they enabled him to achieve highly textured surfaces that caught the play of light, much as in an Impressionist painting. As his career progressed, Rodin's sculptures took on an abstract quality. Distinct features were abandoned in favor of solids and voids that, together with light, constructed the image of a human being. Such works were outrageous in their own day—audacious and quite new. Their abstracted features set the stage for yet newer and more audacious artforms that would rise with the dawn of the twentieth century.

key terms

Planar recession
Linear recession
Neoclassicism
Romanticism
Academic art

Realists
Salon
Salon des Réfusés
Avant-garde
Postimpressionist

Symbolism
Pointillism
Synthetism
Expressionism
Hudson River School

Fin de siècle
Art Nouveau
Steel-cage construction

artists

Jacques-Louis David
Angelica Kauffman
Jean-Auguste-Dominique
   Ingres
Eugène Delacroix
Paul Cézanne
Sylvia Sleigh
Francisco Goya
Adolphe William Bouguereau
Honoré Daumier
Gustave Courbet
Edouard Manet

Marcantonio Raimondi
Titian
Paul Gauguin
Suzanne Valadon
Rosa Bonheur
Claude Monet
Pierre-Auguste Renoir
Berthe Morisot
Edgar Degas
Georges Seurat
Vincent van Gogh
Henri de Toulouse-Lautrec

Edvard Munch
Käthe Kollwitz
Mary Cassatt
James Abbott McNeill Whistler
Thomas Eakins
Thomas Cole
Harriet Powers
Victor Horta
Antonio Gaudi
Auguste Rodin

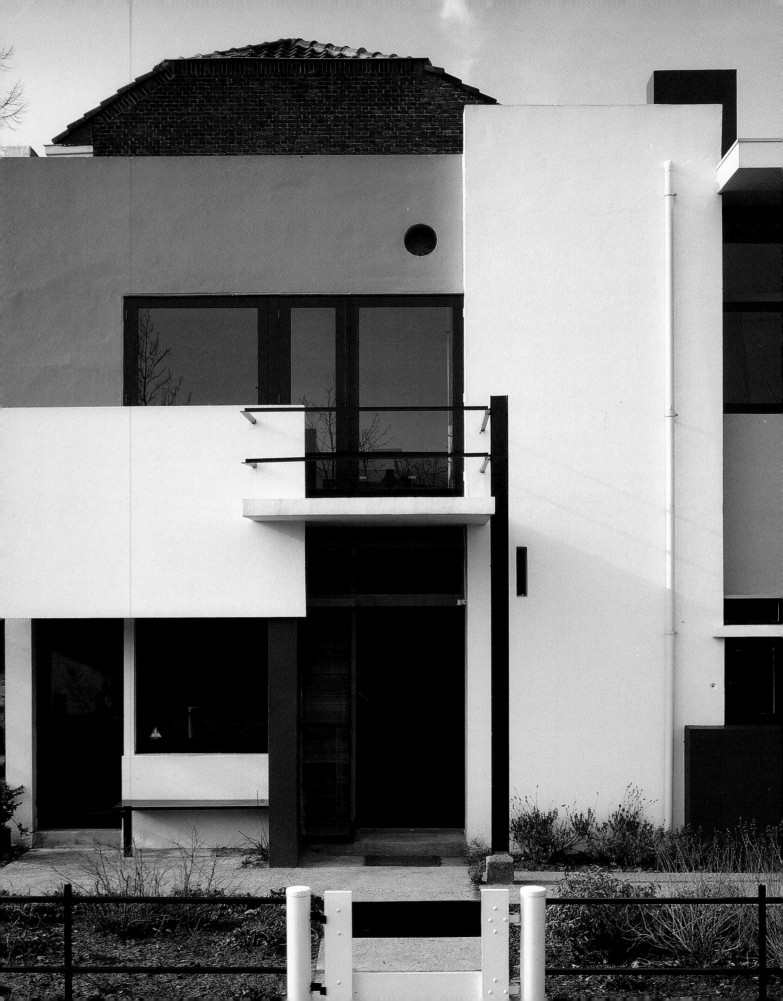

THE TWENTIETH CENTURY: THE EARLY YEARS

PRELIMINARY *Sketch*

- The art world has been in a state of turmoil for the last hundred years.

- The term for one school of modern artists translates from the French as "The Wild Beasts."

- The Fauves saw color as a subject in and of itself, not merely a way of describing nature.

- Matisse believed that painting should be joyous, "something like a good armchair in which to rest."

- Expressionists intentionally distort nature in order to achieve a desired emotional effect.

- Picasso was strongly influenced by African art.

- Picasso and Braque pasted items such as characters cut from newspapers, labels from wine bottles, and even theater tickets onto their canvases.

- One group of twentieth-century artists sought to use art to destroy art.

- Salvador Dalí once tossed open cans of paint at a huge canvas on the Ed Sullivan television show.

Gerrit Rietveldt, *Schroeder House* (detail). See Figure 16–21.

It could be said that the art world has been in a state of perpetual turmoil for the last hundred years. All the important movements that were born during the late nineteenth and early twentieth centuries were met by the hostile, antiseptic gloves of critical disdain. When Courbet's paintings were rejected by the 1855 Salon, he set up his own Pavilion of Realism and pushed the Realist movement on its way. Just eight years later, rejection by the salon jury prompted the origin of the Salon des Réfusés, an exhibition of works including those of Manet. These ornery French artists went on to found the influential Impressionist movement. Their very name—Impressionism—was coined by a hostile critic who degraded their work as mere "impressions"—sort of quick and easy sketches—of the painter's view of the world, rather than the preferred illusionistic realism of Academic painting.

The opening years of the twentieth century saw no letup to these scandalous entrees into the world of modern art. In 1905 the **Salon d'Automne**—an independent exhibition so named to distinguish it from the Academic salons that were traditionally held in the spring—brought together the works of an exuberant group of French avant-garde artists who assaulted the public with a bold palette and distorted forms. One art critic who peeked in on the show saw a Renaissance-type sculpture surrounded by these blasphemous forms. He was sufficiently unnerved by the juxtaposition to exclaim, *"Donatello au milieu des fauves!"* (Donatello among the wild beasts). With what pleasure, then, the artists adopted as their epithet: "The **Fauves**." After all, it was a symbol of recognition.

THE FAUVES

In some respects, the Fauvist movement was a logical successor to the painting of van Gogh and Gauguin. Like these Postimpressionists, the Fauvists also rejected the subdued palette and delicate brushwork of Impressionism. They chose their color and brushwork on the basis of their emotive qualities. Despite the aggressiveness of their method, however, their subject matter centered on traditional nudes, still lifes, and landscapes.

What set the Fauves apart from their nineteenth-century predecessors was their use of harsh, nondescriptive color, bold linear patterning, and a distorted form of perspective. They saw color as autonomous, a subject in and of itself, not merely an adjunct to nature. Their vigorous brushwork and emphatic line grew out of their desire for a direct form of expression, unencumbered by theory. Their skewed perspective and distorted forms were also inspired by the discovery of ethnographic works of art from Africa, Polynesia, and other ancient cultures.

ANDRÉ DERAIN   One of the founders of the Fauvist movement was André Derain (1880–1954). In his *London Bridge* (Fig. 16–1) we find the convergence of elements of nineteenth-century styles and the new vision of Fauvism. The outdoor subject matter is reminiscent of Impressionism (Monet, in fact, painted many renditions of Waterloo Bridge in London), and the distinct zones of unnaturalistic color relate the work to Gauguin. But the forceful contrasts of primary colors and the delineation of forms by blocks of thickly applied pigment speak of something new.

Nineteenth-century artists emphasized natural light and created their shadows from color components. Derain and the Fauvists evoked light in their canvases solely with color contrasts. Fauvists tended to negate shadow altogether. Whereas Gauguin used color areas primarily to express emotion, the Fauvist artists used color to construct forms and space. Although Derain used his bold palette and harsh line to render his emotional response to the scene, his bright blocks of pigment also function as building facades. Derain's oblong patches of color define both stone and water. His thickly laden brushstroke constructs the contour of a boat and the silhouette of a fisherman.

HENRI MATISSE   Along with Derain, Henri Matisse (1869–1954) brought Fauvism to the forefront of critical recognition. Yet Matisse was one of the few major Fauvist artists whose reputation exceeded that of the movement. Matisse started law school at the age of 21, but when an illness interrupted his studies, he began to paint. Soon thereafter he decided to devote himself totally to art. Matisse's early paintings revealed a strong and

16–1 ANDRÉ DERAIN
LONDON BRIDGE (1906). OIL ON CANVAS. 26 × 39".

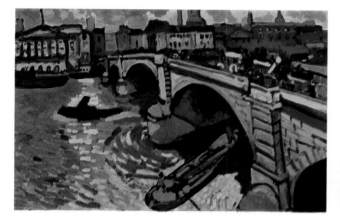

16–2 HENRI MATISSE
RED ROOM (HARMONY IN RED) (1908–9).
OIL ON CANVAS. 69¾ × 85⅞".

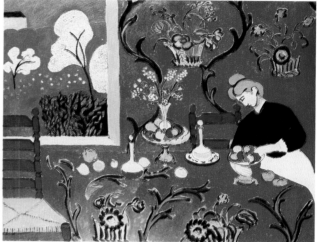

traditional compositional structure, which he gleaned from his first mentor, Adolphe William Bouguereau (see page 381), and from copying Old Masters in the Louvre. His loose brushwork was reminiscent of Impressionism, and his palette was inspired by the color theories of the Postimpressionists. In 1905 he consolidated these influences and painted a number of Fauvist canvases in which, like Derain, he used primary color as a structural element. These canvases were exhibited with those of other Fauvists at the Salon d'Automne of that year.

In his post-Fauvist works, Matisse used color in a variety of other ways—structurally, decoratively, sensually, and expressively. In his *Red Room (Harmony in Red)* (Fig. 16–2), all of these qualities of color are present. The gay mood of the canvas is created by a vibrant palette and curvilinear shapes. The lush red of the wallpaper and tablecloth absorb the viewer in their brilliance. The arabesques of the vines create an enticing surface pattern.

A curious contest between flatness and three dimensions in *Red Room* characterizes much of Matisse's work. He crowds the table and wall with the same patterns. They seem to run together without distinction. This jumbling of patterns propels the background to the picture plane, asserting the flatness of the canvas. The two-dimensionality of the canvas is further underscored by the window in the upper left, which is rendered so flatly that it suggests a painting of a garden scene instead of an actual view of a distant landscape. Yet for all of these attempts to collapse space, Matisse counteracts the effect with a variety of perspective cues:

the seat of the ladderback chair recedes into space, as does the table; and the dishes are somewhat foreshortened, combining frontal and bird's-eye views.

Matisse used line expressively, moving it rhythmically across the canvas to complement the pulsing color. Although the structure of *Red Room* remains assertive, Matisse's foremost concern was to create a pleasing pattern. Matisse insisted that painting ought to be joyous. His choice of palette, his lyrical use of line, and his brightly painted shapes are all means toward that end. He even said of his work that it ought to be devoid of depressing subject matter, that his art ought to be "a mental soother, something like a good armchair in which to rest."[1]

Although the colors and forms of Fauvism burst explosively on the modern art scene, the movement did not last very long. For one thing, the styles of the Fauvist artists were very different from one another, and so the members never formed a cohesive group. After about five years, the "Fauvist qualities" began to disappear from their works as they pursued other styles. Their disappearance was, in part, prompted by a retrospective exhibition of Cézanne's painting held in 1907, which revitalized an interest in this nineteenth-century artist's work. His principles of composition and constructive brush technique were at odds with the Fauvist manifesto.

[1]Robert Goldwater and Marco Treves, eds., *Artists on Art* (New York: Pantheon Books, 1972), p. 413.

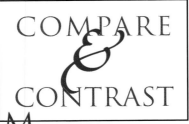

COMPARE & CONTRAST

MATISSE'S
THE GREEN STRIPE
WITH
PICASSO'S
SEATED WOMAN

We have witnessed the stylistic polarity between the intellectual and the emotional numerous times in the history of art. The Hellenistic period of ancient Greece, the Baroque era, the Neoclassical and Romantic periods, and the Postimpressionist period were all rich with artists who preferred one of these modes of expression over the other. Which does Matisse use in *The Green Stripe* (Fig. 16–3)? Which does Picasso use in *Seated Woman* (Fig. 16–4)? How does the palette in each work complement the style employed? How would you describe the figure-ground relationships in each? Who are the artistic ancestors of Matisse and Picasso—Cézanne? Van Gogh? David? Delacroix?

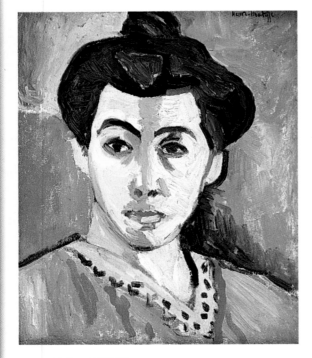

16–3 HENRI MATISSE
THE GREEN STRIPE (MADAME MATISSE) (1905).
OIL AND TEMPERA ON CANVAS. 15⅞ × 12⅞".

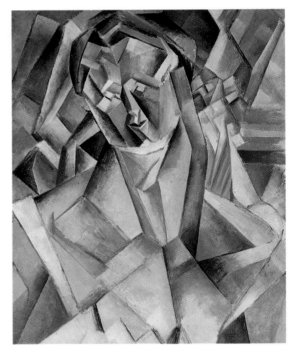

16–4 PABLO PICASSO
SEATED WOMAN (FEMME ASSISE) (1909).
OIL ON CANVAS. 31⅞ × 25⅝".

While Fauvism was descending from its brief colorful flourish in France, related art movements, termed *expressionistic,* were ascending in Germany.

EXPRESSIONISM

Expressionism is the distortion of nature—as opposed to the imitation of nature—in order to achieve a desired emotional effect or representation of inner feelings. According to this definition, we have already seen many examples of this type of painting. The work of van Gogh and Gauguin would be clearly expressionistic, as would the paintings of the Fauves. Even Matisse's *Red Room* distorts nature or reality in favor of a more intimate portrayal of the artist's subject, colored, as it were, by his emotions. Edvard Munch and Käthe Kollwitz were expressionistic artists who used paintings and prints as vehicles to express anxieties, obsessions, and outrage.

Three other movements of the early twentieth century have been termed Expressionistic: Die Brücke, Der Blaue Reiter, and The New Objectivity, or Neue Sachlichkeit. Although very different from one another in the forms they took, these movements were reactions against Impressionism and Realism. They also sought to communicate the inner feelings of the artist.

DIE BRÜCKE (THE BRIDGE)

Die Brücke (**The Bridge**) was founded in Dresden, Germany, at the same time that Fauvism was afoot in France. The artists who began the movement chose the name *Die Brücke* because, in theory, they saw their movement as bridging a number of disparate styles. Die Brücke, like Fauvism, was short-lived because of the lack of cohesion among its proponents. Still, Die Brücke artists showed some common interests in techniques and subject matter that ranged from boldly colored landscapes and cityscapes to horrific and violent portraits. Their emotional upheaval may, in part, have reflected the mayhem of World War I.

EMIL NOLDE   The supreme colorist of the Expressionist movement was Emil Nolde (1867–1956), who joined Die Brücke a year after it was founded. Canvases of his such as *Dance Around the Golden Calf* (Fig. 16–5) are marked by a frenzied brush technique in which clashing

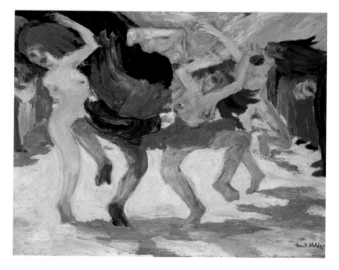

colors are applied in lush strokes. The technique complements the nature of the subject—a biblical theme recounting the worshipping of an idol by the Israelites even as their liberator, Moses, was receiving the Ten Commandments on Mount Sinai. In Nolde's characteristic fashion, both ecstasy and anguish are brought to the same uncontrolled, high pitch.

Nolde was also well known for his graphics. He used the idiosyncratic, splintered characteristics of the woodcut—a medium that had not been in vogue for centuries—to create ravaged, masklike portraits of pain and suffering (see Fig. 5–3).

DER BLAUE REITER (THE BLUE RIDER)

Emotionally charged subject matter, often radically distorted, was the essence of Die Brücke art. **Der Blaue Reiter** (**The Blue Rider**) artists—who took their group name from a painting of that title by Wassily Kandinsky, a major proponent—depended less heavily on content to communicate feelings and evoke an emotional response from the viewer. Their work focused more on the contrasts and combinations of abstract forms and pure colors. In fact, the work of Der Blaue Reiter artists, at times, is completely without subject and can be described as nonobjective, or abstract. Whereas Die Brücke artists always used nature as a point of departure, Der Blaue Reiter art sought to free itself from the shackles of observable reality.

16–6 WASSILY KANDINSKY
SKETCH I FOR COMPOSITION VII (1913).
OIL ON CANVAS. 30¾ × 39⅜″.

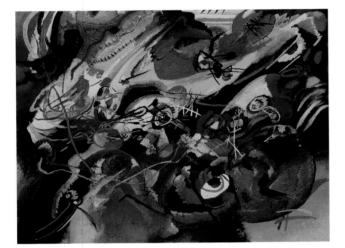

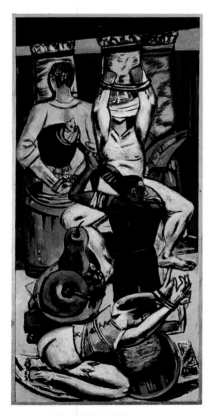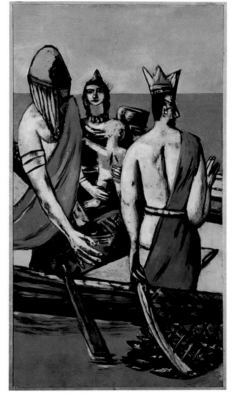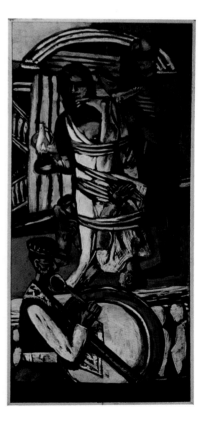

16–7 MAX BECKMANN
DEPARTURE (1932–33). OIL ON CANVAS. TRIPTYCH, CENTER
PANEL 7′¾″ × 3′⅜″, SIDE PANELS EACH 7′¾″ × 3′¼″.

WASSILY KANDINSKY   One of the founders of Der Blaue Reiter was Wassily Kandinsky (1866–1944), a Russian artist who left a career in law to become an influential abstract painter and art theorist. During numerous visits to Paris early in his career, Kandinsky was immersed in the works of Gauguin and the Fauves and was himself inspired to adopt the Fauvist idiom. The French experience opened his eyes to color's powerful capacity to communicate the artist's inmost psychological and spiritual concerns. In his seminal essay, "Concerning the Spiritual in Art," he examined this capability and discussed the psychological effects of color on the viewer. Kandinsky further analyzed the relationship between art and music in this study.

Early experiments with these theories can be seen in works such as *Sketch I for Composition VII* (Fig. 16–6), in which bold colors, lines, and shapes tear dramatically across the canvas in no preconceived fashion. The pictorial elements flow freely and independently throughout the painting, reflecting, Kandinsky believed, the free flow of unconscious thought. *Sketch I for Composition VII* and other works of this series not only underscore the importance of Kandinsky's early Fauvist contacts in their vibrant palette, broad brushstrokes, and dynamic movement; they also stand as harbingers of a new art unencumbered by referential subject matter.

For Kandinsky, color, line, and shape are subjects in themselves. They are often rendered with a spontaneity born of the psychological process of free association. At this time free association was also being explored by the founder of psychoanalysis, Sigmund Freud, as a method of mapping the geography of the unconscious mind.

THE NEW OBJECTIVITY (NEUE SACHLICHKEIT)

As World War I drew to a close and World War II loomed on the horizon, different factions of German Expressionism could be observed. Some artists, like Max Beckmann (1884–1950), calling themselves **Neue Sachlichkeit (The New Objectivity)**, reacted to the horrors and senselessness of wartime suffering with an art that commented bitterly on the bureaucracy and military

with ghastly visions of human torture. In *Departure* (Fig. 16–7), a painting whose subject is exile, two panels depicting such torture flank a central canvas in which a king looks back longingly on his homeland. He stands as a universal symbol for all of those who were forced to flee their native lands with Adolph Hitler's rise to power.

CUBISM

The history of art is colored by the tensions of stylistic polarities within given eras, particularly the polarity of an intellectual versus an emotional approach to painting. Fauvism and German Expressionism found their roots in Romanticism and the emotional expressionistic work of Gauguin and van Gogh. The second major art movement of the twentieth century, **Cubism**, can trace its heritage to Neoclassicism and the analytical and intellectual work of Cézanne.

Cubism is an offspring of Cézanne's geometrization of nature and his abandonment of scientific perspective, his rendering of multiple views, and his emphasis on the two-dimensional canvas surface. Picasso, the driving force behind the birth of Cubism, and perhaps the most significant artist of the twentieth century, combined the pictorial methods of Cézanne with formal elements from native African, Oceanic, and Iberian sculpture.

PABLO PICASSO   Pablo Ruiz y Picasso (1881–1973) was born in Spain, the son of an art teacher. As an adolescent, he enrolled in the Barcelona Academy of Art, where he quickly mastered the illusionistic techniques of the realistic Academic style. By the age of 19, Picasso was off to Paris, where he remained for over forty years—introducing, influencing, or reflecting the many styles of modern French art.

Picasso's first major artistic phase has been called his Blue Period. Spanning the years 1901 to 1904, this work is characterized by an overall blue tonality, a distortion of the human body through elongation reminiscent of El Greco and Toulouse-Lautrec, and melancholy subjects consisting of poor and downtrodden individuals engaged in menial tasks or isolated in their loneliness.

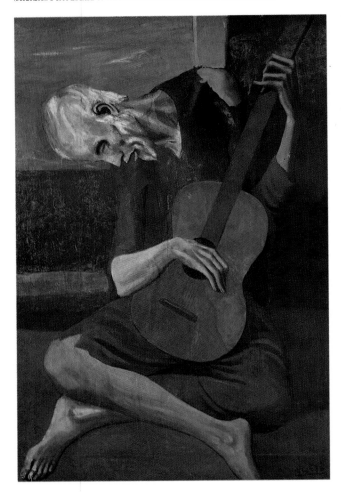

The Old Guitarist (Fig. 16–8) is but one of these haunting images. A contorted white-haired man sits hunched over a guitar, consumed by the tones that emanate from what appears to be his only possession. The eyes are sunken in the skeletal head, and the bones and tendons of his hungry frame are painfully evident. We are struck by the ordinariness of poverty, from the unfurnished room and barren window view (or is he on the curb outside?) to the uneventfulness of his activity and the insignificance of his plight. The monochromatic blue palette creates an unrelenting somber mood. Tones of blue eerily echo the ghostlike features of the guitarist.

Picasso's Blue Period was followed by works that were lighter both in palette and in spirit. Subjects from this so-called Rose Period were drawn primarily from circus life and rendered in tones of pink. During this second period, which dates from 1905 to 1908, Picasso was inspired by two very different art styles. He, like many artists, viewed and was strongly influenced by the Cézanne retrospective exhibition held at the Salon d'Automne in 1907. At about that time, Picasso also became aware of the formal properties of ethnographic art from Africa, Oceania, and Iberia, which he saw regularly at the Musée de l'Homme. These two artforms, which at first glance might appear dissimilar, had in common a fragmentation, distortion, and abstraction of form that were adopted by Picasso in works such as *Les Demoiselles d'Avignon* (Fig. 16–9).

This startling, innovative work, still primarily pink in tone, depicts five women from Barcelona's red-light district. They line up for selection by a possible suitor who stands, as it were, in the position of the spectator. The faces of three of the women are primitive masks. The facial features of the other two have been radically simplified by combining frontal and profile views. The thick-lidded eyes stare stagefront, calling to mind some of the Mesopotamian votive sculptures we saw in Chapter 10.

The bodies of the women are fractured into geometric forms and set before a background of similarly splintered drapery. In treating the background and the foreground imagery in the same manner, Picasso collapses the space between the planes and asserts the two-dimensionality of the canvas surface in the manner of Cézanne. In some radical passages, such as the right leg of the leftmost figure, the limb takes on the qualities of drapery, masking the distinction between figure and ground. The extreme faceting of form, the use of multiple views, and the collapsing of space in *Les Demoiselles* together provided the springboard for **Analytic Cubism,** co-founded with the French painter Georges Braque about 1910.

ANALYTIC CUBISM

The term "Cubism," like so many others, was coined by a hostile critic. In this case the critic was responding to the predominance of geometrical forms in the works of Picasso and Braque. Cubism is a limited term in that it does not adequately describe the appearance of

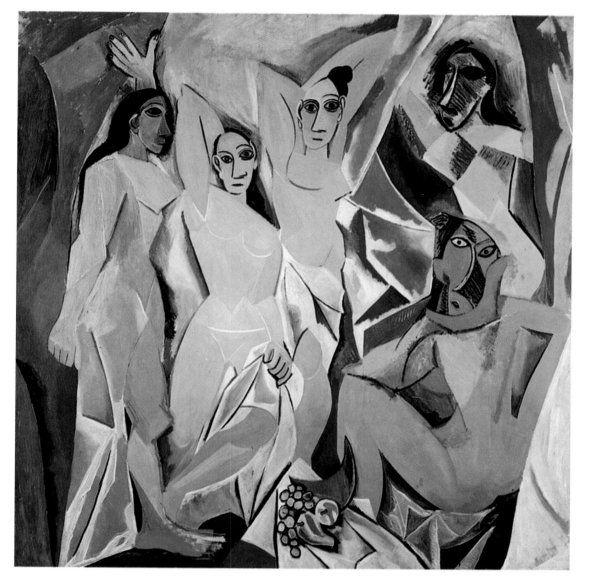

Cubist paintings and it minimizes the intensity with which Cubist artists analyzed their subject matter. It ignores their most significant contribution—a new treatment of pictorial space that hinged upon the rendering of objects from multiple and radically different views.

The Cubist treatment of space differed significantly from that in use since the Renaissance. Instead of presenting an object from a single view, assumed to have been the complete view, the Cubists, like Cézanne,

realized that our visual comprehension of objects consists of many views that we perceive almost at once. They tried to render this visual "information gathering" in their compositions. In their dissection and reconstruction of imagery, they reassessed the notion that painting should reproduce the appearance of reality. Now the very reality of appearances was being questioned. To Cubists, the most basic reality involved consolidating optical vignettes instead of reproducing fixed images with photographic accuracy.

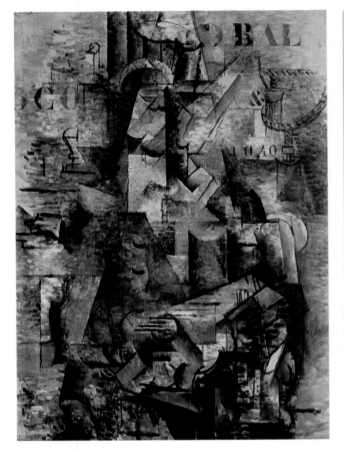

AT THE HEIGHT OF ANALYTICAL CUBISM, MARIE CURIE WON THE NOBEL PRIZE FOR CHEMISTRY AND THE *TITANIC* SANK IN THE NORTH ATLANTIC.

16–10 GEORGES BRAQUE
THE PORTUGUESE (1911). OIL ON CANVAS. 45½ × 31½".

OEFFENTLICHE KUNSTSAMMLUNG, KUNSTMUSEUM, BASEL. © 1998 ARTISTS RIGHTS SOCIETY (ARS) N.Y./ADAGP PARIS.

16–11 PABLO PICASSO
THE BOTTLE OF SUZE (1912–13). PASTED PAPER WITH GOUACHE AND CHARCOAL. 25¾ × 19¾".

WASHINGTON UNIVERSITY GALLERY OF ART, ST. LOUIS. UNIVERSITY PURCHASE, KENDE SALE FUND, 1946. © 1998 ESTATE OF PABLO PICASSO/ARTISTS RIGHTS SOCIETY (ARS), N.Y.

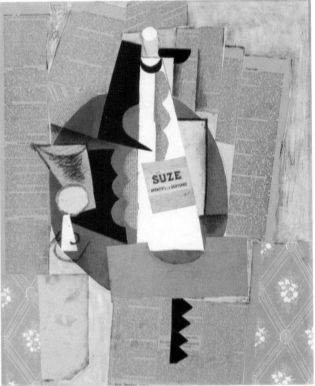

GEORGES BRAQUE   During the analytic phase of Cubism, which spanned the years from 1909 to 1912, the works of Picasso and Braque were very similar. The early work of Georges Braque (1882–1963) graduated from Impressionism to Fauvism to more structural compositions based on Cézanne. He met Picasso in 1907, and from then until about 1914 the artists worked together toward the same artistic goals.

The theory of Analytic Cubism reached the peak of its expression in 1911 in works such as Braque's *The Portuguese* (Fig. 16–10). Numerous planes intersect and congregate at the center of the canvas to form a barely perceptible triangular human figure, which is alternately constructed from and dissolved into the background. There are only a few concrete signs of its substance: dropped eyelids, a moustache, the circular opening of a stringed instrument. The multifaceted abstracted form appears to shift position before our eyes, simulating the time lapse that would occur in the visual assimilation of multiple views. The structural lines—sometimes called the *Cubist grid*—that define and fragment the figure are thick and dark. They contrast with the delicately modeled short, choppy brushstrokes of the remainder of the composition. The monochromatic palette, chosen so as not to interfere with the exploration of form, consists of browns, tans, and ochres.

Although the paintings of Picasso and Braque were almost identical at this time, Braque first began to insert words and numbers and to use **trompe l'oeil** effects in portions of his Analytic Cubist compositions. These realistic elements contrasted sharply with the abstraction of the major figures and reintroduced the nagging question, "What is reality and what is illusion in painting?"

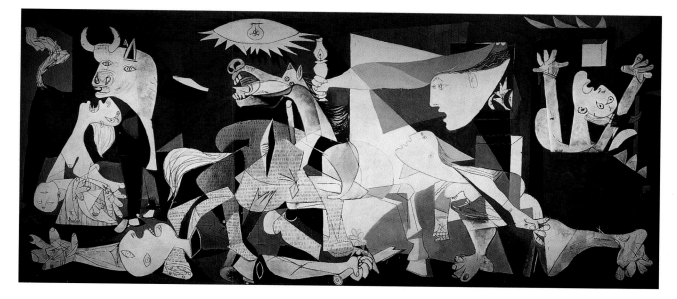

SYNTHETIC CUBISM

Picasso and Braque did not stop with the inclusion of precisely printed words and numbers in their works. They began to add characters cut from newspapers and magazines, other pieces of paper, and found objects such as labels from wine bottles, calling cards, theater tickets—even swatches of wallpaper and bits of rope. These items were pasted directly onto the canvas in a technique Picasso and Braque called *papier collé*— what we know as **collage.** The use of collage marked the beginning of the synthetic phase of Cubism.

Some **Synthetic Cubist** compositions, such as Picasso's *The Bottle of Suze* (Fig. 16–11), are constructed entirely of found elements. In this work, newspaper clippings and opaque pieces of paper function as the shifting planes that hover around the aperitif label and define the bottle and glass. These planes are held together by a sparse linear structure much in the manner of Analytic Cubist works. In contrast to Analytic Cubism, however, the emphasis is on the form of the object and on constructing instead of disintegrating that form. Color reentered the compositions, and much emphasis was placed on texture, design, and movement.

After World War I, Picasso and Braque no longer worked together, and their styles, although often reflective of the Cubist experience they shared, came to differ markedly. Braque, who was severely wounded during the war, went on to create more delicate and lyrical still-life compositions, abandoning the austerity of the early phase of Cubism. While many of Picasso's later works carried forward the Synthetic Cubist idiom, his artistic genius and versatility became evident after 1920 when he began to move in radically different directions. These new works were rendered in Classical, Expressionist, and Surrealist styles.

When civil war gripped Spain, Picasso protested its brutality and inhumanity through highly emotional works such as *Guernica* (Fig. 16–12). This mammoth mural, painted for the Spanish Pavilion of the Paris International Exposition of 1937, broadcast to the world the carnage of the German bombing of civilians in the Basque town of Guernica. The painting captures the event in gruesome details such as the frenzied cry of one woman trapped in rubble and fire and the pale fright of another woman who tries in vain to flee the conflagration. A terrorized horse rears over a dismembered body while an anguished mother embraces her dead child and wails futilely. Innocent lives are shattered into Cubist planes that rush and intersect at myriad angles, distorting and fracturing the imagery. Confining himself to a palette of harsh blacks, grays, and whites, Picasso expressed, in his words, the "brutality and darkness" of the age.

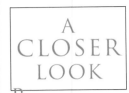

PICASSO'S
GUERNICA
GOES HOME[2]

They called it "Operation Big Picture." Working under tight security, officials at New York's Museum of Modern Art secretly rolled a 26-by-11–foot canvas into a fireproof casing and whisked it off to the hold of a jumbo jet bound for Madrid. There, forty-four years after Picasso painted it, the Spaniards got back *Guernica,* a furious indictment of fascism that evokes a German air raid on the Basque town of Guernica in 1937, during the Spanish Civil War. "This is a moment of great joy, of immense emotion," said Picasso's comrade-at-oils, Joan Miró.

It took Spain five years to convince the New York museum that the Spanish Republic had commissioned the work in 1937. It also had to reassert Picasso's view that he had sent the painting to the United States on loan and that he expected its return to the Prado Museum once democracy returned to Spain. Franco's death in 1975, free elections in 1977, and Spain's new democratic constitution met Picasso's conditions for *Guernica's* return.

The painting hangs in a seventeenth-century annex of the Prado and went on display October 25, 1981, the centenary of Picasso's birth. The Basques would still like to see it moved to Guernica, but it has probably found its home.

16–13 JACQUES LIPCHITZ
STILL LIFE WITH MUSICAL INSTRUMENTS (1918).
STONE RELIEF. 22½ × 28″.

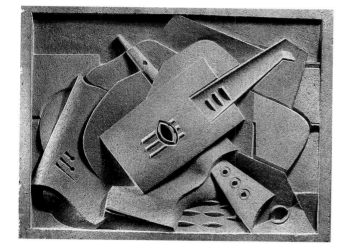

16–14 ALEXANDER ARCHIPENKO
WALKING WOMAN (1912). BRONZE. HEIGHT: 26½″.

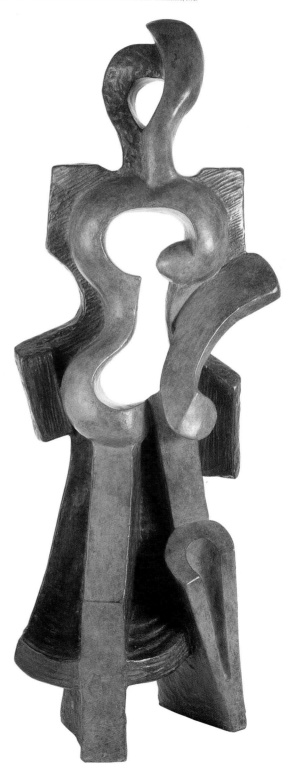

CUBIST SCULPTURE

Cubism was born as a two-dimensional artform. Cubist artists attempted to render on canvas the manifold aspects of their subjects as if they were walking around three-dimensional forms and recording every angle. The attempt was successful, in part, because they recorded these views with intersecting planes that allowed viewers to perceive the many sides of the figure.

Because Cubist artists were trying to communicate all the visual information available about a particular form, they were handicapped, so to speak, by the two-dimensional surface. In some ways the medium of sculpture was more natural to Cubism, because a viewer could actually walk around a figure to assimilate its many facets. The "transparent" planes that provided a sense of intrigue in Analytical Cubist paintings were often translated as flat solids, as in Jacques Lipchitz's (1891–1964) *Still Life with Musical Instruments* (Fig. 16–13).

ALEXANDER ARCHIPENKO   One of the innovations in Cubist sculpture was the three-dimensional interpenetration of cubist planes, as implied in Lipchitz's relief. Another was the use of void space as solid form, as seen in *Walking Woman* (Fig. 16–14) by Alexander Archipenko (1887–1964). True to cubist principles, the figure is fragmented; the contours are broken and dislocated.

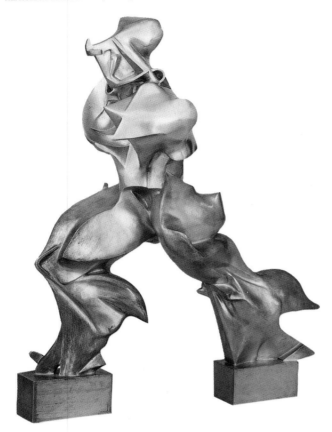

theory, Futurist painting and sculpture were to glorify the life of today, "unceasingly and violently transformed by victorious science." In practice, many of the works owed much to Cubism.

UMBERTO BOCCIONI   An oft-repeated word in Futurist credo is **dynamism**, defined as the theory that force or energy is the basic principle of all phenomena. Umberto Boccioni (1882–1916), a leading Futurist painter and sculptor, said:

> *Everything moves, everything runs, everything turns swiftly. The figure in front of us never is still, but ceaselessly appears and disappears. Owing to the persistence of images on the retina, objects in motion are multiplied, distorted, following one another like waves through space. Thus a galloping horse has not four legs; it has twenty.*[4]

The principle of dynamism is illustrated in *Male Figure in Motion Towards the Left* (see Fig. 3–3). Irregular, agitated lines communicate the energy of movement. The Futurist obsession with illustrating images in perpetual motion also found a perfect outlet in sculpture. In works such as *Unique Forms of Continuity in Space* (Fig. 16–15), Boccioni, whose forte was sculpture, sought to convey the elusive surging energy that blurs an image in motion, leaving but an echo of its passage. Although it retains an overall figural silhouette, the sculpture is devoid of any representational details. The flamelike curving surfaces of the striding figure do not exist to define movement; instead, they are a consequence of it.

But what is new here are the open spaces of the torso and head, now as much a part of the whole as the solid forms of the composition. Although there is a good degree of abstract simplification in the figure, the overall impression of the forms prompts recognition of the humanity of the subject.

FUTURISM

Several years after the advent of Cubism, a new movement sprang up in Italy under the leadership of poet Filippo Marinetti (1876–1944). **Futurism** was introduced angrily by Marinetti in a 1909 manifesto that called for an art of "violence, energy, and boldness" free from the "tyranny of . . . harmony and good taste."[3] In

GIACOMO BALLA   The Futurists also suggested that their subjects were less important than the portrayal of the "dynamic sensation" of the subjects. This declaration manifests itself fully in Giacomo Balla's (1871–1958) pure futurist painting, *Street Light* (Fig. 16–16). The light of the lamp pierces the darkness in reverberating circles; V-shaped brushstrokes simultaneously fan outward from the source and point toward it, creating a sense of constant movement. The palette consists of

---

[3]F. T. Marinetti, "The Foundation and Manifesto of Futurism," in Herschel B. Chipp, ed., *Thieves of Modern Art* (Berkeley, Calif.: University of California Press, 1968), pp. 284–88.

[4]Robert Goldwater and Marco Treves, eds., *Artists on Art* (New York: Pantheon Books, 1972), p. 35.

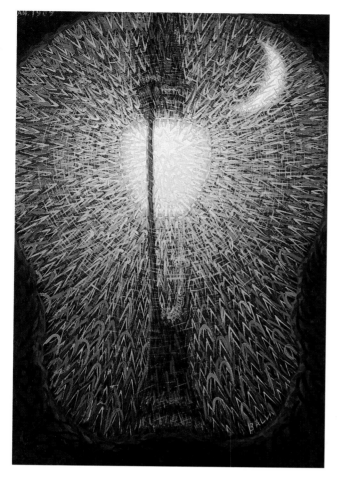

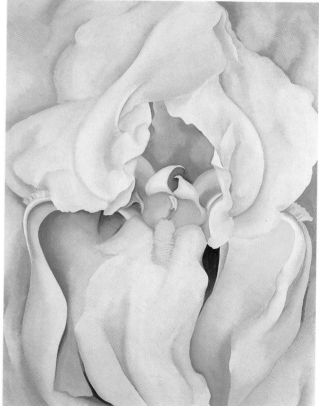

complementary colors that forbid the eye to rest. All is movement; all is sensation.

Cubist and Futurist works of art, regardless of how abstract they might appear, always contain vestiges of representation, whether they be unobtrusive details like an eyelid or a moustache, or an object's recognizable contours. Yet with Cubism, the seeds of abstraction were planted. It was just a matter of time until they would find fruition in artists who, like Kandinsky, would seek pure form unencumbered by referential subject matter.

EARLY TWENTIETH-CENTURY ABSTRACTION IN THE UNITED STATES

The Fauvist and German Expressionist artists had an impact in the United States as well as in Europe. It was the American photographer Alfred Stieglitz who propounded and supported the development of abstract art in the United States by exhibiting this work and calling attention to its originality. Among the artists supported by Stieglitz were Georgia O'Keeffe and John Marin.

GEORGIA O'KEEFFE   Throughout her long career, Georgia O'Keeffe (1887–1986) painted many subjects, from flowers to city buildings to the skulls of animals baked white by the sun of the desert Southwest. In each case she captured the essence of her subjects by simplifying their forms. In 1924, the year O'Keeffe married Stieglitz, she began to paint enlarged flower pictures such as *Light Iris* (Fig. 16–17). In these paintings, she magnified and abstracted the details of her botanical subjects, so that often a large canvas was filled with but a fragment of the intersection of petals. These flowers have a yearning, reaching, organic quality, and her botany seems to function as a metaphor for zoology. That is, her plants are animistic; they seem to grow because of will, not merely because of the blind interactions of the unfolding of the genetic code with water, sun, and minerals. And, although O'Keeffe denied any attempt to portray sexual imagery in these flowers

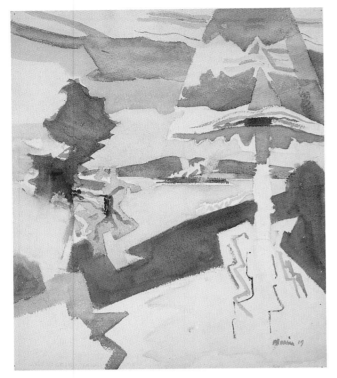

in their ability to render abstractions of the external world. Marin told one biographer that he tried "to give paint a chance to show itself entirely as paint." This love affair with paint also characterizes the Abstract Expressionists of the New York School, as we shall see in the next chapter.

EARLY TWENTIETH-CENTURY ABSTRACTION IN EUROPE

The second decade of the twentieth century witnessed the rise of many dynamic schools of art in Europe. Two of these—**Constructivism** and **De Stijl**—were dedicated to pure abstraction, or **nonobjective art.** Nonobjective art differs from the abstraction of Cubism or Futurism in its total lack of representational elements. It does not use nature or visual reality as a point of departure; it has no subject other than that of the forms, colors, and lines that compose it. In nonobjective art, the earlier experiments in abstracting images by Cézanne and then by the Cubists reached their logical conclusion. Kandinsky is recognized as the first painter of pure abstraction, although several artists were creating nonobjective works at about the same time.

CONSTRUCTIVISM
Whereas nonobjective painting was the logical outgrowth of Analytical Cubism, Cubist collage gave rise to Constructivist sculpture. Born in Russia, Constructivism challenged the traditional sculptural techniques of carving and casting that emphasized mass rather than space.

NAUM GABO   Naum Gabo (1890–1977), a constructivist sculptor, challenged the ascendance of mass over space by creating works in which intersecting planes of metal, glass, plastic, or wood defined space. The nonobjective *Column* (Fig. 16–19) exudes a high-tech feeling. It is somewhat reminiscent of magnetic fields, of things plugged in, of the old vacuum tube. But the subject of the work consists in the constructed forms themselves. The column itself is suggested by intersecting planes that interact with the surrounding space; it does not envelop space, and—true to the Constructivist

(those who saw it, she said, were speaking about themselves and not her), the edges of the petals, in their folds and convolutions, are frequently reminiscent of parts of the female body. The sense of will and reaching renders these petals active rather than passive in their implied sexuality, and so they seem symbolically to express a feminist polemic. This characteristic might be one of the reasons that O'Keeffe was "invited" to Judy Chicago's *Dinner Party* Fig. 1–11).

JOHN MARIN   Like Georgia O'Keeffe, John Marin (1870–1953) showed a fierce individualism in his work. Many of his paintings, however, such as *Deer Island—Marine Fantasy* (Fig. 16–18), show the influences of the fractured planes of Cubism and the distortions and vibrant colors of Expressionism. Because of his tendency to apply swaths of paint to his supports, especially in his later oil paintings, some critics have seen Marin as a forerunner of the post-World War II Abstract Expressionist movement. Certainly Marin was fascinated by the properties of his media in their own right, as well as

16–19 NAUM GABO
COLUMN (C. 1923). PERSPEX, WOOD, METAL, GLASS.
41½ × 29 × 29".
© SOLOMON R. GUGGENHEIM MUSEUM, N.Y. (55.1429)

16–20 PIET MONDRIAN
COMPOSITION WITH RED, BLUE, AND YELLOW (1930).
OIL ON CANVAS. 28½ × 21¼".
COLLECTION MR. AND MRS. ARMAND P. BARTOS, N.Y. MODRIAN ESTATE/HOLTZMAN TRUST.

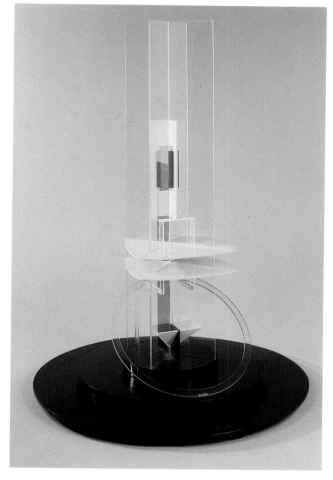

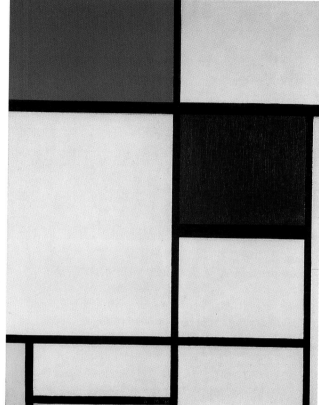

aesthetic—it denies mass and weight. The beauty of *Column* is found in the purity of its elements and in the contrasts between horizontal and vertical elements and translucent and opaque elements.

PIET MONDRIAN Influenced by Vincent van Gogh, fellow Dutch painter Piet Mondrian (1872–1944) began his career as a painter of impressionistic landscapes. In 1910 he went to Paris and was immediately drawn to the geometricism of Cubism. During the war years, when he was back in Holland, his studies of Cubist theory led him to reduce his forms to lines and planes and his palette to the primary colors and black and white. These limitations, Mondrian believed, permitted a more universally comprehensible art.

Mondrian developed his own theories of painting that are readily apparent in works such as *Composition with Red, Blue, and Yellow* (Fig. 16–20):

> *All painting is composed of line and color. Line and color are the essence of painting. Hence they must be freed from their bondage to the imitation of nature and allowed to exist for themselves.*
>
> *Painting occupies a plane surface. The plane surface is integral with the physical and psychological being of the painting. Hence the plane surface must be respected, must be allowed to declare itself, must not be falsified by imitations of volume. Painting must be as flat as the surface it is painted on.[5]*

If Mondrian's views had been a theory of architecture, perhaps they would have found expression in

[5]Robert Goldwater and Marco Treves, eds., *Artists on Art* (New York: Pantheon Books, 1972), p. 426.

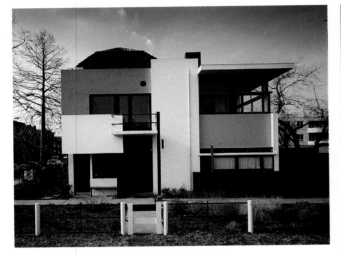

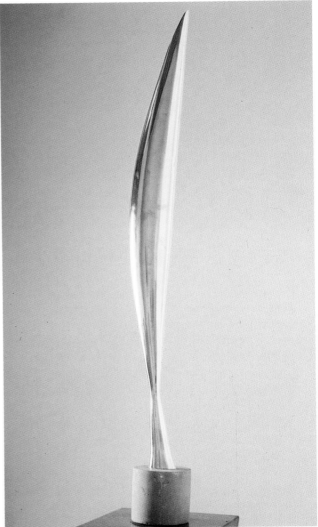

works such as Gerrit Rietveldt's *Schroeder House* (Fig. 16–21) of the same era. Here there is an almost literal translation of geometry to architecture. Broad expanses of white concrete intersect to define the strictly rectilinear dwelling, or appear to float in superimposed planes. As in a Mondrian painting, these planes are accented by black verticals and horizontals in supporting posts or window mullions. The surfaces are unadorned, like the color fields of a Mondrian.

Mondrian's obsessive respect for the two-dimensionality of the canvas surface is the culmination of the integration of figure and ground begun with the planar recession of Jacques-Louis David (see Chapter 15). No longer was it necessary to tilt tabletops or render figure and ground with the same brushstrokes and palette to accomplish this task. Canvas and painting, figure and ground were one.

CONSTANTIN BRANCUSI   The universality sought by Mondrian through extreme simplification can also be seen in the sculpture of Constantin Brancusi (1876–1957). Yet unlike Mondrian's, Brancusi's works, however abstract they appear, are rooted in the figure.

Brancusi was born in Rumania thirteen years after the Salon des Réfusés. After an apprenticeship as a cabinetmaker and studies at the Bucharest Academy of Fine Arts, he traveled to Paris to enroll in the famous École des Beaux-Arts. In 1907 Brancusi exhibited at the Salon d'Automne, leaving favorable impressions of his

work. One of those who saw potential in Brancusi was Auguste Rodin, who asked him to become his assistant. The younger artist rejected the proposal with his now famous comment, "Nothing grows under the shade of great trees."

Brancusi's work, heavily indebted to Rodin at this point, did indeed grow in a radically different direction. As early as 1909 he reduced the human head—a favorite theme he would draw upon for years—to an egg-shaped form with sparse indications of facial features. In this, and in other abstractions such as *Bird in Space* (Fig. 16–22), he reached for the essence of the subject

by offering the simplest contour that, along with a
descriptive title, would fire recognition in the spectator.
Bird in Space evolved from more representational
versions into a refined symbol of the cleanness and
solitude of flight.

FANTASY AND DADA

Throughout the history of art, most critics and patrons
have seen the accurate representation of visual reality
as a noble goal. Those artists who have departed from
this goal, who have chosen to depict their personal
worlds of dreams or supernatural fantasies, have not
had it easy. Before the twentieth century, only isolated
examples of what we call **Fantastic art** could be found.
The early 1900s, however, saw many artists exploring
fanciful imagery and working in styles as varied as
their imaginations.

How do we describe Fantastic art? The word *fantastic*
derives from the Greek *phantastikos,* meaning the ability
to represent something to the mind, or to create a mental
image. Fantasy is further defined as unreal, odd, seemingly impossible, and strange in appearance. Fantastic
art, then, is the representation of incredible images
from the artist's mind. At times the images are joyful
reminiscences, at times horrific nightmares. They may
be capricious or grotesque.

PAUL KLEE   One of the most whimsical yet subtly
sardonic of the Fantastic artists is Paul Klee (1879–1940).
Although influenced early in his career by nineteenth-
century artists such as Goya, who touched upon fantasy,
Klee received much of his stylistic inspiration from
Cézanne. In 1911 he joined Der Blaue Reiter, where his
theories about intuitive approaches to painting, growing
abstraction, and love of color were well received.

A certain innocence pervades Klee's idiosyncratic
style. After abandoning representational elements in his
art, Klee turned to ethnographic and children's art,
seeking a universality of expression in their extreme
simplicity. Many of his works combine a charming navete
with wry commentary. *Twittering Machine* (Fig. 16–23),
for example, offers a humorous contraption composed of
four fantastic birds balanced precariously on a wire
attached to a crank. The viewer who is motivated to

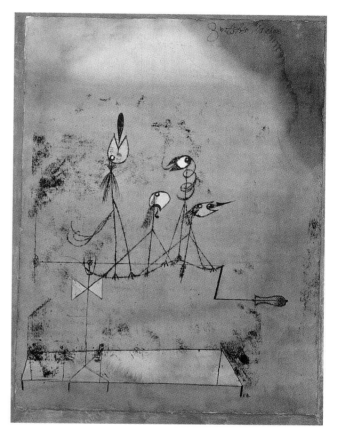

piece together the possible function of this apparatus
might assume that turning the crank would result in
the twittering suggested by the title.

In this seemingly innocuous painting, Klee perhaps
satirizes contemporary technology, in which machines
may sometimes seem to do little more than express the
whims and ego of the inventor. But why a machine that
twitters? Some have suggested a darker interpretation
in which the mechanical birds are traps to lure real
birds to a makeshift coffin beneath. Such gruesome
doings might in turn symbolize the entrapment of
humans by their own existence. In any event, it is
evident that Klee's simple, cartoonlike subjects may
carry a mysterious and rich iconography.

GIORGIO DE CHIRICO   Equally mysterious are the odd
juxtapositions of familiar objects found in the works of
Giorgio de Chirico (1888–1978). Unlike Klee's figures,

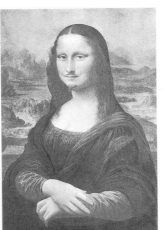

16–25 MARCEL DUCHAMP
MONA LISA (L.H.O.O.Q.)
(1919).
RECTIFIED READYMADE;
PENCIL ON A REPRODUCTION.
7¾ × 4⅞".

PRIVATE COLLECTION. © 1998 ARTISTS
RIGHTS SOCIETY (ARS), N.Y./ADAGP, PARIS.

16–24 GIORGIO DE CHIRICO
THE MYSTERY AND MELANCHOLY OF THE STREET (1914).
OIL ON CANVAS. 34¼ × 28⅛".

PRIVATE COLLECTION, U.S.A. © FOUNDATION GIORGIO DE CHIRICO/LICENSED BY VAGA, N.Y. 1998.

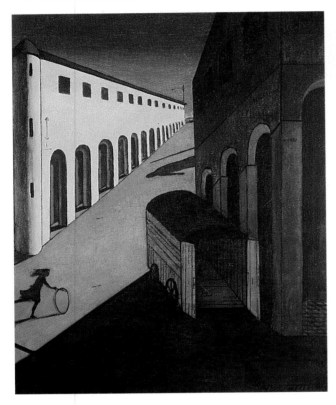

Chirico's are rendered in a realistic manner. Chirico attempted to make the irrational believable. His subjects are often derived from dreams, in which ordinary objects are found in extraordinary situations. The realistic technique tends to heighten the believability of these events and imparts a certain eeriness characteristic of dreams or nightmares. Part of the intrigue of Chirico's subjects lies in their ambiguity and in the uncertainty of the outcome. Often we do not know why we dream what we dream. We do not know how the strange juxtapositions occur, nor how the story will evolve. We may now and then "save" ourselves from danger by awakening.

The intrigues of the dream world are captured by Chirico in works such as *The Mystery and Melancholy of the Street* (Fig. 16–24). Some of his favorite images—the icy arcade, the deserted piazza, the empty boxcar—provide the backdrop for an encounter between two figures at opposite ends of a diagonal strip of sunlight. A young girl, seemingly unaware of the tall dark shadow beyond her, skips at play with stick and hoop. What is she

doing there? Why is she alone? Who is the source of the shadow? Is it male or female? What is the spearlike form by the figure? We quickly perceive doom. We wonder what will happen to the girl and imagine the worst. For example, we are not likely to assume that the girl is rushing to her father standing by a flagpole. Viewers must stew in their active imaginations, pondering the simple clues to a mystery that Chirico will not unlock.

DADA

In 1916, during World War I, an international movement arose that declared itself against art. Responding to the absurdity of war and the insanity of a world that gave rise to it, the Dadaists declared that art—a reflection of this sorry state of affairs—was stupid and must be destroyed. Yet in order to communicate their outrage, the Dadaists created works of art! This inherent contradiction spelled the eventual demise of their movement. Despite centers in Paris, Berlin, Cologne, Zurich, and New York City, **Dada** ended with a whimper in 1922.

The name "Dada" was supposedly chosen at random from a dictionary. It is an apt epithet. The nonsense term describes nonsense art—art that is meaningless, absurd, unpredictable. While it is questionable whether this catchy label was in truth derived at random, the element of chance was indeed important to the Dada artform. Dada poetry, for example, consisted of nonsense verses of random word combinations. Some works of art, such as the Dada collages, were constructed of materials found by chance and mounted randomly. Yet however meaningless or unpredictable the poets and artists intended their products to be, in reality they were not. In an era dominated by the doctrine of psychoanalysis, the choice of even nonsensical words spoke something at least of the poet. Works of art supposedly constructed in random fashion also frequently betrayed the mark of some design.

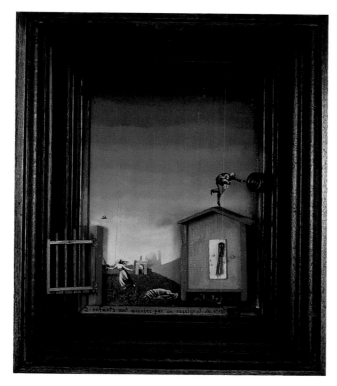

objects. These often menacing paintings also incorporate the realistic technique and the suggestion of dream imagery found in Fantastic art.

SURREALISM

Surrealism began as a literary movement after World War I. Its adherents based their writings on the nonrational, and thus they were naturally drawn to the Dadaists. Both literary groups engaged in **automatic writing,** in which the mind was to be purged of purposeful thought and a series of free associations were then to be expressed with the pen. Words were not meant to denote their literal meanings, but rather to symbolize the often seething contents of the unconscious mind. Eventually the Surrealist writers broke from the Dadaists, believing that the earlier movement was becoming too academic. Under the leadership of the poet Andre Breton, they defined their movement as follows in a 1924 manifesto:

> Surrealism, *noun, masc., pure psychic automatism by which it is intended to express either verbally or in writing, the true function of thought. Thought dictated in the absence of all control exerted by reason, and outside all aesthetic or moral preoccupations.*

> Encycl. Philos. *Surrealism is based on the belief in the superior reality of certain forms of association heretofore neglected, in the omnipotence of the dream, and in the disinterested play of thought. It leads to the permanent destruction of all other psychic mechanisms and to its substitution for them in the solution of the principal problems of life.*

From the beginning, Surrealism expounded two very different methods of working. **Illusionistic Surrealism,** exemplified by artists such as Salvador Dalí and Yves Tanguy, rendered the irrational content, absurd juxtapositions, and metamorphoses of the dream state in a highly illusionistic manner. The other, called **Automatist Surrealism,** was a direct outgrowth of automatic writing and was used to divulge mysteries of the unconscious through abstraction. The automatist phase is typified by Joan Miró and Andre Masson.

MARCEL DUCHAMP   In an effort to advertise their nihilistic views, the Dadaists assaulted the public with irreverence. Not only did they attempt to negate art, but they also advocated antisocial and amoral behavior. Marcel Duchamp offered for exhibition a urinal, turned on its back and entitled *Fountain* (see Fig. 1–34). Later he summed up the Dada sensibility in works such as *Mona Lisa (L.H.O.O.Q.)* (Fig. 16–25), in which he impudently defiled a color print of Leonardo da Vinci's masterpiece with a moustache and goatee. In *Nude Descending a Staircase #2* (Fig. 2–48), Duchamp's simulation of the fourth dimension of time through a series of overlapping images added a new element to the experiments of Cubism.

Fortified by growing interest in psychoanalysis, Dada, with some modification, would provide the basis for a movement called Surrealism that began in the early 1920s. Like Max Ernst's Dada composition, *Two Children Are Threatened by a Nightingale* (Fig. 16–26), some Surrealist works offer irrational subjects and the chance juxtaposition of everyday

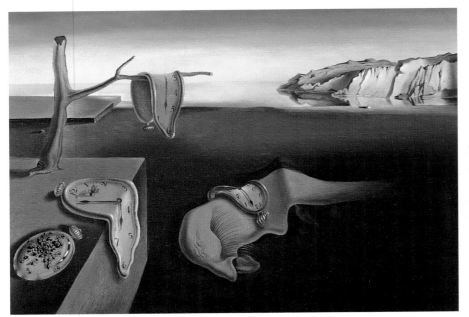

16–27 SALVADOR DALÍ
THE PERSISTENCE OF MEMORY (1931). OIL ON CANVAS. 9½ × 13".

COLLECTION OF THE MUSEUM OF MODERN ART, N.Y. GIVEN ANONYMOUSLY. PHOTOGRAPH © 1998 THE MUSEUM OF MODERN ART, N.Y. © 1998 DEMART PRO ARTE®, GENEVA/ARTISTS RIGHTS SOCIETY (ARS), N.Y.

SALVADOR DALÍ One of the few "household names" in the history of art belongs to a leading Surrealist figure, the Spaniard Salvador Dalí (1904–1986). His reputation for leading an unusual—one could say surrealistic—life would seem to precede his art, for many not familiar with his canvases had seen Dalí's outrageous moustache and knew of his absurd shenanigans. Once, as a guest on the Ed Sullivan television show, he threw open cans of paint at a huge canvas.

Dalí began his painting career, however, in a somewhat more conservative manner, adopting, in turn, Impressionist, Pointillist, and Futurist styles. Following these forays into contemporary styles, he sought academic training at the Academy of Fine Arts in Madrid. This experience steeped him in a tradition of illusionistic realism that he never abandoned.

In what may be Dalí's most famous canvas, *The Persistence of Memory* (Fig. 16–27), the drama of the oneiric imagery is enhanced by his trompe l'oeil technique. Here, in a barren landscape of incongruous forms, time, as all else, has expired. A watch is left crawling with insects like scavengers over carrion; three other watches hang limp and useless over a rectangular block, a dead tree, and a lifeless, amorphous creature that bears a curious resemblance to Dalí. The artist conveys the world of the dream, juxtaposing unrelated objects in an extraordinary situation. But a haunting sense of reality threatens the line between perception and imagination. Dalí's is, in the true definition of the term, a surreality—or reality above and beyond reality.

JOAN MIRÓ Not all of the Surrealists were interested in rendering their enigmatic personal dreams. Some found this highly introspective subject matter meaning-less to the observer and sought a more universal form of expression. The Automatist Surrealists believed that the unconscious held such universal imagery, and through spontaneous, or automatic, drawing, they attempted to reach it. Artists of this group, such as Joan Miró (1893–1983), sought to eliminate all thought from their minds and then trace their brushes across the surface of the canvas. The organic shapes derived from intersecting skeins of line were believed to be unadulterated by conscious thought and thus drawn from the unconscious. Once the basic designs had been outlined, a conscious period of work could follow in which the artist intentionally applied his or her craft to render them in their final form. But because no conscious control was to be exerted to determine the early course of the designs, the Automatist method was seen as spontaneous, as employing chance and accident. Needless to say, the works are abstract, although some shapes are amoebic.

Miró was born near Barcelona and spent his early years in local schools of art learning how to paint like the French. He practiced a number of styles ranging from Romanticism to Realism to Impressionism, but Cézanne and van Gogh seem to have influenced him most. In 1919 Miró moved to Paris, where he was receptive to a number of art styles. The work of Matisse and Picasso along with the primitive innocence of Rousseau found their way into his canvases. Coupled with a rich native iconography and an inclination toward fantasy, these different elements would shape Miró's unique style.

Miró's need for spontaneity in communicating his subjects was compatible with Automatist Surrealism, although the whimsical nature of most of his subjects often appears at odds with that of other members of the movement. In *Painting* (Fig. 16–28), meandering lines join or intersect to form the contours of clusters of organic figures. Some of these shapes are left void to display a nondescript background of subtly colored squares. Others are filled in with sharply contrasting black,

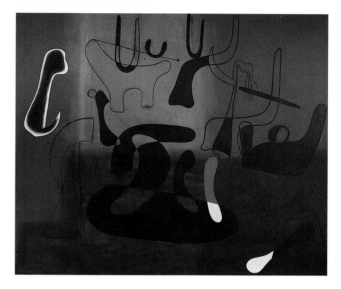

white, and bright red pigment. In this work, Miró applied Breton's principles of **psychic automatism** in an aesthetically pleasing, decorative manner.

By 1930 Surrealism had developed into an international movement, despite the divorce of many of the first members from the group. New adherents exhibiting radically different styles kept the movement alive. As the decade of the 1930s evolved, however, Adolph Hitler rose to power and war once again threatened Europe. Hitler's ascent drove refugee artists of the highest reputation to the shores of the United States. Among them were the leading figures of Abstraction and Surrealism, two divergent styles that would join to form the basis of an avant-garde American painting. The center of the art world had moved to New York.

key terms

Salon d'Automne	The New Objectivity	Synthetic Cubist	Fantastic art
Fauves	(Neue Sachlichkeit)	Futurism	Dada
Expressionism	Cubism	Dynamism	Automatic writing
The Bridge (Die Brücke)	Analytic Cubism	Constructivism	Illusionistic Surrealism
The Blue Rider (Der	Trompe l'oeil	De Stijl	Automatist Surrealism
Blaue Reiter)	Collage	Nonobjective art	Psychic Automatism

artists

André Derain	Alexander Archipenko	Constantin Brancusi
Henri Matisse	Umberto Boccioni	Paul Klee
Pablo Picasso	Giacomo Balla	Giorgio de Chirico
Emil Nolde	Georgia O'Keeffe	Marcel Duchamp
Wassily Kandinsky	John Marin	Max Ernst
Max Beckmann	Naum Gabo	Salvador Dalí
Georges Braque	Piet Mondrian	Joan Miró
Jacques Lipchitz	Gerrit Rietveldt	

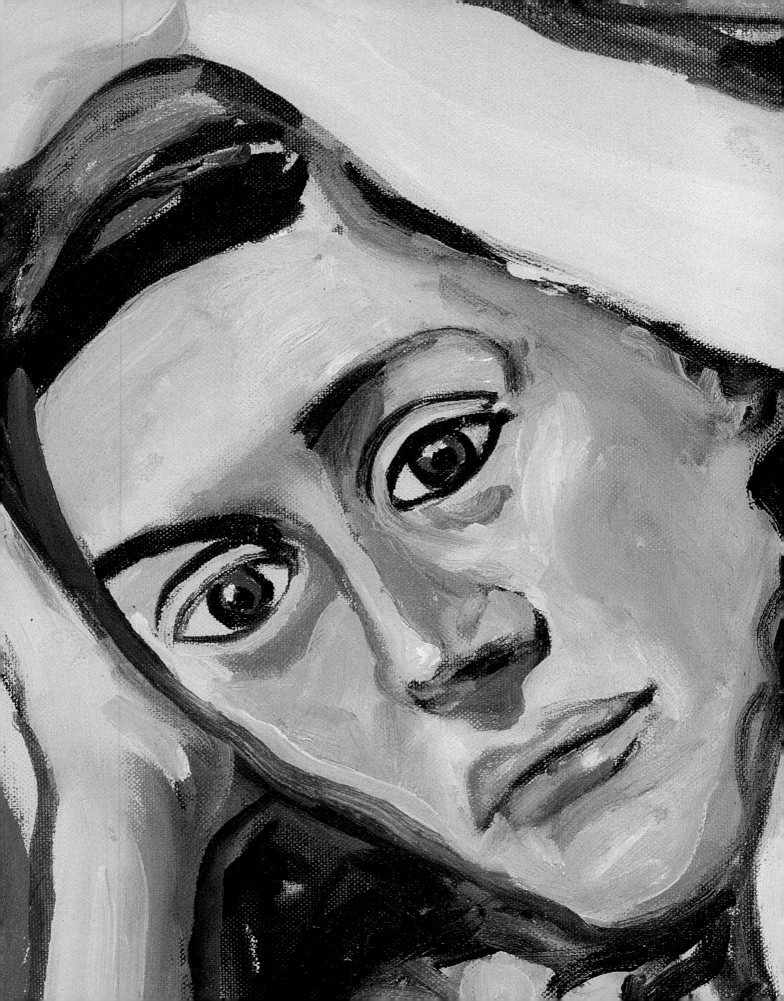

CONTEMPORARY ART

PRELIMINARY *Sketch*

- After World War II, the center of the art world moved to New York.

- Jackson Pollock made drip paintings by placing huge canvases on the floor and then walking over them, splashing paint across their surfaces.

- As painter Mark Rothko grew depressed, the colors of his canvases changed from vibrant reds, oranges, and yellows to somber deep blacks and browns.

- Whereas many artists have strived to portray the beautiful, Pop art intentionally depicts commonplace, familiar, even boring images.

- Painter Robert Rauschenberg would attach objects such as stuffed animals, bottles, articles of clothing, and pieces of furniture to his canvases.

- Pop artist Andy Warhol once earned a living designing packages and Christmas cards.

- Op art manipulates light, color, or patterns of line to produce visual illusions.

- Graffiti artist Jean-Michel Basquiat used crude materials and techniques to enhance compelling images that were often taken from African art.

Alice Neel, *The Pregnant Woman* (detail). See Figure 17–11.

Ah! stirring times we live in—stirring times.

—Thomas Hardy

If Thomas Hardy were writing today instead of a century ago, he might say that we too live in stirring times. If he were writing about art, he would doubtless insist upon it. Never before in history have artists experimented so freely with medium, content, and style. Never before in history have the mass media brought the images wrought by artists so rapidly into our homes. Never before has the general public been so conscious of, and affected by, art.

In this chapter we will talk about the painting and sculpture that has appeared since the end of World War II—the art of recent times and of today. After the war, the center of the art world shifted to New York after its long tenure in Paris. There were a number of reasons. The wave of immigrant artists who escaped the Nazis had settled largely in New York: among them Marcel Duchamp, Fernand Léger, Josef Albers, and Hans Hofmann. The Federal Art Project of the WPA had also nourished the New York community of artists during the Great Depression. This group included Arshile Gorky, Willem de Kooning, Jack Tworkov, James Brooks, Philip Guston, and Stuart Davis, among many others. Together these were known as the first-generation New York School. Even the Mexican muralists Diego Rivera and José Clemente Orozco sojourned and taught in the city.

Just before the Great Depression began, Orozco had already argued that the artists of the New World should no longer look to Europe for their inspiration and their models. In January of 1929 he wrote: "If new races have appeared upon the lands of the New World, such races have the unavoidable duty to produce a New Art in a new spiritual and physical medium. Any other road is plain cowardice." Despite his devotion to the arts and culture of the Mexican Native Americans, Orozco added: "Already the architecture of Manhattan is a new value, something that has nothing to do with Egyptian pyramids, with the Paris Opera, with the Geralda of Seville, or with Saint Sofia, any more than it has to do with the Maya palaces of Chichen-Itzá or with the pueblos of Arizona."[1]

There is no question that the postwar generation produced an art never before seen on the face of the planet. It is a lively art that stirs both adoration and controversy. It is also a fertile art, giving birth to exploration down many branching avenues.

PAINTING

Many vital movements have given shape to contemporary painting. We will begin with painters of the first-generation New York School and their powerful new movement of **Abstract Expressionism.** Then we will consider the work of a younger, second generation of New York School painters, including color-field and hard-edge painters. Finally, we will discuss a number of the other movements in painting that have defined the postwar years, including figurative painting, Pop art, Photorealism, and Op art.

THE NEW YORK SCHOOL: THE FIRST GENERATION

At midcentury the influences of earlier nonobjective painting, the colorful distortions of Expressionism, Cubist design, the supposedly automatist processes of Surrealism, and a host of other factors—even an interest in Zen Buddhism—converged in New York. From this artistic melting pot, Abstract Expressionism flowered. At first, like other innovative movements in art, it was not universally welcomed by critics. Writing in *The New Yorker* in 1945, Robert M. Coates commented:

> [A] new school of painting is developing in this country. It is small as yet, no bigger than a baby's fist, but it is noticeable if you get around to the galleries much. It partakes a little of Surrealism and still more of Expressionism, and although its main current is still muddy and its direction obscure, one can make out bits of Hans Arp and Joan Miró floating in it, together with large chunks of Picasso and occasional fragments of [African-American] sculptors. It is more emotional than logical in expression, and you may not like it (I don't either, entirely), but it can't escape attention.[2]

Abstract Expressionism is characterized by spontaneous execution, large gestural brushstrokes, abstract imagery, and fields of intense color. Many canvases are quite large, lending monumentality to the imagery.

[1]Robert Goldwater and Marco Treves, eds., *Artists on Art* (New York: Pantheon Books, 1972), p. 479.

[2]Robert M. Coates, "The Art Galleries," *The New Yorker,* May 26, 1945, p. 68.

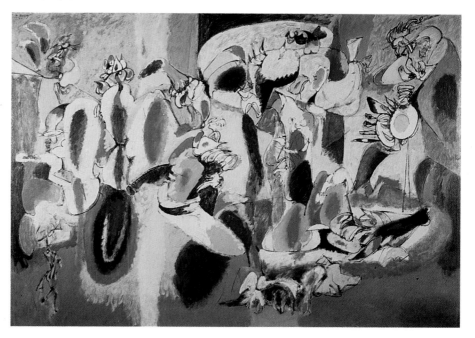

17–1 ARSHILE GORKY
THE LIVER IS THE COCK'S COMB (1944). OIL ON CANVAS. 72 × 98″.

ALBRIGHT-KNOX ART GALLERY, BUFFALO. GIFT OF SEYMOUR H. KNOX, 1956. © 1998 ESTATE OF ARSHILE GORKY/ARTISTS RIGHTS SOCIETY (ARS), N.Y.

The abstract shapes frequently have a **calligraphic** quality found in the painting of the Far East (see Chapter 18). However, the scope of the brushstrokes of the New York group was vast and muscular compared with the gentle, circumscribed brush strokes of Chinese and Japanese artists.

TURNING THE CORNER TOWARD AN ABSTRACT EXPRESSIONISM

Before we discuss the work of the major Abstract Expressionists, let us explore the vibrant canvases of two artists whose work, near midcentury, showed the influence of earlier trends and, in turn, presaged Abstract Expressionism: Arshile Gorky and Hans Hofmann.

ARSHILE GORKY   The vital task was a wedding of abstraction and surrealism. Out of these opposites something new could emerge, and Gorky's work is part of the evidence that this is true.[3]

Born in Armenia, Arshile Gorky (1905–1948) emigrated to the United States in 1920 and became part of a circle that included Willem de Kooning and Stuart Davis. Some of Gorky's early still lifes show the influence of the nineteenth-century painter Paul Cézanne. Later abstract works resolve the shapes of the objects of still lifes into sharp-edged planes that recall the works—and the fascination with native forms—of Pablo Picasso and Georges Braque. Abstractions of the late 1940s show the influence of Expressionists such as Wassily Kandinsky and Surrealists such as Joan Miró.

Gorky's *The Liver Is the Cock's Comb* (Fig. 17–1) is 6 feet high and more than 8 feet long. Free, spontaneous lines pick out unstable, organic shapes from a lush molten background of predominantly warm colors: analogous reds, oranges, and yellows. The shapes are

[3]Adolph Gottlieb, in Introduction to catalog of an exhibition, *Selected Paintings by the Late Arshile Gorky,* Kootz Gallery, New York, March 28–April 24, 1950.

reminiscent of the surrealistic forms of Joan Miró in *The Birth of the World* (see Fig. 2–57).

Many of Gorky's paintings, like those of the Surrealists, are like erotic panoramas. Here and there we can pick out abstracted forms that seem to hark back to dreams of childhood or to the ancestral figures of primitive artists. Transitional works such as this form a logical bridge between early twentieth-century abstraction, Automatist Surrealism, and the gestural painting of Jackson Pollock and Willem de Kooning.

HANS HOFMANN   Born in Bavaria, Hans Hofmann (1880–1966) studied in Paris early in this century. He witnessed at close hand the Fauvists' use of high-keyed colors and the Cubists' resolution of shapes into abstract planes. He emigrated to the United States from Germany in 1932 and established schools of fine art in New York City and in Provincetown, Massachusetts.

Hofmann's early works were figural and expressionistic, showing the influence of Henri Matisse. From the war years on, however, his paintings showed a variety of abstract approaches, from lyrically free, curving lines to the depiction of geometrical masses. Hofmann is considered a transitional figure between the Cubists and the Abstract Expressionists. In his abstract paintings, he shows some

17–2 HANS HOFMANN
The Golden Wall (1961). Oil on canvas. $60 \times 72\frac{1}{2}''$.
PHOTOGRAPH COURTESY OF THE ART INSTITUTE OF CHICAGO. MR. AND MRS. G. LOGAN PRIZE FUND (1962.775).

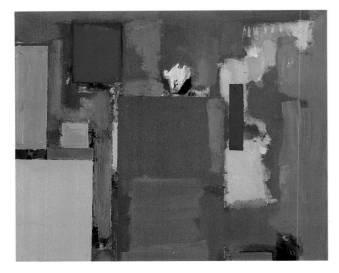

allegiance to Fauvist coloring and Cubist design, but Hofmann also used color architecturally, to define structure.

In *The Golden Wall* (Fig. 17–2), intense fields of complementary and primary colors are pitted against each other in Fauvist fashion, but they compose abstract rectangular forms. The gestural brushstrokes in the color fields of paintings such as these would soon spread through the art world. Hofmann, the analyst and instructor of painting, knew very well that the cool blues and greens in *The Golden Wall* would normally recede and the warm reds and oranges would emerge; but sharp edges and interposition press the blue and green areas forward, creating tension between planes and flattening the canvas. Hofmann saw this tension as symbolic of the push and pull of nature; but the "tension" is purely technical, for the mood of *The Golden Wall,* as of most of his other works, is joyous and elevating.

Later Hofmann would claim that paintings such as these were derived from nature, even though no representational imagery can be found. In their expressionistic use of color and their abstract subject matter, Hofmann's paintings form a clear base for the flowering of Abstract Expressionism.

FOCUS ON GESTURE

For some Abstract Expressionists, such as Jackson Pollock and Willem de Kooning, the gestural application of paint seems to be the most important aspect of their

work. For others, the structure of the color field seems to predominate.

JACKSON POLLOCK

Pollock's talent is volcanic. It has fire. It is unpredictable. It is undisciplined. It spills itself out in a mineral prodigality not yet crystallized. It is lavish, explosive, untidy. . . . What we need is more young men who paint from inner compulsion without an ear to what the critic or spectator may feel—painters who will risk spoiling a canvas to say something in their own way. Pollock is one.[4]

Jackson Pollock (1912–1956) is probably the best-known of the Abstract Expressionists. Photographs or motion pictures of the artist energetically dripping and splashing paint across his huge canvases (Fig. 17–3) are familiar to many Americans. Pollock would walk across the surface of the canvas as if controlled by primitive impulses and unconscious ideas. Accident became a prime compositional element in his painting. Art critic Harold Rosenberg coined the term **action painting** in 1951 to describe the outcome of such a process—a painting whose surface implied a strong sense of activity, as created by the signs of brushing, dripping, or splattering of paint.

Born in Cody, Wyoming, Pollock came to New York to study with Thomas Hart Benton at the Art Students League. The 1943 quote from Clement Greenberg shows the impact that Pollock made at an early exhibition of his work. His paintings of this era (see Fig. 1–44) frequently depicted actual or implied figures that were reminiscent of the abstractions of Picasso and, at times, of Expressionists and Surrealists.

Aside from their own value as works of art, Pollock's drip paintings of the late 1940s and early 1950s made a number of innovations that would be mirrored and developed in the work of other Abstract Expressionists. Foremost among these was the use of an overall gestural pattern barely contained by the limits of the canvas. In *One* (Fig. 17–4), the surface is an unsectioned, unified field. Overlapping skeins of paint create dynamic webs

[4]Clement Greenberg, quoted in Introduction to catalog of an exhibition, *Jackson Pollock,* Art of This Century Gallery, New York, Nov. 9–27, 1943.

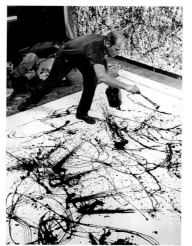

17–3 JACKSON POLLOCK AT
WORK IN HIS LONG ISLAND
STUDIO, 1950.

17–4 JACKSON POLLOCK
ONE (NUMBER 31, 1950) (1950). OIL AND ENAMEL PAINT ON CANVAS. 8′10″ × 17′5⅝″.
THE MUSEUM OF MODERN ART, N.Y. SIDNEY AND HARRIET JANIE COLLECTION FUND (BY EXCHANGE). © 1998 POLLACK-KRASNER
FOUNDATION/ARTISTS RIGHTS SOCIETY (ARS), N.Y.

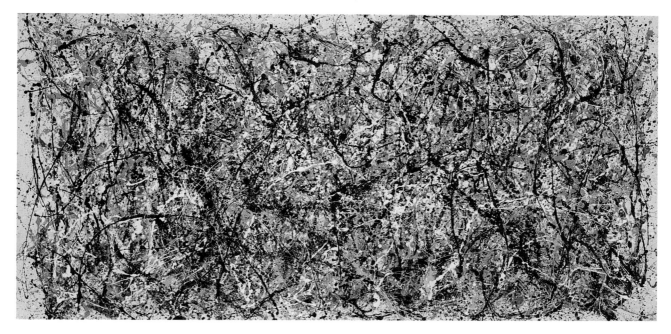

that project from the picture plane, creating an illusion of infinite depth. In Pollock's best work, these webs seem to be composed of energy that pushes and pulls the monumental tracery of the surface like the architectural shapes of a Hofmann painting.

Pollock was in psychoanalysis at the time he executed his great drip paintings. He believed strongly in the role of the unconscious mind, of accident and spontaneity, in the creation of art. He was influenced not only by the intellectual impact of the Automatist Surrealists, but also by what must have been his own impression of walking hand in hand with his own unconscious forces through the realms of artistic expression. Before his untimely death in 1956, Pollock had returned to figural paintings that were heavy in impasto and predominantly black. One wonders what might have emerged if the artist had lived a fuller span of years.

LEE KRASNER   One of only a few women in the mainstream of Abstract Expressionism was Lee Krasner (1908–1984). Yet, in spite of her originality and strength as a painter, her work, until fairly recently, had taken a critical "back seat" to that of her famous husband—Jackson Pollock. She once noted,

> *I was not the average woman married to the average painter. I was married to Jackson Pollock. The context is bigger and even if I was not personally dominated by Pollock, the whole art world was.*[5]

Krasner had a burning desire to be a painter from the time she was a teenager and received academic training at some of the best art schools in the country. She was influenced by artists of diverse styles, including

[5]Lee Krasner, in Roberta Brandes Gratz, "Daily Close-Up—After Pollock," *New York Post,* December 6, 1973.

17–5 LEE KRASNER
EASTER LILIES (1956). OIL ON COTTON DUCK. 48¼ × 60⅛″.
PRIVATE COLLECTION. COURTESY OF THE ROBERT MILLER GALLERY, N.Y. © 1998
POLLACK–KRASNER FOUNDATION/ARTISTS RIGHTS SOCIETY (ARS), N.Y.

17–6 WILLEM DE KOONING
TWO WOMEN (1953). PASTEL DRAWING. 18⅞ × 24″.
PHOTOGRAPH COURTESY OF THE ART INSTITUTE OF CHICAGO. JOSEPH H. WRENN MEMORIAL
COLLECTION, 1955.637. © 1998 WILLEM DE KOONING REVOCABLE TRUST/ARTISTS RIGHTS SOCIETY
(ARS), N.Y.

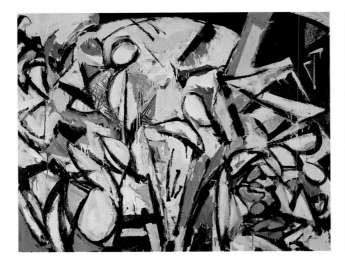

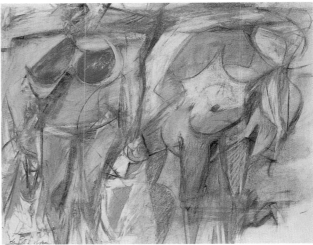

Hoffman—under whom she studied—Picasso, Mondrian, and the Surrealists. Most important, like Pollock and the other members of the Abstract Expressionist school, she was exposed to the work of a number of European emigrés who came to New York in the 1930s and 1940s.

Both Pollock and Krasner experimented with allover compositions around 1945, but the latter's work was smaller in scale and exhibited much more control. Even after 1950, when Krasner's work became much freer and larger, the accidental nature of Pollock's style never took hold of her own. Rather, Krasner's compositions might be termed a synthesis of choice and chance.

Easter Lilies (Fig. 17–5) was painted in 1956, the year of Pollock's fatal accident. The jagged shapes and bold black lines against the muddied greens and ochres render the composition dysphoric; yet, in the midst of all that is harsh are the recognizable contours of lilies, whose bright whites offer a kind of hope in a sea of anxiety. Krasner once remarked of her work, "My painting is so autobiographical, if anyone can take the trouble to read it."[6]

WILLEM DE KOONING   Born in 1904 in Rotterdam, Holland, Willem de Kooning emigrated in 1926 to the United States, where he joined the circle of Gorky and other forerunners of Abstract Expressionism. Until 1940 de Kooning painted figures and portraits. His first

[6]Lee Krasner, in Cindy Nemser, "A Conversation with Lee Krasner," *Arts Magazine* 47 (April 1973): 48.

abstractions of the 1940s, like Gorky's, remind one of Picasso's paintings. As the 1940s progressed, de Kooning's compositions began to combine biomorphic, organic shapes with harsh, jagged lines. By midcentury, his art had developed into a force in Abstract Expressionism.

De Kooning is best known for his series of paintings of women that began in 1950. In contrast to the appealing figurative works of an earlier day, many of his abstracted women are frankly overpowering and repellent. Faces are frequently resolved into skull-like native masks reminiscent of ancient fertility figures; they assault the viewer from a loosely brushed backdrop of tumultuous color. Perhaps they portray what was a major psychoanalytic dilemma during the 1950s—how women could be at once seductive, alluring, and castrating. In our own liberated times, this notion of woman or of eroticism as frightening seems sexist or out of joint. In any event, in some of his other paintings abstracted women communicate an impression of being unnerved, even vulnerable.

The subjects of *Two Women* (Fig. 17–6) are among the more erotic of the series. Richly curved pastel breasts swell from a sea of spontaneous brushstrokes that here and there violently obscure the imagery. The result is a free-floating eroticism. A primal urge has been cast loose in space, pushing and pulling against the picture plane. But de Kooning is one of the few Abstract Expressionists who never completely surrendered figurative painting.

De Kooning's work frequently seems obsessed with the violence and agitation of the "age of anxiety." The abstract backgrounds seem to mirror the rootlessness many of us experience as modern modes of travel and business call us to foreign towns and cities.

FOCUS ON THE COLOR FIELD

For a number of Abstract Expressionists, the creation of pulsating fields of color was more important than the gestural quality of the brushstroke. These canvases are so large that they seem to envelop the viewer with color, the subtle modulations of which create a vibrating or resonating effect. Artists who subscribed to this manner of painting, such as Mark Rothko and Barnett Newman, had in common the reworking of a theme in an extended series of paintings. Even though the imagery often remains constant, each canvas has a remarkably different effect due to often radical palette adjustments.

MARK ROTHKO   Mark Rothko (1903–1970) painted lone figures in urban settings in the 1930s and biomorphic surrealistic canvases through the early 1940s. Later in that decade he began to paint the large, floating, hazy-edged color fields for which he is renowned. During the 1950s, the color fields consistently assumed the form of rectangles floating above one another in an atmosphere defined by subtle variations in tone and gesture. They alternately loom in front of and recede from the picture plane, as in *Blue, Orange, Red* (Fig. 17–7). The large scale of these canvases absorbs the viewer in color.

Early in his career, Rothko had favored a palette of pale hues. During the 1960s, however, his works grew somber. Reds that earlier had been intense, warm, and sensuous were now awash in deep blacks and browns and took on the appearance of worn cloth. Oranges and yellows were replaced by grays and black. Light that earlier had been reflected was now trapped in his canvases. Despite public acclaim, Rothko suffered from depression during his last years. In 1968 he was diagnosed as having heart disease and one year later his second marriage was in ruins. He committed suicide the following winter. His paintings of the later years may be an expression of the turmoil and the fading spark within.

COMBINED GESTURE AND COLOR FIELD PAINTING

For some artists of the Abstract Expressionist era, the most original work lay in the bridging of gesture and color field. Artists such as Adolph Gottlieb, Robert Motherwell, and Clifford Still enlarged simple forms and made them the predominant themes of their compositions. Often these forms were set in large expanses of washed color, their contours eroded by the resonating hues.

ADOLPH GOTTLIEB   Adolph Gottlieb (1903–1974) is preeminent among those artists who chose to combine the two styles of Abstract Expressionism. He was born in New York and studied under American realist painter John Sloan at New York City's Art Students League. During the 1940s and early 1950s, he painted a series of "Pictographs" in which the canvases were sectioned into rectangular compartments filled with schematized or abstract forms such as ancestral images, sinuous shapes of reptiles and birds, pure geometric forms, anatomic parts, and complex shapes suggestive of

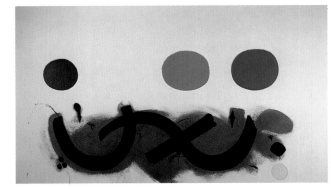

17–8 ADOLPH GOTTLIEB
GREEN TURBULENCE (1968). OIL ON CANVAS. 94 × 157″.
PHOTOGRAPH COURTESY OF ADOLPH AND ESTHER GOTTLIEB FOUNDATION, INC., N.Y.
© ADOLPH AND ESTHER GOTTLIEB FOUNDATION/LICENSED BY VAGA, N.Y.

cosmic symbols or microscopic life forms. He denied that the Pictographs had any meaning beyond their interesting shapes, but much of the enjoyment in viewing them stems from trying to decipher the content.

Some of Gottlieb's most successful paintings belong to the "Bursts" series that began in 1957. In the Bursts, there is an implied horizontal division of the canvas. An orb of color pulsates in the upper part of the canvas, while broad, gestural strokes burst beneath it against a washed field of color. Visually, the Bursts are studies in contrast between pure closed forms and amorphous open forms. On a symbolic level, they seem to reflect the opposites in human nature.

Green Turbulence (Fig. 17–8), painted in 1968, is a variation on the Bursts theme. Below an implied horizon line, a simple black pictograph floats against a field of green, while three pristine orbs hover above. Smaller, and less perfectly formed spheres seem to break out of the chaotic, "earthly" zone, and await their voyage to the celestial realm. The pictograph is strongly calligraphic, as if the baser history of our species is being broadly recorded in swaths of paint. By comparison, the orbs seem immaculate in conception. These pulsating shapes imply a pure but obscure symbol that is close at hand yet unreachable.

Abstract Expressionism may be the major movement in painting of the postwar era, but contemporary painting has been a rich and varied undertaking, with tentative strokes and brilliant bursts of fulfillment in many directions.

THE NEW YORK SCHOOL: THE SECOND GENERATION

Abstract Expressionism was a painterly movement. Contours and colors were loosely defined, edges were frequently blurred, and long brushstrokes trailed off into ripples, streaks, and specks of paint. During the mid-1950s, a number of younger abstract artists, referred to as the "second generation" New York School, began either to build upon or to deemphasize this painterly approach; some furthered the staining technique that Pollock used in his last years, while others focused increasingly on clarity of line and clearness of edges. Beyond a few common features, their styles were quite different, and they modified and extended in a number of ways the forces that had led to Abstract Expressionism. Some of these artists, such as Morris Louis, Helen Frankenthaler, and Kenneth Noland became known as **color-field painters.** Others, like Ellsworth Kelly, whose work focused on clear geometric shapes with firm contours that separated them from their fields, were known as **hard-edge painters.** Many of this new crop of abstract painters, Noland and Kelly among them, also pioneered the shaped canvas, which challenges the traditional orientation of a painting and often extends the work into three-dimensional space. Some artists in the 1980s would use the shaped canvas exclusively in their works.

COLOR-FIELD PAINTING

HELEN FRANKENTHALER Kenneth Noland once said of Helen Frankenthaler (b. 1928) that "She was a bridge between Pollock and what was possible." He claimed that it was Frankenthaler who showed him and Morris Louis a way to push beyond Pollock, showed them "a way to think about and use, color."[7] In fact, it is works like *Lorelei* (Fig. 17–9) that best describe the manner in which Frankenthaler built on Pollock's legacy. The canvas is awash in color. Broad expanses of thinned pigment are allowed to seep into the fibers of the canvas, thus softening the edges of the varied shapes. The shapes themselves are interspersed with flowing lines and paint spatters that make reference to Pollock's techniques. The roles of accident and spontaneity are not diminished. *Lorelei* is in many ways a reconciliation between gesture and color field abstract expressionism; yet its uniqueness lies in its combination of a vibrant palette, staining technique, and above all, strong

[7]Kenneth Noland, in James McC. Truitt, "Art-Arid D.C. Harbors Touted 'New' Painters" *Washington Post,* December 21, 1961, p. A20.

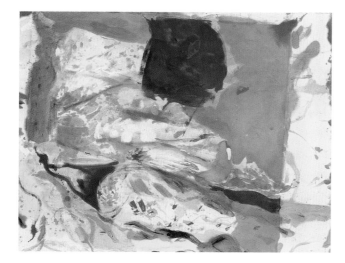

17–9 HELEN FRANKENTHALER
LORELEI (1957). OIL ON CANVAS. 70¾ × 87".
THE BROOKLYN MUSEUM; GIFT OF ALAN D. EMIL (58.39).

17–10 AGNES MARTIN
UNTITLED (1989). ACRYLIC AND GRAPHITE ON CANVAS. 12 × 12".
COURTESY OF PACE WILDENSTEIN.

abstract image in a structurally sound composition. Her fascination with the color field and her ability to suggest space through subtle color modulations has already been noted in *Magic Carpet* (Fig. 2–9). By pouring fields of thinned vibrant color onto unprimed canvas, the resulting central image is open, billowing, and abstract, free of gestural brushing.

MINIMAL ART

Paintings involving the shaped canvas, color field, and images derived from mathematical systems, gave rise to an art form known as **minimal art**, or simply **minimalism.** Alexander Calder, Dorothea Rockburne, and Agnes Martin, among many others in the 1960s, purified their images and painting processes to reflect their commitment to intellectual theory and mathematics as bases for their compositions. Common to all is the sense of the contradictory: an extraordinary lightness and transience that belies the solidity and permanence of their shapes.

AGNES MARTIN *Untitled* (Fig. 17–10) by Agnes Martin (b. 1912) is a quintessential example of the minimalist style. A tiny 12 × 12" canvas provides a luminous backdrop for finely wrought bands of shimmering graphite. The absolute square of the canvas is softened by the delicacy of technique. Martin said of her paintings, "When I cover the square with rectangles, it lightens the weight of the square, destroys its power."[8]

Similarly, the translucent, folded, geometric shapes of Rockburne's work that we saw in Chapter 2 (Fig. 2–14) and in the later work of Calder, which relied upon simplified industrial forms, appeal to both the intellect and to the senses.

---

[8]H. H. Arnason, *History of Modern Art*, 3rd ed. (New York: Prentice-Hall/Abrams, 1986), p. 520.

FIGURATIVE PAINTING

Although abstraction has been a driving force in American painting since the years just prior to World War II, a number of **figurative** painters have remained strong in their commitment to nature, or reality, as a point of departure for their work. De Kooning's *Women* series remains figurative, although he was an active participant in the Abstract Expressionist movement. Other artists have portrayed human and animal figures in any number of styles—realistic, expressionistic, even abstracted. In the thick of Abstract Expressionism, and in the decade following, when artists sought to create new forms of expression within its canon, painters like Alice Neel and Francis Bacon used the figure, respectively, in compositions of extreme verity and surrealist juxtaposition.

ALICE NEEL One of the most dramatic figurative painters of the era was a portrait painter named Alice Neel (1900–1984). The designation, "portraitist," however, in no way prepares the viewer for the radical nature of Neel's work: She took no commissions, but rather hand-picked her sitters from all strata of society

17–11 ALICE NEEL
THE PREGNANT WOMAN (1971). OIL ON CANVAS. 40 × 60″.
COURTESY OF THE ROBERT MILLER GALLERY, N.Y. © THE ESTATE OF ALICE NEEL.

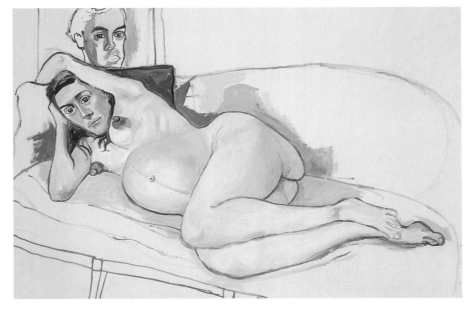

and often painted them in the nude, or semi-nude. The drama, curiously, lies in the very *un*dramatic character of her work—stark, unflinching realism. Neel's sitters were wildly diverse (from painter Andy Warhol to her housekeeper, Carmen), but her harsh style remained constant, as did her belief that she could convey something of a person's inner self through a meticulous rendering of their physical embodiment.

The Pregnant Woman (Fig. 17–11) is one in a series of canvases devoted to the nude pregnant woman. Although her subject reclines in a pose traditionally reserved for the Renaissance goddess, her facial features prevent us from reading the work as either stereotypical or archetypal. They are specific; they belong to this woman and no one else. Her pregnancy is a physical fact; unlike a work such as the Goddess Tlatzolteotl (see Fig. 1–12), Maria does not symbolize maternity or childbirth for all women. This experience is hers alone.

FRANCIS BACON   Many of the figurative canvases of Francis Bacon (b. 1910) rework themes by masters such as Giotto, Rembrandt, and van Gogh. But Bacon's personalized interpretation of history is expressionistically distorted by what must be a very raw response to the quality of contemporary life.

Head Surrounded by Sides of Beef (Fig. 17–12) is one of a series of paintings from the 1950s in which Bacon reconstructed Velásquez's portrait of Pope Innocent X. The tormented, open-mouthed figure is partially obscured, as if seen through a curtain or veil. The brilliantly composed slabs of beef, which stand like totems richly threaded with silver and gold, replace ornamental metalwork posts that rise from the back corners of the papal throne in the Velásquez portrait. Profiles can be seen in the sides of beef, and a goblet of noble proportions is constructed from the negative space between

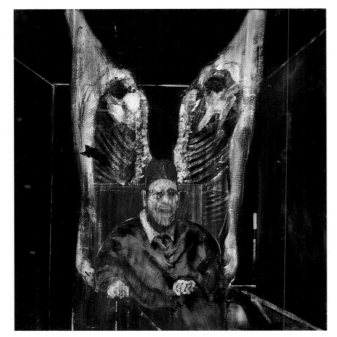

17–12 FRANCIS BACON
HEAD SURROUNDED BY SIDES OF BEEF (1954).
OIL ON CANVAS. 50⅞ × 48″.
PHOTOGRAPH COURTESY OF THE ART INSTITUTE OF CHICAGO. HARRIOTT A. FOX FUND 1956.1201.

17–13 ROBERT RAUSCHENBERG
The Bed (1955). Combine painting:
oil and pencil on pillow, quilt,
and sheet on wood supports.
75¼ × 31½ × 6½".

them. The bloody whisperings shared by the profiles are anybody's guess. Whereas the background of Velásquez's subject was a textured space of indefinite depth, Bacon's seated figure and the sides of beef are set by single-point perspective within an abstract black box.

POP ART

If one were asked to choose the contemporary art movement that was most enticing, surprising, controversial, and also exasperating, one might select **Pop art.** The term "Pop" was coined by English critic Lawrence Alloway in 1954 to refer to the universal images of "popular culture," such as movie posters, billboards, magazine and newspaper photographs, and advertisements. Pop art, by its selection of subject matter that is commonplace and familiar—subjects that are already too much with us—also challenges commonplace conceptions about the meaning of art.

Whereas many artists have strived to portray the beautiful, Pop art intentionally depicts the mundane. Whereas many artists represent the noble, stirring, or monstrous, Pop art renders the commonplace, the boring. Whereas other forms of art often elevate their subjects, Pop art is often matter-of-fact. In fact, one tenet of Pop art is that the work should be so objective that it does not show the "personal signature" of the artist. This maxim contrasts starkly, for example, with the highly personalized gestural brushstroke found in Abstract Expressionism.

RICHARD HAMILTON   Despite the widespread view that Pop art is a purely American development, it originated during the 1950s in England. British artist Richard Hamilton (b. 1922), one of its creators, had been influenced by Marcel Duchamp's idea that the

mission of art should be to destroy the normal meanings and functions of art. Hamilton's tiny collage *Just What Is It That Makes Today's Homes So Different, So Appealing?* (see Fig. 1–28) is one of the earliest and most revealing Pop art works. It is a collection of objects and emblems that form our environment. It is easy to read satire and irony into Hamilton's work, but his placement of these objects within the parameters of "art" encourages us to truly *see* them instead of just coexisting with them. The artist's selection or portrayal of these images imbues them with a larger meaning. It is up to us to divine what we will.

ROBERT RAUSCHENBERG   American Pop artist Robert Rauschenberg (b. 1925) studied in Paris and then with Josef Albers and others at the famous Black Mountain College in North Carolina. Before developing his own Pop art style, Rauschenberg experimented with loosely and broadly brushed Abstract Expressionist canvases. He is best known, however, for introducing a construction referred to as the **combine painting,** in which stuffed animals, bottles, articles of clothing and furniture, and scraps of photographs are attached to the canvas.

Rauschenberg's *The Bed* (Fig. 17–13) is a paint-splashed quilt and pillow, mounted upright on a wall as any painting might be. Here the artist toys with the traditional relationships between materials, forms, and content. The content of the work is actually its support; rather than a canvas on a stretcher, the quilt and pillow are the materials on which the painter drips and splashes his pigments. Perhaps even more outrageous is Rauschenberg's famous 1959 work, *Monogram,* in which a stuffed ram—an automobile tire wrapped around its middle—is mounted on a horizontal base that consists of scraps of photos and prints and loose, gestural painting. In more recent

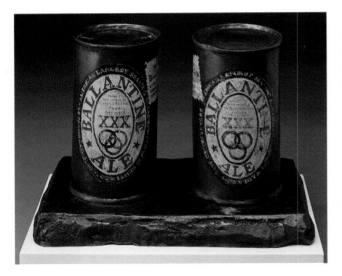

17–14 JASPER JOHNS
Painted Bronze (Ale Cans) (1960).
PAINTED BRONZE. 5½ × 8 × 4¾".
KUNSTMUSEUM (LUDWIG COLLECTION), BASEL. © RHEINISCHES BILDARCHIV.
© JASPER JOHNS/LICENSED BY VAGA, N.Y.

years, Rauschenberg's interests have expanded to include projects ranging from photo-silkscreen works (see Fig. 8–25) to set and costume design. His frequent use of gestural brushing, which he took from Abstract Expressionism and never really abandoned, seems designed to integrate the disparate elements of his constructions. Perhaps it also expresses the human impulse to integrate bits and pieces of experience.

JASPER JOHNS   Jasper Johns (b. 1930) was a classmate of Rauschenberg at Black Mountain College, and his appearance on the New York art scene was simultaneous. His early work also integrated the overall gestural brushwork of the Abstract Expressionists with the use of found objects, but unlike Rauschenberg, the object soon became central to Johns's compositions. His works frequently portray familiar objects such as numbers, maps, color charts, targets, and flags (see Fig. 2–18), integrated into a unified field by thick gestural brushwork.

One "tenet" of Pop art is that imagery is to be presented objectively, that the personal signature of the artist is to be eliminated. That principle must be modified if we are to include as Pop the works of Rauschenberg, Johns, and others, for many of them immediately betray their devotion to expressionistic brushwork.

A work by Johns that adheres more to Pop Art dogma is his *Painted Bronze (Ale Cans)* (Fig. 17–14).

In the tradition of Duchamp's **ready-mades**, Johns has bronzed two Ballantine beer cans and painted facsimile labels thereon. As with works like the Dadaist's *Fountain* (Fig. 1–34) or *Mona Lisa (L.H.O.O.Q.)* (Fig. 16–25), the questions concerning what defines a work of art are raised: Is it art because the artist chooses the object? Because he or she manipulates it? Or because the artist says it is art? One difference separates the Dada and Pop aesthetics, however: While Duchamp believed that art should be destroyed, Johns firmly believes in the creative process of art. Whereas it was left for Duchamp to stop making art (he devoted his life to the game of chess), Johns remains first and foremost an artist.

ANDY WARHOL   Andy Warhol (1930–1987) once earned a living designing packages and Christmas cards. Today he epitomizes the Pop artist in the public mind. Just as Campbell's soups represent bland, boring nourishment, Andy Warhol's soup cans (Fig. 5–17), Brillo boxes (Fig. 9–37), and Coca-Cola bottles (Fig. 17–15) elicit comments that contemporary art has become bland and boring and that there is nothing much to be said about it. Warhol also evoked contempt here and there for his underground movies, which have portrayed sleep (see Chapter 8) and explicit eroticism *(Blue Movie)* with equal disinterest. Even his shooting (from which he recovered) by a disenchanted actress seemed to evoke yawns and a "What-can-you-expect?" reaction from the public.

Warhol painted and printed much more than industrial products. During the 1960s he reproduced multiple photographs of disasters from newspapers. He executed a series of portraits of public figures such as Marilyn Monroe (Fig. 1–10) and Jackie Kennedy in the 1960s, and he turned to portraits of political leaders such as Mao Tse-Tung in the 1970s. Although his silkscreens have at least in their technique met the Pop art objective of obscuring the personal signature of the artist, his compositions and his expressionistic brushing of areas of his paintings achieved an individual stamp.

It could be argued that other Pop artists owe some of their popularity to the inventiveness of Andy Warhol. Without Warhol, Pop art might have remained a quiet movement, one that might have escaped the notice of the art historians of the next century.

17–15 ANDY WARHOL
GREEN COCA-COLA BOTTLES (1962). OIL ON CANVAS. 82¼ × 57″.

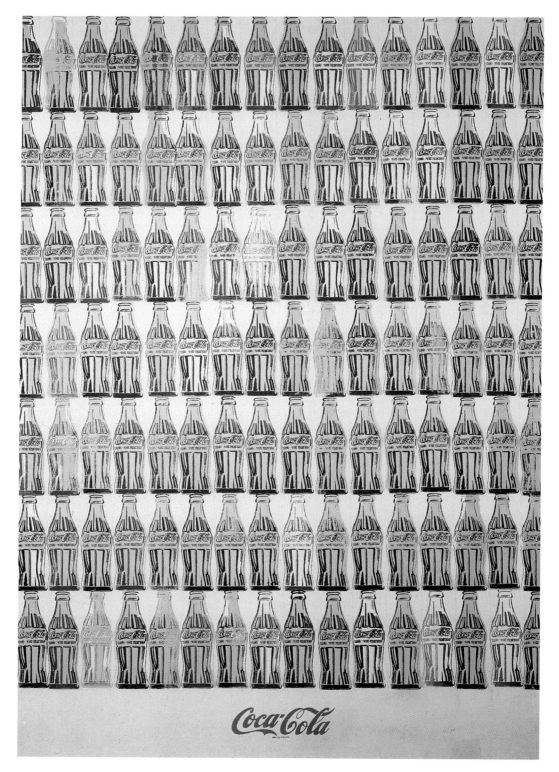

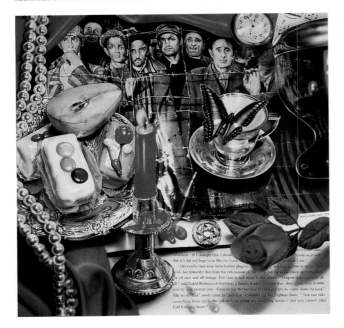

What, then, do we make of Pop Art? Is it a cynical gesture to place expensive but meaningless objects in a gullible marketplace? Is it the sincere expression of deeply felt experience? Is it, perhaps, the only contemporary art movement that is a reflection of its times? Is it an attempt to countermand the unreachable and esoteric in the art of the 1940s and 1950s and provide the public with an art that, on some level, it can relate to?

PHOTOREALISM

Photorealism, or the rendering of subjects with sharp, photographic precision, is firmly rooted in the long, realistic tradition in the arts. But as a movement that first gained major recognition during the early 1970s, it also owes some of its impetus to the Pop artist's objective portrayal of familiar images. Photorealism is also in part a reaction to the expressionistic and abstract movements of the twentieth century. That is, Photorealism permits artists to do something very new to the public eye even while they are doing something very old.

AUDREY FLACK   Audrey Flack (b. 1931) was born in New York and studied at the High School of Music and Art, at Cooper Union, and at Yale University's Graduate

School. During the 1950s she showed figure paintings that were largely ignored, in part because of the popularity of Abstract Expressionism, in part because women artists, in general, had not been privy to the critical attention that their male colleagues had received. Yet throughout these years she persisted in a sharply realistic, or **trompe l'oeil** style. Her illusionistically real canvases often result from a technique involving the projection of color slides onto her canvases, which she then sketches and paints in detail. Since the 1970s, Flack's focus has largely shifted away from the human figure to richly complex still-life arrangements.

One of Flack's best-known works from the 1970s is *World War II (Vanitas)* (Fig. 17–16), a painting that combines Margaret Bourke-White's haunting photo, *The Living Dead of Buchenwald* (see Fig. 8–16), with ordinary objects that teem with life—pastries, fruit, a teacup, a candle, a string of pearls. The subtitle of the work, "Vanitas," refers to a type of still-life composition frequently found in the sixteenth and seventeenth centuries. The content was selected specifically to encourage the viewer to meditate on death as the inescapable end to human life. Flack's items are all the more poignant in their juxtaposition since they suggest lives cut short—abruptly and drastically—by Hitler's Holocaust. The painting further functions as a memorial to those who perished at the hands of the Nazis and as a tribute to survivors. Flack is fascinated by the ways in which objects reflect light, and in this painting and others she uses an airbrush to create a surface that imitates the textures of these objects. She layers primary colors in transparent glazes to produce the desired hues without obvious brushstrokes. The resulting palette is harsh and highly saturated, and the sense of realism stunning.

OP ART (OPTICAL PAINTING)

In **Op art,** also called **optical painting,** the artist manipulates light or color fields, or repeats patterns of line, in order to produce visual illusions. The effects can sometimes be disorienting. Hungarian-born Victor Vasarely (b. 1908) may be the best-known Op artist. In many paintings of recent decades, Vasarely has experimented with the illusion of three dimensions in two-dimensional

17–17 RICHARD ANUSZKIEWICZ
ENTRANCE TO GREEN (1970). ACRYLIC ON CANVAS. 9 × 6′.
PRIVATE COLLECTION. © RICHARD ANUSZKIEWICZ/LICENSED BY VAGA, N.Y. 1997.

17–18 SUSAN ROTHENBERG
DIAGONAL (1975). ACRYLIC AND TEMPERA ON CANVAS. 46 × 60″.
PRIVATE COLLECTION. COURTESY SPERONE WESTWATER, N.Y.

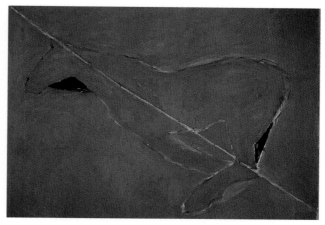

CONTEMPORARY TRENDS

The decade of the 1970s witnessed a strong presence of realism in the visual arts that was, in part, a virulent reaction against the introspective and subjective abstract tendencies that had gripped American painting since World War II.

NEW IMAGE PAINTING

At the tail end of that decade—in 1979—New York's Whitney Museum of American Art mounted a controversial, though significant, exhibition called "New Image Painting." The participants, including Jennifer Bartlett (see Fig. 2–55), Susan Rothenberg (b. 1945), and eight other artists, were doing something very different: They were, in their own way, reconciling the disparate styles of abstraction and representation. The image was central to their compositions, much in the tradition of realist artists. The images were often so simplified, however, that they conveyed the grandeur of abstract shapes. These images never dominated other aesthetic components of the work, such as color, texture, or even composition. Rather, they cohabited the work in elegant balance.

Susan Rothenberg's *Diagonal* (Fig. 17–18) stands as a prime example of **new image painting**, bringing together representational and abstract art. The highly simplified and sketchy contours of a horse in full gallop barely separate the animal from the lushly painted field. While the subject is strong and inescapable, its reality is diminished by the unified palette, the bisecting

space through the use of linear perspective and atmospheric effects (see Fig. 2–19).

RICHARD ANUSZKIEWICZ   *Entrance to Green* (Fig. 17–17), a composition by Richard Anuszkiewicz (b. 1930), is a fine example of the sense of movement that can be achieved in Op art. Finely drawn rectangles that decrease in size as we move from the outer edges of the canvas to its center create the optical illusion of openings that recede into space. This recession, however, is balanced by the use of warm and cool colors that typically have their own tendency to advance or recede. Thus, the warm yellow and orange of the center rectangles push forward, while the greens and blues fade into the background. The resultant tension creates a vibrating effect. We read foreground as background, and vice-versa.

17–19 KIM MacCONNEL

17–19 KIM MacCONNEL
LE TOUR (1979). ACRYLIC SILKSCREEN ON FABRIC. 86½ × 87½″.
COLLECTION OF ANITA GROSSMAN. HOLLY SOLOMON GALLERY.

17–20 ELIZABETH MURRAY
SAIL BABY (1983). OIL ON CANVAS. 126 × 135″ (3 PANELS).
COLLECTION OF WALKER ART CENTER, MINNEAPOLIS, WALKER SPECIAL PURCHASE FUND, 1984.

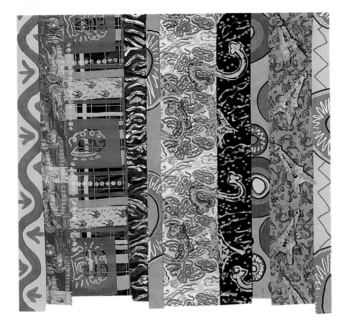

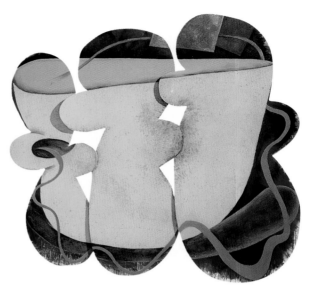

diagonal line, and the structured composition with its repetitive triangles. Rothenberg favored the horse as image in the 1970s, although in the 1980s she turned to the human form. The artist has said of her earlier compositions that "The horse was a way of not doing people, yet it was a symbol of people, a self-portrait, really."[9]

PATTERN PAINTING

Though painted at the same time, it would seem that no two works could be more drastically at odds with one another than Rothenberg's epitome of the "new image" aesthetic and Kim MacConnel's (b. 1946) riotous **pattern painting.** The stylistic and pictorial heritages of these artists are completely different; while Rothenberg's originality lies in her ability to work within and expand the possibilities of representational and abstract constructs, MacConnel allowed his early experiments with rigid geometric forms to be subsumed by a vast and more lively array of evocative signs, symbols, and patterns. What had heretofore been a term of degradation in the arts—"decorative"—became the cornerstone of his compositions. *Le Tour* (Fig. 17–19) is composed of patterned strips that are silkscreened onto

[9]Susan Rothenberg, in Grace Glueck, "Susan Rothenberg: New Outlook for a Visionary Artist," *The New York Times Magazine,* July 22, 1984, p. 20.

fabric and stitched together. A remarkable balance and contradictory reserve are achieved through the juxtaposition of simple and complex patterns and the almost architectural placement of the vertical panels. MacConnel's art form attacks all conventions, from the banality of decoration to the materials and methods associated with women's artistic endeavors.

THE SHAPED CANVAS

The art of the 1980s was nothing if not pluralistic. Painters of extraordinary talent and innovation affirmed their love of the medium and put an end to the speculation of the late 1960s and 1970s that "painting was dead." Many artists, including Frank Stella, Judy Pfaff, and Elizabeth Murray, have obscured the lines between painting, sculpture, and installations by radically changing the shape of their canvases.

In Elizabeth Murray we find a painter who has affirmed a belief in abstraction as a viable style, in the midst of trends that find it sterile and unreachable. Coupling clear-cut, abstract shapes that nonetheless are suggestive of organic forms, or taking specific objects—such as a teacup or a table—and treating them as isolated abstract shapes, Murray has created an artform that is personal and reachable in spite of its emphasis on formal concerns. *Sail Baby* (Fig. 17–20) is a huge work composed of three shaped canvases. Although the somewhat repetitive shapes have strong, separate identities because of their prominent contours, the entire work is unified by the painting of a teacup that traverses all three supports. Beyond the common imagery, Murray has explained that the painting functions as a narrative: "[it is] about my family. It's about myself and my brother and my sister, and I think, it is also about my own three children, even though Daisy (her youngest daughter) wasn't born yet."[10] The individual identities of the separate shapes may, in this context, represent the individuality of the siblings, while their interconnectedness is established by the image that overrides them as well as the snake-like green line (an umbilical cord?) that flows from the smallest shape and wends around to the right, behind the largest. Though essentially an abstract work, its references to human experience cannot be ignored or minimized. They are essential to our comprehension of the piece.

Neo-Expressionism

The center of the art world moved to New York in the 1940s for historical as well as artistic reasons. The first-generation Abstract Expressionists developed a style that was viewed worldwide as highly original and influential. They laid claim to the tenet that the *process* of painting was a viable alternative to subject matter. In the early 1980s, a group of artists who were born during the Abstract Expressionist era—though on other shores—wholeheartedly revived the gestural manner and experimentation with materials that the Americans had devised four decades earlier, but with an added dimension. These young German and Italian artists, who came to be called **Neo-Expressionists**, detested painting "about nothing." Born as they were during the darkest years of postwar Europe, when Germany and Italy stood utterly defeated, these artists would mature to portray the bitter ironies and angst of their generation in emotionally fraught images that are rooted in history, literature, and expressionistic art.

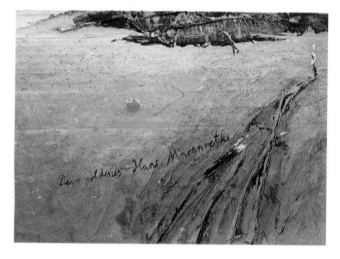

17–21 ANSELM KIEFER
Dein Goldenes Haar, Margarethe (1981). Mixed media on paper. 14 × 18¾".
Courtesy of the Marian Goodman Gallery, N.Y.

The most remarkable of these Neo-Expressionists is certainly Anselm Kiefer (b. 1945). Kiefer has been able to synthesize an expressionistic painterly style with strong abstract elements in a narrative form of painting that makes multivalent references to German history and culture. The casual observer cannot hope to decipher Kiefer's paintings; they are highly intellectual, obscure, and idiosyncratic. But, at the same time, they are overpowering in their scale, their larger-than-life subjects, and their textural, encrusted surfaces.

Kiefer's *Dein Goldenes Haar, Margarethe* (Fig. 17–21) serves as an excellent example of the artist's formal and literary concerns. The title of the work, and others of this series, refers to a poem by Paul Celan entitled "Your Golden Hair, Margarethe," which describes the destruction of European Jewry through the images of a golden-haired German woman named Margarethe and a dark-haired Jewish woman, Shulamith. Against a pale grey-blue background, Kiefer uses actual straw to suggest the hair of the German woman, contrasting it with thick black paint that lies charred on the upper canvas, to symbolize the hair of her unfortunate counterpart. Between them a German tank presides over this human destruction, isolated against a wasteland of its own creation. Kiefer here, as often, scrawls his titles, or other words across the canvas surface, sometimes veiling them with his textured materials. The materials function as content; they become symbols to which we must emotionally and intellectually respond.

[10]*Elizabeth Murray: Paintings and Drawings,* exhibition catalogue organized by Sue Graze and Kathy Halbreich, essay by Roberta Smith (New York: Abrams, in association with the Dallas Museum of Art and the MIT Committee on the Visual Arts, 1987), p. 64.

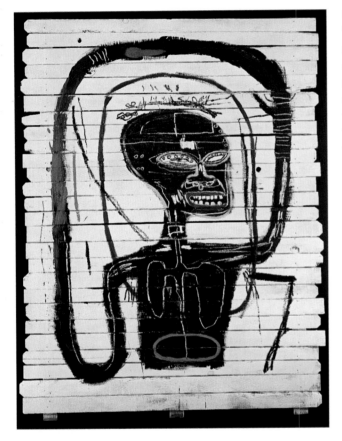

17–22 JEAN-MICHEL BASQUIAT
FLEXIBLE (1984). ACRYLIC AND OILSTICK ON WOOD. 102 × 75″.
COURTESY OF THE ROBERT MILLER GALLERY, N.Y. © THE ESTATE OF JEAN-MICHEL BASQUIAT./
© 1998 ARTISTS RIGHTS SOCIETY (ARS), N.Y./ADAGP, PARIS.

GRAFFITIST ART

The art movements of the 1980s brought anything and everything into the realm of possibility; art was stripped of convention, and the aesthetic lines that were long ago drawn in the sand were smudged, even erased. In what other way could you explain the fine art entries of cartoonists and graffitists in New York's art galleries—the "taggers and bombers" (those who wrote messages and those who used spray paint) who lived in the streets and tried, illegally, to communicate their ethnic rage?

Jean-Michel Basquiat (1960–1988) was a Haitian-Hispanic artist who dropped out of school at age 17. He is now considered to have been the most talented of the graffiti artists who garnered the attention of the art world. Works like *Flexible* (Fig. 17–22) employ crude materials and techniques to enhance potent images that are often culled from African art. In this work, the arms of a schematic figure are joined in a loop that enframes its mask-like head. The torso, shown in half-length, is overpainted with simplistic markings indicating the stomach, lungs, esophagus, and larynx. Spatters of paint and thick brushstrokes of bright color grant the work a directness of expression. Basquiat was known for his uncanny ability to balance the primitive and the sophisticated; he was a savvy artist who never abandoned his connection to the streets.

SCULPTURE

Contemporary sculpture, like contemporary painting, has taken many forms. First we shall look at the sculpture of Henry Moore, which spans the earlier part of the twentieth century and the postwar years. Then we shall survey the figurative and abstract sculpture of the postwar years.

SCULPTURE AT MIDCENTURY

At midcentury there were two major directions in sculpture: figurative and abstract. In a moment we shall follow these two paths over the years. First let us have a look at British artist Henry Moore, whose work encompasses both the figurative and the abstract and who, more than any other individual, epitomizes sculpture in the twentieth century.

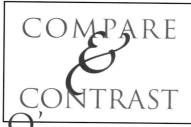
O'KEEFFE'S *RED HILLS AND BONES* WITH GRAVES'S *VARIABILITY AND REPETITION OF SIMILAR FORMS II*

Both Georgia O'Keeffe and Nancy Graves, at a point in their careers, had a fascination with animal bones and skeletons. O'Keeffe found the bones in the desert landscape of New Mexico, bleached white by the blazing sun (Fig. 17–23). Graves first appeared on the New York art scene in 1968 with an exhibition of life-sized camels, which began a long-term interest in the skeletons of these desert creatures. How, and why, does each artist use animal bones in her work? What is more important for each artist: The subject matter? The shapes or forms? Do the bones seem to express life? Death? Does Graves's composition (Fig. 17–24) imply motion? How would you compare Graves's sculpture with the motion photography of Muybridge (see Fig. 2–47)?

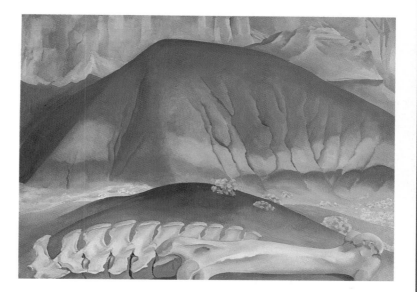

17–23 GEORGIA O'KEEFFE
RED HILLS AND BONES (1941). OIL ON CANVAS. 30 × 40″.

PHILADELPHIA MUSEUM OF ART. THE ALFRED STIEGLITZ COLLECTION. © THE GEORGIA O'KEEFFE FOUNDATION/ARTISTS RIGHTS SOCIETY (ARS), N.Y.

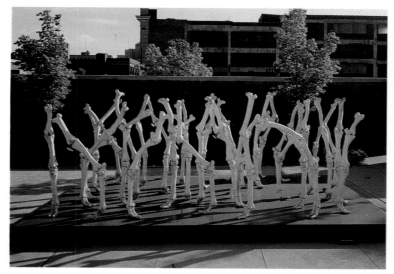

17–24 NANCY GRAVES
VARIABILITY AND REPETITION OF SIMILAR FORMS II (1979). BRONZE WITH WHITE PATINA AND CORTEN STEEL BASE. 72 × 144 × 192″.

COLLECTION OF AKRON ART MUSEUM, PURCHASED WITH THE AID OF THE MARY AND LOUIS S. MYERS FOUNDATION, THE FIRESTONE FOUNDATION, THE NATIONAL ENDOWMENT FOR THE ARTS, AND THE MUSEUM ACQUISITION FUND. © NANCY GRAVES FOUNDATION/LICENSED BY VAGA, N.Y.

17–25 HENRY MOORE
Lincoln Center Reclining Figure (1963–65).
BRONZE. HEIGHT: 16′; WIDTH: 30′.
LINCOLN CENTER FOR THE PERFORMING ARTS, INC., N.Y.

17–26 GEORGE SEGAL
Cézanne Still Life #5 (1982).
PAINTED PLASTER, WOOD, AND METAL. 37 × 36 × 29″.
PHOTOGRAPH © 1984 VIRGINIA MUSEUM OF FINE ARTS, RICHMOND. GIFT OF SYDNEY AND
FRANCES LEWIS FOUNDATION. © GEORGE SEGAL/LICENSED BY VAGA, N.Y.

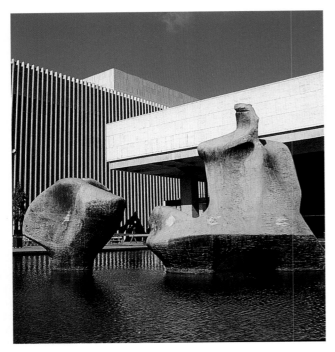

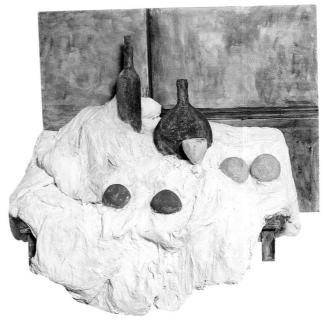

HENRY MOORE   Henry Moore (1898–1986) had a long
and prolific career that spanned the seven decades since
the 1920s, but we introduce him at this point because,
despite his productivity, his influence was not generally
felt until after World War II.

In the late 1920s, Moore was intrigued by the massiveness of stone. In an early effort to be true to his
material, he executed blocky reclining figures reminiscent of the Native American art of Mexico. In the 1930s,
Moore turned to bronze and wood and was also influenced
by Picasso. His figures became abstracted and more
fluid. Voids opened up, and air and space began to flow
through his works.

At midcentury, Moore's works received the attention
they deserve. He continued to produce figurative works,
but he also executed a series of abstract bronzes in the
tradition of his early reclining figures, such as the one
at Lincoln Center for the Performing Arts in New York
City (Fig. 17–25). No longer as concerned about limiting
the scope of his expression because of material, he could
now let his bronzes assume the massiveness of his

earlier stonework. However, his continued exploration
of abstract biomorphic shapes and his separation and
opening of forms created a lyricism that was lacking in
his earlier sculptures.

CONTEMPORARY FIGURATIVE SCULPTURE

Figurative art continues to intrigue sculptors as well as
painters. Some figurative works have the utter realism
of Fumio Yoshimura's (b. 1926) *Dog Snapper* (Fig. 6–16).
Others are highly abstracted, such as the recent reclining figures of Henry Moore.

GEORGE SEGAL   George Segal (b. 1924) was a student
of Hans Hofmann and painted until 1958. During the
1960s he achieved renown as a Pop art sculptor. As in
The Diner (Fig. 6–8), he casts his figures in plaster from
live models and then surrounds them with familiar
objects of the day—Coke machines, Formica and chrome

17–27 MARISOL
WOMEN AND DOG (1964). FUR, LEATHER, PLASTER, SYNTHETIC
POLYMER, WOOD. 72 × 82 × 16″.

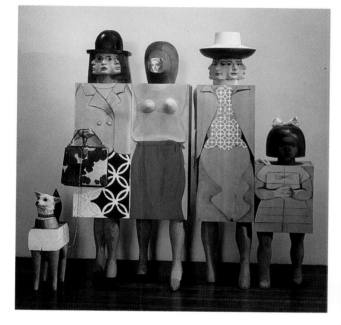

17–28 DUANE HANSON
TOURISTS (1970). POLYESTER RESIN/FIBERGLASS. LIFE-SIZE.

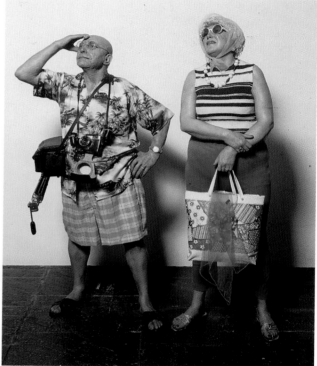

tables, chairs, shower stalls, bathtubs, porcelain sinks
and copper pipes, mirrors, window shades, neon signs,
telephone booths, television sets. In Segal's able hands,
these Pop items clearly proclaim the horrors of the age.

Segal has also made sensuous reliefs of women,
and, more recently, still lifes, as in *Cézanne Still Life #5*
(Fig. 17–26). The plaster of the drapery is modeled extensively by the sculptor's fingers in these reliefs, giving
large areas an almost gestural quality. In many of his
recent works, Segal has used primary colors, eliminating the ghostlike quality of his earlier works.

MARISOL   Venezuelan artist Marisol Escobar (b. 1930),
known to the world as Marisol, creates figurative assemblages from plaster, wood, fabric, paint, found objects, photographs, and other sources. As in *Women and
Dog* (Fig. 17–27), Marisol frequently repeats images of
her own face and body in her work. She has also used
these techniques to render satirical portraits of world
leaders.

DUANE HANSON   Duane Hanson (b. 1925) was reared
on a dairy farm in Minnesota. His *Tourists* (Fig. 17–28)
is characteristic of the work of a number of contemporary

sculptors in that it uses synthetic substances such as
liquid polyester resin to closely approximate the visual
and tactile qualities of flesh. Such literal surfaces allow
the artist no expression of personal signature. In the
presence of a Hanson figure, or a John De Andrea nude,
viewers watch for the rising and falling of the chest.
They do not wish to stare too hard or to say something
careless on the off-chance that the sculpture is real.
There is an electricity in gallery storerooms where these
sculptures coexist in waiting. One tries to decipher
which ones will get up and walk away.

Duane Hanson's liberal use of off-the-rack apparel
and objects such as "stylish" sunglasses, photographic
paraphernalia, and shopping bags lend these figures a
caustic, satirical edge. But not all of Hanson's sculptures have been lighthearted. Like Andy Warhol, Hanson has portrayed disasters, such as death scenes from
the conflict in Vietnam. In recent works he has focused
more on the psychological content of his figures, as
expressed by tense postures and grimaces.

17–29 DEBORAH BUTTERFIELD
HORSE #6–82 (1982). STEEL, SHEET ALUMINUM, WIRE, AND
TAR. 76 × 108 × 41".

DALLAS MUSEUM OF ART. FOUNDATION FOR THE ARTS COLLECTION, EDWARD S. MARCUS FUND
(1982.96.FA).

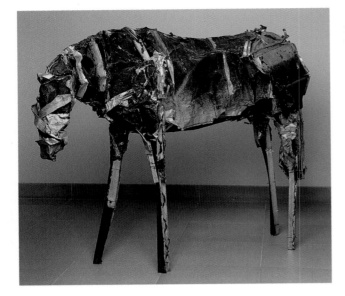

DEBORAH BUTTERFIELD Montana sculptor Deborah
Butterfield (b. 1949) has been interested in horses since
her childhood in California. Horses, of course, are
powerful creatures, and there is a history of equestrian
sculptures that commemorate soldiers. Such horses are
usually stallions that are vehicles of war, but Butterfield
turns to mares. In this way, like Susan Rothenberg,
she uses horses to create something of a symbolic
self-portrait:

> *I first used horse images as a metaphorical*
> *substitute for myself—it was a way of doing a*
> *self-portrait one step removed from the specificity*
> *of Deborah Butterfield. . . . The only horse sculpture*
> *I'd ever seen was very masculine. . . . No knight or*
> *soldier would ever be caught riding a mare into*
> *battle, it was just not done. . . . [What] I wanted to*
> *do [was] to make this small reference to the*
> *[Vietnam] war [with a] big sculpture that was*
> *very powerful and strong, and yet, very feminine*
> *and capable of procreation rather than just*
> *destruction.[11]*

Horse #6–82 (Fig. 17–29) is constructed from scrap
metal derived from a crushed aluminum trailer. Ribbons of shiny metal wrap surfaces splattered with tar,
giving form to the animal. Although her horses are figural, Butterfield notes that their meaning "isn't about
horses at all."[12]

CONTEMPORARY ABSTRACT SCULPTURE

Abstract sculpture remains vital, ever varied in form
and substance. Contemporary abstract sculptures range
from the wrappings of Christo (see Fig. 7–38) and the
earthworks of Smithson (see Fig. 6–31) to the mobiles
of Alexander Calder (see Fig. 6–28), the mysterious
wooden walls of Louise Nevelson (see Fig. 6–22), the
machined surfaces of David Smith's cubes (see Figs. 2–8
and 17–30), and the anti-art machines of Jean Tinguely
(see Fig. 6–29).

DAVID SMITH American artist David Smith (1906–1965)
moved away from figurative sculpture in the 1940s.
His works of the 1950s were compositions of linear
steel that crossed back and forth as they swept through
space.

Many sculptors of massive works create the designs
but then farm out their execution to assistants or to
foundries. Smith, however, took pride in constructing
his own metal sculptures. Even though Smith's shapes
are geometrically pure, his loving burnishing of their
highly reflective surfaces grants them the overall gestural quality found in Abstract Expressionist paintings.

TONY SMITH Tony Smith (b. 1912) has fashioned massive angular black forms from steel and other materials.
They are frequently shown in painted plywood before
being rendered in steel. His *Die* (the singular of *dice*)
executed in 1962 is a monumental black steel cube,
6 feet on a side. *Die* shocks because of its explicitly

---

[11]Excerpts from Deborah Butterfield in *Deborah Butterfield* (Winston-Salem, N.C.:
Southeastern Center for Contemporary Art, 1983; and Providence, R.I.: Rhode
Island School of Design Museum of Art, 1981).

[12]Deborah Butterfield, in Graham W. J. Beal, "Eight Horsepower," in *Viewpoints:
Deborah Butterfield: Sculpture* (Minneapolis: Walker Art Center, 1982).

17–30 DAVID SMITH
CUBI SERIES. STAINLESS STEEL.
(LEFT) CUBI XVIII (1964). HEIGHT 9′8″. MUSEUM OF FINE ARTS,
BOSTON. *(CENTER)* CUBI XVII (1963). HEIGHT 9′. DALLAS
MUSEUM OF FINE ARTS. *(RIGHT) CUBI XIX* (1964). HEIGHT 9′ 5″.
TATE GALLERY, LONDON.
DAVID SMITH PAPERS, ARCHIVES OF AMERICAN ART, SMITHSONIAN INSTITUTION.

17–31 JACKIE FERRARA
A207 RECALL (1980). PINE. 76½ × 37½ × 37½″.
MICHAEL KLEIN, INC., N.Y.

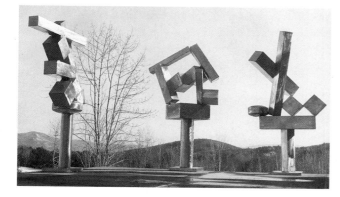

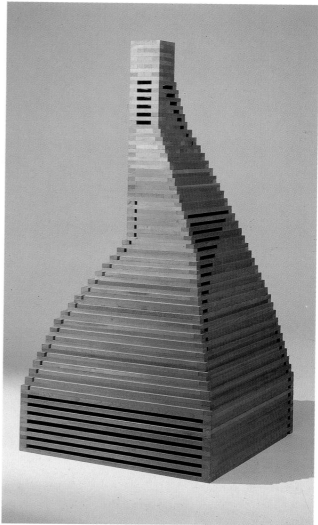

simple expression of form. Other pieces are more
involved, jutting and arching into the air and then turning back on themselves.

Moses (see the nearby "Compare and Contrast"
feature), constructed from black painted steel, stands
15 feet high on the Princeton University campus. Out in
the open, with its metal points, it is something of a
dangerous object. Its massiveness is somewhat compromised by the flow of space throughout. The parallel
edges lend the work a certain rhythm, but it does not
seem quite balanced: the parallel stacks give the piece a
jutting, top-heavy appearance. The imbalance makes
the sculpture seem poised, ready for action.

The stacks are probably a reworking of the horns
that adorn earlier representations of Moses, including
that of Michelangelo. According to the Bible, when
Moses descended from Mt. Sinai with the Commandments, he had an "aura" about him. The word *aura* had
been mistranslated in earlier centuries as "horns." Note
also that if Smith's *Moses* seems poised for action, this
implied movement may reflect the dynamism of the
Michelangelo statue.

JACKIE FERRARA During the 1960s, Jackie Ferrara's
works during the 1960s employed fetishistic materials
such as feathers, fur, and rope, which were often suspended from the ceiling. In the 1970s she began to deal
with gravity from the other end, so to speak, and
created a number of pyramidal forms set firmly on the
floor. *A207 Recall* (Fig. 17–31) has something of the
appearance of a Postmodern chimney and is constructed
from pieces of pine that are glued together. Her concern
with the interior as well as the exterior of the work is
suggested by the series of patterned glimpses within
that alternately complement the shape of the exterior
and set it further awry. While the wooden surface renders her work warm, and the partial revelations make
it mysterious, the sculpture was created with attention
to precise mathematical relationships.

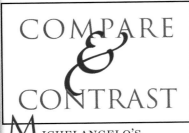

COMPARE
&
CONTRAST

MICHELANGELO'S
MOSES
WITH
SMITH'S *MOSES*

Michelangelo's *Moses* (Fig. 17–32) stands as the most important rendering of the prophet in the history of art. It is the central work in the ambitious tomb of Pope Julius II.

Tony Smith's contemporary *Moses* (Fig. 17–33) is dramatically different from the Renaissance sculpture of Michelangelo, yet there are also similarities. For example, what iconographic details do the works share? How do the works differ in style? How does each artist make his work appear poised for action? How does Smith's sculpture "earn" its title? How does the work impart a sense of leadership or of law, if indeed it does? Is there something of the feeling of what we know of Moses in the work's severe formality, in its somber monumentality?

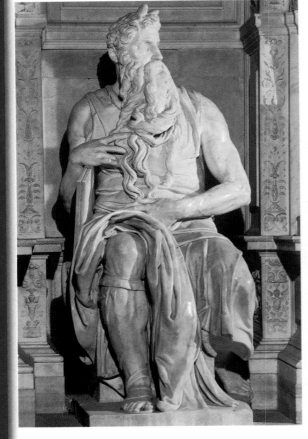

17–32 MICHELANGELO
MOSES (C. 1515–16). MARBLE. HEIGHT: 91½".

SAN PIETRO IN VINCOLI, ROME.

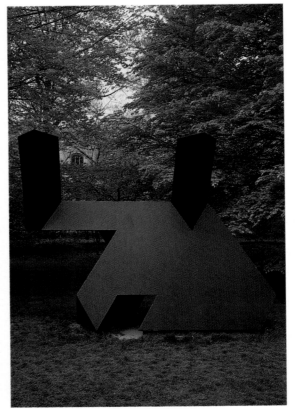

17–33 TONY SMITH
MOSES (MODEL EXECUTED 1967–68; FABRICATED AND INSTALLED 1969). PAINTED MILD STEEL. NUMBER 1 OF EDITION OF 2. HEIGHT: 15′1″; LENGTH: 11′6″.

THE JOHN B. PUTNAM, JR. MEMORIAL COLLECTION, PRINCETON UNIVERSITY.

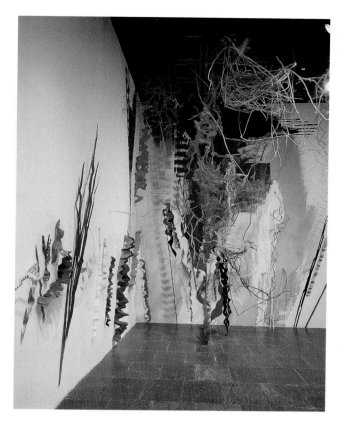

JUDY PFAFF   Another contemporary sculpture form
is the **installation**, in which materials from planks
of wood to pieces of string and metal are assembled to
fit within specific room-sized exhibition spaces.
Installations are not necessarily intended to be permanent. In *Dragons* (Fig. 17–34), by Judy Pfaff (b. 1946),
the viewer roams around within the elements of the
piece, an experience that can be pleasurable and
overwhelming among the vibrant colors and assorted
textures. Many of the elements of Pfaff's installations
hang down around the viewer, creating an atmosphere
reminiscent of foliage, sometimes of an underwater
landscape.

NANCY GRAVES   Nancy Graves (b. 1940) has worked
both in figural and abstract styles and is comfortable
with ignoring the traditional boundary between them.
In addition to sculpture, she has also created drawings,
prints, paintings, and films. When she was only 29 years
old, the Whitney Museum exhibited her life-sized, naturalistic camels.

Tarot (Fig. 17–35) is made of traditional bronze
but is directly cast, such that the original object is
destroyed as it is reborn into the metal. In a sense,
Graves redoes nature. Much of the innovativeness
of the piece is derived from the juxtapositions and
coloration. Graves has focused much of her attention
on the development of polychrome (multicolored) patinas with poured acrylic and baked enamel. *Tarot* (the
word refers to a set of allegorical cards used in
fortune-telling) is an assemblage of sundry humanmade
and natural elements—strange flowers, lacy plants,
noodles, dried fish, lampshades, tools and machinery,
even packing materials. With this concoction—or
perhaps this history—humankind is cast an eccentric
fortune indeed.

JEAN TINGUELY

> *The only stable thing is movement.*
> —Jean Tinguely

Swiss-born kinetic sculptor Jean Tinguely (b. 1925) is
an able satirist of the machine age who shares the
Dadaist view of art as anti-art. He is best known for his

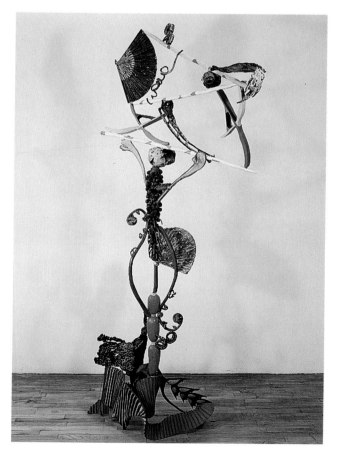

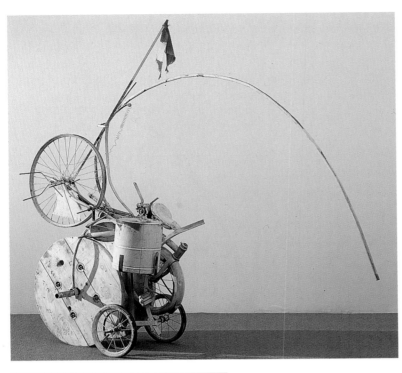

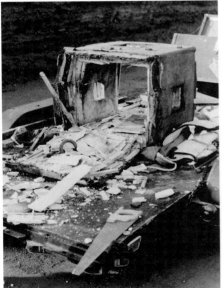

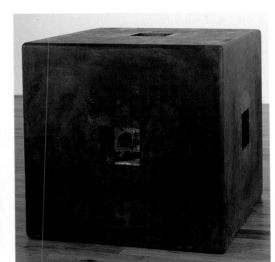

Homage to New York (Fig. 17–36), a motorized, mixed-media construction which self-destructed (intentionally) in the garden of the Museum of Modern Art. But an unexpected fire within the machine necessitated the intervention of the New York Fire Department, which provided a spontaneous touch without charge. Tinguely's machines, more than those on which his work comments, frequently fail to perform precisely as intended.

As a further reflection of his philosophy of art, in the 1950s Tinguely introduced kinetic sculptures that served as "painting machines." One of them produced thousands of "Abstract Expressionist" paintings—on whose quality, perhaps, we need not comment.

JACKIE WINSOR Canadian-born Jackie Winsor (b. 1941), like many of her contemporaries, is taken with the primal aesthetics of simple geometric forms. Yet unlike the machined smoothness employed by David Smith, her works are more likely to have a weathered, organic, handmade look. Winsor's works are a while in the making, and though she has the resources to have others construct them from her design, hers is an art of the hand as well as of the heart and the mind.

Exploded Piece (Fig. 17–37) is one of the sculptures that Winsor also sees as a performance piece. Winsor is not destructive in the mold of Tinguely. (In fact, the culmination of the "performance" was her reconstruction of

17–38 MIRIAM SCHAPIRO,
IN COLLABORATION WITH SHERRY
BRODY
THE DOLL HOUSE (1972) FROM
WOMANHOUSE, THREE–
DIMENSIONAL CONSTRUCTION. MIXED
MEDIA. 84 × 40 × 41 . COLLECTION OF
THE NATIONAL MUSEUM OF
AMERICAN ART, SMITHSONIAN
INSTITUTION, WASHINGTON, D.C.
COLLECTION OF THE ARTIST. COURTESY OF THE
STEINBAUM KRAUSS GALLERY, N.Y.

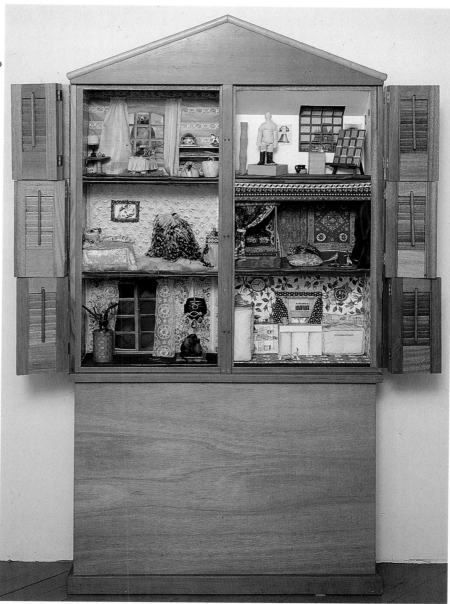

the exploded parts into a perfect whole.) Rather, she seems pre-occupied with the nature and the potentials of her materials. Another work, *Burnt Piece,* seemed to pose and answer the question, "What will happen to a half-concrete, half-wood cube when it is set afire?" *Exploded Piece,* similarly, explores the results of detonating an explosive charge within a cube made of wood, reinforced concrete, and other materials.

It seems appropriate to leave the section on abstract sculpture with a bang.

FEMINIST ART

While on the East Coast Pop art was on the wane and photoreal-ism on the rise, happenings on the West Coast were about to change the course of women's art, history, and criticism for-ever. In 1970, a midwestern artist named Judy Gerowitz—who would soon call herself Judy Chicago—initiated a feminist studio art course at Fresno State College in northern California. One year later, she collaborated with artist Miriam Schapiro on a feminist art program at the California Institute of Arts in Valencia. Their in-terests and efforts culminated in another California project—a communal installation in Hollywood called *Womanhouse.*

What was *Womanhouse?* Beyond being a milestone in the history of women's art, it was a fantastic under-taking, a daring project. Teaming up with students from the University of California, Chicago and Schapiro took over a dilapidated mansion and refurbished each room in a theme built around women's experiences: The "Kitchen," by Robin Weltsch, was covered from walls to ceiling with breast-shaped eggs; a "Menstruation

Bathroom," by Chicago, included the waste products of female menstruation cycles in a sterile white environ-ment; another room housed a child-sized dollhouse, in which Schapiro and Sherry Brody juxtaposed mundane and frightening objects to effect a kind of black humor (Fig. 17–38). The now-famous installation became a much-needed hub for area women's groups and was itself the impetus for the founding a year later of the Los Angeles Women's Building, still active today.

Why was *Womanhouse* important? The reasons are as varied as they are numerous. At the very least, it called attention to women artists, their wants, their needs. In some ways it was an expression of anger toward injustice of art world politics that many women artists experienced—lack of attention by critics, curators, and historians; pressure to work in canonical styles.

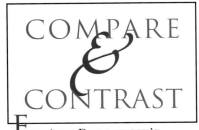

COMPARE & CONTRAST

EUGÈNE DELACROIX'S
*LIBERTY LEADING
THE PEOPLE*,
KÄTHE KOLLWITZ'S
OUTBREAK, AND
FRANCISCO GOYA'S *AND
THEY ARE LIKE WILD
BEASTS*

The evolution of feminist art finds its parallel in the evolution of feminist art history. The dust jacket of a text entitled *Women, Art, and Power and Other Essays* by the nineteenth-century art scholar, Linda Nochlin, bears a detail of Eugène Delacroix's *Liberty Leading the People* (Fig. 17–39). At its center is the allegory of Liberty—a fast-striding woman bearing the tricolor in one hand and a bayonet in the other—looking for all the world like an Amazon of Ancient Greece. An archetypal figure set within an archetypal setting of an archetypal revolution. So, where's the rub?

Nochlin, who also explored the uncharted territory of feminist issues in art history and criticism, notes in her text that "Delacroix's powerful figure of Liberty is, like almost all feminine embodiments of human virtue—Justice, Truth, Temperance, Victory—an allegory rather than a concrete historical woman, an example of what Simone de Beauvoir (French existential philosopher and author of *The Second Sex*) has called Woman-as-Other." By contrast, the forceful figure who inspires courage and motivates action in Kollwitz's *Outbreak* (Fig. 17–40) is an historically documented leader of the sixteenth-century German Peasant's War. She was known as Black Anna. Delacroix's Liberty does not portray the role of women in the French Revolution, but rather embodies the intangible spirit that fueled the burning desire

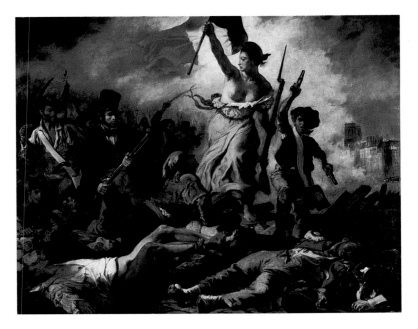

17–39 EUGÈNE DELACROIX
LIBERTY LEADING THE PEOPLE (1830).
OIL ON CANVAS. 8'6" × 10'10".
LOUVRE MUSEUM, PARIS.

for freedom. Kollwitz's Anna is at the front. It is through her example—her indomitable spirit at the cost of her own life—that we experience, firsthand, the quest for justice.

The Spanish artist, Francisco Goya, also turned his attention to the subject of women and aggression (Fig. 17–41) in one of a suite of prints entitled *Disasters of War*. At first glance we observe a group of women, one with an infant astride her hip, defending themselves with rocks and sticks against the swords and guns of male soldiers. Theirs is a valiant effort, inspired by raw courage and maternal instinct. And yet, if we make note of the title of the work, we come to understand that Goya equates this desperate attempt to protect themselves and their children with the animal instincts of "wild beasts."

In all three works, we witness the images of women astride or in the midst of chaos and destruction. How does each artist use vantage point in the composition (frontal, profile, rear) to involve the observer in the action of the scene? What is our relationship to the female figures, and indeed to the action as a whole, in each of these works? Are we observers? Participants? Stylistically, how does each artist use the medium to enhance the subject of the work? How do the use of perspective and compositional arrangement intensify the narrative? Can you speculate as to the gender ideologies reflected in or reaffirmed by the artists of each of these compositions?

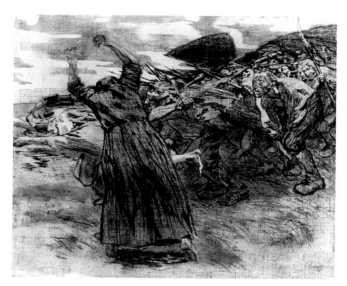

17–40 KÄTHE KOLLWITZ
OUTBREAK (1903). PLATE NO. 5 FROM
THE PEASANTS' WAR.
ETCHING AND AQUATINT. LIBRARY OF CONGRESS, WASHINGTON, D.C.

17–41 FRANCISCO GOYA Y LUCIENTES
AND THEY ARE LIKE WILD BEASTS
(SPANISH TITLE: *Y SON FIERAS*).
FROM *DISASTERS OF WAR*. ETCHING AND
BURNISHED AND DRYPOINT. AQUATINT.
15.5 × 20.1 CM.

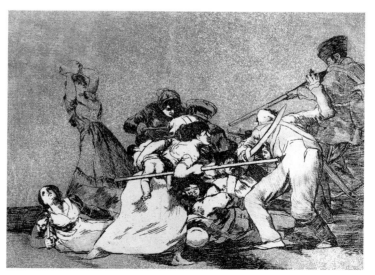

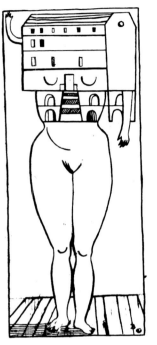

It announced to the world, through shock and exaggeration, that men's subjects are not necessarily of interest to women; that women's experiences, while not heroic, are significant. And, perhaps of most importance, particularly in light of the subsequent careers of its participants, the exhibition exalted women's ways of working.

We have already seen a number of works by women that might be considered feminist (Laurie Simmons's *Red Library,* Fig. 1–22; Jenny Holzer's *Inflammatory Essays,* Fig. 1–19; Suzanne Lacy and Leslie Labowitz's *In Mourning and in Rage,* Fig. 1–31) that highlight women's accomplishments (Judy Chicago's *The Dinner Party,* Figs. 1–11 and 9–9), that speak to women's experiences (Judith Shea's *Inaugural Ball,* Fig. 1–29),

or that assimilate traditional women's craft (Miriam Schapiro's *Wonderland,* Fig. 1–33 and Faith Ringgold's *Tar Beach,* Fig. 1–26). In this section we shall examine several of other works by women artists. They too have been chosen because they make sharp feminist statements, speak directly to women's experiences, or raise to the level of fine art materials and methods that have been employed by women for centuries.

Long before there was a *Womanhouse,* long before the concerns of women artists were addressed, or even heard, sculptor Louise Bourgeois created her drawing entitled *Femme Maison* (Fig. 17–42). It is a disturbing image of a headless, faceless woman, trapped in a house that becomes the center of her intellectual and emotional being. Much of Bourgeois's work is

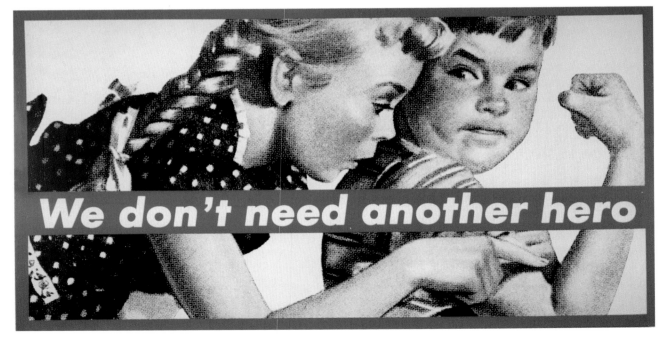

17–43 BARBARA KRUGER
UNTITLED (WE DON'T NEED ANOTHER HERO) (1987).
PHOTOGRAPHIC SILKSCREEN, VINYL LETTERING ON PLEXIGLAS. 109 × 210″.

COLLECTION: EMILY FISHER LANDAU, N.Y. COURTESY MARY BOONE GALLERY, N.Y.

17–44 LAURIE SIMMONS
ARMS UP/PYRAMID (1982). COLOR PHOTOGRAPH. 39 × 29″.
PRIVATE COLLECTION. COURTESY OF METRO PICTURES, N.Y.

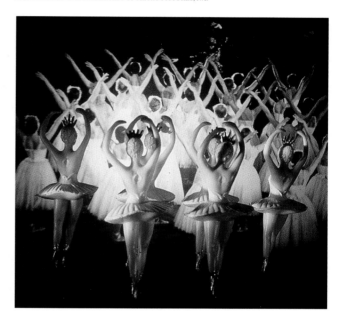

explicitly and violently sexual, and perhaps has provided a role model for other women artists whose work focuses on female anatomical forms.

Many women artists have tried to call attention to stereotypes that influence the way women are perceived. Laurie Simmons's "Stepford Wife" in her *Red Library,* like Bourgeois's *Femme Maison,* shows a woman locked into the compulsive care of her home, to the exclusion of more worthwhile and rewarding activity. Barbara Kruger, in *Untitled (We Don't Need Another Hero)* (Fig. 17–43), confronts her male and female viewers with stereotypical epithets for the "dominant sex," seeming to criticize females for feeding male expectations as much as males for having them. Simmon's *Arms Up/Pyramid* (Fig. 17–44) poignantly addresses gender stereotypes, role models, and the young girl's need for approval. For this color photograph, the artist staged a company of ballerina dolls, *en pointe* with arms raised, behind a photo of real dancers in finale. All have their backs turned toward the viewer, putting us in the position of imitating the imitators, as well as seeking the approval of the audience. Simmons seems to be saying that the little "doll," disciplined in conformity and reaching for nothing less than perfection, is a disturbing characterization that has led girls to live in dread of erring, of disappointing.

Other artists use their medium to overtly counter stereotypes. In *With Love from A to B* (Fig. 17–45) by Nancy Buchanan and Barbara T. Smith, a fixed camera and color videotape were used to record a simple and eventually horrifying—though staged—encounter between a man and a woman. In essence it is a one-sided, tabletop love affair. Two sets of hands meet on a wrinkled white tablecloth. Those of the man offer tokens of affection—rings, flowers, a glass of wine, and so on. One by one the small gifts are refused by the woman's hands, leading the man to commit suicide.

The work of women artists can be fiercely angry, as is Jenny Holzer's *Inflammatory Essays* (see Fig. 1–19). It can also be uplifting and celebratory, as is Schapiro's *Wonderland* (see Fig. 1–33), a work of so-called "femmage," which interweaves memorabilia specific to women's experiences with stitching and quilting techniques that are a part of women's collective traditions. It can also draw attention to women's accomplishments,

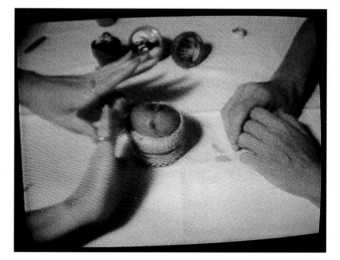

17–45 NANCY BUCHANAN AND BARBARA T. SMITH
WITH LOVE FROM A TO B. (1977).
COLOR VIDEOTAPE, 10 MIN., ADAPTED FROM FIXED CAMERA PERFORMANCE FOR VIDEO AT COLLEGE ART ASSOCIATION, LOS ANGELES, 1976.
COLLECTION OF THE ARTISTS.

17–46 JOAN SNYDER
SMALL SYMPHONY FOR WOMEN #1 (1974). OIL AND ACRYLIC ON CANVAS.
THREE PARTS, EACH 24 × 24″; 24 × 72″ OVERALL.
COLLECTION OF SUELLEN SNYDER. COURTESY OF THE ARTIST.

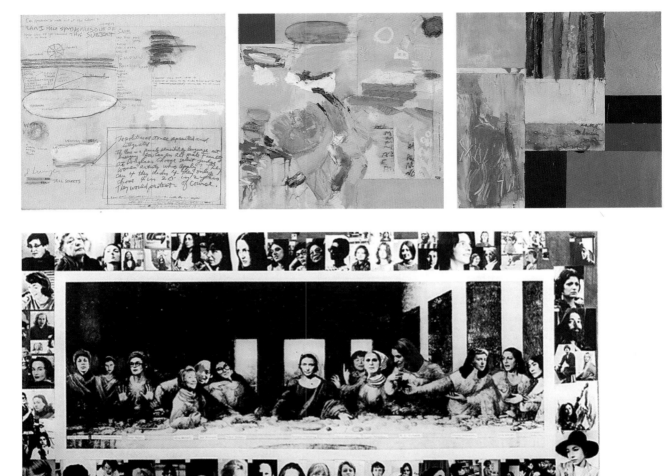

17–47 MARY BETH EDELSON
SOME LIVING AMERICAN WOMEN ARTISTS (LAST SUPPER) (1972). POSTER.

as in Chicago's *The Dinner Party* or Joan Snyder's *Small Symphony for Women #1* (Fig. 17–46). From the early 1970s onward, Snyder focused on women's issues in her work, unifying her narrative content with lush brushwork and an often dramatic palette. *Small Symphony* is broken into three sections, or variations on a theme. The first square presents, according to Snyder, "political ideas, dreams, colors, materials, angers, rage," that are written, scratched out, or emphatically boxed. The center square offers a kind of directory of Snyder's signature images, words and brushstrokes; the third is

a resolution or consolidation of the other two sections. The painting, three times as long as it is high, reads from left to right like a codified narrative. It is at once unique and universal, telling something of woman's plight as well as Snyder's private view of the world.

Let us also call attention to the humor—often a double-edged sword—in much of feminist art. Mary Beth Edelson's *Some Living American Women Artists* (Fig. 17–47) of 1972 is a grand and multivalent spoof. Using perhaps the most famous Old Master composition of all time—Leonardo's *The Last Supper*—as the basis

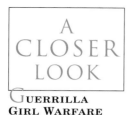
During the 1980s something of a backlash against inclusion of women and ethnic minorities in the arts could be observed.[13] For example, a 1981 London exhibition, *The New Spirit in Painting,* included no women artists. A 1982 Berlin exhibition, *Zeitgeist,* represented forty artists, but only one was a woman. The 1984 innaugural exhibition of The Museum of Modern Art's remodeled galleries, *An International Survey of Recent Painting and Sculpture,* showed the works of 165 artists, only 14 of whom were women. The New York exhibition *The Expressionist Image: American Art from Pollock to Now,* included the works of twenty-four artists, only two of whom were women. And so it goes.

To combat this disturbing trend, an anonymous group of women artists banded together as the Guerrilla Girls. The group appear in public with gorilla masks and proclaim themselves to be the "conscience of the art world." They have mounted posters on buildings in Manhattan's SoHo district, one of the most active centers in the art world today. They have taken out ads of protest.

Figure 17–48 shows one of the Guerrilla Girls' posters from the late 1980s. This particular poster sardonically notes the "advantages" of being a woman artist in an art world that, despite the "liberating" trends of the postfeminist era, continues to be dominated by men. It also calls attention to the blatant injustice of the relative price tags on works by women and men that persists as this millenium comes to a close. A 1993 cover story for *The New York Times Magazine* pictures the "art world all stars" of dealer Arnold Glimcher (Fig. 17–49). Women artists and artists of color are conspicuous by their absence.

[13]Whitney Chadwick, *Women, Art, and Society* (London and New York: Thames and Hudson, 1990).

THE ADVANTAGES OF BEING A WOMAN ARTIST:

Working without the pressure of success.
Not having to be in shows with men.
Having an escape from the art world in your 4 free-lance jobs.
Knowing your career might pick up after you're eighty.
Being reassured that whatever kind of art you make it will be labeled feminine.
Not being stuck in a tenured teaching position.
Seeing your ideas live on in the work of others.
Having the opportunity to choose between career and motherhood.
Not having to choke on those big cigars or paint in Italian suits.
Having more time to work after your mate dumps you for someone younger.
Being included in revised versions of art history.
Not having to undergo the embarrassment of being called a genius.
Getting your picture in the art magazines wearing a gorilla suit.

Please send $ and comments to: **GUERRILLA GIRLS** CONSCIENCE OF THE ART WORLD
Box 1056 Cooper Sta. NY, NY 10276

WHEN RACISM & SEXISM ARE NO LONGER FASHIONABLE, WHAT WILL YOUR ART COLLECTION BE WORTH?

The art market won't bestow mega-buck prices on the work of a few white males forever. For the 17.7 million you just spent on a single Jasper Johns painting, you could have bought at least one work by all of these women and artists of color:

Bernice Abbott	Elaine de Kooning	Dorothea Lange	Sarah Peale
Anni Albers	Lavinia Fontana	Marie Laurencin	Ljubova Popova
Sofonisba Anguisolla	Meta Warwick Fuller	Edmonia Lewis	Olga Rosanova
Diane Arbus	Artemisia Gentileschi	Judith Leyster	Nellie Mae Rowe
Vanessa Bell	Marguérite Gérard	Barbara Longhi	Rachel Ruysch
Isabel Bishop	Natalia Goncharova	Dora Maar	Kay Sage
Rosa Bonheur	Kate Greenaway	Lee Miller	Augusta Savage
Elizabeth Bougereau	Barbara Hepworth	Lisette Model	Vavara Stepanova
Margaret Bourke-White	Eva Hesse	Paula Modersohn-Becker	Florine Stettheimer
Romaine Brooks	Hannah Hoch	Tina Modotti	Sophie Taeuber-Arp
Julia Margaret Cameron	Anna Huntingdon	Berthe Morisot	Alma Thomas
Emily Carr	May Howard Jackson	Grandma Moses	Marietta Robusti Tintoretto
Rosalba Carriera	Frida Kahlo	Gabriele Münter	Suzanne Valadon
Mary Cassatt	Angelica Kauffmann	Alice Neel	Remedios Varo
Constance Marie Charpentier	Hilma af Klimt	Louise Nevelson	Elizabeth Vigée Le Brun
Imogen Cunningham	Kathe Kollwitz	Georgia O'Keeffe	Laura Wheeling Waring
Sonia Delaunay	Lee Krasner	Meret Oppenheim	

Information courtesy of Christie's, Sotheby's, Mayer's International Auction Records and Leonard's Annual Price Index of Art Sales.

Please send $ and comments to: **GUERRILLA GIRLS** CONSCIENCE OF THE ART WORLD
Box 1056 Cooper Sta. NY, NY 10276

17–48 GUERRILLA GIRLS POSTER (C. 1987).

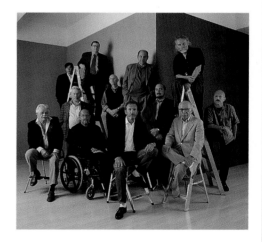

17–49 *ARNOLD GLIMCHER AND HIS ART WORLD ALL-STARS.* USED ON THE COVER OF *THE NEW YORK TIMES MAGAZINE* OCT. 3, 1993.

17–50 CHARLES WHITE
PREACHER (1952). INK ON CARDBOARD. 21⅜ × 29⅝".
COLLECTION OF THE WHITNEY MUSEUM OF AMERICAN ART, N.Y.

17–51 FAITH RINGGOLD
MAMA JONES, ANDREW, BARBARA, AND FAITH (1973).
MIXED MEDIA. LIFE SIZE. FROM THE FAMILY OF WOMEN SERIES.
© BY FAITH RINGGOLD INC.

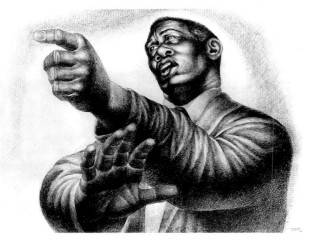

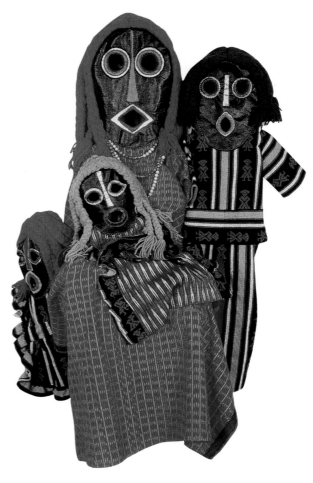

of her composition, Edelson inserted the photographs of the heads of her colleagues in place of the faces of Jesus and his apostles, and bordered the work with a patchwork arrangement of yet other women artists. Georgia O'Keeffe presides over all, but the company includes virtually everyone of note—from Helen Frankenthaler to Edelson herself. Not only is this work an attack on male-generated and male-dominated art styles, but it is an attack on the history of art in general—until recently written by men and perpetuated by men in its exclusion of women.

ARTISTS OF COLOR

As with women artists, artists of color often focus on experiences that are unique to their ethnic groups. These artists bridge contemporary experience and styles from their countries of origin with an eclectic and highly expressive style.

The art produced by artists of color is rich and varied. Some artists of color, like some writers of color, focus on themes of racial injustice and social protest or dedicate themselves to portraying the experiences of their ethnic group in America. Others, like their literary counterparts, have worked without particular reference to ethnicity.

Charles White, like many other artists of the 1930s, was sponsored by the Works Projects Administration. His *Preacher* (Fig. 17–50) is an exciting study of the projection of personality through hands. This ink-on-cardboard drawing is daring in its perspective and exquisite in its implication of light and shade. The textures of flesh and fabric are masterfully portrayed in spite of the monochromatic palette.

Faith Ringgold was born in Harlem in 1930 and educated in the public schools of New York City. In the 1960s she painted murals and other works inspired by the civil rights movement. In the 1970s her art took a feminist turn because of her exclusion from an all-male exhibition at New York's School of Visual Arts.

MESTIZO (1987). CHARCOAL AND PASTEL ON PAPER. 29 × 41″.

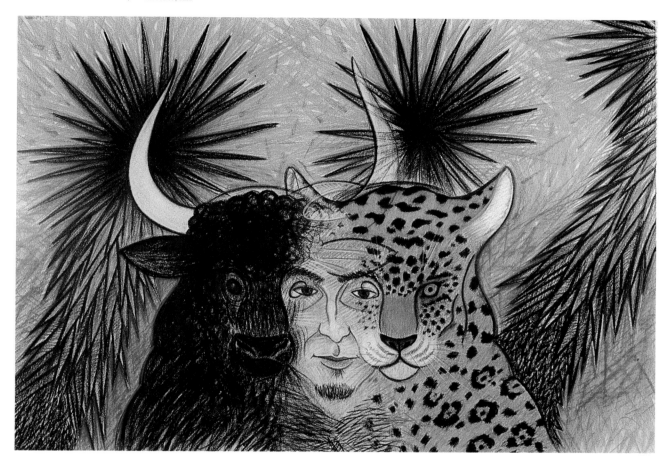

Her mother, a fashion designer, was always sewing, as the artist recalled it, and at this time Ringgold turned to sewing and related techniques—needlepoint, beading, braided ribbon, and sewn fabric—to produce soft sculptures such as those in *Mama Jones, Andrew, Barbara, and Faith* (Fig. 17–51), which is from her series *The Family of Women*. The clothing of these figures is inspired by African garments, and the faces are reminiscent of African masks. More recently, Ringgold has become famous for her narrative quilts (see Fig. 1–26), which combine traditions common to African Americans and women—storytelling and quilting.

In *Mestizo* (Fig. 17–52), César A. Martinez creates a powerful trinity of images symbolizing the clash of the Spanish and Mexican cultures with the arrival of Cortez in the sixteenth century. *Mestizo* was the word used to describe Mexicans of mixed Spanish and indigenous ancestry. He juxtaposes the bull, a symbol of Spain, with the pre-Columbian jaguar and his own portrait. The fiery, passionate background of charcoal strokes, assaulted by the sharpened tongues of native yucca plants, seems to symbolize the violent encounter that gave birth to this Hispanic-American culture.

17–53 LINDA NISHIO
KIKOEMASU KA (CAN YOU HEAR ME?) (1980). PHOTO-TEXT.
COURTESY OF THE ARTIST.

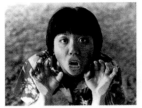

My name is Linda Nishio. I am 28 years old. I am a third generation (sansei) Japanese/American. I grew up in Los Angeles in a house-

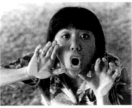

hold where very little Japanese was spoken, except of course by my grandmother, who spoke very little English. During those early years I

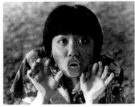

picked up some Japanese phrases, a few of which I still remember today. Then I went to art school of the east coast. I attended classes in

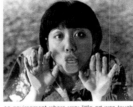

an environment where very little art was taught but where iconoclastic rhetoric (intellectualism) replaced "normal" art education. Before long I

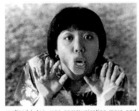

realized I, too, was communicating more and more in this fashion. Ho hum. Upon returning to Los Angeles I found myself misunderstood by

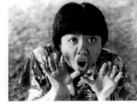

family and friends. So this is the story: A young artist of Japanese descent from Los Angeles who doesn't talk normal.

KI-KO-E-MA-SU KA
(Can you hear me?)

© 1982 Linda Nishio

Art as a form of communication is subverted in Linda Nishio's *Kikoemasu Ka (Can You Hear Me?)* (Fig. 17–53). The story, explained by the artist in a caption within the work, is simply this: "A young artist of Japanese descent from Los Angeles who doesn't talk normal." The work consists of a series of photographs of Nishio, a conceptual and performance artist, behind a pane of glass. She desperately tries to communicate with the viewer, gesturing emphatically, and pressing her lips against the glass. She attempts to explain the difficulties encountered in describing her art to her Japanese family and friends, but the work also resonates with meaning concerning the frustrations of those who speak a language foreign to those among whom they live.

CONCEPTUAL ART

This book began with the question, What is art? That is, what is meant by the concept of art? In bringing our discussion of contemporary art around to **Conceptual art,** we come more or less full circle. For in Conceptual art the work exists in the mind of the artist as it is conceived—just as we could say that the concept of art has no specific requirements for execution or expression but is known or understood by those who think about art.

In any event, if the public has sometimes reacted negatively to contemporary movements such as Pop art or Minimalist art, this response has been magnified in the case of Conceptual art. In Conceptual art, the transitory act of creation is said to have taken place in the artist's mind. A painting or a sculpture is but a poor, dumb record of the actual creative event. Imagery in Conceptual art is deemphasized, frequently in favor of suggestive verbiage.

Conceptual art is perhaps the ultimate separation of the artistic concept from its execution. Traditionally, artists have been noted not only as creative visionaries, but also as masters of their media. Michelangelo not only conceived *David,* but also personally "released" him from his captive stone. Van Gogh not only conceived his *Sunflowers,* but also personally brought them into being by means of his masterful brushstrokes. Consider also the creative process in Abstract Expressionism: To Pollock, "being in" the act of executing a painting somehow caused its form and content to leap into being. By contrast, the contemporary sculptors Tony Smith and Alexander Calder have allowed technicians to actualize their sketches in metal—and Rubens at times assigned the detailed renderings of his paintings to well-schooled assistants. And so, works of art have not always been fully executed by the artists who conceived them. In Tony Smith's *Moses,* where lies the art? Is the "art" in the artist's mind or on the green Princeton campus in central New Jersey, across Nassau Street from P. J.'s Pancake House? The Conceptual artist seems to be making the point that the essence of a work of art is conceived and dwells within the mind of the artist. The rest is communication.

But what grand communication it is!

key terms

Abstract Expressionism
Calligraphic
Action painting
Color-field painters
Hard-edge painters

Minimal art
Minimalism
Figurative
Pop art
Combine painting

Ready-mades
Photorealism
Trompe l'oeil
Op art
New image painting

Pattern painting
Neo-Expressionists
Installation
Conceptual art

artists

Arshile Gorky
Hans Hofmann
Jackson Pollock
Lee Krasner
Willem de Kooning
Mark Rothko
Adolph Gottlieb
Helen Frankenthaler
Agnes Martin
Alice Neel
Francis Bacon
Robert Rauschenberg
Jasper Johns
Andy Warhol
Audrey Flack
Richard Anuszkiewicz
Susan Rothenberg
Kim MacConnel

Elizabeth Murray
Anselm Kiefer
Jean-Michel Basquiat
Georgia O'Keeffe
Nancy Graves
Henry Moore
George Segal
Marisol
Duane Hanson
Deborah Butterfield
David Smith
Tony Smith
Michelangelo
Jackie Ferrara
Judy Pfaff
Nancy Graves
Jean Tinguely
Jackie Winsor

Eugène Delacroix
Käthe Kollwitz
Francisco Goya y Lucientes
Miriam Schapiro
Sherry Brody
Louise Bourgeois
Barbara Kruger
Laurie Simmons
Nancy Buchanan
Barbara T. Smith
Joan Snyder
Mary Beth Edelson
Guerrilla Girls
Charles White
Faith Ringgold
César A. Martinez
Linda Nishio

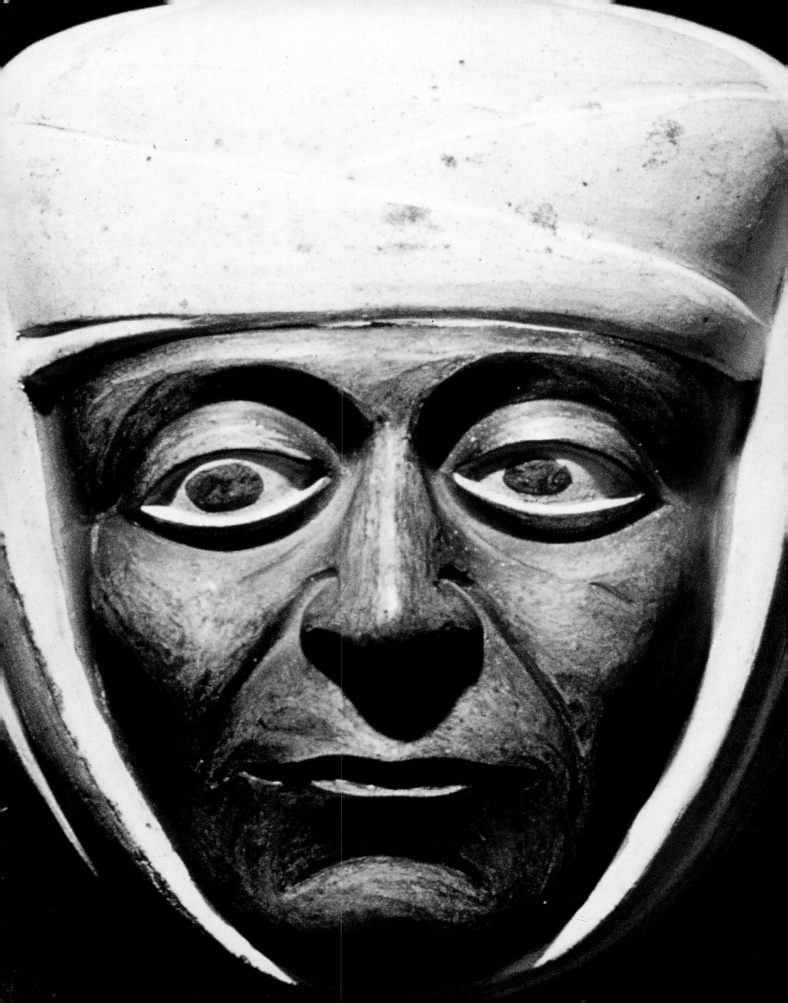

18

BEYOND EUROPE AND THE UNITED STATES: A WORLD OF ART

PRELIMINARY *Sketch*

- ❏ The great mosques of the world of Islam and the cathedrals of Christian Europe share the same Judaic tradition.

- ❏ The Spanish conquest of Mexico was facilitated by the Aztec's belief that the Spaniards were descendants of one of their gods.

- ❏ The Incas of Peru built a walled "royal road of the mountains" that was 30 feet wide and 3,750 miles long.

- ❏ Native Americans created an earthwork in the form of a serpent that meanders for more than one-quarter of a mile in the Ohio countryside.

- ❏ Hinduism considers sexual activity to be a path to virtue, and sculptures of sexual acts adorn many temple walls.

- ❏ For nearly 2,000 years, the Japanese have been razing wooden Shinto shrines every 20 years and replacing them with exact duplicates.

Ceramic Portrait Jar from Peru (detail). See Figure 18–21.

As members of Western civilization, we share an extensive and varied heritage. Western art originated in ancient Egypt and Greece and then developed in Europe and the United States. Its richness cannot be encompassed in a single course, nor in a lifetime.

As citizens of the world, (Map 8) we share a yet more extensive and varied heritage. Just as there is a Western culture and a Western tradition in art, there are many other cultures and many other traditions in art. Artistic expression is found in the ancient wooden sculpture and crafts of Africa, and among Black Africans and African Americans today. Art, like the catamarans of the islanders of Oceania, has spanned the realms of the Pacific. Great Mexican stone sculptures, South American metropolises, Native American cliff palaces, crafts, and earthworks all preceded the European explorers and settlers by many centuries.

ON ETHNOGRAPHIC ART

Many terms have been used to describe the art of societies in parts of Africa, the South Pacific, and the Americas. This art was first referred to as "barbarous" or "savage," then as "primitive" and, in the twentieth century, as "native." Scholars today by and large prefer the word "ethnographic." The reasons for the change in terms are fairly self-evident. For one thing, terms like these are disparaging. They also reflect, historically, the Westerner's desire to measure this unfamiliar work according to familiar—yet inappropriate—standards.

In a word, we know better now. We understand that the art called "ethnographic" embodies ways of life that have developed along their own courses, outside those of historic civilizations. It reflects societal organizations based on the village or the tribe, which are rural and self-sufficient and which continue from generation to generation with little change. It represents peoples who are often isolationist and wary of the intrusions of "civilized" societies.

The art of such societies is original, highly skilled, and meaningful to the community in which it is created. Most importantly, it serves to express the values and beliefs of a people, and it plays a pivotal role in the continuation of customs and traditions in societies dependent on oral rather than written history. Europeans who colonized these territories between the sixteenth and twentieth centuries did not think much of the fetishes, idols, and other curiosities upon which they gazed. Yet today ethnographic, or native, art is avidly collected throughout the Western world.

ON THE ART OF THE EAST

The Islamic art of the Near, Middle, and Far East; Indian art; and the art of China and Japan may be somewhat more familiar to Westerners than native, or ethnographic, art. The great mosques of the world of Islam and the cathedrals of Christian Europe share the same Judaic tradition. Persian rugs are popular, and the Western eye need not be especially schooled to appreciate

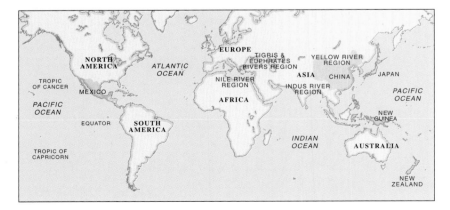

Map 8 A World of Art

them. Some of the great works of the Indian subcontinent are also familiar, and the influence of China and Japan on Western art has been felt since the explorations and beginnings of trade in the early part of this millennium. The refined ceramics of the Chinese, for example, were known to European potters, and the perspective techniques and delicacy of Japanese drawings and paintings influenced many modern artists of the nineteenth century.

In this chapter we shall explore the world of art beyond Europe and the United States. The breadth of the material precludes detailed discussion of the historical aspects of this work, but we shall enjoy a sampling of the widely diverse styles these cultures have to offer.

AFRICAN ART

African art is as varied as the cultures that have populated that continent. The earliest African art, like the earliest art of Europe and North America, consists of rock paintings and engravings that date to the Neolithic period. In tropical Africa—the central portion of the continent—the lost-wax technique was developed to cast small bronze sculptures as early as the ninth century.

The kingdom of Benin, which, during the fourteenth through nineteenth centuries occupied what is now Nigeria, was rich in sculptures of many media, including iron, bronze, wood, ivory, and terra cotta. Works such as the *Altar of the Hand* (Fig. 18–1) illustrate the skill with which the Benin manipulated bronze, as well as the importance of symbolism to their art. The many figures that are cast in relief around the circumference of this small work are meant to venerate the king and glorify his divine office. The king is the central figure in both the relief and in the free-standing figures on top of the altar. He holds the staffs of his office in his hands, and his head is larger than those of his attendants. This purposeful distortion signifies the head as the center of being and source of intelligence and power. The king's importance is further underscored by his placement within a triangular frame of sorts, his head at the apex. The entire altar is cast with symbolic forms or incised with decorative motifs, all arranged in a symmetrical pattern. The monumentality that this altar achieves in its mere 17 inches or so is remarkable and impressive.

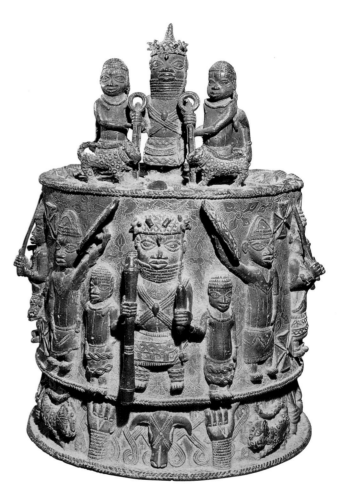

18–1 *ALTAR OF THE HAND,* BENIN, NIGERIA. BRONZE. HEIGHT: 17½″.
BRITISH MUSEUM, LONDON.

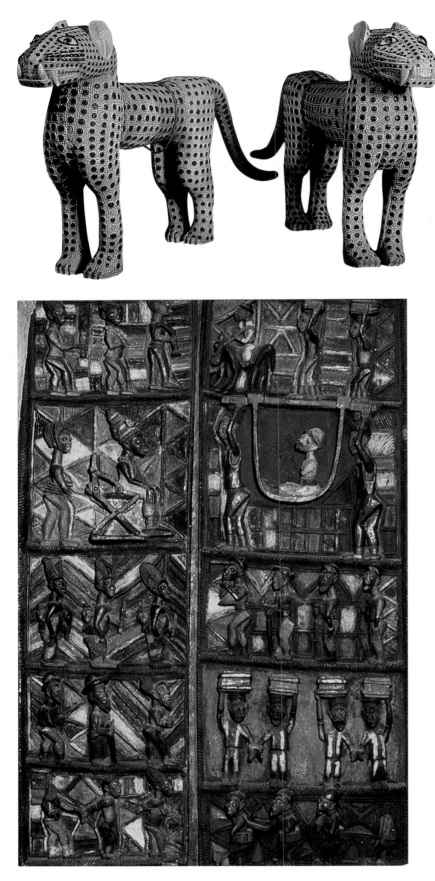

18–2 *LEOPARDS*, BENIN, NIGERIA (C. 16TH–17TH CENTURIES). IVORY WITH BRASS INLAY, LENGTH 32⅝". BRITISH MUSEUM, LONDON.

The decorative nature of Benin art, as well as its powerful symbolism, are fully captured in a sculpture of a leopard (Fig. 18–2), found in a palace when the city of Benin was destroyed in 1897. The stylized beast, carved of ivory and embellished with brass disks, is one of many symbols of royal power. This penchant for ornament can also be seen in more recent tribal art from Nigeria, such as that of the Yoruba. The carved wooden doors in Figure 18–3 depict scenes of tribal life and ritual. The figures are angular and stylized; as in the *Altar of the Hand,* the king, who is seated on a throne, is shown larger than his attendants. The work reads rather like a comic strip, with parts of the narrative confined to small compartments. In most sections, a geometric patterned background adds a rich, tapestrylike quality to the work. These doors continue artistic traditions established in much older works.

The Yoruba are famous for their mix of the old and the modern in fanciful objects crafted for ceremonial or ritualistic purposes. Masks and headdresses like the one in Figure 18–4 are used in performances called masquerades. They incorporate music, dance, and elaborate costuming in a combination of theater and ritual that often involves social criticism. The helmet is placed on top of the head, and the masquerader aims his head downward so that the face of the mask confronts the audience. Such helmets or headdresses are often very elaborate; our example incorporates a detailed mask and cactus leaves that sprout from a central core and culminate in a rough-hewn animal head. Crouching

18–3 DOOR, YORUBA, FROM IDERRE, NIGERIA. WOOD.
BRITISH MUSEUM, LONDON.

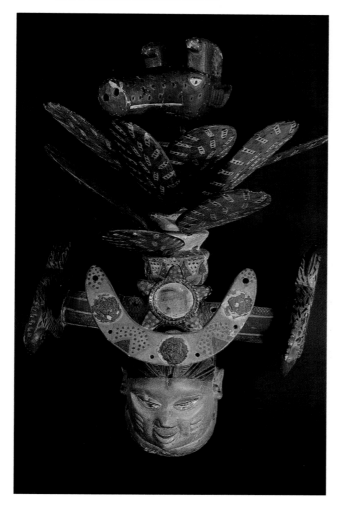

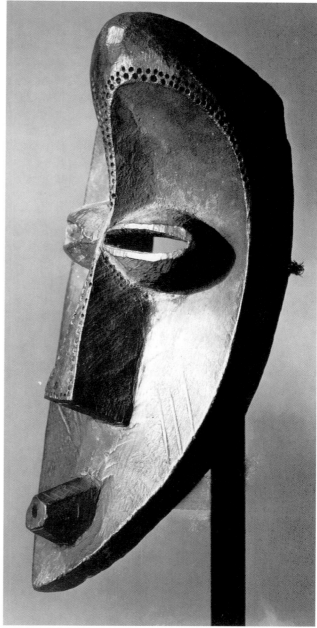

birds look like the runners of a catamaran; a crescent
moon and five-pointed star complete the ornamentation.
The masked performers represent a broad spectrum of
characters from motorcyclists and prostitutes to
hunters, animals, and the king himself.

Masks and headdresses are found in other regions
of Africa as well, and their symbolism is as widely varied as their style. The simplest of these, like the
Etoumbi mask (Fig. 18–5), have facial features resolved
into abstract geometric shapes. They are also sometimes punched and slashed with markings intended to
represent body scarification. More intricate pieces such
as the *mboom* helmet mask from the Kuba people of

18–5 MASK, ETOUMBA
REGION, BRAZZAVILLE, ZAIRE.
WOOD. HEIGHT: 13″.
MUSÉE BARBIER-MILLER, GENEVA.

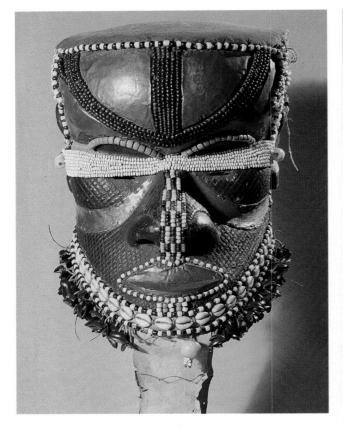

18–6 *MBOOM* HELMET MASK, KUBA, FROM ZAIRE (19TH–20TH CENTURIES). WOOD, BRASS, COWRIE SHELLS, BEADS, SEEDS. HEIGHT: 13″.
MUSÉE ROYAL DE L'AFRIQUE CENTRALE, TERVUREN, BELGIUM.

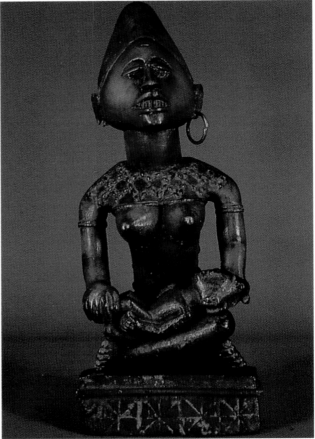

18–7 ANCESTRAL FIGURE, KONGO, FROM ZAIRE. (19TH–20TH CENTURIES). WOOD AND BRASS. HEIGHT: 16″.
MUSÉE ROYAL DE L'AFRIQUE CENTRALE, TERVUREN, BELGIUM.

Zaire (Fig. 18–6) might be embellished with brass, shells, beads, seeds, feathers, and furs. These contrasting textures, along with the protruding chin and prominent forehead, are symbols of royalty. The mask itself represents a primordial ancestor that oversees the passage of boys into adulthood.

Other work from Zaire is more conventional in form. A so-called ancestral or power image from the Kongo peoples (Fig. 18–7) is a delicate wood carving of a mother and child, most likely intended as a repository of the soul of a deceased noblewoman. (Do you recall the Ka figures of Old Kingdom Egypt?) The function of the sculpture was probably to receive prayers for the woman's continuing guardianship and care of the community, but other such figures served to channel ancestral powers from "medicines" placed within or on the sculptures to those in need—warriors in battle, farmers planting crops, or people trying to cure disease.

In many Western societies, Christians light votive candles to request favors from God, to seek the intervention of saints on their behalf, and to thank them for help. In a number of African societies, medicine men have hammered nails into so-called **fetish figures** such as that in Figure 18–8 to ask help from the gods, to ward off evil, and to vanquish enemies. It appears as though this artist has chosen his materials to liken the object to a porcupine. It has also been suggested that, since Christianity was the state religion in this region during most of the sixteenth and seventeenth centuries, the use of nails may refer to the crucifixion of Jesus Christ.

The seated primordial couple in Figure 18–9 are characteristic of another well-known style of African art—that of the Dogon people of Mali, in the western part of the continent. Although the Dogon artist often

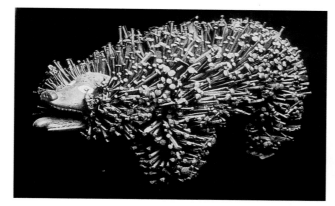

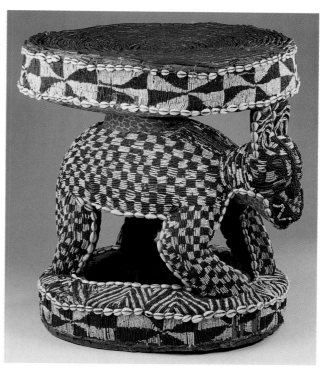

18–8 FETISH FIGURE, FROM ZAIRE (19TH–20TH CENTURIES). WOOD WITH IRON NAILS AND BLADES. LENGTH: 35″.
MUSÉE DE L'HOMME, PARIS.

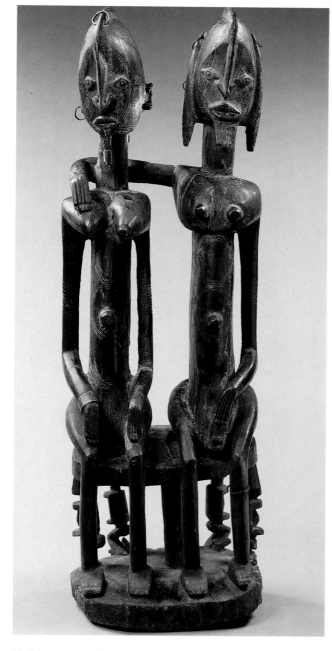

18–9 ANCESTRAL COUPLE, DOGON, FROM MALI. WOOD. HEIGHT: 28¾″.
THE METROPOLITAN MUSEUM OF ART, N.Y. GIFT OF LESTER WUNDERMAN, 1977 (1977.394.15)

18–10 ANIMAL STOOL, BAMUN, FROM CAMEROON (19TH–20TH CENTURIES). WOOD, GLASS BEADS, COWRIE SHELLS, BURLAP, COTTON CLOTH. HEIGHT: 19⅛″.
THE METROPOLITAN MUSEUM OF ART, N.Y. THE MICHAEL C. ROCKEFELLER COLLECTION. BEQUEST OF NELSON A. ROCKEFELLER, 1979 (1979.206.167).

worked in a more naturalistic style, here the artist has opted for a highly stylized, rigid, and elongated figure, incised with overall geometric patterns. This treatment removes the subjects from contemporary reality. The group represents the mythical ancestors of the human race, a kind of Adam and Eve of all of us.

From sculptures intended to house souls of the deceased to power images, masks, and helmets, we have witnessed a sampling of African art that helps us to understand its nature. Like the *Animal Stool* (Fig. 18–10) from the Cameroon, created as a resting place for the soul of a departed individual and adorned with beads and cowrie shells, the art is diverse in style and rich in decoration. Most importantly, it is often empowered to function between the realms of human existence and the unknown, carrying ritual and tradition from generations past to that of the present.

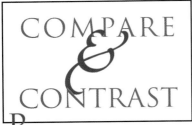

COMPARE & CONTRAST

PICASSO'S *NUDE WITH DRAPERY*
WITH
A FUNERARY FETISH
FROM GABON

In the early years of the twentieth century, painter Pablo Picasso saw two large exhibitions in Paris. One was of ancient sculpture from his native Spain, carved by the Iberians before their conquest by the Romans; the other was of the native art of African peoples. Both would have a lasting impression on his art.

Compare Picasso's painting (Fig. 18–11) with an African piece like the one he may have seen at the Musée de l'Homme in Paris (Fig. 18–12). What lines and shapes has Picasso adopted? What other conventions or stylizations of native art has he used? How has the painter captured the simplicity and strength of the small sculpture in his modern painting? Why do you think this type of work appealed to Picasso?

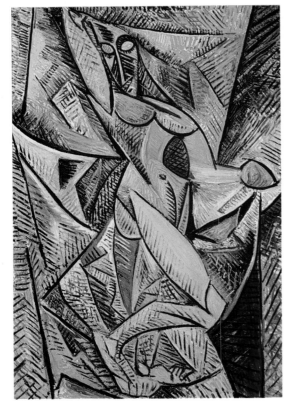

18–11 PABLO PICASSO
NUDE WITH DRAPERY (1907).
OIL ON CANVAS.

THE HERMITAGE, LENINGRAD. © 1998
ESTATE OF PABLO PICASSO/ARTISTS RIGHTS
SOCIETY (ARS), N.Y.

18–12 FUNERARY FETISH FROM GABON
(19TH–20TH CENTURIES).
WOOD, BRASS, COPPER, IRON.
HEIGHT: 28⅞".

METROPOLITAN MUSEUM OF ART, NEW YORK.
PURCHASE 1983 (1983.18).

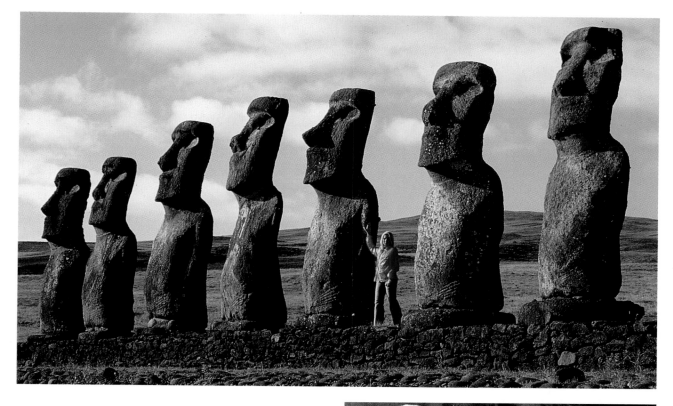

OCEANIC ART

The peoples and art of Oceania are also varied. They span millions of square miles of ocean, ranging from the continent of Australia and large islands of New Guinea and New Zealand to small islands such as the Gilberts, Tahiti, and Easter Island. They are divided into the cultures of Polynesia, Melanesia, and Micronesia. We shall discuss works from Polynesia and Melanesia.

POLYNESIA

The Polynesian artists are known for their figural sculptures, such as the huge stone images of Easter Island (Fig. 18–13). More than 600 of these heads and half-length figures survive, some of them 60 feet tall. Polynesian art is also known for its massiveness and compactness. Carved between the fifth and seventeenth centuries CE, their jutting, monolithic forms have the abstracted quality of African masks and ancestor figures. Figure after figure has the same angular sweep of nose and chin, the severe pursed lips, and the overbearing brow.

Archaeologists have determined that these figures symbolize the power that chieftains were thought to derive from the gods and to retain in death through their own deification. Political power in Polynesia was believed to be a reflection of spiritual power. The images of the gods were thought to be combined with those of

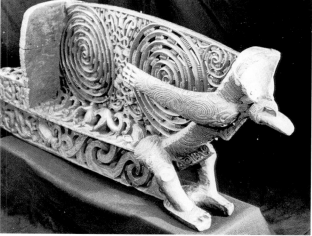

18–14 CANOE PROW, MAORI TRIBE (PRE-1935). WOOD. 70⅞ × 29½″.
MUSÉE D'HISTOIRE NATURELLE, ETHNOGRAPHIE ET PREHISTOIRE, ROUEN, FRANCE.
© RMN.

their descendants in the carvings and other art works like those on Easter Island.

The Polynesian Maori of New Zealand are known for their wooden relief carvings. The plentiful nature of tough durable pine woods allowed them to sculpt works with the curvilinear intricacy and vitality of the nearly 6-foot-long canoe prow shown in Figure 18–14. The figure at the front of the prow is intended to have an earthy phallic thrust.

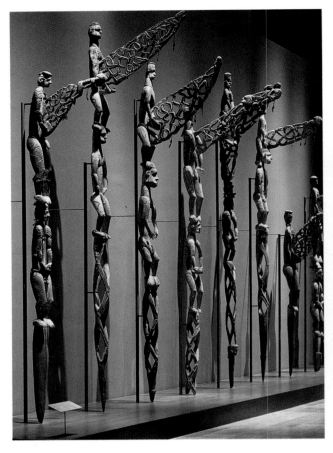

18–15 OCEANIC-MELANESIA, ANCESTOR POLES, NEW GUINEA (ASMAT TRIBE). WOOD, PAINT, AND FIBER. HEIGHT OF TALLEST POLE: 17'11".

THE METROPOLITAN MUSEUM OF ART, N.Y. THE MICHAEL C. ROCKEFELLER MEMORIAL COLLECTION. PHOTOGRAPH © 1982 THE METROPOLITAN MUSEUM OF ART.

18–16 COLOSSAL HEAD, VILLAHERMOSA, MEXICO (OLMEC CULTURE). (C. 500 BCE–200 CE). BASALT. HEIGHT: 8'.

The winding snake pattern on the mythic figure and scrollwork of the eighteenth-century canoe prow is like that found on the Maori's tattooed bodies. Body painting and tattooing are governed by tradition and are believed to link the individual to the spirits of ancestors. Ancestor figures are intended to appear menacing to outsiders, but they are perceived as benevolent within the group. Other Maori carvings are found on assembly houses, storehouses, and stockades.

MELANESIA

Melanesian art is generally more colorful than that of Polynesia. The cloth masks of New Britain are woven with a certain flair, and the mixed-media ancestral poles of New Guinea (Fig. 18–15) are painted in vivid hues. The intricate poles are carved from single pieces of wood and adorned with palm leaves and paint. Space flows around and through the ancestral poles as it could not pass through the figures at Easter Island. The expressionistically elongated and attenuated bodies again represent ancestors. The openwork banners are phallic symbols, intended to give courage to community men in ceremonies before combat with other tribes.

Practical, ceremonial, and decorative uses of art swept across the Pacific into the New World. Many historians and archaeologists believe, in fact, that the Americas were first populated many thousands of years ago by migrations across the Pacific.

NATIVE ART OF THE AMERICAS

The art of the Americas was rich and varied before the arrival of European culture. We shall briefly explore the native arts of North America and Peru.

NATIVE ARTS OF MEXICO

Some of the earliest, and certainly the most massive, art of the Americas was produced by the Olmecs in southern Mexico, long before the Golden Age of Greece. In addition to huge heads such as that in Figure 18–16, the Olmecs produced small stone carvings, including reliefs.

More than a dozen great heads up to 12 feet in height have been found at Olmec ceremonial centers. The hard basalt and jadeite from which they were carved had to be carted nearly 100 miles. The difficulty of working this material with primitive tools may to

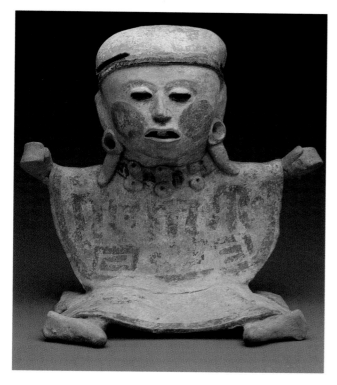

18–17 Effigy vessel, girl on swing, from Remojadas region, Veracruz, Mexico (7th–9th centuries). Ceramic. 9¾".

THE METROPOLITAN MUSEUM OF ART, N.Y. THE MICHAEL C. ROCKEFELLER MEMORIAL COLLECTION. BEQUEST OF NELSON A. ROCKEFELLER, 1979 (1979.206.574). PHOTOGRAPH © 1991 THE METROPOLITAN MUSEUM OF ART.

some degree account for the works' close adherence to the original monoliths. The heads share the same tight-fitting helmets, broad noses, full lips, and wide cheeks. Whether these colossal heads represent gods or earthly rulers is unknown, but there can be no doubting the power they project.

Henry Moore stated that Mexican sculpture is known for its massiveness. But contrast the Olmec heads with the sprightliness of the kinetic sculpture of the swinging girl (Fig. 18–17). This small piece is actually a whistle. The swinging girl was created many hundreds of years after the Olmec heads and was found in the same region of southern Mexico. We can find a continuity of tradition in the oversized head, but note the delicacy of the curved body. The entire length of the body is nothing but a spread-eagled, draped abstraction.

The Mayans, whose civilization reached its height in the Yucatán region of Mexico and the highlands of Guatemala from about 300 to 600 CE, built many huge limestone structures with **corbelled** vaults. Mayan temples were highly ornamented with figural relief carvings that represent rulers and gods, and with commemorative and allegorical murals. The temple discovered at Bonampak in 1947 is decorated with murals of vivid hues such as that in Figure 18–18, in which prisoners are being presented for sacrifice.

The placement of the reasonably realistic figures along the receding steps symbolizes the social hierarchy. At the bottom are the common people. On the upper platform are noblemen and priests in richly embellished headdresses, as well as their personal attendants, and symbols of the heavens. The prisoners sit and kneel on various levels, visually without a home, whereas the Mayans are rigidly erect in their ascendance. There is no perspective; the figures on the

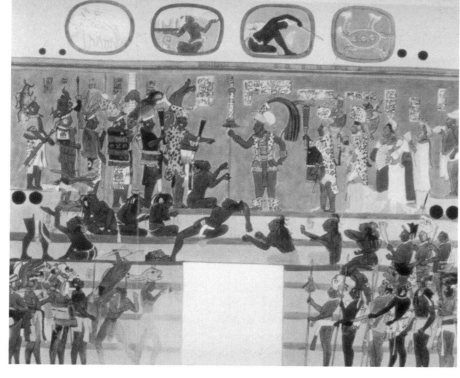

18–18 Mural from Mayan temple at Bonampak, Mexico (c. 6th century). Watercolor copy by Antonio Tejeda.
PEABODY MUSEUM, HARVARD UNIVERSITY.

THE EARLIEST CULTIVATION OF MAIZE OCCURRED IN MEXICO BETWEEN 4500 AND 3500 BCE. NUMEROUS, WIDESPREAD ARCHAEOLOGICAL FUNDS INDICATE THAT SEVERAL VARIETIES OF MAIZE WERE EXPERIMENTED WITH AND IMPROVED AROUND THIS TIME THROUGHOUT MESOAMERICA.

18–19 TEMPLE OF QUETZALCÓATL, TEOTIHUACÁN, MEXICO (300–700).

18–20 STATUE OF COATLCUE (AZTEC, TOLTEC CULTURE). (15TH CENTURY). HEIGHT: 99″.
NATIONAL MUSEUM OF ANTHROPOLOGY, MEXICO CITY.

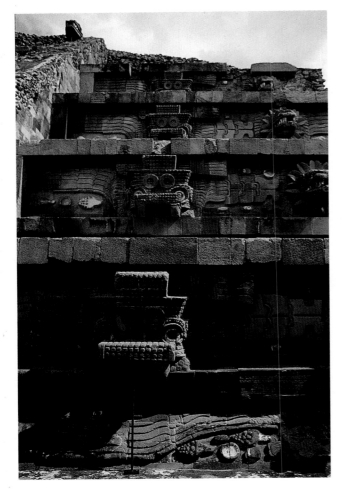

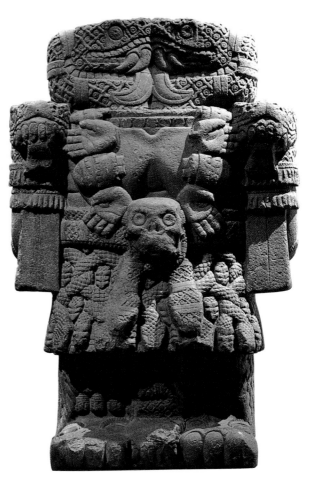

upper registers are not smaller, even though they are farther away. The eye is drawn upward to the center of the composition by the pyramidal shape formed by the scattered prisoners. The figures face toward the center of the composition, providing symmetry, and the rhythm of the steps provides unity. The subject of human sacrifice is repugnant to us, and well it should be. The composition of the mural, however, shows a classical refinement.

While the Mayans were reaching the height of their power in lower Mexico, the population of the agricultural civilization of Teotihuacán may have reached 100,000. The temples of Teotihuacán, harmoniously grouped in the fertile valley to the north of modern-day Mexico City, include the massive 250-feet-high Pyramid of the Sun and the smaller Temple of Quetzalcóatl

(Fig. 18–19). The god Quetzalcóatl was believed to be a feathered serpent. The high-relief head of Quetzalcóatl projects repeatedly from the terraced sculptural panels of the temple, alternating with the square-brimmed geometric abstractions of Tlaloc, the rain god. Bas reliefs of abstracted serpent scales and feathers follow sinuous paths on the panels in between.

The warlike Aztecs were a small group of poor nomads until they established their capital, Tenochtitlán, in about 1325 CE on the site of modern Mexico City. Once established in Tenochtitlán, the Aztecs made great advances in art and architecture, as well as in mathematics and engineering. But they also cruelly subjugated peoples from surrounding tribes. Prisoners of war were used for human sacrifice in order to compensate the sun god, who was believed to have sacrificed

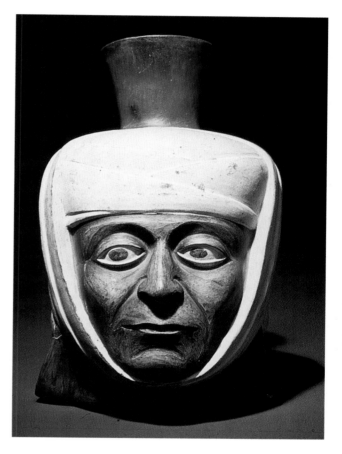

himself in the creation of the human race. It is not surprising that in the early part of the sixteenth century the invading Spaniards found many neighbors of the Aztecs more than eager to help them in their conquest of Mexico. The Aztecs also helped seal their own fate by at first treating the Spanish with great hospitality, because they believed that the Spanish were descended from Quetzalcóatl. The Spanish were thus able to creep into the hearts of the Aztecs within the Trojan Horse of mistaken identity. The Spanish, needless to say, did not rush to disabuse their hosts of this notion.

Coatlcue was the Aztec goddess of earth and death. In the compact, monumental stone effigy shown in Figure 18–20, Coatlcue takes the form of a composite beast that never was. Her head consists of facing snakes. Her hands are also snakes, her fingers fangs. Hands, hearts, and skull compose her necklace. Coiled human figures hang from her midsection. Her gargantuan toes repeat the abstracted serpent fangs above. If one does not take into account the fearsome symbolic content of the statue, Coatlcue is a fascinating basalt assemblage of organic forms. But it is difficult to ignore the work's meanings.

NATIVE ARTS OF PERU

The native arts of Peru include pyramid-shaped structures that form supports for temples, as in Mexico; stone carvings, mostly in the form of ornamental reliefs on ceremonial architecture; ceramic wares; and astounding feats of engineering.

The ceramic portrait jar shown in Figure 18–21 was created in about the fifth or sixth century CE by the Mochica culture along the Pacific coast of northern Peru. These realistic jars were modeled without benefit of a potter's wheel and probably accompanied the departed person into the grave. This particular jar is thought to be a portrait of a high-placed person, perhaps a warrior or a religious figure. It has a typical flat bottom and stirrup-shaped spout. Similar jars show their subjects grinning, sneering, or showing other expressions which must have impressed the artist as characteristic of their dominant traits. Still other jars show entire human or animal figures, some of them caught in erotic poses.

The grand ruins of Machu Picchu, the fortress that straddled the Peruvian Andes, were noted in

Chapter 7 (Fig. 7–3). This structure, built by the Incas in about 1500 CE, shows an engineering genius that has been compared to the feats of the Romans. The tight fit of the dry masonry walls seems to reflect the tightness of the totalitarian fist with which the Incan nobility regulated the lives of their own masses and subjugated peoples from Ecuador and Chile. The conquering Spaniards were amazed by the great Incan "Royal Road of the Mountains"; 30 feet wide and walled for its entire 3,750 miles, it had no parallel in Europe.

NATIVE ARTS OF THE UNITED STATES AND CANADA

Some native art objects in the United States and Canada date back nearly 12,000 years. As with African art, much of it is practical craft, much is ceremonial, all is richly varied.

18–22 Eskimo mask representing a moon goddess
(before 1900).
PHOEBE A. HEARST MUSEUM OF ANTHROPLOGY, THE UNIVERSITY OF CALIFORNIA AT BERKELEY.

18–23 Kwakiutl headdress from Vancouver Island,
British Columbia, Canada (c. 1895–1900). 52 × 46″.
COURTESY OF THE NATIONAL MUSEUM OF THE AMERICAN INDIAN, SMITHSONIAN INSTITUTION.

18–24 Elon Webster
False Face mask, Iroquois (The artist was an Onondaga
of the Tonawanda Reservation) (1937). Wood.
COURTESY OF CRANBROOK INSTITUTE OF SCIENCE, BLOOMFIELD HILLS, MI.

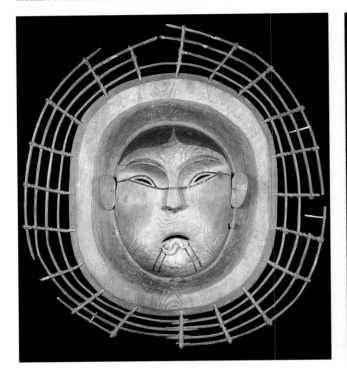

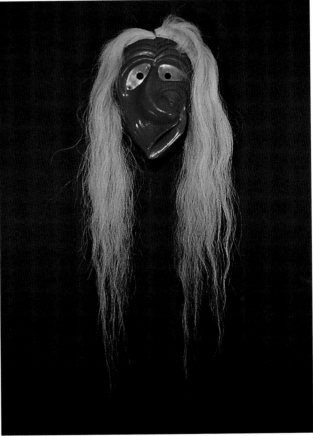

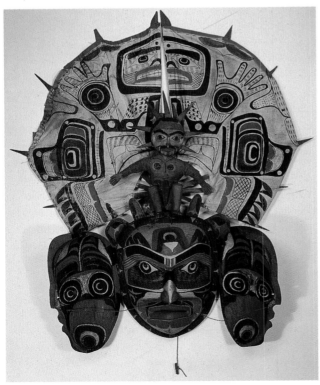

Eskimo, or Inuit, sculpture exhibits a simplicity of
form and elegant refinement in both its realistic and
abstract designs. It can also be highly imaginative, as
in a mask representing a moon goddess (Fig. 18–22).
Such masks, worn by shamans in ritual ceremonies,
were carved of ivory or wood and often had movable
parts which added to the drama and realism of the
object.

Prehistoric sites in what is now the United States
also have yielded many interesting works. One of the
larger ceremonial sculptures to survive is an earthwork
called the Serpent Mound, a snakelike form of molded
earth that meanders some 1,440 feet in the Ohio countryside. Pyramidal temple platforms reminiscent of
those of Mexico and South America have also been
unearthed, as has the magnificent Cliff Palace of
Colorado's Mesa Verde National Park (see Fig. 7–1).

18–25 *Custer's Last Stand* (Sioux, Crow tribe) (late 19th century). Teepee lining. Painted muslin. 35 × 85″.
NATIONAL MUSEUM OF NATURAL HISTORY, SMITHSONIAN INSTITUTION, WASHINGTON, D.C. (358425).

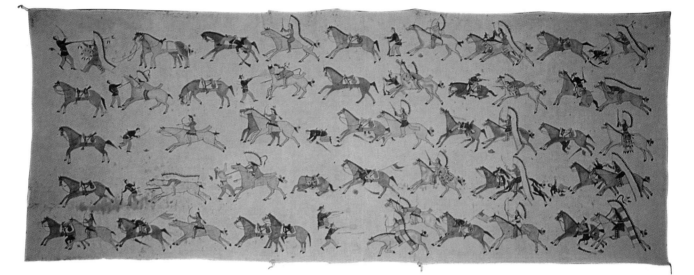

Among Native Americans, the Navajos of the Southwest are particularly noted for their fiber artistry and sand paintings that portray the gods and mythic figures in a stylized manner. Some of these works are believed to be empowered to heal; the ill person sits in the center of the painting while a priest chants ritualistic prayers intended to speed well-being.

Peoples of the Northwest Coast have produced masks used by shamans in healing rituals, totem poles not unlike the ancestor poles of Oceania, bowls, clothing, and canoes and houses that are embellished with carving and painted ornamentation. The Chilkat blanket discussed in Chapter 9 (see Fig. 9–21) was worn during ceremonies and consists of highly abstracted animal designs. The wood and muslin of a 4-foot-high Kwakiutl headdress from British Columbia (Fig. 18–23) is vividly painted with abstracted human and animal forms. Like the Inuit moon goddess mask, it too has movable parts: When the string hanging from the inner mask is pulled, the two profiles to the sides are drawn together, forming another mask. The symbols represent the sun and other spirits. It is an extraordinary composition, balanced by the circular flow of fabric above the heads and by the bilateral symmetry in the placement of the shapes. As is often the case in ethnographic art, the embellishment of the work reflects traditional body decoration, like painting, tattooing, or scarification.

Native Americans in the Eastern Woodlands, such as the Iroquois, are also known for their ceremonial masks (Fig. 18–24). Created for use by False Face Society members in rituals intended to heal sickness or rid communities of destructive forces, these masks feature gross distortions and exaggerations of human anatomy. The faces portray supernatural beings whose deeds are recounted in Iroquois mythology. Other works by Eastern Woodlands artists include feathered and beaded handicrafts.

The highly nomadic tribes of the Great Plains poured their artistic energies into embellishing portable items, such as garments and teepees. The muslin teepee lining of the Crow peoples of the Plains (Fig. 18–25) is a multi-hued and fairly realistic portrayal of nineteenth-century warfare with the United States cavalry. In this symbolic collection of events, Crow warriors advance rhythmically from the right. Many chieftains sport splendid feather headdresses. The cavalry is largely unhorsed and apparently unable to stop the implied momentum of the charge, which is very much like the sequence of frames in a motion picture.

Now that we have glanced at the native arts of Africa, Oceania, and the Americas, let us look once more across the Atlantic to the East. We will work our way across southern Europe and Asia so that we may sample the artistic contributions of the Islamic, Indian, Chinese, and Japanese cultures.

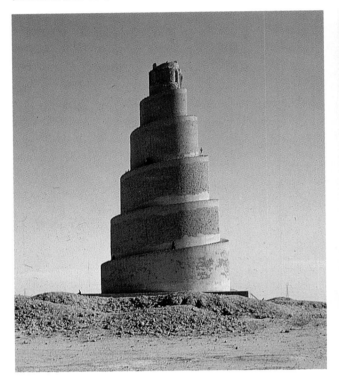

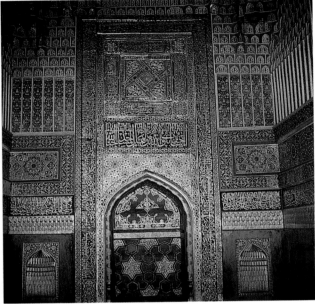

ISLAMIC ART

The era of Islam (also known as Moslem) was founded in Arabia by Mohammed in 622 CE. Within a century, the Moslem faith had been spread by conquering armies westward across North Africa to the Atlantic Ocean. It also spread to the east. So it is that many of the great monuments of Islamic art and architecture are found as far west as Spain and as far east as Agra in India. Muslims look upon the Old and New Testaments as well as the Koran as holy scriptures, and they number Abraham, Moses, and Jesus among their prophets.

The Great Mosque at Samarra, Iraq (Fig. 18–26) was constructed between 848 and 852 CE. Once the largest mosque in the world of Islam, it now lies in ruins. Its most striking feature is the spiral **minaret,** from which a crier known as a **muezzin** called followers to prayer at certain hours. Mosques avoid symbols, and early mosques in particular do not show ornamentation. Nor, in Islam, is there the clerical hierarchy found in many Christian religions. The leader of gatherings for worship, called the **imam,** stands on a pulpit in the Mosque, near the wall that faces Mecca, the spiritual capital of Islam.

The mosque at Samarra was a simple building, 800 feet long and 520 feet wide, covered in part by a wooden roof, with a great open courtyard. The roof was supported by the **hypostyle** system of multiple rows of columns that could be expanded in any direction as the population of the congregation grew. By bowing toward Mecca in the same yard, worshippers were granted equal psychological access to Allah, the Islamic name of God.

The interior of the mosque at Córdoba, Spain, which we used as an example of rhythm in Chapter 2 (Fig. 2–60), shows the system of arches that spans the distances between columns in the hypostyle system. A system of vaults, supported by heavier piers, overspreads the arches. There is not the grand open space of the western cathedral; rather, air and light flow through as in a forest of high-crowned, sturdy trees. The interiors of mosques traditionally have been decorated with finely detailed mosaics, as in that of a mosque in Isfahan, Iran (Figure 18–27). Our photograph is of the area of the

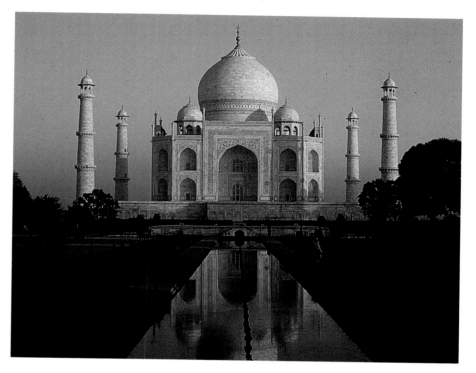

mihrab, a niche in the mosque wall facing Mecca that provides a focus of worship.

The Taj Mahal at Agra (Fig. 18–28) is a mausoleum built by the Shah Jahan in the seventeenth century in memory of his wife. In sharp contrast to the plainness of early Islamic architecture, tree-lined pools here reflect a study in refined elegance. The three-quarters sphere of the dome is a stunning feat of engineering. Open archways, with their ever-changing play of light and shade, slender minarets, and spires unify the composition and give the marble structure a look of weightlessness. Creamy marble seems to melt in the perfect order.

Islamic culture has also produced a wealth of fine craft objects. Persian carpets like that shown in Figure 9–20, which was woven during the century in which the Taj Mahal was built, have set a high standard for the worldwide textile industry since the tenth century. Richly ornamented ceramics, enameled glass, highly embellished metalworks, and fine manuscript illumination also characterize the visual arts of the Moslem world.

INDIAN ART

Indian art, like that of the Americas, shows a history of thousands of years, and it too has been influenced by different cultures. Stone sculptures and **seals** that date to the second or third millennium BCE have been discovered. In low relief, the seals portray sensuous, rounded native animals and humanoid figures that presage the chief Hindu god, **Shiva**.

India once encompassed present-day Pakistan, Bangladesh, and the buffer states between modern India and China. Many religious traditions have conflicted and sometimes peacefully coexisted in India, among them the Vedic religion, Hinduism, Buddhism, and Islam. Today Islam is the dominant religion of Pakistan, and Hinduism predominates in India. Indian art, like Islamic art, is found in many parts of Asia where Indian cultural influence once reigned, as in Indochina.

Buddhism flowered from earlier Indian traditions in the sixth century BCE, largely as a result of the example set by a prince named Siddhartha. In his later years Siddhartha renounced his birthright and earthly luxuries to become a **buddha**, or enlightened being. Through meditation and self-denial, he is believed to have reached a comprehension of the universe that Buddhists call **nirvana.** The Great Buddhist **stupa** at Sanchi, whose architecture was discussed in Chapter 7, was completed in the first century CE. The stupa houses religious relics and also symbolizes the harmony of the universe, stimulating meditation by the visitor.

For many hundreds of years there were no images of the Buddha, but sculptures and other representations began to appear in the second century CE. Some sculpted

18–29 BUDDHA, BENGAL, INDIA. (PALA PERIOD, 9TH CENTURY). BLACK CHLORITE. HEIGHT: 37″.
© THE CLEVELAND MUSEUM OF ART. DUDLEY P. ALLEN FUND (35.146).

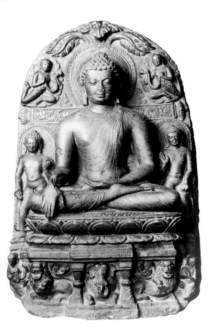

18–30 NATARAJA: SHIVA AS LORD OF DANCE (SOUTH INDIAN) (CHOLA PERIOD, 11TH CENTURY). 43⅞″; WIDTH: 40″.
© THE CLEVELAND MUSEUM OF ART. PURCHASE FROM THE J. H. WADE FUND. (30.331).

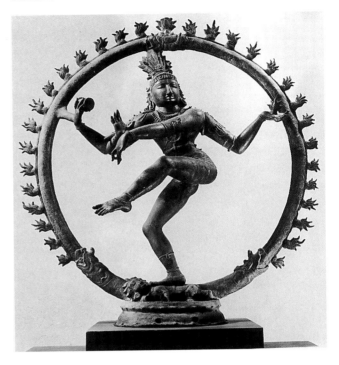

Buddhas show a Western influence that can be traced to the conquest of northwestern India by Alexander the Great in 327 BCE. Others (as in Fig. 18–29) have a sensuous, rounded look that recalls the ancient seals and is decidedly Indian. This slender chlorite Buddha shows delicate fingers and gauzelike, revealing drapery. The face exhibits a pleasant cast that is as inscrutable as the expression of La Gioconda in Leonardo's *Mona Lisa* (see Fig. 1–1).

In the sixth and seventh centuries CE, Hinduism rose to prominence in India, perhaps because it permitted more paths for reaching nirvana, including the simple carrying out of one's daily duties. Another reason for the popularity of Hinduism may be its frank appreciation of eroticism. Western religions impose a distinction between the body or flesh, on the one hand, and the soul or mind, on the other. As a consequence, sex is often seen as unrelated or antagonistic to religious purity. Hinduism considers sexual expression one legitimate path to virtue; explicit sexual acts in high reliefs adorn temple walls and amaze Western visitors.

There are many Hindu gods, including Shiva, the Lord of Lords and god of creation and destruction, which, in Hindu philosophy, are one. Figure 18–30

shows Shiva as Nataraja, the Lord of the Dance. With one foot on the Demon of Ignorance, this eleventh-century bronze figure dances within a symbolically splendid fiery aura. The limbs are sensuous, even erotic. The small figure to the right side of his head is Ganga, the river goddess. This periodic dance destroys the universe, which is then reborn. So, in Hindu belief, is the human spirit reborn after death, its new form reflecting the sum of the virtues of its previous existences.

Hindu temples are considered to be the dwelling places of the gods, not houses of worship. The proportions of the famous Kandariya Mahadeva Temple at Khajuraho (Fig. 18–31) symbolize cosmic rhythms. The gradual unfolding of spaces within is highlighted by the sculptural procession of exterior forms. The organic, natural shapes of the multiple roofs are in most sections separated from the horizontal registers of the base by sweeping cornices. The main tower is an abstracted mountain peak, reached visually by ascending what appear to be architectural and natural hurdles. All this can be seen as representing human paths to oneness

18–31 Kandariya Mahadeva Temple, Khajuraho, India (10th–11th centuries).

18–32 Ceremonial vessel (guang), from a royal tomb at Anyang, Henan (Shang dynasty, 12th century BCE). Bronze. Length: 12¼″.
COURTESY OF THE FREER GALLERY OF ART, SMITHSONIAN INSTITUTION, WASHINGTON, D.C. (38.5).

with the universe. The registers of the base are populated by high reliefs of gods, allegorical scenes, and idealized men and women in erotic positions.

Other Hindu temples are even more intricate. Vast pyramidal bases contain forests of towers and spires, corniced at the edges as they ascend from level to fanciful level. They are thick with low and high reliefs. In the Buddhist temples of Indochina, the giant face of Buddha looms from the walls of imposing towers and gazes in many directions. Indian art, including Indian painting—of which little, sad to say, survives—teaches us again how different the content of the visual arts can be. Still, techniques such as that of stone carving and bronze casting, as well as elements of composition, seem to possess a universal validity.

CHINESE ART

China houses more than a billion people in a country not quite as large as the United States. Nearly 4,000 years ago, inhabitants of China were producing primitive crafts. Beautiful bronze vessels embellished with stylized animal imagery were cast during the second millennium BCE, such as the one shown in Figure 18–32. During the feudal period of the Late Chou Dynasty, which was contemporaneous with the Golden Age of Greece, royal metalworks were inlaid with gold, silver, and polished mirrors. Elegant carvings of fine jade were buried with their noble owners.

Confucianism ascended as the major Chinese way of life during the second century BCE. It is based on the moral principles of Confucius, which argue that social behavior must be derived from sympathy for one's fellows. Paintings and reliefs of this period show the conceptual space of Egyptian painting and create the illusion of depth by means of overlapping. Missionaries

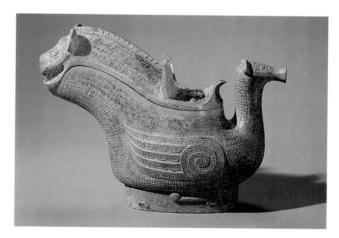

from India successfully introduced Buddhism to China during the second century CE, and many Chinese artists imitated Indian models for a few centuries afterward. But by the sixth century, Chinese art was again Chinese. Landscape paintings transported viewers to unfamiliar, magical realms. It was believed by many that artist and work of art were united by a great moving spirit. Centuries after the introduction of Buddhism, Confucianism again emerged. The present-day Peoples Republic of China is officially atheistic, but many Chinese still follow the precepts of Confucius.

18–33 FAN K'UAN
TRAVELERS AMONG MOUNTAINS AND STREAMS (C. 1000).
HANGING SCROLL, INK AND COLORS ON SILK. HEIGHT: 81¾″.
COLLECTION OF THE NATIONAL PALACE MUSEUM, TAIWAN.

18–34 MU CH'I
SIX PERSIMMONS (SOUTHERN SUNG DYNASTY, C. 1270). INK ON
PAPER. WIDTH: 14¼ . (©) RYUKOUIN–TEMPLE.
DAITOKU-JI TEMPLE, KYOTO, JAPAN.

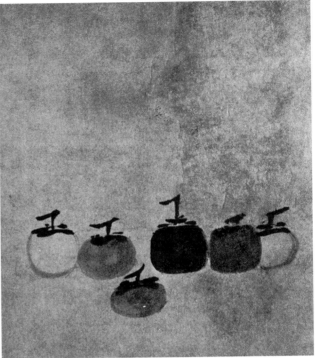

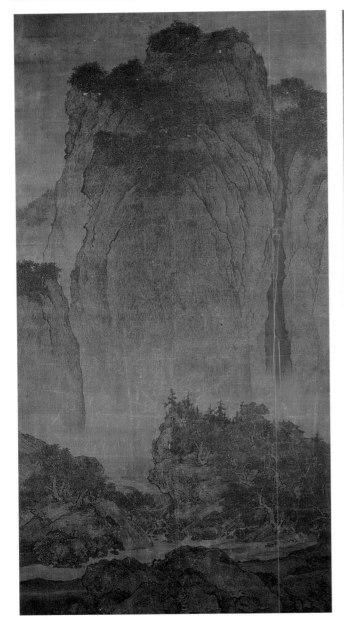

into the painting. Rounded forms rise in orderly, rhythmic fashion from foreground through background. Sharp brushstrokes clearly delineate conifers, deciduous trees, and small temples on the cliff in the middle ground. The waterfall down the high cliffs to the right is balanced by the cleft to the left. A high contrast in values picks out the waterfall from the cliffs. Human figures are dwarfed by distant mountains. In contrast to the perspective typical of Western landscapes, there is no single vanishing point or set of vanishing points. The perspective shifts, offering the viewer a freer journey back across the many paths and bridges.

Six Persimmons (Fig. 18–34) was painted in blue-black ink by Mu Ch'i some two centuries later. It is considered a masterful study of the way in which brushstrokes and different values imply mass and textures. Note how the flatter base of the central persimmon lends it the greatest mass. The placement of the persimmons is extraordinarily delicate and precise. They stand alone in space and are thus given an abstract quality, with the suggestion that their relationships to one another were more important to the artist than

Fan K'uan's *Travelers Among Mountains and Streams* (Fig. 18–33) was painted on a silk scroll during the early part of the eleventh century. Years of political turmoil had reinforced the artistic escape into imaginary landscapes. It is executed in the so-called Monumental Style. Rocks in the foreground create a visual barrier that prevents the viewer from being drawn suddenly

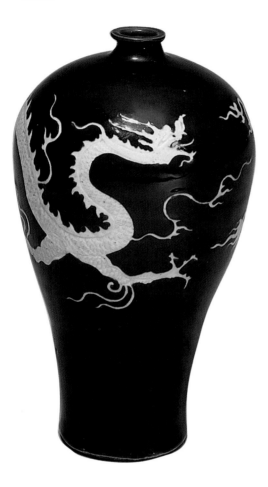

their relationship to external objects. The second and fifth persimmons along the line overlap the fruit at the extremes, one barely and the other noticeably. The third and fourth persimmons may or may not touch, creating a tension between the two, whereas there is a decided distance between the second and third. The lower persimmon stands alone. What subtle variations on a compositional theme! Note, too, how stems and leaves are created with swift, calligraphic strokes of the brush. *Six Persimmons* is executed in the Spontaneous Style, which is characterized by a paucity of rapid brushstrokes that resemble **calligraphy** and a monochromatic palette.

The blue and white porcelain vase from the Ming Dynasty (Fig. 18–35) speaks eloquently of the refinement of Chinese ceramics. The crafting of vases such as these was a hereditary art, passed on from father to son over many generations. Labor was also frequently divided so that one craftsman made the vase and others glazed and decorated it. The vase in Figure 18–35 has a blue underglaze decoration—that is, a decoration molded or incised beneath rather than on top of the glaze. Transparent glazing increases the brilliance of the piece. In many instances the incising or molding was so subtle that it amounted to "secret" decoration.

Li K'an's courageous fourteenth-century ink painting, *Bamboo* (Fig. 18–36), possesses an almost unbearable beauty. The entire composition consists of minor variations in line and tone. On one level it is a

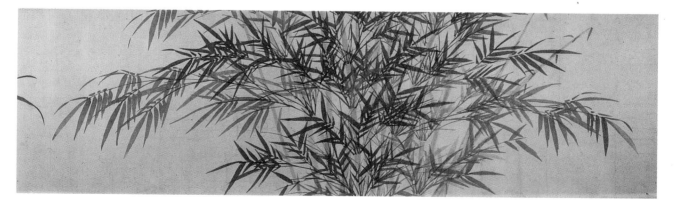

18–36 LI K'AN
BAMBOO (DETAIL OF 1ST SECTION) (1308). HANDSCROLL. INK ON PAPER. 14¾ × 93½".

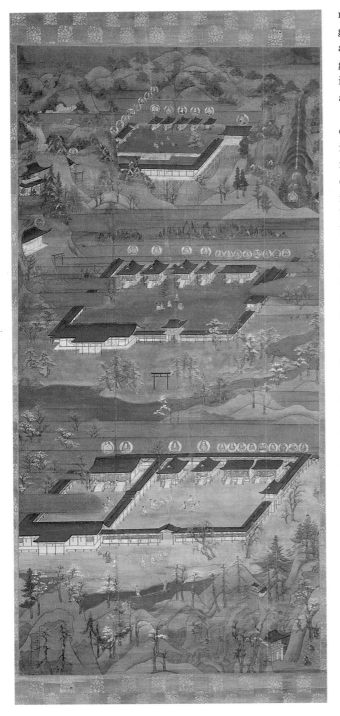

18–37 KUMANO MANDALA
(JAPAN, KAMAKURA PERIOD, C. 1300) HANGING SCROLL. COLOR
ON SILK. 53¾ × 24⅜".

realistic representation of bamboo leaves, with texture gradient providing a powerful illusion of depth. On another level, it is a nonobjective symphony of calligraphic brushstrokes. The mass of white paper showing in the background is a symbolic statement of purity, not a realistic rendering of natural elements such as haze.

In much of Chinese art there is a non-Western type of reverence for nature in which people are seen as integral parts of the order of nature, neither its rulers nor its victims. In moments of enlightenment, we understand how we create and are of this order, very much in the way Li K'an must have felt that his spirit had both created and been derived from these leaves of bamboo and the natural order that they represent.

How can we hope to have spoken meaningfully about the depth and beauty of Chinese philosophies and Chinese arts in but a few sentences? Our words are mean strokes, indeed, but perhaps they point in the right direction.

JAPANESE ART

Japan is an island country off the east coast of Asia, holding more than 120 million people in an area not quite as large as California. The islands were originally formed from porous volcanic rock, and thus they are devoid of hard stone suitable for sculpture and building. Therefore, Japan's sculpture tradition has focused on clay modeling and bronze casting, and its structures have been built from wood.

Ceramic figures and vessels date to the fourth millennium BCE. Over the past 2,000 years, Japanese art has been intermittently influenced by the arts of nearby China and Korea. In the fifth and sixth centuries CE, the Japanese produced **haniwa,** hollow ceramic figures with tubular limbs modeled from slabs of clay. Haniwa were placed around burial plots, but their function is unknown.

By the beginning of the seventh century, Buddhism had been exported from China and established as the state religion in Japan. Many sculptors produced wooden and bronze effigies of the Buddha, and Buddhist temples reflected the Chinese style. Shinto, the native religion of Japan, teaches love of nature and the existence of many beneficent gods, who are never symbolized in art or any other visual form.

For nearly 2,000 years, wooden Shinto shrines, such as those shown in Figure 18–37, have been razed every twenty years and replaced by duplicates. The landscapes, portraits, and narrative scrolls produced by the Japanese during the Kamakura Period, which spanned the late twelfth through the early fourteenth centuries CE, are highly original and Japanese in character. Some of them express the contemplative life of Buddhism, others express the active life of the warrior, and still others express the aesthetic life made possible by love of nature.

The *Kumano Mandala* (Fig. 18–37), a scroll executed at the beginning of the fourteenth century, represents three **Shinto** shrines. These are actually several miles apart in mountainous terrain, but the artist collapsed the space between them to permit the viewer an easier visual pilgrimage. The scroll pays homage to the unique Japanese landscape in its vivid color and rich detail. The several small figures of the seated Buddha portrayed within testify to the Japanese reconciliation of disparate spiritual influences. The repetition of forms within the shrines and the procession of the shrines themselves afford the composition a wonderful rhythm and unity. A **mandala** is a religious symbol of the design of the universe. It seems as though the universe of the shrines of the *Kumano Mandala* must carry on forever, as, indeed, it did in the minds of the Japanese.

Some periods of Japanese art have given rise to an extraordinary realism, as in the thirteenth-century wood sculpture of *The Sage Kuya Invoking the Amida Buddha* (Fig. 18–38). From the stance of the figure and the keen observation of every drapery fold, to the crystal used to create the illusion of actual eyes, this sculptor's effort to reproduce reality knew no bounds. The artist even went as far as attempting to render speech; six tiny images of Buddha come forth from the sage's mouth, representing the syllables of a prayer in which the name of Buddha is repeated. A remarkable balance between the earthly and the spiritual is achieved through the use of extreme realism to portray a subject that refers to religion.

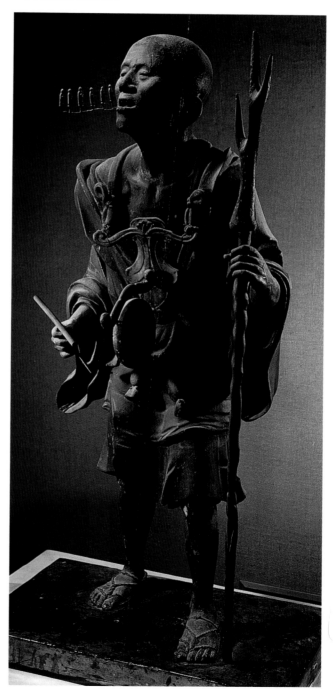

18–39 HASEGAWA TOHAKU
PINE WOOD (1539–1610). DETAIL FROM A PAIR OF SIX-FOLD
SCREENS. INK ON PAPER. HEIGHT: 61″.
TOKYO NATIONAL MUSEUM, JAPAN.

18–40 TORII KIYONAGA
INTERIOR OF A BATHHOUSE (EDO PERIOD). WOODBLOCK PRINT.
OBAN, INK, AND COLOR ON PAPER. 30 × 20½″.
COURTESY OF MUSEUM OF FINE ARTS, BOSTON. BIGELOW COLLECTION, BY EXCHANGE.

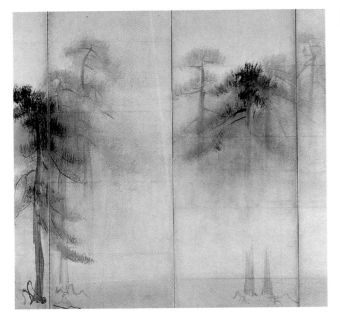

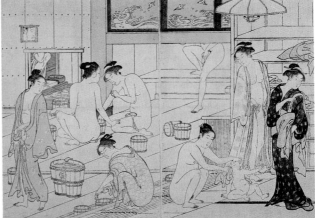

Some three centuries later, Hasegawa Tohaku painted his masterful *Pine Wood* (Fig. 18–39) on a pair of screens. It is reminiscent of Li K'an's study of bamboo in that the plant life stands alone. No rocks or figures occupy the foreground. No mountains press the skies in the background. Like *Bamboo,* it is also monochromatic. The illusion of depth—and, indeed, the illusion of dreamy mists—is evoked by subtle gradations in tone and texture. Overlapping and relative size also play their roles in the provision of perspective. Without foreground and background, there is no point of reference from which we can infer the scale of the trees. Their monumentality is implied by the power of the artist's brushstrokes. The groupings of trees to the left have a soft sculptural quality and the overall form of delicate ceramic wares. The groupings of trees within each screen balance one another, and the overall composition is suggestive of the infinite directional strivings of nature to find form and express itself.

Torii Kiyonaga's *Bathhouse Scene* (Fig. 18–40) is a modern print that influenced European artists during the second half of the nineteenth century. French Impressionist Edgar Degas, in fact, hung the print in his bedroom. Other noted modern Japanese printmakers include Ando Hiroshige (see Fig. 5–2) and Katsushika Hokusai (see Fig. 3–17). In Figure 18–40, strong outlines depict unposed women in a communal bathhouse. There is none of the subtle variation in tone or texture that we find in *Pine Wood.* The charm of the picture in large part derives from the mundane but varied activities and positions of the women. The robes and hair to some degree document the styles of the day. The choice of subject—average people engaged in daily routines—is also a decidedly modern departure from earlier Japanese tradition.

The Japanese tradition, like the Western tradition, has various periods and styles. In Japanese art, as in Western art, we find a developing technology, the effect of native materials, indigenous and foreign influences, a mix of religious traditions, and disagreement as to what art is intended to portray. Despite its vast differences from Western art, Japanese art shows similar meanings and functions. Japanese artists also use the same elements of art, in their own fashion, to shape brilliant compositions.

Art is a visual language that seems to transcend national boundaries, tongues, and customs. It seems that we can begin to understand Japanese art, Chinese art, and other types of non-Western art by using the same language that applies to our own art. In understanding the art of peoples from sundry cultures, we begin to fathom the aesthetic and expressive potential that we bear within ourselves.

key terms

Fetish figures	Hypostyle	Nirvana	Mandala
Minaret	Mihrab	Stupa	
Muezzin	Shiva	Haniwa	
Imam	Buddha	Shinto	

artists

Elon Webster	Mu Ch'i	Hasegawa Tohaku
Fan K'uan	Li K'an	Torii Kiyonaga

GLOSSARY

A

a-b-a-b alternate support system A support system in which every other nave wall support sends up a supporting rib that crosses the vault as a transverse arch.

abrade To scrape or rub off.

abstract A simplified or sometimes distorted rendering of an object that has the essential form or nature of that object (*abstracted*); a work of art whose forms make no reference to visible reality (*nonobjective*).

abstract art Art whose forms make no reference to visible reality; nonobjective art.

abstracted art Art that departs significantly from the appearance of objects, but whose subject is derived from visible reality; art that emphasizes what the artist perceives as the essential forms of objects, de-emphasizing superficial characteristics.

Abstract Expressionism A style of painting and sculpture of the 1950s and 1960s, in which artists expressionalistically distorted abstract images with loose, gestural brushwork. See *expressionistic*.

abstraction The essential form of an object; a process in which the artist focuses on and exaggerates the forms of objects for aesthetic and expressive purposes.

Academic Art A neo-classical, nonexperimental style promoted by the Royal French Academy during the eighteenth and nineteenth centuries.

Achilles The famed mythical Greek warrior and hero of the Trojan War.

achromatic Without color.

acquisitioning Buying (a work of art).

Acropolis The fortified upper part of a Greek city; literally, "city on a hill."

acrylic paint A paint in which pigments are combined with a synthetic plastic medium that is durable, soluble in water, and quick-drying.

Action painting A contemporary method of painting characterized by implied movement in the brushstroke and the splattering and dripping of paint on the canvas.

actual mass The mass of an object, as determined by its weight. Contrast with *implied mass*.

actual texture The texture of an object or picture, as determined by the sense of touch. Contrast with *implied texture*.

additive process A process in which a sculpture is created by adding or assembling materials, as in modeling and constructing. Contrast with *subtractive process*.

afterimage The lingering impression made by a stimulus that has been removed. Afterimages of colors are their complements.

allegory A narrative in which people and events have consistent symbolic meanings; extended metaphor.

altar A raised platform or stand used for sacred ceremonial or ritual purposes in a place of worship.

alternate support system An architectural system in which alternating structural elements bear the weight of the walls and the load of the ceiling.

ambulatory A continuation of the side aisles of a Latin cross plan into a passageway that extends back behind the choir and apse and allows traffic to flow to the chapels, which are often placed in this area; from the Latin *ambulare*, to walk.

amorphous Without clear shape or form.

amphitheatre A round or oval open-air theater with an arena surrounded by rising tiers of seats.

amphora A two-handled vessel with a long neck and an egg-shaped body.

analogous hues Hues that lie next to one another on the color wheel and share qualities of hue due to mixture of adjacent hues; harmonious hues.

Analytic Cubism The early phase of Cubism (1909–1912), during which objects were dissected or analyzed in a visual "information-gathering" process and then reconstructed on the canvas.

Annunciation The angel Gabriel's announcement to Mary that she was going to give birth to Jesus.

aperture Opening.

Apocalypse The ultimate triumph of good over evil foretold in Judeo-Christian writings.

applied arts Arts whose primary aims are utilitarian.

apse A semicircular or polygonal projection of a building with a semicircular dome, especially on the east end of a church.

aquarelle A watercolor technique in which transparent films of paint are applied to a white, absorbent surface.

aquatint An etching technique in which a metal plate is colored with acid-resistant resin and heated, causing the resin to melt. Areas of the plate are then exposed by a needle, and the plate receives an acid bath before being printed.

aqueduct A bridgelike structure that carries a canal or pipe of water across a river or valley. (From Latin roots meaning "to carry water.")

arabesque Descriptive of an intricate and elaborate design of geometric forms, intertwined flowers, and foliage.

arch A curved or pointed structure consisting of wedge-shaped blocks that span an open space and support the weight of material above by transmitting the load outward and downward over two vertical supports, or piers.

Archaic period A period of Greet art dating roughly 660–480 B.C. The term "archaic" refers to "old," or the art created prior to the Classical period.

Architectural style A style of Roman wall painting in which a wall was painted to give the illusion of opening onto a scene.

architecture The art and science of designing aesthetic buildings, bridges, and other structures to help us meet personal and communal needs.

architrave In architecture, the lower part of an entablature, which may consist of one or more horizontal bands.

archivolts In architecture, concentric moldings that repeat the shape of an arch.

arcology Solari's term for designs that combine architecture and ecological planning.

armature In the sculpture method of modeling, a framework for supporting plastic material.

Art Nouveau (French for "new art.") A highly ornamental style of the 1890s, characterized by floral patterns, rich colors, whiplash curves, and vertical attenuation.

assemblage A work of art that consists of the assembling of essentially three-dimensional objects to create an image. Artists often manipulate these pre-existing objects in various ways and incorporate them with other media such as painting or printmaking.

asymmetry Lack of similarity between the left and right sides of a compensation; placement of equivalent rather than identical visual forms to either side of an axis. Asymmetrical balance creates the pictorial equivalent of symmetry without the literal replication of the same image on either side of the axis.

Athena Greek goddess of wisdom, skills, and war.

atmospheric perspective The creation of the illusion of depth through techniques such as texture gradient, brightness gradient, color saturation, and the use of warm and cool colors; an indistinct or hazy effect produced by distance and its illusion in visual art. Its name derives from the acknowledgment that the intervening atmosphere causes the effect.

Atreus An ancient king in Greek mythology.

atrium A hall or entrance court.

automatic writing The written expression of free associations.

Automatist Surrealism An outgrowth of automatic writing in which the artist attempts to derive the outlines of images from the unconscious through free association.

avant-garde The leaders in new, unconventional movements; the vanguard. (A French term meaning "advance guard.")

B

balance The distribution of the weights, masses, or other elements of a work of art such that they achieve harmony.

balloon framing In architecture, the construction of the wooden skeleton of a building from prefabricated studs and nails.

balustrade A railing held up by small posts, or balusters, as on a staircase.

Baroque style A seventeenth-century style of art in Europe characterized by ornamentation, curved lines, irregularity of form, dramatic lighting and color, and exaggerated gestures.

barrel vault A roofed-over space or tunnel that is constructed by placing arches behind one another.

basalt A dark, tough volcanic rock.

bas-relief Relief sculptures that project only slightly from their backgrounds. Contrast with *high relief*. (*Bas* means "low" in French.)

batik The making of designs in cloth by waxing the fabric to prevent a dye from coloring certain areas; a cloth or design made in this way.

bay The area of space spanned by a single unit of vaulting that may be marked off by piers or columns.

Ben Day process Dots or stripling used to add tone or shadow to a line drawing.

berm A shoulder or ledge of earth.

bevel To cut at an angle.

bilateral symmetry Similarity between the left and right sides of a composition.

binder A material that binds substances together.

biomorphic Having the form of a living organism.

bisque firing In ceramics, a preliminary firing that hardens the body of a ware.

bitumen Asphalt.

black-figure painting technique A three-stage firing process that gave vases black figures on a reddish ground. In the first phase of firing (*oxidizing phase*), oxygen in the kiln turns the vase and slip red. In the second phase of firing (*reducing phase*), oxygen is eliminated from the kiln and the vase and slip turn black. In the third phase of firing (*reoxidizing phase*), oxygen is reintroduced into the kiln, turning the vase red once more.

bohemian Literally, of Bohemia, a section of Czechoslovakia. However, the term signifies a nonconformist, unconventional style of life because gypsies had passed through Bohemia in transit to Western Europe.

brass A yellowish alloy of copper and zinc.

brick A hard substance made from clay, fired in a kiln or baked in the sun, and used in construction.

brightness gradient The rendering of nearby objects as having greater intensity than distant objects.

Buddha An enlightened man.

buon fresco True fresco, as executed on damp lime plaster. Contrast with *fresco secco*.

burin A pointed cutting tool used by engravers.

burnish To make shiny by rubbing or polishing.

buttress To support or prop up construction with a projecting structure, usually built of brick or stone; a massive masonry structure on the exterior wall of a building whose function is to press inward and upward to hold in place the stone blocks of arches. Flying buttresses connect the exterior buttresses with the vaults of the nave arcade.

Byzantine style A style associated with eastern Europe that arose after the year 300 A.D. when the emperor Constantine moved the capital of his empire from Rome to Byzantium (he renamed the capital Constantinople; present-day Istanbul). The style was concurrent with the Early Christian style in Western Europe.

C

calligraphy Beautiful handwriting; penmanship.

camera obscura An early camera consisting of a large dark chamber with a lens opening through which an image is projected onto the opposite surface in its natural colors.

candid Unposed, informal.

canon A set of rules.

capital The area at the top of the shaft of a column that provides a solid base for the horizontal elements above. Capitals are decorative transitions between the cylinder of the column and the rectilinear architrave above.

caricature A picture of a person or event that exaggerates predominant features or mannerisms for satirical effect.

Carolingian Relating to Charlemagne or his period.

cartoon A prepatory drawing made for a fresco, usually on paper and drawn to scale with the finished work; a drawing that caricatures or satirizes an event or person of topical interest.

carving The process of cutting away material.

casting The process of creating a form by pouring a liquid material into a mold, allowing it to harden, and then removing the mold.

cast iron A hard alloy of iron that contains silicon and carbon and is made by casting.

catacomb A vault or gallery in an underground burial place.

celadon In ceramics, a pale, grayish-green glaze.

cella The inner room of a Greek temple, used to house the statue of the god or goddess to whom the temple is dedicated. The cella is small and located behind solid masonry walls; it was accessible only to the temple priests.

centering In architecture, a wooden scaffold used in the construction of an arch.

ceramics The art of creating objects made of baked clay, such as pottery and earthenware.

chalk A form of soft limestone that is easily pulverized and can be used as a drawing implement.

charcoal A form of carbon produced by partially burning wood or other organic matter; can be used as a drawing implement.

Charlemagne Emperor of the Holy Roman Empire 800–814 A.D.

chiaroscuro From the Latin roots meaning "clear" and "dark," an artistic technique in which subtle gradations of tone or a gradual shift from light to shadow create the illusion of rounded three-dimensional forms in space; also called modeling.

china A whitish or grayish porcelain that rings when struck.

chinoiserie An eighteenth-century ornate European style based on Chinese motifs.

chisel A sharp-edged tool used for cutting or shaping materials such as wood and stone.

cinematography The photographic art of creating motion pictures.

cinerary urn A vessel for keeping the ashes of people who have been cremated.

circular plan A circle-shaped, centralized plan in which the main central space is dominant and all other spaces are subordinate in function and serve merely to feed into the central space.

clapboard In architecture, siding composed of thin, narrow boards placed in horizontal, overlapping layers.

Classical period The period of Greek art spanning roughly 480–400 B.C.; also known as the Hellenic period, after "Hellas," the Greek name for Greece.

clerestory In a Latin cross plan, the area above the triforium in the elevation of the nave, which contains windows to provide direct lighting for the nave.

close-up In cinematography or video, a "shot" made from very close range, providing intimate detail.

coffer A decorative sunken panel.

coiling A pottery technique in which lengths of clay are wound in a spiral fashion.

college The assembling of essentially two-dimensional objects to create an image; works of art in which materials such as paper, cloth, and wood are pasted to a two-dimensional surface such as a wooden panel or a canvas. (From the French *coller*, meaning "to paste.")

colonnade A series of columns placed side by side to support a roof or a series of arches.

color negative film Color film from which negatives are made.

color reversal film Color film from which color prints (positives) are made directly (without using negatives).

combine painting A contemporary style of painting that attaches other media—frequently, found objects—to the canvas.

complementary color Those specific pairs of colors (red and green, yellow and violet, and blue and orange) that most enhance one another by virtue of their simultaneous contrast. Each pair contains one primary color plus the secondary color made by mixing the other two primaries. Since the complements do not share characteristics of hue, and are as unlike as possible, the eye does not need to alter them, and rather readily distinguishes them.

composition The act of organizing or composing the plastic elements of art. The organization of the plastic elements in a work of art.

compound pier In the Gothic style, a complex-shaped vertical support, often to which are attached a number of colonnettes, or thin half-columns.

compressive strength The degree to which a material can withstand being squeezed or pressed together.

computer graphics The use of the computer to create images.

concave Curved like the inside of a ball.

conceptual Portrayed as a subject is known or thought to be, not as it appears. (Not to be confused with the contemporary style called *Conceptual art*.)

Conceptual art An anticommercial art movement begun in the 1960s in which works of art are conceived and "executed" in the

mind of the artist. The commercial aspect of the "work" is frequently a written description of what exists in the artist's mind.

concrete A building material made from sand and gravel bonded with cement.

Confucianism An ethical system based on the teachings of Confucius, emphasizing devotion to family and friends, ancestor worship, and the seeking of justice and peace.

conservator A person who protects or repairs damaged works of art.

constructed sculpture A type of sculpture in which forms are built from materials such as wood, paper and string, and sheet metal and wire.

Constructivism A sculptural outgrowth of the Cubist collage in which artists attempted to use a minimum of mass to create volumes in space.

contact print Photographic print that is made by placing the negative in contact with a second sheet of photosensitive paper and exposing both of them to light.

conté crayon A wax crayon with a hard texture.

content All that which is contained within a work of art—the plastic elements, the subject matter, and its underlying meaning or themes.

convex Curved like the outside of a ball.

cool colors Blues, greens, and violets; colors that appear to recede spatially behind advancing, or warm, colors and are therefore used to differentiate foreground and background.

corbel A supportive, bracket-shaped piece of metal, stone, or wood.

corbelling In architecture, a technique in which stones are placed above piers in such a way that each new course of masonry projects out slightly more than the one below until the courses on both sides of the arch opening meet at the top (like a staircase in reverse).

Corinthian order The most ornate of the Greek architectural styles, adopted by the Romans and characterized by slender, fluted columns and capitals consisting of acanthus leaf design.

cornice In architecture, a horizontal molding that projects along the top of a wall or a building. The uppermost part of an entablature.

cosmetic palette A palette for mixing cosmetics, such as eye makeup, with water.

craft A special skill; a skilled trade.

crayon A small stick of colored wax, chalk, or charcoal.

crosshatching Shading a drawing through the use of two sets of parallel lines that cross each other.

crossing square The area that defines that right-angle intersection of the vaults of the nave and the transept of the church.

cross-section A diagram of the interior space of a building as seen with the façade removed (section) or side removed (lateral section).

cubiculum In architecture, a chapel in a burial chamber. Plural: cubicula.

Cubism A twentieth-century art style developed by Picasso and Braque, which emphasized a new treatment of pictorial space. Cubism was characterized by multiple views of the same object, the geometric cubelike essential of form, and the two-dimensionality of the canvas.

Cubist Of or similar to Cubism; an artist who uses this style.

cuneiform Wedge-shaped; descriptive of the characters used in ancient Akkadian, Assyrian, Babylonian, and Persian alphabets.

curator The person in charge of a collection of works or of a museum.

D

Dada A post-World War I style of art that attempted to use art to destroy art, thereby underscoring the paradoxes and absurdities of modern life.

daguerreotype Named after Louis Daguerre, a photograph made from a silver-coated copper plate.

Dark Ages The Middle Ages in Europe (approximately in fifth through tenth centuries A.D.). Some scholars consider this period as characterized by intellectual and cultural stagnation.

deaccession Selling (a work of art).

dentil molding In architecture, a molding with a series of small rectangular blocks that project like teeth, as from under a cornice.

Der Blaue Reiter (The Blue Rider) A twentieth-century German Expressionist art movement that focused on the contrasts between and combinations of abstract forms and pure colors.

design The art of making designs or patterns.

diagonal rib In architecture, a rib that connects the opposite corners of a groin vault.

Die Brücke (The Bridge) A short-lived twentieth-century German Expressionist art movement characterized by boldly colored landscapes and cityscapes and violent portraits.

diptych A painting consisting of two panels hinged together.

direct-metal sculpture Metal sculpture that is assembled by techniques such as welding and riveting, instead of being cast.

dissolve In cinematography and video, a fading technique in which the current scene grows dimmer as the subsequent scene grows brighter.

dome In architecture, a hemispherical structure that is round when viewed from beneath.

Doric order The earliest and simplest of the Greek architectural styles, consisting of relatively short, squat columns, sometimes unfluted, and a very simple capital shaped like a square. The frieze of the Doric order is usually divided into triglyphs and metopes.

drawing The act of running an implement that leaves a mark over a surface; a work of art created in this manner.

dry masonry Brick or stone construction that does not use mortar.

dry media Drawing materials that do not involve the application of water or other liquids. Contrast with *fluid media*.

drypoint A variation of engraving in which the surface of the matrix is cut with a sharp needle in such a way that rough edges are made. Rough edges make soft rather than crisp lines in the prints.

dynamism The futurist view that force or energy is the basic principle underlying all events.

E

earthenware Reddish-tan, porous pottery fired at a relatively low temperature (below, 2,000 degrees F).

earth sheltered Descriptive of buildings that are protected from inclement weather and insulated against extremes of heat and cold by earth.

earthwork A work of art in which large amounts of earth or land are shaped into a sculpture.

Eastern Orthodox The Christian church dominant in Eastern Europe, Western Asia, and North Africa.

eclecticism An approach characterized by selecting from various styles and doctrines.

editing Rearranging a film or television record to provide a more coherent or desirable narrative or presentation of images.

egg tempera A medium in which ground pigments are bound with egg yolk.

emboss To decorate with designs that are raised above the surface.

embroidery The art of ornamenting fabric with needlework.

Empire period The Roman period from about 27 B.C. to 395 A.D., when the empire was divided.

Empire style An early nineteenth-century style characterized by massiveness and dignity, reflective of the Napoleonic era.

emulsion A suspension of a salt of silver in gelatin or collodion that is used to coat film and photographic plates.

enamel To apply a hard, glossy coating to the surface. A coating of this type.

encuastic A method of painting in which the colors in a wax medium are burned into a surface with hot irons.

engraving Cutting; in printmaking, an intaglio process in which plates of copper, zinc, or steel are cut with a burin and the ink image is pressed onto paper.

entablature In architecture, a horizontal structure supported by columns which, in turn, supports any element, such as a pediment, placed above. The entablature consists, reading from top to bottom, of a cornice, a frieze, and an architrave.

entasis In architecture, a swelling in a column.

equestrian In sculpture, represented on horseback.

etching An intaglio process in which the matrix is first covered with an acid-resistant ground. The ground is then removed from certain areas with a needle, and the matrix is dipped in acid, which eats away at the areas exposed by the needle. These areas become grooves that can be inked and printed.

Etruscans Natives of ancient Etruria, who dwelled along the northwestern shores of modern Italy.

Expressionism A modern school of art in which an emotional impact is achieved through agitated brushwork, intense colors, and the use of violent, hallucinatory imagery.

expressionistic Descriptive of art that emphasizes the distortion of form and color in order to achieve an emotional impact.

extrude To force metal through a die or through very small holes in order to give it shape.

F

façade A French word meaning the front or face of a building.

fading In cinematography and video, the gradual dimming or brightening of a scene, used as a transition between scenes.

fantastic art The representation of fanciful images, sometimes joyful and whimsical, sometimes horrific and grotesque.

Fauvism An early twentieth-century style of art characterized by the juxtaposition of areas of bright color, distorted linear perspective, and drawing that is unrelated to color.

fenestration The arrangement of windows and doors in a structure.

ferroconcrete Same as reinforced concrete.

Fertile Crescent The arable land lying between the Tigris and Euphrates rivers in ancient Mesopotamia.

Fertile Ribbon The arable land lying along the Nile River in Egypt.

fetish figure An object believed to have magical powers.

fiber A slender, threadlike structure that can be woven.

fiberglass Finespun glass filaments that can be woven into textiles.

figurative Representing the likeness of a human figure.

film A thin sheet of cellulose material that is coated with a photosensitive substance.

fin de siècle A phrase generally referring to the waning of the nineteenth century; literally, the French phrase for "end-of-century."

fine arts Arts whose primary aims are aesthetic and expressive.

finial A decorative part or piece at the top of a lampshade support, spire, gable, or piece of furniture.

flashback In cinematography or video, interruption of the story line by portrayal of an earlier event.

flashforward In cinematography or video, interruption of the story line by portrayal of a future event.

flint glass A hard, bright glass that contains lead oxide.

fluid media Drawing materials that involve the application of water or other liquids. Contrast with *dry media*.

fluting The vertical grooves on the shafts of columns or pilasters.

flying buttress A structure that connects a buttress on the exterior of the building with the interior vault it supports.

foreshortening Diminishing the size of the parts of an object represented as farthest from the viewer. Specifically, diminishing the size of parts of an object rendered as receding away from the viewer at angles oblique to the picture plane, so that they appear proportionately shorter than parts of the object that are parallel to the picture plane.

forge To form or shape (usually heated) metal with blows from a hammer, press, or other machine.

free association In psychoanalytic theory, the process of allowing one's consciousness to flow naturally from thought to thought, without interference from intention or censorship. The free expression of thoughts as they occur.

free-blown Referring to glass that is blown into a bubble by means of a hollow tube.

free-standing sculpture Sculpture that is carved or cast in the round, unconnected to any architectural member, which can be experienced from the 360 possible points of view achieved by walking around it in a circle. Free-standing sculpture can also be designed for a niche, which would necessarily limit one's point of view.

fresco From the Italian word "fresh," a type of painting in which pigments are applied to a fresh, wet plaster surface or wall and thereby become part of the surface.

fresco secco Dry fresco, painting executed on dry plaster. Contrast with *buon fresco*.

frieze In architecture, a horizontal band between the architrave and the cornice that is often decorated with sculpture.

F-stop A setting on a camera that determines the size of the aperture.

Futurism An early twentieth-century style of art that portrayed modern machines and the dynamic character of modern life and science.

G

gadrooning Oval-shaped beading used to decorate silverware.

gallery A long, narrow corridor or room; a place for exhibiting or selling works of art.

gates In the lost-wax technique, these are wax rods connected to the mold. As the molten bronze flows into the mold, the gates allow air to escape.

gauffrage An inkless intaglio process.

genre painting Simple human representations; realistic figure painting that focuses on themes from everyday life.

geometric Shapes that are regular, easy to measure, and easy to describe (as distinguished from organic or biomorphic shapes, which are irregular, difficult to measure, and difficult to describe).

Geometric period A Greek art style that roughly spanned the years 900–700 B.C. During this period, works of art emphasized the geometric patterns suggested by forms.

gesso Plaster of Paris that is applied to a wooden or canvas support and used as a surface for painting, or as the material for sculpture. (Italian for "gypsum.")

Gestalt A German word meaning "shape" or "form." The name of a school of psychology that emphasizes the tendency to perceive whole forms rather than the elements that compose or suggest the form.

gestural Brushwork that is loose and spontaneous, indicative of the bodily gesture that produced it.

gilding The art or process of applying gold leaf or thin sheets of a goldlike substance to a surface.

glazing In painting, the coating of a painted surface with a semitransparent color to provide a glassy or glossy finish; in ceramics, the application of a liquid suspension of powdered materials to the surface of a ware. After drying, the ware is fired at a temperature that causes the ingredients to melt together to form a hard, glossy coating.

Golden Section Developed in ancient Greece, a specific mathematical formula for determining the relationships of parts to the whole, based on the replication of a module or its multiples.

Gothic International Style A refined style of painting in late fourteenth- and early fifteenth-century Europe that was characterized by splendid processions and courtly scenes, ornate embellishment, and attention to detail.

Gothic style A style of Western European art and architecture developed between the twelfth and sixteenth centuries. In architecture, characterized by ribbed vaults, pointed arches, flying buttresses, and high, steep roofs.

gouache A type of watercolor paint that is made opaque by mixing pigments with a particular gum binder.

graphic design Design for advertising and industry according to the specific needs of the client.

graphite A soft, black form of carbon. (From a Greek word meaning "to write.")

graver A cutting tool used by engravers and sculptors. A tool used in stone carving.

Greek cross plan A cross-shaped plan (particularly of a church) in which the arms (nave and transept) are equal in length.

griffin A mythical creature with the body and back legs of a lion and the head, wings, and talons of an eagle.

groin vault A vault that is constructed by placing barrel vaults at right angles so that a square is covered.

ground The surface on which a two-dimensional work of art is created; a coat of liquid material applied to a support that serves as a base for drawing or painting.

gum A sticky substance found in many plants.

gum arabic A gum obtained from the African acacia plant.

H

haniwa A hollow ceramic figure placed at an ancient Japanese burial plot.

hard-edge painting A contemporary art style in which geometric forms are rendered with precision but there is no distinction between foreground and background.

hatcher An engraving instrument that leaves a metal matrix printed.

haute couture A French phrase meaning "high fashion."

heliography From the Greek "Helios," meaning the sun, a photographic process in which bitumen is placed on a pewter plate to create a photosensitive surface that is then exposed to the sun.

Hellenism The culture, thought, and ethical system of ancient Greece.

high relief Relief sculptures that project from their backgrounds by at least half their natural depth. Contrast with *bas relief*.

holography A lensless photography method in which laser light produces three-dimensional images by splitting into two beams and recording both the original subject and its reflection in a mirror.

horizon In linear perspective, the imaginary line (frequently, where the earth seems to meet the sky) along which converging lines meet. Vanishing points are placed on the horizon.

Horus The ancient Egyptian sun god.

Hudson River School A group of nineteenth-century artists whose favorite subjects included the scenery of the Hudson River Valley and the Catskill Mountains of New York State.

hue Color; the distinctive characteristics of a color that permit us to label it (as red or blue, for example) and to assign it a place in the visible spectrum.

Humanism A system of belief in which mankind is viewed as the standard by which all things are measured.

hypostyle In architecture, a structure whose roof is supported by rows of piers or columns.

I

iconoclast A person opposed to the use of religious symbols or icons.

iconography In a work of art, the conventional meanings attached to the images used by the artist; as an artistic approach, representing or illustrating by using the visual conventions and symbols of a culture.

iconology The study of visual symbols in art, which frequently have literary or religious origins.

idealism In art, the representation of forms according to a concept of perfection.

idealistic Based on the artist's conception of how the subject ought to appear.

illumination Illustration and decoration of a manuscript with pictures or designs.

illusionistic surrealism A method of surrealism that renders the irrational content, absurd juxtapositions, and changing forms of dreams in a highly illusionistic manner that blurs the distinctions between the real and the imaginary.

imam The leader in prayer at a Moslem mosque.

impasto Application of media such as oils and acrylics so that an actual texture is built up on a surface.

implied mass The apparent mass of a depicted object, as determined, for example, by the use of forms or of fields of color. Contrast with *actual mass*.

implied motion The use of plastic elements, composition, or content to create the impression of the passage of time.

Impressionism A late nineteenth-century style of art characterized by the attempt to capture fleeting effects of light by applying paint in short strokes of pure color.

incise To cut into with a sharp tool.

incrustation style A style of Roman wall painting in which a wall was divided into solid-colored panels by painted pilasters and columns.

indigenous Native.

industrial design The planning and artistic enhancement of industrial products.

intaglio A printing process in which metal plates are incised, covered with ink, wiped, and pressed against paper. The print receives the image of the areas that are below the surface of the matrix.

intarsia A style of decorative mosaic inlay.

interior design The aesthetic organization and furnishing of interior spaces to serve human needs.

International style A post-World War I school of art and architecture that used modern materials and methods and expressed the view that form must follow function.

intricate style A style of Roman wall painting that created the illusion of open areas and framed them with elaborate architectural motifs.

investiture The fire-resistant mold used in metal casting.

Ionic order A moderately ornate Greek architectural style introduced from Asia Minor and characterized by spiral scrolls (*volutes*) on capitals, and a continuous frieze.

J

jamb In architecture, the side post of a doorway, window frame, fireplace, etc.

jasper A kind of porcelain developed by Josiah Wedgwood. Jasper (also called Jasperware) is characterized by a dull green or blue surface and raised white designs.

junk sculpture A contemporary style of sculpture that assembles industrial debris and other discarded objects.

K

Ka figure An image of a body in which the ancient Egyptians believed that the soul would dwell after death.

keystone The wedge-shaped stone placed in the top center of an arch.

kiln An oven used for drying and firing ceramics.

kinetic sculpture Sculpture that moves.

kiva A circular, subterranean structure built by Native Americans for community and ceremonial functions.

kore The Greek word for "maiden"; this refers to the female figure represented in the sculpture of the geometric and Archaic styles.

kouros The Greek word for "youth"; this refers to the male figure represented in the sculpture of the geometric and Archaic styles.

krater A vessel with a wide mouth and hemispherical body used by the ancient Greeks for mixing water and wine.

L

labyrinth A structure containing an intricate network of passages, as a maze.

laminate To make by building up in layers.

language A means of communicating ideas and feelings that uses symbols and/or plastic elements that are organized according to certain rules or customs.

lapis lazuli An opaque blue, semiprecious stone.

Latin cross plan A cross-shaped church plan in which the nave is longer than the transept.

lavender oil An aromatic oil derived from plants of the mint family.

legitimate theater Professionally produced stage plays.

lens A transparent substance with at least one curved surface that causes the convergence or dispersal of light rays that are passing through. In the eye and camera, lenses are used to focus images onto photosensitive surfaces.

lift-ground etching An etching technique in which a sugar solution is brushed onto a resin-coated plate, creating the illusion of a brush and ink drawing.

light Electromagnetic energy that composes the part of the spectrum that excites the eyes and produces visual sensations.

line The mark left by a moving point.

linear Determined or characterized by the use of line.

linear perspective A system of organizing space in a work wherein lines that in reality are parallel and horizontal are represented as diagonals converging at a point. It is based upon foreshortening; the space between the lines grows smaller until it finally disappears. Linear perspective is made possible by the fact that objects appear to grow smaller as they recede from the eye.

lintel In architecture, a horizontal member supported by posts.

lithography A surface printing process in which an image is drawn onto a matrix with a greasy wax crayon. The matrix is dampened, but the waxed areas repel water. The matrix is then inked, but the ink adheres only to the waxed areas. When the matrix is pressed against paper, the paper receives the image of the crayon.

living rock Natural rock formations, as on a mountainside.

local color The hue of an object as created by the colors reflected by its surface under normal lighting conditions (contrast with *optical color*); colors that are natural for the objects they describe, rather than symbolic.

logo A distinctive company trademark or signature. (Short for "logotype.")

longitudinal plan A church plan in which the nave is longer than the transept and in which parts are symmetrical against an axis.

longshot In cinematography and video, a "shot" made from a great distance, providing an overview.

loom A machine for the weaving of thread into yarn or cloth.

lost-wax technique A bronze casting process in which an initial mold is made from a model (usually clay) and filled with molten wax. A second, fire-resistant mold is made from the wax, and molten bronze is cast in it.

Lucite An acrylic plastic that is cast or molded into transparent or translucent sheets and other shapes; frequently used in contemporary sculpture.

lunette A crescent-shaped space. (A French word meaning "little moon.")

M

magazine In architecture, a large supply chamber.

mandala In the Hindu and Buddhist traditions, a circular design symbolizing the wholeness or unity of life.

mandorla An almond-shaped halo which sometimes surrounds the entire body of a divine figure.

Mannerism A post-Renaissance sixteenth-century style of art characterized by artificial poses and gestures, harsh color, and distorted, elongated figures.

manuscript illumination The decoration of books and letters with designs and color.

masquerade A staged event in which performers wear masks signifying persons who play various social and communal roles.

mass In painting, a large area of one form or color. Also see *implied mass* and *actual mass*.

matrix In printmaking, the working surface of the block, slab, or screen. In sculpture, a mold or hollow shape used to give form to a material that is inserted in a plastic or molten state.

mausoleum A large, imposing tomb.

medium Latin for "means," refers to the materials and techniques used to create an image; in two-dimensional art, the medium is normally a liquid vehicle, or means of applying pigment to the ground.

megalith A huge stone, especially as used in prehistoric construction.

megaron A rectangular room with a two-columned porch.

Mesolithic Referring to the Middle Stone Age.

metope In architecture, the panels containing relief sculpture which appear between the triglyphs of the Doric frieze.

mezzotint A nonlinear engraving process in which the matrix is pitted with a hatcher.

mihrab A niche in the wall of a mosque that faces toward Mecca.

minaret A high, slender tower of a mosque from which the faithful are called to prayer.

Minimal art A contemporary art style that adheres to the Minimalist philosophy.

Minimalism A twentieth-century style of nonobjective art in which a minimal number of visual elements are arranged in a simple fashion.

mixed media The use of two or more traditional or non-traditional media to create a single visual image.

mobile A type of kinetic (moving) sculpture that moves in response to currents of air.

modeling In two-dimensional works of art, the creation of the illusion of depth through the use of light and shade (*chiaroscuro*); in sculpture, the process of shaping a pliable material such as clay or wax into a three-dimensional form.

Modernism A contemporary style of architecture that deemphasizes ornamentation and uses recently developed materials of great strength.

moiré pattern A wavy pattern that appears to vibrate because of the juxtaposition of similar lines whose changes are subtle and progressive.

mold A hollow shape or matrix used to give form to a material that is inserted in a plastic or molten state.

monochromatic Literally, "one-colored," it describes images that are executed in a single color or with so little contrast of colors as to appear essentially uniform in hue; opposite of polychromed.

monolith A single large block of stone; in sculpture, monolith refers to a work that strongly retains the original shape of the block of stone.

monotype A technique in which paint is brushed onto a matrix which is then pressed against a piece of paper, yielding a single print.

montage In cinematography or video, the use of flashing, whirling, or abruptly alternating images to convey connected ideas, suggest the passage of time, or provide an emotional effect.

mortar Plaster or cement that binds bricks or stones together in construction.

mortuary temple An Egyptian temple of the New Kingdom in which the pharaoh worshipped during his or her lifetime and at which the pharaoh was worshipped after death.

mosaic A medium in which the ground is wet plaster on an architectural element (such as a wall), and the vehicle consists of small bits of colored tile, stone, or glass (*tesserae*) that are assembled to create an image.

mosque A Moslem temple or place of worship.

motif A repeated visual theme.

muezzin A crier who calls the faithful to prayer at the proper hours, as from a minaret.

mummification The process of preserving a dead body by embalming.

mural painting Any painting either literally painted on the wall or intended to completely cover a wall.

mural quality From the Latin *muralis*, meaning "of a wall," it refers to solidity.

N

narrative ending In cinematography or video, selection from multiple images of the same subject to advance a story.

narthex A church vestibule leading to the nave, constructed for use by the catechumens (individuals preparing for baptism into Christianity). This space ceased to be built once Christianity had spread throughout Europe.

nave The central aisle of a church constructed for use by the congregation.

negative In photography, an exposed and developed film or plate on which light and shade are the reverse of what they are in the actual scene and in the print, or *positive*.

Neoclassical style An eighteenth-century style that revived the classical character of Greek and Roman art and is characterized by simplicity and straight lines.

Neolithic Referring to the New Stone Age.

neutrals "Colors" (black, white, gray) that do not contribute to the hue of other colors they are mixed with.

newel post The post that supports the rail at the top or bottom of a flight of stairs.

nib The point of a pen; the split and sharpened end of a quill pen.

Nihilism In art, the view that existing styles and institutions must be destroyed.

Niobid painter Anonymous vase painter of the Classical Period in Greece.

nirvana In Buddhist belief, a state of perfect blessedness in which the individual soul is absorbed into the supreme spirit.

nocturne A painting of a night scene; a musical composition with a dreamy, romantic character.

nonobjective art Art that does not portray objects. Art that does not have real models or subject matter.

nonporous Not containing pores that allow the passage of fluids.

O

ocher A dark yellow color derived from an earthy clay.

oculus Latin for eye; in architecture it refers to any round window, particularly one placed in the apex of a dome.

oil paint Paint in which pigments are combined with an oil medium.

oneiric Of dreams.

one-point perspective A type of linear perspective in which one vanishing point is placed on the horizon.

Op painting A style of art (Op or Optical art) begun in the 1960s that creates the illusion of vibrations through afterimages, disorienting perspective, and the juxtaposition of contrasting colors.

optical color The perception of the color of an object, which may vary markedly according to atmospheric conditions. Contrast with *local colors*.

orant A praying figure.

organic Composed of interrelated parts that are usually soft, curvilinear, and irregular, as of living things found in nature.

Orientalizing phase A transitional period in Greek art (circa 700–600 B.C.) during which emphasis was shifting from geometry to the human figure.

ornate Heavily ornamented or adorned.

ornate style A style of Roman wall painting in which areas that gave the illusion of opening onto a scene were confined in frames on a solid-colored background.

orthogonal A line placed at right angles to another line.

Ottonian Of the period defined by the consecutive reigns of the German kings named Otto, begun in 936 A.D.

oxidizing phase See *black-figure painting technique*.

P

paint A mixture of a pigment with a vehicle or medium.

painting The applying of a pigment to a surface; a work of art created in this manner.

palette A surface on which pigments are placed and prepared and from which the artist works; the artist's choice of colors as seen in a work of art.

pan To move a motion picture or television camera from side to side to provide a comprehensive or continuous view of the subject.

Panathenaic procession The celebration, taking place every four years, during which the statue of Athena Parthenos was presented with a new robe.

panel painting A painting whose ground is a wooden panel. The vehicle is usually tempera, but may also be oil.

papyrus A writing surface made from the papyrus plant.

parallel editing In cinematography or video, shifting back and forth from one event or story line or another.

pastel A drawing implement that is produced by grinding up coloring matter, mixing it with gum, and forming it into a crayon.

pastoral Relating to idyllic rural life, especially of shepherds and dairy maids.

patina A fine crust or film that forms on bronze or copper because of oxidation and which usually provides a desirable green or greenish-blue tint to the metal.

Pax Romana A century and a half of peace that was enforced by the power of the Roman Empire. (A Latin phrase meaning "Peace of Rome.")

pediment Any triangular architectural shape surrounded by cornices, especially one that surmounts the entablature of the Greek temple portico facade. The Romans frequently placed pediments without support over windows and doorways.

pencil A rod-shaped drawing instrument with a center stick that is usually made of graphite.

pendentive A spherical triangle that fills the wall space between the four arches of a

groin vault in order to provide a circular base on which a dome may rest.

peplos In Greek Classical art, a heavy woolen wrap.

photography The creation of images by the exposure of a photosensitive surface to light.

Photorealism An art movement that began in the late 1960s in which subjects are rendered with hard, photographic precision.

photosensitive Descriptive of a surface that is sensitive to light and therefore capable of being changed by light and recording images.

piazza An open public square or plaza.

picture plane The flat, two-dimensional surface on which an image is created. In much Western art, the picture plane is viewed as a window opening onto a deep space behind it.

pier In architecture, a support member that is vertical like a column, but whose profile is rectilinear rather than cylindrical. Piers generally support arches.

pigment Coloring matter that is usually mixed with water, oil, or other substances in order to form paint.

pilaster A purely decorative element that recalls the shape of a structural pier. Pilasters are attached to the wall plane and project very little from it; they are, in effect, piers in relief. They have all the visual elements of piers (base, shaft, capital, and often entablature above).

pile weave A type of weave in which knots are tied, then cut, forming an even surface.

plain weave A type of weave in which the woof thread passes above one warp fiber and beneath the next.

planar recession A type of perspective in which the illusion of depth is created through parallel planes that appear to recede from the picture plane.

planography Any method of printing from a flat surface, such as *lithography*.

plastic elements Those elements of a work of art—line, form, color, texture, and so on— that artists manipulate in order to express themselves and achieve desired effects.

plasticity A quality of a material that gives it the capacity of being molded or shaped.

plebeian In ancient Rome, a common person.

plywood Sheets of wood that resist warping because they are built up from layers that are glued together.

pointed arch An arch that comes to a point at the top rather than being rounded.

Pointillism Also called Divisionism, a systematic method of applying minute dots of unmixed pigment to the canvas to be mixed solely by the eye when the painting is viewed.

polygon A many-sided geometric figure.

polyptych A painting constructed of a number of panels, hinged together.

Pop art An art style that originated in the 1960s and uses commercial and popular images and themes as its subject matter.

porcelain A hard, white, translucent, non-porous clay body. The bisque is fired at a relatively low temperature and the glaze at a high temperature.

portico Greek for porch; usually refers to the entrance façade of a Greek temple. The Greek temple portico façade also has been used extensively as a decorative entrance for other types of buildings. It consists of a colonnade, an entablature, and a pediment.

post and beam A type of construction in which vertical (posts) and horizontal timbers (beams) are pieced together with wooden pegs.

post and lintel A type of construction in which vertical posts are used to support horizontal crosspieces (lintels); also called *trabeated structure.*

Postimpressionists A group of late nineteenth-century artists who relied upon the grains made by the Impressionists in terms of use of color and spontaneous brushwork, but who began to use these elements as expressive devices. The Postimpressionists also rejected the essentially decorative aspects of Impressionist subject matter.

Postmodernist A contemporary style of architecture that draws from classical and historical sources to provide ornamentation.

pottery Pots, bowls, dishes, and similar wares made of clay and hardened by heat. A shop at which such objects are made.

Poussiniste Descriptive of neoclassical artists who took Nicolas Poussin as their model. Contrast with *Rubeniste.*

Pre-Columbian Referring to art objects created in the Western hemisphere prior to the arrival of Columbus in 1492.

prefabricate To build beforehand at the factory rather than to make at the building site.

Pre-Hellenic Of ancient Greek culture prior to the eighth century B.C.

primary colors The hues (red, blue, yellow) that are not obtained by the mixing of other hues. Other colors are derived from primary colors.

print A picture or design made from pressing or hitting a surface with a plate, block, etc., as in an etching, woodcut, or lithograph. In photography, a photograph, especially one made from a negative.

prism A transparent, triangular body that disperses white light into the colors of the visible spectrum.

proportion The relationship of parts to the whole in terms of size.

propylaeum A gateway building leading to an open court before a Greek or Roman temple; specifically, such a building on the Acropolis.

proto-Baroque Descriptive of works of art that immediately preceded the Baroque movement and which show characteristics of High Renaissance art and Baroque art.

psychic automatism A process of generating imagery in which artists attempt to allow themselves to receive ideas from the unconscious mind and to express them in an unrestrained manner.

pure abstraction Same as *nonobjective art.*

pylon A massive, towering structure that can be used to support a building or to flank an entrance; the entrance façade to the precincts of an Egyptian temple.

quarry tile Reddish-brown tile, similar to terra cotta.

quill A pen made from a large, stiff feather.

R

radiating chapel An apse-shaped chapel located beyond the ambulatory of a Latin cross plan. There are usually several of these, which appear to radiate outward from the ambulatory.

rasp A rough file that has raised points instead of lines.

ready-made Found objects that are exhibited as art, frequently after being placed in a new context and given a new title.

realistic A method of representing subject matter emphasizing accurate, truthful portrayal of that which is observed by the artist.

rectangular bay system A church plan in which rectangular bays serve as the basis for the overall design. Contrast with *square schematism.*

reducing phase See *black-figure painting technique.*

Reformation A social and religious movement of the sixteenth-century in which various and often unconnected groups attempted to reform the Roman Catholic Church both from within and via the establishment of rival religions—the various Protestant sects.

register A horizontal segment of a work of art or structure.

reinforced concrete Concrete that is strengthened by steel rods or mesh. Also called *ferroconcrete.*

relief printing Any of several printing techniques in which the printing matrix is carved with knives so that the areas not meant to be printed (to leave an image) are below the surface of the matrix.

relief sculpture Sculpture that is carved as ornament for architecture or furniture, as opposed to free-standing sculpture.

Renaissance Literally, rebirth. A period spanning the fourteenth and fifteenth centuries, the Renaissance was a rejection of medieval art and philosophy which first turned for inspiration to classical antiquity and then developed artistic forms and philosophical attitudes which paved the way for the modern world.

reoxidizing phase See *black-figure painting technique*.

repoussé Formed in relief, like a pattern on a metal sheet that is formed by hammering from beneath.

representational Descriptive of art that presents natural objects in recognizable form.

Republican period The Roman period lasting from the victories over the Etruscans to the death of Julius Caesar.

resolution In video, the sharpness of a picture as determined by the number of lines composing the picture.

rhythm The orderly repetition or progression of elements.

rib In architecture, a structural member that reinforces the stress points of groin vaults; seen in Gothic buildings.

Rococo style An eighteenth-century phase of the Baroque era that is characterized by lighter colors, greater wit, playfulness, occasional eroticism, and yet more ornate decoration.

Romanesque style A style of European architecture of the eleventh and twelfth centuries characterized by thick, massive walls, the Latin cross plan, the use of a barrel vault in the nave, round arches, and a twin-towered façade.

Romanticism A movement in the nineteenth century that rebelled against academic neoclassicism in the sense that it turned to sources of inspiration for subject matter and artistic style other than those promoted in the academics.

rosette A painted or sculpted circular ornament with petals and leaves radiating from the center.

rose window A large, circular window in a Gothic church. Rose windows are assembled in segments resembling petals of a flower and are usually adorned with stained glass and plantlike ornamental work.

rotunda A round hall or room, especially a domed hall or room.

Rubeniste Descriptive of romantic artists who took Peter Paul Rubens as their model. Contrast with *Poussiniste*.

S

salon During the eighteenth and nineteenth centuries, an annual exhibition of the French Academy held in the spring.

Salon d'Automne An independent exhibition of experimental works held in 1905—so named to distinguish it from the Academic salons that were usually held in the springs.

sampler A cloth embroidered with various designs and stitches, showing the artisan's skill.

sarcophagus A coffin or tomb, especially one made of limestone.

satin weave A type of weave in which the woof passes above and below several warp threads.

saturation The degree of purity of hue, as measured by its intensity or brightness.

scale The relative size of an object as compared to other objects, the setting, or people.

sculpture The art of carving, casting, modeling, or assembling materials into three-dimensional figures or forms; a work of art made in one of these manners.

S-curve Developed in the Classical style as a means of balancing the human form, and consisting of the distribution of tensions so that tension and repose are passed from one side of the figure to the other and back again, resulting in S-shape; contrapposto.

seal A distinctive design.

secondary colors Colors that are derived from mixing pigments of primary colors in equal amounts. They are orange (red and yellow), violet (red and blue), and green (blue and yellow).

serigraphy A printing process in which stencils are applied to a screen of silk or similar material stretched on a frame. Paint or ink is forced through the open areas of the stencil onto paper underneath.

service systems In architecture, mechanical systems that provide structures with transportation, heat, the elimination of waste products, and so on.

shade The degree of darkness of a color, as determined by the extent of its mixture with black.

shaft grave A vertical hole in the ground where one or more bodies are buried.

shaped canvas A canvas that may be an irregular polygon, as opposed to the traditional rectangle, and that may project considerably from the wall on which it is hung.

Shinto A major religion of Japan, which emphasizes nature and ancestor worship.

Shiva The Hindu god of destruction and reproduction.

shutter In photography, a device for opening and closing the aperture or a lens in a camera so that the film or plate is exposed to light.

siding In architecture, a covering for an exterior wall.

silica A hard, glassy mineral compound of silicon and oxygen.

silverpoint A drawing medium in which a silver-tipped instrument inscribes lines on a support that has been coated with a ground or pigment.

slow motion A cinematographic process in which action is made to appear fluid but slower than normal by exposing a greater-than-normal number of frames per second but then projecting the film at normal speed.

soft-ground etching An etching technique in which a ground of softened wax yields effects similar to those of pencil or crayon drawings.

soft sculpture Sculpture made from soft materials like fabrics and vinyl rather than traditional hard materials like stone, wood, and metal.

sound track An area on the side of a strip of motion picture film that carries a record of the sound accompanying the visual information.

square schematism A church plan in which the crossing square serves as the basis for determining the overall dimensions of the building. Contrast with *rectangular bay system*.

squeegee A T-shaped tool with a rubber blade used to remove liquid from a surface.

stabile A type of winglike, nonmoving sculpture that strongly implies movement through soaring lines.

staccato Composed of abrupt, distinct elements.

stainless steel Steel made virtually immune to corrosion by being alloyed with chromium or other metals.

stamp To impress or imprint with a mark or design.

standing mobile A mobile that is supported on a base rather than hung.

steel A hard, tough metal composed of iron, carbon, and other metals, such as nickel or chromium.

steel cable A strong cable composed of multiple steel wires.

steel cage A method of building that capitalizes on the great strength of steel by piecing together slender steel beams to form the skeletons of structures.

stele An engraved stone slab or pillar that serves as a marker.

step pyramid An ancient Egyptian tomb consisting of squares of diminishing size stacked upon one another.

stereoscopy The photographic process of creating the illusion of a three-dimensional images by simultaneously viewing two photographs of a scene that are taken from slightly different angles.

Stoicism The philosophy that the universe is governed by natural laws and that mankind should follow virtue, as determined by reason, and remain indifferent to passion and emotion.

stonewar In ceramics, a slightly porous or nonporous ware fired at a high temperature.

stroboscopic motion The creation of the illusion of movement by the presentation of a rapid progression of stationary images—such as the frames of a motion picture.

style A characteristics manner or mode of artistic expression or design.

stylobate A continuous base or platform that supports a row of columns.

stylus A pointed, needlelike tool.

subject matter The objects or ideas depicted in a work of art.

subtractive process A process in which a sculpture is created by the removal of unwanted material, as in carving. Contrast with *additive process*.

sunspace In architecture, an area within a solar building that allows light to penetrate and builds up heat, which is usually conducted to cooler areas of the structure.

support A surface on which a two-dimensional work of art is made.

Suprematism Malevich's approach to nonobjective art, characterized by "the supremacy of pure feeling."

Surrealism A twentieth-century art style whose imagery is believed to stem from unconscious, irrational sources and therefore takes on fantastic forms. Although the imagery is fantastic, it is often presented in an extraordinarily realistic or illusionistic manner.

surrealistic Of or similar to Surrealism.

Synthetic Cubism The second phase of Cubism, which emphasized the form of the object, and constructing rather than disintegrating that form.

Synthetism Gauguin's theory of art, which advocated the use of broad areas of unnaturalistic color and primitive or symbolic subject matter.

systemic painting Any form of painting that follows a specific system of rules or principles of organization.

T

telephoto Descriptive of a lens that produces large images of distant objects.

tenebrism A style of painting that uses very little modeling. The artist goes rapidly from highlighting to deep shadow without using a subtle gradation of tones.

tensile strength The degree to which a material can withstand being stretched.

terra cotta A hard, reddish brown earthenware that is used in sculpture and pottery and usually left unglazed.

tertiary colors Colors derived from mixing pigments of primary and adjoining (on the color wheel) secondary colors.

texture The surface character of materials as experienced primarily by the sense of touch.

texture gradient The rendering of nearby objects as having rougher, more detailed surfaces than distant objects.

tholos In architecture, a beehive tomb.

throwing In ceramics, the process of shaping that takes place on the potter's wheel.

tie-dying The making of designs by sewing or tying folds in cloth to prevent a dye from reaching certain areas.

tier a row or rank.

tint The degree of lightness of a color, as determined by the extent of its mixture with white.

transept The "arms" of a Latin cross plan, use by pilgrims and other visitors to allow access to the area behind the crossing square.

transverse rib In architecture, a rib that connects the midpoints of a groin vault.

tribune gallery In architecture, the space between the nave arcade and the clerestory used for traffic above the side aisles on the second stage of the elevation.

triglyph Panels incised with vertical grooves (usually three, hence triglyph) which serve to divide the scenes in the Doric frieze.

trombe wall In solar architecture, a thicker masonry wall that collects heat during the day and releases it through the night.

trompe l'oeil A French phrase meaning "fool the eye." It refers to a painting or other art form that creates such a realistic image that the viewer at first glance wonders whether the image is real or a representation.

trumeau In Romanesque and Gothic architecture, a dividing element in the center of a portal below the tympanum which serves as an area for sculpture.

truss A rigid, triangular frame used for supporting roofs, bridges, and other structures

trglyph In architecture, a sculpted panel in a Doric frieze.

tryptych A set of three panels with pictures or other embellishment, often hinged so that the side panels may be folded over the center panel.

tufa A kind of porous stone.

twill weave A type of weave with broken diagonal patterns.

two-point perspective A type of linear perspective in which two vanishing points are placed along the horizon.

tympanum The semicircular space above the doors to a cathedral.

typography The arts of designing, arranging, and setting types for printing.

U

umber A kind of earth that has a yellowish or reddish brown color.

unity The oneness or wholeness of a work of art.

Upper Paleolithic The late years of the Old (Paleolithic) Stone Age.

V

value The lightness or darkness of a color.

vanishing points In linear perspective, points on the horizon where parallel lines appear to converge.

vantage point The actual or apparent spot from which a viewer observes an object or picture.

vault Any series of arches other than an arcade used to create space. Barrel vaults are created by the placement of arches one behind the other; groin vaults are created by the intersection of barrel vaults at right angles to one another.

vehicle A liquid such as water or oil with which pigments are mixed for painting.

veneer In architecture, a thin layer of fine-quality material used to enhance the appearance of the façade of a structure.

Venus Roman goddess of beauty; also refers to prehistoric fertility sculptures such as the Venus of Willendorf.

Venus pudica A Venus with her hand held over her genitalia for modesty.

video A catch-all term for several arts that use the video screen, including, but not limited to, commercial and public television, video art, and computer graphics.

video art Use of the video screen in works of art. Video art refers to images on these screens and the use of video screens in assemblages.

videotape Magnetic tape that records images that can be instantly replayed and cannot be discriminated from originals ("live pictures") when played on the video screen.

vinescroll A design in which circular forms are embedded in vines that double back upon themselves.

vinyl A leathery material made from one of various synthetic resins and plastics.

visual arts Arts that appeal primarily to the visual sense, such as drawing, painting, sculpture, architecture, many crafts, photography, cinematography, and video art; also called space arts, to distinguish them from the time arts (music, live theatre, etc., whose forms progress primarily through time).

vitrify To become hard, glassy, nonporous.

volute A spiral scroll forming a feature of Ionic and Corinthian capitals.

volute krater A wide-mouthed vessel (*krater*) with scroll-shaped handles.

votive Refers to the quality of being worshipful and is usually employed to describe figures associated with the worship of a deity.

voussoir A wedge-shaped stone block used in the construction of an arch.

W

wainscoting A wood paneling or lining along the walls of a room, particularly along the lower parts of walls.

ware Pottery or porcelain; a good to be sold by a merchant.

warm colors Reds, oranges, and yellows; colors that appear to advance spatially before cool colors (greens, blues, violets).

warp In weaving, the threads that run lengthwise in a loom and which are crossed by the weft or woof.

wash A thin, watery film of paint—especially watercolor—applied with even, sweeping movements of the brush.

watercolor A paint with a water medium. Watercolors are usually made by mixing

pigments with a gum binder and thinning the mixture with water.

weaving The making of fabrics by the interlacing of threads or fibers, often on a loom.

webbing In architecture, a netlike structure that comprises that part of a ribbed vault that lies between the ribs.

weft In weaving, the yarns that are carried back and forth across the warp. Also called *woof*.

weight shift The situating of the figure so that the legs and hips are turned in one direction and the chest and arms in another. This shifting of weight causes a diagonal balancing of tension and relaxation.

wide-angle Descriptive of a lens that covers a wider angle of view than an ordinary lens.

woodcut A type of relief printing in which the grain of the wooden matrix is carved with a knife.

wood engraving A type of relief printing in which a hard, laminated, nondirectional wood surface is used as the matrix.

woof See *weft*.

woodworks Contemporary works of art whose imagery consists of words.

Zen Buddhism An antirational Buddhist worldview that enlightenment is to be sought through introspection and intuition.

zoogyroscope An early motion picture projector.

zoom To use a zoom lens, which can be rapidly adjusted to provide distance shots or close-ups while keeping the image in focus.

INDEX

PHOTO CREDITS